Archaeological Survey of the Kerak Plateau

American Schools of Oriental Research

Archaeological Reports

editor
Larry G. Herr

Number 01
Archaeological Survey
of the Kerak Plateau

edited by
J. Maxwell Miller

Archaeological Survey of the Kerak Plateau

Conducted during 1978-1982
under the direction of
J. Maxwell Miller and Jack M. Pinkerton

edited by
J. Maxwell Miller

Scholars Press
Atlanta, Georgia

Archaeological Survey of the Kerak Plateau

edited by
J. Maxwell Miller

Library of Congress Cataloging in Publication Data

Archaeological survey of the Kerak Plateau / edited by J. Maxwell Miller.
p. cm. — (archaeological reports / American Schools of Oriental Research ; no. 1)
Includes bibliographical references.
ISBN 1-55540-642-4
1. Kerak Plateau (Jordan)—Antiquities. 2. Excavations (Archaeology)—Jordan—Kerak Plateau. I. Miller, James Maxwell, 1937- . II. Series: ASOR archaeological reports ; no. 1.
DS154.9.K47A7 1991
933—dc20 91-32533
CIP

Printed in the United States of America
on acid-free paper

CONTENTS

ABBREVIATIONS

AAA	*Annals of Archaeology and Anthropology* (Liverpool)
AASOR	*Annual of the American Schools of Oriental Research*
ADAJ	*Annual of the Department of Antiquities of Jordan*
AJA	*American Journal of Archaeology*
ANET	*Ancient Near Eastern Texts Relating to the Old Testament*, ed. J. B. Pritchard, Princeton: Princeton University Press, 3rd ed., 1969
AOr	*Archiv Orientálni*, Prague
ARAB	*Ancient Records of Assyria and Babylonia*, ed. D. D. Luckenbill, Chicago: University of Chicago Press, 1926-27
ARA	*Annual Review of Anthropology*
AUSS	*Andrews University Seminary Studies*
BA	*Biblical Archaeologist*
BAH	*Bibliothèque archéologique et historique*, Paris
BAR	*British Archaeological Reports*
BASOR	*Bulletin of the American Schools of Oriental Research*
BN	*Biblische Notizen*
BTAVO	*Beihefte zum Tübinger Atlas der Vorderen Orients*
DMG	*Deutsche morgenländische Gesellschaft*
EI	*Eretz-Israel*
HAW	*Handbuch der Altertumswissenschaft*, Munich
IEJ	*Israel Exploration Journal*
JBL	*Journal of Biblical Literature*
JEA	*Journal of Egyptian Archaeology*
JNES	*Journal of Near Eastern Studies*
JPOS	*Journal of the Palestine Oriental Society*
JSOT	*Journal for the Study of the Old Testament*
LA	*Liber Annuus. Studii biblici franciscani*, Jerusalem
MuNDPV	*Mitteilungen und Nachrichten des deutschen Palästina-Vereins*
NEASB	*Near East Archaeological Society Bulletin*
PEFA	*Palestine Exploration Fund Annual*
PEFQS	*Palestine Exploration Fund Quarterly Statement*
PEQ	*Palestine Exploration Quarterly*
PPTS	*Palestine Pilgrims' Text Society*
QDAP	*Quarterly of the Department of Antiquities in Palestine*
QMIA	*Qedem: Monographs of the Institute of Archaeology*, Jerusalem
RB	*Revue Biblique*
SAOC	*Studies in Ancient Oriental Civilization*, Chicago
SBF	*Studium Biblicum Franciscanum*
VT	*Vetus Testamentum*
WO	*Welt des Orients*
ZAW	*Zeitschrift für die Alttestamentliche Wissenschaft*
ZDMG	*Zeitschrift der deutschen morgenländischen Gesellschaft*
ZDPV	*Zeitschrift des deutschen Palästina-Vereins*

LIST OF FIGURES

LIST OF PHOTOGRAPHS

PREFACE

This volume reports the results of an archaeological survey of the Kerak plateau in southern Jordan. Codirected by J. Maxwell Miller and Jack M. Pinkerton, the fieldwork was conducted in three seasons, during 1978-1982, under the joint sponsorship of Emory University, the American Schools of Oriental Research, and the Department of Antiquities of Jordan. Special credit must go to Jim Waits, dean of Emory's Candler School of Theology, who encouraged the initiation of the project and was of tremendous help in the search for funding, to Drs. James A. Sauer and David McCreery, directors of ASOR's American Center for Oriental Research in Amman, who helped work out the physical arrangements for each season, and to Dr. Adnan Hadidi, Director-General of the Department of Antiquities, who gave the full support of his office.

Funding for the fieldwork came primarily from four sources: Emory University's Research Fund, the Franklin Foundation, the Day Companies Foundation, and the Near East Engineering Corporation (a Jordanian firm). Significant contributions were made also by the IBM Corporation, the Pinkerton and Laws Company, Mr. and Mrs. Jack M. Pinkerton, Mr. Drew Fuller, Mr. Arthur P. Laws, and Mr. and Mrs. Joseph Mattingly. The Hewlett-Packard Corporation provided a 3820 distance meter for the use of the survey, and Heery International provided office space in Amman. All of the persons who participated in the survey, except for the representatives of the Department of Antiquities (indicated below with *), did so at their own expense, or at the expense of their respective academic institutions. In addition to the codirectors, Miller and Pinkerton, these participants were:

1978 Season (July 20 - August 30)

Charles Cashion
James R. Kautz
Michael R. Pinkerton
Sami Rabadi*

1979 Season (July 15 - August 25)

John R. Bartlett
Robin M. Brown
J. Andrew Dearman
James W. Grant
James R. Kautz
Burton MacDonald
W. Harold Mare
Gerald L. Mattingly
James H. Pace
Michael R. Pinkerton
Stephen B. Reid
Sami Rabadi*
Mohammed Khasisby*
Munawer Rwashdeh*

1982 Season (July 23 - September 3)

Patrick M. Arnold
John R. Bartlett
J. Daniel Bing
Patricia Bing
Colin H. Brooker
Robin M. Brown
Phillip R. Callaway
J. Andrew Dearman
M. Patrick Graham
Catherine Klipple
Gerald L. Mattingly
Pamela K. Mattingly
David W. Miller
James H. Pace
Michael R. Pinkerton
Donald G. Schley Jr.
Jane R. Sutter
Linda Schearing
Andreas Reichert
Antoon Schoors
Emanuel Williams
Sami Rabadi*
Munawer Rwashdeh*

Dr. James A. Sauer read the pottery for the 1978 season. Robin Brown took over this responsibility in 1979, correlating their readings and terminology.

All of the persons listed contributed, directly or indirectly, to the preparation of this volume. However, certain ones deserve special mention. Miller served as general editor and authored much of the text. Arnold, Bartlett, Dearman, and Mattingly contributed significantly to the preparation of the individual site descriptions. The pottery analysis is Robin Brown's work, and represents a personal investment in the project which involved many months of research long after the actual fieldwork was completed. Dr. Ernst Axel Knauf, in addition to writing the chapter on the toponymy of the survey area, served as consultant regarding the spelling and transliteration of Arabic names for the whole volume. Brian Jones, Rusty McKeller, and Duane Calhoun prepared the maps. The enlarged satellite photograph of the region east of the Dead Sea was provided by Historical Productions, Inc. Finally, a special word of appreciation is due to Julene Miller, Elizabeth Whipple, and Pat and Betty Pattillo for their patience and encouragement.

The final compilation and editing of this volume was made possible in part by a grant from the National Endowment for the Humanities, an independent federal agency. Publiction costs were subsidized by the American Schools of Oriental Research

J. Maxwell Miller
Jack M. Pinkerton

Chapter I

THE SURVEY

by

J. Maxwell Miller

Limits of the Survey Area and Physical Characteristics of the Region

The narrow strip of cultivable land east of the Dead Sea, sandwiched between the rugged slopes of the Dead Sea escarpment and the Syrian (or North Arabian) desert, is referred to in ancient written records as "Moab." Actually Moab represents a relatively small section of the northwestern edge of the Arabian desert-plateau—the edge, namely, where the gradual northwestern incline of this vast plateau is interrupted by the Jordan Rift and where rains from the Mediterranean encroach on the desert, providing enough moisture for agriculture. Moab is bisected by the deep Wadi el-Mujib and interrupted in the south by the equally formidable Wadi el-Ḥasa canyon, both of which approach the Dead Sea from the east.

The survey reported here focused on that portion of the Moabite/Arabian plateau between Wadi el-Mujib and Wadi el-Ḥasa, referred to henceforth as the "Kerak plateau." Kerak is the largest city between Wadi el-Mujib and Wadi el-Ḥasa, and is situated near the center of the survey area. Although excursions were conducted into the Wadi el-Mujib and Wadi el-Ḥasa canyons, down the Dead Sea escarpment, and into the desert fringe, systematic survey was confined to the plateau proper, an area of approximately 875 sq. km (see fig. 1 and fig. 3).

A secondary division within the Kerak plateau is created by Wadi el-Kerak which provides relatively easy ascent to the plateau from the Lisan, the city of Kerak which is situated at the head of Wadi el-Kerak, and the Kerak-Qaṭranah road which follows the most convenient route eastward from Kerak across Wadi ed-Dabbah to the Qaṭranah oasis. Thus one may think of Moab as divided into three parts with the Kerak plateau corresponding to central and southern Moab.

Northern Moab	—the area north of Wadi el-Mujib, continuous with the Balqaᵓ region, and dominated by the ancient city of Madaba.
Central Moab	—the area between Wadi el-Mujib and the juncture at Kerak of Wadi el-Kerak and the Kerak-Qaṭranah road.
Southern Moab	—the area south of the above, to Wadi el-Ḥasa.

Since the concentration of the first two seasons of survey was on the area between Wadi el-Mujib and the Kerak-Qaṭranah road, the survey came to be called the "Central Moab Survey." This name was rendered inappropriate with the third season, however, during which the survey was extended to include the area south of the Kerak-Qaṭranah road.

The Kerak plateau is gently rolling terrain for the most part, averaging 1,100 m in elevation, but with a gradual

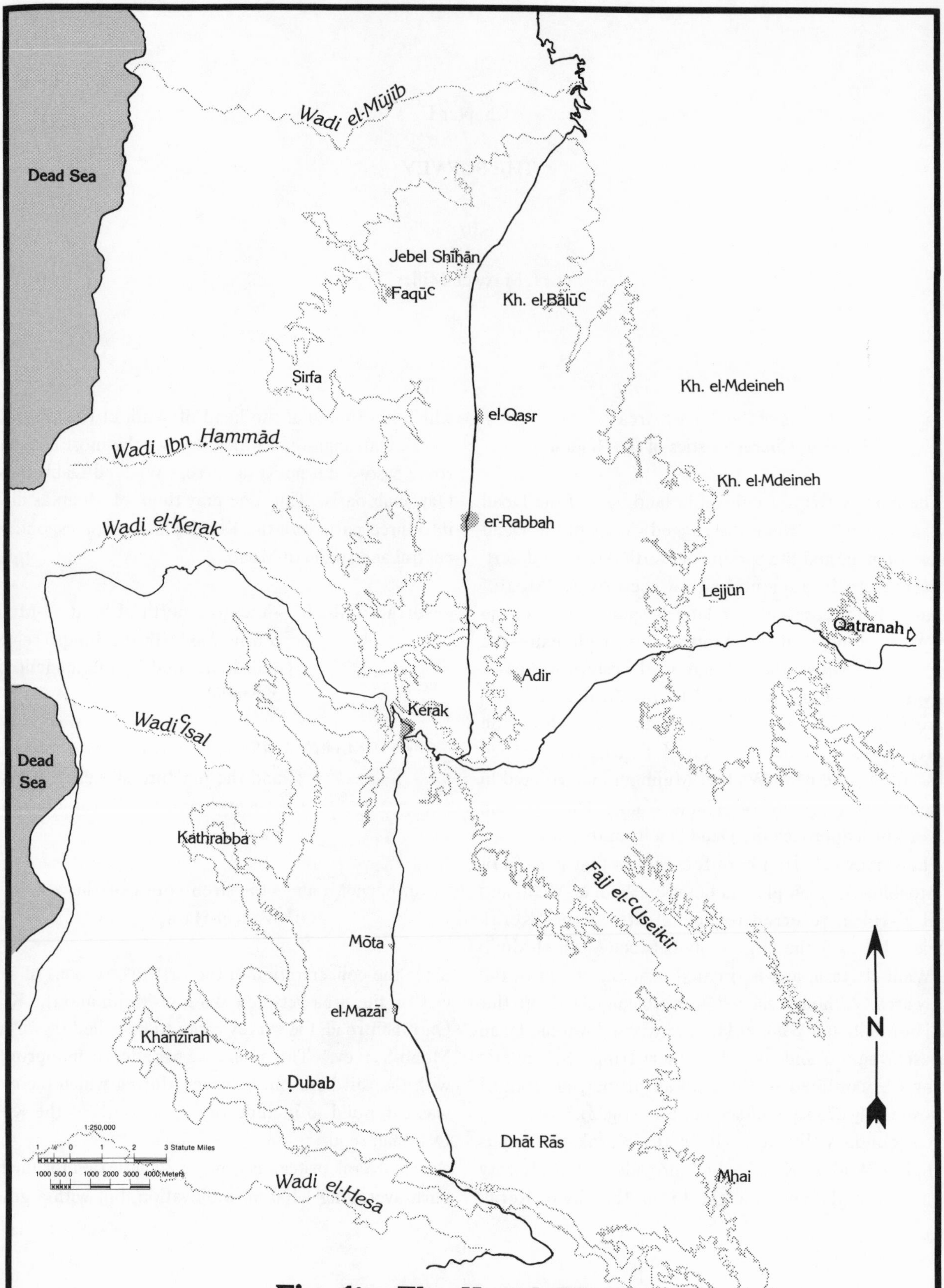

Fig. 1: The Kerak Plateau

Maps by D.Cal's Studio

rise to the south. Thus Jebel Shiḥan stands out prominently in the north-central plateau at 965 m, while Jebel Ḍubab is a less conspicuous elevation on the southwestern edge at 1,305 m. The surface of the plateau is composed of three major geological formations: (a) Volcanic flows, mainly basalt, dominate the northern tip of the plateau with continuation down the eastern side. (b) These flows overlay marine deposits of the Belqaᵓ Series (Middle Cretaceous to Eocene) which account for the surface of most of the survey area. (c) The Belqaᵓ Series deposits overlay in turn ᶜAjlun Series marine deposits (Lower Cretaceous and Jurassic). The latter are exposed along the Dead Sea escarpment, especially where Wadi el-Kerak and Wadi Ibn Ḥammad cut deep into the plateau, and in the Wadi el-Mujib and Wadi el-Ḥasa canyons. Beneath the three formations indicated above are sandstone deposits from Lower Cretaceous and even earlier periods. The dominant rock-types of the Belqaᵓ and ᶜAjlun formations are variations of limestone—chalk, chert, and marls. Red and yellow Mediterranean soils (including *terra rossa*) dominate, produced by the weathering of limestone. Naturally there is loess soil as well, because of the proximity to the desert. The soils tend to be shallow on the plateau, with bedrock occasionally breaking the surface.

The climate of the Kerak plateau, as Palestine in general, is characterized by mild and wet winters balanced with hot and dry summers. However, the elevation of the plateau, along with the increased distance from the Mediterranean and exposure to the icy desert winds, produces somewhat colder winters than in the Cisjordan. The temperature often drops below freezing. The elevation also removes the plateau from the almost tropic heat of the Jordan Valley. Relatively high movement of winds is another notable characteristic of the Kerak plateau. Icy winds from the desert are common in the winter months, but the winter winds, from late October into April, are predominantly from the southwest. During the summer months, from April through October, dry, westerly winds prevail. The hot, dusty *sirocco* or *khamsīn* arrives in the spring, again from the desert, burning up the green landscape, and often reappears in the fall.

Precipitation occurs mainly as rain, although snow is not uncommon on the Kerak plateau. The rain and occasional snow is brought by the prevailing southwestern winds during the winter months. These winds derive moisture from the Mediterranean and then lose it when they rise to pass over the Transjordanian highlands. Although the winter rains may begin already in late October and continue into early May, the largest monthly rainfall comes in February, and the amount can vary significantly from year to year—from as low as 100 mm in an exceptionally dry year to as high as 500 mm in an unusually wet year. The average on the plateau is 350 mm with the Dead Sea escarpment, the Mujib and Ḥesa canyons, and of course the desert frontier, receiving much less (see fig. 2). Much of the rainfall is quickly drained off by the numerous wadis which cut into the plateau from all sides. Yet much also is absorbed by the porous Mediterranean soil and gradually seeps downward into the limestone strata from which some of it reemerges as springs.

Most of these springs are to be found in the ᶜAjlun Series formations. The embedded limestones and marls of this series serve respectively as aquifers and aquicludes, the former absorbing the water and the latter preventing it from seeping deeper and thus forcing it to the surface as springs. Aquicludes prevail in the Balqaᵓ Series, which render it less conducive to springs. In short, the only springs of significance on the Kerak plateau are to be found in the Wadi el-Mujib and Wadi el-Ḥasa canyons and along the wadis of the Dead Sea escarpment.

In spite of disadvantages such as thin soils and relatively few springs, the abundant rainfall spread over five or six months, combined with the absorbent character of the soils, allows a fairly productive yield of rainfall-dependent farming on the Kerak plateau. The broad rolling terrain of the plateau proper is particularly conducive to grain crops such as wheat and barley. Spots where the soil is deeper and springs available, especially along the edge of the Dead Sea escarpment and shelves above Wadi el-Ḥasa, produce fruit trees and vineyards. The Kerak plateau is reasonably good agricultural land, therefore, and is covered with village sites which show evidence of having been occupied off and on throughout the centuries. For a more detailed description of the regional environment of the survey area see Mattingly (1983b), Koucky (1987a), and Donahue and Beynon (1988).

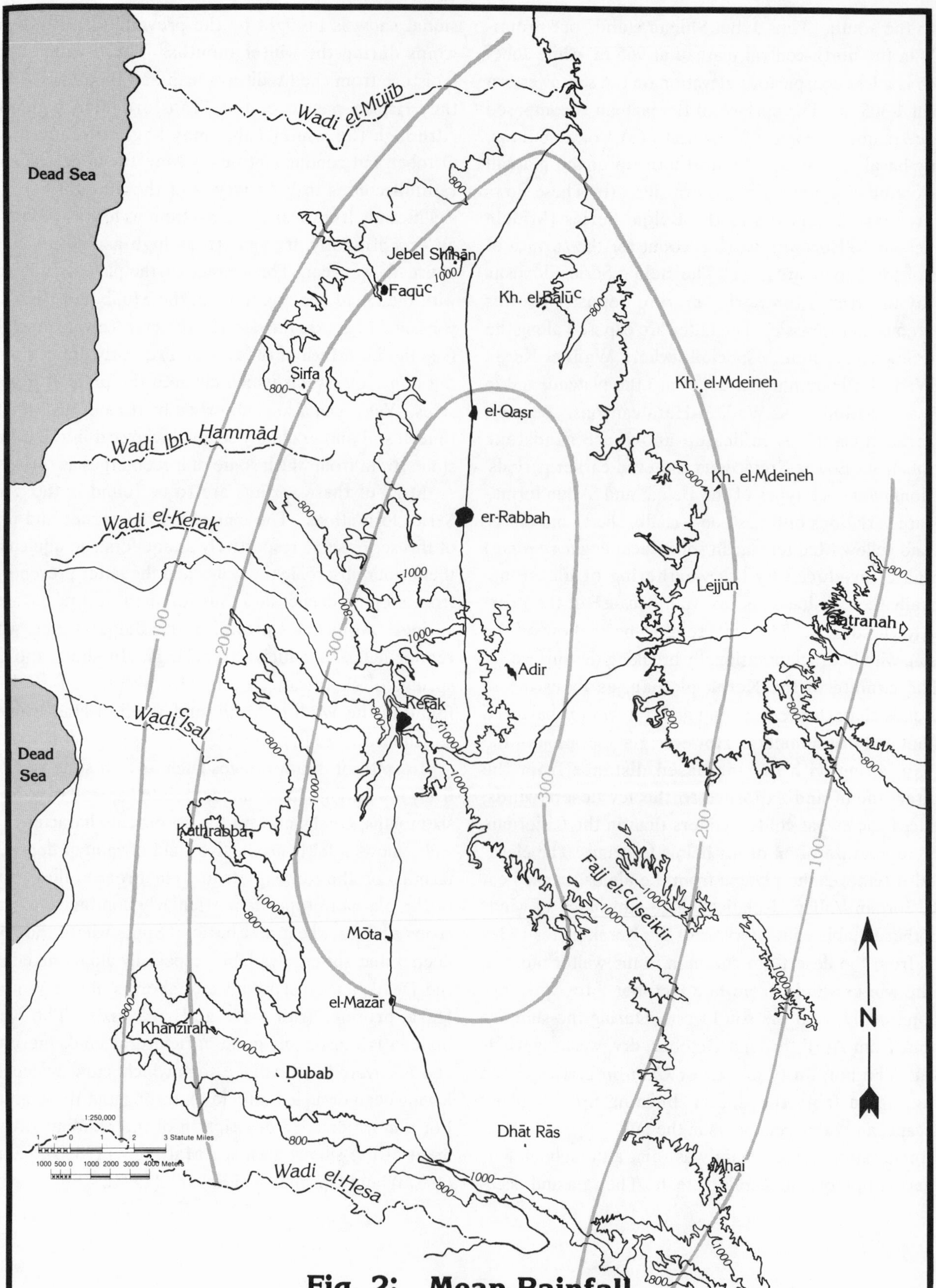

Fig. 2: Mean Rainfall

Maps by D.Cal's Studio

Villagers, Nomads, and Urban Dwellers

The villages which dotted the Kerak plateau in earlier times will have consisted, as typically the villages of the plateau do today, of a small cluster of houses, unfortified, with some sort of water supply, and within walking distance of cultivable ground. Occasionally the water supply is a spring. For the interior of the plateau, however, where there are virtually no springs, village sites often are found where ground rock surfaces above the soil. These rock surfaces usually are slightly elevated above the surrounding fields, can be utilized for the village plot without any loss of cultivable land, and can be hewn out for cisterns.

At the same time, the Kerak plateau is good grazing land and open to the desert which itself favors nomadism. Thus a most important factor to be taken into account for understanding the archaeological situation of the Kerak region is the age-old dynamic between "the desert and the sown," between the lifestyle of the village farmer who requires some degree of security for planting and cultivating crops, and that of the nomad in constant search of pasturage. At the most general level, this dynamic may be understood as one of competition––a competition reflected throughout history in the ebb and flow of villages along the desert frontier. During certain periods of history, villages have increased in number along this frontier and encroached on the desert as far as the rainfall would allow cultivation. During other periods, village economy has tended to retreat, with villages declining in number and cultivable land along the frontier reverting to pasturage.

Yet one must guard against an oversimplified understanding of this ancient competition between village farmers and desert nomads. Some distinction must be made in the first place between the great camel-breeding nomadic tribes which range the desert interior and the pastoral nomads who graze their sheep and goats along the desert frontier. Along this frontier—the transitional zone between the good farm land and the desert, where the rainfall declines from amounts barely sufficient for agriculture to still lesser amounts productive nevertheless of rich seasonal pasturage––the lifestyles of village farmers and pastoral nomads tend to converge. Villagers also raise sheep and goats, and may take to their tents during the summer months and range over relatively extensive territory in search of pasturage. An essentially pastoral nomad, on the other hand, may cultivate a small bit of ground during the growing season. Indeed, during transitional periods when village economy is expanding or retreating along the desert frontier, the villager often is a recently sedentarized pastoral nomad, or vice versa.

Second, it should be kept in mind that the relationship between village farmers and pastoral nomads along the desert frontier usually is symbiotic to some degree as well as competitive. While nomadic tribes from the desert have presented a constant threat through the ages to villages within their reach, they also have come to the villages and towns to trade. After harvest, farm land surrounding the villages provides grazing for the animals of the nomadic tribes. The animals, in turn, fertilize the soil. Often alliances have developed in which nomadic tribes provided "protection" to villages in return for tribute of one kind or another. While such arrangements often were nothing less than exploitation, they represented symbiotic relationships nevertheless that no doubt enabled villages to survive which otherwise would have been abandoned. Moreover, such alliances between nomads and villagers have not always been exploitative. Sometimes the same tribe has included within its constituency both non-sedentary nomads and villagers.

Finally, any attempt to understand the dynamic between villagers and nomads along the desert frontier must take into account the presence of towns and cities in the given region and the power structures which these urban centers represent. The contrast between the lifestyle of the villager and that of the townsman probably is greater than that between the villager and the pastoral nomad—and in many cases the villager has looked upon the townsman as posing an equally serious threat to the viability of the village. The town, in addition to supplying items which the subsistence economy of the village could not produce, was also the seat of governmental authority, the tax collector, the money lender, and the absentee landlord. An overly exploitative tax structure administered from the nearest town or city could destroy the vitality of villages in an area just as effectively as plundering raids from desert tribes.

Throughout history, this third item probably more than anything else has determined when the villages would expand in number along the desert frontier and approach maximum utilization of the cultivable land and when they would be abandoned. When the power structures represented by the urban centers (whether local rulers or local representatives of more distant authorities) have been able to maintain security in a region and have done so without excessive exploitation of the village farmers, the villages have tended to multiply. But when these authorities have provided inadequate security and were themselves excessively exploitative, the villagers have had no choice but to abandon their homes and fields.

A full cycle of the preceding pattern can be documented from medieval and modern records. During the early years of Mamluk rule, beginning in the mid-13th century, Kerak served as the administrative center of *Mamlakat al-Karak* which comprised most of the Transjordan. The Kerak plateau was secured by garrisons of Mamluk soldiers and dotted with active villages (Bakhit 1982). As the Mamluk government began to encounter hard times during the course of the 14th century, however, it became increasingly less able to protect the villagers from raids. At the same time, in their own economic desperation, the Mamluk Sultans placed an increasingly heavier tax burden and other sorts of demands on the villagers. Gradually the villages began to disappear (Brown 1984). Under Ottoman rule the situation continued to deteriorate. The Kerak plateau fell into Ottoman hands in 1516, but already during the reign of Suleiman (1520-66) it became apparent that the Ottoman government would be unable to maintain a tight grip on the region, and following Suleiman's reign only sporadic efforts were made toward that end (see esp. Peake 1958: 81-91). Thus the number of villages continued to decrease, so that when Ulrich Seetzen and Johann Burckhardt passed through at the beginning of the 19th century (see below) they observed only four permanent settlements with mud and stone houses on the whole plateau. These were Kerak, ᶜIraq, Kathrabba, and Khanzirah (Seetzen 1854-55: 416; Burckhardt 1822: 389), all tucked away along the rugged edge of the Dead Sea escarpment. The whole region, including the four settlements, was dominated by Bedouin tribes.

The trend has reversed itself during the present century (see esp. Gubser 1973), again related directly to the power structures represented locally by officials in Kerak. In 1894 the Ottoman government reasserted its authority in the region between Wadi el-Mujib and Wadi el-Ḥasa, placing a military governor with a garrison of soldiers in Kerak (see esp. Mousa 1982). Security naturally was disturbed in the region between the eruption of the Kerak revolt in 1910 and the end of World War I. With the end of the war, however, and the establishment of the Emirate of the Transjordan, the plateau was again policed and administered from Kerak, as it still is today. Some thirty or more villages had reemerged on the Kerak plateau by the early 1920s. There were more than eighty by the early 1970s. Today the count would be more than a hundred and is increasing rapidly. Even during the process of our survey we noted villages springing up on sites which had presented only abandoned ruins when we began our work.

The Kerak Plateau in Ancient, Classical, and Medieval Sources

This is not the place to recount the history of the region in any detail. It is reasonable to hope, in fact, that the results of the survey, when analyzed fully, will contribute significantly to our understanding of that history. The following, therefore, is intended only as a very general overview with primary attention to the available written sources.

Egyptian Sources: The earliest written references to the region are provided by Egyptian sources. Unfortunately these Egyptian references are rare and usually difficult to interpret for one reason or another. First to be considered are the so-called Execration Texts from the 19th or 18th centuries B.C.E. which include "rulers of the Shutu" among Egypt's Asiatic enemies (Posener 1940: 88-90). "Shutu" may be the Egyptian equivalent of "Sheth" which in turn is paralleled with Moab in Num 24: 17-18. It does not follow, of course, that the Shutu of the Middle Bronze Age were specifically Moabites, but only that the biblical poet, composing at a much later time, regarded the Moabites as belonging to Shutu stock.

Egypt maintained a strong presence in Syria-Palestine during the Late Bronze Age, beginning especially with the reign of Tuthmosis III (ca. 1482-1450 B.C.E.). Contact

Photograph 1: Sheep grazing on the south slope of Jebel Shiḥan and wheat fields in the distance

Photograph 2: Miḥnā (Site 273), a modern village emerging on an ancient settlement site

seems to have been primarily with towns and villages along the main roads, but the Egyptians also encountered non-sedentary folk throughout Syria-Palestine whom they referred to generally as "Shasu." None of the Shasu references in the Egyptian texts points specifically to the region east of the Dead Sea. Yet the Egyptians no doubt would have considered this region, at least its desert frontier, as Shasu territory. One of the topographical lists from the reign of Tuthmosis III, the so-called "Palestinian List" (also called the "Megiddo List"), may indicate that he passed through the Moabite plateau on one of his Asiatic campaigns. This possibility depends on the accuracy of the following identifications proposed by Donald Redford (1982b) for numbers 97-101 of the list (but see Kafafi 1985).

97	*betaᵓe*	Jalul
98	*tipun*	Dhiban
99	*ᵓubir*	Wadi el-Mujib
100	*yarutu*	Khirbet Yarut
101	*harkur*	Kerak

Two other inscriptions suggest that Ramesses II (ca. 1304-1237 B.C.E.) may have campaigned in the general region two centuries later. The first of these, a brief topographical list inscribed on a statue of Ramesses II which stands before the northern pylon of the Luxor temple, includes what appears to be the name "Moab" (Simons 1937: 70-71, 155-56). Unfortunately the list is brief and largely destroyed, so that the context is not very helpful. The second is actually a grouping of three texts, two of them original lines of palimpsests, from the inscriptions on the outer face of the east wall of the Court of Ramesses II of the Luxor temple. K. A. Kitchen identified, reconstructed, and combined the three texts to read as follows (Kitchen 1964: 50-53; 1982: 67, 250):

> Town which the mighty arm of Pharaoh, L.P.H., plundered in (the) land of Moab: *b[w]trt*.
> Town which the mighty arm of Pharaoh, L.P.H., plundered: *yn*[?]*d*..., in the mountain of *mrrn*.
> The t[own which] the mighty arm of Pharaoh, L.P.H., [plundere]d, of *tbniw*.

Bwtrt would be a town in Moab if Kitchen's reconstruction is correct, and Axel Knauf (1985a) has suggested its identification with present-day Batir (our Site 300). Kitchen identifies *tbniw* as Dibon (present-day Dhiban), which seems likely even though this identification encounters some archaeological difficulties and has been challenged on other grounds as well (Aḥituv 1972).

Finally, the Baluᶜ Stele deserves attention in connection with the Egyptian sources from the Late Bronze Age, even though it does not qualify specifically as an Egyptian monument and cannot be dated with certainty. This conical shaped stele, discovered in 1930 among the ruins at Kh. el-Baluᶜ (Site 35) on the northeastern edge of the plateau, bears both an inscription and a raised relief. Unfortunately the inscription is so poorly preserved that even the language cannot be established, much less a convincing translation. The relief is very clear, however, with composition and details derived from Egyptian prototypes. It consists of three figures, probably a king (center) flanked by a god (left) and a goddess (right). The god wears the double crown of upper and lower Egypt, while the goddess wears a crown similar to that of Osiris. Since the king's headdress is similar to that worn by certain Asiatics in Egyptian reliefs from Dynasties 19 and 20, it has been argued that this was a specifically Shasu headdress and that the king of the Baluᶜ stele was therefore a Shasu king (Drioton 1933; Worschech 1999: 97). But while Shasu are clearly depicted with this sort of headdress in the Egyptian reliefs, it is less clear that all of those so depicted were Shasu. Ward and Martin (1964) dated the Baluᶜ stele to approximately the end of the Late Bronze Age, in which case it is confirming evidence that Egyptian influence extended to the Kerak plateau at that time. Recently, however, H. Weippert (1988: 666-67) has proposed an Iron IIC date.

Widespread disturbances at the end of the Late Bronze Age, involving migrations of peoples, collapse of the Hittite empire, and radical curtailment of Egyptian international influence, created a power vacuum in Syria-Palestine and allowed for the emergence of several small and essentially independent city-states and kingdoms. References to Moabite kings in the Hebrew Bible imply that a Moabite monarchy emerged rather early in the Iron Age. The Mesha Inscription confirms that a kingdom which encompassed at least a portion of Moab existed by the mid-9th century B.C.E. Assyrian records provide additional references to Moabite rulers who would have lived during the 8th and 7th centuries B.C.E. The standard treatment of Moabite history by Van Zyl (1960) is dated and should be read in conjunction with the more recent studies by Miller (1989a) and Timm (1989).

The Hebrew Bible: The Hebrew Bible is the only one of these sources which pertains to Moabite affairs prior to the 9th century B.C.E. Unfortunately its references to Moab are sporadic and not entirely trustworthy on matters of historical detail. A case in point is Num 21:10-30 which describes the Israelite passage through (or around ?) the Kerak plateau to northern Moab and conquest of northern Moab. In addition to its ulterior motive of providing the Israelites with historical claim to Transjordanian territory as far south as the Arnon River (Wadi el-Mujib), the passage shows evidence of having been compiled from multiple sources (Miller 1989b).

One can conclude from the biblical texts that the Israelites looked upon the Moabites as a closely related people and that there was considerable interchange between the Israelites and Moabites—peaceful relations as well as moments of conflict. One of the narratives in the book of Judges, for example, describes a Moabite raid on Jericho with the result that the city remained in Moabite hands for several years (Judg 3:15-30). The book of Ruth, on the other hand, has as its setting an occasion of famine in Judah when a Bethlehemite family went to Moab in search of food. Saul is reported to have defeated the Moabites in battle (1 Sam 14:47). David, identified as a great grandson of the Moabitess Ruth (Ruth 4:18-22; 1 Chr 2:9-20), is said to have taken his parents to Moab for safety while he was a fugitive from Saul's court, and then later to have defeated the Moabites and executed two-thirds of the captured prisoners (1 Sam 22:3-4; 2 Sam 8:2). Solomon is said to have accommodated in Jerusalem the worship of Kemosh, the Moabite god (1 Kgs 11:7).

Moabites generally are viewed in the poetical sections of the Hebrew Bible, the Psalms and the prophetic books, as enemies of Israel along with the Ammonites, Edomites, Philistines, and other neighboring peoples. Psalms 60 (compare Ps 108:7-9) and 83; Amos 2:1-3; Isaiah 15-16; and Jeremiah 48 deserve special attention in any study of Moabite history or toponymy. In the latter regard, it is significant to note that virtually all of the Moabite towns and villages mentioned in the Hebrew Bible were located north of the Arnon. This suggests that the Moab known to the biblical writers was essentially northern Moab, not the Kerak plateau.

The Mesha Inscription and Kerak Fragment: The famous Mesha Inscription, discovered among or near the ruins of ancient Dibon (present-day Dhiban) in 1868, provides a brief glimpse of Moabite affairs during the latter half of the 9th century B.C.E. (See Dearman 1989 for a full discussion and bibliography). This inscription of more than 34 lines was commissioned by King Mesha of Moab in connection with the building of a sanctuary dedicated to Kemosh. Mesha ruled from Dibon and reported in the inscription what he regarded as the major achievements of his reign. Foremost among these achievements was his liberation of northern Moab from Israelite control. We learn from the inscription that King Omri of Israel had conquered that region and that it had remained under Israelite domination for a time after Omri's death. Mesha was able to espand his own realm as far north as the vicinity of Nebo and Medeba, however, and set about to restore the villages, fortifications, cisterns, highways, etc. throughout northern Moab.

Related information from an Israelite perspective is supplied by 1 Kgs 3:4-27 (see also 1 Kgs 1:1). We read there that Mesha had been required to deliver to the Israelite court an annual tribute of a hundred thousand lambs and the wool of a hundred thousand rams, but that he rebelled after the death of King Ahab (Omri's son). Thereupon King Jehoram (Ahab's son), supported by Jehoshaphat king of Judah and an anonymous king of Edom, marched against Moab, ravaged the land, and laid siege to Kir-hareseth (usually identified with Kerak, but on very weak grounds) to which Mesha himself had retreated. For some reason (the meaning of the closing verse of the biblical narrative is unclear) the city escaped capture. The literary character and historicity of this biblical narrative is much debated (see esp. Miller 1967; de Vries 1978; Bartlett 1983). Whatever one concludes on that score, it seems clear that Mesha was successful in restoring autonomy to his Moabite kingdom.

A small inscription fragment, apparently discovered at Kerak in 1958, provides the last four characters of the name of another Moabite king. This basalt fragment, only 14 x 12.5 cm, seems to have a close parallel in a funerary stele discovered near Aleppo in 1891. If so, the inscription was written in horizontal lines across the garment of a standing figure. Parts of only four lines survive in a script similar to that of the Mesha Inscription. The reconstruction of the king's name in the translation below (proposed by Reed and Winnett 1963) in based on the conjectures that this king of the Kerak fragment was none other than Mesha's father, whose name is also only partially legible in the Mesha Inscription (*Kmsh*[..]).

> ...*K]mshyt*, king of Moab, the ...
> ...of Kemosh (to serve) as an altar (?) because he ...
> ...his... And behold I made ...

Moab in the Assyrian Texts. With the campaigns of Tiglath-pileser in 734-732 B.C.E. all of Syria-Palestine, including the Moabite region, fell under Assyrian domination. Thus the royal Assyrian documents provide occasional glimpses of Moabite affairs. The first is provided by a fragment of a clay tablet discovered at Nimrud which provides a long list of kings who paid tribute to Tiglath-pileser shortly after 734 B.C.E. Among the kings listed is one Shalamanu of Moab (British Museum no. 3751; *ARAB* 1, §§787-804/*ANET* 282). From the reign of Sargon II (721-705 B.C.E.) is a prism fragment which mentions Moab among certain Palestinian kingdoms implicated in an anti-Assyrian revolt led by Ashdod in 713 B.C.E. (Prism A, fragment D; *ARAB* 2, §§193-95/*ANET* 287). The revolt, signaled by Ashdod's refusal to pay the required annual tribute to Assyria, was quickly crushed. Presumably Moab paid off Sargon and escaped punishment.

Two letters, which cannot be dated specifically but belong approximately to the period of Tiglath-pileser and Sargon, also mention Moab. One records the delivery of horses, presumably as tribute, to Calah by officials from Egypt, Judah, Moab, and Ammon (Nimrud Letter no. 2765; Saggs 1955). The other, from an Assyrian official and delivered to Nineveh by a messenger named Ezazu and identified as a "Dabilite," reports a raid on Moabite territory by men of *Gidir*-land (Nimrud Letter no. 2773; Saggs 1955). It has been suggested that "Dabilite" is a scribal error for "Dibonite" (Saggs 1955; but see Donner 1957 and Mittmann 1973).

Among the local Palestinian kings who rushed with presents to assure Sennacherib of their loyalty when he marched against Philistia and Judah in 701 B.C.E. was Kamoshnadab from Moab (Oriental Institute and Taylor Prisms; *ARAB* 2, §233/*ANET* 287). A much shorter text from the reign of either Sennacherib or his successor Esarhaddon reports further tribute from the Ammonites, Moabites, Judeans, and possibly Edomites (British Museum no. K 1295; *ANET* 301). A King Musuri of Moab is listed among others (including Manasseh of Judah and Qausgabar of Edom) who transported building materials to Nineveh during the reign of Esarhaddon (Prism B; *ANET* 291). Musuri, Manasseh, and Qausgabar are listed again among local Palestinian rulers who delivered presents to Ashurbanipal and provided military service for the latter's wars against Egypt (Cylinder C; *ARAB* 2, §876/*ANET* 294).

Finally, two texts from the reign of Ashurbanipal are instructive in that they (a) presume that the kingdoms of the Transjordan were loyal Assyrian vassals and thus due Assyrian protection, and (b) witness to the fact that protection was needed against attacks from the direction of Arabia. One of these texts reports a campaign conducted by Ashurbanipal against Yuhaithi[c], identified in this particular text as king of Arabia but elsewhere as son of Haza'il, king of Qedar:

> He persuaded the inhabitants of Arabia (to join) him and then plundered repeatedly those peoples which Ashur, Ishtar, and the (other) great gods had given to me to be their shepherd and had entrusted into my hands. Upon the oracle-command of Ashur and Ishtar, (I called up) my army and defeated him in bloody battles, inflicting countless routs on him (to wit) in the *girû* of the towns of Azaril (and) Hirata(-)kasaia, in Edom, in the pass of Iabrudu, in Beth-Ammon, in the district of Haurina, in Moab, in Saʾarri, in Harge, in the district of Zobah. In the(se) battles I smashed all the inhabitants of Arabia who had revolted with him, but he escaped... (Rassam Cylinder; *ARAB* 2, §§817-31/*ANET* 297-98).

In the other text, Ashurbanipal claims credit for a victory over ᶜAmmuladdi, king of Qedar, although one Kamoshᶜaśa king of Moab seems to have been the actual victor.

> With the help of Ashur, Sin, Shamash, Adad, Bel, Nebo, the Ishtar of Nineveh--the Queen of Kidmuri—the Ishtar of Arbela, Ninurta, Nergal (and) Nusku and by pronouncing my name which Ashur has made powerful, Kamashaltu [Kamoshᶜaśa], king of Moab, a servant belonging to me, inflicted a defeat in an open battle upon Ammuladi, king of Qedar who, like him [i.e., like Abyathaᶜ, another defeated Arabian ruler mentioned earlier in the text], had revolted and had continuously made razzias against the kings of the Westland (Cylinder B; *ARAB* 2, §870/*ANET* 298).

Thus the Assyrian texts provide the names of four additional Moabite kings: Shalamanu, who paid tribute to Tiglath-pileser; Kamoshnadab, who pledged loyalty to Sennacherib; Musuri, a contemporary of Manasseh of Judah, Esarhaddon, and Ashurbanipal; and Kamoshᶜaśa, who defeated the Qedarites later on in Ashurbanipal's reign. Precise dates are unavailable for any of these four kings. (On the transliteration of their names, see Knauf 1989).

Josephus: We are dependent almost entirely upon Josephus for specific information about the region east of the Dead Sea during the Persian, Hellenistic, and early Roman periods. According to Josephus, the Ammonites and Moabites were brought under Babylonian subjection five years after the destruction of Jerusalem [*Ant*., 10.9.7 (181)]. Presumably the peoples of the Transjordan submitted to Persian occupation as well, although there are no direct references to Moab or the Moabites in available documents from the Persian period. Persian authority will have given way to Nabataean influence, perhaps gradually, perhaps abruptly, following Alexander's conquest. A 3rd century B.C.E. Aramaic inscription from Kerak is dated to "year 15," probably the 15th year of the reign of Ptolemy II (Milik 1958/59; Knauf 1985c: 251 n.31, 252 n.40). This may suggest that the Kerak plateau remained outside the Nabataean realm until the Seleucid conquest of Palestine. That the whole Transjordan was regarded as part of Arabia (i.e., Nabataean realm) by the beginning of the 1st century B.C.E. is presupposed by Josephus' account of the warfare between Alexander Jannaeus (103-76 B.C.E.) and the latter's Nabataean contemporary, Obodas I. Josephus reports, namely, that Alexander "overcame the Arabians, such as the Moabites and Gileadites, and made them bring tribute" [*Ant*. 13.13.5 (374)]. Later on, according to Josephus, Alexander "was forced to deliver back to the king of Arabia the land of Moab and Gilead, which he had subdued, and places that were in them" [*Ant*. 13.14.2 (382)]. This leaves the reader somewhat unprepared for Josephus' account of the negotiations between Hyrcanus II and Aretas III after Alexander's death, at which time Hyrcanus supposedly offered to return the Moabite cities if Aretas would support his bid for the Judean throne:

> Moreover, Hyrcanus promised him, that when he had been brought thither, and had received his kingdom, he would restore that country, and those twelve cities which his father Alexander had taken from the Arabians; which were these: Medaba, Naballo, Libyas, Tharabasa, Agala, Athone, Zoar, Orone, Marissa, Rudda, Lussa, and Oruba [*Ant*. 14.1.4 (18)].

Possibly Oruba (*'Arabâtha*) is to be equated with Rabbathmoba (present-day er-Rabbah) known from Roman and Byzantine sources, although this is not at all certain. Otherwise, the geographical range of the cities listed, plus the fact that the only other details supplied by Josephus regarding Alexander's activities in the Transjordan point to the vicinity of Amathus (Tell ᵓAmtah) and Gadara (Um Qeis), suggest that Alexander's encroachment was confined to northern Moab (north of Wadi el-Mujib). The Kerak plateau, in other words, had remained in Nabataean hands.

Pompey's eastern campaign in 64-63 B.C.E. brought all of Syria-Palestine under the shadow of Rome. Nabataea, including the Kerak plateau, became a client kingdom and vulnerable to the greed of local Roman officials. Josephus reports that Aemilius Scaurus, whom Pompey left in charge of affairs when he returned to Rome in 62 B.C.E., marched on Petra, but was bought off with 300 talents of silver [*Ant*. 14.5.1 (81)]. It is Josephus also who reports that Gabinius, a Roman governor of Syria, invaded and defeated the Nabataeans in a battle, an event which would have occurred in 55 B.C.E. [*Ant.* 14.6.4 (103); *Wars* I.8.7 (178); Wissmann 1976]. Strabo's account of an unsuccessful Roman expedition into the Arabian Peninsula ca. 26 B.C.E. is further evidence that the Roman grip on Nabataea was firm (*Geography* 16.4.24). The Nabataeans supplied approximately a thousand soldiers for this campaign.

There is some evidence to suggest that Nabataea was reduced to the status of a Roman province for a brief time immediately following the death of Herod the Great in 4 B.C.E. (Bowersock 1983: 55-56). If so, this was a temporary arrangement. Aretas IV (ruled 9/8 B.C.E. to 40 C.E.) clearly enjoyed royal status during the bulk of his reign, which moreover represented the zenith of Nabataean prosperity and influence. Josephus' account of the conflict between this Aretas and Herod Antipas [*Ant.* 18.5.1 (109-115)] indicates that Machaerus (present-day el-Mukawer, north of Wadi el-Mujib) was on the frontier between their respective realms.

Sources from Late Roman and Byzantine Times: Nabataea maintained its status as a client kingdom for another century, until 106 C.E. when Trajan joined it with Perea and the Decapolis cities to form the administrative province of Arabia Petraea. Thus the Kerak plateau, annexed with Nabataea, became officially a part of the Roman empire. With the annexation of Nabataea, the whole southeastern frontier of the Roman empire was now lined with provinces—Cyrenaica, Aegyptus, Judaea, Arabia Petraea, and Syria.

Already Rabbel II, whose death in 106 apparently prompted the annexation of Nabataea, had shifted the Nabataean capital from Petra to Bostra (present-day Buṣra). Bostra became the administrative capital of the new Roman province, therefore, and home base for the III Cyrenaica legion. Work probably began immediately on a new Roman road, the *Via Nova Traiana*, although the earliest milestones date from 111 C.E. The *Via Nova Traiana* connected Bostra with Aela (present-day ᶜAqaba), and for the most part followed an ancient route which passed north-south through the Kerak plateau. Much remains to be learned about the *Limes Arabicus*, the system of forts and watchtowers which protected Arabia Petraea on its desert side. Recent investigations suggest that this system emerged gradually during the first three centuries of the Common Era, was reorganized and strengthened by Diocletian at the beginning of the 4th century, and began a noticeable decline in the late 5th and 6th centuries (see esp. Parker 1986b). The buildup of defenses at the beginning of the 4th century accompanied another change in the province divisions. Specifically, the region south of Wadi el-Ḥasa was separated from the province of Arabia Petraea and joined with territory west of the Ghor to form the province of Palaestina Tertia. The Kerak plateau remained with Arabia Petraea (or simply "Arabia," as it came to be called) during the Byzantine period (see esp. Bowersock 1983: 142-44; Gutwein 1981). By the mid-6th century, however, Byzantine military control of the southern Transjordan had deteriorated to the extent that the region south of Wadi el-Mujib was essentially frontier. (Parker 1986b: 152-54).

Written sources pertaining specifically to the Kerak plateau while it was under Roman rule are not very revealing. About the only thing to be learned is that the two main cities on the plateau were Rabbathmoba (present-day er-Rabbah) and Charachmoba (also Charakmoba, present-day Kerak). Seal impressions found at Kurnub (ancient Mamphis) witness to the fact that both were cities of some prominence during the reign of Hadrian (Negev 1969: 89-106). The archive of Babatha from the so-called "Judean Desert Caves," also from the 2nd century, reveals that she had to declare her property to a Roman commander who was based at Rabbathmoba (Polotsky 1962: 258-62). Ptolemy lists Rabbathmoba and Charachmoba among the cities and villages of Arabia Petraea (*Geography* 5.16.4). Coins were struck at both cities in the early 3rd century; those recovered from Rabbathmoba/er-Rabbah date from the reign of Septimius Severus (193-211 C.E.) to that of Elagabalus (218-22 C.E.), while those recovered from Charachmoba/Kerak date from the reign of Elagabalus (Hill 1922: pl.30-31, 42-43; Spijkermann 1978: 108-10, 262-63, pl.20, 59-61; 1984). The Peutinger Map from the 3rd or 4th century introduces "Rababathora," which may be a corrupt form of Rabbathmoba or some combination of Rabbathmoba and Betthoro (Bowersock 1983: 175). Betthoro appears in the *Notitia Dignitatum* from the 4th century which reports that *sub dispositione viri spectabilis ducis Arabiae* is the *praefectus legionis quartae Martiae, Betthoro* (*Not. dign.* Or. 37.22). Brünnow and Domaszewski (1905: vol.II, p.36) were the first to connect Betthoro with Lejjun, an identification which, although not absolutely certain, is widely accepted (Bowersock 1983: 175).

Areopolis emerged as an alternate name for Rabbathmoba probably as early as the 2nd century (Knauf 1984c), and Eusebius uses both names in his *Onomasticon* (10:17; 36:20, 25; 122:28; 124:17). He does not have individual enties for these two names, of course, since neither is a biblical name. Specifically, Eusebius' entries which may relate to the Kerak plateau are: Arnon (*Onom.* 10:17-24), Ar (*Onom.* 10:25), Horonaim (*Onom.* 36:17-18), Eglaim (*Onom.* 36:19-21), [Beer-]elim (*Onom.* 36:22-23), Luhith (*Onom.* 122:28), and Moab (*Onom.* 124:15-17). Neither does Eusebius mention Charachmoba, but both it and Rabbathmoba/Areopolis continue to appear in other Christian sources from the Byzantine period. Also the Madaba Mosaic Map from the 6th century includes Charachmoba, unfortunately with only the letters ...*chmoba* fully preserved. The Tharias, which appears near the River Zered on the Madaba map, has been associated with Dhat Ras (our Site 427; see esp. Germer-Durand 1897: 574; Avi Yonah 1954: 41). However H. Donner (1982) equates it with Tar^{c}īn (present-day el-^{c}Iraq, our Site 292) which seems more likely. Aia, which appears between Charachmoba and the Dead Sea on the map, has been identified with present-day ^{c}Ai (our Site 262) by Donner (1964) and with present-day el-^{c}Aina on the north bank of Wadi el-Ḥasa by Avi Yonah (1954: 41). Again, Donner's proposal seems more likely.

In addition to the sources mentioned above as pertaining to the Roman and Byzantine period are numerous inscription fragments, mostly tomb inscriptions, which have been discovered on the plateau (see esp. Canova 1954; Zayadine 1971a and b).

Arab and Medieval Sources: The first clash between Islamic and Byzantine armies occurred on the Kerak plateau near Mota in 629 C.E. By 640, all of Palestine was in Muslim hands, and would remain so for the next four centuries (see esp. Walmsley 1987). Under the Umayyad caliphs (661-750), the Kerak plateau found itself strategically located between the chief political and religious centers, Damascus and Mecca. This situation changed under the Abbasids, however, who ruled from Baghdad and dominated Syria-Palestine from 750 to the mid-9th century. By the mid-9th century, the Abbasid realm had begun to fragment into three blocs: (1) Persia, (2) Egypt and Syria-Palestine, and (3) North Africa and Spain. Specifically, Palestine was dominated by Egyptian rulers (Tulunids, Ikhshids, Fatimids) from 868 to the coming of the Crusaders in 1099. From this period of Egyptian domination come the earliest Arabic references to the Kerak region. "Maāb" is the name typically used, referring to both the region and to its chief city (present-day er-Rabbah). Maāb is mentioned by al-Ya^{c}qubi, for example, who authored the earliest known Arab history and also a geography of sorts (Le Strange 1890: 494; Marmardji 1951: ix-x). Al-Ya^{c}qubi apparently was born in Egypt and spent much of his life there. His geography, titled *Kitāb al-Buldān* (Book of Countries), was completed in 891 and is essentially a list of provinces with their chief cities.

A more important source from this period, however, is al-Muqaddasi from Jerusalem (lived ca. 946-88). Drawing upon his own observations during extensive travels, al-Muqaddasi described the geography of Syria and surrounding regions as well as the social and religious situation of his day. Associating Maāb with the District of ash-Sharah, he mentioned almonds as its main produce.

> The Fourth belt [of Syria] is that bordering on the Desert. The Mountains here are high and bleak, and the climate resembles that of the Waste; but it has many villages, with springs of water and forest trees. Of the towns therein are Maāb, ^{c}Ammān, Adhra^{c}āh, Damascus, Ḥims, Tadmur, and Aleppo (*PPTS* vol.III, p.85).

> ...the District of ash-Sharāh, and for its capital we should put Ṣughar. Its chief towns are: Maāb, ^{c}Ainānā, Mu^{c}ān, Tabūk, Adhruḥ, Wailah, Madyan (*PPTS* vol.III, p.11).

> Maāb lies in the mountains. The district round has many villages, where grow almond trees and vines. It borders on the desert. Mūtah is counted among its hamlets, where are the tombs of Ja^{c}far aṭ-Ṭayyār, and Abd Allah ibn Rawāḥah (*PPTS* vol. III, p.63; see also pp. 97-98).

Al-Bakri from Marsiyah, who wrote *Mu^cjam ma sta^cjama* (Dictionary of Strange Things) in 1094, also mentioned Maāb as a place in Syria (Marmardji 1951: 191) and singled out Mota among its towns.

The Latin kingdom of Jerusalem was established in 1099, and Kerak was fortified in 1139-42. Called Kerak of Moab (or simply Le Crac) by the Franks and, with Montreal (present-day Shaubak), controlling the Crusader domain in the Transjordan (Oultre Jourdain), Kerak played a prominent role in Crusader-Arab affairs until it fell to Saladin in 1188. The primary source for the period is William of Tyre's *Historia Rerum in Partibus Transmarinis Gestarum*. William of Tyre was born in the East, educated in France, and lived in Palestine from ca. 1160 to 1184. Another important source is *Chronique d'Ernoul et de Bernard le Trésorier*, an old French chronicle which continues William of Tyre's account. It is the latter chronicle, for example, that reports the marriage feast held at Kerak in 1183 when Lady Stephanie sent food from the feast to Saladin and he in turn ordered his troops not to bombard the tower in which the bridal couple was housed (Ernoul 102-6). Gabrieli (1969) provides a useful collection of non-Christian sources for the Crusader period.

Kerak continued to figure prominently in political affairs after 1188, especially in the conflicts following Saladin's death between his Ayyubid descendants in Syria and the Mamluk sultans in Egypt. Specifically, Kerak served as an Ayyubid stronghold against the Mamluks until 1263 when it was conquered by Baybars. Then, under the Bahrī line of Mamluk rulers which began with Baybars, it served as the administrative center of a *Mamlakah* which comprised most of the Transjordan and part of the Hejaz (Bakhit 1982). Indeed, it served as a kind of second capital for political exiles from Cairo. Baybars' son, Sa^cid, forced to abdicate by Qalawun in 1279, retired to Kerak where he lived until his death. Qalawun's son, Naṣir, was elected sultan in 1293, deposed to Kerak in 1298, then recalled to the throne in Egypt the following year. He abdicated in 1309 and returned to Kerak until 1310, when he again was recalled to the throne in Cairo. Later Naṣir banished his oldest son, Aḥmed, to Kerak. After Naṣir's death, intrigues between Aḥmed and Ismail, another of Naṣir's sons, led eventually to Ismail's successful siege of Kerak in 1342 and Aḥmed's execution.

Mamluk strength had begun to decline already before 1382 when the Bahrī line was displaced by a line of Burjī (Circassian) sultans. This trend continued under the Burjī who, while finding it increasingly difficult to provide security for their realm, nevertheless were increasingly exploitative of their subjects. The sedentary population of southern Transjordan began to decrease. The Kerak castle continued to serve as a place of political refuge from the court in Cairo, but even it succumbed to a bedouin attack in 1502. For more details regarding the role of Kerak in political affairs under the Mamluks, see especially Peake (1958: 79-82), Baratto (1978: 134-36), and Brown (1984). Literary references to Kerak and its vicinity during the Mamluk period are collected by Le Strange (1890) and Marmardji (1951).

The Ottoman government, wishing to provide security along the pilgrim route from Damascus to Mecca, attempted for a time to control southern Transjordan. However rebellion broke out among the bedouin of the Kerak plateau near the end of Suleiman 's reign (1520-66), and order was never entirely restored. The last Ottoman census of the region was conducted in 1596/97 (Hütteroth and Abdulfattah 1977; Hütteroth 1978). For three centuries, therefore, until December of 1893, the Kerak plateau was essentially free of outside authority. In fact, the Ottoman government made annual payments to the bedouin sheiks of the region in return for the safety of pilgrims passing through. The villages and agricultural base, already declining under the Mamluks, virtually disappeared during the Ottoman period. As indicated above, when European travelers began to pass through the plateau at the beginning of the 19th century they found only four villages remaining between Wadi el-Mujib and Wadi el-Ḥasa. One of these was Kerak, from which the Majali tribe dominated the region (Gubser 1973).

Previous Archaeological Explorations in the Survey Area

Because of its geographical isolation and the absence of security, the Kerak plateau tended to be by-passed during the 19th century while other parts of Palestine were being mapped and explored systematically for archaeological remains. The Majali sheiks apprehended and extracted payment from travelers who entered their territory. Ulrich Seetzen and Johann Burckhardt were the first modern travelers to penetrate the region and leave accounts of their journeys. Both followed the route of the old Roman road, the *Via Nova Triana*, from north to south. Seetzen, who crossed Wadi el-Mujib in March of 1805, was waylaid and robbed as he climbed out of the wadi onto the plateau. Burckhardt reached Kerak without difficulty in July of 1812, making careful notes regarding the lay of the land and ancient ruins which he observed along the way. Then he was detained in Kerak for three weeks before being allowed to continue. Both men died in the course of their travels, and portions of their accounts, published posthumously, were misunderstood by the publishers. Some of the resulting confusion regarding the topography of the Kerak plateau still is evident in maps from the last decade of the 19th century (see below, the entry for Ariḥa, Site 22).

Charles Irby and James Mangles were able to travel with more freedom when they crossed the Kerak plateau in May, 1818, following the Roman road from south to north. Commanders in the British navy, they were well armed and accompanied by a small troop of bodyguards. Also, as an extra precaution, they presented themselves to the local sheiks as mercenary soldiers of Mohammed Ali. (Mohammed Ali's son, Ibrahim Pasha, would attempt to take Kerak in 1832 and succeed in 1840.) Captain W. F. Lynch, in connection with his exploration of the Dead Sea in April-May of 1848, led a small party of armed men via Wadi el-Kerak to Kerak. Hostilities occurred and they barely escaped capture. Felician de Saulcy was less fortunate in January of 1851. Approaching from around the southern end of the Dead Sea, he and a small party of companions ascended the plateau along the northern slopes of Wadi Ibn Ḥammad and camped one night near a ruin called Rujm el-ᶜAbd where they discovered the so-called Shiḥan Stele (Warmenbol 1983; see also the entry below for Faquᶜ, Site 14). They were intercepted the next day and detained at Kerak until satisfactory payment was made. De Saulcy made very detailed notes regarding the archaeological remains which he encountered before being intercepted, but his notes are understandably less detailed and useful thereafter.

J. R. Roth passed through Kerak in March of 1858, having approached via Wadi el-Kerak, and then departed southward via Kathrabba to Wadi el-Ḥasa. Albert duc de Luynes conducted an expedition to the Dead Sea region in 1864 which involved two visits to Kerak. He also acquired the so-called Shiḥan Stele, discovered by de Saulcy at Rujm el-ᶜAbd, and arranged for its transport to Paris. C. Mauss and H. Sauvaire also approached Kerak via Wadi el-Kerak in the spring of 1866, and then continued southward to Shobak. Rev. F. A. Klein, a German missionary active among the bedouin tribes in the Transjordan, visited Kerak the following year and published a brief account which appeared two years later. In the meantime, in August of 1868, he discovered the Mesha inscription at Dhiban (Graham 1989).

The discovery of the Mesha Inscription inspired two follow-up expeditions into the region east of the Dead Sea, both sponsored by the Palestine Exploration Fund. During the summer of 1870, on the return trip from a more extensive expedition into the Sinai, E. H. Palmer and C. F. T. Drake cut across the northwestern corner of the Kerak plateau. Then, in 1872, H. B. Tristram, accompanied part of the way by Klein, undertook an expedition which originally was intended to focus on the region between Wadi el-Mujib and Wadi el-Ḥasa. Unfortunately, the expedition was doomed to failure. Having approached Kerak from the Dead Sea side, and having been detained in Kerak until payment demands were met, Tristram and his party headed north in blinding rainstorms which precluded any serious exploration until they had crossed Wadi el-Mujib. Moreover, close examination of Tristram's published account and map reveals that his party was confused much of the time as to where they were (see entry for Jadᶜat el-Jbur, Site 34).

Other travelers passed through the Kerak plateau during the latter quarter of the 19th century, including Charles Doughty and Grey Hill. As the century drew to a close, however, the topography of the Kerak plateau, to say nothing of its archaeological treasures, remained largely unknown. This is abundantly evident from the PEFQS map of Palestine published in 1890. For the area between Wadi el-Mujib and Wadi el-Ḥasa this map depends on Tristram's map, adjusted somewhat to fit Burckhardt's account.

In December of 1893, the Ottoman government began to take a more aggressive role in governing and policing the region. Kerak itself, where the Majali sheiks had enjoyed the safety of the Crusader and early Mamluk castle walls, was taken by force. Sections of the wall were destroyed to prevent its future use as a stronghold for rebels. Also a military governor was installed in Kerak with a garrison of soldiers. There followed, for approximately a decade, until the Shobak uprising in 1905 (Gubsner 1973; Mousa 1982), a flurry of archaeological activity in the region. F. J. Bliss began this new phase with an excursion around the desert side of the plateau in March of 1895, at which time he was able to clarify the considerable confusion which still existed regarding the relative positions of the upper branches of Wadi el-Mujib. Rudolf Brünnow and Alfred von Domaszewski made a systematic study of the Roman road system and associated fortifications in the course of three expeditions (1895, 1897, 1898). They published the results of their explorations in a three volume-work, *Die Provincia Arabia*, which included plans of the more prominent Nabataean, Roman, and Byzantine ruins, some of the earliest photographs of these sites, and sketch maps. Alois Musil had access to their notes, made several excursions of his own in 1896-1902, and devoted the first volume of his *Arabia Petraea* to the area east of the Dead Sea. Musil also prepared a 1:300,000 scale map which, although it still included some distortions, indicated the approximate locations of well over a hundred ruins between Wadi el-Mujib and Wadi el-Ḥasa.

Among other travelers who passed through the Kerak region during the decade which followed 1893 were H. Vincent, C. W. Wilson, A. Hornstein, L. Gautier, W. Libbey and F. E. Hoskins. George Adam Smith's report on his trip from Kerak to Madaba along the old Roman road in 1904 may be seen as a concluding statement to this exceedingly fruitful decade of exploration. As a result of this brief flurry of activity, the confusion regarding the topography of the region, resulting largely from misreadings of Burckhardt's notes and Tristram's misleading map, was cleared up. Several of the more prominent ruins, mostly from Nabataean and Roman times, had been planned and photographed. Traveler after traveler had observed that hundreds of other village and city ruins were scattered throughout the plateau, and Musil had noted many of these on his map. Otherwise, the ruins remained uncharted and unexplored. (See fig. 7 on page 28 for a summary list of 19th century travelers whose published accounts are indexed in our site descriptions. Unless otherwise indicated, the relevant publications are entered under the travelers' respective names in the bibliography at the end of this volume.)

The next 25 years, from 1905 to 1930, were as uneventful in terms of archaeological exploration of the Kerak plateau as the preceding decade had been active and fruitful. This would be expected, of course, in view of the turbulent political circumstances surrounding World War I. One item worthy of note was W. F. Albright's brief expedition in February of 1924 to the southern end of the Dead Sea by way of the Kerak plateau. Along the way he explored the surface ruins and pottery at Jebel Shiḥan, Faqu^c, Adir, er-Rabbah, Khanzirah and Kerak. At Adir, moreover, he identified what he thought to be an early Iron Age Moabite temple (Albright 1924).

A second brief flurry of archaeological exploration in the Kerak region occurred during the decade following 1930, initiated and inspired by the discovery that year, by Reginald Head of the newly established Transjordanian Department of Antiquities, of the Balu^c Stele. Political circumstances had once again brought a degree of security to the region, now a part of the Emirate of the Transjordan; and, even though the inscription on the stele could not be deciphered, this monument called attention again, as had the Mesha Inscription discovered over a half century earlier, to the abundant archaeological remains on the Kerak plateau. Horsfield and Vincent published a sketch plan of Khirbet Balu^c in 1932. The next year J. W. Crowfoot and Albright made soundings at Balu^c and Adir respectively, the latter (our Site 227) made conspicuous by three huge standing monoliths (Crowfoot 1934; Albright 1934; Cleveland 1960). Also in 1933, N. Glueck began his important survey of the southern Transjordan.

Actually Glueck spent only about three weeks in the area between Wadi el-Mujib and Wadi el-Ḥasa, and he visited fewer sites than Musil had charted on his map 30 years earlier. The new feature which characterized Glueck's work was not the thoroughness of his coverage, therefore, but the fact that he examined the surface pottery of a significant sampling of sites. Relying on the ceramic evidence, moreover, he developed far-reaching theories regarding settlement patterns in the southern Transjordan. Glueck's survey records and theories, published in the *Annual of the American Schools of Oriental Research* (vols. 14 and 18-19), have had considerable influence on the study of the history of ancient Palestine.

In 1935, while Glueck was still involved with his survey, M. -R. Savignac, Horsfield and Mrs. Horsfield examined the surface ruins at several sites south and southeast of Kerak (Savignac 1936: 247-55). The following year, 1936, Reginetta Canova and her husband joined the staff of the Italian hospital in Kerak (he as director) where they would remain in residence for more than two decades. She used the opportunity to search out and examine Roman and Byzantine inscriptions (mostly tombstones) in Kerak and the surrounding villages. In 1954 she published *Iscrizioni e monumenti protocristiani del Paese di Moab*, which provides full bibliography for inscriptions from the Kerak plateau which had been published earlier, the texts and photographs of more than 400 additional inscriptions and inscription fragments which she examined, plus descriptions and photographs of numerous architectual fragments.

Except for Canova's work, the Kerak plateau received little focused attention from archaeologists between the 1930s and 1976 when Olávarri conducted soundings at Khirbet el-Mdeineh (see below). During the interim, however, several important excavations were undertaken in the surrounding regions. One thinks especially of the excavations at Dhiban (Winnett and Reed 1964; Tushingham 1972; Morton 1957), ᶜAraᶜir (Olávarri 1965, 1969), Bab edh-Dhraᶜ (Lapp 1966; 1968a; 1968b; Rast and Schaub 1974; 1978; 1980; 1981), Tell Hesban (Boraas and Horn 1975; Boraas and Geraty 1976, 1978; Ibach 1987) and Buṣeirah (Bennett 1973; 1974; 1975).

Another important development during the interim was the preparation of detailed topographical maps of the Transjordan based on aerial photography. Specifically, 1:25,000 and 1:50,000 scale maps were produced during the 1950s and 1960s, respectively (North 1979: 143-49). The 1:50,000 map, prepared by the United States Army Map Service for the United States International Cooperation Agency and referred to below as the K737 series, served as the basic map for our survey. It has been reprinted several times with minor changes (see, e.g., the discussion of Sites 313 and 427). Unfortunately this map is not yet widely available.

Goals and Methods of the Survey

As will be apparent from the preceding summary of previous archaeological explorations in the survey area, archaeologists had tended to bypass the Kerak region before 1976, except for two brief flurries of activity—the first at the turn of the century when the Ottoman government reasserted its authority in the region for approximately a decade (Brünnow and Domaszewski, Musil), and the second in the early 1930s following the discovery of an ancient inscription at Khirbet Baluᶜ (Crowfoot and Albright, Glueck). Nineteenth century explorers could enter the region only at considerable personal risk. Three reasons may be given for the continued lack of attention by 20th century archaeologists: (1) Southern Transjordan remained politically volatile during the opening decades of this century. (2) Palestinian archaeologists during the present century have tended to focus attention on "tells," the stratified ruins of major ancient cities. However there are no prominent tells between Wadi el-Mujib and Wadi el-Ḥasa. (3) Archaeologists working in Palestine have also tended to concentrate west of the Jordan because of that region's biblical associations.

Thus, while the Kerak region has a long and rich history and is literally strewn with archaeological remains from virtually every period, the number, exact locations, and surface features of most of these sites remained largely unknown in 1976 when we began planning the survey reported here. Fieldwork was begun in July of 1978, which was the first of three main seasons (1978, 1979, 1982). Each season lasted approximately seven weeks, and the size of the survey team ranged from six in 1978 to twenty-five in 1982. Essentially, we worked the plateau from north to south:

1978	- Base camp at Kerak; concentrated on the sites reported by Glueck in the area between Wadi el-Mujib and the Kerak-Qaṭranah road.
1979	- Base camp at er-Rabbah; completed survey of the area between Wadi el-Mujib and the Kerak-Qaṭranah road.

1982 - Base camp at Kerak; surveyed between the Kerak-Qaṭranah road and Wadi el-Ḥasa.

1983 - Three members of the survey team (Miller, Mattingly, Rabadi) returned to reexamine and rephotograph some of the sites.

The primary goal of the survey was to develop an accumulative and comprehensive gazetteer of the archaeological sites on the plateau. This involved two tasks.

First, while the Kerak plateau had received relatively little focused attention from archaeologists before we began our work, its more conspicuous ruins had been reported and some of them had been described in considerable detail. Occasional mistakes had slipped into the reports, however, especially with regard to the locations and names of the sites reported. The first task of the survey, therefore, was to relocate the sites previously reported, establish their exact positions in terms of map grid coordinates, and disentangle the various names which had been recorded for them. Accordingly, before beginning fieldwork, we sifted through the published reports, catalogued the ruins mentioned, and made some tentative correlations with the sites marked on recent maps. Then, during the course of the fieldwork, we referred to these reports again and again, revised the tentative correlations when necessary, and gradually made additional correlations.

Confusion regarding site locations and names is especially noticeable in reports which were transcribed by editors unfamiliar with the region, as in the cases of Seetzen and Burckhardt whose records were published posthumously. Yet even in the cases of Musil and Glueck, some simple but crucial errors occurred––"northeast" sometimes was recorded for "northwest," for example, or was misread that way when the field notes were transcribed for publication. The fact that the earlier explorers were working without accurate maps (or no maps at all) created additional problems. When reporting sites, therefore, they located them in relative sequence. Each new site reported, in other words, was located in relation to the one mentioned previously (site x is a 10 minute walk from site y which is 20 minutes from site z, and so on). Glueck also followed this practice except that he estimated distances in kilometers. One mislocated site throws the whole sequence off. Finally, there are the inevitable problems with local names. Sometimes more than one ruin in the same general vicinity has the same name—e.g. Khirbet el-Medeiyineh, pronounced locally as Khirbet el-Mdeineh (Site 129 and Site 143), and Um el-Qleib (Site 21 and Site 31). Conversely, a single site may be known to the local inhabitants of the region by more than one name—e.g., el-Franj = esh-Shihabiyyah (Site 201) and Khirbet Ḥwale = Eshjar (Site 281)—or its name may change for some reason for another—e.g., Beit el-Kerm became Qaṣr Rabbah and eventually simply Qaṣr (Site 86). Examples may be cited, in fact, where a traveler recorded the same ruin twice under two different names, apparently having seen it from different directions on different occasions and deriving the names from different informants. This seems to have happened in the case of Jdeiyidah (Site 119), as explained below in the site description.

The second task associated with our primary purpose to produce a comprehensive gazetteer of the Kerak plateau was to search out sites which earlier investigators had missed. This required systematic coverage of the plateau which, as indicated above, we conducted in an essentially north-south direction. We worked in groups of four or five, each group with a vehicle, and each assigned to a sub-region for the particular field season. As each group worked through its sub-region, previously known sites (which usually were the more conspicuous ones) were examined first. Then the territory between the known sites was explored. As one might expect, the harvest of previously unrecorded sites consisted mostly of small ones with relatively inconspicuous surface remains. Specifically, we examined and assigned field numbers to more than 600 features during the process of the survey, ranging from extensive ruins to less prominent features such as isolated building ruins, cairns, small sherd scatters, old roadway beds, caves, cisterns and the like. Some of these were later combined—i.e., sometimes two or more features in close proximity are treated as a single site in this report. Others, nondescript stone heaps for the most part, are not included in this report because they seemed incidental to the purposes of a survey of this scope.

Throughout the plateau—in edges of the fields, on wadi slopes, on isolated knolls, on the outskirts of villages, wherever one looks—there are heaps of stones. These heaps may be relatively isolated or appear in large clusters (thus giving the impression of a khirbeh). Some of them are mounds (*rujūm*) which may be roughly circular or rectangular at the base and could possibly represent collapsed buildings; others are long lines of rubble which could represent collapsed walls. In many cases, however, they will have resulted from field clearing or some similar activity; and it is very difficult to tell which are which without excavating. Usually there is no pottery concentration around these stone heaps, although one can find a few sherds scattered about almost anywhere on the plateau. These stone heaps belong to the archaeological record, of course, whether they are collapsed structures or field clearings. Nevertheless, given the scope of the project, we decided to report only those which could be identified with some degree of certainty as structural remains or which were associated with a more than incidental scattering of sherds.

In conjunction with the primary goal of developing a comprehensive gazetteer of the archaeological sites on the Kerak plateau, we also prepared a descriptive report for each site and collected a sampling of surface pottery. One will notice some unevenness in the degree of detail in the site descriptions as published. As indicated above, the Kerak plateau is undergoing rapid modern development with the result that many of the ancient ruins are disappearing or becoming inaccessible—i.e., they are being systematically robbed for stone or being covered by modern settlements with concrete houses, paved streets, and the like. Beginning about the turn of the century, this process of modern development has increased momentum especially since the 1950s. Thus the 19th and early 20th century explorers saw in undisturbed condition ruins which today are covered over with villages. We, in turn, were able to examine sites which will be inaccessible to future investigators. Correspondingly, there is little or nothing to add regarding some of the major sites which were examined and described by earlier explorers before resettlement; other less prominent but previously unknown sites are treated more fully.

The survey team did not include specialists for prehistoric periods so we cannot claim any degree of comprehensiveness in that regard. When discovered, possible Paleolithic or Neolithic sites were recorded and reported to specialists in appropriate disciplines. Moreover, it will be obvious from the comments above that we make no claim to have recorded every feature or assemblage relevant to the historical periods. This was a general survey, it must be emphasized, an attempt to get better control of the vast amount of archaeological data scattered over some 875 square kilometers. Rather than rendering further survey projects in the region unnecessary, therefore, it is hoped that our work will provide the context for more concentrated examinations of smaller sections of the plateau.

Regarding the ceramic evidence, our intention was to produce a comprehensive archive of pottery from the Kerak plateau, a good sampling of sherds from every site between the Mujib and the Hesa, and make it available to interested scholars for examination and research. Our procedure was to collect sherds as evenly as possible over each site and then discarded at the site all those which seemed to have no potential diagnostic value. The remainder were read by Robin Brown, registered, and (except for a few additional discards in order to avoid extensive duplication) are available for examination and research at Emory University. Interested scholars should apply to the director of the Emory University Museum. The statistical results of Brown's readings are reported in the site descriptions in chapter II of this volume. A detailed discussion of the ceramic evidence which documents her readings is provided in chapter III. Chapter V provides site lists arranged according to the periods represented by their pottery. Many of the potentially diagnostic sherds could not be assigned with any degree of confidence to a particular period. These were registered and saved, however, and are designated in the site descriptions as UD (undetermined) or UDE (undetermined, but probably pre-Hellenistic).

It must be emphasized that Brown's readings are tentative and that the resulting list of sites according to periods should be used very cautiously. Ceramic typology is not an exact science to begin with, and surface sherds often are in poor condition, having been exposed to erosional processes. Two additional factors increase the uncertainties on the Kerak plateau. First, there have been relatively few excavations in southern Transjordan, to say nothing of the Kerak plateau itself, to provide control. This limited amount of comparative data increases the necessity to conjecture regarding particular variations that could be the result of regionally specific forms and fabrics. Second, particularly with regard to the Bronze and Iron Ages, the pottery collected in the course of our survey tended to be mostly utilitarian and domestic in nature. Specialized forms and imported wares so important for dating purposes generally are absent. Thus, while we distinguish in this report between "diagnostic" and "non-diagnostic" sherds, it must be understood that "diagnostic" does not necessarily mean "absolutely certain."

There are also other difficulties inherent to surface sherding in addition to the uncertainties of ceramic typology. The sherding of occupational sites inevitably varies in thoroughness, for example, depending on such factors as the amount of time applied in relation to the size of the site, control procedures, and even the time of day. Small sites with few surface sherds tend to be collected more thoroughly than large sites with heavy coverage; and anyone with field experience knows that the best work is not done when a survey team is tired and laboring under the hot, summer, mid-day sun. Intensive sherding according to grids is an attempt to overcome some of the variables. But random grid sherding would not have been practical for our purpose, which was to gain an overview of the main archaeological features of a large and relatively unexplored area in a reasonably short length of time, and it is not useful at all for dealing with ancient sites which are currently occupied. Obviously we disagree with purists who insist that sites which cannot be sherded in accordance with random grid methodology should be left undisturbed for future archaeologists. Whatever disturbance our sampling might have caused is incidental compared to the disturbance which is taking place daily due to rapid development in the area. Moreover, again because of rapid development, future archaeologists will not have access to most of these sites.

Difficulties such at those described above explain why the same site sherded more than once (sometimes by the same persons) may produce different results. Thus S. Mittmann found no pre-Byzantine pottery at Kathrabba when he sherded the site in 1979, although he was convinced on other grounds that it must have been occupied during the Iron Age and by the Nabataeans (Mittmann 1982). We did find both Iron Age and Nabataean sherds (admittedly only one or two "diagnostic" examples of each) when we worked Kathrabba more intensively in 1982. It should be kept in mind, moreover, that while the surface sherds of a site obviously relate to its occupational history, the one does not necessarily correspond exactly to the other. A number of clearly diagnostic sherds from a period may be taken as good evidence that the site was occupied during that period, but the reverse is not necessarily true. The situation at el-ᶜAl is a case in point. Soundings at the site in 1962 produced Early and Middle Bronze Age pottery (Reed 1972). Yet a surface sherding of the site in 1973 by the Hesban team produced nothing earlier than Iron I (Ibach 1987: 11). Neither is there necessarily a direct correlation between the number of sites in a region which produce pottery from a given period and the population density of the period. The settlement patterns in some periods may have tended toward large urban centers with relatively few outlying hamlets, for example, in contrast to other periods which favored a network of medium-size villages. Theoretically the latter situation would produce more sites for the surveyors statistics. All of this is not to suggest that results of surface sherding are useless, but rather to warn against drawing overly precise conclusions from this sort of evidence.

Neighboring Archaeological Projects

As indicated above, the survey focused on the plateau between Wadi el-Mujib and Wadi el-Ḥasa—that is, from the southern rim of Wadi el-Mujib to the northern rim of Wadi el-Ḥasa, and from the ragged edge of the Dead Sea escarpment to an essentially north-south line indicated by (a) the continuation of the rim of Wadi el-Mujib, following its main southeastern branch (Wadi en-Nukheilah, Wadi Lejjun) to Khirbet el-Mdeineh (Site 143) at the juncture of Wadi ed-Mukheiris and Wadi ed-Dabbah; (b) the track which leads southward from Lejjun to the southeastern entrance of Fajj el-ᶜUseikir; and (c) the track which leads from Rujm Khashm eṣ-Ṣirah (Site 370) at the southeastern end of the Fajj via Khirbet el-Mḍeibiᶜ (Site 435) to Mḥai (Site 436). Several neighboring archaeological projects should be mentioned. These neighboring

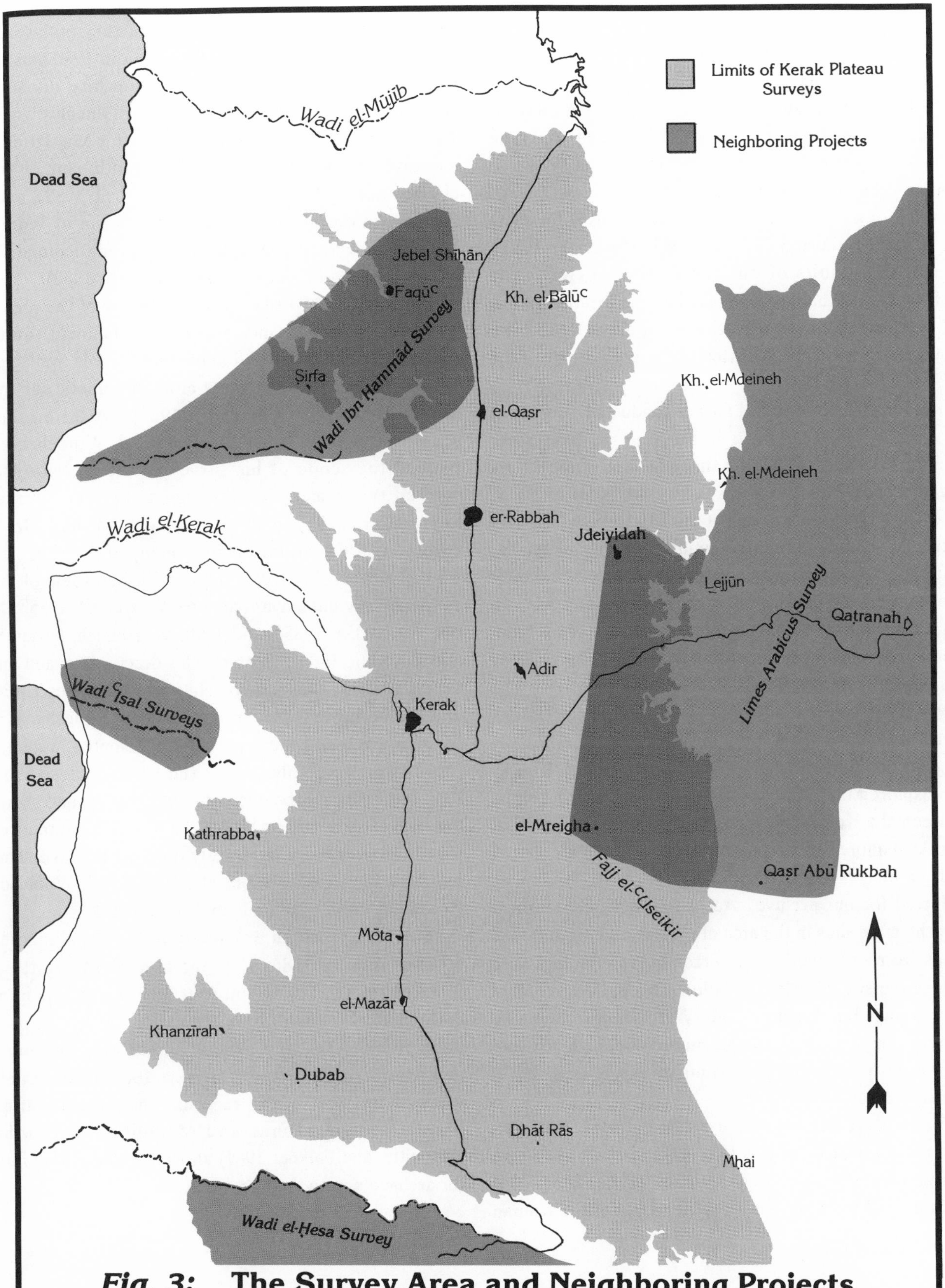

Fig. 3: **The Survey Area and Neighboring Projects**

Maps by D.Cal's Studio

projects provide a basis for comparison and control of our work. Our project, in turn, serves as a central geographical link between all of them (see fig. 3).

In 1976, a Spanish team directed by Emilio Olávarri conducted soundings at Khirbet el-Mdeineh (our Site 129), an early Iron Age fortification overlooking Wadi el-Mujib on the northeastern edge of the plateau. Olávarri returned for a two-week season of excavations at the same site in 1982 (Olàvarri 1977-78, 1983; Menéndez 1983). One of the results of our survey was to clarify the confusion which had arisen regarding the location of this Mdeineh in relation to five other sites, all with the same name, which had been reported in the region east of the Dead Sea (Miller 1990).

Also in 1976, S. Thomas Parker conducted a survey of the Roman *Limes Arabicus* in the Transjordan. Since then he has concentrated on that segment of the *Limes Arabicus* between Wadi el-Mujib and Wadi el-Ḥasa. Specifically, Parker excavated at the late Roman legionary fortress of Lejjun and made soundings at several smaller contempory fortifications in an effort to understand their strategic relationship to the main fortress. Also in connection with the Lejjun project, members of his team conducted intensive surface surveys of the Lejjun vicinity and desert fringe (see esp. Parker 1986b; 1987b). The survey of the Lejjun vicinity, led by Frank Koucky (1987b), overlaps somewhat the area designated for our survey —i.e., in addition to the immediate Lejjun vicinity, Koucky also explored the region southwest of Fityan and Lejjun, between the Kerak-Qaṭranah road and Fajj el-ᶜUseikir. Koucky explored this area of overlap prior to us, shared with us his results, and gave us the pottery which he collected for our archive. Accordingly, we reexamined only the main sites in the area of overlap and, for the sites which we reexamined, have correlated his findings with ours in the site descriptions below. Note, however, that the readings for Koucky's pottery provided in these site descriptions are *our* readings, made independently and prior to his published report (compare esp. Koucky 1987b appendix 1).

Fauzi Zayadine excavated a 1st century C.E. Nabataean tomb near Dhat Ras (Site 427) in 1968. Siegfried Mittmann (1982) and Linda Jacobs (1983) conducted separate and brief surveys along the route of the Roman road which followed Wadi ᶜIsal from the southwestern corner of the plateau to the Dead Sea in 1979 and 1981 respectively. Although not actually touching our survey area, mention should be made also of Glueck's work at Tannur in 1937 (Glueck 1965), Burton MacDonald's intensive survey of a segment of the south bank of Wadi el-Ḥasa during 1979-83 (MacDonald et al. 1988), and of the excavations at Leḥun, on the north rim of Wadi el-Mujib, conducted by Denyse Homès-Fredericq and Paul Naster (Homès-Fredericq and Naster 1979; 1980).

During the 1979 season of our survey of the plateau, we made a reconnaissance of Wadi Ibn Hammad, saw that it had much potential, and made our records available to Udo Worschech who began a more systematic survey of this wadi in 1983 (Worschech 1984). After an initial season of work in Wadi Ibn Hammad, Worschech expanded the scope of his survey to the plateau itself, worked two seasons (July-August, 1984 and August-September, 1985) in territory which we had already covered in 1978-79, reexamined many of the sites which we had already sherded, and has published some of them as "previously unknown" (see esp. Worschech 1985b: 173, but also 1985a, 1985c, and 1990; Worschech, Rosenthal, and Zayadine 1986). Worschech's descriptions and numbering of these sites are correlated with our descriptions and numbering in the site reports below. Typically, as will be seen, we found more periods represented among the sherds which we collected at the various sites than he reported. This may be due to the fact that we had sherded the sites soon before he visited them or that we tended to sherd the sites more intensively than did he. Worschech has since begun excavations at Kh. el-Baluᶜ (Worschech, Rosenthal, and Zayadine 1986; Worschech 1990).

Beginning with an examination of several medieval Islamic sites in 1986, J. Johns and A. McQuitty are focusing on Khirbet Tadun (our Site 56) and its immediate vicinity for intense investigation. It has been our hope all along that our general survey would encourage and provide a framework for more focused and intense work of this sort in the region. Their results after a second season (Johns and McQuitty 1989; Johns, McQuitty, and Falkner 1989) anticipate an exciting future for archaeology on the Kerak plateau.

Chapter II

THE SITES

by

J. Maxwell Miller, et al.

Explanation of the Site Descriptions

As each new site was explored in the course of the survey, it was assigned a four-digit *field number*. Those explored during the 1978 season have field numbers in the 8000s; those explored during 1979 have field numbers in the 9000s; those explored in 1982 have field numbers in the 2000s. Sites with field numbers in the 8000s and 9000s are located north of the Kerak-Qaṭrana road, since that was the area worked during 1978 and 1979. Sites with field numbers in the 2000s usually are located south of the Kerak-Qaṭrana road with those in the 2000-2300s situated southwest of Kerak and with those in the 2300-2600s situated southeast of Kerak. Other than that, the field numbers do not reflect any geographical pattern. Neither do they represent an unbroken sequence.

It is necessary to preserve the field numbers because they are basic to our field notes, pottery registration, and published preliminary reports. In order to render this final report more easily understandable, however, we have assigned each site a second number, a *site number*. The site numbers follow a geographical pattern (from northwest to southeast), are assigned in unbroken sequence (1 to 443), and are plotted on the map of the survey area (which itself is subdivided into 14 sections; see figs. 4 and 5). The individual sites are treated below in the order of their site numbers.

Each description begins with a three-line heading, the first line of which indicates the site number and the name of the site, if we could determine a name. The second line indicates the map section on which the particular site is to be found and its field number. The third line indicates the Palestinian Grid (PG) and Universal Transverse Mercator Grid (UTMG) coordinates. The site names are transliterated as accurately as possible to reflect local pronunciation in the heading and in the site lists at the end of this volume. Otherwise we do not distinguish between short and long vowels when transliterating Arabic place names. Also the transcriptions are not consistent in their treatment of the reduced vowel. The Palestinian Grid and Universal Transverse Mercator Grid coordinates are abbreviated to the last three digits with the east coordinate given first and the north coordinate given second (e.g., the PG coordinates for Kh. Shiḥan, 220.1 east by 087.7 north, become PG 20.1/87.7; the UTMG coordinates, 760.4 east by 475.2 north, become UTMG 60.4/75.2).

Following the heading, the site descriptions typically consist of three paragraphs. The first characterizes the visible archaeological features in a word or phrase, locates the site in relation to the main towns and roads of the plateau (the kilometer estimates are "as the crow flies"), indicates whether the site is marked on the series K737 map, and reports our findings regarding the surface pottery. The second paragraph summarizes references to the site and comments regarding it by early travelers and provides other pertinent bibliographical information. The third paragraph reports our own findings. Exceptions to this three-paragraph format occur with sites which are being reported for the first time and require little or no comment beyond the "overview" information.

Listed below are terms and phrases often used to characterize the sites. These should be understood very loosely. Moreover, they pertain primarily to what one

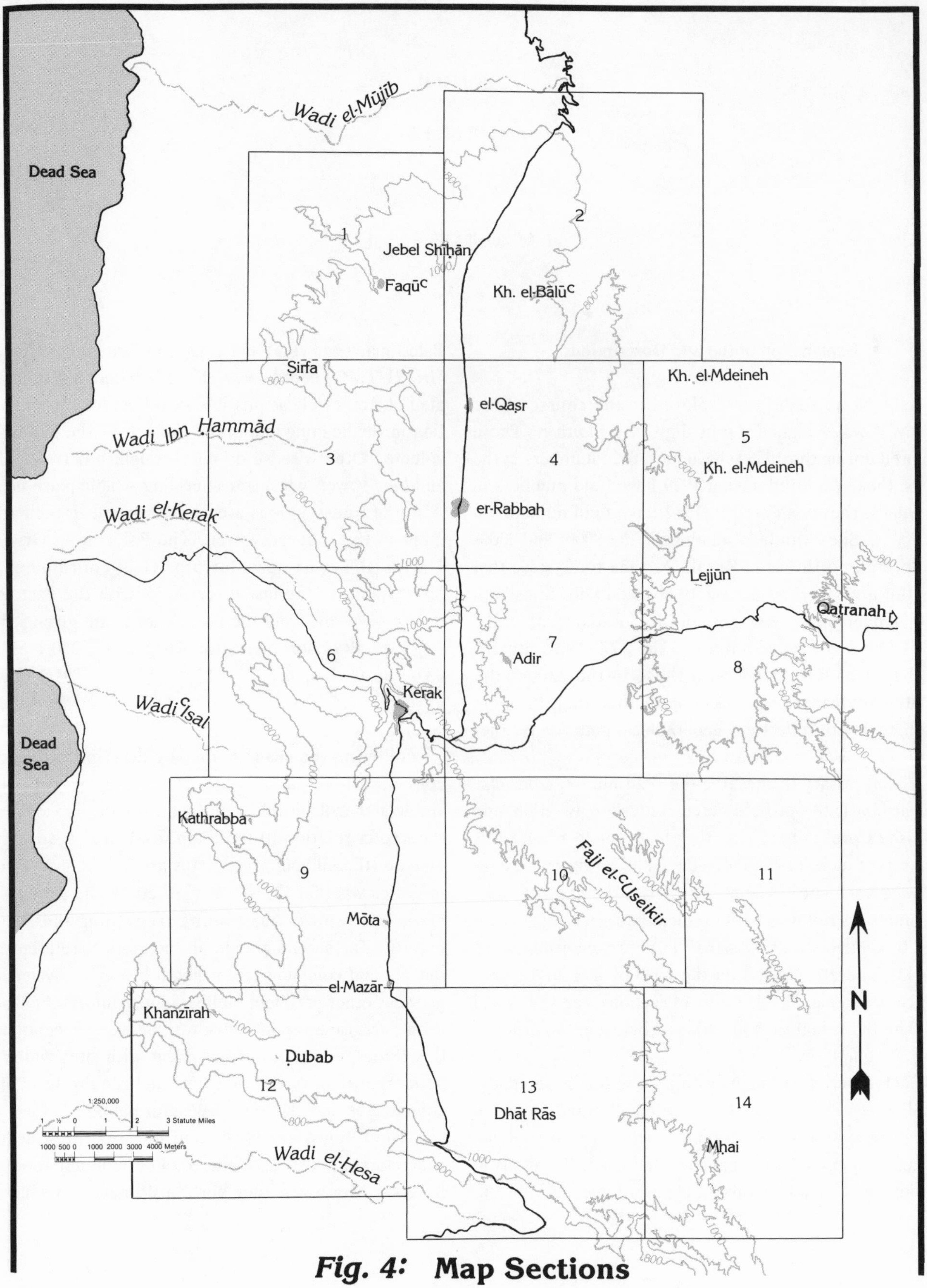

Fig. 4: **Map Sections**

Maps by D.Cal's Studio

Fig. 5: **Satellite Photograph of the Kerak Plateau**

sees on the surface of the ground, which may have little bearing on the overall archaeological profile of the site—e.g., a single building ruin from the Ottoman period may be the most prominent feature of a site which supported large settlements during earlier periods. Thus any realistic assessment of the character of a site must take the ceramic evidence into account as well as surface ruins, and even then any certain conclusions must await excavation.

Cairns - Small stone heaps, usually slightly oval in shape and found mostly on knolls and ridges along the edges of the plateau. Typically there is no pottery. Many, perhaps most, of these represent bedouin burials.

Partitioned cairns - A particular type of cairn often found among those described above, but usually larger, composed of more massive stones, round rather than oval, and with clearly discernible walls. The walls consist of a carefully laid circle of large stones bisected by a line of still larger stones. Typically these partitioned cairns are 5 to 8 m in diameter. Often there are double, concentric circles, possibly representing the interior and exterior faces of a single circular wall. The bisecting line may consist of a single long block or of two long stone blocks laid end to end. Also there may be more than one cross wall. These partitioned cairns appear to be much older than the bedouin cairns described above. Specifically, they seem to correspond to Koucky's "R-III Ring Structures" (Koucky 1987b:58-61; see also Clark 1979:57-77, who suspects them to be Chalcolithic, and Worschech 1985a:28-31, who suspects MB). Usually there is no surface pottery.

Stone heap - A pile of stones, usually larger than a cairn, which may or may not represent the collapsed remains of a building. The Arabic term *rujm* refers to stone heaps of all sorts, including cairns. See comments on page 18.

Building ruin - Although usually presenting itself as a heap of stones, a building ruin has clearly discernible wall lines suggesting a single structure. We also use the phrase "ruined structure," especially when remnants of walls rise above the ground and tumbled stones.

Khirbeh - Visible ruins usually indicating more than a single structure and sometimes representing a settlement site of considerable size.

Settlement site - A site, not necessarily with visible ruins, but presenting evidence of having supported settlements in times past. Usually this is indicated by an abundance of surface pottery, often from various periods. Many settlement sites support modern towns and villages.

Wall lines - Segments of stone walls visible at ground level or standing one or more courses above the ground. Wall lines often are not traceable to the extent that one can identify or understand the structures to which they pertain.

Stone enclosure - Usually a single line of stones enclosing an area. In some cases, the stones may have served as the foundation for a mud brick wall.

As emphasized on chapter I of this volume, the pottery readings reported in the site descriptions below should be regarded as tentative. The total number of sherds collected at a site is reported first, then the separation of diagnostic sherds according to periods, then the number of sherds registered UD ("undetermined") or UDE ("undetermined" but almost certainly pre-Hellenistic). The latter two categories represent sherds which we are unable to assign to a period, but which were registered and saved because of their potential deagnostic value. Since many sherds are not useful for dating purposes and not all unidentified sherds were registered, the sum of the diagnostics, UDEs, and UDs reported for a site usually will be less than the total sherds collected.

See fig. 6 for the chronology and corresponding culture-historical period abbreviations used in the site descriptions. See fig. 7 for a summary list of 19th and early 20th travelers whose published reports are indexed in the site descriptions. Bibliographical entries normally begin with the travelers name, followed by the name of the site under consideration exactly as he transliterated it, followed by the relevant page references in his travel report. Unless otherwise indicated, the relevant publication is entered under the traveler's name in the bibliography at the end of this volume.

Fig. 6: Chronological Divisions and Abbreviations*

Chalco	CHALCOLITHIC	4500-3300 B.C.E.
EB	EARLY BRONZE	3300-1950
EB I	Early Bronze I	3300-2900
EB II	Early Bronze II	2900-2300
EB III	Early Bronze III	2300-2100
EB IV	Early Bronze IV	2100-1950
MB	MIDDLE BRONZE	1950-1550
	Middle Bronze I	1950-1750
	Middle Bronze II	1750-1550
LB	LATE BRONZE	1550-1200
	Late Bronze I	1550-1400
	Late Bronze II	1400-1200
IR	IRON	1200-300
IR I	Iron I	1200-900
IR II	Iron II	900-332
Pers.	Iron IIC/Persian	540-332
Hell	HELLENISTIC	332-64
Nab	NABATAEAN	300 B.C.E.-106 C.E.
Rom	ROMAN	64 B.C.E.-324 C.E.
ERom	Early Roman	64 B.C.E.-135 C.E.
LRom	Late Roman	135-324 C.E.
Byz	BYZANTINE	324-640 C.E.
EByz	Early Byzantine	324-491
LByz	Late Byzantine	491-640
EIsl	EARLY ISLAMIC	640-1174
Um	Umayyad	640-750
Abb	Abbasid	750-969
Fat	Fatimid	969-1071
	Seljuq-Zengid	1071-1174
LIsl	LATE ISLAMIC	1174-1918
A/M	Ayyubid/Mamluk	1174-1516
Ay	Ayyubid	1174-1263
Mam	Mamluk	1263-1516
Ott	Ottoman	1516-1918
EOtt	Early Ottoman	1516-1703
LOtt	Late Ottoman	1703-1918
Mod	MODERN	1918-present

*All of these dates are approximate, including the more precise dates indicated for IR II and following. The latter represent political chronology and must be regarded as "guideline" dates at best for the corresponding pottery types.

Fig. 7: 19th and Early 20th Century Travelers Cited in the Site Descriptions

The travel reports of the following 19th and early 20th century travelers are indexed in the site descriptions. Typically an entry begins with the name of the traveler, followed by the name of the site under consideration as he identified and transliterated it, followed by the page references in his travel report. *Note that the dates given in the list below are for the year(s) in which the particular traveler visited the Kerak plateau*, not the date of publication for the travel report. Unless indicated otherwise, the relevant publication is entered under the traveler's name in the bibliography.

1805	Ulrich Jasper Seetzen (Page references attributed to Seetzen in the site descriptions are to the 1854-55 publication listed under his name in the bibliography.)
1812	Johann Ludwig Burckhardt
1818	Charles Leonard Irby and James Mangles (T. Leigh, who accompanied Irby and Mangles, provided a less detailed account in G. W. Macmichael, *Journey from Moscow to Constantinople*.)
1840	Henry Layard
1848	William F. Lynch
1851	Félicien de Saulcy
1858	J.R. Roth
1864	A. Duc de Luynes (Page references attributed to Duc de Luynes in the site descriptions are to volume 1 of the publication listed under his name in the bibliography.)
1866	C. Mauss and H. Sauvaire (Page references are to their account in Bulletin de la Société de Geographie)
1867	F. A. Klein (Kline also traveled part of the way with Tristram's party in 1872.)
1870	E. H. Palmer
1872	Henry Baker Tristram
1873	Charles Hamilton
1875	Charles M. Doughty
1890	Gray Hill (returned in 1895)
1895	Frederick Jones Bliss
	Rudolf Ernst Brünnow and Alfred von Domaszewski (returned in 1897 and 1898)
	Alexander Hornstein
1896	Alois Musil (returned 1897, 1898, 1900, 1901 and 1902)
	Siméon Vailhé
	M. -J. Lagrange
	Hughes Vincent
1899	C. W. Wilson (Unless otherwise indicated, references to Wilson in the site descriptions are to C. W. Wilson)
	Lucien Gautier
1901	Johannes Bacher
1902	William Libby and Franklin E. Hoskins
1904	George Adam Smith

Site descriptions

Site 1
(Map section 1; field no. 9161)
PG: 20.6/92.0; UTMG: 60.8/79.5

Caves near the northern rim of the plateau, slightly less than 3 km NNW of Misᶜar. 13 caves were counted within a range of ca. 100 m along the west side of Wadi el-Mdeineh (a tributary to Wadi ed-Dafali). Remains of walls along the sides and fronts of several of the caves indicate that they may have served as dwellings in the not too distant past. Now they appear to be used as sheep-folds. No surface pottery.

Site 2
(Map section 1; field no. 9122)
PG: 18.3/91.3; UTMG: 58.4/78.6

Stone heap with no discernible architectural features on a broad terrace with cultivated fields which slope down to the rim of Wadi el-Mujib, ca. 4 km WNW of Misᶜar. 45 sherds were collected, including: Nab 4; UDE 1; UD 4.

Site 3 - **ᶜAwarwareh**
(Map section 1; field no. 8013)
PG: 19.0/91.4; UTMG: 59.2/78.6

Heavy sherd scatter with occasionally discernible wall lines on a terrace which overlooks Wadi ed-Dafali from the southwest, ca. 2 km northwest of Kh. Freiwan. The site, as indicated by the sherd coverage, is ca. 60 x 150 m, oriented parallel to the wadi. 864 sherds were collected, including: EB 10; EB II-III 10; MB 5; LB 7; Pers(?) 1; Nab 6; A/M 1; LIsl 4; UD 16.

This site was identified to us as ᶜAwarwareh by informants in Misᶜar, conflicting with Glueck's report which locates a site by that name, Umm ᶜAwarwareh/#124, WSW of Kh. Freiwan (our Site 5). "About four kilometres west-southwest of Freiwân is Rujm Umm ᶜAwarwareh (?), where there are some indistinguishable small ruins and a large cistern" (1934: 58). Probably Glueck did not actually visit the site, which is reached by a long and difficult trail along the south bank of Wadi ed-Dafali. The distance from Kh. Freiwan indicated above, 2 km, is "as the crow flies." 4 km would be a more reasonable estimate for the actual walking distance. For the "ḫirbet el-Mdejjene" reported in this vicinity by Musil, (19, 137) see Worschech, Rosenthal and Zayadine (1986: 285-87, 290) and Miller (1990).

Site 4 - **Um eṭ-Ṭawābīn**
(Map section 1; field no. 9117)
PG: 18.6/90.3; UTMG: 58.8/77.7

Cave and stone-lined pit, possibly a lime kiln, ca. 2 km west of Khirbet Freiwan. 93 sherds were collected, including: Nab 5; ERom 1; LRom 1; UD 7.

Ruins of two crudely-built houses, probably no earlier than the Ottoman period, mark this site. As indicated by the sparse scatter of sherds around the buildings, however, the site was active to some degree as early as Nabataean and Roman times. In an orchard east of the houses there is a cave with walls extending in straight lines to either side of the entrance. Ca. 42 m east of the cave (90 m from houses) is a stone-lined pit which approximates a circle and is about 3.5 m in diameter. The top of the pit is at ground level and it is ca. 1 m (4-5 courses) deep. A break in the circle on the northwest side with a trench leading to it may have been an entrance. A local informant explained that the pit was a "Roman lime kiln," which may be an essentially correct interpretation—if we take into account that the local inhabitants of the region tend to refer to anything old as "Roman."

Site 5 - **Freiwān**
(Map section 1; field no. 8012)
PG: 20.7/90.1; UTMG: 60.8/77.6

Settlement site indicated by building ruins, caves and cisterns on a slope overlooking Wadi ed-Dafali, slightly less than 2 km WNW of Misᶜar. 263 sherds were collected, including: MB/LB 4; Nab 2; Nab/ERom 4; A/M 1; LIsl 70; UD 4.

See Musil: ḫirbet Frêwân (137, 376); Glueck: Freiwân/#123 (1934: 58); and Worschech: Freiwān/#83 (1985b: 171-72). Glueck reported a few sherds from the same periods that he had identified at nearby Misᶜar

(Early Bronze and Middle Bronze I, Early Iron, Nabataean, early Arabic), but noted that the site was "so covered with modern débris that it was impossible to find much. It may well be that the earlier sherds found at Freiwân were carried over, somehow or other, from Kh. Mis^car." Worschech, who visited the site after we were there, reported "Nab, Nab-R, ER, LR, Byz, and Ayy/Mam pottery."

Specifically, the Freiwan slope overlooks Wadi ed-Dafali (Glueck identifies this as Wadi Jedeirah, but the K737 map places Wadi Jedeirah further west) from the southwest and is bounded on the southeast by a lesser wadi (Glueck's Wâdī Freiwân) which joins the Dafali between Kh. Freiwan and Misᶜar. Collapsed ruins of some 10-12 individual buildings can be identified, several of them incorporating caves and cave cisterns. The buildings were small, apparently dwellings; the largest had no more than six rooms. No doubt these ruins represent a small village and are to be associated with the Late Islamic pottery which dominates. However, the site will have had an earlier settlement history also, as the surface pottery also indicates.

Site 6
(Map section 1; field no. 9119)
PG: 15.7/89.5; UTMG: 56.2/76.9

Partitioned cairn on the northwestern edge of the plateau, ca. 3 km NNW of Faquᶜ. Two concentric circles of stones are clearly visible. The external circle measures 8 m in diameter and is preserved one course above the ground; the internal circle is 4.5 m in diameter with two courses still in place.

Site 7
(Map section 1; field no. 9120)
PG: 17.6/89.6; UTMG: 57.8/76.9

Stone heap with cistern nearby (recently cleared of fill) on the southwest bank of Wadi Juheirah, near the northwestern edge of the plateau. 68 sherds were collected from around the stone heap, including: Ott 23; UD 2.

Site 8
(Map section 1; field no. 9121)
PG: 20.4/89.3; UTMG: 60.5/76.8

Rectangular configuration of stones (6 x 4 m; oriented east-west) ca. 1.5 km southwest of Misᶜar and immediately north of the track from Misᶜar to Faquᶜ. Although we could not determine whether the configuration represents a platform base or an enclosure, its rectangular shape and the surrounding surface pottery suggest some sort of structure rather than field clearing. 47 sherds were collected, including: Nab 1; LIsl 4; UD 1.

Site 9
(Map section 1; field no. 9118)
PG: 15.4/88.3; UTMG: 55.4/75.6

Partitioned cairn on a narrow ridge which extends west from the main plateau, ca. 2 km NNW of Faquᶜ. Two concentric circles of stones are clearly visible representing either a double circular wall foundation or a single wall with distinct external and internal faces. Large rough stones were used. The external circle measures 6 m in diameter and is preserved one course above the ground; the internal circle measures 4 m in diameter and is preserved two courses. 22 sherds were collected, all registered UD.

Site 10
(Map section 1; field no. 9095)
PG: 17.6/88.3; UTMG: 57.8/75.7

Isolated stone heap ca. 2 km northeast of Faquᶜ. The heap is ca. 10 m in diameter and includes some well-dressed stones. 5 sherds were collected, including: LIsl 3.

Site 11 - Abū Ḥalīb
(Map section 1; field no. 9116)
PG: 17.7/88.4; UTMG: 58.0/75.9

Sherd scatter ca. 2 km northeast of Faquᶜ. 44 sherds were collected, including: ERom 4; LIsl 7; UD 2.

Abu Ḥalib ("Father of Milk") is a flat area of exposed bedrock on top of a hill and surrounded by wheat fields. A large cistern cut into the bedrock has a basalt head. There are also cupmarks in the bedrock as well as a cave with an artificially enlarged entrance. The cave may have served as a tomb.

Site 12 - **Kh. Shīḥān**
(Map section 1; field no. 8020, 8021, 9227, 9229, 9238)
PG: 20.1/87.7; UTMG: 60.4/75.2

Building ruin with out-lying walls on the summit of Jebel Shiḥan, which itself is a conspicuous mountain dominating the region between Wadi el-Mujib and el-Qaṣr. Additional occupational remains are scattered along the slopes (especially the southern and eastern slopes) of the mountain. Marked Khirbat Shīḥān on the K737 map. 960 sherds were collected, including: MB(?) 1; IR 5; Nab 17; ERom 2; LRom 4; Byz (15); LByz 15; Abb 1; Fat(?) 1; A/M 34; LIsl 34; OTT 4; Mod 35; UDE 9; UD 28; 6 tesserae.

See Seetzen: Schihhân (411, 16); Burckhardt: Djebel Shyhhan (375); Irby and Mangles: Sheikh Harn (141); de Saulcy: Schihan (280-84); de Luynes: Schihân (170); Palmer: Shíhán (1871b: 482-83, 91; 1871a: 67); Tristram: Shihan (136-39); Bliss: Jebel Shihan (216, 221); Gautier: schihān (120); Libby and Hoskins: Shihan (319); Brünnow and Domaszewski: Šîḥân (I: 46, 52-53); Musil: ḳar^ca Šîḥân (7, 16, 31, 34-36, 124-25, 137, 204, 248, 267, 303, 306, 339, 373, 375-76); Smith: Ḳări^cat Shīḥān (371-72); Albright (1924: 9-10); Worschech: Shiḥān/#81 (1985b: 171; 1990: 13-15). Seetzen's "Kréha" (411) may be Kh. Shiḥan (compare the forms of the name given by Musil and Smith), but more likely is el-Kharya^c (Site 78).

As is obvious from the numerous citations above, the Jebel Shiḥan ruin has been visited and described many times. De Saulcy, Brünnow and Domaszewski, and Smith provide the fullest descriptions. Glueck did not mention it, which is surprising in view of the fact that he reported several other sites in the immediate vicinity. Glueck's Kh. eḍ-Ḍribbân/#117 (1934: 57) must have been on or near the eastern slope of Jebel Shiḥan, for example, and probably is to be equated with el-Jad^cah (Site 30). Worschech, who sherded the site after we were there, reported "(Ir I?), Ir II, Nab, Nab-R, ER, LR, Byz, Um, Ayy/Mam, Tesserae."

The main Jebel Shiḥan ruin (field no. 8020) consists of a large building complex on the southeast side of the summit with wall lines extending westward to form enclosures or courtyards. Brünnow and Domaszewski provided a plan, which may be compared now with a more recent drawing by Worschech. The ancient wall lines can be traced only partially today because of modern building activities on the site. Specifically, the western and southern walls of the building measure 44 m and 52.7 m respectively; the eastern and northern walls are ca. 47 and 45 m respectively. (These are approximations since the northeast corner is not clearly defined). The north and south walls are parallel; but the east and west walls not entirely so. The western wall of the building is especially thick, measuring ca. 7 m wide. Projecting westward from approximately midway along the western wall is what appears to have been some sort of entrance structure. This structure is 9.4 m wide and projects 10.5 m to the west. Remains of what may have been a tower are discernible at the southwest corner of the building and perhaps one also at the southeast corner. There are some column fragments, but none *in situ*. A room in the northeast quadrant of the building measures ca. 7 x 20 m, and one in the southeast quadrant ca. 8 x 8 m. We observed nothing that could be taken for an "apse of a small church" (reported by Bliss), unless the projection which we interpreted as an entrance structure could have been an apse. Neither did we find the Ionic capital mentioned by several travelers, though there is a pillar or column, possibly part of a Roman milestone, standing upright inside the building ruin.

On the east slope of Jebel Shiḥan, immediately west of the Kerak-Dhiban highway, are the foundation remains of some 15 to 20 crudely constructed buildings (field no. 8021) surrounded by an abundance of surface pottery. These buildings are founded on bedrock, several of them incorporate caves, and some of them appear to have reused stones from earlier, more massively built structures. The pottery is predominantly Late Islamic and there is nothing to suggest that the buildings date any earlier. However, earlier periods are surprisingly well represented in the pottery which we collected in this area, many of the sherds no doubt having eroded down the slope from the main site above. Specifically, from an area measuring ca. 330 m (N-S) by 230 m (E-W) on the east slope of Jebel Shiḥan, we collected 1345 sherds including: Chalco 1; IR II 1; Hell 1; Nab 23; ERom 3; Byz 21; EByz

8; LByz 8; LIsl 132; A/M 16; Abb 6; Fat(?) 4; A/M 30; Mod 8; UDE 10; UD 170; also tesserae.

A cistern and caves with remains of walls and doorways at their entrances—i.e., showing evidence of human occupation although they serve now as sheepfolds—are to be found on the south slope of Jebel Shiḥan (field no. 9227) not far from the summit. Again, the volume of the pottery is far more impressive than the architectural remains and probably is to be understood largely as erosion from above. 600 sherds were collected in an area measuring ca. 150 m (E-W) by 75 m (N-S). These sherds included: MB 1; IR 2; IR I 1; IR II 2; Pers(?) 1; Nab 13; ERom 2; EByz 4; LByz 3; Um 2; LIsl 73; A/M 34; Mod 7; UD 9; UDhandle 6; and tesserae.

West of the cistern and caves mentioned above—i.e., on the southwest slope of Jebel Shiḥan ca. 400 m from the summit—are the black basalt remains of a building compound (field no. 9229). Situated in a rocky area of the hillside, the compound measures ca. 27 x 29 m. Its walls, which vary in width up to 0.5 m, are still standing three courses high in some places. Parts of the building serve now as a sheepfold. Other wall lines are noticeable at ground level outside the compound. 145 sherds were collected from around the compound including: Byz 2; LIsl 19; A/M 13.

Approximately midway between the compound reported above and the summit of Jebel Shiḥan is another cistern and two caves surrounded by an oval stone wall, apparently a sheepfold of recent vintage (field no. 9238). Immediately north of the enclosure are the barely distinguishable walls of a structure, ca. 28 x 24 m, which seems to have included at least two rooms and a courtyard. The courtyard encompasses a third cave. 345 sherds were collected in this area including: LB 1; Nab 15; Byz 6; EByz 1; LIsl 1; UD 3; UDhandle 10.

Site 13 - **Rujm Um Ḥlāl**
(Map section 1; field no. 8015)
PG: 16.4/86.9; UTMG: 56.7/74.3

Building ruin with out-lying wall lines and cisterns immediately north of Faqu[c] and separated by a branch of Wadi Muneikhirin. 497 sherds were collected, including: LByz 36; LIsl 1; and 34 tesserae.

See Glueck: Rujm Umm el-Ḥelâl/#125. "There are some small ruined buildings there and a masonry *birkeh* at the northeast corner of the site. A large white-washed tomb distinguishes the site. Several Nabataean sherds were found and quantities of Byzantine and medieval Arabic sherds" (1934: 58-59).

Situated on one of the highest points in the region are the wall remains of an east-west oriented building which measured 30 x 30 m. The walls of the building itself are ca. 1 m thick. Two other walls ca. 0.5 m thick extend from corners of the building. One attaches to the northeast corner, extends eastward, and can be traced ca. 20 m. The other attaches to the southeast corner, extends southward, and can be traced some 30 m. These may have been courtyards and/or adjacent sections of the building. In addition to a cistern ca. 45 m northeast of the building (probably the *birkeh* mentioned by Glueck), there is another cistern near the center of the building. The tomb, a typical "weli," is 10 m east of the building at its southeast corner.

Site 14 - **Faqū[c]**
(Map section 1; field no. 8016)
PG: 16.5/86.5; UTMG: 56.8/73.8

Modern town on an ancient settlement site at the head of Wadi Muneikhirin. Marked Faqū on the K737 map. 962 sherds were collected, including: IR 2; IR II 4; Nab 9; ERom 4; Byz 15; EByz 2; LByz 7; LIsl 32; Fat(?) 1; A/M 2; Mod 6; UDE 1; UD 20.

See Seetzen: Wáphakuéh (416); de Saulcy: Kharbet-Fouqaûa (278-89); de Luynes: Fiqou and Redjom-el-Aàbed (170-71); Palmer: Fugú[c]a (1871b: 483; 1871a: 67); Musil: ḫirbet Faḳû[c]a (19, 375); Albright: Fuqû[c]ah (1924: 9); Glueck: Faqû[c]ah/#128 (1934: 60). De Saulcy's party camped "in the midst of stupendous ruins" identified to them as "Kharbet-Fouqaûa." Nearby was "a circular mound, formed of squared blocks of lava, partly covered over with earth, which seem to constitute the base of a small round tower. This ruin is called the Redjom-el-Aabed." Among the stones of the rujm (stone heap) a stele, which has come to be known as the Shiḥan Stele, was pointed out to de Saulcy—see Warmanbol (1983) for a description, recent analysis, and bibliography. Albright's party also camped at Faqu[c] at the time of his 1924 expedition, pitching their tents "only a stone's throw from Rujm el-ᶜAbd." He described Faquᶜ as "a late ruin, in which some houses have recently been built" and interpreted Rujm el-ᶜAbd as a tumulus burial. A village had emerged on the site when Glueck visited a decade later. "The modern village of Faqûᶜah was carefully examined. Only a few Byzantine architectural stones were found there, embedded in the walls of the modern houses. A short distance away is Rujm el-ᶜAbd, a small tumulus..."

A thriving and rapidly expanding town covers the whole area now. Rujm el-ᶜAbd has long since been dismantled. Some of the older residents of Faquᶜ remember it, however, and told us that it stood where the public school stands today. Two of the men, interviewed independently, recalled that someone removed a "negro statue" while they were boys. Actually the Shiḥan Stele was taken to the Louvre by de Luynes in 1864. Except for the surviving shell of an Ottoman-style building (ca. 25 x 40 m; roofless, but with walls and some of the arches which supported the roof still intact) the only architectural remains from earlier times are sculptured stones from earlier buildings reused in some of the present-day houses. As Glueck indicated, the designs are often suggestive of the Byzantine period, which is also heavily represented by the surface pottery collected in open spaces among the present-day houses and streets. Water is piped to the town now, but one encounters numerous cisterns from earlier times. Water is also available from springs in the nearby wadis.

Site 15 - **Imraᶜ**
(Map section 1; field no. 8017)
PG: 15.3/84.5; UTMG: 55.6/71.7

Modern town on an ancient settlement site at the head of Wadi Imraᶜ (which itself joins Wadi Muneikhirin at Faquᶜ). Marked Imra on the K737 map. 1040 sherds were collected, including: EB II-III 12; EB IVA 21; LB 1; IR 8; IR I 3; IR II 8; IR II C/P 1; Hell 5; Nab 49; ERom 14; LRom 7; Byz 2; EByz 19; LByz 9; Um 1; A/M 1; LIsl 77; Mod 1; UDE 8; UD 20; UDhandle 34.

See Burckhardt: Meraa (389); de Saulcy: Kharbet Emrâah (276-77); Musil: ḫirbet Mraᶜ (88, 374-75); Glueck: Mrâᶜ/#129 (1934: 60, 62). Glueck describes it as a small Arabic village and reports "several ornamented lintels ...built into the walls of the houses, ... probably medieval Arabic in origin. One piece of sigillata ware was found, but otherwise the pottery was medieval Arabic."

Imraᶜ has grown to a town of considerable size. The long settlement history of the site is evidenced by the abundance of sherds to be found along the southern fringe of the town, especially in the garbage and ash scattered over the slopes down to Wadi Imraᶜ. Also, occasional wall lines of previous structures are to be seen in the town.

Site 16 - **Majdalein**
(Map section 1; field no. 8022, 9046, 9058, 9312)
PG: 18.1/82.6; UTMG: 58.5/70.0

Extensive ruins at the head of Wadi Abu Jubeiba, ca. 3 km northwest of el-Qaṣr on the Qaṣr-Faquᶜ road. Marked Majdalein on the K737 map. 1514 sherds were collected, including: IR I 45; IR II 12; Hell 5; Nab 18; ERom 3; LRom 3; Byz 43; A/M 38; LIsl 145; Ott 1; UDE 23; UD 129; pipe fragments; 10 tesserae.

See Seetzen: Müdschdelên (416); Burckhardt: Medjdelein (389); de Saulcy: Kharbet-Medjeleïn (290-91); Palmer: Mejdelain (1871b: 491; 1871a: 67); Tristram: Mejdelein (136); Musil: ḫirbet Meǧdelên (87-88, 375); Glueck: Mejdelein/#132 (1934: 62). De Saulcy spoke of "the vast ruins of a city" and observed: "The ruins by which we are surrounded consist of houses that look as if they had been suddenly crushed, notwithstanding the solidity of their construction, and three parts of which are buried under ground. All seem to be provided with large cellars, whilst these apparent cellars are nothing more than the ground-floors of the original dwelling-places." Glueck confirmed the vastness of the ruins and concluded that they are fairly recent. "The entire site is covered with modern débris. ...intensive search revealed only a few sherds, mostly mediaeval Arabic. On the southeast slope towards the spring several pieces of plain and rouletted sigillata ware were found and a few painted Nabataean sherds." Worschech (Ḫirbet Meǧdelēn/#53, 1985a: 43) resherded Majdalein in 1984, six years after we were there, and reported the following periods represented: "Chalco/EB; E/LR, Byz, Mam."

The area of concentrated ruins stretches some 400 m along the northeast bank of Wadi Abu Jubeibah, and extends some 200 m northeastward from the wadi rim and

Photograph 3: Majdalein ruins (Site 16) with Qaṣr Ḥimmeh (Site 55) in the foreground

Photograph 4: Majdalein ruins

beyond the Qaṣr-Faquᶜ road. Sherd coverage and occasional wall lines which fade into the surrounding fields indicate that the site actually is much larger than this area of concentrated surface ruins. Collapsed remains of six or more large building complexes are discernible as well as partially preserved sections of several other buildings. In some places the lower courses and corners are much more solidly built—limestone ashlars laid in header-stretcher fashion—than the upper walls superimposed upon them. This suggests that rebuilding has occurred on old foundations. There are cisterns throughout the ruin. Along the wadi rim is a wall of well-fitted stones which could have been either a terrace or a defensive wall. If there was a parallel defensive wall on the northeastern side of the ruin, it probably was covered or displaced by the Qaṣr-Faquᶜ road. Across the wadi to the southeast is Qaṣr el-Ḥimmeh (Site 55), a large square tower from which the site may have derived its name.

Site 17
(Map section 2; field no. 9144)
PG: 22.3/93.6: UTMG: 62.5/81.0

Partitioned cairn overlooking Wadi el-Mujib from the north rim of the plateau, 3 km northwest of Ariḥa. The cairn consists of large rough stones laid in concentric circle pattern; an external circle ca. 5 m in diameter and an internal circle ca. 2.5 m in diameter. The internal wall (or wall face) was still preserved two courses above the ground when examined in 1979. It was largely destroyed, presumably having been robbed for stone, when we reexamined it in 1983. 6 sherds were collected, including: Nab/ERom 1; UD 5.

Site 18 - **Mḥaṭṭat el-Ḥājj/Karakūn**
(Map section 2; field no. 8001)
PG: 25.7/93.7; UTMG: 65.8/81.2

Ruin of an ancient fort situated immediately east of the Kerak-Dhiban road at the point where the road begins its descent from the northern edge of the plateau into the Wadi el-Mujib canyon. The Roman road also began its descent into the wadi at this point and the fort no doubt was in use during the Roman and Early Byzantine periods. 1142 sherds were collected, including: Nab 37; ERom 8; LRom 29; Byz 66; EByz 11; LByz 7; Fat(?) 2; A/M 5; LIsl 2; UD 11; UDhandle 8.

Usually this ruin has been reported with some variation of the name Mḥaṭṭat el-Ḥajj, which suggests, probably incorrectly in view of the low percentage of Islamic pottery, that it once served as a pilgrim stop along the route to Mecca. See Seetzen: Mhatta (410); Burckhardt: Mehatet el Hadj (375); Brünnow and Domaszewski (I: 43-45: eš-Šeğera/Muḥâtet el-Ḥağğ; Musil: ḫirbet Mḥaṭṭet el-Ḥâğğ (376); Smith: Maḥaṭṭet el-Hajj (374); and Glueck: Meḥaṭṭet el-Ḥâjj/#119 (1934: 57). Although Tristram mentions "Muhatet el Haj" (139), there is some problem with his notes at this point (see discussion under Jadᶜat el-Jbūr/Site 34). Klein (1869: 153) and Palmer: (1871a: 69; 1871b: 491) mention the ruined fort, but provide no name. Soon after 1894, when the Ottoman government reasserted its authority in the Kerak region, a guardhouse was built immediately west of the ruin. Wilson noticed this building when he passed through in 1899 (311). Three years later, Libby and Hoskins stopped briefly and shared tobacco with two soldiers (315-16). "We visited the guard-house and found three gloomy rooms; one occupied by the soldiers, one for the postman, and one for wayfarers." They heard the place called "Kerakol Ras Mujib," which in Turkish would mean "the police station of Ras Mujib." The alternate name provided by Brünnow and Domaszewski, "eš-Šeğera," referred to a conspicuous tamarisk tree which stood near the guardhouse. Brünnow and Domaszewski also provided a plan of the ruin with photographs. Glueck reported "comparatively few sherds, and most of them seemed to belong to the late Roman period. Several painted Nabataean sherds were also picked up." Parker (1976b) reported: IR 2; Nab/ERom 61; ER IV 12; LRom I-III 2(?); LRom IV 15; EByz I-IV 16; LByz I-III 17; LMam/Ott 7; Mod 3.

The essential layout of the fort, which is ca. 45 m square, is still obvious among the tumbled stones; but the towers are no longer so clearly discernible as they seem to have been when Brünnow and Domaszewski visited the site at the turn of the century. Also some clandestine digging has occurred in the southwest corner of the fort. There are two cisterns nearby, one currently in use. Immediately west of the fort are wall remains of a rectangular three-room building, and near that foundations of a one-room structure. Possibly the first of these was the Turkish guardhouse. The name given to us for the whole ruin was Karakūn.

Site 19
(Map section 2; field no. 9165)
PG: 21.9/92.8; UTMG: 62.0/80.3

Stone heap situated slightly less than 1 km north of Ibḥarmala and ca. 75 m from the edge of the Wadi el-Mujib canyon. The heap is ca. 0.5 m high and covers what appears to be the foundations of a structure approximately 4 x 8 m. That this heap represents a collapsed building rather than field clearing is further suggested by scattered potsherds. 22 sherds were collected, including: LOtt 5.

Site 20
(Map section 2; field no. 9162)
PG: 21.9/91.7; UTMG: 62.0/79.0

A cluster of more than ten caves immediately south of Ibḥarmala, most of them on the west bank of the wadi which passes through Ibḥarmala toward Wadi el-Mujib. Remains of side walls and fronts with doorways at the entrance of several of these caves suggest earlier use as dwellings. Now they are used as sheepfolds. We found no pottery.

Site 21 - **Um el-Qleib**
(Map section 2; field no. 8008)
PG: 23.3/92.0; UTMG: 63.6/79.7

A ruined, tower-like structure surrounded by an outlying wall, located ca. 1.5 km west of Ariḥa and less than 1 km west of the Kerak-Dhiban road. Specifically, Um el-Qleib is situated on a slope which rises in the fork of two shallow valleys which converge ca. 200 m northwest of the tower to become the wadi marked "Wādī Mis^{c}ar" on the K737 map. 3139 sherds were collected, including: EB I 6; EB II-III 173; EB IV 29; EB IVA 45; LB 1; Nab 18; ERom 6; LRom 3; Byz 1; EByz 2; LByz 2; UDE 7; UD 1.

Glueck recorded the name of the site as Rujm Umm el-Qleib/#121, provided a plan, and described it as consisting "of a small tower about seven metres square, which is surrounded by a circular revetment. There are traces of a wall which once surrounded the entire site and of the ruins of various buildings inside of it. ... A large amount of pottery was found, particularly on the north and northeast sides of the tower, belonging to the end of Early Bronze and to the beginning of Middle Bronze I. ... A number of Nabataean sherds were also found, including a painted piece." Glueck also reported ruined foundations at the western end of the site and a large cistern with two openings at the northwest edge of the site (1934: 57-8, 99).

The ruined tower, occasional sections of its out-lying wall (or revetment, according to Glueck's interpretation), and the foundation walls at the west end of the site are still visible. The wall/revetment surrounds the tower at distances from 2 to 10 m. An olive grove surrounded by a stone fence now separates the tower from the western foundations. No doubt most of the stones for the fence were taken from the collapsed tower. We observed two large cisterns, the one noted by Glueck near the western foundation walls and another immediately west of the tower. See also Mattingly (1984: 71).

Site 22 - **Arīḥa**
(Map section 2; field no. 8007)
PG: 24.8/92.0; UTMG: 65.0/79.5

A modern village situated on an ancient settlement site, approximately 2 km south of the Wadi el-Mujib canyon and 1 km east of the Kerak-Dhiban road. Marked Arīḥā on the K737 map. 1641 sherds were collected, including: Nab 28; LRom 14; Byz 26; EByz 9; LByz 4; Fat(?) 2; A/M 2; LIsl 16; Mod 1.

See Seetzen: er Ríhha (410); Burckhardt: el Ryhha (376); Tristram: Er Riha (135); Brünnow and Domaszewski: er-Rîḥâ (I: 45); Musil: ḫirbet Rîḥa (p.376); Smith: Erīha/Er-rīha (373). Nineteenth century maps usually place Ariḥa too far south—i.e., southeast of Jebel Shiḥan—a misconception which can be traced to an incorrect inference from Burckhardt's account. Burckhardt spent the night at a Bedouin camp near Mḥaṭṭat el-Ḥajj and noted that Jebel Shiḥan was visible "to our right, about three quarters of an hour" (375). The next morning, continuing south along the route of the old Roman road, he reported: "At half an hour from the encampment we passed the ruined village El Ryhha" (376). The editors of

Photograph 5: Um el-Qleib (Site 21)

Photograph 6: Site 31, similar in appearance to Site 21 and also called Um el-Qleib

Burckhardt's notes, unfamiliar with the region, naturally assumed that Jebel Shiḥan and Ariḥa were roughly west and south of Mḥaṭṭat el-Ḥajj respectively. Brünnow and Domaszewski cleared up the problem, but Glueck introduced another less serious one—i.e., he placed Ariḥa SSE of Mḥaṭṭat el-Ḥajj rather than SSW as is actually the case. Ariḥa was still unoccupied when Glueck examined it in 1933. Glueck recorded the name as er-Rîḥā/#120 and explained that the site "is situated on the top of a hill and commands an extensive view to the east; it consists of a number of foundations of houses and walls and numerous cisterns, caves, and small mounds. There was a small quantity of Nabataean sherds, as well as some pieces of sigillata and some sherds belonging to the Byzantine and medieval Arabic periods" (1934: 57).

The present-day village covers the ruins which were visible to Glueck and earlier travelers. The main concentration of sherds is on the northeast slope of the slight hill on which the village is located. There are also several caves and cisterns on this slope, some of the cisterns still in use. Some of the caves have been blocked with basalt stone walls with doorways, evidence that they have served as dwellings. Now they serve only as sheepfolds and, in at least one case, as a "ṭābūn" (oven). A prominent track from Mḥaṭṭat el-Ḥajj, with occasional small sherd scatters along the way, passes immediately east of Ariḥa. Probably this is the route of the old Roman road which was clearly visible to nineteenth century travelers. Unfortunately, largely as a result of extensive farming with heavy equipment during the past half-century, most of the traces of the ancient road system have disappeared from the Kerak plateau. On the NNE side of Ariḥa is a planted grove surrounded by a stone fence. Reused in the fence are some 10 or 12 carved limestone pieces which served earlier as part of a decorative facade. Represented, for example, is the same frieze pattern which appears often at Petra (on ed-Deir, the so-called Roman Soldier's Tomb, the Urn Tomb, the Obelisk Tomb, etc.).

Site 23 - **Abū Trābah**
(Map section 2; field no. 8009)
PG: 25.1/90.8; UTMG: 65.2/78.4

Modern village situated on an ancient settlement site, ca. 3 km south of the Wadi el-Mujib canyon, 1 km south of Ariḥa, and 1.5 km east of the main Kerak-Dhiban road. Marked Abū Turābah on the K737 map. 743 sherds were collected, including: Nab 7; Byz 41; EByz 17; LByz 18; LIsl 4; UD 11.

See Musil: ḫ. abu Trâba (138, 376), who incorrectly places it too far south (between Kh. Balu^c and Wadi Uḥaymer). Glueck found Kh. Abū Trâbeh/#118 still unoccupied, and reported two main compounds. "They are approximately square, with the ruins of a number of buildings in them. Immediately to the southwest is a small wādī, which is dammed up on three sides to form a reservoir. No pottery was found. It seems to be an early Arabic site" (1934: 57).

The present-day village, having grown from three houses in 1948 to approximately thirty houses when we visited in 1978, was built over the compounds observed by Glueck. Unusually large, dressed stones in some of the house walls witness to the fact that the ancient ruin supplied building material for the modern houses. This was verified by an elderly resident of the village who stated that stones from a *qaṣr* had been reused in some of the first houses. Occasional large basalt walls are visible at ground level along the southern edge of the village. Also, we observed in a courtyard nearer the center of the village one course of an ancient wall near a cistern. There were a number of cisterns in and around the village, as well as what appears to have been a wine or olive press ca. 200 m southeast of the village. Although filled with sediment and debris which prohibited close examination, the installation was described by the villagers as consisting of two vats connected by a channel, one vat for pressing and the other for sedimentation and collection. Two terraces which cross a small wadi ca. 200 m southwest of the village have collected deep deposits of sediment. This would be the reservoir which Glueck mentioned. Another possible terrace lies ca. 100 m further east—i.e., almost directly south of the village. According to one of the village elders, there was a stand of large bushes (large and thick enough to hide a camel, according to his description) in the area of these terraces when they resettled the site in the 1940s. We saw no stumps, but the roofs of several of the older dwellings incorporate branches which may have come from this thicket. That the Roman road passed less than a kilometer west of the site is suggested by a milestone fragment.

Site 24
(Map section 2; field no. 9216)
PG: 26.5/91.4; UTMG: 66.5/78.9

Intersecting wall lines, apparently representing the corner of a building, situated near the edge of the plateau ca. 1.5 km ENE of Abu Trabah. Although the two walls do not project above ground level, they can be traced 13 m and 20 m respectively. 36 sherds were collected, including: Nab 1; LIsl 3; UD 3.

Site 25 - **Mis^{c}ar**
(Map section 2; field no. 8011)
PG: 21.5/90.0; UTMG: 61.8/77.5

Modern village on an ancient settlement site, situated at the head of Wadi ed-Dafali. Marked Mis^{c}ar on the K737 map. 499 sherds were collected, including: EB II-III 23; EB IV 27; EB IVA 10; EB IVB 1; MB/LB 27; LB 21; LB/IR I 8; IR II 1; Nab 2; LRom 5; Byz 6; A/M 3; Ott 11; UDE 14; Mod 1.

See Seetzen: Mássar (416); Brünnow and Domaszewski: el-Mis^{c}ar (I: 45); Musil: ḫirbet Miṣ^{c}ar (138); Glueck: Kh. Miṣ^{c}ar/#122 (1934: 58). Glueck, who saw the site before modern reoccupation, provided the following description: "... a large ruined settlement, which consists of a complex of ruined houses and foundation walls, with a large number of cemented cisterns and caves. It is divided into two sections by a small wâdī, which joins the Wâdī Jedeirah. In the eastern section, near a cistern, there was found a large stone watering trough, similar to those of the Nabataean site of Ekhwein el-Khâdem [PG: 34.0/54.9; UTMG: 74.8/42.6]. A number of Nabataean sherds were found, and some of the ruins probably go back to the Nabataean period. Most of the ruins, however, belong to the early Arabic period, to judge from the large number of early Arabic sherds found. These ruins are evidently built on top of a much earlier site, which they completely cover. A considerable number of typical Early Bronze and Middle Bronze I sherds were found, extending approximately from the twenty-third to the nineteenth centuries B.C. There were also sherds from Early Iron I."

Occupational remains are still evident on the slopes of two hills which face each other (roughly north-south) across a shallow tributary which joins Wadi ed-Dafali (which Glueck identified as Wâdī Jedeirah) from the east. The present-day village is situated on the northern slope (apparently what Glueck referred to as the "eastern section") and had grown to approximately 25 dwellings when we visited in 1978. Most of this growth, according to a local informant, had occurred during the past seven years. Residents of the village have reused some of the ancient walls and caves. We found few surface remains on the southern slope, which is actually a knoll situated between the tributary mentioned above and another which joins it from the southeast to form Wadi ed-Dafali. However, we did find most of the Bronze Age sherds on this southern slope.

Site 26
(Map section 2; field no. 9243)
PG: 25.7/89.3; UTMG: 66.1/77.0

Building ruin situated 50 m north of Wadi el-Mindassa and ca. 1.5 km southeast of Abu Trabah. Marked Um Qulayb on the K737 map, possibly by mistake; see entry for Site 31. 49 sherds were collected, including: Nab 2; LRom 1; LByz 2; EIsl 1; Ott 4; UD 5.

The wall lines indicate a rectangular structure 13 m (N-S) by 8 m (E-W). No internal walls are discernible, and the external walls, composed of irregularly shaped black stones, have not survived more than one course above the ground. A cistern ca. 40 m east of the structure contains water, and there is a cave ca. 10 m to the ESE.

Site 27 - **el-Harbaj**
(Map section 2; field no. 9244)
PG: 25.9/89.3; UTMG: 66.2/77.1

Cisterns and caves showing evidence of previous human habitation, located just northeast of Site 26 along the north bank of Wadi el-Mindassa. The K737 map identifies this area as Umm Qulayb. 192 sherds were collected, including: Nab 13; ERom 1; EByz 1; LByz 2; A/M 1; LIsl 9; UDE 1; UD 6.

Musil reports a site named "ḫirbet Harbaǧ" in this vicinity, placing it at the beginning of a ravine called the "ammu ḳlejb" (138, 376). Local informants gave us the name el-Harbaj for this site, but identified yet another ruin on the north bank of Wadi Ṣuwar (Site 31) as Rujm Um Qleib.

At least seven caves along the north slope of Wadi el-Mindassa show evidence of having served as human dwellings in times past—e.g., remains of stone walls with doorways at the entrances of some of the caves. Now they serve as sheepfolds.

Site 28
(Map section 2; field no. 9267)
PG: 29.0/89.9; UTMG: 69.1/77.4

Building ruin situated on a shelf below the northern tip of the es-Sanina ridge. 28 sherds were collected, including: IR 1; Byz 1; UDE 3; UD 23.

This is a small square structure (24 m on a side) with at least two building phases. The lowest courses of the walls, which are especially visible in the southwest corner, are very solidly built and composed of large field-dressed basalt slabs laid in header-stretcher fashion. Superimposed are courses more crudely built from small, basalt stones.

Site 29
(Map section 2; field no. 9265)
PG: 29.3/88.8; UTMG: 69.4/76.5

Two rectangular building ruins situated near the northeastern edge of the es-Saninah ridge. 34 sherds were collected, including: Nab 2; Byz 2; LIsl 1.

The structures are side-by-side, with the larger one on the west. A long enclosure wall connects with both buildings and extends ca. 100 m to the south. The western structure measures 15 m (E-W) by 22 m (N-S). The other measures 15 m (E-W) by 19 m (N-S) and is best preserved in the northeast corner where it is composed of stone blocks laid in header-stretcher fashion. Some internal walls are discernible in this eastern structure, and there is a courtyard (15 x 10 m) on its south end. Clandestine digging in a depression 8 m to the west of the western structure has exposed a wall under ca. 1 m of overburden.

Site 30 - **el-Jad^ca** (Kh. eḍ-Ḍribbān)
(Map section 2; field no. 9214)
PG: 22.0/87.8; UTMG: 62.2/75.3

Modern village on an ancient settlement site, immediately ENE of Jebel Shiḥan and less than 1 km east of the Kerak-Dhiban road. Marked Jad^{c}ah on the K737 map. 325 sherds were collected, including: Nab 12; LRom 1; Byz 5; LByz 2; A/M 1; LIsl 28; Mod 1; UD 3; UDhandle 3.

Musil, traveling north from Kh. Balu^c toward Ariḥa, reported "ḫ. eḍ-Ḍribân" at a distance to the left of his trail (376). Glueck provides the only other reference to a site by this name in the vicinity: "Ruins of a similar nature (to those of Jad^{c}a el-Jbūr/Kh. es-Samra^ɔ; our Site 34) were found on the same straight line northward toward the Wâdī el-Môjib at Kh. eḍ-Ḍribbân [Glueck's # 117] and at Kh. Abū Trâbeh [Glueck's # 118]. Kh. eḍ-Ḍribbân is two kilometres north of Kh. es-Samrā, and Kh. Abū Trâbeh is about five kilometres northeast of Kh. eḍ-Ḍribbân" (1934: 57). The old settlement site occupied by the present-day village of Jad^{c}a seems the most likely candidate for Musil's and Glueck's eḍ-Ḍribbān even though we did not hear the latter name used.

The present-day village was begun in the 1950s and is situated on the western slope of a slight foothill to Jebel Shiḥan. An earlier but still fairly recent settlement which was situated on the eastern slope of the hill is indicated by the remains of some 30-40 crudely built stone houses and caves which show evidence of human habitation. We were told by the villagers that people lived in these caves and houses about 70 years ago. The pottery, collected for the most part on the southern side of the earlier settlement, indicates that the hill was also occupied in ancient times.

Site 31
(Map section 2; field no. 8010)
PG: 25.5/87.9; UTMG: 65.7/75.6

Collapsed building (tower?) surrounded by segments of out-lying walls. Located south of the place marked Umm Qulayb on the K737 map—i.e., on the north bank of the wadi marked Wadi Ṣuwar, not on Wadi el-Mendassah. 61 sherds were collected around the central mound including: EB I(?) 1; EB II-III 2; MB 2; Nab 2; Byz 1; UDhandle 1.

This site is called Um el-Qleib locally, and, similar to the other Um el-Qleib reported above (Site 21), its main feature is a conspicuous mound of stone (thus the local explanation for the name, "place of the woman's breast"). With a radius of ca. 13 m, the mound rises abruptly to ca.

4 m at the center. Occasional segments of out-lying wall foundations are also discernible, one of which can be traced 18 m. Approximately 150 m WNW of the central mound is another smaller stone heap, ca. 6 m in diameter. Some digging has occurred at the center of this smaller mound which exposed the inside face of a wall. No pottery was found near the smaller stone heap. See also Mattingly (1984: 72-73).

Site 32
(Map section 2; field no. 9241)
PG: 25.1/86.8; UTMG: 65.3/74.5

Wall lines indicating a large building compound on a terrace with moderate sherd coverage overlooking Wadi Uḥaymir. The compound measures 30 by 40 m and includes ten or more rooms. The walls average 0.7 m thick and still stand 2 m high in places. There is a rocky hillside to the north, a higher terrace to the west, and a lower one to the east. A small area on a lower eastern terrace is under cultivation, as is the area immediately across the wadi to the south. 149 sherds were collected, including: LB 1; Byz 2; LByz 1; A/M 1; LIsl 9; UDE 1; UD 1.

Site 33
(Map section 2; field no. 9266, 9270)
PG: 28.2/87.4; UTMG: 68.4/75.0

Wall lines indicating at least two building complexes overlooking Wadi el-Baluᶜ/esh-Sheqeifat from the western edge of the es-Saninah ridge. 169 sherds were collected, including: Nab 2; ERom 1; LRom 2; Byz 1; LByz 2; LIsl 2; UDE 3; UD 4.

The walls and associated sherd scatter cover an area ca. 30 x 35 m. Unfortunately, a silo recently built among the ruins has disturbed the site considerably. 150 m further south along the edge of the es-Saninah ridge are the collapsed remains of a square structure, 7 m on a side, composed of large, undressed stones. The sherd count indicated above pertains to the main site. There was very little surface pottery at the second building and no diagnostic pieces.

Site 34 - **Jadᶜa el-Jbūr/Kh. es-Samrāʾ**
(Map section 2; field no. 8028)
PG: 21.3/86.0; UTMG: 61.5/73.5

Present-day village occupying an ancient site ca. 2 km SSE of Jebel Shiḥan. Marked Jadᶜat el Jubūr/As Samrāʾ on the K737 map. 291 sherds were collected, including: IR II 2; Nab 3; Byz 9; EByz 2; LByz 2; Um 2; LIsl 35; UD 21; 34 tesserae.

Tristram reports that, after exploring the ruins on Jebel Shiḥan, "we descended in a north-eastern direction by another ancient road, riding at a smart pace, and in twenty-five minutes passed through the ruins of Balʾhua, perhaps the poorest and most featureless we have seen, and all leveled with soil. After this, seventy minutes more of slow and heavy riding through wet and unsound ground ... we reached Kirbet es Sumʾhra, a mere castle, apparently of Saracenic origin, near Muhatet el Haj, the remains of a city of yet older date than the castle..." (139). The names are familiar: compare Kh. Baluᶜ (Site 35), Kh. es-Samraʾ (Site 34), and Mḥaṭṭat el-Ḥajj (Site 18). However Tristram's descriptions do not fit the sites and such a route from Shiḥan to the Mujib does not make sense. Glueck placed Kh. es-Samrā/#116 1 km north of Kh. ed-Denn (our Site 36) and reported "extensive ruins from the Nabataean, Byzantine, and mediaeval Arabic periods" with "characteristic sherds from all of these periods found" (1934: 57).

The modern village of Jadᶜa el-Jbur is built over the ruins of more than 15 earlier buildings on an eastern-sloping hill. Cisterns, some still in use, provided water. Also there are caves which apparently have served as dwellings in fairly recent times. Among the ancient buildings disturbed by modern development is a curving, apsidal wall ca. 4 m across on the east end of a building, possibly the remains of a Byzantine church. The surrounding land is flat, fertile, and well-drained. Also there is some agricultural terracing to the north of the site.

Site 35 - **Kh. el-Bālūᶜ**
(Map section 2; field no. 8014,8004)
PG: 24.4/85.5; UTMG: 64.5/72.9

Extensive ruins on the north and south banks of Wadi Qurri. Marked Khirbat al Bālūᶜ on the K737 map. 988

Photograph 7: Kh. el-Balūʿ (Site 35) with Kh. es-Samrāʾ/Jadʿah el-Jbūr (Site 34) in the distance

Photograph 8: Kh. el-Balūʿ ruins north of Wadi Qurri

sherds were collected on the main site (south of Wadi Qurri) including the following diagnostics: EB 2; EB I 1; EB II-III 2; EB IVA 1; MB 1; LB 42; IR 82; IR I 37; IR II 77; Pers(?) 1; Hell 6; Nab 16; Nab/ERom 12; ERom 24; Byz 18; EByz 3; A/M 7; LIsl 97; UDE 149; UD 11. 545 sherds were collected on the north bank including: EB IV 21; EB IVA 80; EB IVB 1; LB 3; IR 7; IR I 1; Ott 3; UDE 36.

See Seetzen: Bellué/Bälué (410-11); Burckhardt: Kalaat Baloua (374); Bliss: Balua^c (221); Brünnow and Domaszewski: el-Balû^{c}a (I: 46); Musil: ḫirbet Bâlû^{c}a (138, 376); and Smith: Balu^{c}a (372-73). Although Tristram reports a visit to "Bal^{ɔ}hua" (139), his description does not fit the site and there are also some other problems in his account at this point; see discussion of Jad^{c}at el-Jbūr/Kh. es-Samra^ɔ (Site 34). R.G. Head's discovery of the famous stele at Kh. Balu^c in 1930 accounts for the special attention which Kh. Balu^c received over the next few years. Horsfield and Vincent published a plan of the site and the "qaṣr" in 1932 (417-22). Glueck examined it in July of the following year (Bālû^{c}ah/#110; 1934: description on pp. 53-56, but see also pp. 1-16, 18, 19, 24-27, 66-67 and 1939: 32, 35, 90, 179, 265). Four months later, in November, Crowfoot (1934: 76-84) conducted soundings at Kh. Balu^c. Glueck reported a broad chronological range of surface pottery: "The sherds gathered at Bālû^{c}ah ranged from the late Early Bronze to medieval Arabic. Most of the sherds ... were found on ancient dump-heaps on the hillsides below the northern walls of the city. They belong exclusively to two periods, namely, from the last phase of the Early Bronze to the end of the first phase of Middle Bronze I, that is, from about 2200 to about 1800 B.C., and from the beginning of EI I down to the first part of EI II. ... No pottery whatsoever was found belonging to the periods between the end of Middle Bronze I and the very end of Late Bronze, that is, between the eighteenth and the thirteenth centuries B.C. The Early Iron Age pottery found extended from not before the middle of the thirteenth century B.C. to about the ninth century B.C." (1934: 55-56). Except for a few possible Early Bronze sherds, Crowfoot's soundings produced remains indicative of the Iron Age to the Roman period. Kh. Balu^c escaped the attention of archaeologists for the next half century. We reexamined the site in 1978, and U. Worschech began excavations there in 1985 (Worschech, Rosenthal, and Zayadine 1986: 285-310; Worschech 1990: 71-90).

Our work at Kh. Balu^c was limited to a resherding of the already well known ruins south of Wadi Qurri (field no. 8014; map grids indicated above) and investigation of the less conspicuous ruins north of the wadi (field no. 8004; UTMG: 64.5/73.5; PG: 24.5/86.0). We also found a wide chronological range represented among the sherds collected south of the wadi, but with less EB representation than Glueck seems to imply and no conspicuous MB-LB gap. Also in agreement with Glueck, we found the heaviest concentration of sherds from the later periods (Hell and later) at the western end of the ruin. North of Wadi Qurri, sherd coverage and occasional wall lines extend ca. 800 m along the wadi rim—i.e., opposite and to the north and northeast of the main Kh. Balu^c ruins. The walls, which are oriented generally N-S/E-W, are often constructed from stones as large as 1 m across. Two unusual features were noted, a circle of orthostats enclosing an area of ca. 5000 sq. m, and a cave situated immediately over the wadi rim with orthostats screening it from the wadi. On the inner scarp of the cave was a possible petroglyph. A path descends from the western end of the ruin area to pools in the wadi, one of which contained water when we were there in early August. The pottery collected among the ruins north of the wadi contrasted with that collected at the main site south of the wadi in that the former is heavily EB IV. See also Mattingly (1984: 70-71, 73-74).

Site 36 - **ed-Denn wa-l-Baradān**
(Map section 2; field no. 8025)
PG: 21.4/85.1; UTMG: 61.9/72.4

An unoccupied settlement site with standing ruins nearby of a recently abandoned farmstead, ca. 1 km south of Jad^{c}at ed-Jbur/es-Samra^ɔ, 1 km east of the Kerak-Dhiban road, and immediately north of er-Rib^{c}i (Site 37). 580 sherds were collected, including: Nab 14; LRom 11; Byz(?) 3; EByz 14; LByz 1; Um 1; A/M 5; Ott 3; Mod 3; UD 28; 8 tesserae.

Tristram included "^{ɔ}Am^{ɔ}rah el Bourdan" in a list of unlocated ruins in the region (120). Brünnow and Domaszewski reported "el-Burdân" (I: 46); Glueck reported Kh. ed-Denn/ed-Denneh/#115 (1934: 57); and we were given the compound name ed-Denn wa-l-Baradan for the site reported here. Musil, however, reported riding in a southeast direction from the east slope of Jebel Shiḥan, crossing the "Sulṭâni-Strasse" (predecessor of the Kerak-Dhiban road), and reaching "the small destroyed village, ḫ. Denn." From there he headed ESE and followed the left bank of Wadi el-Qurri to Kh. Balu^{c}. Leaving Balu^{c} and riding north, he observed "el-Burdân" and "eḍ-Ḍribbân" to the left of his route. In short, Musil recorded "ḫ. Denn" and "ḫ. el-Burdân" as separate sites; also he treated them as separate places on his map. There may be a kernel of truth to this; our Kh. ed-Denn wa-l-Baradan actually is a double ruin (see below). Yet they are not so widely separated as Musil's map implies. Note further that Musil saw "el-Burdân" only from a distance, probably pointed out to him by a local informant, and that, since he had turned north after Kh. Balu^{c}, the "ḫ. Denn" which he had reported earlier in the day (as well as our ed-Denn wa-l-Baradan) would have been in the distance to his left. The possibility must be considered, therefore, that Musil recorded the same site twice, that the "el-Burdân" pointed out to him in the distance was the same "ḫ. Denn" which he had passed through earlier in the day. Glueck's description of Kh. ed-Denn(eh) as "another indistinguishable ruin two miles north of Kh. er-Rub^{c}ī" is also misleading. The two sites are no more than a half kilometer apart.

As indicated above, ed-Denn wa-l-Baradan consists of two distinct ruins. The north ruin apparently represents the remains of a small village which was situated on flat, rocky terrain surrounded by fertile land. In addition to the numerous sherds which cover the site, occasional wall lines can be traced and possibly a perimeter wall. Also there are two cisterns. The southern ruin, ca. 150 m away, appears to be a recently abandoned farmstead. One building is still roofed, another is partially covered. However, these fairly recent structures clearly were founded on the ruins of an earlier building complex of much more solid construction. Some of the stones composing the latter reach .75 m in length. On the east side and partially covered by the recent structure is a long room with an apsidal east end. The apsidal shape, along with tesserae collected in this area, suggest the remains of a monastery or church.

Site 37 - **er-Rib^{c}ī/es-Samrā$^{\circ}$**
(Map section 2; field no. 8026)
PG: 21.5/84.8; UTMG: 61.9/72.2

Unoccupied settlement site 1.5 km south of Jad^{c}at el-Jbur/es-Samra$^{\circ}$, immediately south of Kh. ed-Denn wa-l-Baradan (Site 36) and 1 km east of the Kerak-Dhiban road. This site is also marked As Samrā$^{\circ}$ on the K737 map. 425 sherds were collected, including: Hell 2; Nab 8; LRom 4; Byz 18; LByz 1; Um 2; A/M 4; LIsl 75; UD 32.

This is Glueck's Kh. er-Rub^{c}ī/#114 (1934: 56) which he describes as "a small ruined site ... where a few Nabataean sherds were found and numerous pieces of mediaeval Arabic ware." We heard the name pronounced er-Rīb^{c}ī and were told that it was the name of a man who lived in one of the caves many years ago.

The most recent occupation of this site seems to have involved semi-permanent dwellings, perhaps used seasonally, and with heavy dependence on cave shelters. The site covers an area of approximately 50 x 125 m on a barren hilltop surrounded by fertile fields. Ten caves are visible, most of which show signs of alteration for use as dwellings or sheepfolds. Remains of a ca. 20 x 20 m building are also detectable, with a smaller ca. 5 x 5 m foundation nearby. Several cisterns are cut in the limestone, one in the center of the larger building complex.

Site 38 - **Kh. es-Sa^{c}adūnī/Um Dimis**
(Map section 2; field no. 8027)
PG: 21.4/84.0; UTMG: 61.8/71.4

Unoccupied village site east of the Kerak-Dhiban road approximately midway between el-Qaṣr and Jebel Shiḥan. Marked Umm Dims on the K737 map. 373 sherds were collected, including: IR I 1; Nab 2; LRom 1; Byz 14; EByz 1; LByz 1; Fat(?) 1; A/M 24; LIsl 119; UD 19.

See Tristram: Sahdouneh (120); Musil: ḫirbet es-Sa^{c}dûni (140); and Glueck: Kh. es-Sa^{c}adûnī/#113 (1934: 56). Glueck describes it as "a small Arabic ruin."

Situated on bedrock and overlooking a shallow wadi from its south bank are the foundation walls of six or more crudely constructed building complexes, presumably dwellings, of fairly recent vintage. Typically these buildings contained 6-12 rooms or clustered dwellings. There are a number of caves in the bedrock, some of which had been converted to dwellings by the addition of walls with doorways at the entrances—some, in fact, had been incorporated into the freestanding houses. Several cisterns provided water. The total area covered by the ruins is ca. 35,000 sq. m. There is some terracing, and wheat is planted in nearby fields.

Site 39 - **Naṣīb**
(Map section 2; field no. 8032)
PG: 22.4/83.1; UTMG: 62.7/70.6

Settlement site, currently unoccupied but with surviving walls of some 15 or more houses, situated approximately midway between el-Qaṣr and Jadᶜat el-Jbur and slightly more than a kilometer east of the Kerak-Dhiban road. Marked Naṣīb on the K737 map. 486 sherds were collected, including: IR I 14; Nab 10; ERom 1; Byz 27; Um 4; A/M 2; LIsl 98; UD 43.

See Tristram: N'assit (120); Brünnow and Domaszewski: en-Naftīb (I: 46); Musil: ḫirbet Nṣîb (140); and Glueck: Kh. Naṣîb/#112 (1934: 56). Glueck reported only that the site was located in a cultivated area and that "several Nabataean sherds were found, one piece of sigillata ware, and several pieces of mediaeval Arabic pottery."

The settlement area, a rocky knoll surrounded by fertile land, is ca. 700 m in circumference. This is indicated by the sherd coverage and occasional walls, some still standing up to three courses high. There are numerous caves on the knoll, some of which apparently served as dwellings. More than 20 cisterns were counted, some still in use. A grove surrounded by a stone fence now covers the western end of the site, the stone for the fence no doubt having come from the ruin.

Site 40
(Map section 2; field no. 9272)
PG: 25.7/84.3; UTMG: 65.9/71.4

Heavy sherd coverage indicating an ancient settlement site on the western rim of Wadi el-Baluᶜ, ca. 2 km southeast of Kh. Baluᶜ. 550 sherds were collected, including: EB I 3; EB II-III 28; EB IV 22; MB 2; LB 2; IR 15; IR I 3; IR II 2; Hell 2; ERom 2; Byz 14; EByz 8; LByz 10; UDE 9; UDEhandle 4; UD 14.

The sherds are spread over a large field (ca. 150 x 150 m) which straddles a small wadi tributary to Wadi el-Baluᶜ. Numerous large stones are strewn over the site, but there are no distinguishable wall lines. A modern house with a tree and two small outbuildings serve as landmarks at the northwest corner of the field.

Site 41
(Map section 2; field no. 9269)
PG: 26.3/83.9; UTMG: 66.7/71.4

A stone heap, probably a collapsed building, on the western edge of the es-Saninah ridge, ca. 1.5 kms WSW of ᶜAzzur (Site 43). 27 sherds were collected, including: Nab 2; ERom 2; LByz 2; UDE 1.

That the heap is a collapsed building rather than the result of field clearing is suggested by its roughly squared shape, indicated especially by the large, uncut stones at the outer edges of its base. If so, the structure would have been ca. 5 m on a side. 15 m to the northeast is another, smaller heap of stones with no discernible architectural shape.

Site 42
(Map section 2; field no. 9271)
PG: 27.7/84.3; UTMG: 68.0/71.9

Building ruin and moderate sherd coverage on a hillside 200 m west of ᶜAzzur (Site 43). 212 sherds were collected, including: LB 3; IR 1; Nab 5; ERom 6; LRom 2; Byz 1; LIsl 2; UD 2.

The hillside location of this site provides a good view over the east side of the es-Saninah ridge. While the tumbled walls of the building ruin are difficult to trace, the site having been disturbed by cultivation, visible wall lines on the east end of the ruin indicate that the east end of the building measured 17 m (N-S) by 9 m (E-W). Other less clearly visible wall lines suggest that the whole building complex may have been more than twice that large.

Site 43 - **ᶜAzzūr**
(Map section 2; field no. 8029)
PG: 28.1/84.3; UTMG: 68.4/71.9

Ancient settlement site, currently unoccupied, on the es-Saninah ridge (between Wadi el-Baluᶜ/Wadi esh-

Shqeifat on the west and Wadi el-Ghuweir on the east). Marked ᶜAzzūr on the K737 map. 581 sherds were collected, including: EB II-III 1; Nab 18; ERom 3; LRom 2; Byz 19; EByz 7; LByz 6; LIsl 57; UD 35; UDhandle 3.

See Seetzen: Ashûr (416); Tristram: Azour (120); Musil: ᶜAzzûr (139); and Glueck: Kh. ᶜAzzûr/#111 (1934: 56). Glueck reports the site as follows: "Four kilometres northeast of Bālûᶜah are the ruins of a small site called Kh. ᶜAzzûr. It is at the edge of the plateau overlooking the Wâdī esh-Sheqeifât from the east. A few Nabataean and Byzantine sherds were found there, as well as a well-preserved coin of Constantine the Great." Actually ᶜAzzur is ESE of Kh. el-Baluᶜ (Site 35).

The ruins consist of collapsed buildings, courtyards, and cisterns covering an area of ca. 200 x 350 m on two adjacent hills separated by a shallow ravine. Otherwise the terrain slopes gradually southward toward a wadi (a branch of Wadi el-Ghuweir) which drains ESE. The site is flanked by wheat fields, and there is evidence of terracing along the slopes paralleling the wadi. Approximately 25 separate buildings can be distinguished, each with several rooms. Many walls and archways are still standing, suggesting that the settlement has not been long abandoned. Probably the houses are to be associated with the LIsl sherds which account for most of the pottery collected. Some of the buildings incorporated caves as dwelling or storage space, and one cave not associated with a building had been provided with an arched entrance. Numerous cisterns supplied water, and the adjacent wadi may have been a seasonal source. There are some recent burials among the ruins, and clandestine digging has exposed older burials.

Site 44
(Map section 2; field no. 9194)
PG: 31.0/84.2; UTMG: 71.3/71.9

A large stone heap with several wall lines extending from it in different directions, located near the north end of the ridge between Wadi el-Ghuweir and Wadi el-Mujib. Apparently the stone heap represents the remains of a collapsed building, although the only clearly discernible architectural features are the outlying walls. These probably pertained to open enclosures and were constructed of large field-dressed limestone slabs along with smaller undressed stones. At the northeastern edge of the central heap are two large (ca. 0.8 m high) standing stones. Along a wall which extends northward from this northeastern side of the heap is a small offset chamber in which was found a small stone with a flat face (20 x 9 x 4 cm), broken into two pieces and bearing a Thamudic /Safaitic inscription fragment (identified and transcribed by David F. Graf).

Front side:	*[l] wm bn'lm*	By *WM* son of *'LM*
	l 'bd-tm' bn 'm	By *'BD-TM'* son of *'M*
Back side:	*l bwj*	By *BWJ*

No surface pottery was observed except for two nondescript body sherds.

Site 45
(Map section 2; field no. 9195)
PG: 31.3/84.2; UTMG: 71.5/71.9

Several cairns on the the northern end of the ridge between Wadi el-Ghuweir and Wadi el-Mujib, including two "partitioned cairns" near the east rim overlooking Wadi el-Mujib. The largest is ca. 5 m. in diameter.

Site 46
(Map section 2; field no. 9196)
PG: 31.1/84.0; UTMG: 71.4/71.7

Collapsed remains of a rectangular structure (ca. 6 x 2 m) and an adjacent stone heap (6.5 m in diameter) situated near the north end of the ridge between Wadi el-Ghuweir and Wadi el-Mujib. The rectangular structure has a possible interior cross wall and is situated ca. 60 m from the west edge of the ridge—i.e., overlooking Wadi el-Ghuweir. Nearer to the edge are three prominent cairns—two ca. 40 m WNW of the rectangular structure and the third ca. 30 m WSW. The two largest are ca. 7 m in diameter and appear to be partitioned cairns.

Site 47 - **Kh. es-Sanīnah**
(Map section 2; field no. 8030)
PG: 29.6/83.4; UTMG: 69.8/70.8

Ruins of two solidly-built structures on the eastern slopes of the ridge between Wadi el-Baluᶜ/esh-Shqeifat and Wadi el-Ghuweir. This ridge is marked as-Sanīnah on the K737 map. The site itself, not marked on the map, is located approximately 2 km SSE of ᶜAzzur (Site 43). 471 sherds were collected, including: Nab 46; ERom 9; LRom 1; Byz 4; A/M 1; UDE 2; UD 27.

The two structures, both built from field-dressed, squared stones, stand 15 m apart with no visible connecting or surrounding walls. The northern structure measures 20 m (N-S) by 26 m (E-W), includes a possible courtyard or large hall on its east side, and presents a complex network of walls (.80-1.00 m thick) on its west side. Apparently the entrance was from the west. The southern structure is smaller, measuring 15.6 x ca. 12 m, but also has walls .80-1.00 m thick and includes several rooms. The sturdy construction of these two buildings and their location on the eastern edge of the plateau suggest that they may have served a military purpose. The es-Saninah ridge provides good farm land, on the other hand, and there is evidence of terracing along the slopes surrounding Kh. es-Saninah.

Site 48
(Map section 2; field no. 9197)
PG: 30.8/82.7; UTMG: 71.2/70.8

Numerous cairns on a spur which extends SSW from the ridge between Wadi el-Ghuweir and Wadi el-Mujib. Most of these cairns have distinctly circular foundation walls and several are "partitioned cairns." The largest is 8 m in diameter with a round foundation of basalt stones still standing two courses high. It is filled with tumbled stones, as is another adjacent and similar cairn (5 m in diameter).

Site 49
(Map section 2; field no. 9193, 9198-9202)
PG: 31.2/83.1; UTMG: 71.4/70.8

Large stone heap, possibly the remains of a rectangular structure, and several cairns on a southern spur of the north end of the ridge between Wadi el-Ghuweir and Wadi el-Mujib. The stone heap measures ca. 5 x 10 m and has no surrounding surface pottery.

Site 50
(Map section 2; field no. 9203, 9204)
PG: 30.8/82.7; UTMG: 71.1/70.3

Building ruin, a partitioned rectangular structure (15 x 3 m) and attached enclosure situated on the north slope of a saddle in the ridge between Wadi el-Ghuweir and Wadi el-Mujib. The structure was composed of large white stones and, while interior rubble makes features difficult to distinguish, there appears to be a crosswall which would have divided the building into chambers 7 and 8 m long. A crude enclosure wall (ca. 15 x 6 m) extends from the structure. 8 sherds were collected, none of diagnostic value. Nearby is a cairn ca. 4 m in diameter.

Site 51
(Map section 2; field no. 9191, 9192)
PG: 31.2/82.6; UTMG: 71.5/70.4

Stone heap in a saddle of the ridge between Wadi el-Ghuweir and Wadi el-Mujib. Although no wall lines are clearly discernible, the stones are large and appear to have been dressed for building purposes. Also the site provides a clear view in all directions except north and NNE, which makes it an excellent place for a watch tower. Ca. 100 m to the southwest is another small stone heap which probably represents a collapsed structure. One nondescript body sherd was found near the second heap.

Site 52 - Ṣirfa
(Map section 3; field no. 9059, 9022)
PG: 12.4/81.8; UTMG: 52.4/69.3

Modern developed area covering ancient sites, overlooking Wadi Ibn Hammad from the north, ca. 4.5 km southwest of Imra. Marked Maqam en Nabī Yūshaᶜ/Ṣirfa on the K737 map. 419 sherds were collected, including: Hell 1; Nab 8; ERom 5; EByz 9; LByz 16; A/M 4; LIsl 131; LOtt 1; Mod 5; UD 8; UDhandle 16.

See Seetzen: Wasürrpha (416); Burckhardt: Seraf (389); de Saulcy: Kharbet-Sarfah (273-76); Palmer: Sarfat el Mál (1871b: 482; 1871a: 67); Musil: ẖirbet Ṣarfa (2, 88, 374). From Mazraᶜa at the Dead Sea, de Saulcy followed the Wadi Ibn Ḥammad eastward and ascended the plateau at Ṣirfa. "Before us appears a mass of scattered ruins, covering the remainder of the ascent. The Bedouins call them Kharbet-Sarfah; but, as I have said already, the mountain is named Djebel-en-Nouêhin. By forty-two minutes past eight, after some windings amongst the ruins, we reach the high level of the land of Moab. We are marching due east, in a line parallel to the direction of Ouad-ebni-Hammid, which is scarcely one hundred and fifty yards distant to our right. The upper ledge of this ouad is literally covered throughout with ruined walls, undoubtedly the remains of a very considerable town." Having ascended the plateau, de Saulcy and his party followed an ancient roadway which itself appears to have traced essentially the same route as the present-day road from Maqam en-Nabi Yusha[c] through Ṣirfa to Imra[ɔ]. He reported ancient ruins all along the way. "By nine o'clock we notice, about forty yards to our left, a considerable ruin. Fifteen yards to our right, passes the wall crowning the ledge of the Ouad-ebni-Hammid, and we now enter upon cultivated grounds. On our right is a well called Bir-Sirfah, and a little further on the left a square cistern, excavated in the rock. Lastly, a hundred paces further on, we halt before a curious building... By nineteen minutes past nine we leave this place and resume our march, proceeding southeast. We pass a wall built as usual with blocks of lava, stretching perpendicularly across our road, and edging, on our right, the brink of the ouad. About five hundred yards from the ruin I have just described, a circular elevation, of no great height, presents itself before us. It seems artificial, and entirely covered with the remains of half-buried houses. A town has formerly stood here. The ruins are called by the Arabs Kharbet-Sarfah. By thirty-two minutes past nine we leave the mound of Sarfah. At the spot where we clear the ruins, a wall, still in tolerable preservation, and built with blocks of lava, turns inwards to our left, most likely to connect the other wall we have lately passed, forming the crown work of the upper level of the Ouad-ebni-Hammid. Here stood, in all probability, the gate of the ancient city, for the track we are following passes between two uninterrupted lines of lava blocks, forming one of those strange avenues which bounded most unquestionably the high roads leading through the plains of Moab." Palmer visited the Ṣirfa ruin twenty years later: "Passing through a number of fields enclosed by ancient walls, and called Hákúrát Huseiní, we came to a ruined village called Sarfat el Mál, where we had been told of the existence of a stone with writing on [it]. This turned out to be nothing more than a broken boulder of black basalt with natural markings. The buildings were not unlike those at Dátráiyeh, the arches being of the same pattern, but all composed of the black basalt spoken of. We found a millstone of the same in one of the wells, in the shape like those discovered at Pompeii" (1871a: 67).

The modern and rapidly expanding town of Ṣirfa covers the ruins reported by de Saulcy and Palmer. We found the heaviest concentration of sherds along the slopes south of the most recent part of town (the section marked Ṣirfa on the K737 map) and overlooking Wadi Ḥammad. The sherd count indicated above pertains to these slopes. The western part of Ṣirfa (identified on the K737 map as Maqam en Nabi Yūsha[c]) consists of houses of fairly recent vintage but now largely abandoned. Apparently these houses represent an earlier phase of the modern resettlement of the area. 79 sherds collected among these houses (field no. 9022) included LByz 2; LIsl 10; A/M 2; UD 1. There is also a cemetery in this western part of Ṣirfa.

Site 53 - **Ḥimmeh**
(Map section 3; field no. 9035)
PG: 14.5/82.0; UTMG: 54.8/69.6

Three building ruins, numerous stone heaps, and sherd scatters along the eastern rim of Wadi ed-Daḥila, ca. 2 km ENE of Ṣirfa. 532 sherds were collected, including: LB(?) 2; IR I 1; Hell 1; Nab 16; LRom 1; Byz 3; EByz 3; A/M 4; LIsl 30; UDE 2; UD 19; UDhandle 7.

See de Saulcy: Redjom-el-Hammah (277); Palmer: Hammet [c]Aneinah (1871a: 67); Musil: ruǧm el-Ḥamma (88). The form of the name reported by de Saulcy and Musil suggests that Ḥimmeh was a rujm, a stone heap. However Palmer described it as a fort. "Riding along beside an old road which ran between two walls we passed sundry other ruins, Hammet [c]Aneinah and Mejdelain, two forts on the right..." It does not appear that any of the three actually stopped to investigate.

In fact this site appears more impressive from a distance than it does upon close examination. Scattered and random stone heaps stretch almost a kilometer along the edge of the wadi. One large rujm stands out, measuring over 20 m in diameter and 5 m high. Near the western edge of the site and ca. 75 m from the rim of Wadi ed-Daḥilah are the partially standing remains of three building compounds. One of them, composed of several rooms, measures 43 m (E-W) by 23 m (N-S). The other two were smaller, 12 x 14 m and 7 x 23 m. There are numerous cisterns, terraces, and some caves in the area. Actually the sherds are relatively sparse. The large number indicated above were collected over a large area.

Site 54 - **Shaḥtūr**
(Map section 3; field no. 9026)
PG: 17.5/81.7; UTMG: 57.7/69.3

Building ruin on a knoll overlooking Wadi Abu Jubeibah, southwest of Majdalein. 55 sherds were collected, including: IR I 1; Byz 2; A/M 1; LIsl 5; UDE 2.

See Musil: ḫirbet Šaḫtûr (p.88).

The foundation remains indicate a NW-SE oriented building complex measuring 20 x 33 m. Its external walls average ca. 1 m thick and are solidly built. There are also internal divisions, although the plan cannot be determined entirely from the surface remains. An apsidal projection from the southeast wall, 6 m in diameter, may be the base of a tower.

Site 55 - **Qaṣr el-Ḥimmeh**
(Map section 3; field no. 9023)
PG: 18.2/82.0; UTMG: 58.6/69.4

Partially preserved tower on the south bank of Wadi Abu Jubeibah, opposite Majdalein. Marked "Ruins" on the K737 map. 60 sherds were collected, including: LB 4; ERom 1; Byz 2; UDE 3; UD 3.

De Saulcy referred to "an old square tower" near Majdalein (290-91). Also Glueck reported: "To the southeast [of Majdalein], on the left bank of the *wâdī*, is a small, rectangular tower, oriented north and south, with an entrance on the east side. It is made of large, roughly dressed limestone blocks. No sherds were found near this tower which could have been of assistance in dating it" (1934: 62). No doubt both de Saulcy and Glueck refer to Qaṣr el-Ḥimmeh.

The tower stands on a bedrock outcropping. It measures 5 m (E-W) by 6 m (N-S) and its walls, which are 1 m thick, stand 5 m high in the northeast corner. The entrance is on the east side, and there may have been a stairway on the collapsed northwest side. The roof is supported in corbel fashion.

Site 56 - **Tadūn**
(Map section 3; field no. 8033)
PG: 19.2/81.2; UTMG: 59.5/68.6

Partially standing ruins of three buildings on earlier wall lines, and a nearby rectangular mound. Ca. 2 km northwest of el-Qaṣr, between the Qaṣr-Faqu[c] road and the rim of Wadi Zuqeibah. Khirbat Tadūn on the K737 map. 527 sherds were collected, including: MB 1; LB 2; IR I 23; IR II 3; Nab 13; LRom 3; Byz 9; EByz 4; LByz 24; Um 4 AB 1; Fat(?) 2; A/M 2; LIsl 62; UD 60; 2 roof tiles; 31 tesserae.

See de Saulcy: Kharbet-Tedoum (291-93); Musil: ḫirbet Tedûn/Tedûm (16, 19, 87, 375); Glueck: Kh. Tedûn/#133 (1934: 62). De Saulcy described in some detail a structure, built of fine hewn stone, on the northern front of a large enclosure. According to de Saulcy, the structure was "a square edifice, of rather more than thirty feet on each side; its walls are two feet and a half in thickness, and still above six feet and a half in height. Openings of gates are visible on three of its faces—the northern, the eastern, and the southern; but one, the northern, is at present blocked up." De Saulcy described the adjacent mound as "a small, circular hillock" and interpreted it as the ruin of a Byzantine church. This was indicated, in his view, by a column fragment which he observed on the summit, a Byzantine style capital at the foot of the mound, and another column fragment not far away. Glueck reported only that there were "two modern abandoned buildings, standing among several ruined buildings" and that he found "a few Nabataean sherds and some mediaeval Arabic sherds." Worschech (1985a: 43-45; 1990: 15-20) has examined Tadun since our survey and distinguished four subsites: Tedūn/#54; Tedūn II = Ḫ. Fāris/#55; Tedūn III/#55.1 and #55.2. From Tedūn/#54 he reports LR and Byz sherds; from Tedūn III/#55.1 he reports pottery from LB II through Ir IIC; from Tedūn III/55.2 he reports Chalco/EB; Ir I/II; LR; Byz; Mam. In 1986, J. Johns and A. McQuitty began an intensive investigation of the site and its immediate

Photograph 9: Qaṣr el-Ḥimmeh (Site 55)

Photograph 10: Dolmen near Site 59

vicinity, including excavations at Kh. Fāris (Johns and McQuitty 1989; Johns, McQuitty, and Falkner 1989).

We saw the remains of three buildings, two of them with walls surviving over 4 m high and with roof arches still in place. The third building is less well preserved and not immediately obvious without close examination of the site. Apparently further building occurred at Tadun after de Saulcy's visit in 1851—probably about the turn of the century when the Ottoman government reasserted its authority and brought increased security to the Kerak plateau. The site had been abandoned again by the time of Glueck's survey, however, and he noticed only the two more conspicuous buildings. Around and beneath the shell of the three buildings are wall lines of numerous apparently earlier structures. In all, this part of the Tadun ruin covers ca. 70,000 sq. m. There are numerous cisterns among the wall remains. Also there is an Islamic period tomb which incorporates a sculpted limestone lintel.

The mound is ca. 200 m to the SSE of the building ruins and covers an area of ca. 3,800 sq. m. On it we found predominantly Byzantine pottery, numerous tesserae, and two roofing tiles, which seem to support de Saulcy's view that the mound represents the remains of a Byzantine church.

Site 57 - **Beit Lajjah**
(Map section 3; field no. 9014)
PG: 19.0/79.8; UTMG: 59.4/67.3

Settlement site at the head of Wadi ez-Zuqeiba and marked Khirbat ez-Zuqeiba on the K737 map. However Zuqeiba appears to be the name of the area and Beit Lajjah the local name for the site itself. 485 sherds were collected, including: EB II-III 1; IR 1; IR II 4; Nab 8; EByz 1; LByz 5; Abb 1; A/M 34; LIsl 87; Mod 1; UD 14; 1 glass fragment.

See Seetzen: Bêt Lidschá (416) and Musil: ḫirbet Bejt Leǧǧa (87, 375). Beit Lajjah is also the most likely candidate for Klein's Jherra: "At some distance to the right I was shown Yerud, an ancient ruin near a river, and another ruin, Jherra, also close to a small river, but none of these places are inhabited" (1869: 153). Worschech (Ḫ. zuqēba/#57, 1985a: 47) has resherded this site since we were there and reported LR, Byz and Mam pottery. Also he examined several archaeological features ca. 500 m southwest of the main site (see below).

The site is a low mound, measuring ca. 160 x 120 m and consisting of some 3-5 m overburden on bedrock, which overlooks Wadi ez-Zuqeiba from its southern rim. The mound is strewn with sherds. Also scattered over the site are some 10-15 large depressions, within which wall lines are occasionally visible. Apparently this mound represents the remains of a village with the depressions corresponding to the interior parts of buildings. One has the impression that the whole lay-out of a village is accessible immediately beneath the surface. A cistern and two wells were noted on the site, a presently occupied house on the west side of the mound, and cultivated fields to the east, south, and west. Approximately 500 m southwest of the main site is a large stone enclosure (85 x 85 m) where Worschech collected "some LR and several pieces of Ayy/Mam pottery." Since there were no internal walls visible and a probe revealed that the external wall was founded on a single row of stones sunk into the ground, he concluded that the compound probably "served only as a protective walled enclosure for tents." Worschech also excavated two tombs near the compound, which he identified as Roman tombs reused during the Mamluk period, and reports certain other archaeological features nearby (see his sites #58 [1985a: 58] and #74 [1985b: 163]).

Site 58 - **Abū el-Wsheish**
(Map section 3; field no. 9313)
PG: 16.4/79.9; UTMG: 56.7/67.4

Wall lines indicating a building compound on a narrow, rocky ridge overlooking Wadi Abu Jbeibah, slightly more than 2 km northwest of ed-Dimnah and el-Yarut. No pottery.

The shape of one room, 20 m (N-S) by 10 m (E-W), can be determined from the remains of walls situated for the most part on bedrock. Although the east and west walls extend beyond the room northward, a third crosswall to complete a second room is not discernible. SSW of the building compound, on an outcrop over the wadi, is a cistern.

Site 59
(Map section 3; field no. 9007)
PG: 16.7/79.4; UTMG: 57.1/66.6

A small square structure on the western edge of the plateau overlooking Wadi Ḥammad, 2 km WNW of el-Yarut. 77 sherds were collected, including: Chalco 1; EB II-III 30; EB IV 6; Nab 2; A/M 1; LIsl 1; Mod 2; UDE 8; UD 3.

Situated ca. 150 m from the edge of the plateau, this enigmatic structure is 2.8 m square, ca. 1.5 m high, and has walls 0.5 m thick. The foundation of a wall attached to the northeast corner can be traced several meters eastward. Another, attached to the southwest corner, can be traced westward. Nearby are a dolmen-like structure and a stone slab with cupholes, which correspond to Worschech's Sites #73 and #73.1 (Mattingly 1984: 76; Worschech 1985b: 163).

Site 60 - **Kh. el-Kharziyyah**
(Map section 3; field no. 9027)
PG: 18.0/79.2; UTMG: 58.2/66.7

Tumbled walls, foundations, and building rubble near ᶜAin Yarut, less than 1 km northwest of el-Yarut. 394 sherds were collected, including: EB II-III 1; EB IV 5; LB 6; IR 2; ERom 2; Mod 1; UDE 7; UDhandle 2.

The area of scattered ruins covers ca. 150 m (E-W) by 75 m (N-S). An important spring, ᶜAin Yarut, the site of a modern pumping station, is located on the floor of the steep Wadi Yarut, just a short distance below the edge of this site's basalt ruins.

Site 61 - **Um Sidreh**
(Map section 3; field no. 9013)
PG: 16.8/78.6; UTMG: 57.2/66.1

Building ruin, apparently a tower with two attached rooms, at the western edge of the plateau slightly less than 2 km west of el-Yarut. 110 sherds were collected, including: EB 1; Nab 3; LRom 1; EByz 3; LIsl 1; UD 5; 1 perforated glass disk; 1 glass bracelet fragment.

This seems the most likely candidate for Musil's "ruǧm al-Maᶜrâḍ." "I rode northeastward [he must mean northwestward!] with Tawfiḳ from ar-Rabba at 4:23 [p.m.] to ruǧm al-Maᶜrâḍ, a knoll on the left bank of w. el-Jârût, where, at 4:57, I climbed a collapsed tower, about 1.5 km northeast of ḫ. Dimne, in order to take in the countryside. One can view the whole area, from ḳaṣr el ᶜÂl in the northeast and ḳarᶜa Šîḥân in the north to šaǧarat el-Mêse. The ammu Ḥbele ridge obstructs the view to the ESE [again he must mean WSW, with reference to Jebel el-Ḥudeib]" (373). Another possible candidate is Site 59. Worschech (Umm Sidreh/#72, 1985b: 161) examined Um Sidreh six years after we were there and reported Chalcolithic and EB flints in addition to Nab, Nab-R, ER/LR and Byz sherds. Note the typographical error in his report: the PG is 16.8/78.6, not 16.8/76.8.

The partially collapsed walls of a roughly square tower, 6.5 m on a side, rise about 1 m above the tumbled ruins of a building complex. The eastern end of the complex is a large room oriented north–south (11.5 x 9 m). The tower joins this room on its northwest side and shares part of the latter's western wall. In the corner formed by the tower and the large room is a smaller room, this second room sharing the tower's south wall and the remainder of the large room's west wall (5 m). West of the tower and small room the wall lines become unclear. The northeast and southwest corners of the square tower have been reused for modern burials. There is a cistern nearby.

Site 62
(Map section 3; field no. 9009, 9028, 9142)
PG: 18.4/78.8; UTMG: 58.7/66.3

Wall lines indicating three stone structures within 0.5 km northwest of el-Yarut, in a roughly straight line. 26 sherds were collected, including: EB 3; Nab 2; UD 1; 2 glass fragments.

The most prominent of the three structures (field no. 9009) appears as a two-level platform extending (like terracing) from the side of a hill. Both levels of the platform are 5 m wide across the front. The lower level projects 9 m and the upper level 11 m from the slope of the hill. The pottery indicated above was collected around this platform. Several hundred meters northwest of it is a building ruin (field no. 9028) which included an "L-shaped" chamber (ca. 3.5 x 1.7 m). The back wall, set into the slope, is composed of large stone blocks and nearly 3 m thick. The other walls are from 1.6 to 1.8 m thick and composed of stones dressed on both faces. There was no surface pottery of consequence near this building ruin. The third structure (field no. 9142), also giving the impression of a terrace extending from the side of a hill, is situated immediately to the northwest of the building ruin and composed of partially dressed stones. It measures 8 m (EW) by 14 m (NS), and the center of its front wall has collapsed, forming a major break. Again there was no pottery.

Site 63 - **el-Yārūt**
(Map section 3; field no. 9002)
PG: 18.8/78.7; UTMG: 59.0/66.1

Present-day village on an ancient settlement site at the head of Wadi el-Yarut, slightly more than 3.5 km NNW of er-Rabbah and 2 km west of the Kerak-Dhiban road. El Yarut on the K737 map. 126 sherds were collected, including: EB II-III 1; MB(?) 1; IR 3; IR II 1; IR II C/P 1; Pers(?) 1; Nab 8; ERom 3; Byz 1; EByz 1; LByz 2; A/M 4; LIsl 11; Mod 1; UDE 6; UD 4; UDhandle 18.

See Seetzen: Järûd/Jarûd (411, 16); Burckhardt: El Yaroud (377); Klein: Yerud (1869: 153); Tristram: Yaroud (120); Musil: ḫirbet el-Jârûṯ (16-17, 87, 156, 373-74); Smith: el-Yarut (370); Worschech: Yarūt (1990: 20-27). Note that Burckhardt identifies "El Djebeyba" and "El Yaroud" as "two copious springs" southeast of er-Rabbah, when surely he means northwest of er-Rabbah. Burckhardt also lists a "Yarouk" among the ruins in the Kerak region. Redford (1982a: 115-20) identifies el-Yarut as the site of *yarutu*, one of the places mentioned in the so-called "Palestinian List" (also called the "Megiddo List") from the reign of Thuthmosis III.

The modern town of el-Yarut overlooks Wadi el-Yarut from the wadi's southeast end. The spring which Burckhardt and others mentioned is NNW of the town, in the wadi bed, and has been converted to a pumping station (marked on the K737 map). The sherds indicated above were collected on the southern slopes of the wadi, beginning just below the northwestern edge of the modern village. Most of the sherds were found high on the slopes, above the road to the pumping station. Remnants of walls are discernible here and there along the slopes. It is difficult to determine which are building remains and which are terrace walls. The situation is further complicated by bedrock outcroppings and scattered boulders. Also the area is under cultivation in spots and serves as a local quarry. Actually the main area of settlement in earlier times is probably covered by the modern town. There are cisterns and wells in the town, and also two caves near its center.

Site 64 - **ed-Dimnah**
(Map section 3; field no. 9017)
PG: 17.1/77.9; UTMG: 57.4/65.3

Modern village on an ancient settlement site situated on the western edge of the plateau, ca. 4 km northwest of er–Rabbah. Ed Dimna on the K737 map. 679 sherds were collected, including: LB 1; IR 1; Per(?) 1; Nab 5; LRom 2; Byz 1; EByz 1; A/M 4; LIsl 98; Mod 7; UD 23.

See Tristram: Dimnah (120) and Musil: ḫirbet Dimne (15, 19, 157, 374). The place name *dîmôn*, which appears twice in Isa. 15:9 but nowhere else in the Hebrew Bible, usually is emended to read *dîbôn* or otherwise interpreted as a reference to the more often mentioned Moabite city Dibon. However it may have been this place or a site nearby (see, e.g., Worschech and Knauf 1986: 70-94; Worschech 1990: 49-53).

The modern settlement has obscured all indications of ancient occupation except for surface sherds which are to be found primarily in the area of the village dump—i.e., on the east side of the village and north of the road to Yarut.

Site 65
(Map section 3; field no. 9256)
PG: 18.3/76.2; UTMG: 58.7/63.6

Large rock-cut pool and associated basins situated on a rise overlooking Wadi Manasib, slightly less than 2 km WNW of er-Rabbah. 4 sherds were collected, including: Byz 1; UD 3.

The whole system, which consists of three small basins attached to the south side of a rectangular pool, measures 7 x 7 m. Each basin is attached to the pool by a drain, and the basin in the southwestern corner has three internal steps. Part of the western end of the large pool is broken away. There has been a considerable amount of quarrying in this area.

Site 66 - **Batīr**
(Map section 3; field no. 9073)
PG: 17.2/74.8; UTMG: 57.5/62.3

Modern village on an ancient settlement site, ca. 3.5 km WSW of er-Rabbah. Batīr on the K737 map. 512 sherds were collected, including: Chalco 1; MB(?) 1; LB(?) 1; IR 2; Nab 7; ERom 2; Byz 1; LByz 10; A/M 11; LIsl 36; Mod 1; UDE 2; UD 12; UDhandle 18.

See Seetzen: Batîr (416); Tristram: Betêr (120); Musil: Betîr (21, 87, 373). See also now Worschech (1985b: 166-67) who reports under the name Butayyīr/#77 some cisterns and "exposed foundation walls" on the slight knoll ca. 500 m southeast of the modern town and separated from it by a small wadi. One of the cisterns has been excavated by a villager, according to Worschech, and produced pottery from "exclusively ER and LR, with only a few pieces from Byzantine times."

The present-day settlement has obscured all traces of earlier occupation except for surface pottery which can be collected in open areas in the village and along the slopes on its northern, eastern, and western sides.

Site 67 - **Kh. el-Ḥdeib**
(Map section 3; field no. 2588)
PG: 12.5/75.3; UTMG: 52.9/62.6

Extensive building ruins on a spur of Jebel el-Ḥdeib, overlooking Wadi el-Kerak. Marked "Ruins" on the K737 map, although the ruins are nearer the crest of Jebel Ḥdeib than the map implies (there are no significant ruins further below). 117 sherds were collected, including: Byz 1; EByz 2; A/M 1; LIsl 32; UDhandle 5; 1 glass fragment.

Probably this is Musil's ḫirbet el-Ḥdêb (156).

Building ruins cover an area of ca. 100 x 40 m (NW-SE) on a narrow spur which extends from Jebel Ḥdeib and then drops precipitously into Wadi el-Kerak. Notable are the collapsed remains of a recent and crudely built square tower on the northwest end of the site and a well-constructed building (10 x 10 m) of beautifully dressed stones on the southeast end. Numerous other walls, some of which stand four courses high, are interspersed with modern sheepfolds. Several cisterns dot the site, and there is an unusually large cistern near the center of the ruins. Also among the tumbled walls are part of a column drum and stone door sockets.

Site 68
(Map section 3; field no. 2589)
PG: 12.9/75.0; UTMG: 53.3/62.3

A cistern, wall remains of a rectangular building, and sparse covering of sherds in plowed fields on the Jebel Ḥdeib ridge. 163 sherds were collected, including: IR 1; Nab 9; ERom 2; LRom 1; Byz 2; LIsl 2; UD 4.

The cistern is large and well-cut with an opening ca. 1 m in diameter. Near the opening is a cuphole. At the northwest end of the plowed area surrounding the cistern are the wall remains of a solidly built structure, possibly a tower, which measures 7 m (E-W) by 4 m (N-S). The walls were composed of large, roughly shaped blocks and have survived only one course high. The sherds were collected in the plowed field near the wall remains.

Site 69
(Map section 3; field no. 2590, 2591, 9315)
PG: 13.6/73.12; UTMG: 54.2/60.4

Numerous cairns of various sizes were observed along the whole length of the mountain ridge which begins immediately west of Rakin and becomes Jebel Ḥdeib (marked Jebel el Ḥudeib on the K737 map). At least two of the cairns are of the "partitioned" type. Five are distinctively circular in shape and four rectangular. Occasional sherds were found near some of the cairns, but there were no diagnostic pieces and never was there any concentration of sherds.

Site 70 - **Kh. Zabūbah**
(Map section 3; field no. 2593)
PG: 13.1/72.7; UTMG: 53.6/60.0

Building ruins on a narrow shelf between the Jebel Ḥdeib ridge and Wadi el-Kerak. Appears as Khirbat Zabūba on the K737 map—note, however, that the name is slightly misplaced on the map. Actually Kh. Zabubah is situated on the northwest side (rather than the southeastern side) of the hill whose summit bears the 666 m elevation marker. 100 sherds were collected, including: Nab 6; LByz 1; LIsl 27; A/M 5; UD 1.

See Seetzen: Sübbûba (416); de Saulcy: Aÿn-Zeboub (331-32). Worschech (Ḫ. Zabbūba/#68, 1985a: 61) examined the site five years after we were there, reported only ER and LR pottery, and identified it as the ruin of "a Roman tower or small castellum."

Apparently representing the remains of a small village, the ruins cover an area of ca. 80 m (N-S) by 40 m (E-W). The Jebel Ḥdeib ridge rises steeply on one side of the site while the slope to Wadi el-Kerak becomes precipitous on the other. Especially notable among the ruins are the collapsed remains of a solidly constructed building with a superb view toward the Dead Sea. This building, which may have been a tower, measures 7 m sq, is of better construction than the surrounding houses, and possibly is older than they. There is a large cistern ca. 50 m below the site on the north, and also a spring ca. 100 m from the site.

Site 71 - **ed-Deir**
(Map section 3; field no. 9070)
PG: 14.8/73.3; UTMG: 55.3/60.6

Unoccupied settlement site on the summit of an isolated peak ca. 4 km northwest of Rakin. 2572 sherds were collected, including: Chalco 1; EB I 1; LB 5; IR(?) 4; IR 22; IR I 14; IR II 27; Hell 1; Nab 134; ERom 22; LRom 19; Byz 20; EByz 18; LByz 28; Um 2; A/M 46; LIsl 99; Mod 1; UDEhandle 9; UD 34; UDhandle 57.

See Seetzen: et Dêr (416); Musil: ed-Dejr (19, 153-54, 157); Canova: ed-Deir (14-17). Worschech (1990: 44-49) has examined the site since we were there and published a fairly extensive description. Also, with Knauf, he proposes it as the site of Horonaim mentioned in Isa. 15:6-5 and the Mesha Inscription (Worschech and Knauf 1986: 70-94).

The steep hill (elevation 1038 m) on which this extensive ruin is situated provides a clear view west toward the Dead Sea and an overview of approaches from the sea to the plateau. One approaches the site itself from the south along a narrow ridge. The ruins stretch over an area ca. 150 x 165 m. What probably is the latest phase of ruins at ed-Deir is fairly well preserved, with some walls standing several courses high. On the western and northern perimeters are buildings and/or chambers measuring up to ca. 5 x 5 m. Considerably larger buildings are located in the central area. One of the central buildings preserves a limestone lintel from its entrance and part of a vaulted roof. Its dimensions are ca. 24.25 m (EW) by 9.5 m (NS) and it appears to have been subdivided into three rooms. In the southeastern corner of the site is a pool (2 x 3 m x 1.5 m deep) with plastered steps. Near the western perimeter is exposed bedrock with remains of a press and two collecting vats. Earlier wall lines are discernible beneath the latest phase of ruins, which is consistent with the ceramic evidence that this site has a long occupational history.

Site 72 - **el-Qabū**
(Map section 3; field no. 9098)
PG: 16.0/74.0; UTMG: 56.5/61.5

Building ruin on the ridge southwest of Batir on the opposite bank of Wadi eṣ-Ṣuwwan. 124 sherds were collected, including: IR I 1; ERom 1; LRom 3; EByz 1; LByz 1; LIsl 5; UD 2; one tessera.

Worschech's Kh. Qabū/#75 (1985b: 166) must be the same place in spite of the fact that his PG coordinates (17.3/73.3) would place it further to the southeast. Compare his Ġabū/#75 (1990: 28) which he places at (16.1/74.0). Worschech reports "Ir I, II, Nab, ER, LR, Byz, Um, Mam" pottery.

This 13 x 16 m structure rests on bedrock and includes 3 rooms. A room on the west extends the entire 13 m length and has walls 1.5 m thick. A smaller room in the northeastern sector of the structure is roughly square and contains a cistern in its southwestern corner. A still smaller room (5 x 8 m ?) in the southeastern sector has a curved wall on its eastern side (possibly a chapel?). The walls of the two smaller rooms are ca. 1 m thick. A large stone heap against the western wall may have been part of the structure also, possibly a tower. At the northeastern corner of the building is another cistern and a corner segment of a wall which may have enclosed the building. The foundation line of another wall extends 28 m south from the southeast corner of the building; then it turns west for 17 m; and then north for 20 m. While it is difficult to trace the wall line beyond that point, there seems to be another corner with the wall turning eastward. Apparently this was also an external enclosure wall of some sort.

Site 73 - **Rujm Birjis**
(Map section 3; field no. 9047, 9072)
PG: 17.2/73.9; UTMG: 57.7/61.2

A low mound covered with pottery 1 km south of Batir, immediately west of the road from Batir to Rakin.

Photograph 11: Approach to ed-Deir (Site 71)

Photograph 12: Apse (?) at el-Qabū (Site 72)

1167 sherds were collected, including: Chalco 2; EB I 9; EB II-III 177; EB IV 54; MB 1; LB 2; IR 1; IR I 2; IR II 1; Hell 1; Nab 14; UDE 14; UD 8.

See Musil: ruğm Barğas (156).

The mound is ca. 95 m (N-S) by 155 m (E-W) and situated in an intensely cultivated area. Its eastern end was disturbed during the construction of the Batir-Rakin road. Sections of a wall which may have surrounded the whole mound are visible. In a large terrace which extends 130 m south from the mound is a fallen menhir with the stone socket in which it stood. Ca. 1.75 m wide and nearly 5 m long (high), this pillar has been broken into two parts since we first observed it in 1979.

Site 74 - **Kh. Zughriyyeh**
(Map section 3; field no. 9074)
PG: 16.0/73.2; UTMG: 56.6/60.6

Ancient settlement site, currently unoccupied except for three modern houses, ca. 2 km SSW of Batir. Khirbat Zugheiriya on the K737 map. 345 sherds were collected, including: Nab 13; Nab(?) 1; ERom 1; LRom 2; Byz 3; LByz 145; UM(?) 1; LIsl 2; UD 1; UDhandle 11.

See Musil: ḫirbet ez-Zṛejrijje (156). Apparently this is the same site which Worschech (1985b: 166) reports under the name eẓ-Ẓahirīye/#76, although we must disagree with his PG coordinates (17.7/72.5). Worschech, who visited the site in 1985, reports "Nab-R, ER, LR, Byz, Um, Mam" pottery. It will be apparent from his description, moreover, that the modern settlement had grown considerably since we had examined it six years earlier.

On the top of a hill overlooking Wadi Qahush are three modern houses and an abandoned building with walls and arched doorways still standing. Occasional walls are observable at ground level. Possibly there were more conspicuous ruins at the site when Musil reported it. If so, these ruins have been robbed for building stones by modern villagers in the area. Most of the sherds indicated above were collected on the south and east slopes of the hill. A winepress carved in bedrock on the northwest side of the site consists of a main vat (2.75 x 2.75 m) and attached smaller vat (0.75 x 1.25 m). Another larger winepress (with the main vat measuring 8 x 2.5 m) was observed on the northeast side of the site. Also there is a large pool, or open cistern, on the northeast side which measures 13 x 12 m.

Site 75
(Map section 3; field no. 9067)
PG: 16.8/73.2; UTMG: 57.6/60.6

Sherd scatter and wall remains of a small house ca. 1.5 km south of Batir, immediately north of the branch road to Zughriyyeh near the intersection of this road with the Batir-Rakin road. A sparse scatter of sherds covers an area ca. 25 m (E-W) by 15 m (N-S), and faint traces of walls suggest a small house in the sherd area. 72 sherds were collected, including: EB 1; ERom 1; Byz 1; UD 4.

Site 76 - **Bteiyir**
(Map section 3; field no. 9068)
PG: 18.3/73.5; UTMG: 58.7/61.0

Sherd scatter, traces of wall lines, and stone heaps on a ridge overlooking Wadi el-Manasib/Wadi ᶜUweir, slightly less than 3 km southwest of er-Rabbah. 426 sherds were collected, including: LB 1; IR II 1; Nab 24; ERom 6; Byz 14; EByz 2; LByz 4; A/M 1; LIsl 4; UD 14; UDhandle 7.

See Seetzen: Btéïjir (416). The name Bteiyir actually pertains to the vicinity, which accounts for the fact that Worschech (1985b: 166-67) reports under the same name, Butayyīr/#77, some exposed foundation walls ca. 1 km further to the northwest of this site and on the outskirts of the modern settlement Betir.

Sherds scattered over an area ca. 100 x 150 m are the strongest evidence that this is an ancient site. One foundation wall can be traced a few meters. Also there are several stone heaps, none of which presents clearly discernible architectural features.

Site 77 - **Rujm Abū Zaᶜrūrah**
(Map section 4; field no. 8031)
PG: 23.9/82.2; UTMG: 64.3/69.5

Building ruins ca. 3.5 km northeast of el-Qaṣr, near the head of Wadi Baluᶜ. 277 sherds were collected, including: IR 1; IR I 21; IR II 8; Nab 12; ERom 1; Byz 6; LIsl 6; UDE 3; UD 13.

A ruin covering ca. 100 sq. m on a hillside, this khirbeh consists of two small stone fenced courtyards connected to the ruin of one house. Two cisterns on the site will have supplemented water from a nearby wadi (ca. 100 m to the west) which flows north toward Wadi Abu Za^crura. Occupational debris is shallow (ca. 50 cm). Probably this was a farmstead.

Site 78 - **el-Kharī^c**
(Map section 4; field no. 9041)
PG: 26.5/81.5; UTMG: 66.7/69.2

Sherd scatter on a knoll overlooking Wadi Ghneim, 2 km north of es-Smakiyyah. 372 sherds were collected, including: EB 7; EB II-III(?) 6; EB II-III 43; EB IV 16; LB(?) 1; Nab 10; ERom 1; LRom 2; Byz 1; A/M 1; LIsl 1; UDE 5; UD 4.

See Seetzen: Kréha (411) and Tristram: Keriyeh (120). Smith thought that Seetzen's Kréha may have been identical with Shiḥan (the full name of which Smith reported as Ḳări^cat Shīḥān; 371). However, Seetzen apparently saw both sites from a distance and clearly distinguished between them: "Wir kamen neben einem ruinirten Orte Bellúe hin, von welchem westwärts drey Viertelstunden entfernt auf einem hohen Hügel der ruinirte Ort Schihhân lag. Eine halbe Stunde weiter lag das ruinirte Kréha, und weider eine halbe Stunde weiter Hhmeimât..." It seems equally unlikely, on the other hand, that Seetzen and Tristram would have noted a site with so few visible surface ruins as the one reported here. Actually the name el-Kharya^c is attached also to the knoll between es-Smakiyyah and Wadi Ghneim and may have been attached to some more prominent ruin in their day, possibly es-Smakiyyah. The fact that Seetzen included both "Smakije" and "Esmekiéh" in a list of sites with unspecified locations, while Tristram included both "Keriyeh" and "Tzemakiyeh" in a similar list, is not a strong argument to the contrary. Seetzen and Tristram will have collected the names for these lists from several informants, and different informants may have given different names for the same site.

The sherds cover a relatively large area, ca. 200 x 225 m. Also there are several cisterns and caves in the rocky, hilly terrain.

Site 79 - **Rujm Ghneim**
(Map section 4; field no. 9033)
PG: 27.3/81.2; UTMG: 67.6/68.8

Building ruin, a small square structure overlooking Wadi Ghneim from the north, ca. 1.5 km NNE of es-Smakiyyah. 74 sherds were collected, including: EB II-III 1; Nab 1; Byz 2; UD 2.

See Tristram: Oneim (120); Musil: ẖrejbe Ṛnêm (139).

The building, possibly a farmstead, measured ca. 10 m square with walls surviving three courses high. There are some ten or twelve recent burial mounds (cairns) in the area immediately surrounding it. The skeletons were not totally covered; 16 separate ones were counted.

Site 80
(Map section 4; field no. 9263)
PG: 28.0/82.0; UTMG: 68.3/69.7

Building ruin (13 x 6 m) with attached enclosures situated on the north bank of a tributary to Wadi el-Ghweir, ca. 3 km NNE of Smakiyyah. Probably the remains of a farmstead. 9 sherds were collected, including Byz 1; LIsl 1; UD 7.

Site 81 - **Dalāleḥ**
(Map section 4; field no. 9084, 9090, 9261, 9264)
PG: 28.0/81.5; UTMG: 68.3/69.2

Numerous rubble wall-lines covering an area ca. 75 x 45 m on the west slope of Wadi el-Ghweir, ca. 2.5 km NNE of es-Smakiyyah. 180 sherds were collected, including: EB II-III 1; Nab 1; ERom 1; A/M 2; LIsl 76; UD 1.

See Tristram: Ed D^ɔlalhye (120); Musil: ẖirbet ed-Dlâleḥ (34, 139).

Ca. 100 m northwest of the khirbeh is a large cistern with supporting arches known locally as Bir Qneiṭreh ("well of arches"). Ca. 200 m north of the khirbeh, on a steep slope above Wadi el-Ghweir, are more building rubble, some caves, and several cisterns (some of them in use). This latter complex covers ca. 25 x 35 m and produced diagnostic sherds only from the Late Islamic period (51 sherds were collected, including 13 LIsl). Ca. 250 m southeast (further down the slope) from the Islamic ruins, beyond two stone enclosures, is a "partitioned cairn" (field no. 9261), ca. 4.5 m in diameter, constructed of large, field-dressed limestone blocks and bisected by a single stone slab.

Site 82
(Map section 4; field no. 9262)
PG: 29.6/81.4; UTMG: 69.9/69.1

Building ruin on a low hill in the bed of Wadi el-Ghweir. 15 sherds were collected, including: IR 2; UDE 2; UD 1.

Wall lines visible at ground level suggest a northeast-southwest oriented building complex which measured 23 x 13 m and was partitioned by at least one interior wall. Small rooms (4 x 4 m and 5 x 5 m) were appended to the east and south corners.

Site 83
(Map section 4; field no. 9184)
PG: 29.5/81.1; UTMG: 69.9/68.6

Building ruin, a 11 x 11 m structure with attached enclosures on the east bank of Wadi el-Ghweir (west slopes of the ridge between Wadi el-Ghweir and Wadi el-Mujib), ca. 3 km northeast of es-Smakiyyah. The walls are ca. 1 m thick and composed of large basalt stones. Probably this is a farmstead of fairly recent times (see also several other similar structures with attached enclosures in the same vicinity—e.g., sites 120, 122, and 123). 40 m farther north is a partitioned cairn 5 m in diameter, bisected by a single stone slab and filled with large stone rubble.

Site 84
(Map section 4; field no. 9182)
PG: 29.4/80.5; UTMG: 69.8/68.1

Two cairns of large, field-dressed, limestone blocks on a knoll overlooking Wadi el-Ghweir, ca. 3 km ENE of es-Smakiyyah. Several of the blocks are over 1 m long. There are terrace walls in the wadi.

Site 85 - **Shajarah**
(Map section 4; field no. 8034)
PG: 19.8/80.5; UTMG: 60.1/67.9

Ruins of a church, probably Byzantine, ca. 1 km west of el-Qaṣr. 100 sherds were collected, including: Byz 10; LIsl 6; UDE 6; UD 8.

See Seetzen: Bêt állah (416). Musil described a circular stone enclosure with a huge stone slab underneath an olive-tree. It was regarded as a sacred spot by one of the local tribes who, according to Musil, called it "Bêt állah" or "šaǧarat Bejt Allâh" and on certain occasions sacrificed sheep on the stone slab. Outside the tribe, the name "šaǧara ᶜObejdallâh" seems to have been preferred (87, 375). This is Glueck's site #134 for which he reported: "Half a kilometre farther east [from Tedun] we came to a site called Sejerah (?). There are traces of the foundations of a large walled enclosure, with more distinct ones of a large church at the east end of it. The apse is recognizable from a few of its foundation stones, which are still in place. A line of column bases, oriented east and west, is visible to the left of the apse. A Corinthian capital was found inside the church area. The church may have been built over the site of an earlier Roman building." He reported no pottery (1934: 62). Worschech (Ḫ. Šeǧerat Bēt Allāh/#56, 1985a: 47) has resherded the site since we were there and reported LR, Byz and Mam pottery .

The ruins cover an area ca. 35 x 40 m, and the building mound which Glueck identified as a church is still visible. We were unable to distinguish an apse. A carved, round limestone baptistry (?) at the east end of the building mound is the clearest evidence that it was a church (Worschech provides a photograph in 1985a: pl. XX).

Site 86 - el-Qaṣr
(Map section 4; field no. 9273)
PG: 21.2/80.5; UTMG: 61.3/67.9

Modern town at the site of an ancient Nabataean temple. El Qaṣr on the K737 map. 1587 sherds were collected, including: MB(?) 3; LB 3; IR I 2; IR II 1; Hell 1; Nab 32; ERom 10; LRom 3; Byz 12; EByz 5; LByz 1; A/M 26; LIsl 100; UDE 8; UD 63; tesserae; 1 clay button.

See Seetzen: Bêt el Kerm/Küssr Ubba (411, 16); Burckhardt: Beit Kerm (376); Irby and Mangles: Beit-Kerm (141); Macmichael: Bart-el-Carn (241); de Saulcy: Beit-el-Kerm (293-96); de Luynes: Beit-el-Kurn (172); Klein: Kasr-beit-el-Kerm (1869: 153); Tristram: Kasr Rabba/Beit el Kurm (133-34); Hill: Beit el Kurn (1891: 212; 1896: 40); Bliss: Beit el Kuhn/Kasr Rabba (217); Gautier: ḳaṣr rabba (120); Libby and Hoskins: Kasr Rabba (317, 319); Brünnow and Domaszewski: Ḳaṣr Rabba/Bêt el-Kerm (I: 46-52); Musil: ḫirbet el-Ḳaṣr/bejt el-Karm/ḳaṣr er-Rabba (35, 87, 140, 239, 274, 340); Smith: Beit el-Karm/Ḳaṣr Rabba (371); Glueck: Qaṣr Rabbah, /#135 in 1934 (62), #147 in 1939 (46, 48, 65, 67-68, 107-13).

It will be apparent from the citations above that virtually every traveler who passed through the Kerak plateau during the nineteenth century mentioned this site which was dominated by a conspicuous temple. Many of them stopped to investigate and included descriptions of the temple in their published reports. Gautier, Libby and Hoskins, and Brünnow and Domaszewski published the first photographs. Brünnow and Domaszewski published a plan. The modern village was just beginning to emerge around the temple when Glueck visited, and he observed that "many of its stones, particularly the ornamental pieces, have been inserted into the rude walls of the modern houses." Comparing the temple to other similar structures on the Transjordan, particularly the temples at Kh. et-Tannur and Kh. edh-Dheriḥ, he dated it to the first quarter of the second century A.D.

The temple still stands, as photographed by Glueck (1939: 107), although surrounded now by one of the largest towns on the Kerak plateau. As Glueck observed, reused decorative stones are to be seen in many of the older houses. Exposed walls also are to be seen here and there at open places, especially in the northern and eastern part of town —i.e., east of the Kerak-Dhiban road. Most of the sherds indicated above were collected in this area. Soon before we examined Qaṣr in 1979, excavations in connection with building construction had exposed a major wall ca. 50 m northeast of the temple and some 50 cm below ground level. Another foundation wall east of the "Turkish mill" can be traced several meters in a northeast-southwest direction.

Site 87 - **el-Misdāḥ**
(Map section 4; field no. 9001)
PG: 20.9/79.4; UTMG: 61.2/66.8

Unoccupied settlement site 1 km south of el-Qaṣr and immediately south of the "Police post" marked on the K737 map. The K737 map notes "Ruins" at approximately the spot, although actually el-Misdaḥ is situated on the east side of the Kerak-Dhiban road rather than the west side. 514 sherds were collected, including: IR I 1; Nab 27; ERom 1; LRom 2; Byz 9; EByz 9; LByz 13; A/M 4; LIsl 3; UD 13; UDhandle 20; 2 roof tiles.

See Tristram: Missdehh (132); Brünnow and Domaszewski: el-Misde (I: 53-54); Smith: el-Misdaḥ (371).

The ruin consists of mounds of dirt and rocks covering an area approximately 90 x 90 m. While it has been robbed for building stones (e.g., by the residents of nearby el-Qaṣr), the site also serves as a clearing dump for the surrounding fields. Architectural features are no longer clearly discernible, therefore, except for a cistern filled now with debris immediately west of the site. The surrounding terrain is generally flat with wheat fields. Further to the west, at the spot marked "Ruins" on the K737 map, are two cisterns still in use. Foundation walls of a rectangular structure near the cistern are, according to a local informant, from a building begun about ten years ago and never finished.

Site 88 - **Um el-Habāj**
(Map section 4; field no. 9012)
PG: 23.0/81.0; UTMG: 63.4/68.4

Unoccupied settlement site ca. 2 km ENE of el-Qaṣr. 2922 sherds were collected, including: EB I 2; EB II-III 317; EB IVA 110; EB IVB 1; MB/LB 1; LB 4; IR II 1; Hell 4; Nab 52; ERom 11; LRom 16; Byz 3; EByz 6; LByz 1; A/M 1; LIsl 5; UDE 78; UDEhandle 28; UD 27; UDhandle 35.

Traces of wall lines and an abundance of surface pottery are noticeable over an area of ca. 300 m (N-S) by 150 m (E-W) on a low-lying, rocky hill. The wall lines are especially concentrated on the south central part of the hill. As one moves down the slopes it becomes increasingly difficult to distinguish between wall lines and natural rock formations. Several depressions in the southwest quadrant of the site may be filled cisterns.

Site 89 - **Ḥmeimāt (NW)**
(Map section 4; field no. 9004)
PG: 22.6/80.3; UTMG: 63.0/67.8

A low mound of occupational debris slightly less than 2 km east of el-Qaṣr. Marked "Ruins" on the K737 map. 572 sherds were collected, including: EB II-III 14; EB IV 70; MB 3; IR 1; IR I 1; Hell 1; Nab 12; ERom 1; LRom 6; Byz 3; EByz 6; LByz 5; A/M 4; LIsl 33; UD 17; UDhandle 10.

See Seetzen: Hhmeimât/Chmeimât/Hhémeimât (411, 16); Burckhardt: Hemeymat (376); Tristram: Hameitât (132); Brünnow and Domaszewski: el-Ḥamêmât? (I: 53); Musil: ḫirbet Ḥmêmât (18, 35, 141); Smith: Hemēmāt (371). With the exception of Musil, these travelers did not distinguish between the four prominent ruins in close proximity to each other (Sites 89, 90, 91 and 92), and Musil reported only three of these ruins (141). Tristram incorrectly equated Ḥmeimāt with the Hammet ᶜAneineh reported by Palmer (1871a: 67) and notes that Ḥmeimāt is "laid down in all the maps as the remains of the ancient Ham mentioned in Gen. xiv.5 as the place where Chedorlaomer defeated the Zuzim."

Remnants of walls, some standing up to three courses above the ground, are concentrated in the center of this ca. 275 m (N-S) by 175 m (E-W) mound. A central building with walls ca. 1.5 m thick is discernible. Also there are three partially collapsed cisterns in the northeast quadrant of the site.

Site 90 - **Ḥmeimāt (SW)**
(Map section 4; field no. 9005)
PG: 25.7/79.8; UTMG: 63.1/67.4

A small knoll covered with stone heaps and occasional wall lines ca. 2 km ESE of el-Qaṣr and ca. 0.5 km north of the Qaṣr-Ḥmud road. Marked "Ruins" on some editions of the K737 map. 1194 sherds were collected, including: EB II-III 9; EB IV 1; IR 2; IR I 1; IR II(?) 1; IR II 1; IR II C/P 1; Nab 56; ERom 7; LRom 17; EByz 6; LByz 7; LIsl 12; UD 9; UDhandle 26.

See Site 89 for bibliographic references.

This site is located only 0.5 km south of Site 89 and measures ca. 300 m (N-S) x 115 m (E-W). Occasional wall lines and the collapsed remains of one building are discernible among nondescript stone heaps. There are two threshing floors at the north edge of the site, several cisterns, and some cleared areas (apparently for Bedouin camps). The eastern slope of the knoll is terraced.

Site 91 - **Ḥmeimāt (NE)**.2
(Map section 4; field no. 9008)
PG: 23.5/79.9; UTMG: 63.9/67.4

Unoccupied settlement site ca. 3 km east of el-Qaṣr. 652 sherds were collected, including: Hell 1; Nab 23; ERom 5; LRom 4; Byz 2; LByz 2; EIsl (?) 2; Um 2; Abb 7; FAT (?) 1; A/M 34; LIsl 82; UDE 2; UD 26; UDhandle 3.

See Site 89 for bibliographic references.

On a low mound ca. 150 m (N-S) x 200 m (E-W) are numerous wall lines, cisterns, and caves. Some of the caves evidently served as dwellings (indicated by remnants of walls at their entrances). Ruins of a substantial building complex at the southeastern corner of the mound gives the impression of a small acropolis.

Site 92 - **Ḥmeimāt (SE)**
(Map section 4; field no. 9006)
PG: 23.2/79.0; UTMG: 63.6/66.4

Unoccupied settlement site located ca. 2.5 km southeast of el-Qaṣr and immediately south of the Qaṣr-Ḥmūd road. Ḥumaymat on the K737 map. 679 sherds were collected, including: LB(?) 3; IR 3; IR I 2; Hell 1; Nab 18; ERom 3; LRom 10; Byz 1; EByz' 13; LByz 4; Um 2; Fat(?) 2; A/M 39; LIsl 114; UD 23; UDhandle 13.

See Site 89 for bibliographic references.

Numerous tumbled structures and exposed wall lines cover a slight rise, ca. 200 x 200 m, surrounded by fertile fields. Seasonal water is available from a small wadi ca. 125 m to the west, and there are collapsed cisterns on the site. Two small columns, both ca. 35 cm in diameter and one of which was still standing, were found on the site.

Site 93
(Map section 4; field no. 9018)
PG: 23.3/78.2; UTMG: 63.8/65.7

Building ruin, a small, square structure on the crest of a ridge slightly less than 1 km SSE of Site 92. The building, possibly a watchtower, would have measured 8.5 x 9 m at its base. 98 sherds were collected, including: Nab 1; Nab/ERom 2; LRom 1; LRom 1; UD 4.

Site 94 - **es-Smākiyyah**
(Map section 4; field no. 9037)
PG: 26.5/79.6; UTMG: 66.9/67.2

Occupied settlement site 6 km east of el-Qaṣr. Marked Simākīyah on the K737 map. 660 sherds were collected, including: IR 11; IR I 1; IR II 1; Hell(?) 4; Nab 19; ERom 4; LRom 4; Byz 9; EByz 7; LByz 2; A/M 6; LIsl 71; Mod 21; UD 21.

Seetzen included "Smakije" and also "Esmekiéh" in a list of ruins with unspecified locations (416). Tristram included "Tzemakiyeh" in a similar list (120). See also Musil: ḫirbet es-Smâčijje (19, 34, 139); Glueck: es-Smakîyeh/#139 (1934: 63) and Canova: Smākiyeh (192-97). Seetzen's reference to "Kréha" (411) and Tristram's reference to "Keriyeh" (120) may pertain to es-Smakiyyah (see bibliographic notes for Site 78: field no. 9041). Es-Smakiyyah was still an unoccupied khirbeh when Musil passed near it at the turn of the century. Glueck found it resettled by Christians and reported "a few Nabataean sherds." Canova provided a photograph of a large stone, cut in the shape of a cross (1.37 x 1.20 m), in an open field near Smakiyyah.

The modern settlement, which began about 90 years ago according to local informants, has completely displaced the earlier khirbeh. As is often the case in the Kerak region, this modern settlement itself has experienced two building phases. At the lower (southeastern) end of town is an older section of "Turkish" houses, now either deserted or reused. The heaviest concentration of surface pottery was found in this older section.

Site 95
(Map section 4; field no. 9226)
PG: 26.9/79.4; UTMG: 67.4/66.8

Rubble, a cistern, and surface pottery on a knoll ca. 0.3 km ESE of es-Smakiyyah, separated from the town by a small wadi. 117 sherds were collected, including: IR 4; Nab 15; LByz 1; A/M 3; UD 1.

Several piles of stone and dirt rubble (with no discernible wall lines) and a very moderate scattering of surface pottery cover an area ca. 35 m (E-W) by 75 m (N-S). There is a partially collapsed cistern near the center of the site and currently used threshing floors to the north and south of site.

Site 96 - **Kh. ᶜAleiyān**
(Map section 4; field no. 9218)
PG: 25.6/78.7; UTMG: 66.0/66.2

Caves, cisterns, and surface pottery on a rocky hillside ca. 1 km NNW of Ḥmud and immediately west of the power line. 778 sherds were collected, including: Nab 10; LRom 2; Byz 1; A/M(?) 6; A/M 8; LIsl 162; UDE 1; UD 4; UDhandle 12.

See Tristram: Alayan (120); Musil: ḫirbet ᶜAlejjân (139).

The sherd scatter covers an area ca. 150 x 75 m. In addition to three clearly visible cisterns, three other depressions in the ground surface may represent filled cisterns. There were no surface ruins. Although generally rocky, much of the surrounding area is under cultivation.

Site 97 - **Kh. Mḥeisin**
(Map section 4; field no. 9225)
PG: 28.1/78.7; UTMG: 68.5/66.3

A small khirbeh ca. 1.5 km ESE of es-Smakiyyah, near the north end of the ridge marked Muḥaysin/Muheisin on the K737 map and at approximately the spot marked "Ruins" on some editions of the map. Specifically, the khirbeh is situated on the south slope of the saddle which separates the main ridge from the knoll bearing the 814 elevation marker on the K737 map. 146 sherds were collected, including: MB 1; Nab 3; EByz 1; LByz 4; Um 1; A/M 5; LIsl 2; LOtt 1; UD 1.

Building rubble, several caves, and a large cistern constitute this khirbeh which covers an area some 100 by 200 m. The outlines of several buildings can be traced, none of them particularly impressive but some with walls two courses wide. Some areas in the khirbeh appear to have been cleared for cultivation.

Site 98 - **Rujm Qneiṭrah**
(Map section 4; field no. 9223)
PG: 28.3/79.2; UTMG: 68.8/66.8

Collapsed remains of a building complex on the north end of a ridge less than 2 km ESE of es-Smakiyyah; at approximately the 814 m elevation marker on the K737 map. 119 sherds were collected, including: IR 5; Nab 2; LIsl 8; UDE 2; UD 9.

See Musil: ruǧm Ḳnêṭra (34).

Walls of a 6 x 9 m room are visible with the east wall standing five courses high at one point and Bedouin burials in the interior rubble. Remnants of walls extending west and south indicate adjacent rooms. A well with a pump station is visible ca. 500-600 m north of the ruin. Qnēṭra ("arches") seems to refer to the region east of es-Smakiyyah.

Site 99 - **Kh. el-Makhārīm**
(Map section 4; field no. 8035, 9219)
PG: 28.9/78.9; UTMG: 69.7/66.5

Stone heaps and occasionally discernible wall lines along the slopes of the east bank of Wadi el-Ghweir, ca. 2.5 km ESE of es-Smakiyyah and 3 km ENE of el-Ḥmūd. Marked "Ruins" on some editions of the K737 map. 31 sherds were collected, including: ERom 1; Byz 1; UDE 2; UD 27.

See Musil: die Hürden Maḫârîm (34).

Stone heaps and occasional traces of wall lines cover an area ca. 0.5 sq. km. One would assume that the heaps are the result of field clearing, except that this is not agricultural terrain. An especially prominent rujm at the southern end of the site, ca. 10 x 10 m, produced a number of sherds (23 collected, including Nab 2 and EByz 1). Although this stone heap is without distinct wall lines, it is joined on the north and partially enclosed by what appears to be a fence of small stones. More numerous than surface sherds scattered over the khirbeh were lithics. From an area overlapping, but not corresponding exactly to that of the stone heaps, 417 flints were collected, including 5 bifaces (handaxes) from Lower Paleolithic or beginning of Middle Paleolithic (see Miller 1979a: 48).

Site 100 - **Ḥmūd**
(Map section 4; field no. 9020)
PG: 26.2/77.8; UTMG: 66.5/65.4

Modern village on an ancient settlement site ca. 5.5 km ESE of el-Qaṣr and ENE of er-Rabbah. Al Hamūd on the K737 map. 614 sherds were collected, including: Nab 17; ERom 3; Byz 1; EByz 2; LByz 5; A/M 9; LIsl 47; Mod 4; UDE 2; UD 13.

See Tristram: Hhomoud (120); Musil: ḫirbet Ḥmûd (34, 139); Glueck: Ḥamûd/#138 (1934: 63). Glueck described it as "a small inhabited site" and reported no pottery.

The modern village is itself now largely deserted. Most of the sherds reported above were found on the east and northeast sides of the present-day settlement, particularly in the dump.

Site 101 - **Kh. el-Minsaḫlāt**
(Map section 4; field no. 9049)
PG: 25.8/77.3; UTMG: 66.0/64.6

Low mound with occupational debris ca. 1 km southwest of Ḥmūd and on the west bank of Wadi Ḥamūd. 1349 sherds were collected, including: Chalco 2; EB I 2; EB II-III 124; EB IV 40; MB 1; Nab 8; ERom 1; LByz 2; A/M 1; Mod 1; UDE 6; UD 2.

The mound measures ca. 150 m (N-S) by 140 m (E-W) and has been plowed extensively on its lower, northeastern slopes. Traces of two walls on its summit and a cistern (still in use) at its southwestern edge are the only visible architectural features. Surface pottery is especially abundant on the east slopes where there has been digging, apparently in search of antiquities.

Site 102 - **Kh. el-Ḥinū**
(Map section 4; field no. 9025)
PG: 25.1/76.8; UTMG: 65.7/64.3

Building ruin situated on the southwest side of a ridge which itself overlooks Wadi Ḥmud, ca. 1.5 km southwest of Ḥmud. 81 sherds were collected, including: LB 1; IR 2; Nab 4; A/M 4; LIsl 17; UD 2.

The building itself, probably a farmstead, is situated just below the crest of the ridge and seems to be of recent origin. No doubt it corresponds to the LIsl pottery. A good dirt track crosses near the southeast corner of the building, and three depressions farther down the southwest slope of the ridge may have been cisterns.

Site 103
(Map section 4; field no. 9309)
PG: 25.8/77.3; UTMG: 66.2/64.9

Several small stone heaps on a hilltop west of the road from Ḥmud to Jdeiyidah, less than 1 km southwest of Ḥmud. While the situation does not suggest field clearing or burials, neither are there any distinguishable architectural features. There were occasional nondescript sherds, but not in any significant concentration (three were collected near one of the rujms) and none of them with diagnostic potential.

Site 104 - **Qaṣr Ḥamdān**
(Map section 4; field no. 9021)
PG: 26.1/77.2; UTMG: 66.5/64.5

Building ruin, collapsed debris of a small, square structure situated immediately below the crest of a ridge and slightly less than a kilometer south of Ḥmud. 194 sherds were collected, including: Nab 2; LRom 7; LByz 5; LIsl 3; UDE 1; UD 7.

Possibly a farmstead, the building measured 7 x 7 m at its base and was constructed of roughly hewn stones (ca. 0.4 x 0.6 x 1.2 m; two courses still in place). Nearby are three cisterns: two of them collapsed, the third lined with plaster, none of them in use.

Site 105 - **el-Jilimeh**
(Map section 4; field no. 9003)
PG: 21.1/77.0; UTMG: 61.6/64.5

Stone heaps at the southern end of a swell on the plateau slightly less than 2 km NNE of er-Rabbah and less than 1 km east of the Kerak-Dhiban road. Near the 937 m elevation marker on the K737 map. 106 sherds were collected, including: IR 1; Nab 5; LByz 1; LIsl 4; Mod 1. See Brünnow and Domaszewski: eğ-Ğilime (I: 54); Musil: ḫirbet el-Ğilime (35).

Surface pottery is sparse (the sherd count indicated above required intense search) and the stone heaps present no discernible architectural features. These mounds are ca. 50 m apart and may be the result of field clearing. Several spots are cleared for modern threshing floors.

Site 106 - **Miṣna^c**
(Map section 4; field no. 8024)
PG: 22.3/76.7; UTMG: 62.8/64.2

A small "tell" ca. 2.5 km northeast of er-Rabbah. Marked "Ruins" on the K737 map. 348 sherds were collected, including: EB 2; EB II-III 16; EB IVA 11; MB 12; LB 4; LB II 8; IR 16; IR I 13; IR II 8; Nab 12; Byz 4; EByz 3; LByz 3; A/M 1; LIsl 6; UDE 51; UD 10.

See Tristram: Misnar (120); Musil: ḫirbet el-Miṣna^c (141, 370); Glueck: el-Miṣna^c/#137 (1934: 62-63, 67, 82, 102). Glueck described the site and provided a plan of the vague wall lines on its summit. Also he reported pottery primarily from the Bronze and Iron Ages. "The Bronze Age sherds extend from the end of Early Bronze to Middle Bronze I, from about 2200 to about 1800 B.C. The Iron Age sherds extend from the beginning of Early Iron I down to about the middle of Early Iron II, that is, from after the middle of the thirteenth century to about the ninth, possibly the eighth century B.C. There were several elaborately profiled rims at el-Miṣna^c, which seem to belong to Middle Bronze II, being similar to those found in the E-D levels at Tell Beit Mirsim. A few Nabataean sherds were also found. ... One black Hellenistic sherd was also found." Miṣna^c has been proposed as a possible candidate for Ar Moab (e.g., Van Zyl 1960: 71-73).

Photograph 13: Qaṣr Ḥamdān (Site 104)

Miṣna^{c} seems to have remained essentially unchanged since Glueck described it and sketched the traces of walled compounds on its northern side.

Site 107 - **el-Miyāl**
(Map section 4; field no. 9143)
PG: 20.4/76.5; UTMG: 60.7/64.0

Tristram reported that "a mile [north] from Rabba, a tolerably perfect little Roman temple abuts on the road on the left. The bases of the columns of the portico remain *in situ*, and the shafts lie broken and prostrate by them. The adytum at the west end is only partially ruined, and the lower cornices are still remaining" (132). Brünnow and Domaszewski also reported this temple, recorded the name of the site as "el-Miyâh," and noted that only the foundations of the temple remained (I: 54). Smith, the last traveler to mention the temple, recorded "el-Meyāl" as the name of the site (370). No traces of the temple remain today, but we were able to verify its earlier location; the site is occupied now by an agricultural station.

Site 108 - **er-Rabbah**
(Map section 4; field no. 9123-9141)
PG: 20.3/75.5; UTMG: 60.8/63.0

Modern town on the site of an ancient city ruin. Er Rabba on the K737 map. 9611 sherds were collected, including: EB 2; MB(?) 4; LB(?) 3; IR 7; IR I 22; IR II 28; IR II C/P 2; Hell 13; Nab 352; ERom(?) 4; ERom 85; LRom(?) 1; LRom 66; Byz(?) 3; Byz 75; EByz(?) 3; EByz 104; LByz(?) 1; LByz 129; UM(?) 2; Um 6; Abb 4; Fat(?) 2; A/M(?) 3; A/M 375; LIsl 781; LOtt 3; Mod 98; UDE 18; UDEhandle 7; UD 160; UDhandle 152.

See Seetzen: Róbba (411, 16); Burckhardt: Rabba (377); Irby and Mangles (141); Macmichael: Rubbah (240-41); de Saulcy: Er-Rabbah (297-300); Klein: Er-rabba (1869: 153); Tristram: Rabba (123-30); Doughty (21-22); Hill (1891: 212; 1896: 40); Bliss (217); Wilson (310); Libby and Hoskins (319); Brünnow and Domaszewski (I: 54-59); Musil: ḫirbet er-Rabba (5, 15, 20-21, 25, 35, 44, 87, 112, 142, 156, 370; note also Musil's reference to "marma el-ᶜEjr" near er-Rabbah, 369); Smith (369-70); Glueck: #136 (1934: 62, 66; see also 1939: 63, 249); Canova: ar-Rabba (lix-lxi, 198-208). As is apparent from the numerous citations above, er-Rabbah caught the attention of virtually every traveler who passed through the Kerak plateau during the nineteenth century. When Musil and Brünnow and Domaszewski visited the vast ruin at the turn of the century it was still unoccupied and thus easily accessible. Musil prepared a plan of the whole ruin (376, reproduced in Spijkerman: pl. 80) and published photographs. Brünnow and Domaszewski planned the temple (I: 54) and also published photographs. The modern settlement had begun to emerge when Glueck visited in 1933: "At er-Rabbah, generally associated with Rabbah-Moab, an extensive search was undertaken for Early Iron Age pottery. Not a sherd was found which could be identified as belonging to the Early Iron Age or earlier. A very large quantity of Nabataean sherds of all kinds was found, and one Hellenistic sherd. There were numerous Roman sherds, and also a large number of mediaeval Arabic sherds."

Although often identified as Ar Moab of the Hebrew Bible, this is very uncertain (Olivier 1989a; Miller 1989b). Josephus knew this place as Arabatha (*Ant*. 14.1.18). From the "Cave of Letters" (Polotsky 1962: 258-60) dating from the 2nd century C.E., we learn that Babatha had to declare her property to a Roman commander at Rabbathmōba. The name appears as Rabbathmoōb in the seal impressions from Kurnub (Negev 1969: 96-99), also dating from the 2nd century. Ptolemy listed Rabathmōba among the cities and villages of Arabia Petraea (*Geographia* V. 16.4). Rababatora on the Peutinger Map is either a variant (corrupt?) form of Rabbath Moab or some combination of Rabbah and Betora. The latter name appears in the *Notitia Dignitatum* (37:22) and probably is to be identified with Lejjūn (site 240). Eusebius rendered it Rabbath Mōab with Areopolis as an alternate name (*Onom*. 10:17; 36:24; 124:15-17). Rabbah and Areopolis continue as alternate names for the city in Byzantine texts (see Avi Yonah 1976: 90; Canova lix-lxi).

The modern settlement at er-Rabbah, which had begun to emerge when Glueck visited, has since grown to a town of considerable size and continues to expand rapidly. Paved streets and modern buildings have obscured most traces of the ancient ruins. There are exceptions, the most notable being the small Roman temple often mentioned by the nineteenth century travelers. Built in the time of Diocletian and Maximanus according to an inscription (Brünnow and Domaszewski I: 54-5), it still stands, isolated in a small patch of ruins which was cleared by the Department of Antiquities in 1962-3. Yet comparison of the present structure with the photograph provided by Brünnow and Domaszewski reveals that even this monument has not escaped modern development entirely. Internal arches, not to be seen in the photographs, witness to the fact that this building was modified and reused during the early decades of present century. In addition to three inscription fragments published by Canova (198-208), Zayadine (1971a and b) has published two almost complete inscriptions; one referring to the restoration of a building after an earthquake in 597-598, the other referring to the construction of a building in 687.

Less spectacular reminders that er-Rabbah once was a place of importance in times past are at hand wherever one walks in the town––exposed walls in open places, ancient water reservoirs, pieces of columns, decoratively carved stones reused in modern houses, etc. Near the center of town to the east of the highway is an underground chamber with its entrance located in the courtyard of a private home. The town is strewn with potsherds, largely but not entirely from the Nabataean, Roman, Byzantine, and Late Islamic periods. Recent construction of a gas station across the highway from the agricultural school exposed what appears to have been a Nabataean /Roman pottery dump. In contrast to Glueck, we did find sherds from the Iron Age and earlier.

Site 109 - **Kh. Um Kharīᶜah**
(Map section 4; field no. 9113, 9318)
PG: 23.7/74.9; UTMG: 64.0/62.4

Wall lines, cisterns, and sherd scatter on a slight knoll ca. 3 km ESE of er-Rabbah. 174 sherds were collected, including: IR 2; Nab 10; LRom 2; Byz 3; EByz 1; LByz 1; LIsl 5; UD 4; UDhandle 6.

The features indicated above are found in an area ca. 50 m (E-W) by 125 m (N-S) on a slight knoll in the fork of two branches of Wadi Ḥmud. The surrounding area is rocky with cultivated fields in wadi beds. There are no standing structures. Some 250 meters to the west of Um Khariᶜah and separated from it by a small wadi is a cave surrounded by a 20 x 10 m enclosure.

Site 110
(Map section 4; field no. 9221, 9222)
PG: 28.4/76.4; UTMG: 68.9/63.9

Two rectangular building ruins, along the track from Ḥmud to Kh. Mdeinet ᶜAliya (Site 143), ca. 2.5 km southeast of Ḥmud. 91 sherds were collected, including: IR II 1; Nab/ERom 5; Byz 2; UD 2.

Situated on a slight knoll south of the track from Ḥmud to Kh. Mdeinet ᶜAliya and between two branches of Wadi Muḥeisin are the remains of a small rectangular structure (4 x 6 m). 27 sherds were collected, but only two of them could be dated with any degree of certainty (ERom). The sherds reported above were collected around the ruin of a second building ruin located ca. 250 m further to the southeast, immediately south of the same track and on a second knoll. Surrounding fields are under cultivation.

Site 111
(Map section 4; field no. 9091, 9157)
PG: 29.2/76.3; UTMG: 69.7/63.8

Building ruin (ca. 8 x 8 m) on a high point approximately midway between Ḥmud and Kh. Mdeinet ᶜAliya (Site 143). The site is immediately north of the track from Ḥmud to Mdeineh, at the point where a second track branches off to Jdeiyidah. 38 sherds were collected, including: Nab 3; ERom 1; LByz 2; UD 1.

Other possible wall lines are discernible at ground level 10 m to the NNE. Ca. 0.5 km to the northeast is another smaller stone heap with two visible wall lines and an attached enclosure. The latter produced 4 sherds (UD and UDE).

Site 112
(Map section 4; field no. 9307, 9308)
PG: 28.0/75.8; UTMG: 69.0/63.5

Stone heap, apparently the collapsed remains of a small building, ca. 2.5 km NNE of Jdeiyidah. Situated north of a track which leads from er-Rabbah to Kh. Mdeinet ᶜAliya (Site 143), this ruin is ca. 6 m square and reveals lower courses of walls ca. 80 cm wide. Only 10 nondescript body sherds were found near it. Some 200 m to the southwest, on the opposite (south) side of the track (PG: 28.4/75.6; UTMG: 68.9/63.2), is another stone heap which also may be the ruin of a small building, but this is not at all certain.

Site 113 - **Rujm et-Teis**
(Map section 4; field no. 9089, 9306)
PG: 28.0/75.0; UTMG: 68.5/62.6

Rubble remains of an enclosure, possibly including a room and cistern, on the crest of a hill slightly more than 1 km NNE of Jdeiyidah. Near the 905 m elevation point on the K737 map. 25 sherds were collected, including LIsl 2.

See Musil: ruğm et-Tejs (34, 139).

The whole complex measures 20 x 13 m. Extending from the 20 m wall on the south side is a possible room (ca. 5 x 6 m). A depression within the tumble of stones at the north corner suggests a collapsed cistern. Ca. 200 m further down the southwest slope of the hill is a small stone heap (ca. 5 x 5 m). Two unusually large stones (ca. 1 m long) in the north corner, one of them standing on end, raise the possibility that this may be a collapsed structure of some sort. Some 200 m east of Rujm et-Teis, at the end of a spur of the same hill, is a stone heap with no discernible wall lines or associated pottery.

Site 114 - **Mḥarraqāt (N)**
(Map section 4; field no. 9115)
PG: 21.6/73.3; UTMG: 62.1/60.9

Wall lines and sherd scatter ca. 2.5 km southeast of er-Rabbah; at the 980 m elevation marker on the K737 map.

392 sherds were collected, including: Chalco 1; EB II-III 8; EB IVA 18; LB 4; IR I 1; IR II 1; Nab 7; Byz 3; LByz 1; UDE 24; UD 2.

Farther down the northern slope of the same ridge on which Site 115 is situated are traces of building ruins covering an area ca. 33 m (N-S) by 23 m (E-W) and surrounded by surface sherds. These ruins are not very impressive, some of the stone heaps among the ruins are the result of field clearing, and it is difficult sometimes to distinguish one from the other.

Site 115 - **Mḥarraqāt** (S)
(Map section 4; field no. 9114)
PG: 21.7/72.9; UTMG: 62.2/60.3

Small khirbeh ca. 3 km southeast of er-Rabbah, on the north end of a ridge which parallels the Kerak-Dhiban road. 370 sherds were collected, including: EB 1; EB II-III 9; EB IV 9; IR I 7; Nab 13; ERom 1; Byz(?) 3; LIsl 1; UDE 4; UD 6.

See Tristram: Mekhersit (124) and Smith: el-Muḥār-aḳāt (369).

Surface sherds and numerous wall fragments, some of them standing several courses above the ground, cover an area ca. 200 m (N-S) by 75 m (E-W) at the north end of the crest of this rocky ridge. The walls, including a perimeter wall, are largely confined to the western side of the site. Heaps of stones at various points along the walls may be structural remains (small towers?).

Site 116
(Map section 4; field no. 9185)
PG: 22.2/73.9; UTMG: 62.6/61.4

Two stone heaps, possibly collapsed structures, ca. 2.5 km southeast of er-Rabbah. 42 sherds were collected including: Nab 4; LRom 1; LByz 3; UDE 1; UD 2.

One of the stone heaps is ca. 5 m square with distinct wall lines and corners. The other, ca. 20 m ENE of the first, is more rounded in shape (ca. 15 m in diameter) and also reveals remnants of a circular wall in its east side. Both heaps are ca. 1.5 high and situated on rocky ground.

Site 117
(Map section 4; field no. 9176)
PG: 22.3/73.8; UTMG: 62.8/61.2

Collapsed ruin of a small (5 x 5 m) building on a small knoll ca. 2.5 km southeast of er-Rabbah. The building was constructed of large stones, and there has been some unauthorized digging at its northeast corner. 51 sherds were collected, including: ERom 3; LRom 1; UD 3.

Site 118
(Map section 4; field no. 9177)
PG: 22.2/73.7; UTMG: 62.8/61.1

Rujm ca. 2.5 km southeast of er-Rabbah and ca. 200 m south of site 117. While no distinct architectural features are discernible, there is surface pottery. 26 sherds were collected, including: Nab 1; LByz 1; UD 3.

Site 119 - **Jdeiyidah**
(Map section 4; field no. 9045)
PG: 27.3/73.6; UTMG: 67.8/61.3

Modern village on an ancient settlement site, ca. 7 km ESE of er-Rabbah. Judaydah on the K737 map. 106 sherds were collected, including: Nab 9; ERom 2; LByz 1; LIsl 12; Mod 5; UD 4.

See Seetzen: Körriét el Grâb (416); Musil: ruǧm umm Čedâde and ḫ. el-Ṛurâb (35-36); Brünnow and Domaszewski: Ḫirbet el-Ġurâb (Vol. II: 41); and Glueck: Jedeideh/#140 (1934: 63). Passing south of Ḥmud (Site 100) while traveling west toward Ḥmeimat (Site 92), Musil reported "ruǧm umm Čedâde" to the left (south) of his route. This fits the location of Jdeiyidah in spite of the fact that the "ḫ. el-Ṛurâb," which Musil saw the following day from a different direction, is even more obviously Jdeiyidah. Specifically, he recorded "die Ruinen des großen Dorfes ḫ. el-Ṛurâb, das zur Erntezeit die Fellâḥîn und Ḥâreṯîn von ǧebel Nâblûs bewohnen." In short, Musil's "ruǧm umm Čedâde" must have been part of, or very near to, "ḫ. el-Ṛurâb," both displaced now by the modern village of Jdeiyidah. Looking at the same ruin area from different directions on different days and receiving different names, probably from different informants, he failed to realize that they were so closely related. Brünnow and Domaszewski also described

"Ḫirbet el-Ġurâb" as a large ruin and spoke of "ein vorspringender Absatz" at the foot of the wall at a northwest corner of the site. Glueck, who passed but apparently did not stop to investigate, described it as "a small, indistinguishable ruined site."

A local informant who had grown up in Jdeiyidah observed that there had been a khirbeh at the site, that its reoccupation still consisted of only two or three houses and some Bedouin tents in the early 1920s, and that the stones from the khirbeh had been reused in the earlier houses of the relatively large village which stands there today. Some of the earlier "Turkish" houses still exist in various states of disrepair near the center of the village. Otherwise there is nothing to suggest that the site was occupied in earlier times. Sherding in open places and along the slopes on all sides of the current village produced a relatively low yield.

Site 120
(Map section 5; field no. 9186)
PG: 29.9/81.6; UTMG: 70.3/69.3

Building ruin on the west slopes of the ridge between Wadi el-Ghuweir and Wadi el-Mujib, ca. 3.5 km northeast of es-Smakiyyah. 24 sherds were collected, including: IR I 1; LIsl 3; UD 20.

The building was a rectangular structure oriented north-south (17 x 8 m) with external walls ca. 1.5 m thick, constructed of large stones, and still standing 5 courses high in some places. A door on the east side opened onto an enclosure almost as large as the building itself. Ca. 30 m NNE of the building was a cistern. Probably this was a farmstead of fairly recent vintage. The same is probably true of several other isolated building ruins in the immediate vicinity (Sites 83, 121, 122, 123, and 124).

Site 121
(Map section 5; field no. 9188)
PG: 30.0/81.5; UTMG: 70.4/69.2

Building ruin on the west slopes of the ridge between Wadi el-Ghuweir and Wadi el-Mujib, ca. 3.5 km northeast of es-Smakiyyah and ca. 150 m higher up the slope (i.e., southeast) of site 120. 4 sherds were collected, including: IR 1; UD 3.

Oriented east-west and with walls of small stones preserved only one course above the ground, the building measured 8 x 11 m. The north wall appears to have been two courses wide while the others were only one course wide. Also there was an attached enclosure wall.

Site 122
(Map section 5; field no. 9189, 9190)
PG: 30.1/81.4; UTMG: 70.4/69.0

Building ruin on the west slopes of the ridge between Wadi el-Ghuweir and Wadi el-Mujib, ca. 3.5 km northeast of es-Smakiyyah. Situated on the ridge above (southeast) of site 121. 34 sherds were collected, including: ERom 4; UDE 1; UD 24.

The building measured ca. 14 m (E-W) by 5 m (N-S). Its walls are constructed of small stones, two courses wide, and preserved one course above the ground. 40 m southeast is a large rujm yielding a few unidentifiable sherds.

Site 123
(Map section 5; field no. 9187)
PG: 29.8/81.3; UTMG: 70.1/68.9

Building ruin on a rocky spur (a continuation of the knoll on which site 124 is located) which extends northwest from the ridge between Wadi el-Ghuweir and Wadi el-Mujib, ca. 3.5 km northeast of es-Smakiyyah. 21 sherds were collected, including: Byz 1; UD 20.

The main section of the building measured 16 m (E-W) by 13 m (N-S). An internal north-south wall extends part way across, partially dividing it into two rooms. Against the outside of the southern wall, except at its eastern end, is a large tumble of rocks, apparently a collapsed appendage of some sort. Extending ca. 40 m. from the southeast corner of the ruin is an enclosure wall.

Site 124
(Map section 5; field no. 9183)
PG: 29.9/81.0; UTMG: 70.2/68.2

Building ruin on a sloping ridge which extends NNW from the west side of the ridge between Wadi el-Ghuweir and Wadi el-Mujib, ca. 3.5 km northeast of es-Smakiyyah. 41 sherds were collected, including: LIsl 9; UDE 2.

Photograph 14: Building ruin (Site 127) northeast of es-Smakiyyah

The building was a rectangular structure (ca. 11 x 16 m) built with small, undressed field stones. Some internal walls are discernible amid the rubble which is less than a meter deep. Probably this was a farmstead contemporary with the Late Islamic pottery scattered about.

Site 125
(Map section 5; field no. 9205, 9206)
PG: 31.2/82.1; UTMG: 71.5/69.7

Building ruin, a round structure situated on a spur which extends southeast (pointing toward Kh. Mdeinet el-Mu^{c}arrajeh (Site 129) from the ridge between Wadi el-Ghuweir and Wadi el-Mujib. The structure was ca. 17 m in diameter, composed of large stones, and several courses of its exterior wall are visible in the tumble (ca. 2 m high). From this site one has a good view of the Wadi el-Mujib basin, the western and northern slopes of Kh. Mdeinet el-Mu^{c}arrajeh. It is in line of vision also with Kh. Mdeinet ^{c}Aliya (Site 143). In short, the situation suggests a watchtower used in conjunction with the settlements at the two Mdeinehs. Nearby and higher on the ridge are several cairns ranging from 6 to 15 m in diameter. Two of them are of the "partitioned" type.

Site 126
(Map section 5; field no. 9210)
PG: 31.0/81.7; UTMG: 71.4/69.4

Oval stone enclosure (ca. 22 x 29 m) on a rocky knoll overlooking Wadi el-Mujib from the ridge between Wadi el-Ghuweir and Wadi el-Mujib. Situated ca. 40 m from the rim of the Mujib, the wall is visible at ground level and composed of small stones (ca. 20-40 cm). Internal walls mark off the northwestern quadrant. This may be the remains of a bedouin encampment. No sherds were found.

Site 127
(Map section 5; field no. 9211)
PG: 31.8/82.0; UTMG: 72.0/69.7

Building ruin, a small square building (6 x 9 m) along the modern road which leads from the western rim of Wadi el-Mujib to the base of the canyon immediately north of Kh. Mdeinet el-Muᶜarrajeh (Site 129). The building was constructed with large stone slabs. Two interior pillars are aligned parallel to its western wall. No sherds were found.

Site 128
(Map section 5; field no. 9212)
PG: 32.0/81.9; UTMG: 72.3/69.6

A circular enclosure on a low-lying knoll overlooking the Wadi el-Mujib bed at the foot of Kh. Mdeinet el-Muᶜarrajeh (Site 129). The enclosure is ca. 18 x 14 m with its walls in collapse (never more than two courses in place or higher than .75 m). Adjacent to the enclosure are the tumbled remains of a small structure (ca. 5 x 5 m). 46 sherds were collected, including: UDE 5; UD 5.

Site 129 - **Kh. Mdeinet el-Muᶜarrajeh**
(Map section 5; field no. 8018)
PG: 32.2/81.3; UTMG: 72.5/69.0

Fortified settlement on a steep-sided promontory overlooking Wadi el-Mujib, ca. 6 km ENE of es-Smakiyyah. 199 sherds were collected, including: EB IVA 1; IR 3; IR I 11; UD 2.

One of the important discoveries of our survey is that there are two Khirbet Mdeinehs overlooking Wadi el-Mujib where it marks the northeastern frontier of the Kerak plateau. Both sites are very similar in appearance and hardly more than 4.5 km apart (as the crow flies; ENE and ESE of es-Smakiyyah respectively). Musil (ḫirbet el-Mdejjene; 34) passed near one of them, possibly the one reported here; and it is this Mdeineh which Olávarri excavated in 1976 and 1982 (Sauer 1979b: 9; Olávarri 1977-78: 136-49; 1983: 165-78; Menéndez 1983: 179-84). Glueck (Kh. el–Medeiyineh /#141; 1934: 52-53) reported the other one which is farther south. Following Olávarri, we refer to the northern Mdeineh as Khirbet Medeinet el-Muᶜarrajeh and to the southern Mdeineh (Site 143) as Khirbet Medeinet ᶜAliya.

Kh. Mdeinet el-Muᶜarrajeh is a double-walled settlement protected on all sides, except for a narrow land bridge at the south end, by the steep sides of the promontory on which it is situated. The walls encompass a north-south oriented area of ca. 25,000 sq. m. A dry moat has been cut into bedrock on the site's south end, thus protecting against access via the landbridge mentioned above. A tower and gate, partially excavated by Olávarri, stood above the moat. Several houses constructed with standing monoliths have also been investigated by Olávarri. Although the matter is open to further study, there is reason to believe that the site was primarily a military post. While it is not near a main road or in a good agricultural situation, it is, with Kh. Mdeinet ᶜAliya, strategically located for defending the northeast frontier of the Kerak plateau.

Site 130
(Map section 5; field no. 9207)
PG: 31.1/81.0; UTMG: 71.5/68.7

Circular stone enclosure, ca. 16 m in diameter, at the crest of the rocky spur which leads to Kh. Mdeinet el-Muᶜarrajeh (Site 129); at the 786 m elevation marker on the K737 map. Some of the enclosure wall consists of large, flat stones standing in orthostat fashion (similar to contemporary fences in the region). 13 sherds were collected, none datable with any degree of confidence.

Site 131
(Map section 5; field no. 9220, 9209)
PG: 31.5/80.9; UTMG: 71.9/68.6

Two partitioned cairns on the rocky knoll which leads to Kh. Mdeinet el-Muᶜarrajeh (Site 129). Marked "Ruins" on some editions of the K737 map.

Both cairns consist of double (concentric) circular walls, measure ca. 8 m in diameter, and are bisected with large stone slabs (each ca. 1 m long and laid end-to-end).

Three oval terraces extend eastward in stairstep fashion from one of the cairns. The other cairn is situated further down the eastward slope of the knoll, and 12 m to the east of it are the foundation remains of a 12 x 16 m rectangular structure. Of 38 sherds collected in the vicinity of the two cairns, only one could be dated with any degree of confidence (ERom).

Site 132
(Map section 5; field no. 9160)
PG: 31.5/80.3; UTMG: 71.9/68.0

A cave and rock shelters on the east side of the ridge between Wadi el-Ghuweir and Wadi el-Mujib, ca. 5 km ENE of es-Smakiyyah. 79 sherds were collected, including: EB I 76; EB IV 1.

The cave and rock shelters are shallow recesses just beneath the rim of the ridge and overlook Wadi el-Mujib. The sherds reported above were collected in the shallow cave and shelters, and also along the slopes of the Mujib canyon immediately below the shelters.

Site 133
(Map section 5; field no. 9213)
PG: 29.9/79.6; UTMG: 70.2/67.2

Small, unoccupied settlement site ca. 3.5 km east of es-Smakiyyah. Situated on the slopes immediately northwest of the 797 m elevation marker on the K737 map. 100 sherds were collected, including: IR(?) 1; Pers(?) 1; Nab 4; LIsl 9; UD 3.

Several wall lines are visible amid rock heaps and tumble on bedrock of a hill sloping west and facing es-Smakiyyah. The ruins cover an area ca. 50 x 80 m with debris and tumble up to 2 m high in places. There is a cistern ca. 30 m further down the slope (northwest) from the ruins.

Site 134
(Map section 5; field no. 9159)
PG: 30.7/79.4; UTMG: 71.0/67.0

An isolated building ruin on a hilltop ca. 4 km east of es-Smakiyyah and 1 km ESE of site 133. The building measures ca. 7 x 7 m. No internal walls are visible, much of the stone having been robbed. 26 sherds were collected and UD 13 registered.

Site 135
(Map section 5; field no. 9158)
PG: 29.8/77.8; UTMG: 70.3/65.5

Two stone heaps on a hilltop ca. 3.5 km east of Ḥmud, less than 1 km east of the 840 m elevation marker on the K737 map. Although no wall lines are discernible, some of the stones are unusually large for fieldstone and appear to have been worked. 56 sherds were collected, including ERom 5; UD 3.

Site 136
(Map section 5; field no. 9147)
PG: 30.6/77.6; UTMG: 70.9/65.3

Building ruin, a 5 m square structure built from large stones, on the south side of the crest of a hill across the wadi east of site 135 and slightly more than 4 km east of Ḥmud. Attached to and extending from the north side of the structure was a circular stone enclosure ca. 16 m in diameter. 25 sherds were collected, including: IR 1; UD 2.

Site 137
(Map section 5; field nos. 9148-9154)
PG: 30.5/78.0; UTMG: 71.0/65.9

Numerous cairns, including several partitioned cairns along the banks of the wadi system which enters the main Wadi el-Mujib canyon east of Ḥmud. These are concentrated especially on the northwestern slopes of the hill which bears the 816 m elevation marker on the K737 map. Typically these cairns are from 5 to 7 m in diameter and present no surface pottery of consequence. Many of them have been robbed for their stone.

Site 138
(Map section 5; field nos. 9145, 9146)
PG: 31.2/77.6; UTMG: 71.5/65.3

Building ruin, a rectangular structure (ca. 9 x 6 m) slightly more than 300 m south of the 816 m elevation

Photograph 15: Caves and rock shelters (Site 132) with EB I pottery

Photograph 16: Partitioned cairn (Site 137)

marker on the K737 map. Two standing stones in the interior are possible remnants of an interior wall. A small stone heap (field no. 9146) at the 816 elevation marker is probably the work of geographical surveyors, but there is some indication that the stones were piled over the foundation remains of a rectangular structure which would have measured ca. 5 x 7 m.

Site 139
(Map section 5; field no. 9157)
PG: 29.6/77.2; UTMG: 70.0/64.9

Stone heap with at least two wall lines discernible in the tumble. Also there appears to have been a stone enclosure attached to its east side. Only four nondescript body sherds were found.

Site 140
(Map section 5; field no. 9156)
PG: 29.8/76.8; UTMG: 70.3/64.6

Building ruin, a small rectangular structure (ca. 9 x 5 m) situated on a spur ca. 3.5 km ESE of Ḥmud. Northeast of the structure, only 5 m away, is a circle of large stones (ca. 5 m in diameter). Possibly the latter is the remnant of a partitioned cairn.

Site 141
(Map section 5; field no. 9155)
PG: 30.4/76.3; UTMG: 70.9/63.9

Building ruin, a rectangular structure (ca. 4.5 x 5.5 m), and nearby cistern situated slightly more than 4 km ESE of Ḥmud and ca. 75 m north of the track from Ḥmud to Kh. Mdeinet ^{c}Aliya (Site 143). Only one course of the external wall is exposed; the center is filled with tumbled stones. There is a cistern immediately to the south. One A/M sherd was found.

Site 142
(Map section 5; field no. 9305)
PG: 30.3/76.0; UTMG: 70.8/63.7

Building ruin, a small square structure (5 x 5 m), and an attached elliptical enclosure (28 x 18 m) on the north side of the crest of a hill, situated east of the track from Jdeiyidah to Kh. Mdeinet ^{c}Aliya (Site 143) near its juncture with the track from Ḥmud to the latter site. There was no surface pottery.

Site 143 - **Kh. Mdeinet ^{c}Aliyā**
(Map section 5; field no. 8019)
PG: 33.0/76.8; UTMG: 73.4/64.5

Fortified settlement site on a promontory overlooking Wadi el-Mujib, ca. 7 km ESE of es-Smakiyyah and ca. 6 km ENE of Jdeiyidah. 152 sherds were collected including: MB 1; IR I 12; ERom 1; UDE 1.

See discussion of Kh. Mdeinet el-Mu^{c}arrajeh (Site 129). Glueck (Kh. el-Medeiyineh/#141; 1934: 52-53, 63, 82, 98) provided a plan of this southern Mdeineh. Read "(141)" rather than "(140)" on p. 52, line 6. Note also that footnote 60a on p. 63 mistakenly equates the Mdeineh reported here with the Kh. el-Mdeineh which overlooks Wadi eth-Themed (i.e. Glueck's site #68 treated on pp. 13-15, 20, 22-25, 27, 29, 35, 56, 67).

Kh. Mdeinet ^{c}Aliya has remained essentially undisturbed since Glueck described it over a half century ago. It represents the remains of a walled settlement which was situated on a northeast-southwest oriented promontory with steep sides all around except for a narrow land bridge at the southwest end. The walls are better preserved than those of Kh. Mdeinet el-Mu^{c}arrajeh and encompass an area which measures ca. 275 x 110 m. At the southwest end, protecting the land bridge, are the collapsed remains of a gate and massive tower. Large limestone slabs that were probably cut on the site were used in the construction of the walls and houses. Some of these slabs were erected in orthostat fashion to form solid walls. Others were used as pillars to support roof lintels (some still in place). Kh. Mdeinet ^{c}Aliya, as Kh. Mdeinet el-Mu^{c}ar-rajeh, may have served a primarily military function. While both are strategically located for the defense of the Kerak plateau, neither would have provided a very good situation for an agriculturally based settlement.

Site 144
(Map section 5; field no. 9166)
PG: 32.2/76.3; UTMG: 72.6/64.0

Building ruin, a rectangular structure (ca. 7 x 8 m) overlooking Wadi ed-Dabbah, ca. 6 km ESE of Ḥmud and 1 km southwest of Kh. Mdeinet ^{c}Aliya (Site 143). Built from dressed field stones, the external walls are preserved three courses above the ground in some places. The site provides an excellent view to the east, from Kh. Mdeinet ᶜAliya to the Lejjun area, which suggests that the structure may have been a watchtower. 14 sherds were collected, including: IR II 2; UDE 1; UD 11.

Site 145
(Map section 5; field no. 9168)
PG: 32.2/75.7; UTMG: 72.7/63.4

Partitioned cairn ca. 1.5 km southwest of Kh. Mdeinet ᶜAliya (Site 143), on the edge of the plateau overlooking Wadi ed-Dabbah. The cairn is ca. 3 m in diameter with a standing stone in the center.

Site 146
(Map section 5; field no. 9303, 9304)
PG: 29.8/74.5; UTMG: 70.2/62.0

Building ruin, a 4 x 4 m structure on the northeast bank of Wadi Abu Shaᶜr, ca. 2 km ENE of Jdeiyidah. The walls were exposed 1.5 m above the ground (4 courses in some places). 5 sherds were collected, including: IR 1; Nab 2; LRom 1; UD 1.

Some 200 m to the west—i.e., further down the slope into the wadi bed—is a partitioned cairn (field no. 9303). The circular wall, which is exposed 2 courses above the ground, is 5 m in diameter measured from its external faces and 3 m in diameter measured from its inner faces. Monoliths lying lengthwise bisect this circular wall. No pottery was found.

Site 147
(Map section 5; field no. 9310)
PG: 30.0/74.7; UTMG: 70.6/62.4

Two cairns (or possibly tumbled structures) slightly more than 2 km ENE of Jdeiyidah and on the small ridge which extends west from the 857 m elevation marker on the K737 map. The two features of site 146 are further down the slope to the southwest. The two stone heaps are between 4 and 5 m in diameter and connected. There are no distinct wall lines and no surface pottery.

Site 148
(Map section 5; field no. 9169)
PG: 31.5/74.7; UTMG: 72.1/62.5

Cairn on the north slope of the main ridge which forms the north bank of Wadi Abu Shaᶜr, approximately midway between the 857 m and 776 m markers on the K737 map. This is an especially prominent cairn and oblong in shape (ca. 10 x 7 m). A large standing stone in the center is surrounded by the stone heap.

Site 149
(Map section 5; field no. 9170)
PG: 32.4/74.5; UTMG: 72.8/62.3

Partitioned cairn reused for a recent burial ca. 0.5 km east of site 148 and on the eastern slope of the same ridge. The cairn is exposed from 0.3 to 1.3 m above the ground, having been robbed for stones. The circular wall is two courses wide and measures ca. 3 m in diameter. There is a large standing stone in the center along with disarticulated human bones and snail shells.

Site 150
(Map section 5; field no. 9171)
PG: 31.2/74.3; UTMG: 71.7/62.0

Ruin of a rectangular structure (ca. 4 x 4 m), two partitioned cairns, and various heaps of stone rubble along the spine of a narrow ridge which overlooks Wadi Abu Shaᶜr from the north. This ridge is immediately ESE of the 857 m marker on the K737 map and separated from it by a branch of Wadi Abu Shaᶜr. The partitioned cairns measure between 4 and 5 m in diameter and have been robbed for stones to the extent that they are hardly visible above the ground.

Site 151
(Map section 5; field no. 9167)
PG: 31.8/74.3; UTMG: 72.2/61.9

Small building ruin (4.5 x 10 m) on a knoll which extends south from the main ridge which forms the north bank of Wadi Abu Shaᶜr, ca. 5 km east of Jdeiyidah. Only one course of the external wall is clearly discernible in places amid the tumbled stones. 14 sherds were collected, including: LIsl 1; UD 7.

Various stone heaps and circular enclosure walls appear along the bed of Wadi Abu Shaᶜr. There was no pottery associated with them or anything to suggest antiquity.

Photograph 17: Partitioned cairn (Site 146)

Photograph 18: Partitioned cairn (Site 149)

Site 152
(Map section 5; field no. 9245)
PG: 31.6/73.3; UTMG: 72.4/61.4

Five prominent cairns, ranging from 4 to 7 m in diameter, along the rocky hillside between Fityan and Wadi Abu Sha^{c}r. No surface pottery.

Site 153 **Rujm el-Qanāṭir**
(Map section 5; field no. 9052)
PG: 30.3/72.8; UTMG: 70.9/60.5

Stone heap (ca. 8 m in diameter) representing a collapsed building or, perhaps more likely, a cairn. Situated on a high point immediately north of the dirt track from Jdeiyidah to Fityan. Both Jdeiyidah and Fityan are visible from the site, the latter ca. 1.5 km to the east. 15 sherds were collected, including: UD 2.

Site 154 - **Fityān**
(Map section 5; field no. 9317)
PG: 31.6/72.6; UTMG: 72.1/60.2

Roman *castellum* overlooking the Roman fortress Lejjun from the northwest. Fityan is included here only for reference. We did not investigate the site since S. Thomas Parker examined it closely in connection with his *Limes Arabicus* survey (see especially 1986b: 74-79). For earlier reports of the site see Seetzen: Chürrbet el Phüttiân (416); Tristram: El Fityan (120); Vincent: plan (1898: 436-39); Brünnow and Domaszewski: Ḫirbet el-Fityân (Vol. II: 38-41); Musil: el-Ftijân (21, 28, 30, 36-37, 142, 144); and Glueck: Kh. el-Fityân/#150 (1934: 47-48). Brünnow and Domaszewski provided a plan and photograph. Bliss reported: "On the hill to the west of the springs [of Lejjûn] I saw a ruin which I had no time to visit" (223). Probably this ruin was Kh. el-Fityan.

Site 155
(Map section 6; field no. 2217)
PG: 10.5/72.1; UTMG: 51.3/59.5

Building ruin, apparently a caravansary or small inn, ca. 9 km northwest of Kerak on the road to el-Mazra^{c}a (at the Dead Sea). 194 sherds collected, including: MB 1; LB 10; IR I 5; Hell 1; Nab 3; LIsl 5; UDEhandle 6; UD 5.

Situated approximately 150 m north of the road, between it and Wadi el-Kerak which is ca. 0.75 km away, are the foundation remains of a square (28 x 28 m) building. Its external walls are 1 m thick while the internal walls average .80 m. Typical of caravansarais, the plan consists of narrow rooms (4 m deep) surrounding an open courtyard (18 x 18 m). A depression in the southwest corner of the courtyard probably was a cistern, while a large tumble of stones appended to the south wall and another in the northeast corner may represent towers. The wall lines of the courtyard are barely discernible and the cross walls dividing the rooms usually cannot be traced at all.

Site 156
(Map section 6; field no. 2592)
PG: 14.4/72.6; UTMG: 54.9/59.9

Possible foundations of a circular structure on the Jebel Ḥudeib ridge. Stones of irregular size and shape compose a somewhat circular pattern (16 m in diameter) visible at ground level on the ridge line. The pattern is suggestive of a circular foundation wall perhaps as much as a meter wide. There is a slight buildup of rubble on the west side, but not enough tumbled stones to indicate that the wall ever stood very high. 21 sherds were collected, including: Nab 1; UD 20.

Site 157
(Map section 6; field no. 9076)
PG: 15.4/72.4; UTMG: 55.8/59.7

Small building complex with a cistern and possibly a grape or olive press located at the north end of a ridge which extends northwest from Rakin. Specifically, the site is ca. 2.5 km northwest of Rakin, 0.5 km WSW of Site 158, and overlooks Wadi esh-Shalalikah. 9 sherds were collected, including: LIsl 1.

Site 158 - **Kh. Um Rummānah**
(Map section 6; field no. 9069)
PG: 15.6/72.4; UTMG: 56.1/59.9

Wall lines indicating a building complex at the north end of a ridge which extends northwest from Rakin.

Specifically, the site is ca. 2.5 km northwest of Rakin and overlooks Wadi Qahush. Note that the K737 map places "Khirbat Um Rummāna" ca. 1 km southeast of where we found it to be. 106 sherds were collected, including: Nab 3; Byz 17; LIsl 2; Mod 1; UD 8.

While several of the walls can be traced, one for more than 20 m, the overall plan of the building cannot be determined without further investigation. Musil's eš-Šâᶜeb (87) must have been somewhere in this vicinity.

Site 159
(Map section 6; field no. 2594)
PG: 13.9/71.3; UTMG: 54.4/58.6

Large stone centered in a rectangular enclosure on a small hilltop under the ridge overlooking Wadi el-Kerak, ca. 1 km north of Badhdhan. Indicated by a dot on the K737 map. 50 sherds were collected, including: Nab 18; ERom 1; UD 18.

Although most of the stones are missing, enough remain in place to indicate a single-line, rectangular pattern (18 x 12 m) oriented northwest-southeast. Roughly centered in the rectangle is a large stone, standing semierect ca. 1 m high. A group of large stones outside the rectangle at its southeast end included a rounded pillar segment (40 cm long; 20 cm diameter).

Site 160 - **el-Minqaṭᶜah**
(Map section 6; field no. 9107)
PG: 19.2/72.6; UTMG: 59.8/60.0

Unoccupied settlement site 3 km south of er-Rabbah and less than 1 km west of the Kerak-Dhiban road. 269 sherds were collected, including: LB 1; Hell 2; Nab(?) 4; Nab 9; LRom 1; Byz 3; LByz 1; A/M 4; LIsl 4; Mod 2; UD 6; UDhandle 9.

Musil's "ḫirbet el-Ḳanaᵓ" (87) would have been in this vicinity.

The sherds were collected on a low mound, ca. 130 m (E-W) by 140 m (N-S), with no distinguishable building ruins. There are several cisterns, however, and a rock-cut tomb on the mound's southeastern side. The tomb has an arched entrance and is semi-circular in shape. Ca. 0.5 km to the northeast of the mound are the ruins of two buildings which Worschech interprets as Roman farm houses (his #59 and #60; 1985a: 48).

Site 161 - **Um Najīl**
(Map section 6; field no. 9044)
PG: 17.2/71.1; UTMG: 57.8/58.4

Sherd scatter in a field ca. 0.75 km north of Rakin, just west of the road from Rakin to Batir. 333 sherds were collected, including: IR(?) 1; IR 34; IR I 11; IR II 7; Nab (?) 1; Nab 2; A/M 1; UDE 8; UD 2; UDhandle 1.

Site 162 - **Rākīn**
(Map section 6; field no. 9062)
PG: 17.3/70.4; UTMG: 57.8/57.8

Modern town on an ancient settlement site, ca. 4 km north of Kerak and near the western escarpment of the plateau. Marked Rākīn on the K737 map. 135 sherds were collected, including: LB 2; IR 3; IR I(?) 3; IR I 3; IR II 1; Nab(?) 4; ERom 2; LRom 1; Byz 2; EByz 3; Um 1; A/M 3; LIsl 9; UDEhandle 22; UD 2; UDhandle 4. Also 1 loom weight and 1 roof tile.

See Seetzen: Rakîn (416); Tristram: Rakun/Rakim (120, 124); Musil: Râčîn (19, 154, 369).

Although it is clear that the surface on which the present-day settlement has emerged consists largely of ancient occupational debris, we noted only two sections of ancient wall. The most impressive of these, referred to by the local inhabitants as a "Roman castle," was constructed of stones which range in size up to 0.75 m long, stands about 2 m high, and runs east-west through a back alley for ca. 15 m. We were told that the village now covers much of it. The other section of old wall was found on the south side of the town, while most of the sherds indicated above were collected on the slopes north and east of the town.

Site 163
(Map section 6; field no. 9101, 9102, 9103)
PG: 18.2/71.0; UTMG: 58.5/58.5

Remains of several square structures in a field ca. 0.75 km northeast of Rakin, at the head of Wadi Uweir and north of the road which branches to Rakin from the

Kerak-Dhiban road. 55 sherds were collected at the largest of these, including: Nab 1; LRom 1; LByz 1; UDE 2; UD 3.

The largest and best preserved of the structures (field no. 9103), where the sherds indicated above were collected, presents a double-faced foundation wall (external face measuring 9 x 9 m, internal face measuring 6 x 6 m). The wall faces consist of single rows of large stones. 38 m to the northeast are the remains of another square structure of smaller dimensions (3.5 x 3.5 m) and with walls constructed of large stone blocks. One block on its north side is 2 m long. Wall lines indicating two more square structures lie further east and southeast. Both measure ca. 8 x 8 m, one of them with a possible entrance on the western side. Few sherds with diagnostic potential were found around them. 27 sherds were collected at the one with the possible entrance, for example, including: Nab 1; LIsl 2; UD 1. A structure 4.5 m square still farther to the southeast is treated separately (Site 164). Other stone heaps nearby may represent field clearing.

Site 164
(Map section 6; field no. 9099)
PG: 18.7/70.9; UTMG: 59.1/58.4

Building ruin, a small structure in a field ca. 1.5 km NNE of Rakin, north of the road which branches to Rakin from the Kerak-Dhiban road. The building was constructed of large stone blocks and measures ca. 4.5 x 4.5 m. There was an entrance on the north side, evidenced by a threshold and hinge socket. 66 sherds were collected, including: Nab 2; Byz 1; UDE 2; UD 1.

Site 165 - **Kh. el-Minḥār**
(Map section 6; field no. 9063)
PG: 19.5/70.5; UTMG: 59.9/58.0

Wall lines, a cave, and a cistern on the summit of a hill ca. 2 km east of Rakin and 0.75 km west of the Kerak-Dhiban road. Marked Khirbat el Minḥar on the K737 map. 64 sherds were collected, including: IR 1; Nab 24; LRom 4; EByz 3; LByz 2; UDEhandle 5; UD 28.

See Musil: ruǧm el-Minḥar (87, 369).

The wall lines are very faint, barely exposed above the surface of the ground. But they are noticeable at several places on the site which, judging from the sherd scatter, covers an area ca. 60 x 75 m. The cave had a well-carved entrance and steps. Cut in the rock just south of this site is a large cistern and what appears to have been a watering trough for animals.

Site 166 - **Qreifilla**
(Map section 6; field no. 9031)
PG: 19.4/69.4; UTMG: 60.0/56.8

Emerging modern village on an ancient settlement site, located ca. 2 km southeast of Rakin and less than 1 km west of the Kerak-Dhiban road. Marked Khirbat Qureifilla on the K737 map. 789 sherds were collected, including: LB 1; EByz 2; LByz 14; Fat(?) 2; A/M 37; LIsl 31; Mod 3; UD 7.

See Seetzen: Kräphîlla (411); Seetzen: Gräphîlla (416); Burckhardt: Kereythela (377); Tristram: Hhrofillat (120); Brünnow and Domaszewski: Ḳrêfilla (I: 59); Musil: ḫirbet Ḳrêfilla (19, 86, 369); Smith: Ḳreifla (369).

On the southern side of the small village are the partially standing remains of some abandoned buildings, one of which the villagers said was 100 years old. Similar in style to the structures at Tadun (Site 56) which date from approximately the turn of the century, it has walls still standing up to 2.5 m high and a surviving ceiling arch. There is a large, plastered cistern with two openings to the east of the village. The plaster has been impressed with a rouletted design to produce a herringbone pattern.

Site 167 - Ḥabāsh/Ḥabāj
(Map section 6; field no. 2595)
PG: 14.9/69.9; UTMG: 55.5/57.3

Settlement site on a large terrace overlooking Wadi el-Kerak, ca. 4 km NNW of Kerak and 1.5 km ESE of Badhdhan. 790 sherds were collected, including: LB 1; IR 1; Byz 3; A/M 108; LIsl 242; UD 14.

See de Saulcy: Daouarat-el-Habs (330); Musil: ḫirbet Ḥbêš? (154).

Building ruins cover an area ca. 200 m square. Walls of some 10-12 adjacent dwellings are well preserved at the center of the site. Walls around the perimeter are largely tumbled, having been robbed for building materials and cleared for sheep pens. At the northern edge of the site is a dome-shaped cistern ca. 5 m in diameter and 4 m deep, built of stone and plastered. It seems reasonable to associate these visible building remains with the A/M and LIsl pottery which dominates the site.

Site 168
(Map section 6; field no. 9105)
PG: 15.9/69.8; UTMG: 56.7/57.3

Building ruin, a rectangular structure ca. 1.5 km southwest of Rakin, situated on one of two peaks (the westernmost) immediately south of the road from Rakin to Badhdhan. 31 sherds were collected, including: IR I 1; Nab/ERom 2; UDE 1; UD 3.

Situated on an isolated hilltop, the structure measures ca. 19 m (E-W) by 10 m (N-S) overall and is divided into two chambers. The smaller (7 x 10 m) chamber on the western end was built of larger stones and had thicker walls than the eastern (12 x 10 m) chamber, and may represent a roofed building (possibly a tower) with an attached courtyard. Kerak is visible to the SSE as is much of the Wadi Kerak system (particularly the sections marked Wadi el-Khawāja, Wadi eṭ-Ṭawāhīn, and Wadi ed-Dafāli on the K737 map).

Site 169 - **Badhdhān**
(Map section 6; field no. 9277)
PG: 12.1/71.5; UTMG: 54.2/57.4

Currently occupied village on the east bank of Wadi el-Kerak, ca. 4 km west of Rakin and 6 km northwest of Kerak. Marked Badhdhān on the K737 map. No pre-modern pottery was found at the site.

Seetzen included two similar names, "Bedân" and "Beddân," in a list of ruins for which he provided no specific location other than that they were situated between Wadi el-Mujib and Wadi el-Ḥesa. See also Tristram: Bedthan (120); and Musil: ḫirbet Beḏḏân (65-66, 154).

The villagers speak of a time when sacrifices were offered here; now there is only a "holy tree." Otherwise the only indications of antiquity are worked stones incorporated into the entrances to some of the houses.

Site 170 - **Kh. el-Mrabbaᶜah**
(Map section 6; field no. 9275)
PG: 13.9/68.7; UTMG: 54.6/56.4

Small khirbeh on a hilltop overlooking Wadi el-Khawaja from the east, ca. 3.5 km southwest of Rakin and 1.5 km SSE of Badhdhan. 285 sherds were collected, including: IR 3; Nab 19; LRom 5; Byz 4; EByz 4; LByz 7; UD 13.

This is probably Musil's eṭ-Ṭrunǧe (154), although we were given the name Kh. el-Mrabbaᶜah (derived from a nearby cave) for it and received the name eṭ-Ṭrunjeh for the less conspicuous remnants of some walls in a vineyard ca. 200 m further to the WSW (Site 171).

The vague outlines of several small structures are discernible in this complex of tumbled ruins. Some of the walls are almost a meter wide, as in the north-south wall of a 10 x 12 m room near the northeast corner of the site. The heaviest concentration of collapsed walls is ca. 70 m further south from this room, however, at the south-eastern end of the khirbeh. One wall in this area is still standing three courses high. Two adjacent rooms (10 x 14 m and 10 x 8 m) can be identified. There is also a cistern at this end of the khirbeh which would have supplemented the water from a nearby spring. The cave mentioned above is just east of the khirbeh and not easily accessible since it is cut into the side of a cliff ca. 10 m above the present ground level. Soot on the ceiling indicates that it has been used as a shelter or habitation.

Site 171 - **Kh. Ṭrunjeh**
(Map section 6; field no. 9276)
PG: 13.7/68.6; UTMG: 54.2/56.3

Wall lines in a vineyard on the east bank of Wadi el-Khawaja, ca. 4 km southwest of Rakin and ca. 200 m WSW of Kh. el-Mrabbaᶜah (Site 170). Some of the walls are still standing up to a meter (5 courses) high. A total of 12 sherds was collected, none of which could be dated.

See Musil: eṭ-Ṭrunǧe (154) and discussion of site 170.

Site 172 - **Um ed-Dajāj**
(Map section 6; field no. 2218)
PG: 11.9/70.2; UTMG: 53.5/56.7

Abandoned Ottoman period houses on the outskirts of the modern settlement of Um ed-Dajaj, ca. 5.5 km northwest of Kerak along the road from Kerak to el-Mazra^{c}a. Marked Um ed Dajāj on the K737 map. 28 sherds were collected, including: LIsl 11.

The modern settlement is shifting positions under the influence of the new Kerak-el-Mazra^{c}a road and thus leaving houses from approximately the turn of the century abandoned. For the moment these old houses are still intact, providing an excellent example of village layout from the Ottoman period.

Site 173 - **^{c}Ain Um Jam^{c}ān**
(Map section 6; field no. 2219)
PG: 12.0/69.5; UTMG: 52.7/56.6

Building ruin ca. 6 km northwest of Kerak on the southwest bank of Wadi el-Kerak and immediately southwest of the road from Kerak to el-Mazra^{c}a. Marked ^{c}Ain Um Jam^{c}ān on the K737 map. Foundation walls of a 5 x 5 m building stand up to two courses high in a terraced area above the spring. Below are beautiful orchards and vegetable fields. 2 LIsl sherds were collected.

Site 174 - **Kh. Sakka**
(Map section 6; field no. 2204)
PG: 12.5/69.0; UTMG: 53.2/56.0

Building ruin, a small but substantial structure (ca. 6 x 5 m), and other less distinct wall lines on a prominent rock outcrop ca. 0.5 km northwest of the modern village of Sakka. Marked "Ruins" on the K737 map; note however that the ruins are actually on the north bank of Wadi Sakka, between Wadi Sakka and the Kerak-el-Mazra^{c}a road. 201 sherds were collected, including: EB II-III 13; LB 3; IR I 6; IR II 4; Nab 1; Byz 1; LIsl 1; UDE 9.

De Saulcy mentioned Aÿn-el-Sekkeh (331) and Musil ^{c}ajn Sakka (65). Musil's ḥ. el-Mikbas and ḫ. el-Mefâḫît were somewhere in the vicinity (65).

The ruins and sherd scatter cover an area ca. 30 x 20 m bounded on the south and west by Wadi Sakka. There are steep terraces on the eastern slope and an open field to the north.

Site 175 - **Samrā$^\circ$**
(Map section 6; field no. 2205)
PG: 12.2/67.5; UTMG: 52.7/54.8

Modern village on an ancient settlement site ca. 5 km WNW of Kerak. Marked Samra on the K737 map. Not to be confused with Jad^{c}at ed-Jbur/Kh. es-Samra$^\circ$ (Site 34) or er-Rib^{c}i/Kh. es-Samra$^\circ$ (Site 37) or Kh. es-Samra (Site 199). Samra$^\circ$ is an appellative name which has to do with the dark, basalt stone which dominates certain parts of the plateau. 393 sherds were collected, including: MB 1; LB 1; Nab 5; Byz 3; EByz 3; LByz 7; LIsl 21; Mod 15; UD 1; UDhandle 5.

See Seetzen: Zémra (416); Tristram: Sumrah (120); Musil: ḫirbet Samra$^\circ$ (65); Glueck: Semerā (1939: 98); Canova: Samrah (209-15). Glueck described it as "a modern village" and reported no pottery. Canova reported eight tomb inscriptions, none of them dated.

The modern settlement is surrounded on the north, east, and south by fine agricultural fields. Sherding was conducted in the village refuse heap and adjacent fields on the southeast side of the village. No ancient remains are visible. Local residents showed Byzantine and Arabic coins allegedly found on the site.

Site 176 - **Zeita**
(Map section 6; field no. 2221)
PG: 11.4/66.8; UTMG: 51.9/54.1

Small khirbeh on a mountain ridge ca. 5.5 km west of Kerak and 1 km SSW of Samra$^\circ$. Scattered rubble with occasional traces of foundation walls covers an area ca. 30 x 100 m. 183 sherds were collected, including: LB 1; Nab 11; ERom 2; LRom 3; LIsl 3; UD 3; UDhandle 6.

Site 177
(Map section 6; field no. 2211)
PG: 09.8/65.9; UTMG: 50.5/53.2

Small khirbeh on the north bank of Wadi ^{c}Isal and near the head of Wadi Ṣhalwa, ca. 7.5 km west of Kerak and approximately midway between Kh. Qashab and Kh. Ruṣeifa. 313 sherds were collected, including: MB 2; LB 16; LB/IR I 1; IR II 7; Hell 2; Nab 32; ERom 4; UDE 20; UD 3; UDhandle.

The ruin is situated on a rounded spur which overlooks Wadi ^{c}Isal, and on all sides but the northeast the terrain falls away steeply. A few wall lines are visible but difficult to trace among the tumbled stones and sheepfolds which cover an area ca. 100 x 150 m. There is a cistern filled with debris.

Site 178
(Map section 6; field no. 2068)
PG: 08.8/66.1; UTMG: 49.9/53.3

Three large caves and two plastered cisterns near a spring overlooking Wadi ᶜIsal, ca. 8 km west of Kerak and less than 1 km southwest of Kh. Qashab. 11 sherds were collected, including: EB II-III 1; Nab 2; LIsl 2.

Site 179 - **Kh. el-Qashab**
(Map section 6; field no. 2212)
PG: 09.9/66.7; UTMG: 50.3/53.9

Wall lines, caves, and cisterns on the north bank of Wadi ᶜIsal and near the head of Wadi Ṣhalwa, ca. 8 km west of Kerak. Marked Khirbat el Qashab on the K737 map. 226 sherds were collected, including: Nab 2; ERom 4; Byz 5; A/M 4; LIsl 7; UD 1; UDhandle 2.

The site is almost totally eroded to bedrock slabs. Nevertheless, wall lines pertaining to at least one building and possibly two more can be traced among tumbled stones. Also there are several caves and cisterns. These features and surface pottery are scattered over an area ca. 30 x 100 m.

Site 180 - **el-ᶜĀrūḍ**
(Map section 6; field no. 2213)
PG: 09.0/67.3; UTMG: 49.8/54.5

Partitioned cairns on the crest of the ridge between Wadi Qinaᶜ and Wadi ᶜIsal, ca. 8 km west of Kerak and 1 km northwest of Kh. el-Qashab. 10 sherds were collected, including: Nab 1; UDE 1; UD 8.

The largest and best preserved of these cairns consists of a double circle of stones—the external circle measuring 7.90 m in diameter and the internal circle measuring 5.30 m—partitioned by two cross walls. Nearby are two smaller cairns represented by remnants of single circles, one circle measuring 4 m in diameter the other 5 m. Less than 100 m to the west was a fourth circle, 3 m in diameter, and with a cross wall. The sherds were collected in the general area of the cairns but not concentrated around any one of them.

Site 181
(Map section 6; field no. 2214)
PG: 08.5/68.2; UTMG: 49.2/55.4

Building ruin, possibly a watchtower, on a mountain spur overlooking the Lisan; ca. 3 km WNW of Samra and ca. 300 m southwest of Kh. Btheinah. The building was constructed from large stones, measured ca. 15 x 10 m, and has walls standing two courses high at the southwest corner. 42 sherds were collected, including: Nab 3; EByz 2; UDE 1; UD 4.

Site 182 - **Kh. Btheinah**
(Map section 6; field no. 2215)
PG: 08.9/68.4; UTMG: 49.7/55.5

Abandoned settlement on a hilltop 3 km WNW of Samra. Marked Khirbat Btheinah on the K737 map. 334 sherds were collected, including: IR II 8; Hell 1; Nab 3; Byz 4; EByz 2; Um 1; A/M 13; LIsl 92; UDhandle 16; perforated ceramic disc.

Collapsed building ruins of what appears to have been a relatively recent settlement are spread over an area ca. 40 m (N-S) by 100 m (E-W). Many walls survive several courses high, especially at the eastern end of the ruin, rendering it possible to envision the general plans of several of the houses. On the northeast edge of the site is a circular limestone basin 2 m in diameter and 60 cm high with a central hole 1 cm square. Wadis form the northern and southern sides of the site, and on the southeast a narrow saddle separates the ruins from a steep, rocky hill. The surrounding terrain is very rocky, though some terrace farming is apparent.

Site 183 - **Rujm esh-Shmūs**
(Map section 6; field no. 2216)
PG: 09.1/69.0; UTMG: 49.9/56.2

Sherd scatter on top of a hill between two upper branches of Wadi Btheinah, ca. 3 km northwest of Samra. Marked Rujm esh Shumūs on the K737 map. There is a sheepfold with signs of recent use, but no ancient walls. Only 7 sherds were collected, all UD.

Site 184 - **Kh. ᶜAizār**
(Map section 6; field no. 2002)
PG: 12.9/66.9; UTMG: 53.8/54.1

Unoccupied village site ca. 4 km WNW of Kerak and slightly more than 1 km ESE of Samraᵓ. Marked Khirbat ᶜAizar on the K737 map. 504 sherds were collected, including: IR II 2; Nab 16; ERom 2; Byz 2; EByz 2; LByz 6; Fat(?) 1; A/M 11; LIsl 118; Mod 4; UDEhandle 2; UD 3; UDhandle 10.

See Seetzen Eisâr (416); Tristram: ᵓIzzar (120); Musil: ḫirbet ᶜEjzâr (65); and Glueck: el-ᶜIzâr/#129 (1939: 98). Glueck described Kh. ᶜAizar as consisting "of a few modern houses, built on the ruins of a small site, where fine Nabatean sherds, and also Roman and Byzantine sherds were found."

The surface ruins of Kh. ᶜAizar are largely indistinguishable except for the remains of three abandoned and collapsed houses which probably are the "modern houses" to which Glueck referred. Their walls remain standing, but the arches which supported their roofs have fallen. Walls of another small square building are discernible at the northern end of the site with army trenches and a bunker nearby. Many cisterns dot the site. Plowed fields surround the ruin on all sides.

Site 185 - **Um Kharūf** (Maᶜmūdiyyeh)
(Map section 6; field no. 2001)
PG: 14.3/67.3; UTMG: 54.9/54.7

Building ruins, probably the site of a Byzantine church, ca. 3 km WNW of Kerak and 100 m south of the Kerak-el-Mazraᶜa road. 78 sherds were collected, including: Hell 1; ERom 2; LByz 5; UD 3. Also many tesserae and marble fragments.

Probably this is De Saulcy's Deir-el-Mokharib (331) and certainly Glueck's Maᶜamūdîyeh/#130. Glueck reports: "Turning s.w. off the road that leads from Kerak to Mezraᶜah, we ascended the Wâdī Suḥûr, coming upon some tremendous stone wine (?)-presses, carved out of huge blocks of stone, measuring more than a metre in diameter. Several of them had been turned on their sides by the winter freshets that rush down the *wâdī*, and overflow its banks. One of these great basins is called the Maᶜamûdîyeh" (1939: 98).

What appears to have been the north wall of a substantial building can be traced ca. 10 m. Situated on a hillside terrace which has been disturbed by bulldozing in recent years, the wall included a doorway. A doorframe block (with a hollowed out space to receive the bar) was found 4 m north of the wall. Farther north (20 m from the wall), in a much bulldozed area, was found a round baptistry carved from a single stone, possibly Glueck's Maᶜamûdîyeh. It measures 1.3 m high and 1.5 m across. Stairs are incised in a cruciform fashion in the block. A local informant stated that the original position of the baptistry was ca. 50 m farther east. Other large stone building blocks are scattered around and what appears to have been the face of a north-south wall can be traced for some 4-5 m between the baptistry and the wall described above. The modern road cuts the site on the north, exposing more wall lines and what appears to have been a watercourse. There is a spring 0.5 km to the east.

Site 186
(Map section 6; field no. 9258)
PG: 15.7/67.9; UTMG: 56.3/55.1

Abandoned mill in the bed of Wadi el-Kerak, immediately south of the wadi stream and less than 1 km NNW of ᶜAin Sarah; ca. 2 km northwest of Kerak. Marked "Mill" on the K737 map. No pottery.

A building (ca. 8 x 12 m) remains standing with walls of large worked stone, a stone vaulted ceiling, and two arched entrances. Apparently it is of fairly recent vintage. That it served as a mill is indicated by two mill stones in the building and an aqueduct (ca. 4 m wide, 2 m deep, and plastered on the inside) which circles around a low hill south of the Wadi el-Kerak stream bed and ends above the roof of the building. Presumably the water would drop into the building through two vertical shafts and exit through an opening in one of the exterior walls. The exit could not be determined because of overburden which has accumulated in and around the building.

Site 187 - **Kh. Sārah**
(Map section 6; field no. 2003, 9259)
PG: 16.3/67.3; UTMG: 57.0/54.6

Large stone wall (possibly a dam), a mill complex, and other nondescript building rubble near ᶜAin Sara, NNW of Kerak along the road from Kerak to the Dead Sea.

Marked ᶜAin Sāra on the K737 map, this is the site of a modern water pumping station. 36 sherds were collected near the "dam," including: IR 2; LByz 1; A/M 3; UDE 6; UD 5. 12 sherds were collected at the mill house, including: EB I 1; IR I 1; IR II 1; Nab/ERom 1; Byz 1; UDE 5; UD 2.

See Burckhardt: Ain Sara (379); de Saulcy: Aÿn-Sara (330); Glueck: ᶜAin Ṣarâḥ/#131 (1939: 98). Glueck reported: "On top of the ridge [above ᶜAin Sarah] was a small, flat, rectangular area, with some few traces of former occupation. Several Nabataean-Roman sherds were found. ... There are remnants of a dam-wall above ᶜAin Ṣarâḥ, where water was impounded for the now abandoned mill below it, which has been replaced by a chortling gasoline pumping station."

The wall which Glueck interpreted as a dam (probably correctly) is southeast of a bow in the Wadi el-Kerak stream bed (this section marked Wadi eṭ-Ṭawāhīn on the K737 map), extends some 25 m in a roughly north-south direction, is constructed of large stones, and remains standing some 10 m high. The mill complex is immediately below the "dam," between it and the wadi bed, near where the wadi flows under the Kerak-Dead Sea road. Here the wadi has cut a canyon ca. 40 m wide and 10 m deep. The water apparently was channeled by an aqueduct from the reservoir behind the dam to a point several meters above the mill house and then dropped down a vertical shaft supplying power. Portions of the aqueduct can be traced to the mill house, and the house is still standing. A secondary aqueduct may have continued the water flow from the mill house to another mill on the opposite (west) side of the wadi bed.

Site 188
(Map section 6; field no. 9108)
PG: 17.7/67.2; UTMG: 58.4/54.7

Building ruin NNE of Kerak on the opposite rim of Wadi ez-Zaiyatin. At the 1068 m elevation marker on the K737 map. 121 sherds were collected, including: Nab 5; ERom 2; A/M 4; LIsl 3; Mod 1; UD 4; UDhandle 5.

The building measured ca. 15 m (E-W) by 14 m (N-S) with internal walls dividing it into at least three chambers. Except for scattered rubble from the collapsed walls, there is no accumulation of debris on the site. Farther down the slope to the south are low wall lines, probably representing animal enclosures.

Site 189
(Map section 6; field no. 9110)
PG: 18.4/67.0; UTMG: 59.1/54.3

Wall lines and caves ca. 1.5 km northeast of Kerak, on a hilltop at the northwest end of a ridge formed by a bend in Wadi el-Kinnar. Marked Khirbat el Kinnar on some editions of the K737 map. 169 sherds were collected, including: Nab 7; LIsl 3; Mod 2; UD 4.

See Seetzen: Szweiníje (412); Tristram: Suweiniye (124); and the entry for site 190.

The ruins and sherds are spread over an area ca. 100 x 50 m. Although the site has been defaced considerably by modern construction, several old wall lines remain visible.

Site 190 - Ẓweihirah
(Map section 6; field no. 9109)
PG: 18.9/67.1; UTMG: 59.7/54.5

Unoccupied settlement site ca. 2 km northeast of Kerak, on the northern rim of Wadi el-Kinnār. The site consists of a scatter of tumbled stones, with few wall lines clearly discernible, covering an area ca. 120 x 75 m. 488 sherds were collected, including: LB 3; IR II 1; Hell 1; Nab 17; ERom 2; Byz 3; EByz(?) 1; LByz 1; UM(?) 3; A/M 2; LIsl 4; Mod 1; UDE 3; UD 4; UDhandle 13.

Seetzen, having gained sight of Kerak as he approached from the northeast, observed that before reaching it "we still had to traverse some unusually deep ground, on whose slopes are to be found the ruined villages Duéheréh and Szweiníje" (412). Tristram, departing Kerak toward er-Rabbah, noted: "On the way we passed the ruins of Suweiniye, Duweineh, Rakim, and Mekhersit" (124). Smith (369), departing Kerak via "the new Turkish road laid across the deep Wady ᶜAin es Sitt [the wadi immediately east of Kerak]," noted the following landmarks: "6.30: Crossed the Wady bed; 6.45: Reached ridge on north side of Wady, the limit of the Turkish road; 6.55: Eẓ-Ẓeweiher a cistern and a few ruins;..." Smith then equates his Eẓ-Ẓeweiher with Seetzen's Duéheréh. Their Duéheréh/Duweineh/eẓ-Ẓeweiher apparently corresponds to our Ẓweihirah/site 190 while their Szweiníje /Suweiniye corresponds to our site 189.

Site 191 - **Kh. er-Rṣeifah**
(Map section 6; field no. 2209)
PG: 11.4/65.4; UTMG: 52.2/52.6

Khirbeh on a hillside terrace at the head of Wadi er-Rṣeifah (a tributary of Wadi ᶜIsal), ca. 5.5 km WSW of Kerak. Marked Khirbat er-Ruṣeifa on the K737 map. 300 sherds were collected, including: LByz 10; A/M 1; LIsl 92; tesserae.

Building ruins are spread over an area ca. 150 x 150 m. Few ancient wall lines can be traced with confidence, the site having been defaced by sheepfolds and robbed for building stones, especially on the west and south where the debris is deep. Most of the remaining stones are unworked, but some have been roughly squared. There is a cistern on the east side of the village and two springs within 0.5 km. Some plowing of fields is in evidence, but the ground surface is mostly rocky. Kathrabba and ᶜAi (Sites 261 and 262) are visible to the south, across the upper branches of Wadi ᶜIsal.

Site 192 - **Qaṣr er-Rṣeifah**
(Map section 6; field no. 2210)
PG: 11.9/64.8; UTMG: 52.7/51.9

Building ruin, apparently a Byzantine church, at the head of one of the upper tributaries of Wadi ᶜIsal, ca. 5 km WSW of Kerak and 1 km southeast of Kh. Rṣeifah. 59 sherds were collected, including: Nab 3; ERom 2; Byz 2; LByz 4; LIsl 10; UD 1.

Situated on a terrace beneath the steep ridge which separates the Wadi el-Kerak and Wadi ᶜIsal systems, and accessible by a narrow path from the road along the crest of the ridge, the Qaṣr er-Rṣeifah ruin measures ca. 20 x 30 m overall. Although the plan is not entirely certain, there seems to have been a rectangular building (ca. 12 x 18 m, oriented roughly east-west) with a smaller structure or attached chambers on the south side. The main rectangular building was constructed of medium-sized, unhewn limestone rocks. At its eastern end was an apsidal wall forming an arc ca. 6 m in diameter. At the opposite end are six or more huge, finely dressed monoliths (averaging 1 x 1 x 0.5 m). Apparently these monoliths are the remains of the facade at the western end of the building, and three of them in particular seem to have formed the sides and top of the entrance frame. Two of the three will have served as the sides of the frame —one stands over 2 m high; the second has fallen and is broken, but was of corresponding dimensions and would have stood 1.5 m away. The third, the lintel, lies between the other two with the door hinge socket visible. A depression just outside the building at its southwestern corner may be a collapsed and filled cistern. Discovered in the tumbled ruins was an inscription fragment with the Greek letter *delta* followed on a second line by the letters *kappa*, *iota*, *tau*, *epsilon*. A raised point separates the *iota* and *tau* (KI·TE). All of this, along with the pottery, suggests that the building was a Byzantine church possibly reused during fairly recent (LIsl) times.

Site 193 - **el-ᶜUmyān**
(Map section 6; field no. 2108)
PG: 11.0/63.7; UTMG: 51.8/51.0

Present-day settlement on an ancient site located ca. 1 km north of Jauza on the north bank of Wadi ᶜIsal. Marked El ᶜUmyān on the K737 map. 131 sherds were collected, including: LB 3; IR 1; IR II 1; IR II/Pers 3; Nab 12; LByz 2; LIsl 6; Mod 5; UDEhandle 4; UD 2; UDhandle 2.

The present-day village, small to begin with, seems to be in a process of abandonment. Some houses are occupied by families, others have been converted to sheep pens. Only the light sherd scatter among the houses witnesses to earlier phases of occupation at the site. There is a spring nearby and olive orchards on a shelf farther down the slope of the wadi bank.

Site 194 - **Kh. el-ᶜOkbar**
(Map section 6; field no. 2004)
PG: 13.2/64.3; UTMG: 53.8/51.6

Khirbeh ca. 2.5 km WSW of el-Ifranj, along the road from el-Ifranj to ᶜAi and in the angle of the road where it changes directions from NNW to south. 595 sherds were collected, including: Nab 35; ERom 1; LRom 3; EByz 2; LByz 7; A/M 16; LIsl 28; Mod 4; UD 9; UDhandle.

See Musil: ḫirbet ᶜOčbor (255, 261, 364); and Glueck: Kh. el-ᶜOkber/#128 (1939: 100). Glueck reported "numerous ancient boundary walls, terraces and heaps of stones which had of old been removed from the fields" but no actual ruins or pottery.

Kh. ᶜOkbar is a complex of tumbled stone walls covering an area ca. 100 x 40 m on the northwest slopes of a hill. A small depression runs east to west through the site dividing it into two parts; the northern part consists primarily of a 33 m square structure built of medium sized blocks and containing several rooms. The southern section also contains visible wall lines. There are three cisterns on the western slope of the site. The Dead Sea and Lisan are visible to the west.

Site 195 - **Mseimṭah** (S)
(Map section 6; field no. 2207)
PG: 13.5/64.7; UTMG: 54.3/52.0

Small khirbeh on a hilltop ca. 3.5 km WSW of Kerak and 2 km west of el-Ifranj. At the 1197 m elevation marker on the K737 map. 232 sherds were collected, including: Nab 29; LRom 1; LIsl 1; UD 4; UDhandle 6.

Is this Musil's el-Mčêmin (65)?

Foundation remains of approximately 10 small buildings are clustered in an area ca. 50 x 30 m. The largest measures ca. 10 m square, while the smallest measures ca. 5 m square. A large wall comprises the southwest side of a series of these buildings and is composed of fairly large blocks 3-4 courses high. Also the outline of a street is visible between some of the houses. Site 196 is not far away, ca. 0.5 km farther down the slope toward Wadi el-Kerak, and likewise is dominated by Nabataean pottery.

Site 196 - **Mseimṭah** (N)
(Map section 6; field no. 2208)
PG: 13.6/65.1; UTMG: 54.3/52.5

Several building ruins, perhaps the remains of a small settlement, on a mountain terrace above a slope which drops precipitously toward Wadi el-Karak, ca. 3.5 km WSW of Kerak and less than 2 km west of el-Ifranj. 214 sherds were collected, including: LB 2; IR 2; IR II 2; Hell 2; Nab 27; Nab/ERom 1; ERom 1; LRom 1; Byz 4; EByz 2; LIsl 4; UDEhandle 4; UD 5; UDhandle 26.

Foundation walls pertaining to some four or five separate structures are spread over an area ca. 50 x 100 m. The largest one measured ca. 12 x 20 m and was divided into three chambers. Another structure nearby measured ca. 8 x 8 m. Both were built of large, roughly-hewn blocks, some now laid on their sides. Foundations of another sturdy structure on the west side of the site measures 5 x 4 m with a small segment of wall extending from it. This may have been a tower of some sort. Smaller buildings on the site were constructed of smaller stones and have left less pronounced surface remains. Three cisterns provided water. Note that this site is situated within 0.5 km of site 195 and that both are dominated by Nabataean pottery.

Site 197 - **Mgheir**
(Map section 6; field no. 2202)
PG: 14.1/65.9; UTMG: 54.7/53.1

Small khirbeh on a rocky terrace 3 km west of Kerak, flanked by two branches of Wadi el-Kerak—Wadi el-Mafariq and Wadi Shuᶜeib en-Nar. 411 sherds were collected including: EB 3; IR 1; IR II/Pers 1; Nab 1; Byz 12; LByz 4; A/M 32; LIsl 112; Ott 1; UDE 5; UD 4; UDhandle 3.

See Musil: ḫirbet Mḳêr (65, 365).

Tumbled building ruins are scattered over an area ca. 100 m square. Wall lines are difficult to distinguish except for the remains of a relatively recent 7 x 10 m house near the center of the site. Its walls are still standing but the roof arches have fallen. A carved stone lintel with socket was found in the southeastern quadrant of the ruin near two cisterns. Terraced fields surround the site.

Site 198 - **Ibn Ayyūb**
(Map section 6; field no. 2201)
PG: 14.8/66.2; UTMG: 55.6/53.4

Building ruins and a column fragment on a north-facing spur overlooking Wadi el-Kerak, ca. 2 km west of Kerak. Marked "Ruins" on the K737 map. 143 sherds were collected, including: MB 1; IR II/Pers 6; Nab 3; LRom 1; Byz 6; LByz 7; Um 3; A/M 5; LIsl 3; Mod 1; UD 3; UDhandle 4.

Photograph 19: Door frame at Qaṣr er-Rseifah (Site 192)

Photograph 20: Inscription fragment at Qaṣr er-Rseifah

Bits of nondescript stone and dirt rubble cover an area ca. 40 x 60 m. One corner of house wall is visible near the center of the site and another possible wall line on the east side. Near the latter is a depression, possibly representing a collapsed and filled cistern. The column fragment is 1 m long and 0.5 m in diameter.

Site 199 - **Kh. es-Samrāʾ**
(Map section 6; field no. 2203)
PG: 14.7/65.3; UTMG: 55.2/52.5

Small khirbeh ca. 3 km SSW of Kerak and 1 km northwest of el-Ifranj, situated on a roughly semicircular terrace facing Kerak with a ridge behind. 224 sherds were collected, including: IR 2; IR II 1; Hell 2; Nab 7; LRom 1; Byz 1; EByz 2; LByz 2; UD 4; UDhandle 14.

Tumbled building ruins of large blocks are scattered over an area ca. 100 x 50 m. The collapsed remains of a ca. 14 m square building dominate the center of the ruin. Another collapsed building at the north end of the site measures 7 x 16 m and consists of two rooms. There is abundant farming activity in the area.

Site 200 - **Kaminna**
(Map section 6; field no. 2206)
PG: 15.2/64.2; UTMG: 55.8/51.5

Recently abandoned settlement ca. 2.5 km SSW of Kerak, along the road from el-Ifranj to Jauza. Marked Kaminna on the K737 map. 211 sherds were collected, including: IR 1; IR II 3; Nab 1; ERom 1; LRom 1; Byz 3; EByz 1; LByz 10; A/M 1; LIsl 2; Mod 1; UDhandle 10.

Some 10-12 houses are spread over an area ca. 100 x 200 m on an east-facing, downhill slope and surrounded on the north and south by plowed fields. Eight of the houses had roofs of wattle and mud slate partially preserved when we examined the site in 1982. One of the houses was occupied.

Site 201 - **el-Franj** (esh-Shihābiyyah)
(Map section 6; field no. 2220)
PG: 15.6/64.5; UTMG: 56.1/52.0

Modern town near an important spring ca. 1.5 km southwest of Kerak. Marked El Ifranj on the K737 map. 88 sherds were collected, including: EB II-III 1; LB 1; Nab 4; Byz 1; LIsl 1; Mod 6.

See Burckhardt: Ain Frandjy (379, 395); Irby and Mangles: Ain-el-Frangee (137); Bliss (220); Brünnow and Domaszewski: ᶜAin el-Frenǧî (I: 11); Musil: ᶜajn el-Franǧ (15, 56, 255, 363): Canova: el-Franǵ (219-28). Canova reported nine inscribed tombstones, all from the 6th century.

El-Ifranj is a growing modern settlement astride the road from ᶜAi to Kerak. No ancient ruins are apparent, but sherds were collected in the older, "Turkish" parts of the present-day settlement.

Site 202 - **eth-Thallājah**
(Map section 6; field no. 2122)
PG: 16.8/65.2; UTMG: 57.5/52.7

Modern town on an ancient settlement site, ca. 0.5 km southwest of Kerak. Marked Eth Thallāja on the K737 map. 46 sherds were collected, including: Nab 3; A/M 4; LOtt(?) 2; Mod 4; UDhandle 3.

See Musil: ǧebel umm eṯ-Ṯelâǧe (45, 152, 255, 362).

The modern town covers the site, and no ancient architectural remains were observed. Most of the sherds were collected from the dump on the southeastern slope of the modern settlement.

Site 203
(Map section 6; field no. 2302)
PG: 17.9/65.6; UTMG: 58.5/53.0

Several of the earlier investigators mentioned ruins on the ridge between Kerak and eth-Thanniya. See Brünnow and Domaszewski: Gelamet es-Sabḫa (map); Musil: ruǧm el-Ǧilime (45, 362); Glueck: Rujm el-Jilīmeh/#126 and Kh. Umm Ḥamâd (1939: 98-99); Canova: Kh. Umm el-Ḥāmed (278-280). Glueck provided the only description of any detail: "Immediately across from Kerak to the s.e. is Rujm el-Jilīmeh. It is not a real ruin, as one might suppose from Musil's description, but a pile of field stones flung into a large heap during the course of years and centuries, as ploughmen have attempted to clean somewhat the petraean acres. S.s.e. of Kerak is Kh. Umm Ḥamâd, a small, almost completely destroyed site, with a few wall remnants. The buildings had been constructed of large, rude flint blocks. Nabataean, Roman, Byzantine, and mediaeval Arabic sherds were found. Cave-cisterns supplied water for the small community." Canova reported nondescript remains and three inscribed tombstones at Umm el-Ḥāmad. Highrise apartments have replaced Rujm el-Jilīmeh. The name Um Ḥamâd survives but no traces of the ancient ruin.

Site 204 - **Kerak**
(Map section 6; field no. 2599)
PG: 17.0/66.0; UTMG: 58.0/53.5

Crusader-Ayyubid-Mamluk citadel at the southwestern end of a modern city. Sections of the walls and towers which surrounded the medieval city of Kerak also survive. 3894 sherds were collected within the citadel walls and on the slopes below its walls. These included: EB 2; EB II-III 2; MB 3; LB 15; IR 21; IR I 15; IR II 80; IR II/Pers 2; Hell 4; Nab 145; ERom 26; Byz 13; EByz 16; Fat(?) 7; A/M 2278; LIsl 204; Isl 423; Mod 82; UDE 1; UDEhandle 6; UD 115; UDhandle 90.

Beginning with Seetzen, virtually every traveler-explorer crossing the Kerak plateau has stopped at Kerak. See Seetzen: Kárrak (412-26); Burckhardt (377-95); Irby and Mangles (137, 141); Layard (79-98); Lynch (356-64); de Saulcy (304-29); de Luynes (74-126); Mauss and Sauvaire (471-84); Klein (1869: 153; 1879: 254-55); Tristram (84-113); Doughty (23-25); Hill (1891: 201-11; 1896: 40-41); Bliss (217-20); Hornstein: (95-97); Musil (see esp. 45-62); Lagrange (210); Gautier (119-20); Bacher (109-11); Wilson (310-12); Libby and Hoskins (319-53). Mauss and Sauvaire and Musil provided descriptions with plans; Hornstein, Gautier, and Musil published early photographs. In addition to "Byzantine and Arabic" sherds, Albright found what he identified as "Moabite" ware on "the steep southeastern slopes of the hill, below the citadel" (1924: 11). Glueck found Nabataean pottery as well (1934: 65), an Iron Age figurine (1939: 32, 34-35), and what he took to be "sculptural evidence" of a Nabataean temple (1939: 48, 65-66, 89, 98-100, 107). Canova (3-173) reported the remains of two Crusader churches, occasional architectural remains from the Byzantine period, and 197 inscribed tombstones from three Byzantine cemeteries. A small Iron Age inscription fragment containing parts of three lines in "Canaanite" script was discovered at Kerak in 1958 or soon before and reconstructed to read as follows (Reed and Winnett 1963; see also Freedman 1964: 50-51).

...K]mshyt, king of Moab, the ...
...of Kemosh (to serve) as an altar (?) because he ...
...his... And behold I made ...

Kerak has been proposed as *harkur*, #101 on the so-called "Palestinian List" (also called the "Megiddo List") from the reign of Thuthmosis III (Redford 1982a: 115-20). Kerak is often equated with Kir in Isa. 15:1 and Kir-hareseth/Kir-heres in II Kings 3:25; Isa. 16:7, 11; Jer. 48:31, 36; but on inconclusive grounds. More certain is its identification with Charakmōbapolis represented by second century A.D. seal impressions discovered at Kurnub (Negev 1969: 89-106); Charachmōba listed by Ptolemy among cities and villages in Arabia Petraea (*Geographia*. V,16,4); [Char]achmōba on the Madaba map; and Charakmōba, Charagmouba, Charachmouda, etc. in various Byzantine sources (Thomsen 1907: 114-15; Canova 1954: lxi-lxii; Negev 1969: 89-106; Avi-Yonah 1976: 48; Gutwein 1981: 130-32). There are also coins from Charachmoba /Charakmoba, particularly from the reign of Elagabalus (Spijkerman 1979: 108-14; pls. 22-23).

Our investigation of Kerak was limited to a thorough sherding of the citadel and its slopes. The results indicate that the site has been used by human beings almost steadily since at least as early as the Chalcolithic period. Especially interesting is the fine imported ware from the Ayyubid-Mamluk period, including several pieces of glazed Lu'ang Ch'uan Chinese celadon wares. Robin Brown conducted a sounding in the citadel in 1987, specifically in the Palace Reception Hall, and distinguished two main phases, Mamluk and Ottoman (1989: 287-304).

Site 205 - **ᶜIzra**
(Map section 6; field no. 2090)
PG: 16.0/63.2; UTMG: 56.7/50.5

Modern village on an ancient settlement site ca. 2.5 km SSW of Kerak and 0.5 km west of the Kerak-Tafila road. Marked ᶜIzra on the K737 map. 132 sherds were collected, including: IR 1; Nab 7; Byz 6; A/M 17; LIsl 13; UDE 3; UD 1; UDhandle 15; tesserae.

Canova (1954: 264-274) found sixteen inscribed tombstones with dates ranging from 460 to 577, and we observed a stone with a Greek inscription fragment reused in a retaining wall. This supports the evidence from surface pottery that the site of this modern settlement has been occupied in earlier times. However, it was probably Kh. ᶜIzra nearby which caught the attention of Musil and others (See site 206 for references).

Site 206 - **Kh. ᶜIzra**
(Map section 6; field no. 2083)
PG: 16.3/63.1; UTMG: 57.1/50.3

Khirbeh in the process of resettlement, ca. 2.5 km south of Kerak, immediately west of the Kerak-Tafila road, and north of the juncture of the secondary road to ᶜIzra. 1091 sherds were collected, including: LB 8; LB/IR I 1; IR 2; IR I 4; IR II 3; Hell 2; Nab 41; ERom 11; LRom 3; Byz 1; EByz 1; LByz 1; A/M 2; LIsl 9; Mod 1; UDE 10; UD 41; UDhandle 19.

Although Mauss and Sauvaire do not mention this site, they clearly passed nearby (see 484, 517-18). From the context of his report, it seems clear that this was Tristram's Kirbet Azizah (116): "From Kureitun [our Site 210] we turned S.S.W., and in ten minutes were on the mound of ruins called Kirbet Azizah. The remains are extensive, and with very many wells. Among other traces of older and better times, I came upon a wine-press hewn in the rock—two troughs hewn out of the native rock, with a perforated partition left between them. ... To the left of Azizah runs the Wady Mᵓhheileh, in which there is a remarkable large, open reservoir, formed out of a natural cavity. Fifteen minutes brought us from Azizah to Kirbet Nekad [our site 207] with ruins like the former, on a knoll; and in eighteen minutes more we reached Hhoweiyeh [our Site 270]..." At the spot where one would expect Kh. ᶜIzra, Brünnow and Domaszewski reported a site which they called "Ḫirbet el-ᶜUṭwi" (I: 11, 103). They also depicted "ᶜUṭwi" on their map at approximately the location of Kh. ᶜIzar, but introduced "ᶜAzīza" as a separate site on the opposite side of "Wadi-l-ᶜUṭwi" (marked Wadi eṭ-Ṭuwai on the K737 map). This raises the possibility that ᶜUṭwi and Azizah/ᶜAzīza were separate sites, the former to be equated with Kh. ᶜIzra and the latter with some other site slightly further east or southeast. For the following reasons, however, we suspect that Brünnow and Domaszewski collected different names for the same site without realizing it. (1) ᶜAzīza appears only on their map, not in the text of their report. (2) Our site 209 is the only site which comes into consideration as a candidate for the ᶜAzīza on their map. But even it seems too far north. Moreover it is a rather insignificant ruin to have found a place on their map. (3) Musil, who explored the region about the same time as did they, reported only one site for this immediate vicinity, "ḫirbet ᶜAzra" (362). (4) The local people today know Site 206 only by the name Kh. ᶜIzra, and are unaware of any other sites in the immediate vicinity with names corresponding to either ᶜUṭwi or Azizah/ᶜAzīza. To summarize, we believe that ᶜUṭwi, Azizah/ᶜAzīza, and ᶜAzra were names collected by the early travelers for the same site, present-day Kh. ᶜIzra.

Modern houses are beginning to appear on the site, and there is a considerable amount of agricultural activity surrounding it. Some of the ruins are still visible, however, and the foundation walls of several buildings can be traced. These include a 3.5 x 4 m house in the north-west quadrant of the ruin, traces of a 3 x 7 m structure near the center of the ruin, and some walls of a building which would have been ca. 15 m long in the southern part of the site. Three cisterns and three caves were also noted.

Site 207 - **Kh. en-Neqqāz**
(Map section 6; field no. 2305)
PG: 17.1/62.7; UTMG: 57.8/50.0

Khirbeh 3 km south of Kerak and immediately east of the Kerak-Ṭafilah road. Marked Khirbat en Naqqāz on the K737 map. 2396 sherds were collected, including: Chalco(?) 2; EB II-III 2; LB 6; IR 21; IR I 7; IR II 21; IR II/Pers 10; Hell 3; Nab 160; Nab/ERom 11; ERom 12; LRom 4; EByz 13; Abb 2; A/M 20; LIsl 8; UD 35; UDhandle 133.

See Seetzen: el Nackâs (416); Klein: Khurbet Nakkad (1879: 255); Tristram: Kirbet Nekad (116); Doughty: Negaés (22); Musil: ḫirbet en-Naḳḳâz (45, 362); Glueck: Kh. en-Neqqâz/#123 (1939: 99). Glueck described it as a "small, ruined site with Nabataean-Roman sherds."

This ruin, situated on a hilltop overlooking the Kerak-Ṭafilah road, covers an area ca. 60 x 90 m. It consists largely of tumbled stones, although in some places fairly clear wall lines are visible. Many of the surface stones have been rearranged for sheepfolds. Also the site has been robbed for building stones, and soon it will be even more vulnerable since a new road is being constructed which will pass ca. 30 m to the east. There is a cistern on the site, still in use. Also we were told of a spring nearby which was dry at the time of our visit. To the northeast and south were large plowed fields.

Site 208
(Map section 6; field no. 2301)
PG: 17.3/64.3; UTMG: 58.0/51.6

Small khirbeh on a ridge ca. 1.5 km south of Kerak and immediately east of the Kerak-Ṭafilah road. 593 sherds were collected, including: IR 1; IR I 1; IR II 1; Nab 1; Byz 2; A/M 38; LIsl 167; UD 10; tesserae.

Stone tumble and debris are scattered over an area ca. 130 x 50 m on the rocky top of a spur of the ridge between Kerak and eth-Thanniya. Cultivated fields lie to the north and south. The area to the west, which drops rapidly to the Kerak-Ṭafilah road in Wadi eṭ-Ṭuwai, is terraced. Kh. el-Qaryatein is located ca. 0.5 km to the ENE on the spine of the main ridge. Occasional foundation walls can be traced in the rubble, two of which are preserved up to three courses high. There are two cisterns, one still in use. A new road under construction, which will connect the Kerak-Ṭafilah road with the Kerak-Qaṭranah road, will pass immediately east of the site.

Site 209
(Map section 6; field no. 2364)
PG: 17.6/63.4; UTMG: 58.3/51.0

Stone heaps ca. 2 km south of Kerak and less than 1 km east of the Kerak-Ṭafilah road. At the 1094 m elevation marker on the K737 map.

The largest stone heap measures ca. 18 m in diameter and may be the remains of a collapsed building. There are no clearly visible wall lines, however, and other stone piles in the area seem to be the result of field clearing. If the Azizah/ᶜAzīza reported by Tristram and Brünnow and Domaszewski is not to be equated with Kh. ᶜIzra (Site 206; see comments there), then this seems to be the only possible candidate.

Site 210 - **Kh. el-Qaryatein**
(Map section 6; field no. 2303)
PG: 17.7/64.5; UTMG: 58.4/51.8

Large khirbeh ca. 2 km SSE of Kerak, on the ridge between Kerak and eth-Thanniya. Marked Khirbat el Qurein on the K737 map. 1417 sherds were collected, including: Chalco 2; EB II-III 9; EB IVB(?) 3; MB 6; LB 7; IR I 5; IR II 1; Nab 34; ERom 4; LRom 2; EByz 14; LByz 26; Um 4; Fat(?) 4; A/M 22; LIsl 85; LOtt 2; Mod 2; UDE 5; UD 36; two roof tiles.

Klein: Keryatein (1879: 255); Tristram: Kureitun (114-15).; Musil: ḫirbet el-Ḳarjetên (45, 362); Glueck: Qarytein/#125 (1939: 99); Canova: Kh. el-Qaryataīn (275-77). Glueck reported Nabataean-Roman sherds in addition to cave-cisterns and several artificial cisterns. Canova reported two undated tombstones.

Substantial ruins and a heavy scattering of sherds cover an area ca. 100 x 160 m on this dominating ridge. The tumble of stones is at least 2 m deep in places, and many walls can be traced. There are numerous cisterns and caves. One of the caves has a walled entrance, apparently having served as a dwelling.

Site 211 - **eth-Thaniyyah**
(Map section 6; field no. 2304)
PG: 18.8/64.1; UTMG: 59.5/51.4

Modern town on an ancient settlement site ca. 2 km southeast of Kerak. Marked Eth Thanniya on the K737 map. 1440 sherds were collected, including: EB II-III 4; EB IVA 4; MB 7; LB 15; IR 9; IR I 36; IR II 41; IR II/Pers 10; Hell 4; Nab 63; ERom 6; LRom 4; Byz 2; EByz 1; LByz 8; EIsl 10; Um 4; Fat(?) 7; A/M 135; LIsl 201; Ott 21; LOtt 4; Mod 24; UDE 38; UDEhandle 104; UD 47; UDhandle 42; 1 figurine fragment.

See Seetzen: Tínniéh (416); Burckhardt: Thenye (389); Klein: Chirbet Ta̱tnije/Khurbet Tatiyeh (1879: 255); Tristram: Theniyeh (120); Brünnow and Domaszewski: e̱t-Ṯenîye (I: 11, 60); Musil: ḫirbet e̱t-Ṯenijje (21, 26, 45, 77, 369); Canova: eth-Thaniyyeh (257-62). Klein noted that "tanks and remains of Roman roads" were to be found at the site. Canova reported six inscribed tombstones, two of which could be dated to the 6th century, and a lintel with a poorly preserved Greek inscription.

Eth-Thaniyyah is a large town on a commanding hilltop near the crossing of the main north-south and east-west routes through the Kerak plateau. Note that the modern north-south highway takes a sharp turn before reaching eth-Thaniyah and passes at the foot of Kerak instead. Kerak, of course, enjoys an even more imposing position and probably has overshadowed eth-Thanniya throughout history as it does today. As will be apparent from the K737 map, however, it would have been more direct for an ancient traveler to pass along the eastern slope of eth-Thaniyyah, and a secondary road does so even today. The modern town has completely displaced the ancient ruins, but the heavy scattering of sherds in the town and especially on the slopes of the hill bears evidence of a steady occupation at the site since the Early Bronze Age.

Site 212 - **Kh. ed-Dāwūdiyyah** (N)
(Map section 7; field no. 9061)
PG: 19.3/71.8; UTMG: 60.1/59.2

Building ruins on a low mound ca. 4 km south of er-Rabbah and slightly less than 1 km west of the Kerak-Dhiban road. 340 sherds were collected, including: IR 3; Nab 13; LRom 4; Byz 5; EByz 4; A/M 4; LIsl 1; LOtt 1; UD 6; UDhandle 11.

See Seetzen: Daûd (416); Musil: Dâûdijje (87). Clearly this is the site which Worschech reports as Ẓahret ᶜeyal hārūn/#59 (1985a: 48), in spite of the fact that his UTMG coordinates and pottery findings differ from ours. Correspondingly, his Ruğm ed-Dāᵓūdīye/#60 is the same as our site 213. Worschech's coordinates place both sites ca. 1 km NNE of where we calculate them to be and in fact conflict with his estimate that Zahret ᶜeyal hārūn "is located ca. 800 m off the main road from Kerak to er-Rabba." Regarding the ceramic evidence from Kh. ed-Dāwūdīyah/Zahret ᶜeyal hārūn, he reports only ERom, LRom and Byz. Our broader chronological range probably is to be explained by the fact that we had sherded the site rather intensively not long before he sherded it.

The site consists of a long, low mound, ca. 100 m (E-W) by 200 m (N-S) with several cisterns and the foundation walls of at least two structures in its northeastern quadrant. While some of the walls and corners of the two buildings are clearly visible, their overall plan is difficult to determine. Worschech, who apparently was more successful than we in this regard, interpreted them as a villa, possibly Roman, and a storage building. "The villa measures 21x18 m. It has an apse-like extension (ca. 7 m in diameter) at its east side. ... The storage house is 10x10 m with well dressed walls 1 m thick."

Site 213 - **Kh. ed-Dāwūdīyyah** (S)
(Map section 7; field no. 9064)
PG: 19.4/71.6; UTMG: 60.2/58.9

Building ruin and cistern ca. 4 km south of er-Rabbah and ca. 300 m southeast of site 212. Just west of the spot marked "Ruins" on the K737 map. 80 sherds were collected, including: Nab 1; Byz 20; UD 4.

This is Worschech's Ruğm ed-Dāᵓūdīye (1985a: 48); see entry for site 212. He reported no pottery and described the building as a "Roman farm house."

Roughly centered on a low mound which itself measures ca. 40 x 40 m, foundation walls indicate a structure which measured ca. 30 m (E-W) by 20 m (N-S). A depression (ca. 2.5 m deep) in the southeast quadrant of the building may have been an installation of some sort (Worschech suggests a wine press or a cellar). Several tesserae were found on the east side of the site which, along with the predominantly Byzantine pottery, raises the possibility that this was a church. The cistern is located ca. 25 m northeast of the building and is still in use.

Site 214 - **ez-Zarrāᶜah**
(Map section 7; field no. 9040)
PG: 23.0/72.0; UTMG: 63.4/59.6

Unoccupied settlement site located ca. 4 km southeast of er-Rabbah, 2.5 km east of the Kerak-Dhiban road, and midway along the track from er-Rabbah to Adir. Marked Khirbat az Zarrāᶜah on the K737 map. 370 sherds were collected, including: IR I 1; Hell 1; Nab 2; LRom 1; Byz 1; LByz 1; A/M 21; LIsl 65; Mod 1; UD 12.

Photograph 21: Walls at Kh. ed-Dāwūdiyyah (Site 212)

Photograph 22: Walls at Kh. ed-Dāwūdiyyah

See Seetzen: Serráa (416); Tristram: Zérar (120); Musil: ẖirbet ez-Zerrâᶜa (86, 92, 369). Probably this is Brünnow and Domaszewski's Demûs es-sumr (I: 59).

Foundation walls representing several small buildings, cisterns, and surface pottery are scattered over an area measuring ca. 60 x 70 m. Outlying wall lines may represent an enclosure for the village area, but not a defensive wall. The terrain is essentially flat with rocky but fertile fields to the south and west.

Site 215 - **Qmeir**
(Map section 7; field no. 9030)
PG: 22.0/71.4; UTMG: 62.5/58.8

Wall lines and cisterns on a hilly spur ca. 3 km north of Adir and ca. 2 km east of the Kerak-Dhiban road. Marked Qumayr on the K737 map. 226 sherds were collected, including: LB 1; IR 1; A/M 38; LIsl 28; Mod 1; UD 10.

See Musil: ẖirbet el-Ḳmêr (369).

Surface pottery and rubble are scattered over an area ca. 40 x 80 m at the northwest end of a hilly spur which points to the northwest. Thus the site is bounded by sharp slopes on three sides and provides an open view to the northwest. Rakin and er-Rabbah are both visible. Wall lines indicating a single building complex (ca. 25 x 25 m) dominate the site. Other outlying walls can be traced in places, but there is nothing to suggest a settlement of any size. Possibly these are enclosure walls associated with the central building. There were at least five cisterns, one inside the main building and the others southeast of it.

Site 216 - **Abū er-Ruzz**
(Map section 7; field no. 9048)
PG: 20.0/69.8; UTMG: 60.5/57.3

Unoccupied settlement site located ca. 2.5 km ESE of Rakin and less than 0.5 km west of the Kerak-Dhiban road. 545 sherds were collected, including: MB 1; LB 1; IR 2; IR I 1; Nab 15; ERom 6; LRom 2; Byz 15; EByz 11; LByz 44; Um 1; UD 23; UDhandle 29; 1 glass base; 1 ceramic figurehead.

See Brünnow and Domaszewski: Abû-r-Ruzze (I: 59); Musil: ẖirbet abu Ruzzi (86, 369); Smith: Khurbet Ibn Ruz (369). Smith, incorrectly and in contradiction to Brünnow and Domaszewski and Musil, placed the site south of Qreifilla (Site 166).

This small mound, ca. 85 m (E-W) by 185 m (N-S), is surrounded by fertile, stony fields which slope down to a branch of Wadi eṣ-Ṣaqrah ca. 250 m to the southwest. Most of the sherds were found on its slopes, especially the western slopes, rather than on the summit. A crescent of stone rubble and ruined walls wrap around the northern end of the site. Occasional wall lines are visible elsewhere as well, and two corners are exposed at the south end of the site. One has three courses of dressed stones exposed; the other, located 6 m east of the first and possibly related to the same structure, has one course exposed. One cave cistern has rouletted impressions in the plaster.

Site 217 - **Kh. Qamarein**
(Map section 7; field no. 9051)
PG: 21.3/70.7; UTMG: 61.7/58.0

Caves, cisterns, and heavy concentration of sherds on a slight rocky rise ca. 5 km south of er-Rabbah and 1 km east of the Kerak-Dhiban road. Marked Khirbat Qamarein on the K737 map. 881 sherds were collected, including: LB(?) 1; LB 1; Hell 1; Nab 59; ERom 2; LRom 2; Byz 7; LByz 1; LIsl 19; UDE 2; UD 15; UDhandle 20.

See Tristram: Ghᵓmarein? (120); Doughty: Gamereyn (22); Brünnow and Domaszewski: el-Ḳamarên (I: 59); Musil: ẖirbet el-Ḳamarên (86, 369).

In addition to the several caves and cisterns on this slight rise, numerous large stones are scattered about —larger than one would expect in this natural context. Some of these stones cover cisterns, but others serve no obvious purpose. What appears to be a slight trace of an early road leaves the site in the direction of er-Rabbah.

Site 218
(Map section 7; field no. 9173)
PG: 22.2/70.7; UTMG: 62.9/58.2

Stone enclosure and monoliths on a high point slightly more than 2 km north of Adir. At the 1019 m elevation marker on the K737 map. No surface pottery.

A small enclosure (7 x 10 m) of large stones tops a rise north of Adir. Inside are three large stones, fragments of a fourth, and possibly a fifth, which probably represent a line of monoliths comparable to those at Lejjun (Site 239) and Adir (Site 22). Although none of them is standing now, the stones are larger than normally occurs on this ridge; they lie evenly spaced in an east-west row, and they alternate in color (i.e., white limestone alternating with dark stone). Beginning at the west end, the dimensions are as follows: 1.27 x 3.20 m (white); 1.10 x 2.90 m (dark); 1.20 x 3.90, broken now into two parts (white); 1.35 x 4.00 m (dark); 2.70 x 2.50 fragment (white). The monoliths would have been in line of vision with Rakin and Jdeiyidah (Sites 162 and 119).

Site 219 - Ḥujfah
(Map section 7; field no. 9043)
PG: 24.4/71.0; UTMG: 65.0/58.4

Small khirbeh located ca. 3 km northeast of Adir, on the road from Adir to Jdeiyidah. Marked Hajfā on some editions of the K737 map; marked "ruins" on others. 110 sherds were collected, including: EB I 2; EB II-III 5; LB 1; IR 4; IR I 1; Nab 2; ERom 1; LByz 1; LIsl 28; Ott 4; UDE 5; UD 3.

See Seetzen: Hödschfa (416); Burckhardt: Hedjfa (389); Tristram: Hadjfeh (120); Brünnow and Domaszewski: Ḥeğfa (Vol. II: 41); Musil: ḫirbet Ḥeğfa (19, 142); Glueck: Kh. Hejfeh/#142 (1934: 63). Glueck described it as "a small early Arabic site" and reported no pottery.

Mounds of stone and dirt rubble with a moderate amount of surface pottery cover a slope immediately west of and facing the Adir-Jdeiyidah road. The area of concentrated debris measures ca. 225 m (E-W) by 75 m (N-S). At the top of the slope (i.e., at the west end of the site) is a stone enclosure which measures ca. 30 x 12 m. Only one course of its walls is preserved above ground level. There are faint traces of internal walls, as well as occasional traces of wall lines among the mounds of rubble scattered farther down the slope.

Site 220
(Map section 7; field no. 9088)
PG: 28.3/72.4; UTMG: 68.8/60.0

Stone heap on a hillside slightly less than 2 km southeast of Jdeiyidah and less than 0.5 km northeast of the 892 m marker on the K737 map. While there are no obvious wall lines, we did find a small amount of surface pottery. 30 sherds were collected, none of which could be dated with any confidence. 5 were saved and registered as UD.

Site 221
(Map section 7; field no. 9279)
PG: 27.9/70.9; UTMG: 68.5/58.6

Small settlement site ca. 2.5 km SSE of Jdeiyidah. Less than 0.5 km east of the point marked "Ruins" on the K737 map and on the north bank of the same wadi. 21 sherds were collected, including: A/M(?) 2; LIsl 9; Mod 6; A/M 2.

The houses of this small settlement were built into the hillside and extended to within 2 m of the wadi, which itself is very narrow at this point (no more than 15 m). The front and side walls of at least three separate houses are still evident, but none of the back walls is visible. Possibly the hillside itself served as the back walls. The walls are composed of single courses of field stones. The best preserved unit measures ca. 11 x 11 m and is divided into two rooms. There are at least two cisterns and probably three (the third is filled and thus indicated only by a depression in the ground). Large stones scattered across the wadi at the edge of the site may be the remains of a dam. 60 m farther down the wadi (east) is a cave artificially divided into two chambers.

Site 222
(Map section 7; field no. 9290, 9291, 9292, 9296)
PG: 27.6/70.9; UTMG: 68.2/58.5

Building ruin ca. 2.5 km south of Jdeiyidah. Marked "Ruins" on the K737 map. 16 sherds were collected, including: LIsl 12; UD 4.

This appears to be a farmstead consisting of a small house (14 x 6 m), a courtyard on the eastern side (ca. 14 x 11 m), and a cistern in the courtyard. It is situated on the south bank of a wadi, and most of the sherds were collected below the ruin, on the slopes down to the wadi. On a lower shelf in the wadi bed, to the southwest of and visible from the building ruin, is a stone enclosure (field no. 9291). It is specifically this enclosure, at a fork in the wadi, which is designated as "Ruins" on the K737 map. The enclosure measures ca. 6 x 10 m, is built of large rectangular stone blocks, and is preserved 2 m high in places. No pottery was found at the enclosure. Two other features on the ridge between this wadi (unnamed on the K737 map) and Wadi el-Jazur to the southwest deserve mention, although it is not entirely clear that either has archaeological significance. Near the crest of the ridge, at approximately the 882 m marker on the K737 map, is a circular configuration of stones (field no. 9296)—rather like an enclosure but only 6 m in diameter. The fact that it is suggestive of an enclosure instead of a stone heap seems to rule out the possibility that it was left by surveyors. Some 300 m further to the southwest (PG: 27.3/70.4; UTMG: 68.0/58.0), overlooking Wadi el-Jazur, is a stone heap ca. 10 m in diameter (field no. 9292). Possibly this is a collapsed structure of some sort, but one cannot be certain without dismantling some of the heap.

Site 223
(Map section 7; field no. 9295)
PG: 27.1/70.3; UTMG: 67.8/57.7

Dam across a branch of Wadi el-Jazur ca. 4.5 km northeast of Adir. Constructed from large, dressed field stones, some as large as 1.5 x 0.7 x 0.4 m, the dam was more than 25 m across. Much of it is still in place, the water having found a new route around its southern edge and broken that end of the dam in the process. No pottery was found.

Site 224 - **Rujm el-ᶜAbsī**
(Map section 7; field no. 9092)
PG: 26.2/69.6; UTMG: 66.9/57.2

Building ruin a rectangular structure ca. 4 km ENE of Adir. Marked Rujm ᶜAbsī on the K737 map. The structure measured ca. 20 x 30 m at the base and was situated on a gentle hill which slopes from southeast to northwest. Its walls were one course thick and composed of rough stones. 47 sherds were collected, including: Hell 2; LRom 5; LIsl 4; UD 1.

Site 225
(Map section 7; field no. 2634)
PG: 28.9/69.6 > 29.3/66.8; UTMG: 69.5/57.2 > 70.0/54.6

Remains of a cross-country, north-south wall which bisects the Kerak-Qaṭranah road ca. 6 km east of Adir. This wall line, which is marked on sheet 225/065 of the 1:25,000 Ministry of Economy map and some editions of K737, can be traced ca. 3 km, from the rim of Wadi Adir at PG: 28.9/69.6; UTMG: 69.4/57.2 to the rim of Wadi ed-Dakakin at PG: 29.3/66.8; UTMG: 70.0/54.6. Thus it crosses, and presumably controlled at some point in time, one of the natural corridors between the desert and the interior of the Kerak plateau. The wall was constructed with basalt fieldstones from the area, apparently ranged between two and four meters in width, and remains standing .33 m high in places. Sherds were collected along the wall, but not in any concentration and should not necessarily be associated with it (85 sherds were collected, including: IR 2; Nab 2; ERom 3; LByz 2; UD 76).

Parker's Sites 174a and 174b are near this wall (Koucky 1987b:88-89). We identified the following diagnostic pieces among the sherds collected by his team at 174b: IR 4; Nab 1; ERom 2; UDE 2; UD 4.

Site 226
(Map section 7; field no. 9294)
PG: 27.7/68.6; UTMG: 68.3/56.2

Stone enclosure ca. 5 km east of Adir, between Wadi Adir and the Kerak-Qatrana road. The enclosure is essentially a circle, 11 m across, and formed by basalt field stones which are set into the ground. Basalt stones are plentiful in that area. No surface pottery.

Site 227 - **Adir**
(Map section 7; field no. 9060)
PG: 22.5/68.5; UTMG: 63.1/55.7

Modern town on an ancient settlement site, northeast of Kerak and ca. 2 km east of the Kerak-Dhiban road. Marked Adir on the K737 map. 2191 sherds were collected, including: Chalco 2; EB II-III 74; EB IV 68; LB 3; IR(?) 3; IR 8; IR I 1; IR II 4; Nab 11; ERom 4; LRom 1; Byz 3; EByz 6; LByz 5; A/M 1; LIsl 6; Mod 2; UDE 15; UD 9.

See Burckhardt: Addar (389); Hornstein: Adar (97); Wilson: Adr/Adar (315); Brünnow and Domaszewski: Addir (Vol. II: 41); Musil (see esp. 26-27, but also 19, 143, 369) provided the earliest description of Adir, located the monoliths (Sarbûṭ Ader) 150 m northwest of the actual

Photograph 23: Possible fallen "menhirs" (Site 218)

Photograph 24: Dam (Site 223) across a branch of Wadi el-Jazur

khirbeh (ḫirbet Ader), and included a photograph of the standing monolith. In addition to the standing monolith, he reported what he thought to be an altar between it and another broken monolith lying on its side ca. 10 m further north. Ader was in the early stages of resettlement when Albright stopped there during his 1924 expedition to Moab and the Dead Sea (1924: 10). Examining the khirbeh and concluding that "nearly everything here is Byzantine and Arabic," he observed that there was an older settlement nevertheless "shown by potsherds of the Early Bronze and Early Iron which we picked up around the edges of the ruin." Albright also observed what appears to be a fragment of a third monolith in the Adir group and discovered what he interpreted to be a Moabite temple in the northwestern quadrant of the khirbeh. However, the evidence upon which he identified and dated the temple is not entirely convincing by today's standards. He contended that it belonged to a later period than the monoliths (which he associated with EB) but had to be pre-Hellenistic because of its hammer-dressed masonry. When Albright returned to Adir in 1933, he found that the modern settlement had expanded and that "the site of the temple was partly occupied by an Arab house, while the ancient walls had been almost completely destroyed for the sake of their building stone" (1934: 13-18). Although allowed to dig in the courtyard of the house, he reported no findings and made no further comment on the character or age of the supposed temple. From this and other soundings on the khirbeh (which he called "a small tell") Albright recognized three occupational phases overlapping the end of EB and what he called MB I. Other soundings in what he called "the Byzantine city," apparently the area south of and across a wadi from the main khirbeh/tell, produced Iron II pottery, a Nabataean phase with some Nabataean tombs, a Roman phase, and miscellaneous remains from the Byzantine and early Arabic periods. Glueck (Ader/#143; 1934: 45-47; see also 3, 63, 65), who visited Adir earlier the same year of Albright's soundings, observed that the khirbeh/tell was being plowed and reported large quantities of sherds on it and around it similar to those collected at the monoliths —i.e., "belonging to the last phase of Early Bronze and to the first part of Middle Bronze I." Canova (Ader; 174-91) published fifteen inscribed tombstones from Adir, dating to the 6th and 7th centuries, including six that had been published previously by A. Alt (1928: 218-33).

Adir is one of the largest towns on the Kerak plateau today and still expanding rapidly. The monolith is still standing with what appears to be fragments of two or perhaps three more nearby. Sherds collected in the area around them (figured into the summary above) included EB II-III 35; EB IVA 3; MB (?) 1; IR (?) 3; Byz 6. The modern house which incorporates the "temple" is 95 m southeast (160°) of the monoliths. Large stones at the base of the north wall probably belonged to the former structure. The owner of the house said that foreigners had dug there forty years ago and this was confirmed by a neighbor. Both claimed that the excavators had found gold. Sherds collected in the area of the khirbeh/tell were overwhelmingly EB II-III with the MB, LB, IR, Nab, and Rom periods barely represented. South of the khirbeh /tell and separated from it by a wadi, where one would expect to find Albright's "Byzantine city," was an open, unoccupied area when we investigated in 1979. Bedrock breaks the surface at several places providing threshing floors. There are several cisterns and occasional foundation walls. The pottery from this area was also heavily weighted toward EB II-III. LByz and LIsl were less well represented, along with occasional Nab and Rom sherds. Thus our findings do not agree well with Albright's report of Iron II and Nabataean materials. Possibly he was referring to the currently occupied area west of the road and the church, although this should have been described as "southwest" rather than "south" of the tell.

Site 228 - **Rujm el-Jazūr**
(Map section 7; field no. 2638)
PG: 26.4/67.3; UTMG: 67.0/54.8

Stone heap, possibly a building ruin, ca. 3.5 km ESE of Adir and 300 m south of the Kerak-Qaṭranah road. Marked Rujm al Jazūr on the K737 map. 73 sherds were collected, including: IR II 1; Nab 4; UDE 7; UD 18; UDhandle 2.

See Brünnow and Domaszewski: Ḫirbet ᶜêsir (Vol.II: 41); and Musil: ḫirbet el-Ǧâzur (26-28, 143).

The ruin, which has been greatly disturbed, consists of an oval stone heap on a north-south axis (ca. 32 m N-S). No clear wall lines are visible, but the stones are large (limestones ranging in size from 1 x 0.4 x 0.5 m to 1.5 x 0.6 x 0.3 m and rounded basalt fieldstones ca. 1 x 0.8 m) and of a type not found in the immediate area. There are three depressions (graves?) in the tumble and another a few meters north of the ruin on a slightly lower (ca. 1.5 m) terrace.

Site 229
(Map section 7; field no. 9080)
PG: 07.5/67.3; UTMG: 68.2/57.0

Oval shaped configuration of irregular stones in a rocky but plowed area ca. 5 km ENE of Adir, between Wadi Adir and Wadi el-Jazur. Marked "Ruins" on the K737 map, but the cartographers may have been mistaken. It is not absolutely certain, upon close examination, that this admittedly interesting pattern of stones represents anything more than a natural outcropping augmented by field clearing. However, there is a definite oval pattern, giving the impression of an enclosure (ca. 10 x 14.5 m), with a heavier concentration of stones on the west side. A possible wall line is discernible in the tumbled stones along this west side. There is an unusual tapered stone in the pile (0.35 x 0.3 x 1 m) and another slightly smaller stone that may have broken from it. 42 sherds were collected, including: Nab/ERom 2; UD 18.

Site 230 - **Kh. ᶜArbīd**
(Map section 7; field no. 2635)
PG: 29.2/67.4; UTMG: 69.8/55.0

Ruins of a major, fortified building complex ca. 6 km east of Adir and 1.5 km southeast of the Kerak-Qaṭranah road. Marked ᶜArbīd on the K737 map. 296 sherds were collected, including: EB II-III 1; MB/LB 3; IR 5; IR II 2; Nab 1; A/M 1; LIsl 20; UDE 10.

See Brünnow and Domaszewski: Riğm il-Arbîd (Vol. II: 41); and Musil: ḫirbet ᶜArbîd (28, 143). This is Parker's Site 173 (Koucky 1987b: 88-89). We identified the following diagnostic pieces among the sherds collected by his team at the site: MB (?) 1; IR 1; IR II 4; Hell 1; LRom/EByz 1; LIsl 5; UDE 6.

The ᶜArbid ruin is situated on a low hill 300 m north of the rim of Wadi ed-Dakakin and is surrounded by other low hills to the west and north. Otherwise, the terrain slopes gradually eastward, and a noteworthy feature some 90 m to the northeast is the remnant of a cross-country wall which extends from Wadi ed-Dakakin northward to Wadi Adir (Site 225). The most prominent structure of the ᶜArbid ruin is what appears to have been a tower (10 x 8.5 m at the base) on a terrace, or on a lower "stepped" level of the tower (ca. 15 x 15 m). The tower ruin rises some 2 m above the terrace and was composed of huge limestone blocks (1.40 x 0.45 x 0.45 m). A depression in the middle of the tower contained a skeleton. Seven courses of the terrace wall (composed of local basalt field stones) are clearly visible on the southern side. The tower and terrace are situated in the southeastern quadrant of a much larger area of tumbled walls which itself is enclosed by a well constructed wall (43 x 50 x 47.30 x 42.35 m) surviving six courses high in some places. At least ten rooms can be identified inside and adjoining this enclosure wall; a gap on its east side may have been a gate; and secondary enclosure walls are attached on its northwestern side. So far ᶜArbid has escaped the rapid modern development underway in the region—i.e., it has not yet been robbed for building stones—which renders it a good candidate for further investigation. Obviously, some of the building complex is of relatively recent vintage, corresponding to the LIsl pottery. But its strategic location and the broad chronological range of surface pottery suggest that the site was important in earlier times as well.

Site 231
(Map section 7; field no. 2641)
PG: 28.9/65.9; UTMG: 69.5/53.5

Stone enclosure 6 km southeast of Adir and 5.5 northeast of Zaḥum. Marked "Ruins" on some editions of the K737 map. 18 sherds were collected, including: Chalco/EB 2; Nab 1; UDE 15.

This may be Parker's Site 183 interpreted in the published report as a "building with courtyards" (Koucky 1987b: 88-89). We identified the following diagnostic pieces among the sherds collected by his team at the site: Nab 17; ERom 3; LRom 1.

Photograph 25: Building ruin at Kh. ʿArbīd (Site 230)

Site 232
(Map section 7; field no. 2642)
PG: 29.2/65.6; UTMG: 69.7/53.3

Prominent stone heap (7 x 8 m) among other scattered piles of stone ca. 7 km ESE of Adir and 1 km west of the track from el-Lejjun to el-Mreigha. Marked "Ruins" on the K737 map. Although roughly rectangular in shape and composed of black field stones, the heap presents no definite wall lines. The surrounding configurations of stone probably represent argicultural activity. We collected 9 sherds including: UDE 2; UD 7.

This is Parker's Site 184 (Koucky 1987b: 88-89) described in the report as a "rectangular structure." We were unable to date any of the sherds which they collected at the site, but identified 4 UDE.

Site 233 - **Kinnār**
(Map section 7; field no. 9111)
PG: 19.3/66.7; UTMG: 60.0/54.3

Ancient settlement site with numerous caves and cisterns ca. 2 km ENE of Kerak, at the head of Wadi el-Kinnar. Marked Khirbat el Kinnār on the K737 map. 660 sherds were collected, including: EB 2; IR 2; IR II C/Pers 1; Nab 8; ERom 1; LRom 1; Byz 8; LByz 9; A/M 31; LIsl 40; UDEhandle 2; UD 11; UDhandle 2.

Seetzen includes Schinnâr and also el Kinnâr in a list of ruins on the Kerak plateau (416). See also Brünnow and Domaszewski: Ḫirbet Činnâr (Vol. II: 42); Musil: ḫirbet el-Činnâr (19, 26); Wilson: Chinar (315).

The ruins at this site, which originally covered an area of some 250 x 100 m between two branches of Wadi el-Kinnar, have been largely obliterated by construction of modern facilities (subsequently abandoned).

Site 234
(Map section 7; field no. 9079)
PG: 20.9/65.7; UTMG: 61.6/53.1

Stone heap, possibly the collapsed remains of a structure which would have been slightly more than 4 m square, ca. 0.5 km east of the Kerak-Dhiban road at Abu Ḥammur. 76 sherds were collected, including: Nab 1; LRom 2; Byz 1; UD 10.

Site 235 - **el-Ḥaddādah**
(Map section 7; field no. 9082)
PG: 21.3/65.5; UTMG: 62.0/53.0

Small khirbeh 1 km east of the Kerak-Dhiban road at Abu Ḥammur. Marked "Ruins" on the K737 map. 272 sherds were collected, including: LB 1; IR II 7; Nab 9; LRom 2; LRom(?) 1; A/M 23; LIsl 20; UDhandle 5.

See Seetzen: Haddâde (416); Burckhardt: Hadada (389); Tristram: Hadādah (120); Musil: ḫirbet el-Ḥaddâde (26, 369).

Building rubble with occasionally distinguishable wall lines covers a low mound (ca. 200 x 100 m) on a hillside in this generally hilly area. There are several caves, at least two cisterns, a well, and a power pole on the site. The surrounding area is under cultivation. Most of the sherds were collected at the lower (southeastern) end of the site, where they had been carried by erosion.

Site 236
(Map section 7; field no. 9078)
PG: 20.4/64.3; UTMG: 60.9/51.7

Cistern with a stone cover, two caves, and sherd scatter on a slope immediately north of the Kerak-Qaṭranah road, ca. 1.5 km ENE of eth-Thanniya. 100 sherds were collected, including: Nab 7; A/M 8; LIsl 4; Mod 1; UD 3.

Site 237 - **Rujm esh-Sharīf**
(Map section 7; field no. 2639)
PG: 26.7/64.3; UTMG: 67.3/51.8

Building complex, apparently a watchtower with attached rooms and courtyards, ca. 8 km east of eth-Thanniya. Marked Rujm esh Sharīf on the K737 map. 55 sherds were collected, including: IR 1; A/M 2; LIsl 2; UD 5.

This is Parker's Site 186 (Koucky 1987b: 88-89). We identified the following diagnostic pieces among the sherds collected by his team at the site: IR 3; ERom 1; A/M 1; LIsl 5.

The collapsed ruins of this building complex are situated on a 920 m hill at the northwest end of the esh-Sharif ridge (which itself parallels Fajj el-ᶜUseikir on the northeast). Thus the site was a natural vantage point for the area northwest of the ridge as well as for the lower areas on both sides of the ridge (including Fajj el-ᶜUseikir). At the center of the building complex was a rectangular structure (7 x 10 m) with massive walls (0.85 to 1.45 m thick). These walls were constructed of two parallel rows of partly hewn limestones filled with smaller fieldstones, and remain standing 1 m high (3 courses). The cornerstones are 1.00 x .50 x .50 m monoliths. No inner partitions are visible. Two chambers adjoining the central structure on its south side may have been attached rooms; the masonry style is similar but less massive. Attached to the central structure and rooms on the west and east are what appear to have been courtyards. The walls of the one on the west (ca. 18 x 10 m) were built of upstanding limestone blocks slightly more than 1 m high. The walls of the one on the east form an irregular triangle and were built of small fieldstones. Five recent burials were observed among the ruins.

Approximately 500 m to the southeast and separated from the ruins described above by a saddle in the esh-Sharif ridge (PG: 26.9/63.9; UTMG: 67.5/51.5) are three stone heaps. The largest is an irregular pile of limestone blocks (up to .70 m long) which rises 1 m above ground and suggests a collapsed structure of some sort. The other two are probably burial cairns (ca. 3 m in diameter).

Site 238 - **esh-Sharīf**
(Map section 7; field no. 2643)
PG: 27.6/63.2; UTMG: 68.3/50.8

Ruined building complex 7 km southeast of Adir on the esh-Sharif ridge. 1053 sherds were collected, including: IR 21; IR II/Pers 1; Nab 22; ERom 8; LRom 1; Byz 2; EByz 2; LByz 2; Fat(?) 1; A/M 30; LIsl 44; UDEhandle 5; UD 36; UDhandle 4.

This site encompasses Parker's Sites 187, 188 and 189, which correspond respectively to the main esh-Sharīf ruin, the cistern area, and a stone heap southeast of the main ruin (Koucky 1987b: 88-89). We identified the following diagnostic sherds among those collected by his team. Site 187: IR 23; Nab 7; ERom 3; LByz 2; A/M 8; LIsl 7; Ott 1. Site 188: IR II 4; Nab 8; ERom 5; LByz 6. Site 189: IR 2; Nab 4. Esh-Sharīf may be Musil's ḳṣêr et-Tamra (42) and is almost certainly Glueck's Qeṣeir eṭ-Ṭamrah/#144 (1934: 63). According to Glueck, "From Ader we proceeded south-southeast to Qeṣeir eṭ-Ṭamrah, a small ruined site about seven kilometres from Ader in a straight line. A few painted Nabataean sherds were found and also several Byzantine and mediaeval Arabic sherds. Two kilometres southwest of it lies Kh. el-Moreighah ..." In any case, Glueck's Qeṣeir eṭ-Ṭamrah is not to be equated with the Qaṣr at Tamrah of the K737 map (UTMG: 73.9/44.7). The latter is probably Glueck's Qaṣr Noᶜmân.

The esh-Sharif ruins extend 80 x 60 m over a hill (elevation 940 m) which provides a commanding view of the surrounding area, especially Fajj el-ᶜUseikir. Mreigha (Site 316) is visible ca. 3 km to the SSW. These ruins are dominated by the remains of a central building which would have measured 20 m square. Its walls are almost 2 m wide, survive up to 3 m above the ground, and were constructed of limestone blocks up to 2 m in length. There are interior rooms and doorways with lintels still intact. Remains of outlying walls indicate other smaller buildings and courtyards. A short distance northwest of the central building, for example, are the remains of a rectangular building with two rooms connected by a door. Two depressions in the northeast quadrant of the ruin seem to indicate cisterns. Approximately 200 m northwest of the main esh-Sharif ruins is a cistern and adjacent line of huge stones. On a hill 300 m southeast of the main ruin are a small stone heap and a stone circle composed of local limestone blocks.

Site 239 - **Lejjūn** (Bronze Age)
(Map section 8; field no. 9066)
PG: 31.7/71.9; UTMG: 72.3/59.6

Ruin of a fortified city, apparently from the Early Bronze Age, situated on the northern end of a north-south ridge ca. 4.5 km SSE of Jdeidiyah and 2.3 km north of the Kerak-Qaṭranah road. 589 sherds were collected including: EB I 1; EB II-III 29; EB IV 23; Byz(?) 2; Byz 2; A/M 1; LIsl 2; UDE 10; UD 2.

See Musil: ḥarîm el-Fârde (36); Glueck (1933: 15; 1934: 44-45, 47, 67, 95); and Albright (1934 : 15). Musil reported a row of standing monoliths which are arranged in a row down the northwest slope of the ridge on which the ruin is situated. Comparing these "Steinplatten" to those at Adir and Iskander, he also reported local folk explanations as to how the stones came to be there. According to one of the explanations, God transformed a group of bridesmaids into stone because they insulted the sun. Glueck examined the site in 1933 and provided a full description, a plan, and a photograph of the monoliths. The ruin is oriented east-west, as can be seen from Glueck's plan, and he estimated it to cover an area ca. 700 x 250 m (Albright estimated it 700 by 150 m). Just outside the northeastern corner of the city wall was a major spring, while an acropolis dominated the southwestern corner of the city. "The slope of the hill between the spring and the east wall is strewn thickly with sherds belonging to the end of the Early Bronze and to the beginning of the Middle Bronze, that is, from about the twenty-third to the twentieth centuries B.C." Glueck counted sixteen monoliths, eleven of them still standing in a gently curved row from north to south and the other five having fallen in place. "The monoliths are uncut limestone blocks, most of them being about a metre and a half high." Albright spent a day at the site later the same year (in connection with his soundings at Adir). "At the south end of this great site lies the acropolis, which was occupied synchronously with phases C and B of Ader [i.e. 23rd-21st centuries B.C.E. according to Albright's dates], while the lower city was enclosed only in period B. Phase A [of Adir, which Albright dated 2000-1800 B.C.E.] was not represented at all, suggesting that sedentary occupation extended further out toward the desert before 2000 than after that date."

This is an important site which has escaped the ravages of modern development thus far. Indeed it remains essentially as Glueck and Albright described it, except that we were unable to trace some of the wall lines which they saw. The sixteen monoliths (eleven standing and five fallen) are still in place.

Photograph 26: Bronze Age Lejjūn (Site 239)

Photograph 27: "Menhirs" at Bronze Age Lejjūn

Site 240 - **Lejjūn** (Roman)
(Map section 8; field no. 9316)
PG: 32.7/72.0; UTMG: 73.1/59.7

Roman fort immediately northeast of the barracks marked Al Lajjūn on the K737 map. Included here only for reference; we did not examine the site or its immediate vicinity since it is being excavated by S. Thomas Parker (see esp. Parker 1986b: 58-74; Parker, ed 1987).

For earlier reports of the site see Seetzen: Ledschûn (413, 16); Burckhardt: Tedoun (373); Doughty: Lejûn (20); Bliss: Lejjûn (221-23); Hornstein: Lejûne (97, 102); Vincent: Ledjoun (1898: 436-39); Gautier: ledschūn (120); Wilson (310, 315); Brünnow and Domaszewski: el-Leǧǧûn (Vol.II: 22-38, 41-42, 86); Musil: ḳaṣr el-Leǧǧûn (10-11, 17, 29, 36, 143-44); Glueck: el-Lejjûn/#47 (1934: 40-45, 49, 63, 65, 72; 1939: 84, 90, 100-7, 120-30). Burckhardt's Tedoun clearly is Lejjun, even though his description of the region seems to place Tedoun much further to the northeast. "The principal source of the Modjeb is at a short distance to the N. E. of Katrane, a station of the Syrian Hadj; there the river is called Seyl Sayde, lower down it changes its name to Efm el Kereim, or, as it is also called, Szefye. At about one hour east of the bridge [i.e., the Roman bridge which crossed Wadi el-Mujib below ᶜAroᶜer] it receives the waters of the Ledjoum, which flow from the N. E. in a deep bed; the Ledjoum receives a rivulet called Seyl el Mekhreys, and then the Baloua, after which it takes the name of Enkheyle. Near the source of the Ledjoum is the ruined place called Tedoun; and near the source of the Baloua is a small ruined castle called Kalaat Baloua." There is a glaring error in this description which was to create considerable confusion in early 19th century maps of the region. Wadi Lejjun/Enkheyle approaches Wadi el-Mujib from the southeast rather than from the northeast, which in turn places Tedoun/Leddun too far to the northeast. Surely this error is to be attributed to the editors who published Burckhardt's travel notes posthumously.

Site 241
(Map section 8; field no. 2685)
PG: 31.7/68.2; UTMG: 72.1/56.0

Campsite ca. 3.5 km SSW of Roman Lejjun and slightly more than 1 km south of the Kerak-Qaṭranah road. This is Parker's Site 172 (Koucky 1987b: 88-89) which we did not examine. It is included here because of the interesting pottery. Parker's team collected 83 sherds which included, according to our reading, EB (?) 1; IR 2; ERom 2; LIsl 2; UDE 2.

Site 242 - **el-Bṭeimah**
(Map section 8; field no. 9255)
PG: 30.7/69.9; UTMG: 71.2/57.5

Building ruin ca. 5 km southeast of Jdeiyidah and less than 0.5 km north of the Kerak-Qaṭranah road. Marked "Ruins" on the K737 map. 5 sherds were collected, including: IR 1; UD 4

See Musil: ḫirbet el-Bṭême (28-29, 248); Glueck: el-Beṭeimeh/#149 (1934: 63); and Brünnow and Domaszewski who mentioned el-Bṯême as a region (Vol. II: 41) and marked the spot of el-Bṭeimah as a "Baum" on their map. Glueck reported el-Bṭeimah as "a small, ruined watch-tower" and reported no sherds.

Foundation remains indicate a 6 x 6 m building situated on a prominent hill with good visibility in all directions. Visible to the north are the ruins of Bronze Age Lejjun, for example, as is the entire Lejjun basin to the northeast and east. The exterior walls of the building were constructed of large dressed stones, some of which are more than a meter in length. These walls remain in place three courses above ground at the northeast corner, and the area which they enclose is filled with rubble. The location, size, and strong construction of the building suggest a watchtower.

Site 243
(Map section 8; field no. 2632)
PG: 31.8/68.0; UTMG: 72.4/55.6

Two cairns on a ridge overlooking a branch of Wadi er-Ramla; ca. 3 km ENE of Kh. ᶜArbid, 2 km south of the Kerak-Qaṭranah road, and ca. 500 m northwest of site 244. The largest cairn is essentially rectangular (ca. 12 x 4 m) and composed of large field stones (up to 0.59 x 0.90 x 0.30 m). The other is a circular cairn (ca. 3.5 m in diameter). Also nearby are recent bedouin burials. 4 sherds were collected, none of which could be dated.

Site 244
(Map section 8; field no. 2629)
PG: 32.1/67.8; UTMG: 72.7/55.5

Stone circle (28 x 30 m) ca. 3 km ENE of Kh. ᶜArbīd and 2 km south of the Kerak-Qaṭranah road. Situated at the base of a low hill. 16 sherds were collected, including: EB 2; UD 13. 4 possible retouched flakes.

Parker reports two more "stone rings" in the vicinity —i.e., his Site 171.

Site 245
(Map section 8; field no. 2628)
PG: 32.3/67.3; UTMG: 72.9/54.9

A stone circle (3.5 m diameter) and nearby rectangular shaped stone heap (9 x 5 m) on the north bank of a sharp bend in Wadi er-Ramlah; slightly more than 2 km south of the Kerak-Qaṭranah road and immediately west of the track which leads south from Lejjun, through Wadi er-Ramla, and then turns southwest toward Rujm esh-Sharif. No pottery.

The main site described above as a stone circle actually has a polygonal west side composed of four large stones (ca. 1 x 0.60 x 0.40 m). Smaller stones (ca. 0.50 x 0.50 x 0.50 m) compose the remaining sides. There is a slight depression in the middle of the circle and a bedouin shelter on its south side. This is Parker's Site 175 where his team collected 15 sherds (Koucky 1987b: 88-89). Among these, according to our reading, were 6 EB sherds. Ca. 50 m farther to the NNE and separated from the circle by a minor branch of Wadi er-Ramla is a small, roughly rectangular stone heap (ca. 9 x 5 m).

Site 246
(Map section 8; field no. 2631)
PG: 31.1/66.8; UTMG: 71.9/54.4

Poorly defined configuration of stone circles on a hilltop overlooking Wadi er-Ramlah. Ca. 3 km south of the Kerak-Qaṭranah road; less than 1 km northwest of Kh. Thamayil (Site 248); and near the 797 m elevation point on the K737 map.

Site 247
(Map section 8; field no. 2627)
PG: 32.4/66.7; UTMG: 72.7/54.5

Possible remains of a farmstead along the west bank of Wadi er-Ramlah, ca. 3 km south of the Kerak-Qaṭranah road. 11 sherds were collected in the vicinity including: EB II-III 1; Nab 1; Rom 1; LByz 1; UD 7.

This is Parker's Site 165 from which his team collected 39 sherds (Koucky 1987b: 88-89). Among these we recognized the following diagnostic pieces: EB 4; Byz 1.

An oval circle of stones (ca. 24 x 30 m) and smaller circle inside (6 x 5.5 m) possibly are to be interpreted as the foundations of a mudbrick house and surrounding fence. If so, this would have been a farmstead associated with the agricultural field immediately to the south. The sherds noted above were found in and around the field. Other occasional wall lines and small stone circles also are to be found in the vicinity.

Site 248 - **Kh. Thamāyil**
(Map section 8; field no. 2630)
PG: 31.5/66.3; UTMG: 72.1/53.9

Building ruin (apparently a tower on a constructed system of terraces) situated on a ridge above the juncture of two tributaries to Wadi er-Ramlah; slightly more than 3 km south of the Kerak-Qaṭranah road. Marked "Ruins" on the K737 map. Thamayil is the name of the region. We collected 279 sherds including: IR 22; IR II 7; Nab 2; LRom 1.

This is Parker's Site 166 from which his team collected 120 sherds (Koucky 1987b: 88-89). Among these, we identified the following diagnostics: IR 10; IR II 4.

Kh. Thamayil is situated along a track which leads south from Lejjun, through Wadi er-Ramlah, and then turns southwest in the direction of Rujm esh-Sharif. A commanding view to the east, south, and west is provided by the ridge, but visibility to the north is obstructed by another ridge ca. 80 m higher. The whole ruin, including various outlying terrace walls, covers ca. 80 x 55 m. Foundation walls of a solidly constructed square building (actually 7.15 x 7.60 x 6.70 x 7.50 m) are the central feature. These walls are preserved up to 2 m high and composed of huge, regularly-shaped stones (1.20 x .20 x .25 m) laid in "header-stretcher" style. At least two bedouin burials are embedded in the building ruin, which itself is situated on a constructed terrace. The latter is formed by essentially straight retaining walls on all four sides, is approximately square (ca. 30 x 28 m), and is oriented southwest-northeast. The building was situated at the southwestern end of the terrace ca. 2 m from the southwestern retaining wall, and several depressions in the northwest quadrant of the terrace may be filled cisterns. Attached to the southwestern retaining wall approximately opposite the building is a slanted rampart (ca. 1 m high) built of field stones (20 x 20 x 15 cm). The essential outline of a secondary terrace (ca. 23 x 18 m) can be traced on the southeast side of the one described above. Another secondary terrace on the northwest side is less clearly defined.

Site 249
(Map section 8; field no. 2637)
PG: 30.9/66.0; UTMG: 71.5/53.6

Building ruin, apparently a tower, situated on a steep hill overlooking the track which leads south from Lejjun, through Wadi er-Ramlah, and then turns southwest toward Rujm esh-Sharif; ca. 3.5 km south of the Kerak-Qaṭranah road, less than 1 km southwest of Kh. Thamayil, and marked "Ruins" on the K737 map. 13 sherds were collected, including: UDE 12; UD 1.

This is Parker's Site 167 from which his team collected 16 sherds (Koucky 1987b: 88-89), none of them, according to our reading, clearly diagnostic. Parker's Sites 168 and 169 are a short distance to the northwest.

The hill on which this ruin is located provides broad visibility especially to the east and south: Qaṣr Abu Rukbah is visible ca. 9 km to the SSE, for example, Kh. ᶜArbid to the northwest, and Rujm el-Meriḥ directly to the east. The ruin itself is a stone heap (15 m in diameter and 2.5 m high) which represents the collapsed remains of a building. Roughly square at the base (5.50 x 4.80 m), the building was constructed of large stone blocks (measuring up to 1.40 x 0.50 x 0.60 m). Its exterior walls are still standing five courses (ca. 1.5 m) high at the southeast corner. The stone heap also contains at least one and perhaps more bedouin burials. Two small cairns (ca. 2.5 m diameter) nearby presumably are burials also.

Site 250
(Map section 8; field no. 2626)
PG: 31.8/66.4; UTMG: 72.5/54.2

Two stone circles ca. 3 km south of the Kerak-Qaṭranah road and immediately west of the track which leads south from Lejjun, through Wadi er-Ramlah, and then southwest toward Rujm esh-Sharif. Possible lithic fragments are to be found in the area. 4 sherds were collected, all UD.

The circles are situated on the southeast slope of a ridge between Wadi er-Ramlah and one of its tributaries —i.e., the site overlooks the track mentioned above and faces Rujm el-Meriḥ (Site 251) which is slightly more than 1 km away. The circles are ca. 50 m apart (one to the north and further up the slope than the other) and composed of field stones laid in a single line visible at ground level. The northernmost circle is 10 m in diameter and has two large stones marking a possible entrance on its western side. Immediately outside this circle on the southeast single lines of field stones form a square enclosure (ca. 4 x 4.5 m). The second circle cannot be traced completely, but appears to have been ca. 15 m in diameter. Farther up the slope from the two circles is a small cairn, presumably a bedouin burial.

Site 251 - **Rujm el-Merīḥ**
(Map section 8; field no. 2625)
PG: 33.1/66.1; UTMG: 73.8/53.8

Building ruin, apparently a watchtower, situated on a prominent hill along the track which leads south from Lejjun via Qaṣr Abu Rukbah (Site 377) and Qaṣr et-Tamrah (Site 379) to Um Ḥamaṭ (Site 419). Ca. 11 km ESE of Adir and 4 km south of the Kerak-Qaṭranah road; at the 781 m elevation marker on the K737 map. 168 sherds were collected, including: Nab 14; LRom 4; EByz 2; UD 2.

This is Parker's Rujm Meeker/Site 120 from which his team collected 59 sherds. These included, according to our reading: IR 1; Nab 4; LRom 2; LByz 7; LIsl 1; UDE 3.

Rujm Meriḥ enjoys a commanding view. El-Bṭeimah and Bronze Age Lejjun are visible to the north, for example, and Qaṣr Abu Rukbah to the south. The rujm is a stone heap over 3 m high with the foundations of a well-constructed, square building (ca. 7 x 7 m) clearly visible among the tumbled stones. Its exterior walls, which are most clearly visible on the northwest and southwest sides, are 1.5 m thick and constructed with two faces of hewn stone blocks (ca. 0.20 x 0.50 x 0.30 m) with fill material between. Its interior is filled with tumbled blocks, and the collapsed remains of the building have also tumbled down the surrounding slopes of the hill. Ten or more bedouin graves were noted on the hill, and numerous tracks cross near the site. The ground surface is rocky and sandy, the soil chalky, and the vegetation of grass and thorns sparse. The location of the site, the dimensions and solid construction of the building, and the associated pottery combine to suggest that Rujm Meriḥ represents a Nabataean watchtower which remained in use during the Roman and Early Byzantine periods.

Site 252
(Map section 8; field no. 2640)
PG: 29.7/64.8; UTMG: 70.3/52.4

Building ruin, probably a watchtower, on a low hill 3 km ENE of Rujm esh-Sharif, immediately south of the track which leads from Lejjun to Rujm esh-Sharif, and ca. 4.5 km south of the Kerak-Qaṭranah road. At the 843 elevation marker on the K737 map. 3 sherds were collected, including: Nab 1; LIsl 1; UD 1.

This is Parker's Site 176 from which his team collected 23 sherds (Koucky 1987b: 88-89). These included, according to our reading: IR 1; Nab 4; LIsl 1.

Foundation walls indicate a solidly built square structure (4.40 x 4.25 m) composed of large limestone blocks (largest: 1.3 x 0.4 x 0.3 m). Two courses are still in place on the west side and three courses on the east side. The site has been much disturbed by bedouin tombs. Several of the tumbled blocks bear Arabic inscriptions. Three meters to the north is a small cairn, poorly preserved (ca. 3.5 m in diameter). The hill on which the structure was located provides a commanding view of the low valleys to the east. Kh. Thamayil (Site 248) is visible to the NNE, Rujm el-Meriḥ (Site 251) to the northeast, Qaṣr Abu Rukbah (Site 377) to the southeast, and the esh-Sharif ridges rise to the west and southwest.

Site 253
(Map section 8; field no. 2633)
PG: 31.8/64.2; UTMG: 72.4/51.9

Stone heap (4.2 x 3.2 m), possibly a building ruin, ca. 5 km east of Rujm esh-Sharif and ca. 5.5 km south of the Kerak-Qaṭranah road. Reused for bedouin burials.

Site 254
(Map section 8; field no. 2676)
PG: 33.4/64.1; UTMG: 74.1/51.9

Building ruin along the track which leads south from Lejjun via Qaṣr et-Tamrah (Site 379) and Qaṣr Abu Rukbah (Site 377) to Um Ḥamaṭ (Site 419). Ca. 5.5 km south of the Kerak-Qaṭranah road; marked "Ruins" on the K737 map. The precise dimensions and outline of the walls are difficult to determine because they are covered by debris, but the building seems to have been ca. 4.5 m square and constructed of small limestone blocks. A bedouin tomb rests at the top of the ruin. The site overlooks the Wadi el-Khabrah region to the east.

Site 255 - **Kh. eḍ-Ḍweibi[c]**
(Map section 9; field no. 2103)
PG: 10.1/62.2; UTMG: 50.9/49.4

Sherd scatter on a hill south of [c]Ain Ḍweibi[c], along a track ca. 1.2 km north of Kathrabba and 2 km southwest of Jauza. 801 sherds were collected, including: MB 15; LB 16; LB/IR I 1; IR 2; IR II 1; Nab 19; ERom 2; Byz 3; EByz 2; LIsl 4; Mod 3; UDE 12; UD 12; UD handle 26.

See Musil: ḫirbet eḍ-Ḍwejbî[c] (256, 364).

Site 256 - **Jauza**
(Map section 9; field no. 2006)
PG: 11.4/62.8; UTMG: 52.1/49.9

A modern village on an ancient settlement site, 2.5 km north of [c]Ai. Marked Jauza on the K737 map. 280 sherds were collected, including: IR II 2; Nab 4; LIsl 77; LOtt 3; Mod 1; UDE 10; UDhandle 4.

See Doughty: Khurbet Enjahsah (22); Musil: Ǧôza (15, 19, 256, 364).

Immediately west of the small village is a ruined structure on a small hill, ca. 11 x 7 m. The wall lines are clearly visible in places, and several stones in the tumble are large enough to have served as material for the lower courses of a watchtower, farmstead, or similar structure. On both the north and south the small hill slopes steeply to small wadi beds.

Site 257 - **ᶜAlaqān**
(Map section 9; field no. 2102)
PG: 11.7/61.4; UTMG: 52.5/48.6

Small khirbeh near the spring ᶜAin ᶜAlaqan, ca. 1.5 km northeast of ᶜAi. Marked ᶜAlaqān on the K737 map. 242 sherds were collected, including: LB 3; IR 1; IR I 4; IR II 6; Nab 2; LIsl 1; Mod 1.

Burckhardt: "At the end of two hours and a half [traveling SSW from Kerak] we reached, on the descent of the mountain, Ain Terayn, a fine spring, with the ruins of a city near it. The rivulet which takes its rise here joins that of Ketherabba, and descends along a narrow valley into the Ghor, from which it takes the name of Wadi Assal" (395-96). Although one cannot be entirely certain, Burckhardt seems to be at ᶜAlaqan.

Wall lines, representing at least two structures, and surface pottery cover an area ca. 125 x 35 m. The sherd scatter is light. There is a modern house nearby, and the site is bordered by wadis on three sides.

Site 258
(Map section 9; field no. 2107)
PG: 12.3/61.6; UTMG: 53.1/48.9

A ruined, rectangular structure ca. 1.5 km southeast of Jauza and 0.5 km ENE of ᶜAlaqan (Site 257). The paved Jauza-Franj Road lies 50 m to the west. 51 sherds were collected, including: IR I 1; Nab 2; UDE 2; UDEhandle 4; UDhandle 1.

The ruin consists of a single structure with exterior wall lines, three discernible courses, and at least one interior wall. Situated on a slight slope rising to the east, the ruin is oriented east-west (20 x 12 m) and surrounded by a light sherd scatter.

Site 259 - **Kh. el-Meidān** (NW)
(Map section 9; field no. 2012)
PG: 07.7/60.8; UTMG: 48.6/47:8

An unoccupied walled settlement ca. 1.2 km west of Kathrabba, on the northwestern end of Jebel er-Ras. 438 sherds were collected, including: IR 5; IR I 1; Hell 1; Nab 107; LRom 1; LByz 3; LIsl 1; UDEhandle 4; UD 6; UDhandle 28.

See Irby and Mangles: Medin (113); Musil: ḫirbet ar-Râs and ğebel er-Râs (364); Brünnow and Domaszewski: el-Middîn (I: 9, 60, 79); Glueck: el-Meidân/#115 (1939: 94-96); Schottroff: ḫ. el-Mēdān (207-8); Mittmann: Tall al-Mēdān (175-80). According to Glueck, "There are really two sites, although both go by the same name, one of them being at the s. e. end of the top of the hill [our site 260], and the other on the n. w. end [our Site 259]..." He described the site at the northwest end as the remains of a fairly large Nabataean settlement now completely detroyed except that wall lines of several houses could be made out. He found large quantities of Nabataean sherds and conjectured that the slopes of the hill were cultivated by the Nabataeans.

The site provides a commanding view of the approaches from the Dead Sea to the plateau. Glueck's description is basically accurate. The rectangular ruins measure ca. 65 x 85 m with numerous interior wall lines, some of which survive two to three courses high. Both the exterior and interior wall lines are laid out in rectangular fashion which suggests that the settlement was constructed according to an overall plan.

Site 260 - **Meidān** (SE)
(Map section 9; field no. 2092)
PG: 07.9/60.5; UTMG: 48.8/47.6

A ruined building complex on the southeastern end of Jebel er-Ras. 240 sherds were collected, including: IR I 3; Nab 16; Byz 3; A/M 1; LIsl 1; UDE 2; UD 3.

See references for site 259. Glueck described Meidan as a double ruin (1939: 96), and this obviously is the southeast ruin which he described as the remains of a strongly-walled circular enclosure, measuring roughly 23 m in diameter, with the remains of a blockhouse on the west side. The enclosing wall was 1.2 m thick, according to his measurements, and he observed fragments of walls of several other buildings in the complex as well as several cisterns. On the basis of Iron Age and Nabataean surface pottery, he interpreted Meidan as an originally Moabite fortress which was reused by the Nabataeans.

Glueck's description still applies. In the debris, which appears to be some 2-3 m deep, is the vague outline of a central structure (Glueck's blockhouse?). Immediately north of the main ruin is the base of a small rectangular structure which he failed to note. Glueck probably invested too much in the term "fortress," although this complex (like site 259, or perhaps in conjunction with it) must have served as a lookout/outpost for the settlements immediately to the east. The combination of Meidan's relative isolation and command over the approaches from the Lisan toward the plateau seems to define its purpose.

Site 261 - **Kathrabba**
(Map section 9; field no. 2010)
PG: 09.3/60.8; UTMG: 50.2/48.0

A modern village on an ancient settlement site ca. 9 km southwest of Kerak. Marked Kathrabbā on K737 map. 1098 sherds were collected, including: IR II 1; Nab 2; LRom 1; EByz 6; LByz 23; A/M 8; LIsl 260; Mod 7; UD 13; UDhandle 10; 1 roof tile; 1 Ott pipe fragment; 1 glass bracelet.

See Seetzen: Katrábba (416); Burckhardt: Ketherabba (389, 396); Musil: Kufrabba/Kuṯrabba (22, 68, 73, 77, 168, 254-56, 261, 364); Glueck: Kathrabbā/#116 (1939: 89, 94, 97, 100, 147-48); Mittmann: Kaṯrabba (175-80). The early travelers noted that Kathrabba was one of only a few permanent settlements between the Mujib and the Ḥesa. Musil and Glueck observed that a Roman period roadway ran from the plateau through Kathrabba and descended to the Dead Sea. Mittmann, examining both the relevant literary evidence and the site itself, identified Kathrabba as Nabataean Luhith. He reported a Nabataean horned capital of basalt and a column drum with base, both found in the present-day village. Although he found no Iron Age pottery at Kathrabba, Mittmann proposed it as the site also of Moabite Luhith mentioned in Isaiah 15:5.

Kathrabba extends along the western slopes of Wadi Jayah (or Wadi Kathrabba). There is a strong spring near the modern village, which itself has displaced all ruins from ancient times. Along the wadi slopes are dense sherd scatters, especially in some of the terraced areas. The sherd collection indicated above represented only a sampling.

Site 262 - **ᶜAi**
(Map section 9; field no. 2013)
PG: 11.0/60.4; UTMG: 51.8/47.5

A modern village on an ancient settlement site ca. 2 km ESE of Kathrabba. Marked ᶜAi on the K737 map. 1026 sherds were collected, including: EB II-III 12; LB 10; IR 3; IR I 5; IR II 7; IR II C/Pers 2; Nab 81; ERom 14; LRom 6; Byz 7; EByz 19; LByz 22; Um 5; A/M 4; LIsl 20; Mod 8; UDE 11; UDEhandle 5; UD 11; UDhandle 56.

See Seetzen: Ey (416); Musil: ḫirbet ᶜAjj (73, 256, 364); Donner: ᶜAiy (1964: 90). ᶜAi has been proposed as the Iye-abarim of Num. 21:11 and 33:44, and it may be the Aia of the Madaba Mosaic Map. ᶜAi was an isolated and uninhabited ruin when Musil visited at the end of the nineteenth century, and Glueck did not mention it. Donner, who visited the site in 1963, reported surface pottery from the following periods: Early Bronze, Middle Bronze, Iron II, Roman-Byzantine, and post-Mamluk.

ᶜAi, which now is one of the larger villages in the Kerak district, is situated in a fertile valley with a dependable water supply (a spring). Our sherd collection was limited to the area around the town "dumps" near the slopes of Wadi el-ᶜAmmal.

Site 263 - **Kh. el-Meiseh**
(Map section 9; field no. 2014)
PG: 13.1/60.2; UTMG: 53.8/47.5

Small ruin on a high point (ca. 1252 m above sea level) marked by a lone tree visible from a distance; ca. 2 km east of ᶜAi. 372 sherds were collected, including: IR 4; IR II 4; Nab 17; UD 10.

See Brünnow and Domaszewski: Mêsi-Baum (I: 103); Musil: ḫirbet el-Mêse/šaǧarat el-Mêse (2, 4, 15, 77, 82, 170, 204, 250, 255-56, 364-65, 373); Glueck: Kh. el-Meiseh/#117 (1939: 100). Earlier travelers noted that this highpoint with ruins and a prominent tree were visible from a distance. Glueck mentioned the site only in passing, apparently without visiting it.

The ruins of numerous buildings cover an area ca. 75 x 75 m. Occupation may have extended 75 m further north along the ridge, but cultivation and field clearing render this uncertain. The ruins have heavy stone tumble 2-3 m deep in several places. The stones vary in size; many are rectangular blocks up to 1 m in length. Wall lines are visible in stretches of 2-4 m before disappearing in the tumble. Apparently the site was enclosed by a wall, but our attempt to trace this wall met with little success. The best preserved evidence for a perimeter wall line can be seen on the north side of the ruin. There is a cistern and a well, the latter in current use by shepherds. Immediately north of the main ruins are wall lines representing the base of a small rectangular structure (ca. 12 x 10 m). Just as Kh. el-Meiseh is a landmark which can be seen from a long distance in almost every direction, so also it enjoys an unparalleled view over the plateau south of Kerak. One can see west to the Dead Sea and east to the Kerak-Ṭafileh road. Kathrabba and ᶜAi are both visible, as is the wadi system which surrounds them and flows to the Dead Sea. The site is well known because its tree is virtually the only tall tree in this part of the plateau. The size of the stones which compose the ruins and the location of the site suggest a stronghold of some sort.

Site 264 - **ᶜAinūn**
(Map section 9; field no. 2085)
PG: 15.2/62.7; UTMG: 55.9/49.8

A modern village on an ancient settlement site, ca. 4 km SSW of Kerak and ca. 3 km NNW of Miḥna. Marked ᶜAinun on the K737 map. 975 sherds were collected, including: EB I 1; EB II-III 9; EB IV 7; LB 3; IR 25; IR I 4; IR II 12; IR II C/Pers 3; Hell 4; Nab 62; ERom 3; EByz 16; LByz 10; Fat(?) 5; A/M 30; LIsl 37; Mod 6; UD 36.

Canova (ᶜAinūn; 229-34) reported various architectural fragments and thirty-four inscribed tombstones, seven of which could be dated from the late-5th to the early 7th centuries.

The village is located on a spur surrounded almost completely by a loop in Wadi eḍ-Ḍabᶜah. The north end of the village, which has a few dwellings formed around caves, is largely abandoned. The pottery was gathered on the northern and eastern slopes of the wadi and from the abandoned section of the village.

Site 265
(Map section 9; field no. 2091)
PG: 16.0/62.7; UTMG: 56.8/49.8

Building ruin located near the crest of a hill overlooking a small valley approximately 3 km SSW of Kerak and slightly less than 1 km south of ᶜIzra. 123 sherds were collected, including: IR 6; IR II 1; Nab 1; ERom 1; A/M 4; LIsl 2; UDE 6; UD 6.

Located roughly midway between a high tension tower and the modern Kerak-Ṭafileh road, the ruin suggests an "L-shaped" structure measuring ca. 30 m (EW) x 15 m (NS). The walls remain standing three courses high. Many of the stones are chert blocks. 150 m north of the ruin are two standing stones (ca. 1.5 m high), and immediately south of the ruin are two cisterns.

Site 266 - **Kh. eṭ-Ṭalīsah**
(Map section 9; field no. 2005)
PG: 16.1/62.0; UTMG: 57.2/49.5

Building ruin on a ridge ca. 4 km south of Kerak and immediately west of the Kerak-Ṭafileh road. 900 sherds were collected, including: MB 1; LB II 3; IR 28; IR I 1; IR II 1; Nab 26; Nab/ERom 2; Nab/ERom(?) 1; ERom 1; LRom 1; LIsl 2; UD 36; 1 perforated ceramic disc.

See Musil: ḫirbet Ṭelîsa (362); Glueck: Kh. eṭ-Ṭelîsah/#124 (1939: 99). Glueck, describing it as a large ruined site on a ridge with flint block remains, reported Nabataean and Iron Age pottery.

Several foundation wall lines are visible, all of which may pertain to a single building complex. If so, the complex measured ca. 40 x 18 m. There is a cistern still in use on the east side of the ridge, just outside what appears to have been an external wall of the building.

Site 267 - **Kh. el-Labūn**
(Map section 9; field no. 2008)
PG: 15.3/62.0; UTMG: 56.5/49.3

Unoccupied settlement site immediately ESE of ᶜAinun (on the opposite bank of Wadi eḍ-Ḍabᶜah) and ca. 1 km west of the Kerak-Ṭafileh road. 1148 sherds were collected, including: IR 1; IR I 2; Nab 30; EByz 3; LByz 3; Um 1; A/M 19; LIsl 37; UD 23; 1 Ott pipe fragment.

Doughty: Libbun (22); Glueck: Kh. el-Lebûn/#121 (1939: 99). Glueck described Labun as a ruin with some flint blocks among the tumbled stones and made no mention of pottery.

Occasional wall lines are discernible in much tumbled stone. Also there are several cisterns, some of which are

are still in use. A black basalt bowl was found on the surface. Immediately to the southeast is another ruin (Site 268) which the local people include under the name Labun.

Site 268
(Map section 9; field no. 2084)
PG: 15.8/61.6; UTMG: 56.6/49.2

A ruined building complex located on a small hill ca. 4 km SSW of Kerak and 1 km ESE of ᶜAinun, between Kh. el-Labun (Site 267) and Kh. el-Mṣaṭeb (Site 269). 352 sherds were collected, including: EB II-III 2; IR 4; IR II 2; Nab 12; ERom 1; Byz 1; A/M 2; UD 8.

Glueck's description of Kh. el-Muṣaṭeb (1939: 99) seems to describe this ruin, but local inhabitants called it Labun (with Site 267) and identified as el-Muṣāṭeb other ruins on a ridge still farther ESE (Site 269).

Although tumbled stones cover an area ca. 18 x 35 m, the ruin seems to represent a single building which was oriented NE-SW and measured ca. 15 x 8 m. It is situated on top of a small hill and composed of large limestone blocks with bossed sides and numerous flint blocks. The northwest wall, which is best preserved, appears to have been ca. 1 m thick. There may have been a stairway (4 m wide) leading up to the building on its northeast side. The ruin has been robbed for its limestone blocks—two are used to cover a cistern located ca. 25 m southeast of the ruin. A 3 m section of wall which parallels the building on its southeast side (at a distance of 4 m) was also constructed with limestone blocks and has a bonded corner with a perpendicular wall.

Site 269 - **Kh. el-Mṣāṭeb**
(Map section 9; field no. 2007)
PG: 16.1/61.7; UTMG: 57.0/49.0

Unoccupied settlement site on a prominent ridge ca. 4.5 km south of Kerak and less than 0.5 km west of the Kerak-Ṭafileh road. 634 sherds were collected, including: IR 9; IR II 3; Nab 17; A/M 2; Mod 1; UDE 2; UD 7.

See Klein: Masateb (1987: 255); Musil: ḫirbet el-Mṣâṭeb (15, 45, 362); Glueck: Kh. el-Muṣâṭeb/#122 (1939: 99-100). But see discussion of Site 268.

The ruin consists of a mound of stone rubble (ca. 75 m in circumference) with several large, well-hewn flint blocks. The corner of a structure is clearly distinguishable (two courses high) in the rubble. Also ruins of several, smaller structures are found elsewhere on the ridge, including two wall lines, one on the west side of the ridge and curving to the south, the other higher up on the ridge. There is no modern occupation on the ridge, but some bedouin tents were nearby. A dirt road brushes against the southern edge of the mound.

Site 270 - **Kh. el-Ḥawiyyah**
(Map section 9; field no. 2306)
PG: 15.2/62.7; UTMG: 58.0/48.6

An unoccupied settlement site ca. 5 km south of Kerak and less than 1 km east of the Kerak-Ṭafileh road. Marked Khirbat el Ḥawiya on the K737 map. 5166 sherds were collected, including: Chalco 9; EB II-III 42; MB 6; MB/LB 1; LB 15; LB II 19; IR 2; IR I 9; IR II 8; Hell 5; Nab 81; ERom 6; LRom 7; EByz 4; LByz 3; Fat(?) 1; A/M 242; LIsl 229; Mod 27; UDE 84; UD 85.

See Irby and Mangles: Howeeh (113); Klein: Khurbet Hawiyeh (1879: 255); Tristram: Hhoweiyeh (116-17); Doughty: Howiheh (22); Musil: ḫirbet el-Ḥawijje (19, 44, 362). These earlier travelers mentioned the ruin only in passing, and Glueck apparently overlooked it.

Tumbled ruins of buildings cover an area ca. 75 m (N-S) by 130 m (E-W). Many of the walls remain standing up to four courses high, suggesting fairly recent occupation. Both plastered and carved limestone cisterns are to be seen.

Site 271 - el-Msheirfah
(Map section 9; field no. 2361)
PG: 18.7/60.3; UTMG: 59.4/47.7

Modern village ca. 3.5 km south of eth-Thaniyyah, along the road from eth-Thanniyyah to Mirwid. Marked Musheirifa on the K737 map. 9 sherds were collected: Nab 5; LIsl 1; Mod 3.

The sherd coverage was sparse, and the only other evidences of earlier occupation observed were a few cisterns still in use and two Ottoman period buildings.

Photograph 28: Building ruin (Site 268) near Kh. el-Labūn

Photograph 29: Building ruin near Kh. el-Labūn

Site 272 - **Kh. el-Jūbah**
(Map section 9; field no. 2015)
PG: 16.7/59.6; UTMG: 57.5/46.9

A large pool and sherd scatter ca. 1 km northeast of Miḥna on the west side of the modern Kerak-Ṭafileh road. 477 sherds were collected, including: IR 18; IR II 3; Nab 16; UD 7; UDhandle 6.

See Mauss and Sauvaire: Birket-el-Djoubé (484); Tristram: Jubah (117); Brünnow and Domaszewski: el-Ǧûba (I: 11, 103); Musil: ḫirbet el-Ǧûba (362); Glueck: Kh. el-Jûbah/#119 (1939: 100). Tristram mentioned that the Roman road ran nearby. Glueck described Kh. el-Jubah as an almost featureless ruin and did not mention the pool.

The pool is approximately 40 m deep and 130 m in circumference. On the ridge above (west of) the pool is a moderate-density sherd scatter with a few wall lines preserved.

Site 273 - **Miḥna**
(Map section 9; field no. 2017)
PG: 16.0/59.0; UTMG: 56.8/46.4

A modern village on an ancient settlement site 7 km south of Kerak and less than 1 km west of the Kerak-Ṭafileh road. Marked Miḥnā on the K737 map. 967 sherds were collected, including: LB 1; IR 5; IR I 1; IR II 2; Hell 1; Nab 12; LRom(?) 5; LByz 7; Um 2; Abb 7; Fat(?) 4; A/M 86; LIsl 100; LOtt 3; Mod 10; UD 21; UDhandle 30; 1 roof tile; 1 Ott pipe fragment.

See Seetzen: Möhhna (416); Irby and Mangles: Mahanna (113); Mauss and Sauvaire: El Mehna (484); Klein: Mahna (1879: 255); Tristram: Mahk'henah (117); Doughty: Mehaineh (22); Brünnow and Domaszewski: el-Mḥna (I: 103); Musil: Maḥna (19, 77, 152, 362, 365); Glueck: Meḥnā/#120 (1939: 99-100); Canova: Maḥna (281-84). The early travelers generally referred to it as a large ruined village or otherwise noted its importance. Irby and Mangles and Tristram mentioned the ruins of an old church at the site. Glueck reported predominantly Nabataean sherds. Canova reported lintels with crosses, a Kufic Arabic inscription, and four inscribed tombstones. One of the tombstones could be dated to the mid-6th century. Some local residents call the village ᶜAdnāniyyah.

Several Ottoman period houses have survived in the modern village, some of which seem to overlie earlier ruins. Reused stones appear in some of their walls. For example, the rosette design on one limestone block suggests a Roman-Byzantine setting. Most of the sherds were collected on the slopes west and north of the modern village.

Site 274 - **Kh. el-Jeljūl**
(Map section 9; field no. 2016)
PG: 14.6/59.7; UTMG: 55.3/47.0

An ancient settlement site ca. 1.5 km northwest of Miḥna. 1043 sherds were collected, including: EB II-III 1; IR 2; IR II 1; Hell 2; Nab 15; ERom 1; LRom 2; EByz 6; LByz 9; A/M 37; LIsl 30; UDE 8; UD 22.

See Burckhardt: Djeldjoun (389); Irby and Mangles: Dgellgood (113); Klein Hulhul ((1879: 255); Tristram: Jeljul (118); Doughty: Jeljul (22); Brünnow and Domaszewski: Ǧelǧûl (I: 103); Musil: ḫirbet Ǧalǧûl (364-65); Glueck: Kh. el-Jeljûl/#118 (1939: 100). While Brünnow and Domaszewski described both Ǧelǧûl and Umm eḍ-Ḍurub as situated near el-Meḥna, they failed to mark Ǧelǧûl on their map and placed Umm eḍ-Ḍurub at approximately the location of Kh. el-Jeljul. Glueck described Jeljul as a large, completely destroyed, Nabataean-Roman site, with the usual cisterns.

Prominent ruins cover an area ca. 150 x 75 m on the western edge of the Wadi eḍ-Ḍabᶜah. The site provides a clear view of Miḥna to the southeast. Occasional sections of a surrounding wall can be traced, and some of the walls of internal buildings survive up to five courses high. The sherds were collected from among the ruins and the immediately surrounding slopes and fields. Four cisterns were found. The area around the ruins is also known locally as Jeljul.

Site 275
(Map section 9; field no. 2088)
PG: 14.1/58.7; UTMG: 54.9/46.4

Unoccupied settlement site ca. 1.5 km west of Miḥna. 383 sherds were collected, including: LB 2; Nab 26; Nab/ERom 5; Byz 1; UD 20.

Prominent ruins cover an area ca. 100 x 60 m and include numerous walls representing several structures. Some of the walls survive up to three courses high. No water sources were found in the immediate vicinity of the site, and the sherd density was light.

Site 276
(Map section 9; field no. 2089)
PG: 14.8/58.6; UTMG: 55.8/45.7

Sherd scatter ca. 1 km southwest of Miḥna. 85 sherds were collected, including: IR II 4; Nab 4; Byz 1; LIsl 1; UD 2; UDhandle 6.

Associated with the sherd scatter was a field clearance wall and a dry cistern 5-7 m deep.

Site 277
(Map section 9; field no. 2087)
PG: 14.5/58.0; UTMG: 55.1/45.1

Ruined building complex ca. 2 km southwest of Miḥna, along a dirt track which leads south from Jeljul. 1208 sherds were collected, including: LB 16; Nab 24; ERom 2; LIsl 3; UDE 7; UD 9; UDhandle 33.

Since this site is in an intensely cultivated area, it is difficult to distinguish architectural remains from field clearance. A cluster of wall lines which can be discerned with some confidence suggests a building complex which would have measured ca. 29 x 31 m. Sherds were gathered from the ruins and adjacent fields. We observed one cistern still in use.

Site 278 - **Kfeirāz**
(Map section 9; field no. 2020)
PG: 13.3/57.6; UTMG: 54.1/44.8

Large, unoccupied settlement site ca. 3 km southwest of Miḥna and slightly more than 3 km northwest of el-Mazar. Marked Khirbat Kufeirāz on the K737 map. 968 sherds were collected, including: EB II-III 1; LB 3; IR 2; Hell 1; Nab 46; Rom 4; LRom 2; Byz 15; Fat(?) 2; A/M 16; LIsl 50; Mod 1; UDE 3; UD 2; UDhandle 68; 1 tessera.

See Burckhardt: Djefeiras (389); Brünnow and Domaszewski: Kefeêr Râz (I: 105); Musil: ḫirbet Čfêrâz (19, 364-65); Glueck: Kefeirâz/#114 (1939: 96); Canova: Kefeīrāz (304-5). Glueck described it as a large ruined site, apparently once enclosed by an outer wall, with numerous cisterns. Several of the buildings had flint blocks, he observed, including one in the southwest corner with blocks remaining in place six courses high. Glueck believed some of the buildings dated to Nabataean and Roman times. Canova reported three tombstone fragments.

The ruins cover an area ca. 220 x 120 m. Five cisterns were found, and 200 m west of the ruins is a large well (Glueck's large birkeh). Adjacent to the main section of the ruins is a large threshing floor—the surrounding fields are intensely cultivated. Multiple wall lines, some standing three to five courses high, can be traced in extensive tumble. Some of the limestone slabs in the walls and among the tumble are more than a meter in length.

Site 279
(Map section 9; field no. 2109)
PG: 11.7/58.2; UTMG: 52.6/45.4

Stone heap (ca. 6 x 6 m) and light sherd scatter on a high ridge north of and overlooking the paved road from Mauta to Kathrabba and ᶜAi. Other stone heaps nearby are the result of field clearance and this one may be also. 17 sherds were collected, including: Nab 6; UD 6.

Site 280
(Map section 9; field no. 2128)
PG: 09.7/58.4; UTMG: 50.6/45.6

Two cairns ca. 2 km southwest of ᶜAi and ca. 0.5 km south of the road from Mauta to Kathrabba and ᶜAi. The larger and better preserved of the two is a partitioned cairn ca 10 m in diameter. The other is ca. 8 m in diameter and some of its stones appear to have been relaid to form a corner. 10 sherds were collected, including: Nab 4; UDE 1; UD 5.

Site 281 - **Kh. el-Ḥwāleh** (Kh. Eshjar)
(Map section 9; field no. 2104)
PG: 09.0/58.8; UTMG: 49.9/45.9

Small khirbeh ca. 2 km south of Kathrabba. 192 sherds were collected, including: Nab 4; Byz 2; A/M 1; LIsl 81; UD 1.

See Musil: ḫirbet el-Ḥwâle (73, 258, 364). We received two names for this site: Kh. el-Ḥwāle and Kh. Eshjar. However, Eshjar seems to be the regional name. Note that Musil reported a Kh. Ešǧar slightly further north (4, 256).

Stone tumble and occasional wall lines cover an area ca. 75 x 75 m. Among the ruins was a limestone lintel. There was one family living in a tent just north of the site when we investigated it (seasonal occupation), otherwise there were no settlements within a kilometer in any direction. The wadi slopes become steep to the west and lead eventually to the Dead Sea.

Site 282
(Map section 9; field no. 2086)
PG: 15.1/57.3; UTMG: 56.2/44.5

Building ruins ca. 2 km SSW of Miḥna and 1.5 km NNW of Mauta, on the northwest bank of Wadi es-Saninah esh-Shamali. 9 sherds were collected: Nab 1; LIsl 1; UDE 3; UD 4.

The ruins are located on a stretch of ground that slopes downward to the east and cover an area ca. 20 x 20 m. The main structure was possibly a house (13 x 15 m) with four rooms and some contiguous wall lines. The walls of the house are constructed from chert or flint stones in medium to large sizes. They are preserved up to four courses high in places, the exterior walls over 1 m wide and the interior walls ca. 1 m wide. Outside the exterior walls of the house are four segments of additional walls that may have belonged to other structures. There is a dirt track 200 m to the west of the site.

Site 283
(Map section 9; field no. 2394)
PG: 17.1/57.2; UTMG: 57.9/44.6

Sherd scatter ca. 1.5 km northeast of Mauta. Although this site is marked "Ruins" on the K737 map, the large stones are scattered around in haphazard arrangement and probably do not represent architectural remains. 309 sherds were collected, including: MB 2; IR II 3; Nab 28; EByz 1; LIsl 2; UDE 5; UDEhandle 4; UDhandle 2.

Site 284
(Map section 9; field no. 2393)
PG: 18.5/57.1; UTMG: 59.3/44.5

Light sherd scatter in fields ca. 0.5 km west of Mirwid. Marked "Ruins" on the K737 map, but no architectural remains were observed. 43 sherds were collected: Nab 9; UD 34.

Site 285 - **Mirwid**
(Map section 9; field no. 2309)
PG: 19.1/57.1; UTMG: 59.9/44.5

A modern village on an ancient settlement site ca. 3 km northeast of Mauta. Marked Mirwid on the K737 map. 719 sherds were collected, including: LB 1; Nab 9; ERom 3; A/M 2; LIsl 48; Mod 12; UD 7; UDhandle 14.

Irby and Mangles: Marrowhieh (113); Doughty: Mehrud (22); Musil: ruǧm el-Mradd/ḫirbet Merwed (44, 366).

Whatever ruins were visible to the early travelers have been covered or dismantled by the modern settlement. While no visible ruins remain, however, sherds were collected from several areas in the village. Also in the village are several cisterns still in use and two caves with vaulted stone entrances.

Site 286 - **Um Naṣr**
(Map section 9; field no. 2129)
PG: 10.7/56.7; UTMG: 51.6/43.9

Building ruin (or possibly a small settlement ruin) situated on a hillock of the northwest bank of Wadi ᶜUseifir; ca. 1 km NNW of el-ᶜIraq. 24 sherds were collected, including: Nab 1; LByz 2; LIsl 1; UD 17.

Foundation walls and a door socket indicate an essentially square structure (ca. 8 x 8 m). Also there are occasional wall lines at lower levels along the slope of the hillock, some of them parallel to the main structure and some not. These could be the remains of additional structures, but more likely they represent terrace walls. The site provides good visibility—e.g., the Dead Sea can be seen to the west. The sherds were collected from around the ruined building and the nearby slopes.

Site 287 - **Rujm el-Ḥleileh**
(Map section 9; field no. 2024)
PG: 10.9/56.9; UTMG: 51.8/43.9

Building ruin ca. 1 km north of el-ᶜIraq. Um Naṣr (Site 286) is immediately to the west and separated by a small wadi. 52 sherds were collected, including: IR 2; Nab 3.

Clearly this is Glueck's Rujm Ḥeleileh/#111 (1939: 95), which he described as a ruined building ca. 10 x 8 m, although he placed it 1 km east of ᶜIraq.

The ruin consists of walls, preserved two courses high in some places, of a fortress-like structure. Built with large limestone and chert blocks, it measured ca. 8 x 9 m at the base.

Site 288
(Map section 9; field no. 2119)
PG: 11.0/56.6; UTMG: 51.9/43.8

Light sherd scatter on a hill ca. 1 km north of (and overlooking) el-ᶜIraq. 91 sherds were collected, including: EB 1; EB II-III 4; Nab 3; LIsl 1.

A 6 m segment of wall constructed from large chert blocks was observed along the top of the hill and west of the sherd scatter. Also there are some large cupholes in a limestone outcropping along the ridge.

Site 289 - **Kh. Um el-Qṣeir**
(Map section 9; field no. 2021)
PG: 11.7/56.1; UTMG: 52.6/43.5

Small khirbeh ca. 1 km NNE of el-ᶜIraq and immediately west of the modern road which descends from the plateau to ᶜIraq. 673 sherds were collected, including: EB I 9; MB 1; LB 10; Hell 1; EByz 3; A/M 16; LIsl 93; UDE 12; UD 3.

See Musil: ḳṣejr Ḥazîm (258); Glueck: Kh. Umm el-Qeṣeir/#113 (1939: 95). Musil placed this ruin north of ẖ. Tarᶜîn, itself near el-ᶜIraq (see entry for el-ᶜIraq/site 292). Glueck mentioned it only as a ruin north of el-ᶜIraq.

The site presents multiple wall lines amid rock tumble which covers an area ca. 80 x 60 m. Some of the walls are preserved up to four courses high. There are some caves and cisterns, and part of the site is used now as a threshing floor.

Site 290 - **Kh. Zabdah**
(Map section 9; field no. 2022)
PG: 12.8/56.2; UTMG: 53.7/43.5

Small khirbeh ca. 3.5 km west of Mauta and immediately south of the paved road from Mauta to Kathrabba. Marked Khirbat Zabda on the K737 map. 464 sherds were collected, including: LB 1; IR I 3; IR II 2; Nab 5; Fat(?) 2; A/M 10; LIsl 38; UD 4; UDhandle 6; 1 roof tile.

See Musil: ẖirbet Zabda (256); Glueck: Zabdah/#112 (1939: 96). Glueck described it as a "large, completely ruined site...situated on top of the fertile Moabite plateau. In it are the ruins of several large buildings, built of large, roughly hewn flint blocks, with several almost completely filled-up cisterns between them. There are numerous Nabataean, Roman, Byzantine, and mediaeval painted and glazed Arabic sherds."

The ruins cover an area ca. 70 x 55 m. As described by Glueck, multiple ruined structures are evident amid considerable stone tumble. Some of the walls survive up to four courses high. The rubble includes many chert blocks. Possibly the site was enclosed by a wall at one time, depending on whether certain outlying wall segments represent such a perimeter wall or whether they are exterior walls of individual buildings. Two cisterns were found. The northwestern end of the site is being used as a threshing floor.

Site 291 - **Kh. Ghifrah**
(Map section 9; field no. 2120)
PG: 10.6/55.1; UTMG: 51.4/42.6

Small khirbeh with a light sherd scatter immediately west of el-ᶜIraq. Situated ca. 125 m south of ᶜAin Ghifrah and on the western extremity of a slope which descends west and north toward Wadi el-Beiḍa. 103 sherds were collected, including: Nab 9; Byz 2; LByz 3; LIsl 4; UD 4.

See Musil: ẖirbet Ǧifra (258, 364).

Except for barely visible segments of walls at ground level, virtually nothing remains to indicate previous settlement. Probably the site was robbed for construction in el-ᶜIraq.

Site 292 - **el-ᶜIrāq**
(Map section 9; field no. 2029)
PG: 11.2/55.5; UTMG: 52.1/42.8

Modern town on an ancient settlement site, ca. 5 km west of Mauta. Marked El ᶜIrāq on the K737 map. 144 sherds were collected, including: Nab 2; Byz 7; Um 2; Fat(?) 1; LIsl 23; Mod 4; UD 8.

See Seetzen: Errâk (416, 26); Burckhardt: Oerak (389, 96); Klein: ᶜOrak (1879: 254); Musil: el-ᶜArâḳ (72-73, 75, 151, 257-59); Glueck: el-ᶜIrâq/#110 (1939: 94-96); Canova: el-ᶜArāq (306-7). Musil provided a photograph, described it as a small village surrounded by grottos, and mentioned another village /ruin nearby called Tarᶜîn. In that regard, see Burckhardt (395-96): "At the end of two hours and a half [traveling SSW from Kerak] we reached, on the descent of the mountain, Ain Terayn, a fine spring, with the ruins of a city near it. The rivulet which takes its rise here joins that of Ketherabba, and descends along a narrow valley into the Ghor, from which it takes the name of Wadi Assal." Glueck reported el-ᶜIraq as a modern village. Canova reported two inscribed tombstones, neither of which could be dated. Donner (1964: 90), who visited el-ᶜIraq in 1963 and collected Roman-Byzantine and Late Islamic pottery, observed that the village and ruins known to Musil (258) as Tarᶜîn had been incorporated into the modern town of el-ᶜIraq. Tarᶜin may correspond to Tharais which appears on the mosaic map from Madaba.

The modern town is still growing, with new roads and houses under construction. The sherds indicated above were collected from the slopes on the west side of town. Unfortunately, the survey team had limited access even to these slopes.

Site 293
(Map section 9; field no. 2121)
PG: 11.0/55.2; UTMG: 51.9/42.5

Sherd scatter on a wide shelf ca. 0.5 km southwest of el-ᶜIraq; near a spring and two modern houses just west of the road from el-ᶜIraq via el-Baḥr to Khanzirah. The area is cultivated, including orchards, and this activity would have removed any earlier architectural remains. 101 sherds were collected, including: IR I 15; IR II 2; Nab 4; Byz(?) 2; UDEhandle 10; UD 4; UDhandle 4.

Site 294 - **Fqeiqes**
(Map section 9; field no. 2028)
PG: 11.3/54.9; UTMG: 52.3/42.3

Dense sherd scatter on top of a hill ca. 0.5 km southeast of el-ᶜIraq. 1113 sherds were collected, including: EB 73; EB II-III 38; EB IVA 147; EB IVB 13; MB II(?) 6; LB 1; A/M 12; UDE 7; UD 8.

See Glueck, Feqeiqes/#109 (1939: 94, 96), who described it as a large site whose remains have been worn away or torn down to their foundation levels. It was a strongly built site, he observed, with traces of a thick wall surrounding the top of the hill. He reported large numbers of EB IV-MB I sherds on the top and sides of the hill with large numbers of Nabataean sherds particularly on the northeast and east slopes. Musil's ḫirbet Fḳêḳes (151, 256) is probably Kh. Fqeiqes (Site 301).

The hilltop is actually part of the shelf of the westward slopes from the plateau proper down to Wadi el-Beiḍa. It is intensely cultivated and presents no architectural remains except for an occasional hint of a wall line. However, the large amount of surface pottery in the fields on the rounded summit of the hill, together with Glueck's description, indicate that Fqeiqes was a substantial settlement during the Early Bronze Age.

Site 295 - **Kh. Mishrāqāh**
(Map section 9; field no. 2025)
PG: 13.1/55.4; UTMG: 54.0/42.7

Small khirbeh between Mauta and el-ᶜIraq, along the road from Kathrabba to el-Mazar. Marked Khirbat Mishrāqā on the K737 map. 795 sherds were collected, including: Hell 1; Nab 50; ERom 2; EByz 2; LByz 12; Um 1; A/M 11; LIsl 49; UDE 2; UD 8; UDhandle 50.

Possibly Musil's ḫirbet Zabbûd (256) or ḫirbet en-Niswân (365).

The ruins, which are scattered over an area ca. 100 x 100 m, consist of stone tumble from collapsed houses. Many of the walls can be easily traced amid the tumble, some of them still preserved up to five courses high. Also, almost completely covered by debris, are two intact archways. No doubt these walls and arches represent a fairly recent occupation, associated with the late Islamic pottery. There are several cisterns.

Site 296
(Map section 9; field no. 2093)
PG: 14.0/55.6; UTMG: 54.8/42.8

Building ruin ca. 2 km west of Mauta, along a track from Mauta to Mishraqah. The site overlooks Wadi eth-Thamayil from its south bank. 16 sherds were collected, including: LB 4; EByz 1; UD 11.

Wall lines visible at ground level mark three sides of a rectangular structure 14 m (N-S) by 17 m (E-W). The walls were constructed with large chert blocks and apparently rest on chert bedrock. There is a light sherd scatter and one cistern, now collapsed and filled with debris.

Site 297 - **Rujm Mes^cīd**
(Map section 9; field no. 2026)
PG: 13.0/54.8; UTMG: 53.8/42.2

Stone heap ca. 2 km ESE of el-^cIraq, between Kh. Mishraqah and Kh. Um el-^cAṭaṭ. 215 sherds were collected including: LB 1; IR 1; Nab 12; LIsl 3; UDhandle 9.

Glueck, Rujm Mes^cîd/#105 (1939: 97), described it as an almost totally destroyed building constructed of rude flint blocks and reported surface pottery from Nabataean, Roman and Byzantine times. He also noted a north-south section of the Roman road on the east side of the ruin.

One sees today only a crescent-shaped mound of stones that looks very much like field clearance. There are no discernible wall lines, and we found neither flint blocks nor a section of Roman road. However, there is a cistern nearby. The area is under cultivation, so the stones of the ruin and road probably were removed for agricultural purposes or robbed for construction elsewhere.

Site 298 - **Rujm Um el-^cAṭāṭ**
(Map section 9; field no. 2027)
PG: 13.5/54.5; UTMG: 54.5/41.9

Small khirbeh ca. 3 km southwest of Mauta and northwest of el-Mazar, on the east side of the dirt road from el-Mazar to Kh. Zabdah. Marked Khirbat Um el ^cAṭaṭ on the K737 map. 626 sherds were collected including: EB 2; LB 3; IR 2; Nab 20; ERom 3; LRom 1; EByz 8; LByz 15; EIsl 1; Um 1; A/M 13; LIsl 24; UDE 7; UD 9; UDhandle 49; 1 Ott pipe fragment.

See Musil: ḫirbet umm el-^cAṭaṭ (365); Glueck: Rujm Umm el-^cAṭâṭ/#103 (1939: 97). Glueck described it as completely destroyed, with rough flint blocks and cisterns, and with Nabataean, Roman, Byzantine, and medieval Arabic sherds.

Numerous wall lines and rubble adjacent to a large threshing floor cover an area ca. 100 x 100 m. None of the walls has survived with more than one course above ground. There are four cisterns, two of them still in use.

Site 299 - **Rujm el-Baqr**
(Map section 9; field no. 2033)
PG: 13.8/54.0; UTMG: 54.6/41.5

Small khirbeh ca. 3 km southwest of Mauta and northwest of el-Mazar, ca. 0.5 km south of Rujm Um el-Aṭaṭ. 613 sherds were collected, including: LB 2; IR I 4; IR II 4; Hell 1; Nab 19; ERom 1; EByz 1; LByz 3; A/M 1; UDhandle 67.

Clearly this is Glueck's Rujm el-Beqr/#102 (1939: 96): "About 2 km. west of Mazâr is Rujm el-Beqr. It is a small, completely destroyed site, with several cisterns visible among the ruins. The remains of several buildings constructed of rough flint blocks are visible. A small quantity of Nabataean-Roman sherds was found. About half a kilometre n.n.w. of Rujm el-Beqr is Rujm Umm el-^cAṭâṭ, ..." Note that the name el-Baḥr appears twice on the K737 map, but farther southwest than this site.

The ruins of at least four separate buildings are located in cultivated wheat fields just east of the dirt track from el-Mazar to Kh. Zabdah. Nothing more than wall lines and a moderate sherd scatter remains. There are four cisterns and, ca. 50 m east of the ruins, a possible dolmen.

Site 300 - **el-Bqei^c**
(Map section 9; field no. 2032)
PG: 12.6/53.7; UTMG: 53.4/41.0

One modern house, several vacant Ottoman period houses, and some apparently earlier wall lines ca. 3.5 km WNW of el-Mazar; situated near the western edge of the plateau overlooking the steep descent to Wadi el-^cIraq some 500 m below. Marked El Baqei[c] on the K737 map. 473 sherds were collected, including: EB 4; IR II 3; Nab 85; ERom 5; LRom 1; Byz 4; LByz 10; Um 1; A/M 2; LIsl 42; UDEhandle 3; UD 8; UDhandle 15.

Glueck mentiond el-Beqei[c]/#107 but did not describe it (1939: 93-94).

Site 301 - **Kh. Fqeiqes**
(Map section 9; field no. 2030)
PG: 11.5/53.8; UTMG: 52.4/40.8

Small khirbeh ca. 2 km south of el-[c]Iraq, immediately east of the el-[c]Iraq-Khanzirah road near [c]Ain Fqeiqes. 62 sherds were collected, including: LB 1; Nab 5; ERom 2; Byz 2; LByz 3; LIsl 2; UD 1.

Musil: ḫirbet Fḳêḳes (151, 256).

Although difficult to examine because the site is overgrown with grass and thistles, the ruin seems to represent a multi-roomed structure (ca. 14 x 14 m) with thick (ca. 1.5 m) walls. These walls were constructed from limestone and chert blocks ca. 1 m in length. Other wall lines on the southwest side of this main structure suggest rooms with similar dimensions. [c]Ain Fqeiqes is ca. 30 m to the SSW of the ruin, farther down the slope.

Site 302 - **Kh. el-Beiḍā**
(Map section 9; field no. 2034)
PG: 11.5/53.4; UTMG: 52.0/41.1

Sherd scatter ca. 1.5 km south of [c]Iraq, on the eastern bank of the Wadi Beiḍa near two modern houses. 342 sherds were collected, including: Nab 13; LByz 3; Mod 2; UDE 4.

Glueck, Kh. el-Beiḍā/#108 (1939: 93-94), described it as a small, completely destroyed site, with worn sherds dating from the Nabataean and later periods.

Local inhabitants have been robbing stones from this site to the extent that only traces of possible wall lines remain.

Site 303 - **Beit Sahm**
(Map section 9; field no. 2031)
PG: 08.9/53.9; UTMG: 49.8/41.2

Small khirbeh ca. 2.5 km southwest of [c]Irāq, immediately west of the [c]Iraq-Khanzirah road. Marked Beit Sahm on the K737 map. 274 sherds were collected, including: EB I 9; MB/LB 2; Nab 12; LRom 3; Byz 3; A/M 2; LIsl 69; UD 5; UDhandle.

Musil: ḫrejbe Bejt Sahm (259, 261). Musil described it as a small ruin with olive trees nearby and a few local inhabitants.

The site has multiple wall lines, some preserved up to three courses high, amid rubble which appears to be 1-2 m in depth. There are two springs nearby, and the local inhabitants are developing vineyards in the immediate vicinity of the ruin. Some of the rubble from the ruin has been removed in connection with the cultivation. A broken limestone slab found near the ruin contained a fragmentary Greek inscription.

Site 304 - **Mauta/Mōta**
(Map section 9; field no. 2023)
PG: 16.7/55.8; UTMG: 57.1/43.2

Modern town on an ancient settlement site 8 km south of Kerak on the Kerak-Ṭafileh road. Marked Mauta on the K737 map. 1244 sherds were collected, including: EB 3; MB 1; LB 2; IR I 3; IR II 5; Hell 1; Nab 63; ERom 4; LRom 7; Byz 16; EByz 16; LByz 11; Um 3; A/M 33; LIsl 12; LOtt 1; Mod 14; UDEhandle 10; UD 26; UDhandle 72.

See Seetzen: Môte (412, 416); Burckhardt: Mouthe (389); Irby and Mangles: Harnahta/Mote (113); Mauss and Sauvaire: El Móteh (484-85); Klein: Moteh (1879: 255); Tristram: Modeh (118); Hornstein (97, 102); Brünnow and Domaszewski: el-Môte (I: 60, 68, 104); Musil: Môte (14, 22, 152, 156, 361, 365); Glueck: Môteh (1939: 97); Savignac: Môteh (247); Canova: el-Mōte (285-303). Seetzen described Mauta as a destroyed place. A century later, when Musil visited the site, the modern settlement was just beginning to emerge. Glueck knew Mauta as a modern town and made no mention of its antiquity. Canova reported twenty-one inscribed tombstones, sixteen of which could be dated (ranging from mid-5th to the mid-7th centuries).

According to Muqaddasi, "Maâb lies in the mountains. The district round has many villages, where grow almond trees and vines. It borders on the desert. Mûtah is counted among its hamlets, where are the tombs of Ja[c]far aṭ-Ṭayyār, and [c]Abdallāh ibn Rawâḥah" (PPTS vol.III, p. 63; see also PPTS vol.III, pp.97-98). Al-Bakri reported:

"And Muʾtah is a place in the land of Syria, of the district of al-Balqāʾ. It is there that the Messenger of God sent the expeditionary corps in the year 8. He put his freedman, Zayd ben Ḥārithah, at its head and said: 'If Zayd is killed, it will be Jaᶜfar ben abi Ṭālib who will replace him; if Jaᶜfar is killed, it will be ᶜAbdallah ben Rawāḥah.' Now they were all killed successively, according to his prediction. That very day he went out, at noon, having a sorrowful face. He was talking to the people who were listening to his speech about what had happened to them until he added, 'Now seize the flag of one of the swords of God, Khālid ben al-Walād who fought until God gave him the victory.' On this very day Khālid was named 'the sword of God.' Their encounter with the Rums took place in a village named Mashārif, on the frontier of al-Balqāʾ. Then the musilmans went to Muʾtah. Ibn ᶜUmar says: 'I was among them in that battle. We looked for Jaᶜfar and we found him among the dead, having in his body more than thirty sword and arrow wounds.' This is mentioned on his own authority, by al-Bukhāri" (Marmardji: 196).

Except for the Ayyubid-Mamluk mosque, this is an entirely modern town. The sherds indicated above were collected in the northern section, especially on the edge of town where it meets cultivated fields. Many tesserae and sherds were found along a small wadi there.

Site 305 - **el-Mashhad**
(Map section 9; field no. 2312)
PG: 17.5/55.5; UTMG: 58.4/42.9

Remains of a Muslim shrine situated on the south side of the paved road from Mauta to Mirwid, ca. 1 km east of Mauta. Marked El Mash-had on the K737 map. 124 sherds were collected, including: Nab 3; A/M 5; LIsl 12; Mod 1; UD 1.

Irby and Mangles distinguish between Machad and Arti-Musshut, describing the latter as a "single building supposed to be the tomb of Abou-Taleb" (113). See also Mauss and Sauvaire (485, 517); Tristram: Meshʾhad (119); Hornstein: El Meshʾhad (97, 102); Brünnow and Domaszewski: el-Mešhed (I: 9, 11, 60, 104); Musil: mešhed abi Ṭâleb (77, 361); Savignac: Mešhed abi Ṭâleb (247-8). The early travelers usually observed that the building was in a state of disrepair, and Savignac provides a photograph.

Commemorating the clash between Muslim and Byzantine armies in 629 C.E., el-Mashhad lies on a level plain next to a modern mosque and across the road from the new military college. The shrine, which measured 31 m (N-S) by 21 m (E-W) and had several rooms, is represented now by limestone and flint walls standing six courses high. It has been cleared and partially reconstructed by the Department of Antiquities. Also the Department of Antiquities constructed a platform and arch in the shrine. On the platform are three stone slabs with Arabic inscriptions, one at the left front and two at the right rear.

Site 306
(Map section 9; field no. 2395)
PG: 18.5/55.4; UTMG: 59.4/42.8

Stone heap on a hill ca. 1 km ESE of el-Mashhad and slightly less than 2 km WSW of Mirwid. 332 sherds were collected, including: LB 2; IR 2; Hell 1; Nab 12; ERom 5; LRom 3; LByz 1; UD 1; UDhandle 14.

The rubble of the stone heap consists of large, unworked chert and limestone blocks, along with smaller fieldstones which obscure any previous wall lines. Sherds were gathered from a 30 m radius of the rubble. There is a cistern located nearby. The hill slopes east and south down to Wadi eṭ-Ṭur.

Site 307 - **Kh. el-ᶜEdūl**
(Map section 9; field no. 2396)
PG: 18.8/55.5; UTMG: 59.7/42.9

Large khirbeh on the northwest bank of Wadi Um el-ᶜEdul, ca. 2.5 km ESE of Mauta. 534 sherds collected, including: IR II C/Pers 3; Nab 14; ERom 2; Byz 3; EByz 1; LByz 1; Um 4; A/M 20; LIsl 35; UD 2; UDhandle 7.

See Brünnow and Domaszewski: Umm el-ᶜêdûl (I: 9, 60); Musil: ḫirbet el-ᶜEdûl (366).

Although difficult to see from a distance because of its location in the Wadi Um el-ᶜEdul basin, this khirbeh covers an area ca. 100 x 150 m. Numerous wall lines are visible, some standing up to five courses high, amid considerable stone tumble. There are at least three cisterns, and a well is being drilled immediately south of the site.

Photograph 30: Mosque (Site 308) near el-Meshhad

Site 308
(Map section 9; field no. 2359)
PG: 17.4/54.8; UTMG: 58.3/42.2

Building ruin, a small mosque, slightly less than 1 km south of el-Mashhad; ca. 1.5 km southeast of Mauta and 2 km northeast of el-Mazar. 27 sherds were collected, including: EB 1; Nab 1; Byz 1; A/M 1; LIsl 4; UDE 1; UD 18.

Walls ca. 1 m wide which remain standing three to five courses high indicate an irregularly shaped building which measured ca. 12 m (N-S) by 8 m (E-W). A miḥrāb facing south and a cistern inside, near the western wall, suggest that this was a small mosque—perhaps located here with reference to the 629 C.E. battle between Islamic and Byzantine forces. A lintel block lies on the ground in the interior near the mihrāb and cistern. A north-south dirt road passes immediately west of the site.

Site 309
(Map section 9; field no. 2355)
PG: 17.3/54.3; UTMG: 58.1/41.8

Collapsed cistern and associated sherd scatter on the southwest slope of a low hill ca. 1.5 km southeast of Mauta and northeast of el-Mazar. The hill is used as a threshing floor. This may be Brünnow and Domaszewski's Suḫîtaras/Suḫît er-Râs (I: 105). 213 sherds were collected, including: LB/IR I 1; Nab 10; ERom 3; LIsl 1; UDE 2; UD 5.

Site 310
(Map section 9; field no. 2365)
PG: 17.0/53.7; UTMG: 57.9/41.2

Wall lines and light sherd scatter ca. 1 km NNE of el-Mazar and ca. 0.75 km WNW of Kh. eṭ-Ṭur (Site 312). Note, however, that the K737 map is misleading regarding the precise location of Kh. eṭ-Ṭur. 18 sherds were collected, including: Nab 4; UD 7.

On a hilltop, in view of the Mauta-Mirwid road which passes to the north, are traces of two disturbed wall lines of large chert blocks, and a few surface sherds. The site is used now as a threshing floor, and the immediate area has been cleared of stones for cultivation.

Site 311 - **el-Mazār**
(Map section 9; field no. 2019)
PG: 16.4/52.8; UTMG: 57.3/40.3

Modern town on an ancient settlement site south of Kerak on the Kerak-Ṭafileh road. Marked El Mazār on the K737 map. 87 sherds were collected, including: A/M 8; LIsl 7; LOtt 1; Mod 3.

See Mauss and Sauvaire: Djafar (1864: 208-9; 1867: 485); Doughty: Jarfa (22); Hornstein: Jaʾfar (97, 102); Wilson: Jaafar (312); Brünnow and Domaszewski: Ǧaᶜfar (I: 68, 105); Musil: Ǧaᶜfar (152, 361, 365-66); Glueck: Mazâr/#104 (1939: 93, 96, 100). These early travelers saw a mosque and a tomb at the site. In the mosque they saw three Arabic inscriptions, two of which bear dates of the mid-fourteenth century C.E. The third is fragmentary and refers to Jaᶜfar ibn Abi Ṭalīb. At least three persons are reputed to be buried at the tomb: Jaᶜfar, for whom the tomb (*weli*) is named, Ḥudeib, and Suleiman, all companions of the prophet Muhammed. The early travelers consistently referred to the site by a form of the name Jaᶜfar; only in the early decades of the present century did it come to be known as el-Mazar.

The mosque and tomb are still visible at the center of the modern town which emerged around it and continues to expand. No other ancient structural remains are visible, and collecting sherds was rendered virtually impossible by the modern buildings and paved streets.

Site 312 - **Kh. eṭ-Ṭūr**
(Map section 9; field no. 2316)
PG: 17.8/53.7; UTMG: 58.7/41.0

Large khirbeh slightly more than 1 km northeast of Mazar. Marked Khirbat eṭ Ṭūr on the K737 map—note, however, that the name appears above and to the left of the actual location of the site. 577 sherds were collected, including: EB 1; LB 4; Nab 13; ERom 1; LRom 1; Byz 12; EByz 2; EIsl 5; Abb 3; Fat(?) 1; A/M 4; LIsl 169; UD 11; UDhandle 29; tesserae; 1 possible ceramic loom weight; 1 roof tile.

See Seetzen: et Tûr (416); Irby and Mangles: Toor (113); Brünnow and Domaszewski: eṭ-Ṭûr (I: 10, 11, 60, 68, 105); Musil: ḫirbet eṭ-Ṭûr (6, 21, 78). Brünnow and Domaszewski and Musil observed that the main, north-south Roman road passed immediately west of eṭ-Ṭur—i.e. it ran slightly further east than the modern Kerak-Ṭafileh road.

These prominent ruins cover an area ca. 112 x 220 m on a low hill with good visibility in all directions. Many wall lines are exposed with the eastern side of the site presenting the heaviest concentration of wall lines, rubble, and surface sherds. In places the rubble appears to be as much as 3 m deep. In addition to the surface sherds and tesserae, we noted a mortar fragment, a basalt bowl or basin fragment, and bits of glass. There were at least 15 cisterns.

Site 313 - **Ghuweir**
(Map section 10; field no. 2360)
PG: 22.1/61.1; UTMG: 62.9/48.6

Modern village on an ancient settlement site at the northwest end of Fajj el-ᶜUseikir, 4 km southeast of eth-Thaniyyah and 3 km south of the Kerak-Qaṭranah road. Ghuweir on the K737 map (but see below). 188 sherds were collected, including: EB II-III 1; MB 1; LB 1; IR 1; A/M 5; LIsl 19; Mod 15; UD 2.

See Klein: Khurbet Ghuweir (1879: 255). Brünnow and Domaszewski indicate a Wâdî-l-Ġuwêr at this place on their map, and Musil indicates a site called el-Ṛwêr on w. el-Ṛwêr on his map. One edition of the K737 map reverses the names of Ghuweir and Dhat Ras—i.e., the site treated here is marked Dhat Raʾs while Site 427 is marked al-Ghuwayr. Apparently the names were transposed by mistake, or possibly under the influence of early nineteenth century maps. These early maps do not include Ghuwayr and place "Dâtrâs" immediately ESE of Kerak (See especially Kiepert's map published in Robinson's *Biblical Researches*, 1841; W. and A. K. Johnston's map published in Wilson 1847; and Van de Velde 1866). These early maps are misleading regarding the location of Dhat Ras, however, and the problem was cleared up during the 1850s and 1860s: (1) Actually the topography of the whole region between Kerak and Wadi el-Ḥesa is very much confused in these early maps. (2) The revised edition of Kiepert's map published with Robinson's *Later Biblical Researches in Palestine* (1856) does not indicate the location of Dhat Ras, probably in recognition that the earlier edition had it located incorrectly. (3) E. H. Palmer's map (1871b) has "Zat Rass" located much further south, near Wadi el-Ḥesa, and this new positioning is standard with later nineteenth and early twentieth century maps.

Situated on the west slope of Wadi Ghuweir with plowed fields on the gently rolling hills above, the modern village has displaced virtually all evidence of earlier settlement phases except for some surface pottery. One can distinguish between the older "Ottoman style" houses of the contemporary village and the more recent ones. Also five caves with remnants of walls at their entrances probably served as dwellings at an early stage of the modern resettlement of the site. An old cistern and watering trough likewise belongs to earlier times; now water is piped into the village.

Site 314
(Map section 10; field no. 2677)
PG: 23.4/61.5; UTMG: 64.2/49.0

Building ruin on a low hill ca. 5 km southeast of eth-Thaniyyah and slightly more than 1 km ENE of Ghuweir. At the 954 m elevation marker on the K737 map. 80 sherds were collected, including: IR 2; Nab 2; ERom 2; LRom 2; Mod 1; UD 5.

Traces of walls (never more than one course visible) among tumbled limestone fieldstones indicate a solidly-built building which was roughly square at the base (5.9 x 6.4 m). The setting—at the north end of Fajj el-ᶜUseikir with a commanding view through it to the southeast—suggests that the building may have served as a watchtower and/or checkpoint.

Site 315
(Map section 10; field no. 2678)
PG: 24.9/60.7; UTMG: 65.8/48.2

Ancient settlement site at the north end of Fajj el-ᶜUseikir, ca. 7 km southeast of eth-Thaniyyah and 3 km east of Ghuweir; immediately west of the 932 m elevation marker on the K737 map. 205 sherds were collected, including: Chalco/EB 162; EB I 1; Nab 3; EByz 2; A/M 2; UDE 15; UD 20.

Situated in an area of low hills and wadis, the site sits like a rounded terrace above a minor tributary of the Wadi es-Saninah system which curves around its western side. The ruin itself consists of wall lines which can be traced at ground level among general rubble and scattered sherds. Typically the wall lines are represented by basalt field stones laid in a single line, possibly having served as foundations for mudbrick dwellings. The main part of the ruin is a cluster of circular chambers formed by such walls (from 5 to 17 m in diameter) surrounded by a more substantial enclosure wall. The latter is several field stones in width, and the enclosed area measures ca. 40 x 45 m. Other chambers similar to the ones mentioned above, except that they tend to be slightly smaller and more rectangular in shape, are to be found outside the enclosure and along the very edge of the wadi.

Site 316 - **el-Mreigha**
(Map section 10; field no. 2602)
PG: 26.2/60.8; UTMG: 67.0/48.4

Large ruin of a walled settlement at the northwest end of Fajj el-ᶜUseiker, ca. 7 km ESE of eth-Thaniyyah. Al Murayghah on the K737 map. 3492 sherds were collected, including: EB II-III 1; MB 3; IR 7; IR II 21; Hell 7; Nab 188; ERom 70; LRom 55; EByz 210; LByz 5; Fat(?) 9; A/M 24; LIsl 82; Mod 6; UDE 8; UD 70; UDhandle 63; 1 tessera.

See Seetzen: el Mréiga (416); Irby and Mangles: Imriega (113); Klein: Mugheira (1879: 255); Tristram: Mouriyeh (120); Brünnow and Domaszewski: el-Mrêga (I: 9, 79; II: 41); Musil: el-Morejra (20-21, 43-44, 325); Glueck: Kh. el-Moreighah/#145 (1934: 63-65, 69, 81, 103). Musil provided the first description of this impressive site, comparing the extensive ruins to those of Um er-Rṣaṣ. Glueck described the site in some detail also, provided a plan, and attributed its origin to the Nabataeans. "The origin of the site, however, seems certainly to be Nabataean, to judge from the large numbers of Nabataean sherds of all types which were found. There were also large numbers of Byzantine and mediaeval Arabic sherds, which come from the periods when the walls were built and added to and the size of the city enlarged. Even in the Nabataean period el-Moreighah was a large and thriving city. It was an important station along the busy Nabataean trade route which led northward from Petra to Damascus and westward from Petra to Gaza, and was also located in the midst of a thriving Nabataean district." Canova (1954: 263) identified a church among the ruins. This is Parker's Site 163 (Koucky 1987b: 88-89). Among the sherds which his team collected at the site, we identified the following diagnostics: IR 14; IR II 8; Nab 12; ERom 5; LRom 10; EByz 4; LByz 6; Byz 2; Um 1; A/M 2; and LIsl 1.

El-Mreigha sits on a 950 m hill overlooking the Fajj el-ᶜUseiker and Wadi el-Baṭra. It is surrounded by fertile fields and also, as both Musil and Glueck pointed out, at a natural crossroad. Wadi es-Sani forms a slight natural barrier from northwest to north and Jebel esh-Sharif forms the horizon from north to southeast. Covering an area ca. 100 x 80 m, the ruin remains essentially as described by Musil and Glueck except for recent disturbances: (1) There is some indication of recent military activity—e.g., "foxholes" embedded among the ruins. (2) The ruin is being robbed by local builders for stone; indeed a truck was being loaded while we were at the site on one occasion in 1982. (3) A Byzantine cemetery (ESE of the main ruin) had been discovered by antiquities robbers and was being dug systematically, tomb by tomb, that same year. (It is illegal to buy and sell antiquities in Jordan, so artifacts generally are smuggled into Israel where the regulations are less confining.) The city wall enclosed a roughly rectangular area (ca. 72 x 70 m), is 2 m thick in some places, and survives up to 2.5 m high. It is supported by towers at the corners and by bastions on the west and east walls. The north gate is clearly visible, from which a main street with alleys can be traced into the city. There are numerous cisterns, a complex system of terraces, and several structures located outside the city wall. This site cries out for more intensive investigation. Contrary to Glueck, for example, the pottery suggests that the site is pre-Nabataean in origin.

Site 317
(Map section 10; field no. 2654)
PG: 27.8/60.8; UTMG: 68.6/48.4

Building ruin, possibly a watchtower, on a spur of the esh-Sharif ridge; ca. 1.5 km east of el-Mreigha. One UD sherd collected.

Walls composed of massive stone blocks, with two courses still in place, are discernible in a stone heap. These walls indicate a 5 x 5 m structure. Situated at the WNW end of a WNW-ESE spur of the esh-Sharif ridge, the building would have offered a commanding view to the west including el-Mreigha.

Site 318
(Map section 10; field no. 2653, 2655)
PG: 28.2/60.8; UTMG: 68.9/48.5

Stone enclosure and cairns along a segment of the esh-Sharif ridge; ca. 2 km east of el-Mreigha. The enclosure is ca. 11 m in diameter and composed of unhewn limestone fieldstones up to 0.5 m in length. Only one course of stones is visible; some recent stone robbing has occurred. Also on this segment of the esh-Sharif ridge are numerous small stone heaps, apparently cairns, and two partitioned cairns (ca. 7 m in diameter).

Site 319
(Map section 10; field no. 2644)
PG: 28.4/62.4; UTMG: 69.4/49.9

Building ruin with attached stone enclosure on a spur extending southeast from Jebel esh-Sharif; ca. 3 km ENE of el-Mreigha. 9 sherds were collected, including: EB 2; Nab 3; UD 4.

Although the site has been robbed for stones, apparently recently, the remaining stones and rubble indicate a building which would have measured ca. 6.5 x 12 m and an attached, circular enclosure which measured ca. 22 m in diameter. Nearby is another oval stone heap (ca. 5 x 10 m and 1 m high), and all along the spur are small cairns, most of them probably bedouin burials.

Photograph 31: Chalco/EB I settlement site (Site 315) in Fajj el-ʿUseiker

Photograph 32: El-Mreigha (Site 316)

Site 320
(Map section 10; field no. 2646)
PG: 28.6/61.5; UTMG: 69.4/49.0

Building ruin (5.8 m square), possibly a watchtower, on the esh-Sharif ridge (990 m elevation). This is Parker's Site 191 from which his team collected 6 sherds (Koucky 1987b: 88-89). One of these is LRom according to our reading, the remainder UD. We found no sherds at the site.

Site 321
(Map section 10; field no. 2645, 2647, 2648, 2649)
PG: 29.2/61.4; UTMG: 70.1/48.8

Numerous cairns, including several large partitioned cairns and various stone heaps, along a ridge which extends southeast of Jebel ash-Sharif.

The map grids indicated above mark a large partitioned cairn with double external walls (11 m and 7 m in diameter) and two bisecting walls. One of the bisecting walls consists of three stone blocks placed end-to-end for a total length of 4.1 m. The other, which parallels the first at a distance of 2.4 m, consists of two blocks with a slightly shorter total length. Ca. 200 m further along the ridge to the southeast is another partitioned cairn with double bisecting walls and similar measurements. Higher up the ridge to the northwest (PG: 28.3/61.6; UTMG: 69.1/49.2) is a concentration of cairns, including another good example of the partitioned type (7.7 m in diameter with single partition wall).

Among the cairns and stone heaps on this ridge are Parker's Sites 190, 192, 193, 194, 197 and 198. The latter, a rectangular heap measuring ca. 8 x 8 m and located at PG: 30.1/59.8; UTMG: 70.8/47.8, may represent a structure of some sort, possibly a watchtower. Parker's team collected 85 sherds near this heap (Koucky 1987b: 90-91), among which we identified: IR 3; ERom 3; LRom 2; EByz 1; LByz 1 and LIsl 1.

Site 322
(Map section 10; field no. 2650)
PG: 29.6/60.9; UTMG: 70.4/48.4

Building ruin (ca. 4 x 5 m), possibly a watchtower, situated on a ridge ca. 3.5 km east of el-Mreigha. The site commands an excellent view in all directions except to the south—e.g., Qaṣr Abu Rukbah ca. 5 km to the southeast is visible. The building was constructed with large, rectangular stone blocks (up to 3.9 x 4.9 m). This is Parker's Site 195 (Koucky 1987b: 90-91) where his team collected 7 sherds, one of which we identified as Nabataean. We collected no pottery.

Site 323
(Map section 10; field no. 2651)
PG: 29.7/61.2; UTMG: 70.5/48.8

Stone heap, possibly a building ruin, on a small ridge ca. 3.5 km east of el-Mreigha. The location provides excellent visibility to the north, northeast, and northwest. Nearby to the south, also on the ridge, is a stone ring (ca. 6 m in diameter) on bedrock. We collected no pottery, but this is Parker's Site 196 (Koucky 1987b: 90-91) from which his team collected 7 sherds. None of these, according to our reading, was clearly a diagnostic piece.

Site 324
(Map section 10; field no. 2656)
PG: 28.2/60.1; UTMG: 69.0/47.7

Building ruin ca. 2.5 km ESE of el-Mreigha. 29 sherds were collected, including: IR 2; Nab 2; UDE 7; UD 17.

On a natural bedrock terrace (ca. 50 x 20 m) near the northwestern end of a northwest-southeast ridge are the foundation walls of a rectangular building complex. The ruin has been robbed for stones to the extent that its main features are difficult to determine, yet it is clear that the external walls were ca. 1.2 m thick and constructed of large limestone blocks. Interior walls which seem to have partitioned the southwest quarter of the building were constructed from stone slabs up to 1 m in length. Down the slope of the ridge and ca. 100 m west of the building ruin is a covered cistern (still in use) within a stone-lined half-circle depression designed to channel water into the cistern. Within 100 m to the southeast are two small cairns (ca. 3 m in diameter).

Site 325
(Map section 10; field no. 2661)
PG: 27.2/59.8; UTMG: 67.9/47.5

Foundations of a 5 m square structure at the northwest end of the ridge which forms the northeast side of Fajj el-ᶜUsaykir; slightly more than 1 km southeast of el-Mreigha. 15 sherds were collected, including Nab 2; UD 13.

The foundation consists of nine huge stone blocks, one of which measures 1 x 2 x 0.5 m, forming the base of a square building. A gap on the west side of the square may have been an entrance. Immediately to the north and northeast are other wall lines barely discernible at ground surface. Whether or how these relate to the square structure is unclear.

Site 326
(Map section 10; field no. 2657)
PG: 28.5/59.6; UTMG: 69.4/47.3

Numerous small cairns, most of them presumably burial cairns, along a prominent ridge ca. 2.5 km ESE of el-Mreigha (from UTMG: 68.9/47.8 to 69.6/47.1). These cairns range in diameter or length from 2 to 8 m, and several of them appear to be older burial cairns with secondary graves embedded.

Site 327
(Map section 10; field no. 2658)
PG: 29.0/59.8; UTMG: 69.8/47.4

Partitioned cairn with double external walls and two bisecting walls on a ridge 3 km ESE of el-Mreigha. 53 sherds collected, none identifiable with any degree of certainty.

The external walls are 10.5 and 7.3 m in diameter (measured from the outside) and the bisecting walls are 3 m long. Actually, the "bisecting walls" may represent the long sides of a rectangular, inner chamber oriented east-west and measuring 3 x 2.6 m. Fragments (4.4 and 4.5 m long) of two walls meet in a right angle 3 m north of the cairn. 10 m north of the cairn is another, rectangular cairn (7.70 x 5.50 m) built of limestone slabs (1.2 x 0.4 x 0.3 m) with small field stones in the gaps. The slabs are still in place up to 3 courses high, but the mass of collapsed stones suggests that the original cairn would have been at least twice that high. Ca. 100 m southwest of the first cairn described above is a third cairn with an oval line of limestone blocks at its core. The blocks average 0.5 m in length and are in place up to two courses high.

Site 328
(Map section 10; field no. 2663)
PG: 27.7/59.3; UTMG: 68.5/46.9

Building ruin, possibly a watchtower, overlooking Fajj el-ᶜUseikir from its north bank, ca. 2 km southeast from el-Mreigha. 13 sherds were collected, including: Nab 2; Nab/ERom 4; UDE 1; UD 6.

Walls of a structure (3.5 m square at the base) are discernible in a prominent stone heap. Four courses of the south wall and two courses of the west wall are visible. Bedouin graves are embedded in the collapsed stones on both sides of the south wall. The walls were constructed with large, roughly-dressed limestone blocks usually up to 1.25 m in length (although one is 2 m long). A secondary wall paralleling the north wall may have protected an entrance. The shape of the structure and its commanding view suggest a watchtower.

Site 329
(Map section 10; field no. 2659)
PG: 28.2/59.5; UTMG: 69.0/46.9

Six small, circular cairns along a ridge southeast of el-Mreigha (from UTMG: 68.5/47.4 to 69.1/46.6). All contained graves which have been robbed.

Site 330
(Map section 10; field no. 2669)
PG: 28.7/58.4; UTMG: 69.5/46.0

Building ruin on the ridge which parallels Fajj el-ᶜUsaykir on its northeast side; ca. 3.5 km southeast of el-Mreigha. Near the 1041 elevation marker on the K737 map. 137 sherds were collected, including: IR 9; IR II 2; Nab 2; LIsl 2; UDE 19; UD 18.

Wall lines are barely discernible in a prominent stone heap (17 m in diameter and 4 m high) which itself is situated on a small flat plateau. The plateau overlooks Fajj el-ᶜUseikir and provides a clear view to Adir and Ghuweir. The ruin has been much disturbed, with stones robbed to construct three large sheep pens on its western side. Also there are several bedouin graves embedded in the ruin.

Site 331
(Map section 10; field no. 2660)
PG: 29.5/57.5; UTMG: 70.8/44.8

Numerous cairns (including some of the partitioned type) and small, nondescript stone heaps along the ridge which forms the northeast side of Fajj el-ᶜUsaykir (from UTMG: 67.9/47.5 to 72.0/43.5).

Site 332 - **Kh. el-Weibdeh**
(Map section 10; field no. 2405)
PG: 22.2/59.9; UTMG: 62.9/47.3

Stone heap and two roughly rectangular areas of rubble at the north end of a ridge, slightly more than 1 km south of Ghuweir. Caves in the area have been altered, one plastered for use as a cistern, another provided with an artificial semi-circular entrance. 139 sherds were collected including: A/M 5; LIsl 5; UD 3.

See Musil: ḫirbet el-Lwêbde (366).

Site 333 - **Middīn**
(Map section 10; field no. 2307)
PG: 19.7/58.7; UTMG: 60.5/46.2

Modern village situated on an ancient settlement site, ca. 4.5 km northeast of Mauta and 3.5 km east of Miḥna. Middein on the K737 map. 1060 sherds were collected, including: EB II-III 36; EB IVA 3; MB 4; LB 29; IR 9; IR I 21; IR II 15; Hell 1; Nab 64; ERom 4; LRom 7; EByz 6; LByz 20; A/M 35; LIsl 31; Mod 9; UDE 40; UDEhandle 48; UD 15; UDhandle 89.

See Seetzen: Mûddîn (416); Burckhardt: Meddyn (389); Klein (1879: 255); Tristram: Maudîn (119-20); Doughty: Meddáin (22); Musil: ḫ. Middîn (6, 15, 17, 43-44, 77, 82, 125, 142-43, 250, 366, 368). Klein described Middin as situated on a steep hill and reported "extensive ruins, stones, broken pillars and sarcophagi." Tristram also observed that Middin was "on the crest of a hill—not, like the other cities, on a gentle knoll in a plain. ... The ruins are rather extensive, and more perfect than any others we examined in this ride—squared stones of considerable size, and many old house-walls, still standing, apparently, at their original height, built of dressed stones, without any trace of mortar. Several sarcophagi were lying about; one had been used as the lintel for an old door-way; and there were sculptured fragments of the Roman period, and broken oil-presses. Jebel Shihan stood out clearly, bounding the northern horizon." Presumably Meddein was in the process of resettlement as the nineteenth century drew to a close, since Musil speaks of the people of Meddein using the spring. Musil regarded the Middin spring as an important landmark and noted on one visit that "Sie ist im weiten Umkreise die einzige Quelle, welche noch nicht ganz von Heuschreckenschwärmen, die heuer [1897] besonders zahlrich auftraten, unbrauchbar gemacht war" (143).

Middin is situated on a prominent hill which is bounded on the north, east, and south by upper tributaries of Wadi Middin. Three springs are still active in the wadi bed on the east, although water is now piped into the village from elsewhere. The ancient ruins observed by nineteenth century travelers are completely covered by modern houses, some of them probably dating to Ottoman times. Surface pottery is concentrated in the north, northwest and southeast sections of the village and on the corresponding slopes. Fields are under cultivation to the west of the site, where there are no deep wadis, as well as on some of the more gentle slopes below the site on the other sides. There is a threshing floor at the eastern end of the village.

Site 334
(Map section 10; field no. 2414, 2415, 2416)
PG: 21.6/58.1; UTMG: 62.4/45.5

Cairns, including partitioned cairns up to 5 m in diameter, along the ridge marked Umm Ṭaur on the K737 map; ca. 2 kms ESE of Middin.

Site 335
(Map section 10; field no. 2417)
PG: 23.4/59.3; UTMG: 64.2/46.8

Collapsed remains of a single (5 x 5 m) structure—the external walls composed of large limestone blocks and the interior filled with tumble—situated at the north end of a ridge overlooking Fajj el-Usaykir; ca. 3.5 km southeast of Ghuweir. No surface pottery.

Site 336
(Map section 10; field no. 2391)
PG: 20.1/56.7; UTMG: 60.9/44.2

Partitioned cairn (6 m in diameter) with double exterior walls and single cross wall; ca. 1 km ESE of Mirwid, at the 1110 m elevation marker on the K737 map. 13 sherds were collected, including: EB II-III 1; UDE 1; UD 11.

Site 337
(Map section 10; field no. 2392)
PG: 20.8/57.1; UTMG: 61.6/44.5

Small khirbeh ca. 1.5 km east of Mirwid. 1232 sherds were collected, including: Chalco 5; EB I 7; EB II-III 10; EB IVA 2; MB 25; LB 11; Nab 5; UDE 46; UDEhandle 22.

Occasional wall lines and rubble cover an area ca. 100 x 150 m on a low, gentle slope cut on three sides by wadis. The site has been plowed, and several stone heaps may be the results of field clearing. Nearby is a collapsed cistern.

Site 338
(Map section 10; field no. 2366)
PG: 19.6/65.3; UTMG: 60.4/43.7

Sherd concentration and building ruins ca. 1 km southeast of Mirwid; marked "Ruins" on the K737 map. 423 sherds were collected, including: LB 1; Nab 32; LRom 1; Byz 2; UD 6; UDhandle 7.

Situated on a hilltop surrounded by wadi-dissected terrain, the site measures ca. 25 x 12 m as indicated by the sherd concentration. Although the site is much disturbed, wall lines indicate a large rectangular structure built of medium sized blocks and one, possibly two, smaller structures. There are plowed fields in the vicinity.

Site 339
(Map section 10; field no. 2390)
PG: 20.4/56.2; UTMG: 61.2/43.7

Large cairn, or tumulus, on a prominent hill ca. 4 km east of Mauta and 1.5 km southeast of Mirwid. 31 sherds were collected, including: Nab 4; UDE 2; UD 23.

Consisting of three concentric tiers of limestone blocks (ca. 0.50 x 0.50 x 0.30 m) and rising ca. 1.5 m above the crest of the hill, the tumulus measures ca. 10 m in diameter. It stands at the northern end of a larger (30 x 40 m) area which is strewn with stone blocks and sherds.

Site 340
(Map section 10; field no. 2413)
PG: 22.5/57.9; UTMG: 63.3/45.5

Cairn (5 m in diameter) on a north slope of the ridge marked Umm Ṭaur on the K737 map; slightly less than 3 km ESE of Middin. Nearby are what appear to be faint remnants of two corners of a square stone structure which would have measured ca. 5 m on a side. 7 sherds were collected: 1 ERom and 6 UD.

Site 341
(Map section 10; field no. 2412)
PG: 22.4/57.6; UTMG: 63.2/45.1

Large stone heap with the foundation walls of a solidly built (3 x 3 m) structure at its center, situated on a ridge slightly less than 3 km ESE of Middin. At the 1089 elevation marker on the K737 map. 19 sherds were collected, including: Nab 2; EByz 2.

The structure was built from large stones (up to 1 x 0.5 x 0.25 m) laid in three courses, and its walls stand up to three courses above the surrounding stone heap. The heap itself is 13 m in diameter, with a larger, roughly rectangular area of rubble adjoining along its southwest side and extending beyond it to the northwest. Consisting of smaller stones (typically 0.25 x 0.25 m), the rubble area is divided into two segments of unequal size by remnants of a northeast-southwest wall (1 m wide). The smaller segment is situated along the southwest side of the main heap and measures roughly 12 m (NW-SE) by 8 m (NE-SW). The larger segment, which extends to the northwest from the smaller segment and the north corner of the main heap, measures roughly 15 m (NW–SE) by 12 m (NE-SW).

Site 342
(Map section 10; field no. 2411)
PG: 22.4/57.3; UTMG: 63.2/44.8

Partitioned cairn (ca. 4.5 m in diameter) on a ridge ca. 2.5 m north of Kh. en-Nsheinish and immediately west of the track from en-Nsheinish to the Fajj el-ᶜUseikir.

Site 343
(Map section 10; field no. 2410)
PG: 22.5/56.9; UTMG: 63.4/44.5

Partitioned cairn (4 m in diameter) and faintly visible wall foundations, ca. 2 km north of Kh. en-Nsheinish and immediately east of the track from en-Nsheinish to Fajj el-ᶜUseikir. 6 sherds were collected, including: IR 1; Nab 1.

Site 344
(Map section 10; field no. 2409)
PG: 22.5/56.5; UTMG: 63.4/44.0

Small khirbeh ca. 1.5 km north of Kh. en-Nsheinish, along the road from en-Nsheinish to Fajj el-ᶜUseikir. 23 sherds were collected, including: IR II 1; Nab 3; UDE 1; UD 1.

Situated on a hilltop with good visibility, this khirbeh is being robbed for stones and also is disturbed by bedouin burials. The few wall lines which can be traced with confidence indicate several associated structures. One rectangular area of tumbled blocks (some of them 1 x 2 m) may represent a stronghold of some sort.

Site 345 - **Um Zebel**
(Map section 10; field no. 2397)
PG: 19.1/55.4; UTMG: 60.0/42.8

Sherd scatter and wall lines on a knoll ca. 3.5 km ESE of Mauta and 1 km west of Kh. Um ᶜAlanda. 151 sherds were collected, including: Nab 13; A/M 1; UD 3; UDhandle 4.

See Musil: ḫirbet el-Mzebbel (10, 366).

The wall remains (visible only at ground level in some places) suggest a well-built rectangular structure or enclosure (ca. 22 x 36 m) partitioned into two parts of approximately equal size. There is also a cistern. The site is used now as a threshing floor.

Site 346
(Map section 10; field no. 2400)
PG: 19.3/55.2; UTMG: 60.2/42.7

Two partitioned cairns (ca. 4.5 m in diameter) on a knoll less than 1 km WSW of Kh. Um ᶜAlanda. No pottery was collected.

Site 347
(Map section 10; field no. 2367)
PG: 19.7/55.5; UTMG: 60.6/42.9

Large stone heap with sherd scatter immediately northwest of Kh. Um ᶜAlanda, on an opposite knoll separated by a wadi. Marked "Ruins" on the K737 map. 337 sherds were collected, including: Chalco 1; Chalco/EB 5; EB II-III 3; MB 1; LB 1; Nab 5; ERom 1; Mod 1; UDE 17.

The sherd scatter covers an area ca. 20 x 15 m. There are no architectural remains other than the stone heap, which itself exhibits no discernible wall lines. The surrounding terrain is rocky with minimal topsoil.

Site 348
(Map section 10; field no. 2398, 2399)
PG: 19.2/54.6; UTMG: 60.0/42.1

Stone heap, apparently the collapsed remains of a small (5 x 5 m) structure, situated on the west side of a ridge ca. 1 km southwest of Kh. Um ᶜAlanda. The tumbled stones are large, unworked blocks, mostly limestone. 113 sherds were collected, including: Nab 25; UD 88.

Approximately 300 m to the south is another, smaller stone heap which is possibly the collapse of a 3 x 5 m structure.

Site 349 - **Kh. Um ᶜAlanda**
(Map section 10; field no. 2358)
PG: 20.1/55.1; UTMG: 61.0/42.6

Large khirbeh ca. 3.5 km ESE of Mauta. Kh. Um ᶜAlanda on the K737 map. 1922 sherds were collected, including: Chalco 13; EB I 4; EB II-III 12; MB I 3; LB 4; IR I 1; IR II 1; Hell 1; Nab 21; ERom 9; LRom 3; Byz 17; Um 1; Fat(?) 3; A/M 31; LIsl 277; UDE 45; UD 5; UDhandle 30.

See Irby and Mangles: Behlanah (113); Musil: "die kleine Ruine ruğm und tell umm ᶜAlenda" (10, 366).

Kh. ᶜAlanda is situated on the sloping northwest end of a northwest-southeast ridge. It is an impressive ruin which covers an area of ca. 100 x 75 m. Some sections of walls stand four to five courses high. Extensive stone robbing has occurred, however, so that it is difficult to trace the outlines of particular buildings. There are at least six cisterns among the ruins, a sheep fold further down slope to the northwest, and plowed fields in the wadi bed still farther to the west and northwest. Probably the visible architectural remains correspond to the predominant Late Islamic pottery. Yet it is clear from the broad chronological range of the surface pottery that this place has served as a settlement site throughout the ages.

Site 350 - **Rujm Rafīyeh**
(Map section 10; field no. 2357)
PG: 21.3/55.0; UTMG: 62.2/42.5

Small khirbeh ca. 5 km ESE of Mauta, 5.5 km northeast of el-Mazar, and approximately midway between Kh. Um ᶜAlanda and Kh. en-Nsheinish. 351 sherds were collected, including: Nab 17; Nab/ERom 6; LRom 6; LIsl 1; UD 7; UDhandle 10.

Situated at the north end of a north-south ridge, the khirbeh consists of low lying remains of walls and building rubble. Wadis on the east and west sides of the ridge converge to the north. The khirbeh is not situated on the highest part of the ridge, so visibility is only fair. The walls were constructed of limestone and chert blocks, can be easily traced for the most part, cover an area of ca. 24 x 34 m, and may represent several related structures. There are at least two cisterns among the ruins. Local informants called the place "Rujm Rafiyyeh."

Site 351
(Map section 10; field no. 2407, 2408)
PG: 21.5/54.5; UTMG: 62.4/42.0

Rubble heap with exposed wall ca. 5 km ESE of Mauta and 5.5 km northeast of el-Mazar; approximately midway between, and slightly further south than Kh. Um ᶜAlanda and Kh. en-Nsheinish. 280 sherds were collected, including: MB 3; Hell 1; Nab 25; ERom 4; LRom 2; Byz 1; LByz 1; UD 5; UDhandle 7.

This small rubble heap is concentrated in a 5 x 6 m area and seems to have been excavated intentionally, possibly an unauthorized search for antiquities. Exposed underneath the rubble was a small, corner section of wall, constructed of roughly shaped limestone blocks and small chink stones. Ca. 30 m further south along the ridge is another small, nondescript stone heap of small angular stones and large rectangular blocks. Still further south, on a high point of the ridge (PG: 21.6/54.3; UTMG: 62.4 /41.7), is a partitioned cairn.

Site 352
(Map section 10; field no. 2356)
PG: 22.5/55.1; UTMG: 63.4/42.6

Stone heap, roughly circular in shape (ca. 8 x 10 m) but probably representing the collapsed remains of a rectangular structure built from large limestone blocks. Ca. 250 m southeast of Kh. en-Nsheinish. 53 sherds were collected, including: LB 4; IR 1; Hell 1; Nab 4.

Site 353 - **Kh. en-Nsheinish**
(Map section 10; field no. 2314)
PG: 22.3/55.2; UTMG: 63.1/42.7

Extensive unoccupied ruin ca. 6 km east of Mauta and 6.5 km ENE of el-Mazar. Nusheinish on the K737 map. 697 sherds were collected, including: EB I 1; LB 4; Hell 2; Nab 22; ERom 6; Byz 9; Um 2; Fat(?) 5; A/M 18; LIsl 77; UD 7; UDhandle 28.

See Tristram: En Sheynesh (120); Doughty: Ensheynish (20); Brünnow and Domaszewski: ᶜên Šênš (I: 9, 60); Musil: Nšêneš (19, 28, 42, 366); Glueck: Kh. en-Nesheinish/#148 (1934: 65). Glueck described it as "a small Nabataean site with a complex of ruined houses, foundation walls, and a few large cisterns. The sherds found there were almost all Nabataean, but there were a number of early Arabic sherds also."

Situated on the high point of a north-south ridge with valleys on either side which provide cultivatable land, this large khirbeh (215 x 165 m) presents the lower courses of numerous walls which were built of roughly shaped limestone and chert, unmortared. Clear outlines of

Photograph 33: Kh. en-Nsheinish (Site 353)

Photograph 34: Wall remains at Kh. en-Nsheinish

structures are visible in several places. One which exhibits three limestone column blocks may have been a public building of some sort. There are at least 10 cisterns or caves in the area—several are collapsed and thus difficult to identify.

Site 354
(Map section 10; field no. 2418)
PG: 24.1/56.2; UTMG: 64.9/43.7

Three cairns on a hilltop slightly less than 2 km northeast of Kh. en-Nsheinish. Sherds were collected immediately west of the cairns from a 4 x 8 m depression with one visible wall line along its north side. Apparently this was a building of some sort. 30 sherds were collected, including: Nab 3; LByz 1; UDE 3; UD 2.

Site 355 - **Kh. el-Baṭrāᵓ**
(Map section 10; field no. 2308)
PG: 25.4/58.3; UTMG: 66.2/45.9

Unoccupied settlement site on the northwest end of Jebel el-Baṭraᵓ, ca. 2.5 km SSW of el-Mreigha. Al Batrā on the K737 map. 689 sherds were collected, including: MB 2; IR 4; IR II 10; Hell 9; Nab 174; ERom 25; LRom 6; EByz 4; LByz 2; Um 1; A/M 3; LIsl 3; UDE 2; UD 18; UDhandle 14.

See Seetzen: el Bottra (416); Burckhardt: Batrā (390); Klein: el-Bathra (1879: 255); Brünnow and Domaszewski: el-Batra (I: 9, 79; Vol.II: 41); Musil: ḫirbet al-Batra (368); Glueck: el-Batrah/#146 (1934: 65). According to Glueck, "Kh. el-Batrah is a typical ruined Nabataean village, consisting of a number of ruined houses with vaulted chambers. There are many cisterns and a number of small low mounds. The village is built on the sides and top of a high hill. Large quantities of purely Nabataean sherds were found."

At the center of this site is a massive tumble of stones which covers an area ca. 56 x 130 m. There are many large limestone blocks in the rubble, but it is very difficult to trace any wall lines. Occasional segments of foundation walls can be observed in the areas surrounding the central tumble, however, and north of it are the foundation remains of a large square building (42 x 37 m). Immediately outside the north wall of this building is a collapsed cistern. Along the east slope of the ridge are several caves, presently in use as sheepfolds.

Site 356
(Map section 10; field no. 2387)
PG: 26.2/57.1; UTMG: 67.0/44.6

Rectangular enclosure on Jebel el-Baṭraᵓ, roughly midway between Kh. el-Baṭraᵓ and Naṣir. 100 sherds were collected, including: Nab 5; UD 5.

According to Glueck: "About a kilometre to the w.n.w. [of Naṣir] are the foundation ruins of another *qaṣr*, with Nabataean sherds around it. To the n.w. of it, about a kilometre removed, is a much destroyed site, called Rujm Nâṣer. It consists of several completely demolished, and at times evidently partly rebuilt buildings, of which little more is left now than a confusion of walls and fallen debris. A small number of EI I-II Moabite sherds was found by it, including several plain and painted Nabataean sherds, and several fragments of Nabataean lamps, some fragments of Byzantine ware of the 4th to the 5th centuries A.D., and some painted and glazed mediaeval Arabic ware" (1939: 72-73). Our Site 356 seems to fit Glueck's description of the *qaṣr* but correspond to the location of his Rujm Nâṣer.

The enclosure is oriented northeast-southeast and measures 25 x 30 m. Its walls were ca. 1 m thick and constructed from black basalt and chert blocks. There is a bedouin grave inside the enclosure and some evidence to suggest that bedouin have camped at the site.

Site 357
(Map section 10; field no. 2371, 2377)
PG: 26.9/57.0; UTMG: 67.6/44.7

Numerous stone heaps and cairns, including many partitioned cairns, all along the crest of the Jebel el-Baṭraᵓ. Fifteen were counted between PG: 26.3/57.6; UTMG: 67.2/45.1 and PG: 28.5/55.5; UTMG: 69.7/42.7.

Site 358
(Map section 10; field no. 2386)
PG: 26.0/55.5; UTMG: 66.9/43.0

Building ruin on the northwest end of a knoll, southwest of the Jebel el-Baṭraᵓ ridge; ca. 1 km SSW of

Naṣir. 183 sherds were collected, including: IR 6; A/M 1; LIsl 4; UDE 11; UDEhandle 3; UD 21.

The external walls are composed of large limestone blocks, not neatly laid, and indicate an essentially square ground plan (10 x 11 m). There are interior walls, but they are so covered with collapsed stones that it is difficult to distinguish rooms. Some of the stones from the ruin have been reused for nearby sheepfolds, one being built against the south wall of the ruin; a second was then built against the first and the east wall. While the view from the site is adequate, there are higher spots nearby which provide better vantage points.

Site 359 - **Nāṣir**
(Map section 10; field no. 2385)
PG: 26.3/56.2; UTMG: 67.2/43.8

Building ruin on Jebel el-Baṭraᵓ, ca. 7 km southeast of Ghuweir and 7 km northeast of Um Ḥamaṭ. Naṣṣār on the K737 map. 197 sherds were collected, including: MB 2; LB 1; IR I 1; IR II 3; Hell 3; Nab 2; A/M 3; LIsl 17.

Glueck: Qaṣr Nâṣer/#136 (1939: 72-73). "A short distance west of Rujm el-Mâhrī is Qaṣr Nâṣer, situated on a rise overlooking the small *wâdī* between the two sites. It is a much destroyed building, measuring about 13.50 m. square, and oriented s.w. by n.e. There is a wing on the s.e. side, which measures 9.50 by 7 m. The walls of the building, which are made of large flint blocks, are 1.30 m. thick. A considerable number of EI I-II sherds was found, and also a small quantity of Nabataean-Roman sherds" (72).

The external walls of the main structure described by Glueck remain standing up to five courses high in places. Internal walls separate four rooms. Tumbled stones with occasional traces of outlying walls cover an area ca. 25 m across. Among the tumbled stones on the east side of the ruin are three underground chambers with artificial entrances.

Site 360
(Map section 10; field no. 2384)
PG: 26.9/55.8; UTMG: 67.7/43.4

Building ruin on a ridge southwest of Jebel el-Baṭraᵓ, less than 1 km southeast of Nāṣir and on the same ridge. 539 sherds were collected, including: MB 5; LB 8; IR 14; Nab 3; LRom 1; Um 1; LIsl 20; UDE 38; UDEhandle 7; UD 19; UDhandle 2.

This is a collapsed building complex, the main section being a 12 x 12 m unit with exterior walls constructed from large limestone blocks standing up to three meters high in places. There are interior walls as well, but difficult to trace because of the heavy overlay of stone debris. A second unit, possibly a single chamber, is attached to the southeast side of the main unit and shares a common wall with it. This latter unit measures 6.5 x 9 m and has stone blocks up to two meters long among the debris in its southwest corner. These may have served as rafters for a second floor. More rubble and less clearly defined wall lines extend still farther to the southeast, beyond the second unit. The building complex was situated on the east side of the ridge line; farther down the east slope are a cistern and two rock shelters.

Site 361
(Map section 10; field no. 2371)
PG: 28.5/55.5; UTMG: 69.7/42.7

Stone heap with possible outlying wall lines overlooking Fajj el-ᶜUseikir from Jebel el-Baṭraᵓ. Immediately southeast of the 1007 m elevation marker on the K737 map. The heap seems to be a large burial cairn which was superimposed on the foundation walls of a building of some sort, but it is difficult to tell because the whole site has been badly robbed for stones. 73 sherds were collected, including: EB I 20; EByz 3; UDE 49.

Probably this is the other "Turm" which Brünnow and Domaszewski reported under the name el-ᶜÂli (I: 76, 79; see entry for Site 364 below) and the place which Glueck described as follows: "Immediately on the top of the next rise to the n.n.w. of this site [our Site 363 or 364], about a quarter of a kilometre away, is yet another ruined blockhouse, so completely destroyed, however, that little could be made out of it. No sherds were found by it to help fix the period of its occupation" (1939: 71).

Site 362
(Map section 10; field no. 2372)
PG: 28.7/55.4; UTMG: 69.5/43.0

Building ruin, possibly a fortified watchtower, overlooking Fajj el-ᶜUseikir from Jebel el-Baṭraᵓ. At the

Photograph 35: Kh. el-Baṭrā' (Site 355)

Photograph 36: Nāṣir (Site 359)

1007 m elevation marker on the K737 map. 744 sherds were collected, including: Chalco 1; MB 3; LB 9; IR 23; Hell 2; Nab 16; ERom 4; LRom 7; EByz 13; A/M 2; UD 7; UDhandle 20.

This is probably Brünnow and Domaszewski's eṭ-Ṭarfawîye (I: 79) which they saw only from a distance, and Glueck's eṣ-Ṣîreh/Ṣîret el-Ḥeirân/#133 (1939: 71-73, 88) which he described as follows: "On the top of a rise several kilometres to the n.w. of Meḍeibîᶜ is a small ancient *rujm*, with a cadastral survey cairn on top of it, indicating again how excellently the early settlers chose sites for their fortifications which could be seen from afar, and which necessarily then commanded a wide field of vision. This site is known as Rujm eṣ-Ṣîreh, or Ṣîret el-Ḥeirân. The *rujm* seems to be the ruin of a small fort, oriented n.n.e. by s.s.w., and measuring approximately 10.50 by 9.50 m. A considerable number of plain, burnished, and painted EI Moabite sherds was found by the site, in addition to quantities of Nabataean sherds of all kinds, including several fragments of sigillata of the 'Pergamene' type. The *rujm* seems originally to have been set in the center of a fairly large walled enclosure, in which wall-foundations of houses and pens of sheep or goats are visible" (71-72).

Tumbled stones with occasionally discernible wall lines (up to 1.75 m wide) cover an area ca. 35 x 50 m. The collapsed structure with cadastral survey cairn which Glueck reported is at the northeast end of the ruin.

Site 363
(Map section 10; field no. 2368, 2369)
PG: 29.0/54.7; UTMG: 69.7/42.4

Building ruin on Jebel el-Baṭraᵓ, immediately northwest of the track from Um Ḥamaṭ and Nakhl via Qaṣr et-Tamrah and Qaṣr Abu Rukbah to Lejjun. 68 sherds were collected, including: IR II 1; IR II C/Pers 1; UDE 3; UD 63.

This must be the site which Glueck described as follows: "Below this blockhouse [i.e., Site 364], at the bottom of the slope opposite it to the s.w., are the clear outlines of another *qaṣr*, which has been completely demolished" (1939: 71).

Situated in a saddle between two ridges, the ruin consists of foundation walls (ca. 1 m thick) indicative of a single rectangular building (ca. 20 x 15 m). The external walls are best preserved in the southeast corner (up to 3 courses high). A gap midway along the north wall seems to have been a doorway, and an exceptionally long stone block (ca. 2 x 0.5 m) lying immediately inside the "doorway" may have been the lintel stone. The line of an internal wall parallel to the south external wall can be traced ca. 10 m. Bedouin had camped at the site not long before we examined it. Approximately 700 m to the ESE (UTMG: 70.4/42.3) is a large cistern with a limestone collar and watering trough. A pile of dirt at its mouth indicated that it has been cleared recently. 19 sherds were collected near the cistern: 2 Nab and 17 UD.

Site 364
(Map section 10; field no. 2370)
PG: 29.0/54.9; UTMG: 69.9/42.5

Building ruin, possibly a watchtower, overlooking Fajj el-ᶜUsaykir from the crest of Jebel el-Baṭraᵓ. Immediately southeast of the 1007 m elevation marker on the K737 map. 324 sherds were collected, including: IR 10; IR II 8; Nab 9; ERom 6; LRom 2; EByz 16; UD 10.

Brünnow and Domaszewski reported this ruin along with another one nearby (probably site 361) under a single name, el-ᶜÂli (I: 76-77). In spite of the fact that he found only one surface sherd and we found many, this must be the same site which Glueck described as follows: "About half a kilometre to the n.n.w. of el-Mâhrī are the very large foundation stones of a strongly built blockhouse. It is oriented w.s.w. by e.n.e., and measures 15.70 by 13.40 m. The walls measured originally about 2 m thick. Only one fine Nabataean-Roman sherd could be found. ... The rise on which it is situated has been washed clean of all sherds, except the one we found, and the few which may have escaped our attention" (1939: 71).

The building, which would have been 16.4 x 13.3 m at the base according to our measurements, was constructed from large limestone blocks (some up to 2.0 x 0.5 m). Its external walls are best preserved at the west corner where it stands up to four courses (2 m) high. Probably there was a tower in that corner since, in addition to the wall, the stone tumble is especially high. An internal wall (ca. 1.5 m thick) which can be traced the length of the building partitions a long chamber on the northwest side. Other internal walls are discernible in the south corner.

Photograph 37: Building ruin (Site 364) overlooking Fajj el-ʿUseikir

Photograph 38: Carved stone at Site 364

Site 365
(Map section 10; field no. 2374)
PG: 29.4/54.0; UTMG: 70.3/41.7

Building ruin, a small structure overlooking Fajj el-ᶜUseikir from Jebel el-Baṭraᵓ. Ca. 30 m northwest from, and possibly a watchtower ancillary to, the main el-Mahri ruin, which is marked Ṣirat el Ḥeirān on the K737 map. 42 sherds were collected, including: LB 1; IR 4; Byz 1; LIsl 3; UDE 12.

This is Brünnow and Domaszewski's "el-Mâhri, c: kleiner Wartturm" for which they provided a plan (I: 77). Although one cannot be certain because of the tumbled stones, we calculated the outside dimensions of the building to be slightly less than Brünnow and Domaszewski's measurements which total 8.2 by 8.1 m. The walls were constructed with undressed limestone blocks of varying sizes with no mortar, ca. 1 m thick, and stand ca. 1.25 m high on the south side.

Site 366 - el-Māhrī
(Map section 10; field no. 2375)
PG: 29.5/53.7; UTMG: 70.4/41.5

Building ruins on the crest of Jebel el-Baṭraᵓ, immediately east of the track from Um Ḥamaṭ and Nakhl across the Fajj to Qaṣr Abu Rukbah and Qaṣr et-Tamra. Identified as Ṣirat el Ḥeirān on the K737 map [although Glueck associated the name Rujm eṣ-Ṣîreh/Ṣîret el-Ḥeirân with another site, apparently our site 362]. 479 sherds were collected, including: MB 24; LB 1; Hell 16; EByz 1; LByz 1; A/M 7; LIsl 27; UDE 2; UDEhandle 7; UD 2.

See Musil: ḳṣejr el-Mâhri (6, 81, 367); Brünnow and Domaszewski: el-Mâhri (I: 10-11, 76-77, 79); and Glueck: el-Mâhrī/#135 (1939: 70-71, 73). Musil described it as "ein uralter, zerfaller Beobachtungsposten, von viereckiger Form, aus grossen Steinblöcken erbaut" (367). Brünnow and Domaszewski, describing it as a "Zwischenkastell im Wartturmtypus," provided plans and photographs (76-78). Glueck reported: "A little more than 3 km., n.n.w. of Meḍeibîᶜ is the strong EI border fortress called el-Mâhrī. Situated on top of a ridge, at 1073 m., it commands a view of Meḍeibîᶜ and Maḥaiy to the s.s.e., and of Dhât Râs to the s.w. It is a well built, rectangular structure, measuring 16 by 20.4 m., and is oriented n.e. by s.w. The division of the rooms can be seen inside the building, whose outer walls measure about 1.40 m. thick. The rudely hewn building blocks are laid in dry courses, with the corners laid in headers and stretchers. The e. end of the s.e. wall is still 14 courses high, totalling 5 m. In front of the n.e. wall is a platform in two stages extending 5.90 m. from the wall. The first stage or step of this platform extends 2.35 m. from the w. end to 2 m. at the e. end of the n.e. wall, and is .55 m. above the step of the platform below it, which extends 1.15 m. beyond the e. end of the n.e. wall. ... Close to [the building] was clustered at one time, evidently, a number of small buildings and enclosures, to judge from the wall foundations in its immediate vicinity. ... There are several large cisterns on the s.w. slope of the ridge below el-Mâhrī. A small quantity of EI I-II sherds was found, in addition to a small number of plain and painted Nabataean sherds. There was also a small quantity of Byzantine sherds of the Umm er-Raṣâṣ type, including some interesting fragments of other types of painted Byzantine ware..." (70-71).

The ruin remains essentially as Glueck described it. Among the small buildings and enclosures observed by Glueck as represented by foundation remains clustered around the main ruin were two identified by Brünnow and Domaszewski and treated separately in this report (see sites 365 and 367). While we did not find any clearly diagnostic Iron Age sherds near the main el-Mahri ruin, some were found near site 365.

Site 367
(Map section 10; field no. 2376)
PG: 29.7/53.6; UTMG: 70.6/41.2

Building ruins on Jebel el-Baṭraᵓ, immediately southeast of and possibly associated with the main el-Mahri ruin, which itself is identified as Ṣirat el Ḥeirān on the K737 map. 5 sherds were collected, none of which could be dated with confidence.

Wall lines indicate a cluster of three small structures separated from the main el-Mahri ruin by a saddle in the Jebel el-Baṭraᵓ ridge. The structures measure ca. 3 x 4 m, 3 x 3 m, and 1.5 x 2.5 m respectively. All are constructed from rectangular limestone blocks. One is tempted to think that one of these is tower "a" on Brünnow and Domaszewski's general plan of el-Mahri (I: 77), in spite of

Photograph 39: El-Māhri (Site 366) with secondary building behind

Photograph 40: Interior walls at el-Māhri

the fact that all are considerably more than thirty paces away from the main ruin (see p. 76).

Site 368
(Map section 10; field no. 2378)
PG: 30.3/53.3; UTMG: 71.3/40.8

Building ruin, a small structure, ca. 3 m square and bisected with an interior wall, on Jebel el-Baṭraʾ. Ca. 0.5 km northwest of Rujm Khashm eṣ-Ṣirah, at the 1059 m elevation marker on the K737 map.

Site 369
(Map section 10; field no. 2380, 2381)
PG: 30.4/53.0; UTMG: 71.4/40.5

Building ruin near the southeast end of Jebel el-Baṭraʾ and immediately WNW of Rujm Khashm aṣ-Ṣirah. Marked "Ruins" on the K737 map. 137 sherds were collected including: Nab 1; A/M 12; LIsl 16; LOtt 2; UDE 11; UD 16.

Glueck described the site as follows: "On the next rise above Rujm Khushm eṣ-Ṣîreh, about a quarter of a kilometre distant to the w.n.w., is a small, ruined site, which apparently at one time was partly rebuilt. On its s.w. slope is a large *bîr*, which at the time of our visit still had water in it, someone having recently dug a new channel down the slope leading to it. Numerous tracks can be seen leading to this renovated cistern, which evidently possesses considerable antiquity, being one of the few of many similar cisterns at ancient sites which could very well be cleaned out and reused. A small number of Nabataean sherds was found at this site, including one piece of sigillata of the 'Pergamene' type, as well as several painted and glazed mediaeval Arabic sherds" (1939: 75).

The remains of a single structure (ca. 6 x 6 m) built with roughly hewn chert and limestone blocks is situated on a narrow ridge. The exterior walls of the structure were ca. 1 m thick and appear to have been repaired with smaller stones in several places. No interior wall lines are visible, but what appears to be a wall line extends eastward from near the southeast corner of the structure and perpendicular to its eastern exterior wall. There are also traces of what may have been additional walls connected to the west side of the structure. Several sheepfolds on the site have been built with stones robbed from the ruin. Approximately 100 m to the north, on the northeast slope of the ridge, is a cave with a circular enclosure of stones at its mouth. The cave has an ashy fill, and the ceiling is smudged from smoke. No pottery was found near the cave.

Site 370 - **Rujm Khashm eṣ-Ṣīrah**
(Map section 10; field no. 2382)
PG: 30.9/52.9; UTMG: 71.8/40.3

Fortified building ruin at the southeast end of Jebel el-Baṭraʾ. Rujm Khashm aṣ Ṣīrah on the K737 map. 144 sherds were collected, including: IR II 2; LRom 1; A/M 2; LIsl 10; UD 5.

See Glueck: Rujm Khushm eṣ-Ṣîreh/#134 (1939: 72-73, 75). "Several kilometres n.e.-e.n.e. of Meḍeibîᶜ is Rujm Khushm eṣ-Ṣîreh, for which we were also given the name of Rujm Meḥbes. It is a large, ruined fortress on top of a hill, commanding an excellent view across the approaches from the Fejj el-ᶜAseiker. Rujm el-Mâhrī is visible to the n.w., Meḍeibîᶜ to the s.s.w., and Maḥaiy in the distance to the south. The very strongly built fortress is oriented e.s.e.-s.e. by w.n.w.-n.w., and measures 32 by 23 m. The walls appear to be 1.50 m. thick, and are built of large, rudely hewn flint blocks. Originally a strong glaçis was built against the walls further to strengthen them, a part of it being particularly well preserved at the n. corner. Inside the fortress is a mass of fallen building blocks and debris, which has been dug into to provide sepulchres for the recent dead. ... Water for the garrison of Rujm Khushm eṣ-Ṣîreh was obtained from three large cave-cisterns on the n.e. slope. In view of its general position, its relationship to such sites as Maḥaiy and Meḍeibîᶜ, and el-Mâhrī, the strong nature of its construction, with the addition of glaçis which in Transjordan is to be found only in connection with EI sites, one could identify this site even without pottery evidence as another one of the chain of EI fortresses along the e. border of the Moabite kingdom. A small quantity of EI I-II sherds was found, mainly on the n.e. slope, and also a small number of Nabataean and early Byzantine sherds" (72-73).

The ruin remains essentially as Glueck described it. Note, however, that we found predominantly Late Islamic pottery.

Site 371
(Map section 11; field no. 2675)
PG: 33.7/61.6; UTMG: 74.6/49.6

Rectangular ruin (8.4 x 8.7 m), possibly a watchtower, ca. 4 km north of Qaṣr Abu Rukbah and along the track from Qaṣr Abu Rukbah to el-Lejjun. Marked "Ruins" on the K737 map. Situated on essentially flat terrain but with a good view to the north, the walls of this small rectangular building were 1.5 m thick and composed of limestone blocks laid in two courses with rubble fill between. The walls stand six courses high at one place; possibly three additional courses are hidden beneath the collapse. This is Parker's Site 124, from which he reports 49 sherds: 45 ER/Nab and 4 possibly IR. We collected 8 sherds including: LRom 1; UD 7.

Site 372
(Map section 11; field no. 2681)
PG: 33.1/61.5; UTMG: 73.8/48.8

Building ruin ca 3 km NNW of Qaṣr Abu Rukbah and overlooking Wadi Abu Rukbah from the west. Wall lines indicate a rectangular structure (18 x 15 m) with two rooms. Traces of outlying walls probably represent sheep pens. 96 sherds were collected, including: IR 2; IR II 1; Nab 2; ERom 1; A/M 1; LIsl 1; UDhandle 1; 1 Ott pipe fragment.

Site 373
(Map section 11; field no. 2682)
PG: 33.4/60.2; UTMG: 74.2/47.6

Building ruin ca. 2 km north of Qaṣr Abu Rukbah and overlooking Wadi Abu Rukbah from the west. This is Parker's Site 131 (Koucky 1987b: 84-85), from which his team collected 84 sherds. According to our reading these included: IR 3; Nab 2; ERom 2 and LByz 3. We collected 122 sherds at the site including: IR 4; Nab 3; LByz 2; LIsl 1; UD 1; UDhandle 2.

An essentially rectangular enclosure wall (ca. 18 m [E-W] by 20 m [N-S]), but rounded at the north end, was constructed with roughly shaped limestone blocks and is preserved up to six courses above the ground. The walls are two courses wide (ca. 0.7 m) except where unusually large stones were used. Inside and attached to the west wall are foundation lines which may represent interior rooms. Although it is not entirely certain that the rooms were contemporary with the enclosure, it is tempting to suppose that this was once a small dwelling with an open courtyard. Secondary enclosures, probably sheep pens of fairly recent vintage, extend from the east and west walls. Ca. 200 m further east, leaning against a chain of rocks 5 m above a wadi bed, is another large enclosure which has been rebuilt as a sheep pen. Also there are numerous cairns and nondescript stone heaps in the region. See, for example, Parker's sites 125, 132 and 135 (Koucky 1987b: 84-85).

Site 374
(Map section 11; field no. 2674)
PG: 34.8/59.5; UTMG: 75.6/47.2

Building ruin, possibly a watchtower, ca. 2 km northeast of Qaṣr Abu Rukbah and immediately east of the track from Qaṣr Abu Rukbah to Lejjun. This is Parker's Site 126, from which he reports 11 Nab/ERom sherds. We collected 7 sherds: Nab/ERom 1; UD 6.

Walls composed of limestone slabs, laid two courses wide (ca. 1 m), and standing six to seven courses high, indicate a structure which was roughly square at the base (6.2 x 6.4 m). No doorway is evident. The site provides a commanding view of the surrounding region—Fityan is visible to the north and Qaṣr Abu Rukbah to the south.

Site 375
(Map section 11; field no. 2683)
PG: 32.8/59.3; UTMG: 73.5/46.9

Building ruin on the summit of Jebel Abu Rukbah, ca. 6.5 km ESE of el-Mreigha. Near the 994 m elevation marker on the K737 map. This is Parker's site 137 where his team collected 80 sherds (Koucky 1987b: 84-85). Among these, according to our reading, were IR 1 (?); Nab 6; and Byz 2. We collected 39 sherds at the site including: Nab 4.

A completely ruined structure which probably has been rebuilt and modified several times is laid out in an "L" shape (ca. 16 x 13 m on the long sides). Most recently, the ruin has been used for burials. Situated on the summit of Jebel Abu Rukbah, the site dominates the surrounding region. There are cisterns and a rectangular enclosure (Parker's Site 142; [Koucky 1987b: 86-87]) on the southeast slope of the hill.

Site 376
(Map section 11; field no. 2684)
PG: 33.2/59.0; UTMG: 73.9/46.7

Two prominent cairns on Jebel Abu Rukbah, slightly more than 1 km northwest of Qaṣr Abu Rukbah. This is Parker's Site 135, from which he reports 36 sherds, most of them found near the northernmost cairn: Nab/ERom 30; LRom/EByz 3; LOtt 1; UD 2.

Although composed of large, roughly hewn blocks, neither cairn presents any definite structure. A semicircle of stones flanks the northernmost cairn, ending at bedrock. Also a water channel constructed with stones can be traced some 90 m from a gully east of the cairns to fields south of them.

Site 377 - **Kh. Abū Rukbah**
(Map section 11; field no. 2603)
PG: 33.5/58.9; UTMG: 74.3/46.6

Building ruin at the eastern end of Jebel Abu Rukbah, ca. 1 km NNW of Qaṣr Abu Rukbah. This is Parker's Site 129 from which he reports primarily Nab/ERom sherds with 5 IR II and 5 LRom/EByz (Koucky 1987b: 84-85). We collected 369 sherds including: IR 1; Nab 32; ERom 6; LRom 6; Byz 6; EByz 2; UDEhandle 2; UD 6.

See Brünnow and Domaszewski "Klein Abû Rukbe" (Vol. II: 45); Glueck: Kh. Abū Rukbeh/#145 (1939: 78-79). Glueck reported: "Less than a kilometre away to the n.n.w., situated on a knoll which overlooks Qaṣr Abū Rukbeh, is a much ruined structure, which is called Kh. Abū Rukbeh. It commands a view not only over Qaṣr Abū Rukbeh, but also of Qaṣr Noᶜmân [our Site 379], to the s.s.w. It is oriented w.-w.n.w. by e.-e.s.e. and measures 9.60 by 8.40 m. There is an entrance on the s. side, with an offset extending 3.30 m. to the w. wall from the w. side of the entrance, and jutting out 1.20 m. from the rest of the s. wall. The doorway is one metre wide, and at the present time, measuring from the debris which partly covers the bottom of the doorway, is 1.30 m. high. It must be nearly 2 m. high in reality, but the debris covering the bottom of it will have to be removed before an accurate measurement can be taken. Nabataean sherds of all kinds, including sigillata, were found among and around the ruined structure, the inside of which is littered with fallen building blocks. The occupation of the site probably extended into the Roman period, to judge from the character of a number of the sherds."

The ruin remains essentially unchanged from Glueck's description. The walls average .90 m thick, are constructed with two faces filled with rubble, and are preserved up to six courses high. Internal walls can be traced which divide the building into four chambers. Ca. 30 m to the southwest lies the much more poorly preserved ruin of a second structure which would have measured ca. 7 x 7 m. Both structures have been reused as burials.

Site 378 - **Qaṣr Abū Rukbah**
(Map section 11; field no. 2604)
PG: 33.9/58.0; UTMG: 74.7/45.7

Building ruin located ca. 1.3 km northeast of Qasr et-Tamra. Marked Qaṣr Abū Rukbah on the K737 map. This is Parker's Site 127 where his team collected 18 sherds (Koucky 1987b: 84-85). These included, according to our reading, Nab 1; LRom 1; LIsl (?) 1. We collected 18 sherds at the site: IR 1; Nab 1; LRom 1; UD 15.

See Brünnow and Domaszewski: Abû Rukbe (I: 10, 76: Vol. II: 43-45); Glueck: Qaṣr Abū Rukbeh/#44 in 1934 (71), #144 in 1939 (78). Brünnow and Domaszewski provided a plan with photographs.

A large, almost square (10.3 x 11 m) tower is preserved to 25 courses at the northwest corner. The inside is filled with collapsed masonry. A stairway leads up the inside northwest wall to an upper level of which the floor no longer survives. The walls are heavily mortared on the outside and plastered on the inside.

Site 379 - **Qaṣr et-Tamrah**
(Map section 11; field no. 2605)
PG: 33.0/57.0; UTMG: 73.9/44.7

Building ruin, apparently a watchtower, ca. 8 km southeast of el-Mreigha and 1.5 km SSW of Qaṣr Abu

Rukbah. Marked Qaṣr et Tamrah on the K737 map. This is Parker's Site 140 where his team collected 22 sherds (Koucky 1987b: 86-87), among which we recognized the following clearly diagnostic pieces: Nab 1; ERom 1. We collected 9 sherds including: Nab 1; UD 8.

See Musil: ḳṣêr et-Tamra (42), although he may have associated the name Qaṣr et-Tamrah with esh-Sharif (our Site 238) as did Glueck. The site reported here seems to be Glueck's Qaṣr No^cmân/#43 (1934: 69-71; photograph on p. 70 and plan on p. 104; see also 1939: 78). "A kilometre north-northeast of it [apparently our Site 380] we came to another small ruined watch-tower, probably Nabataean. The type of construction of the walls of Qaṣr Noᶜmân is the same as that of other indubitably Nabataean towers. It is 5.40 metres square. The walls, which are constructed of rectangular, roughly dressed basalt blocks, are preserved to a height of ten and eleven courses on various sides. The height of the wall at the northeast corner is 3.70 metres. In the north side is a door a metre wide, and 1.20 metres high. It gives access to a passage of the same dimensions, running north and south the length of the interior. Over this passage is a ceiling of stone beams. The second last beam at the south end of the ceiling is missing. It seems that access to the interior of the tower was gained through the passage, and then through the space in the ceiling above it, which was blocked up after entrance had been effected. Probably the entrance to the passage proper was blocked up from the inside, after the occupants of the tower had entered. It is uncertain whether or not the walls on either side of the passage way are solid, because the inside of the tower was filled with débris. The outside walls of the tower were carefully examined, and there is no other possible entrance than the one described through the door in the north wall. Qaṣr Abū Rukbeh is visible to the northeast of Qaṣr Noᶜmân. Nabataean sherds were found around Qaṣr Noᶜmân, which established the date of the tower with certainty" (1934: 69-71).

The tower remains standing as Glueck described it. A gap in the south wall (70 cm high) may have been another entrance, although it seems unlikely that Glueck would have failed to see it. Possibly some stone robbing has occurred since he examined the site.

Site 380
(Map section 11; field no. 2607)
PG: 32.2/56.8; UTMG: 73.0/44.4

Building ruin, probably a watchtower, located ca. 7.5 km southeast of el-Mreigha and ca. 1 km WSW of Qaṣr et-Tamrah. Marked "Ruins" on the K737 map. 10 sherds were collected, including: Nab 1; UDE 2; UD 7.

This is Glueck's #42 (1934: 69): "A kilometre north-northeast of it [Bîr Bashbash] we came to another small ruined watchtower. A kilometre to the east of it lies Qaṣr Noᶜmân."

Foundation walls visible in a tumble of stones indicate a structure which was built with large, limestone blocks and measured ca. 10 x 10 m at the base. A stone enclosure at its east corner probably is a modern feature.

Site 381 - **Bīr Bashbash**
(Map section 11; field no. 2608)
PG: 32.0/56.2; UTMG: 72.8/43.9

Faint wall lines and cistern ca. 7.5 km southeast of el-Mreigha and 2.5 km southwest of Qaṣr Abu Rukbah. 22 sherds were collected, including: Nab 8; UD 13.

See Musil: bîr Bašbaš (368); and Glueck: Bîr Bashbash/#41. "Two kilometres to the northeast of Bîr en-Nâyem is a small ruined site with a large cistern called Bîr Bashbash, where some Nabataean sherds were found" (1934: 69). Note, however, that Bir Bashbash is *northwest* rather than northeast of Bîr en-Nâyem, which Glueck placed near Ekhwein el-Khâdem (Qaṣr al Juwayn on the K737 map; UTMG: 74.8/42.6).

Walls barely visible at ground level and some large stone slabs suggest an earlier structure in what now seems to be a bedouin encampment. 300 m further south is a cistern, possibly the one to which Glueck referred, with a stone cover and trough. The cover, now out of place, is 1.2 x 1.8 m with a 0.40 m hole. The trough is 2.6 x .55 x .45 m.

Site 382
(Map section 11; field no. 2383)
PG: 31.2/52.5; UTMG: 72.1/40.1

Remains of a small rectangular structure (ca. 2 x 3 m) and several small burial cairns along the ridge at the southeastern tip of Jebel el-Baṭra'. The building was constructed with large limestone blocks.

Site 383 - **ed-Dabbākah**
(Map section 12; field no. 2036)
PG: 12.3/52.4; UTMG: 53.3/39.6

Modern village on an ancient settlement site, ca. 4 km west of el-Mazar and 1.5 km WNW of el-Jauza. Ed Dabbāka on the K737 map. 299 sherds were collected, including: LB 2; IR II 2; Hell 1; Nab 6; Byz 10; EByz 3; LByz 6; A/M 3; LIsl 37; UD 2; UDhandle 18.

See Tristram: Dubbak (120); Musil: ḫirbet ed-Dabbâče (365); Glueck: ed-Debâkeh/#106 (1939: 93). Glueck, who incorrectly located ed-Dabbakah northeast of el-Jauza (it is northwest), noted one rude, modern house built on a small, completely ruined site, using old blocks from the ruins. He observed Nabataean, Roman, Byzantine and "mediaeval Arabic" sherds.

Rubble and occasional wall lines, never more than one course high, are visible over an area ca. 100 x 200 m at the western edge of the modern village. The village itself is on a ridge at the western edge of the plateau. Beyond the ruins the terrain drops rapidly toward Wadi el-Muqeir.

Site 384 - **el-Jauza**
(Map section 12; field no. 2038)
PG: 13.8/51.9; UTMG: 54.7/39.2

A modern village on an ancient settlement site ca. 2.75 km WSW of el-Mazar. El Jauza on the K737 map. 397 sherds were collected, including: LB 7; IR 2; IR II 2; Nab 9; Byz 5; Fat(?) 1; A/M 2; LIsl 34; Mod 2; UD 3; UDhandle 14.

See Musil: ḫirbet Ğôza' (365).

The village is situated on a ridge that gradually slopes southward toward a branch of Wadi el-Muqeir (ca. 100 m away). The hills between the village and the wadi are currently used for wheat farming. In the southwest corner of the village are the remains of a simple structure (15 x 17 m) built of large limestone blocks. Only one course of stones was visible for the wall lines. Also there are cisterns at the southwestern edge of the village.

Site 385 - **Kh. el-Bāsiliyyah**
(Map section 12; field no. 2037)
PG: 14.5/52.0; UTMG: 55.4/39.4

Building ruins located 2 km southwest of el-Mazar. Kh. el Bāsiliya on the K737 map. 390 sherds were collected, including: Nab 3; A/M 4; LIsl 51; UD 6; UDhandle 4.

See Glueck: Rujm Basalîyeh/#100 (1939: 98). "To the east of Jōzā is a small, completely ruined, flintblock site....where Nabataean, Roman, Byzantine, and mediaeval Arabic sherds were found."

A light to medium sherd scatter with occasionally visible wall lines covers an area ca. 50 x 40 m. The walls, which were built with small to medium-sized chert blocks, are never preserved more than one course high, and few can be traced more than 10 meters. The site is situated on a low hill surrounded by flat wheat fields on all sides. Stones from field clearance have been piled around the edges of the ruins, and a large threshing floor occupies the center of the site.

Site 386
(Map section 12; field no. 2096)
PG: 13.8/51.1; UTMG: 54.8/38.5

Building ruin on a hilltop overlooking Wadi el-Muqeir, ca. 3 km southwest of el-Mazar and slightly less than 1 km SSE of el-Jauza. 26 sherds were collected: Nab 4; LIsl 1; UD 21.

The ruin appears to represent a single structure (8 x 5 m) which was built of large chert blocks. Only one course of stones is visible at ground level.

Site 387 - **Rujm Um Ṣuwwānah**
(Map section 12; field no. 2047)
PG: 13.5/50.3; UTMG: 54.5/37.7

Very light sherd scatter and several abandoned houses on a ridge ca. 3.5 km southwest of el-Mazar and 1 km WSW of el-Manshiya. Um Ṣuwwāna on the K737 map. Only badly worn body sherds were observed, none of which we considered useful for dating purposes, and none were retained.

See Glueck: Rujm Umm Ṣuwânā/#97 (1939: 92), which he described as a small completely destroyed EI I-II site with a few worn EI I-II sherds.

Although unoccupied when we visited the site, the few houses clearly date from modern times. There is a cistern at the northern end of the site.

Site 388 - **Rujm el-Ḥleileh**
(Map section 12; field no. 2044)
PG: 13.1/50.8; UTMG: 54.2/37.8

Small settlement site on a ridge ca. 4 km southwest of el-Mazar, between Um Ṣuwwanah and ᶜAin Ḥleileh. 402 sherds were collected, including: LB 1; Nab 32; Byz 2; LIsl 1; Mod 3; UD 18; UDhandle 28.

See Glueck: Rujm Ḥeleileh/#96 (1939: 92), which he described as a small, completely ruined site with a few worn Nabataean-Roman sherds. Glueck's description seems to fit this ruin better than site 389, although we heard them called Ḥleileh and Rujm el-Ḥleileh respectively.

Occasional wall lines can be traced amid the rubble of chert blocks spread over an area ca. 50 x 75 m. The sherds were gathered from a rectangular pattern around the ruins. The terrain drops slowly from the northeast edge of the site toward Wadi Muqeir. ᶜAin Ḥleileh is located immediately to the west.

Site 389
(Map section 12; field no. 2125)
PG: 12.3/50.8; UTMG: 53.3/38.1

Ruined building complex ca. 1 km NNW of Mudawwarah and ca. 1 km WNW of Rujm el Ḥleileh on the west side of ᶜAin Ḥleileh. 123 sherds were collected, including: Nab 7; ERom 1; LIsl 5; UDE 3; UD 5; UDhandle 3.

See comments for site 288.

A completely ruined, small site on a hill top. The wall lines of one structure are visible to one course and measure ca. 15 x 5 m. On the southwest edge of the hill are a few wall lines with small, chert stones 4-6 courses high.

Site 390 - **Kh. el-Mudawwarah**
(Map section 12; field no. 2048)
PG: 12.7/50.2; UTMG: 53.6/37.4

Unoccupied settlement site on the summit of a hill overlooking Wadi Juḥra, ca. 4.5 km southwest of el-Mazar. Kh. el Mudawwara on the K737 map. 507 sherds were collected, including: EB 73; EB I 1; EB II-III 33; MB 4; IR 5; LRom 1; LByz 1; UD 8.

See Doughty: Mehnuwara (22); Glueck: Mudawwerah /#95 (1939: 89-90, 94). Glueck described Mudawwarah as a "tremendous site occupying the entire, fairly flat top of a completely isolated hill, which is surrounded by small wadis on every side. The entire site, which has the shape roughly of a great truncated triangle, was once enclosed with strong walls." Part of the perimeter wall could be seen by him, particularly on the southwestern side. He described the two long walls of the triangular shape as ca. 300 m in length, and reported large numbers of sherds within the enclosure and on the upper slopes, most of them dating to the Early Bronze period. Elsewhere (94), Glueck described Mudawwarah as one of five large Early Bronze sites in this part of Transjordan. The summit of Mudawwarah had been completely plowed over when he visited in 1936.

Except for extensive surface pottery and traces of the ancient wall which encircled it, there is little to indicate the antiquity of this site. The top of the hill is still under cultivation, having been plowed for wheat when we were there. Constant field clearing has resulted in numerous scattered stone heaps. The perimeter wall was built from chert blocks and never more than one course is visible. As Glueck indicated, the surface of the hill marked by the perimeter wall is roughly triangular in shape with two long sides and one shorter side. The short side of the triangle is at the northwest end, where there is a limestone outcropping and the ground drops sharply. Also there is a cistern at this end of the site. The long sides intersect and point toward the southeast, where the ground slopes more gradually toward a lower ridge line. Wadi Juḥra runs along the southern edge of the hill and Wadi el-Wiḥsha along the northern edge. The ground drops sharply into both wadis. Near the base of the southern slope of the hill, in Wadi Juḥra, are several caves whose openings are blocked with stones.

Photograph 41: Kh. el-Mudawwarah (Site 390)

Site 391 - **Juḥra**
(Map section 12; field no. 2101)
PG: 12.3/49.9; UTMG: 53.3/37.2

Small village, partially abandoned, on the northwest end of the ridge which forms the south bank of Wadi Juḥra, ca. 5 km southwest of el-Mazar. Juḥra on the K737 map. 16 sherds were collected, including: Nab 1; Byz 1; LIsl 2; UD 1.

Possibly Seetzen's Seháhharaᵓ (416).

Only a few families occupied the eastern end of this village when we visited in 1982. Older, abandoned houses at the west end were used as sheep shelters. Occasionally one notices large worked stones in the walls of these older houses, no doubt reused from earlier structures. Otherwise there are no visible ruins. Also there is very little surface pottery, most of it on the northwest side of the site where it slopes down to Wadi Juḥra.

Site 392
(Map section 12; field no. 2126)
PG: 11.7/51.1; UTMG: 52.7/38.4

Building ruins ca. 5 km WSW of el-Mazar and slightly more than 1 km northwest of Kh. el-Mudawwarah. 156 sherds were collected, including: IR 1; IR II 1; Nab 27; ERom 1; LByz 1; UD 3; UDhandle 8.

Wall lines preserved one course above the ground indicate two structures. One is near a large cistern and measures ca. 5 x 5 m. The other, ca. 20 m southeast of the first, measures ca. 12 x 24 m.

Site 393
(Map section 12; field no. 2127)
PG: 11.2/51.1; UTMG: 52.2/38.5

Building ruin ca. 5 km WSW of el-Mazar and 2 km northwest of Mudawwarah. 28 sherds were collected, including: MB 3; Nab 5; UDE 6.

The ruin is located on an isolated hill which affords a clear view in all directions. The rubble includes roughly-cut limestone blocks, many of which are over 1 m long. Two short stretches of wall are visible at ground level, except at one point where two courses are in place. These appear to be the remains of a structure (5.5 m square), possibly a tower.

Site 394 - **Sdeir**
(Map section 12; field no. 2097)
PG: 10.5/50.6; UTMG: 52.1/37.8

Building ruin on the south bank of Wadi Sdeir, ca. 5.5 km WSW of el-Mazar and 1.5 km west of Khirbet el-Mudawwara. 22 sherds were collected, including: Nab 2; Byz 1; EByz 1; UD 1.

The ruin indicates a two-room building constructed with limestone blocks and measuring 7 x 9 m. Since it was built into the hillside, some of the wall lines are not exposed above the current ground surface. However four courses remain in place at the northeast corner of the west room. The building had an east-west axis with a long east-west wall on the south side ending at the east end with a circular apse-like construction (the apse faces east and may indicate the remains of a church). The threshhold on the south side is composed of well dressed limestone *in situ*. The stones in the doorway were cut to accommodate a door frame.

Site 395 - **Khāneq en-Naṣāra**
(Map section 12; field no. 2042)
PG: 10.8/50.8; UTMG: 51.8/38.1

Small khirbeh on an isolated hill immediately north of ᶜAin Sdeir and Wadi Sdeir, ca. 6 km WSW of el-Mazar and 1.5 km north of Kh. Ḍubab. 491 sherds were collected, including: LB II 46; Hell 13; Nab 4; ERom 3; Mod 2; UDE 14; UDEhandle 27; UD 14.

Glueck: Kh. Khâneq en-Naṣârā/#93 (1939: 84, 86). Glueck, observing that the site provides a good view of the spring and approaches to it, reported EI I-II, Nabataean and Roman pottery.

Remains of a rectangular building (8 x 16 m) occupy the highest point on the hill, which itself is situated below the plateau shelf and surrounded by a plowed field. Although the hill is below the plateau, it provides a clear view to the north, south and west. Only one course of the building's stone walls remains in place, surrounded by rubble which is scattered all over the hilltop. Terrace walls can be seen on the north, south, and west sides of the slope. There are cisterns on the east side of the hill.

Site 396 - **Kh. eṭ-Ṭayyibeh**
(Map section 12; field no. 2043)
PG: 09.8/50.7; UTMG: 50.8/38.0

Modern village on an earlier settlement site along the south bank of Wadi Sdeir; ca. 7 km WSW of el-Mazar and 1.5 km northwest of Ḍubab. 97 sherds were collected, including: Nab 1; LIsl 38; Mod 1.

See Musil: ḫirbet eṭ-Ṭajjibe (151, 259). Musil passed this ruin on his way to Ḍubab and noted olive gardens in the vicinity.

The modern village is located just east of the road from ᶜIraq to Khanzirah, at the point where the road makes a sharp turn to the west (i.e., toward Khanzirah). The sherd collection indicated above came from the northern end of the village where there are orchards and numerous field clearance walls separating fields. One of the field walls includes a stone inscribed in Greek, probably a tombstone. The text is illegible.

Site 397 - **Kh. es-Sdeir**
(Map section 12; field no. 2046)
PG: 10.2/50.5; UTMG: 52.0/37.7

Small khirbeh with abandoned houses ca. 6 km WSW of el-Mazar, 1 km NNE of Ḍubab, and 100 m WSW of ᶜAin Sdeir. 107 sherds were collected, including: Nab 4; LByz 6; UDE 2; UDhandle 3.

See Glueck: Kh.es-Sedeir/#91 (1939: 86). Glueck described it as a completely destroyed site a short distance SSW of Khaneq en-Naṣara where he picked up a few Nabataean sherds and a piece of sigillata.

Situated on a ridge along the south bank of Wadi Sdeir are several abandoned houses and a courtyard. The walls stand 1-2 m high, and two of the houses still have roofs. Scattered rubble covers an area ca. 150 x 50 m. A single family occupies the site now.

Site 398
(Map section 12; field no. 2110)
PG: 10.3/49.9; UTMG: 51.3/37.2

Sherd scatter on the top of a rocky hill which itself is situated along the track which leads northwest from the Khanzirah-Majra road to Ṭayyibeh (Site 396); ca. 3.5 km southeast of Khanzirah and slightly less than 1 km northwest of Ḍubab. There is a well in a depression of the hill but no wall lines or structures are visible. The surrounding fields are cultivated. 51 sherds were collected, including: LB 1; Nab 3; EByz 1; LByz 1.

Site 399 - **Kh. Ḍubāb**
(Map section 12; field no. 2049)
PG: 10.5/49.4; UTMG: 51.4/36.7

Unoccupied settlement site immediately north of the Khanzirah-Majra road, and approximately midway between the two. Dabāb on the K737 map. 979 sherds were collected, including: MB 17; LB 38; IR 16; IR I 24; IR II 64; IR II C/Pers 6; Hell 9; Nab 147; ERom 29; LRom 4; LIsl 1; UDE 15; UDEhandle 75; UD 25; UDhandle 63.

Musil referred to ǧebel Ḍubâb (2, 4-5, 151, 257, 259-60)—i.e., to the high hill (1275 m) immediately ENE of Kh. Ḍubab, which itself is situated on a slightly lower hill below the southwest corner of the plateau proper. Glueck reported the khirbeh itself, Kh. edh-Dhubâb/#90 (1939: 84, 86): "The Lisân is visible from this site. Kh. edh-Dhubâb also commands a view of the descent to the Wâdī el-Ḥesā. Below the n.w. base of the hill on which it is situated are some springs at the beginning of the Wâdī eṭ-Ṭaiyibeh. The sides of this hill are terraced anciently, and on top of it, stretching along part of the length of its ridge, are the ruins of this site, which was situated within a long, more or less rectangular walled enclosure. The s.w. wall measures approximately 130 m. long, while the n.w. wall measures approximately 32 m. Among the completely destroyed ruins of the site were found large quantities of EI Moabite sherds of all kinds, and also very numerous Nabataean sherds, including sigillata of the 'Pergamene' type and sigillata with the reddish core. There were also some early Byzantine sherds."

Ḍubab is a large complex of building ruins and wall lines with a dense sherd scatter. Glueck's perimeter wall was not so obvious to us, and the extent of the ruins on the surface of the hill is considerably larger than his estimate of the perimeter wall might suggest—i.e., the ruins and sherd scatter cover an area ca. 205 m (N-S) by 118 m (E-W). On the eastern side of the hill are the remains of at least three houses which were built after Glueck's visit but abandoned before ours, with more ancient wall lines scattered among them. On the western slope are the remnants of ancient walls constructed from large chert blocks. Only a single course of stones could be seen. There are two cisterns and a possible plastered pool near the center of the hill. Most of the sherds indicated above came from the ruins on the hill, but some were collected in a small, cultivated field east of the site, between it and Jebel Ḍubab.

Site 400 - **Merzab Mezraᶜah**
(Map section 12; field no. 2050)
PG: 08.8/49.2; UTMG: 49.8/36.4

Small khirbeh overlooking Wadi el-Ḥesa, ca. 3 km southeast of Khanzirah and 2 km west of Ḍubab. 139 sherds were collected, including: Nab 1; Byz 2; Fat(?) 1; A/M 2; LIsl 58; UDE 1; UDhandle 4; 1 glass bracelet fragment.

Glueck mentioned Merzab Mezraᶜah without assigning it a site number: "...we came to the small site of Merzab Mezraᶜah, with its spring, fig-tree grove, and vineyard. There were some modern Arabic sherds on the ground" (1939: 86).

Merzab Mezraᶜah is a completely destroyed site with a moderate sherd scatter extending over a rocky slope which descends to the southwest. Few wall lines could be traced with any confidence. Immediately north of the site are a few occupied houses and modern stone fences.

Site 401 - **Khanzīrah** (eṭ-Ṭayyibeh)
(Map section 12; field no. 2040)
PG: 07.3/51.6; UTMG: 48.3/38.8

Modern village on an ancient settlement site at the southwestern corner of the plateau, ca. 9 km WSW of el-Mazar and 5 km southwest of el-ᶜIraq. Khanzīra on the K737 map. 842 sherds were collected, including: IR II 2; Hell 3; Nab 4; ERom 1; Byz 4; EByz 3; A/M 20; LIsl 91; LOtt(?) 2; Mod 9; UD 7; UDhandle 21.

See Seetzen: Chansíreh (416, 271); Burckhardt: Khanzyre (389, 96); Irby and Mangles: Khanzyre (137);

Photograph 42: Kh. Dhubāb (Site 399)

Doughty: Khanzîra (25); Musil: Ḫanzîra (22, 70, 72, 151, 204, 254-55, 257-58, 261, 360). Seetzen and Burckhardt reported that Khanzirah was one of four occupied villages between Wadi el-Mujib and Wadi el-Ḥesa at the beginning of the 19th century. Musil reported approximately ten houses with gardens when he stayed there overnight.

The village is set on slopes which descend northward and eastward to Wadi eṭ-Ṭayyibeh. Many of the houses are of Ottoman architecture, the older ones to be found on the northern side of the village where there are also two large cisterns. The antiquity of the site is indicated by its moderate sherd scatter.

Site 402 - **Kh. Medīnet er-Rās**
(Map section 12; field no. 2041)
PG: 05.9/51.1; UTMG: 46.9/38.3

Small khirbeh on a prominent hill less than 1.5 km WSW of Khanzirah. Kh. Madinat er Ras on the K737 map. 77 sherds were collected, including: EB I 14; LB 1; IR II 1; Nab 4; A/M 1; LIsl 5; Mod 6; UDE 5; UD 37.

See Musil: ḫirbet Medînt-er-Râs (72, 260); Glueck: Kh. Medînet er-Râs/#94 (1939: 86, 88-90, 95). While Musil did little more than mention this ruin, Glueck found in it the key to the defense of the southwestern corner of the Moabite plateau during the Iron Age. Specifically, he described it as a ruined fortress with an excellent overview of the descent to Wadi el-Ḥesa and the Dead Sea. "The great walled enclosure which is built along the fairly flat top of the ridge is oriented s.s.w. by n.n.e. The Dead Sea is visible up to beyond the Lisân...The walls are built of large, rudely shaped blocks, and are still one metre high on the average, and 2 m. wide. The walls seem to be 2 m. thick. Inside the walls of the enclosure are the ruins of numerous houses, built against its sides. The w. wall of the enclosure, excluding the w. wall of the ruined fortress itself, which forms the s. continuation of the wall, is 146 m.

long. The w. wall of the fortress measures 18.30 m. The n.n.e. wall of the enclosure measures 5.40 from the w. side to the gateway, which measures 3 m., and then continues for another 8.50 m., making the n. side 16.90 m. in length all told....The e.s.e. wall which has a large bulge in approximately the middle of its length measures 141.60 m. to the point where the e. wall of the ruined fortress begins, which seems to measure about 14 m. There is very little of this part of the wall left. The ruined fortress itself, as it has been seen, is situated at the s. end of the enclosure, its e. and w. walls evidently forming a part of the long walls of the enclosure. The outer s.s.w. wall of the fortress proper, which at the same time forms the outer end of the entire complex, measures about 26 m. Only the w. half of the fortress is preserved to any extent, and it measures 8.30 by 10 m. It is very strongly built, and its walls of large flint and limestone blocks are set in headers and stretchers. Four courses of the wall of the fortress at the s.w. corner measure one metre high. At one time there seems to have been a revetment built against the outer walls of the fortress, which, however, has now fallen away. The fortress proper is situated on a knoll at the s. end of the site, which overlooks the entire enclosure."

Glueck's description is generally accurate. Certainly he was correct in emphasizing the strategic setting and commanding view of Medinet er-Ras, and thereby also identifying its function as a military or police outpost. However, the walled enclosure is a less impressive defensive structure than we had expected from his description. We measured the ruin as a whole to be ca. 150 m (E-W) x 44 m (N-S). Also we observed wall lines either of two structures, perhaps towers, or of two rooms, inside the southwest and southeast corners of the walled enclosure and built into the enclosure walls. At the northern end of the walled enclosure are the remains of two modern buildings apparently constructed after Glueck's visit to the site but abandoned before our visit.

Site 403 - **Rujm er-Rās**
(Map section 12; field no. 2113)
PG: 06.3/50.1; UTMG: 47.4/37.3

Sherd scatter 1.5 km southwest of Khanzirah, on a high point overlooking Wadi el-Ḥesa. Rujm er Ras on the K737 map. 107 sherds were collected, including: IR 2; Nab 9; LByz 1; UDhandle 1.

Site 404 - **Kh. Um Rummānah**
(Map section 12; field no. 2051)
PG: 07.0/49.0; UTMG: 48.1/36.3

Building ruins ca. 2.5 km south of Khanzirah, on the edge of the escarpment overlooking Wadi el-Ḥesa. Kh. Um Rummāna on the K737 map. 173 sherds were collected, including: EB 4; Nab 18; ERom 1; Byz 3; EByz 1; LByz 3; A/M 1; LIsl 37; UD 1; UDhandle 3.

See Glueck: Kh. Umm Rummâneh/#92 (1939: 86). He described it as a small, completely ruined site with a small spring below it.

The building ruins are situated on a steep slope overlooking ᶜAin Rummanah from the NNW. The area has been terraced and the building ruins consist of wall lines with one course visible at ground level. Corners are also visible for a main structure (ca. 21 x 21 m) with interior rooms. Another wall line immediately west of this building suggests a semi-circular structure of some sort (ca. 13 m in diameter).

Site 405 - el-Mjeidel
(Map section 12; field no. 2052)
PG: 12.9/48.7; UTMG: 53.9/35.9

Modern village on an ancient settlement site ca. 5.5 km southwest of el-Mazar and immediately south of the road from Majra to Khanzirah. El Mujeidil on the K737 map. 337 sherds were collected, including: Hell 8; Nab 13; ERom 3; LRom 1; EByz 6; LByz 8; Um 1; A/M 1; LIsl 21; UD 7; UDhandle 17.

See Musil: Mğâdel (19, 360); Glueck: el-Mejâdel/#89 (1939: 80). Glueck described Mjeidel as a completely destroyed site with a modern house on the western end.

The present-day village is situated on a hillside at the beginning of the descent from the plateau southward to Wadi el-Ḥesa. No ruins were observed, but some of the modern houses may include stones from earlier structures.

Site 406
(Map section 12; field no. 2114)
PG: 13.2/48.7; UTMG: 54.2/36.1

Sherd scatter on a ridge of stones ca. 2 km west of Majra and ca. 100 m south of the road from Majra to Khanzirah. 30 sherds were collected, including: Nab 5.

Site 407
(Map section 12; field no. 2116)
PG: 14.4/48.3; UTMG: 55.4/35.8

Building ruin ca. 1 km west of Majra and 0.5 km south of the road from Majra to Khanzirah. Marked "Ruins" on the K737 map. 65 sherds were collected, including: Nab 3; LIsl 1; UDE 3; UD 15.

The ruins indicate a single building which measured ca. 14 m (E-W) by 12 m (N-S). Constructed with large blocks (some more than a meter wide), some sections of the exterior walls stand three courses high. Interior wall lines suggest a 6 x 6 m room (or tower) in the northeast corner.

Site 408
(Map section 12; field no. 2117)
PG: 13.9/48.5; UTMG: 54.9/35.7

Two partitioned cairns on the north rim of Wadi el-Ḥesa, approximately midway between Majra and el-Mjeidel, and ca. 75 m south of the paved road from Majra to Ṣararah. Marked "Ruins" on the K737 map. 24 sherds were collected, including: Nab 3; UDE 1; UD 16.

The better preserved of the two cairns measures ca. 5.5 m in diameter, with the inner circle and bisecting wall standing up to two courses higher than the exterior wall. The other cairn is situated ca. 100 m south of the first, and further down the slope. Only its interior circle is clearly defined, measuring slightly less than 4 m in diameter. A structure of some sort which stood 9 m southeast of this second cairn is represented only by a bit of its corner which rests on bedrock.

Site 409
(Map section 13; field no. 2098)
PG: 15.4/52.4; UTMG: 56.4/39.6

Building ruin and light sherd scatter on a hilltop ca. 2 km southwest of el-Mazar and 1 km west of the road from el-Mazar to Majra. The walls of the building survive ca. 1 m high. Also there is a collapsed cistern. None of the sherds had diagnostic potential.

Site 410 - **el-ᶜAmaqa**
(Map section 13; field no. 2039)
PG: 6.8/51.7; UTMG: 57.8/39.1

Modern village on an ancient settlement site 1 km SSE of el-Mazar. Marked El ᶜAmaqa on the K737 map. 339 sherds collected, including: IR 1; Nab 35; Byz 2; EByz 1; LByz 2; A/M 7; LIsl 53; Mod 3; UD 4; UDhandle 8.

See Brünnow and Domaszewski: el-Ammagâ (I: 106); and Musil: ḫirbet el-ᶜAmaḳa (20, 152, 361). The former described it as "a large village ruin," the latter as a "large, now resettled, ruin." Canova (1954: 316-21) reported six inscribed tombstones, one of which is dated to 537-538.

Several old houses and a moderate sherd scatter at the southwestern edge of the modern village are the only visible remains of earlier phases of settlement. Also in this earlier part of the village are two threshing floors and several cisterns. The surrounding countryside is generally flat and planted with wheat.

Site 411 - Sūl
(Map section 13; field no. 2319)
PG: 19.7/52.4; UTMG: 60.7/39.7

Modern town on an ancient settlement site, slightly more than 3 km east of el-Mazar. Marked Sūl on the K737 map. 992 sherds were collected, including: EB II-III(?) 2; MB 5; LB 12; IR I 16; IR II 6; Hell 2; Nab 22; Rom 4; EByz 2; LByz 2; Fat(?) 1; A/M 5; LIsl 77; UDEhandle 19; UD 11; UDhandle 34.

See Seetzen: Szûl (416); Irby and Mangles: Suhl (113); Mauss and Sauvaire: Kharbet-Soûl (517); Tristram: Suhl (120); Brünnow and Domaszewski: Ṣûl (I: 9, 60); Musil: ḫirbet Sûl (77, 366). Canova (1954: 313-15) reported a lintel with a cross and three inscribed tombstones, two of which dated 577-578 and 585-586.

The nineteenth century travelers cited above saw Sul as an unoccupied ruin. Old "Ottoman style" houses, some of them still in use for livestock, indicate that resettlement began early in the present century—possibly by the time of Glueck's survey in the 1930s, although he did not mention Sūl. The modern village has expanded to the southwest of the older houses. Substantial ancient ruins lie beneath the latter, and villagers report having dug up whole pottery vessels. Sherds were collected over the whole site and down the steep hillsides, particularly on the north and west slopes.

Site 412 - **Rujm Um ᶜAlanda**
(Map section 13; field no. 2045)
PG: 15.7/50.6; UTMG: 56.6/38.0

Modern village on the site of a prominent rujm (stone heap), ca. 2 km SSW of el-Mazar. Marked Rujm Um ᶜAlanda on the K737 map; also called Rujm el-Nameiseh locally. 59 sherds were collected, including: LB 2; Nab 1; LIsl 1; Mod 11; UD 43.

See Musil: ḫirbet umm ᶜAlanda (361); and Glueck: Rujm ᶜAlendā/#98 (1939: 97). Glueck described Rujm Um ᶜAlanda as "situated on top of a rise, in a fertile, cultivated area. The ruins consist of two rooms of a large building. The larger, oriented e.w., measures 20 by 16 m., while the smaller, built against the s. wall of the former, with its w. wall being the continuation of the w. wall of the larger room, measures about 10.50 m. square. The walls are about 1.20 m. thick. The entrance seems to be near the center of the n. side. There are remnants of a strongly built garden wall beyond this side, and of walled-in courtyards all around the site. The walls of the building are constructed of large, roughly hewn flint blocks, the corners being set in headers and stretchers. The s.e. corner of the larger room is still 4 courses high, equalling 1.70 m. On the w. side is a large cistern, another on the e. side, and a cave-cistern on the s. side. In addition to a small quantity of Nabataean-Roman sherds, there were some clear EI I-II sherds. It would seem that the main part of the building belongs to the Early Iron Age."

Except for ancient sherds scattered among the modern dwellings, the present-day village has completely obliterated the ruin seen by Musil and Glueck.

Site 413
(Map section 13; field no. 2095)
PG: 15.7/50.7; UTMG: 57.0/38.2

Stone rubble and light sherd scatter ca. 400 m ENE of Rujm Um ᶜAlanda, at the juncture of the Um ᶜAlanda road with the road from el-Mazar to Majra. 175 sherds were collected, including: LB 17; ERom 1; Mod 1.

This must be the ruin which Glueck described as follows: "A few hundred metres n. of Rujm ᶜAlendā is another small, completely destroyed site, containing the ruins of a small building in a walled enclosure, inside of which there was also a cistern. Nabataean-Roman sherds were found, in addition to several EI sherds. It seems probable that both *rujûm* belong to the same site" (1939: 97).

The site is marked by rocky rubble on a slight rise surrounded by cultivated fields. We were unable to trace wall lines, but occasional large stone blocks suggest past building activity. There is a cleared depression at the top of the rise with a threshing floor and cistern still in use. On the south side of the site is another possibly collapsed cistern.

Site 414 - **Rujm Eshqāḥ**
(Map section 13; field no. 2094)
PG: 16.5/50.5; UTMG: 57.7/37.8

Building ruin ca. 2.5 km south of el-Mazar and slightly more than 1 km ESE of Rujm Um ᶜAlanda. At the 1272 m elevation marker on the K737 map. 40 sherds were collected, including: LB 4; Nab 1; UD 30.

Probably this is Musil's ruğm Eškaḥ (360) and Glueck's Rujm Eshqâḥ/#77 (1939: 97-98), the name preserved in that of Wadi el-Ashqaḥ (see K737 map). According to Glueck, "N.w. of Dhât Râs and s.e. of Rujm ᶜAlendā is Rujm Eshqâḥ, a destroyed building, only the line of the w. wall of which is somewhat intact. It is oriented n.-s., measures about 16.40 by 12.50 m, and contains a number of inner room divisions. It is built of roughly hewn flint blocks. Fragments of garden walls are to be seen arround it. Quantities of Nabataean and Roman sherds were found."

This is a small ruin with several wall lines visible and a light sherd scatter. The walls which can be traced suggest a rectangular building which would have measured ca. 13

m (N-S) by more than 23 m (E-W). The building had multiple rooms, and there is a well ca. 25 m from it.

Site 415 - **Rujm el-Awsaj**
(Map section 13; field no. 2425)
PG: 16.6/50.4; UTMG: 57.5/37.8

Stone heaps and rubble ca. 200 m west of site 414. 310 sherds were collected, including: LB 9; IR I 1; Nab 7; LIsl 4; UDE 1; UDEhandle 1; UD 2; UDhandle 6.

Stone heaps and rubble, much of which probably resulted from modern field clearing, cover an area ca. 80 x 70 m on a low rise surrounded by gently rolling agricultural plains. The site includes several threshing floors, at least three cisterns, and occasionally discernible wall lines. At the east end of the site are the foundation remains of a 13 x 20 m building, filled with stone rubble. The outline of another building, ca. 3 x 3 m, is visible at the west end of the site.

Site 416 - **Dleiqa/el-Umariyyah**
(Map section 13; field no. 2324)
PG: 19.1/49.5; UTMG: 60.1/36.9

Modern village on an ancient settlement site ca. 4.5 km southeast of el-Mazar. Marked Duleiqa on the K737 map; now called el-Umariyyah. 391 sherds were collected, including: LB 1; IR II 1; Nab 6; ERom 1; LRom 4; EByz 1; LByz 3; Fat(?) 1; A/M 8; LIsl 42; Mod 1; UDE 4; UD 7; UDhandle 5.

See Musil: ḫirbet Dlêḳa (78, 360).

The modern village is situated on a natural rise which is surrounded by rolling plains and hills. Several of the older "Ottoman style" houses have reused stones in their walls. Otherwise, earlier phases of settlement at the site are indicated only by surface pottery.

Site 417 - **Rujm eṣ-Ṣakharī/el-Ḥseiniyyah**
(Map section 13; field no. 2326)
PG: 19.1/48.6; UTMG: 60.1/36.0

Modern village on an ancient settlement site, ca. 5 km southeast of el-Mazar. Marked El Huseiniya on the K737 map. 605 sherds were collected, including: Hell 1; Nab 28; ERom 1; Byz 2; EByz 2; LByz 2; A/M 2; Mod 6; UD 3; UDhandle 9.

El-Ḥuseiniyyah is a recent name, replacing Rujm Ṣakhri; compare the 1:25,000 Hashimite Kingdom of Jordan map (sheet 210/045). See also Musil: ruǧm eṣ-Ṣaḫari (360). Canova (1954: 328-29) reported a lintel with a fragmented Greek inscription and an inscribed tombstone that dates to 606.

Earlier phases of occupation at the site are indicated by surface pottery and reused stones in some of the older houses of the village. For example, a fragment of a stone which exhibited a defaced Greek inscription has been reused for a lintel.

Site 418 - **Um Zabāyir**
(Map section 13; field no. 2363)
PG: 20.3/48.8; UTMG: 61.3/36.4

Modern village on an ancient settlement site, ca. 5.5 km southeast of el-Mazar. Marked Um Zabāyir on the K737 map. 757 sherds were collected, including: Hell 1; Nab 16; ERom 1; Byz 1; EByz 1; LByz 2; Um 1; A/M 7; LIsl 86; UD 6; UDhandle 9.

Mauss and Sauvaire refer to Ardh Omm Essabaïr (487), but none of the early explorers mentioned a ruin at this spot. Only the surface pottery collected among the modern dwellings indicates earlier phases of settlement. These dwellings include the remains of some early "Ottoman style" houses.

Site 419 - **Um Ḥamāṭ**
(Map section 13; field no. 2323)
PG: 22.8/49.8; UTMG: 63.8/37.3

Modern village on an ancient settlement site, ca. 7 km ESE of el-Mazar and 4 km southeast of Sul. Marked Umm Ḥamāt on the K737 map. 1571 sherds were collected, including: MB 7; LB 8; IR 7; IR I 5; IR II 37; IR II C/Pers 8; Hell 15; Nab 28; ERom 15; LRom 5; EByz 1; LByz 10; A/M 7; LIsl 31; Mod 3; UDE 8; UDEhandle 21; UD 27; UDhandle 57; and 13 tesserae.

Tristram: Hamad (120); Brünnow and Domaszewski: Umm el-Ḥammâr (I: 60, 78); Musil: ḫirbet umm Ḥamât (6, 80, 322-24). Musil described Um Ḥamaṭ as a rectangular, fortified camp, probably Roman, situated on the east end of an east-west groundswell. Its walls, which he measured to be 50 steps north-south by 100 steps east-west, were very strong. Musil observed a square structure in the northwest part of the ruin which, on the basis of its construction and design, he believed could be assigned to very high antiquity when it possibly served some cultic function. Not much could be made of the remaining buildings of the ruin because their stones had been reused for sheepfolds which covered the site. Tobacco had been planted in the open areas and straw had been stored in the cisterns. Canova (1954: 322-24) reported the remains of the presbytery area of a church with an apse, a nearby circular structure with a stone pavement, and an inscribed tombstone dating to 620.

All traces of the ruin which Musil described have been obliterated by the modern settlement except for the remains of one ancient structure near the center of the village. This building was constructed from worked limestone blocks filled out with smaller chert stones, measures 25 x 30 m at the base, and is preserved up to 5 courses high in places. It may have been rebuilt at least once and is filled with debris. It is unclear how Musil's possible "cultic" structure, Canova's church, and the building which we observed are related, or if they are related at all.

Site 420 - **Nakhl**
(Map section 13; field no. 2320)
PG: 24.5/52.3; UTMG: 65.4/39.8

Extensive unoccupied ruin, ca. 9 km east of el-Mazar and 3 km northeast of Um Ḥamaṭ. Marked Nakhl on the K737 map (one edition has Nikhil). 2178 sherds were collected, including: EB I 4; EB II-III 1; LB 1; IR 3; IR II 1; Hell 3; Nab 134; Nab/ERom 2; ERom 23; LRom 23; EByz 24; LByz 21; EIsl 2; Fat(?) 3; A/M 56; LIsl 255; Mod 3; UD 31; UDhandle 124; 9 tesserae; 1 bomb fragment; 2 pipe fragments.

See Seetzen: Náhhel (416); Irby and Mangles: Nehkill (113); Tristram: Nachal (120); Doughty: Nikkel (20); Brünnow and Domaszewski: Niḫel/Niḫḫel (I: 61, 78); Musil: ḫirbet Naḫl (6, 19, 20, 80, 324, 367); Glueck: Nakhl/#147 (1934: 65-66, 69, 81). Brünnow and Domaszewski observed Nakhl from a distance and mentioned standing columns. Musil, who reported it as one of the most extensive ruins in the area, provided the first description (324). According to him, the ruin covered a flat, semicircular groundswell open to the west. The actual city was situated on the northern part of the groundswell; the city fortification and temple were on the eastern part; and the southern part was covered with extensive foundation walls constructed with ashlar masonry and giving the impression that none of the structures had been completed. Musil was especially impressed with the masonry of some of the walls in the fortification/temple area. These were constructed from well-dressed limestone blocks, without mortar and so well fitted that he compared them to the Egyptian pyramids. In the depression on the west side of the groundswell Musil observed cross walls which provided water reservoirs and numerous cisterns. Glueck also was impressed with the numerous cisterns and walls, compared the ruin to those of el-Mreigha and Um er-Raṣaṣ, and, correctly no doubt, associated the most important phase of the city with the Nabataean period. "The walls of the city, which are most nearly intact on the western and southern sides, are similar to the walls of el-Moreighah and of Umm er-Raṣâṣ. Intermittent towers, or buttresses, built of large, roughly dressed, rectangular limestone blocks, flank the walls. To judge from the large quantities of Nabataean sherds of all kinds found all over the site, the origin of Nakhl was Nabataean. Numerous pieces of sigillata ware were found, similar to those found on other sites with Nabataean sherds. ... The site of Nakhl was extensively built on, certainly from Nabataean-Roman times on. ... In addition to the Nabataean and numerous Roman sherds, large quantities of Byzantine and mediaeval Arabic sherds were found. At the northeastern end of the site is a large building made of excellently cut limestone blocks, similar in the style of its construction to the temple at Qaṣr Rabbah. Inside of this building, which is probably of Nabataean or perhaps Roman origin, a church was built. The apse of the church, facing due east, is clearly visible. On the western side of this building is a large dump-heap, containing Nabataean and mediaeval Arabic sherds" (66). Canova (1954: 325-27) described the church also, giving as its measurements: 18.5 x 14 m.

Nakhl remains very much as Musil and Glueck described it, and in urgent need of more detailed examination. The Nabataean temple, for example, is still

Photograph 43: Nakhl temple (Site 420)

Photograph 44: Nakhl building ruin

clearly discernible at the highest point of the ruin near the northeast corner. Nearby is the large Nabataean/Roman building with a Byzantine church inside.

Site 421 - **Rujm el-Mismar**
(Map section 13; field no. 2433)
PG: 26.8/47.9; UTMG: 67.8/35.5

Building ruin ca. 4 km ESE of Um Ḥamaṭ and immediately south of the road from Um Hamat to Mḥai. 125 sherds were collected, including: LB 2; Nab 3; LIsl 2; UDE 1; UDEhandle 2; UD 1; UDhandle 3.

Situated in a flat area with low rolling hills rising to the south are the foundation remains of a two-room structure. The larger room, oriented north-south, measures 18 x 14 m. The second room, which shares the northernmost 8 m of the western wall of the large room, measures 8 x 6 m. Built of rough limestone and basalt blocks, the walls remain standing 2 courses high in some places. The room interiors contain tumbled blocks.

Site 422
(Map section 13; field no. 2427)
PG: 18.5/45.8; UTMG: 59.6/33.3

Partitioned cairn on the ridge north of Akuzeh, ca. 1 km southeast of el-Hashimiyyah (Kh. ed-Dweikhleh, Site 426).

Site 423 - **Majra**
(Map section 13; field no. 2053)
PG: 15.1/48.3; UTMG: 56.1/35.6

Modern village on an ancient settlement site situated ca. 4.5 km SSW of el-Mazar, on the north rim of Wadi el-Ḥesa. Marked Majrā on the K737 map. 1349 sherds were collected, including: EB 3; IR I 3; Hell 1; Nab 25; Byz 8; Fat(?) 5; A/M 13; LIsl 142; Mod 1; UDE 10; UD 6; UDhandle 18; 1 Ott pipe fragment.

See Musil: ḫirbet Meğra (360); and Glueck: Mejrā/#85 (1939: 80-81, 97). According to Glueck, "Several kilometres to the n.w. [of Juweir] is the small inhabited village of Mejrā, likewise built over Nabataean-Roman and Byzantine ruins, with sherds from these periods. In various places in the village are several stones with Byzantine crosses on them, some of them with faint Greek characters. Several of them seem to be head-stones from graves, and one of them seems to end with the name ANTONINOY. On the s. side of the village is one fairly intact Roman building" (80). Canova (1954: 409-15) reported a mausolem and two probable churches built over by modern houses, along with four inscribed tombstones.

Contrary to Glueck, Majra is situated no more than one km WNW of Juweir. Early phases of settlement at the site are represented by surface pottery, remnants of earlier buildings under modern houses (such as described by Canova) and the visible ruin of one pre-modern building. The latter probably is the "fairly intact Roman building" to which Glueck referred. It is oriented roughly north-south, measures 9 x 9 m, and is bisected by a north-south wall. A doorway near the south end of the bisecting wall, with lintel still in place, connects the east and west rooms. Possibly another east-west interior wall bisected the west room. The east exterior wall of the building is constructed with well-worked stones preserved up to 3 m high in places. An entrance through this wall, near the southeast corner of the building, is filled with debris. Both the west exterior wall and the north-south interior wall have been rebuilt at some point with smaller stones.

Site 424 - **Jweir**
(Map section 13; field no. 2054)
PG: 15.9/48.1; UTMG: 56.9/35.5

Modern village on an ancient settlement site ca. 4.5 km south of el-Mazar, on the rim of Wadi el-Ḥesa. Marked Juweir on the K737 map. 965 sherds were collected, including: EB IVB(?) 1; MB 1; LB 3; Hell 2; Nab 139; ERom 1; LRom 4; Byz 2; EByz 2; LByz 1; LIsl 3; UDE 5; UD 1; UDhandle 54.

See Glueck: Juweir/#81 (1939: 80), which he described as a "small inhabited village ... built over Nabataean-Roman and Byzantine ruins." Canova (1954: 407-8) reported the remains of a small fort, some houses, and one inscribed tombstone dating to 536-537.

Present-day dwellings cover only a portion of the ruin area, which itself extends some 150 x 200 m and is composed of building ruins, scattered wall lines, and stone rubble. Part of the ruin, south of the modern paved road which runs east-west through the village, has been enclosed with a barbed-wire fence. The best preserved building ruin is situated north of this paved road, is oriented roughly north-south, measures 9 x 9 m, and has exterior walls ca. 1 m thick. Interior walls separate three chambers: a large one which corresponds to roughly the western half of the building and two smaller ones (5 x 5 m and 5 x 4 m respectively) which account for the eastern half. All three rooms are filled with tumbled stones. An entrance to the building on its south side still has the lintel in place.

Site 425
(Map section 13; field no. 2426)
PG: 16.2/48.0; UTMG: 57.2/35.3

Unoccupied settlement site on the northern rim of Wadi el-Ḥesa, less than 0.5 km ESE of Juweir and 4.75 km south of el-Mazar. 610 sherds were collected, including: LB 1; Nab 78; LIsl 3; UDEhandle 3; UD 5; UDhandle 15.

Ruins consisting of numerous wall lines with visible corners cover an area ca. 70 x 80 m. Several individual structures are discernible. Also there are several caves, and on the east side of the ruin are two possible terrace walls (running north-south).

Site 426 - **el-Hāshimiyyah/Kh. ed-Dweikhleh**
(Map section 13; field no. 2059)
PG: 18.0/46.7; UTMG: 59.1/34.1

Modern village on an ancient settlement site, ca. 6 km SSE of el-Mazar on the north rim of Wadi el-Ḥesa. Earlier Kh. ed-Dweikhleh, now el-Hashimiyyah; marked El Hāshimiya el Janūbiya on the K737 map. 963 sherds were collected, including: EB 1; IR 2; IR II 4; Hell 1; Nab 101; ERom 6; LRom 6; Byz 8; LByz 16; LIsl 59; Mod 2; UD 10; UDhandle 69.

See Musil: ḫirbet ed-Dwêḫle (360); and Glueck: ed-Deweikhleh/#79 (1939: 80). Glueck described ed-Deweikhleh as "a small modern village ... built over the ruins of previous Nabataean-Roman and Byzantine settlements." He reported sherds from these three periods "in addition to some building blocks of these periods found inserted into modern walls. Over the doorway of one of the houses in the village is a lintel with a Byzantine cross on it." Canova (1954: 404-6) reported various architectural fragments, including the lintel with cross mentioned by Glueck, and three tombstones.

The modern village has almost completely obliterated all traces of earlier settlement phases at this site. There are some old cisterns, one of which has stairs leading to it and possibly occupational debris inside. An early wall line is visible, built of monumental blocks and serving now as the foundation of a modern wall. As Glueck observed, some of the modern dwellings include reused stones. We were shown a stone lintel with what may be a tree carved on it, but the stone is so badly weathered that one cannot be certain.

Site 427 - **Dhāt Rās/el-Ghuweir**
(Map section 13; field no. 2327)
PG: 22.8/46.0; UTMG: 63.8/33.6

Modern village on an ancient settlement site ca. 4 km east of the Kerak-Ṭafileh road and ca. 2 km from the southern rim of the plateau. Marked Al Ghuwayr or Dhat Rās on different editions of the K737 map. 1919 sherds were collected, including: EB II-III 4; EB IVA 2; LB 2; IR I 1; IR II 4; Hell 9; Nab 54; ERom 12; LRom 1; Byz 16; EByz 32; LByz 52; EIsl 1; Um 3; Fat(?) 6; A/M 501; LIsl 194; Ott 12; Mod 29; UDE 2; UD 67; UDhandle 111; 1 pipe fragment; 4 tesserae.

See Seetzen: Dâd Râs (416); Burckhardt: Datras (389); Irby and Mangles: Dettrass (113); Mauss and Sauvaire: Kharbet zat-Rass (487, 514-17); Tristram: Dadras (120); Doughty: Dat Ras (21); Hornstein: Datras (102-3); Germer-Durand: Zat Rass (574); Vincent: Dāt-Râs ("Notes de voyage": 438); Wilson: Datras (310, 315); Vailhé: Dhâs-Ras (110); Brünnow and Domaszewski: D̠ât Râs (I: 10, 60-69, 75, 78, 80); Musil: D̠ât Râs (20-21, 76, 79, 322-23, 361); Glueck: Dhât Râs/#76 (1939: 48, 50, 63-67, 70, 80, 97). Irby and Mangles provided the earliest description, which does such injustice to the site that one questions whether they actually explored the ruin or only observed it from a distance: "At the foot of the hill are many cisterns; the ruins are indistinct and of no interest, except three piles of buildings, which appear to be Roman architecture; one was evidently a temple; the others, though large, are so much ruined that it is impossible to ascertain what they had originally been." The description of Mauss and Sauvaire is more in keeping with what later travelers would observe. Having reached Dhat Ras by following an ancient Roman road with a small wall along each side, they observed the ruins of two temples—a large one with propylaea and a smaller, better preserved one (487). Doughty, Hornstein, Brünnow and Domaszewski, Musil, and Glueck provided additional descriptions; Brünnow and Domaszewski included plans of the small temple and photographs of the site; Musil and Glueck provided additional photographs. Vailhé reported a church, capitals and mosaic fragments. From these early descriptions, Dhat Ras emerges as a massive ruin from primarily the Nabataean-Roman-Byzantine era dominated by three temples. Resettlement at the site, which involved reusing the stones from the ancient ruins, had begun by the turn of the century and was observed by Musil. Three decades later, Glueck observed that "The small temple at the s.e. side of Dhât Râs is fairly well preserved, but the other temples have been almost completely destroyed by constant quarrying operations going on among their ruins for stones to build the miserable houses that characterize the small modern village on the site, and the neighboring villages. ... Numerous rock-cut, pear-shaped cisterns, many of them on the n.w. slope of Dhât Râs, provided water for the site. Large numbers of Nabataean sherds were found, which must represent the Roman as well as the Nabataean periods. There were also Byzantine sherds, testifying to the occupation of Dhât Râs in that period. Savignac [1936: 250] reports the presence of two enormous Byzantine capitals which give the appearance of having originated from a monumental church. They were found in the two eastern-most houses of the village of Dhât Râs." Canova (1954: 330-40) reported various architectural fragments from the Byzantine period, as well as eight in scribed tombstones.

Germer-Durand (574) proposed Dhat Ras as the site of ancient Tharais which appears on the Madaba Mosaic, and this identification has been widely, although not unanimously, accepted (see, e.g., M. Avi-Yonah 1954: 41). Al-Ghuwayr (el-Ghuweir), as the place is called on a recent edition of the the K737 map, apparently is a newly emerging name for the modern village. Possibly this new name corresponds to that of a nearby wadi which Mauss and Sauvaire (514) recorded as "Wâdy-Guerahy." See the discussion of site 313 which is also named Ghuweir but identified as Dhāt Rās on one edition of the K737 map.

The modern settlement continues to expand and now covers the whole area of the ruins which were visible to nineteenth century travelers. Some remains of all three temples still survive, however, and the small temple is protected by a strong wire fence. Numerous cisterns honeycomb the site. F. Zayadine (1970: 117-35) excavated a first century C.E. tomb approximately midway between Dhāt Rās and Shqeirah (Site 434) in 1968.

Site 428 - **Kh. el-ᶜAkūzeh**
(Map section 13; field no. 2331)
PG: 18.6/45.2; UTMG: 59.6/32.6

Small khirbeh, the ruin of an ancient fort, on the southern rim of the plateau at the point where the modern Kerak-Tafileh road begins its descent into Wadi el-Ḥesa. 158 sherds were collected, including: LB 3; IR II 85; LIsl 1; UD 8.

Irby and Mangles: Acoujah (114); Brünnow and Domaszewski: el-ᶜAkûze/el-ᶜAcᶜuze (I: 106); Glueck: Kh. el-ᶜAkûzeh/#78 (1939: 61-62, 84, 90). Irby and Mangles passed Kh. el-ᶜAkuzeh as they proceeded from Dhat Ras and descended into Wadi el-Ḥesa: "We recovered the track which we had quitted, where it falls into a deep ravine, which has steep, rocky sides. At the extremity, where we turned out of this track to follow a more rapid descent into the Wady-el-Ahsa, we saw upon our left hand, on the height, the remains of an ancient fortress, which seems to have commanded the pass. It is of dry masonry and large stones, and is no doubt antique. They give it the name of Acoujah." By the time Glueck explored this region over a hundred years later than Irby and Mangles, a modern road had been built which passed east of the track which they followed and thus bypassed Kh. el-ᶜAkuzeh. Glueck explored the site rather thoroughly, however, and interpreted ᶜAkūzeh as one in a string of forts which protected ancient Moab's southern boundary: "The zigzag line of the new automobile road leads up the steep slope of the Neqb el-Quṣûbah on the n. side of the Wâdī el-Ḥesā in an e.n.e. direction. The footpath, however, which follows the line of the ancient highway, ascends to the w.n.w. at a considerably steeper angle than the automobile road. The path climbs the

Photograph 45: Kh. el-ʿAkūzeh (Site 428)

Photograph 46: Kh. el-ʿAkūzeh wall

Neqb el-ᶜAkûzeh to a point near the top of the slope, where an almost completely isolated outspur juts out from the ridge leading to the very top of the plateau. Stretched across the route of the path, which perforce must go around it, this outspur which is oriented e.-w. and averages about 15 m. in thickness could not have better served the needs and purposes of a fortress if it had been purposely built. And indeed a very strong fortress was found to have been built on top of it, which to judge from the almost exclusively EI I-II Moabite sherds of all kinds which were found on and around it, must have been one of the line of fortresses which guarded the s. boundary of Moab. It is called Kh. el-ᶜAkûzeh, and strongly dominates the entire steep descent of the Neqb el-ᶜAkûzeh down to the Wâdī el-Ḥesā below. ... The entire long area of Kh. el-ᶜAkûzeh is walled, the narrow outspur on which it is built being practically inaccessible except on the e. side. There it is connected with the continuation of the ridge of the rest of the slope which rises very steeply to the tip of the plateau about twenty minutes climb above it. On this e. side, however, the Moabite engineers cut a deep and wide moat, thus completely isolating the spur on which the fortress is built. A ruined watchtower stands over the moat at the e. end of the fortress, guarding the ruins of the gateway, with its winding entrance, at the n.e. corner. The tower is oriented n.-s., and measures about 13 by 10 m. The s. wall of the fortified top of the hill measures about 225 m., while the n. wall which bends at its e. end to allow for the entrance way and natural contours of the hill measures about 240 m. About 55 m. from the e. end of the site, abutting against the n. wall is another ruined tower measuring about 10 m. square. There are traces of ruins of another tower at the w. end of the hill, which narrows from an average width of about 15 m. to less than 12 m. at this point. Between the towers were considerable open spaces, with traces of walls of a few houses. ... The narrow top and steep sides of the fortress made the finding of an adequate collection of sherds difficult, because the rains during the course of the centuries which had elapsed since the site was abandoned had washed most of them away. It was nevertheless possible, as already noted, to find representative sherds of all types belonging clearly to Moabite pottery of the Early Iron Age. In addition a small number of Nabataean sherds was found, indicative of the fact there may have been a small Nabataean settlement there at one time. ... We chanced upon an Umayyad coin of the 8th century A.D., which some wayfarer had dropped perhaps while resting at Kh. el-ᶜAkûzeh. There were no sherds or anything else at Kh. el-ᶜAkûzeh to indicate the presence of even a squatter's settlement there in the 8th century A.D." (61-62).

A new paved road has been built since Glueck's day which follows essentially the route of the old Kh. el-ᶜAkuzeh track. Specifically, as the current Kerak-Ṭafileh road begins its descent from the plateau into Wadi el-Ḥesa, it makes a hairpin curve around the northern, eastern, and southern sides of the ridge on which Kh. el-ᶜAkuzeh is situated. The moat which marks the east end of the site is clearly visible from the road, as well as a small section of wall at the northeast corner of the fort. Although ancient wall lines also are visible elsewhere on the site, including other segments of the defensive wall along the edge of the ridge, the clearly defined surface ruins which Glueck described have largely disappeared. Note also that our reading of the surface pottery associates ᶜAkuzeh with Iron II, whereas Glueck interpreted it as one of a string of forts which supposedly protected Moab during Iron I.

Site 429
(Map section 13; field no. 2402)
PG: 19.2/46.0; UTMG: 60.4/33.4

Stone heap overlooking Wadi el-Ḥesa and one of its tributaries, immediately east of the main Kerak-Ṭafileh highway, ca. 1 km northeast of Kh. el-Akuzeh (Site 428) and 3.5 km west of Dhat Ras/Ghuweir (Site 427). 468 sherds were collected, including: EB II-III 14; MB 19; MB/LB 2; Nab 2; LOtt 2; UDE 20; UD 3.

This is an amorphous heap of large and small stones located on high ground. At its summit is a smaller, circular pile of stones, probably a bedouin marker. There was a fairly heavy concentration of sherds around the heap, and several large blocks north of it may indicate wall lines.

Site 430 - **Rujm ᶜAbdeh**
(Map section 13; field no. 2404)
PG: 19.7/45.3; UTMG: 60.7/32.7

Small khirbeh near the southern rim of the plateau and immediately east of the Kerak-Ṭafileh road. Near the

1165 m elevation marker on the K737 map. 491 sherds were collected, including: Nab 6; Byz 1; LByz 2; A/M 5; LIsl 115; UD 5; UDhandle 6; 1 tessera.

See the references cited for Kfeir/Kh. el-ᶜAbdeh (Site 431). These two sites are very close together, and the travelers prior to Glueck either made no distinction between them or, more likely, were unaware that two sites were involved. Having described Kh. ᶜAbdeh, Glueck continued: "Several hundred metres to the n.n.e. is another much ruined site, really a part of the main site, being also called Kh. el-ᶜAbdeh, the same types of sherds being found there, with the addition of some fairly modern Arabic sherds" (1939: 80).

Building rubble, including a few discernible wall lines, and surface pottery cover an area ca. 80 x 60 m. There are at least five cisterns cut in the bedrock, one of which has a circular depression (12 cm diameter, 20 cm deep), presumably a watering trough, carved near its opening.

Site 431 - **Kfeir/Kh. el-ᶜAbdeh**
(Map section 13; field no. 2403)
PG: 19.3/45.2; UTMG: 60.4/32.6

Small khirbeh on the southern rim of the plateau, immediately east of the hairpin curve in the Kerak-Ṭafileh road (around Kh. el-ᶜAkuzeh) which begins its descent into Wadi el-Ḥesa. 980 sherds were collected, including: LB 8; IR 3; Hell 3; Nab 54; ERom 8; LRom 4; Byz 7; EByz 3; LByz 14; Fat(?) 1; A/M 4; LIsl 44; UDE 1; UD 18; UDhandle 37; 1 pipe fragment; 1 tessera.

See Brünnow and Domaszewski: Ḫirbet el-ᶜAbde (I: 10, 106); Musil: ḫirbet ᶜAbde (78, 361); Glueck: Kh. ᶜAbdeh/#99 (1939: 80). According to Glueck, "About 7.5 km. n.w. of Dhât Râs [actually less than 4 km WSW of Dhat Ras] is Kh. el-ᶜAbdeh, situated in a fertile, agricultural area, not far from the s. edge of the Moabite plateau. It is a rather large, completely destroyed Nabataean-Roman site, with only house and wall-foundations visible. A considerable number of Nabataean sherds of all kinds was found, including sigillata fragments of the 'Pergamene' type, and fine sherds with bands of polishing similar to fragments found for instance at Aila, which may extend down into the Byzantine period. There were also some early Byzantine sherds."

Numerous wall lines indicating both square and rectangular buildings cover an area ca. 75 x 100 m. Most of the walls were constructed with double faces—two rows of large blocks with smaller stones and fill between. Some of the walls are more than 1 m thick, and one survives 4 courses high. At least 12 cisterns have been cut into the limestone at the south edge of the site, overlooking Wadi el-Ḥesa. Cut in the bedrock near the opening of one of these cisterns is a circular depression ca. 15 cm in diameter and 25 cm deep.

Site 432 - **Kh. el-Quṣūbah**
(Map section 13; field no. 2332)
PG: 24.6/43.5; UTMG: 65.7/31.0

Small khirbeh on the south rim of the plateau, ca. 3 km southeast of Dhat Ras/Ghuweir and on the southwest side of the road from Dhat Ras to ᶜAina. 344 sherds were collected, including: EByz 4; Um 4; Fat(?) 15; A/M 9; LIsl 13; LOtt 1; Mod 4; UD 6; 261 tesserae.

Although it cannot be determined with certainty that this is Musil's ḫ. al-Ḳṣuba (see discussion of site 433), it is undoubtedly Glueck's Kh. el-Quṣûbah (1934: 63, 79-80). "A short distance removed from Kh. esh-Sheqeirah is Kh. el-Quṣûbah on the w. side of the road. Kh. el-Quṣûbah is also built on a rise, and evidently consists of a completely filled-in and covered-over *khân*, of rectangular shape. Between it and the road are the remains of a large *birkeh*, in which at one time a considerable amount of water must have been stored, and which apparently without considerable effort could again be restored to its original use. A small number of Nabataean-Roman and Byzantine sherds was found, including a small terracotta bull's head, which, according to Prof. C. S. Fisher, is similar to those found in a cave near Jerash... The bull's head may be late Roman in type, or Byzantine" (63).

A modern settlement is emerging on the north side of the ruin. The ruin itself has been partially cleared by the Department of Antiquities and consists of largely nondescript rubble, occasional wall lines of roughly shaped limestone blocks, and surface pottery. The most distinctive feature is what appears to have been a large rectangular building constructed from finely dressed limestone blocks, presumably the *khan* which Glueck mentioned. The best preserved section of its wall is 7.80

m long and 1.2 m high. Many of the tesserae were collected in the building area—i.e., in the north part of the ruin. On the south side of the ruin were observed two capitals and fragments of a column and column base. The *birkeh* observed by Glueck is east of the ruin and there is a cistern nearby. Two more cisterns were observed on the west side of the ruin. Similar ruins also cover the next hilltop to the east, thus raising the possibility that this site may be Musil's "das doppelte ḫ. eš-Šḳêra" (see discussion of site 433).

Site 433 - **Kh. esh-Shqeirah**
(Map section 13; field no. 2362)
PG: 25.0/43.4; UTMG: 66.1/30.9

Recent settlement on an ancient site, situated on the southern rim of the plateau ca. 3 km southeast of Dhat Ras and immediately east of the secondary road from Dhat Ras to ᶜAina. 866 sherds were collected, including: MB 18; LB 4; IR 1; IR I 2; Nab 96; ERom 16; LRom 10; Byz 9; EByz 10; LByz 14; LIsl 14; Mod 1; UD 6; UDhandle 12; 1 tessera.

See Mauss and Sauvaire: Choqeyra (488); Musil: ḫ. eš-Šḳêra (80, 321); Glueck: Kh. esh-Sheqeirah/#74 (1939: 63, 66, 79). Glueck described the site as follows: "At the very top of the s. end of the Moabite plateau, on the e. side of the modern road at the point where it begins the descent down the Neqb el-Quṣûbah to ᶜAineh and the Wâdī el-Ḥesā, is Kh. esh-Sheqeirah. It is a small, completely destroyed Nabataean site, built on a low rise, and marked by several cave-cisterns, which are extensively employed in Nabataean settlements. There is a modern house standing among the ruins, half of which is built of large flint blocks taken from walls of the Nabataean buildings. Numerous Nabataean sherds of all kinds were found." The modern road to which Glueck refers would have been what is now the secondary road from Dhat Ras to ᶜAina; the corresponding section of the current Kerak-Ṭafileh road had not yet been built. Since this site and site 432 clearly are to be equated with Glueck's Kh. esh-Sheqeirah/#74 and Kh. el-Quṣûbah/#75 (1939: 63, 79-80) respectively, it is tempting to equate them with Musil's ḫ. aš-Šḳêra and ḫ. al-Ḳṣuba, which he mentions together on two different occasions (80, 321). On both occasions, however, Musil refers to ḫ. eš-Šḳêra as a double site, "das doppelte ḫ. eš-Šḳêra," which suggests two ruins near to each other. This raises two possibilities: (1) that sites 432 and 433 were Musil's double ḫ. eš-Šḳêra and that his ḫ. al-Ḳṣuba was some other ruin in the vicinity of Neqb el-Quṣūbah; (2) That Musil's ḫ. aš-Šḳêra and ḫ. al-Ḳṣuba were sites 432 and 433 in reverse order—note that site 432 has ruins on two adjacent hills. Both names, Sheqeirah and Quṣubah, are appellatives derived from local topographical features, which means that they may have been applied to any site in the vicinity.

The ruins are situated on a natural rise, cover an area ca. 125 x 125 m, and consist of largely nondescript stone rubble. The only wall lines clearly discernible are those of a 9 x 9 m structure with a cistern nearby in the northwest quadrant of the ruin. No doubt this is the "modern house" which Glueck reported and which has since been abandoned. A recent cemetery which covers a portion of the site apparently also has emerged since Glueck's visit. We counted four cisterns among the ruins in addition to the one mentioned above, including a large cave cistern on the west side of the ruin. At the time of our visit, the modern settlement consisted of two houses on the southwest side and a few more houses on the east side.

Site 434 - **Shqeirah**
(Map section 13; field no. 2424)
PG: 26.3/43.2; UTMG: 67.4/30.8

Modern village on an ancient settlement site, located on the southern rim of the plateau ca. 4 km southeast of Dhat Ras. Marked Shuqeirā on K737 map. 232 sherds were collected, including: Nab 23; LRom 1; LByz 1; A/M 8; LIsl 48; UDEhandle 3; UD 3; UDhandle 11.

Although this modern village apparently has taken the name Sheqeirah, as indicated on the K737 map, Glueck's esh-Sheqeirah/#74 (1934: 62-63) clearly is to be identified with site 432. The latter would have been along the ancient track described by Glueck which ascends from ᶜAina to Dhat Ras (east of the present-day Kerak-Ṭafileh road and marked as a secondary road on the K737 map). Probably Mauss and Sauvaire followed this track, which means that their "Choqeyra" (488) would also have been along that trail. For the problem of locating Musil's "das doppelte ḫ. eš-Šḳêra" (80, 321), see the discussion under site 433.

The antiquity of the site is indicated by surface sherds scattered on the slopes around the modern village and especially in the area of the village dump.

Site 435 - **Mḍeibi^c^**
(Map section 14; field no. 2322)
PG: 30.6/50.3; UTMG: 71.6/38.0

Fortification ca. 8 km east of Um Ḥamaṭ. Marked Khirbat Mudaybī/Khirbet Mudiebi on the K737 map. 586 sherds were collected, including: EB 1; LB 1; IR 12; IR II 3; Hell 1; Nab 4; Nab/ERom 10; LRom 4; Byz 13; EByz 7; LByz 3; A/M 13; LIsl 97; Mod 1; UD 416.

See Doughty: Medeybîa (20); Brünnow and Domaszewski: el-Medaibîye (I: 76); Musil: ḫirbet Mḍejbi^c^ (80-81, 367); Glueck: Meḍeibî^c^/#45 in 1934 (67-69), #132 in 1939 (69-73, 76). Doughty described it as a "smaller ruined town, the building and the walls of wild massy blocks of lava." Musil reported it as a fortified camp excellently situated to control the surrounding vicinity. "Two gates, in the east and west walls, led to an open space in the interior, around which small rooms were grouped against the surrounding wall." Glueck, also impressed with the strategic position of Mḍeibi^c^, provided a fuller description with photographs and interpreted it as an Iron Age (Moabite) fort which was reused by the Nabataeans. "It is a large, square, walled enclosure on the top of a small knoll. The walls were made of roughly dressed basalt blocks, taken from the adjacent hill-sides. They seem to belong to the Early Iron Age and are similar in construction to the walls of fortress I at Za^c^ferân [see 1934: 30-31] and to the original walls at Qaṣr Bālû^c^ah [our Site 35]. There are two entrances, one each on the eastern and western sides, flanked by two rectangular towers. The gates were constructed of huge limestone blocks. Several large limestone blocks lie outside of the eastern gate, and others are still in position there and also in the western gate. Four square corner towers, a rectangular tower in the center of the north wall, and another in the center of the south wall make up the complete fortification. The towers are constructed with alternating headers and stretchers, as are the intact corners of Qaṣr Bālû^c^ah and the Israelite walls at Samaria and Megiddo. Parts of the walls were evidently rebuilt after having been breached. Thus definite parts of the west wall, for instance, were rebuilt, probably also in the Iron Age, with large, undressed basalt blocks. The spaces between them were filled with smaller stones. ... The relationship of the Iron Age fortresses in Moab with those in Palestine is further attested by a large, proto-Ionic pilaster capital, made of a large limestone block, which we found inside the eastern entrance at Meḍeibî. It measures 1.90 by .87 by .50 metres. ... The entire site was peculiarly destitute of sherds, which might otherwise have been of assistance in determining the date of the Early Iron Age citadel and of the proto-Ionic pilaster capital which belonged to it. ... Beyond the southwest corner of the fortress is a large, cemented cave-cistern, near the mouth of which lies a large limestone pillar which probably belongs to the western gate of the Iron Age fortress. Inside of the walls of the Iron Age fortress is a smaller enclosure, which is probably Nabataean. It is built of smaller stones than the outer enclosure. A few Nabataean sherds were found" (1934: 68-69).

We saw Mḍeibi^c^ essentially as Glueck described it, except that the original plan of the interior has been disturbed by the building of a sheepfold. The overall dimensions of the fort are ca. 65 x 90 m, and its external walls still survive several courses high. The two gates and towers are easily discernible. Also the proto-aeolic capital is still in place just inside the east gate, but having received some Arabic graffiti since Glueck photographed it (1934: 68, fig. 26). Two more carved limestone capitals lie partially buried nearby. There are at least five caves on the eastern slope of the site, all of which may have served as cave-cisterns.

Site 436 - **Mḥai**
(Map section 14; field no. 2328)
PG: 31.9/44.9; UTMG: 73.0/32.6

Modern village on an ancient city ruin, situated on a prominent hill at the southeast corner of the survey area; ca. 10 km ESE of Um Ḥamaṭ. Marked Qaṣr Muḥai on the K737 map. 2274 sherds were collected, including: LB 2; IR 3; IR I 1; IR II 2; Hell 7; Nab 94; ERom 36; LRom 14; EByz 25; LByz 58; Um 9; Fat(?) 12; A/M 20; LIsl 38; Mod 4; UDE 13; UDEhandle 24; UD 41; UDhandle 93; 50 tesserae.

See Seetzen: Em Hey (416); Tristram: Um Hayh (120); Doughty: Mehai (20); Mauss and Sauvaire: Mʾheyij (516-17); Brünnow and Domaszewski: Mḥayy (I: 10, 69-76); Musil: Mḥajj (5-6, 9, 19, 22, 77-78, 80-82, 324, 367); Glueck: Maḥaiy/#69 (1939: 66-70, 72-73, 76, 78, 103). Doughty seems to have been the first of the nineteenth century travelers to visit this impressive ruin: "a little nearer Kerak I visited Mehai, a double rising ground encumbered with wild ruins; there I heard might be seen an effigy, some columns and inscriptions; but of all this I found nothing, and languishing with famine I could not climb on through these fallen desolations of stones. Mehai was a wide uplandish place without any curiosity of building, but all is dry-laid masonry of the undressed limestone and the great tabular flint blocks of these plains." Musil emphasized Mḥai's very favorable strategic location, noting that it is situated on the eastern frontier of the fruitful plain which stretches from Wadi el-Ḥesa northward to the el-Baṭraʾ ridge and northwestward to el-Meiseh (Site 263) and Middin (Site 333). It would have controlled the entrance to this plain from the desert, therefore, and could have protected the numerous watchtowers on the various hills overlooking the plain. Brünnow and Domaszewski provided a full description. Specifically, they reported general city ruins covering the fairly level surface of an essentially north-south oriented hilltop—actually a double hilltop joined by a slight saddle. Estimating the extent of the ruins to be ca. 500 m, they identified three main architectural features: a watchtower (ca. 30 x 21 m) at the highest point near the center of the ruin, a temple (ca. 32 x 16 m) near the northern edge of the ruin, and two connected chambers with vaulted roofs (3.60 m span x 2.30 m height) approximately midway between the watchtower and temple. They provided photographs of all three features and plans of the watchtower and temple. A modern village had begun to emerge among the ruins by the 1930s when Glueck visited Mḥai, but he was able to locate all three items. The temple, he believed, on the basis of its similarity to the el-Qaṣr temple (Site 86), could be attributed to the Nabataean period: "This is further borne out by the fact that by the gate of the temple in Maḥaiy, Brünnow found a sculpture in relief, which to judge from the poor photograph he gives [i.e., Brünnow and Domaszewski, Vol. I: 75, fig. 71], which has evidently been taken upside down, is to be identified with a Helios figure, of the type discovered at Kh. et-Tannûr and not yet published, and at Qaṣr Rabbah. In addition, large numbers of Nabataean sherds of all kinds were found at Maḥaiy testifying to a considerable Nabataean settlement there, which had its own temple. ... In addition to the large quantities of Nabataean-Roman ware mentioned above, which included numerous pieces of creamy-core 'Pergamene' type of sigillata and reddish-core sigillata, there were some sherds which seemed to be early Byzantine in origin. Especially, we were able to record the presence of a number of clear EI I-II Moabite sherds, including both plain and painted varieties. They were found on the s.w. and w. slopes, and also near the s.e. end of the top of the hill." Glueck also reported a "great outer wall surrounding the top of the hill of Maḥaiy," numerous cisterns, and a *birkeh* on the east side of the site. Canova (1954: 341-401) reported two Byzantine cemetaries, one northwest and the other southwest of the village, and sixty-eight inscribed tombstones. Except for one which may date as late as the 8th century, these tombstones date from 505 to 686.

The settlement has continued to expand so that it virtually covered the site when we visited in 1982. Yet we also were able to identify two of the architectural features reported by Brünnow and Domaszewski. At the summit of the hilltop, having been reduced by robbing to a flat platform, the rectangular structure which they interpreted to be a watchtower now supports a modern house. The original structure was of massive block construction, the typical block size being 1.50 x 0.75 x 0.60 m, laid to course as headers and stretchers. A section of battered wall was built against the northwest face. A stone with sculptured relief depicting two gazelles (possibly Byzantine) has been reused in the north facade of the modern building. At a lower level of the hill are foundation remains of a rectangular wall (60 x 55+ m) which enclosed the summit area—presumably the "great outer wall" which Glueck reported. This outer wall was of different masonry than the structure on the summit which it enclosed, and there is some evidence of rectangular subdivisions (small rooms?) built against its inside face. The whole area is so badly eroded and robbed of stones that it was impossible to establish the actual dimensions of the enclosure wall. Approximately 150 m to the northwest, at the crest of the hilltop, are the remains of the temple. Its masonry was of

Photograph 47: Mdeibiᶜ (Site 435)

Photograph 48: Proto-aeolic capital at Mdeibiᶜ

excellent quality, well dressed limestone blocks laid to course (typical size 1.50 x 0.30 to 0.45 m high). Musil observed two building phases for this temple, the latter of which included a rotunda: "...dann überschritten wir einen breiten Wall und stiegen hinauf zu den abgeschrägten Quadermaurern eines Tempels. Auf diesen massiven Unterbau hat man wohl erst in späterer Zeit aus behauenen Steinen einen festen Rundbau aufgesetzt, welcher mit vielen gewölbten Räumlichkeiten versehen war" (82). We also observed what appeared to be secondary wall lines superimposed on the original structure, and belonging to the latter, at the eastern end, what we interpreted to be an apse (Musil's "Rundbau") —i.e., the Nabataean-Roman temple may have been reused as a church during the Byzantine period. The apse is of irregular and roughly laid blocks and only partially visible.

Site 437
(Map section 14; field no. 2431)
PG: 29.6/45.1; UTMG: 70.7/32.7

Partitioned cairn situated on a small knoll overlooking the plain which stretches northwest from Mḥai; ca. 2.5 km WNW of Mḥai and 5.5 km SSW of Mḍeibiᶜ. The cairn measures ca. 5 m in diameter and consists of two concentric circles of large undressed limestone blocks bisected with a north-south crosswall of large slabs. The east side of the cairn is covered with field clearing stones. Immediately northeast of the cairn are the foundation remains of a rectangular structure (ca. 7 x 5 m).

Site 438
(Map section 14; field no. 2432)
PG: 29.3/45.2; UTMG: 70.4/32.8

Stone heap ca. 5.3 km SSW of Mḍeibiᶜ and 2 km west of Mḥai. Two wall lines are visible, a 9 m section running north-south along the west side of the heap, and a 7 m section running east-west along the nouth side of the heap. Near their intersection is a recent burial.

Site 439
(Map section 14; field no. 2429)
PG: 29.7/44.5; UTMG: 70.8/32.1

Two partitioned cairns ca. 3.5 km northeast of Shqeira and 2.5 km WSW of Mḥai. Both are ca. 5 m in diameter and filled with tumble. On a nearby spur is a stone heap.

Site 440
(Map section 14; field no. 2430)
PG: 30.0/44.4; UTMG: 71.1/32.1

Building ruin ca. 2 km WSW of Mḥai and 4 km ENE of Shuqeira. The ruin suggests a rectangular structure (ca. 4 x 4.5 m) with a door in the western wall. A small stone heap inside its walls probably represents a burial.

Site 441 - Qfeiqef
(Map section 14; field no. 2428)
PG: 29.2/44.4; UTMG: 70.3/32.0

Building ruin ca. 3 km WSW of Mḥai. Marked Rujm Qufeiqif on the K737 map; the actual spot indicated by the 1104 m elevation marker. 520 sherds were collected, including: LB 1; IR 2; IR II 1; Nab 38; ERom 1; LRom 1; LByz 5; LIsl 5; LOtt 1; UD 4; UDhandle 3.

See Mauss and Sauvaire: Qofâïqef (488); Brünnow and Domaszewski: el-Ḳufaiḳef (I: 69, 75); Musil: ḫirbet Ḳfejḳef (19, 80, 82); Glueck: Qefeiqf/#73 (1939: 66). Brünnow and Domaszewski referred to it as a watchtower. Glueck described it as a "small, completely ruined, Nabataean-Roman site ... in the midst of which a cadastral survey cairn has been erected. Numerous Nabataean sherds of all kinds were found."

Situated on a rocky knoll between rich agricultural plains to the west and more barren land to the east is the ruin of a solidly built structure which measured 6 x 7 m at the base. Its walls are composed of roughly shaped limestone blocks, ca. 0.5 m thick, and survive several courses high in some places. Someone has dug a small trench against the exterior face of the east wall and exposed its lower foundations; otherwise the structure is filled and surrounded with tumbled stones. Broken segments of an outlying wall parallel the structure on its east and south sides. Apparently these are remnants of a stone enclosure in which the building (watchtower?) was situated. Down the slope to the east is an area of exposed limestone with a large plastered cistern and a *birkeh*.

Site 442
(Map section 14; field no. 2389)
PG: 30.3/43.3; UTMG: 71.4/30.9

Building ruin ca. 7.5 km southeast of Ghuweir/Dhat Ras and 4 km east of Shqeira. 121 sherds were collected, including: Nab 6; EByz 1; 1 Ott pipe fragment.

Wall remains still standing up to four courses high indicate a 10 m square building in the southwest corner of an attached courtyard. The overall measurements of the building with courtyard are ca. 16 x 16 m. There are terrace walls below the building site and a cistern ca. 150 m east of it. Also there are several bedouin burials near the ruin, most of which have been disturbed.

Site 443
(Map section 14; field no. 2388)
PG: 30.4/43.1; UTMG: 71.5/30.7

Two partitioned cairns (ca. 100 m apart and both ca. 4.5 in diameter) on small rises in hilly area near the edge of Wadi el-Ḥesa; slightly less than 2.5 km southwest of Mḥai and 4 km east of Shuqeira. 71 sherds were collected, including: Nab 8; UD 1.

One has north-south bisecting slabs; the other, which is located ca. 100 m northeast of the first, is surrounded by snail shells.

Chapter III

CERAMICS FROM THE KERAK PLATEAU

by

Robin M. Brown

Introduction

This review of selected sherds from the survey assemblage is presented in sixteen chronologically ordered sections spanning the Chalcolithic through the Modern eras. Each section contains: (1) a brief description of the physical attributes of the pottery associated with the period; (2) a description of vessel forms with notes on comparative typology and chronology; and (3) a brief summary discussion. This chapter is intended to provide an introduction to the ceramic history of the region, as well as a basis for interpreting the raw sherd counts and sherd distributions reported elsewhere in this volume. There have been significant refinements in ceramic chronology and typology over the decades following Glueck's pioneering survey of the Transjordan (Glueck 1934, 1935, 1939, 1951), and one purpose of this study is to introduce some of these recent advances in classification in the context of a discussion of ceramics from the Kerak plateau. With respect to the presentation of the ceramics included in this sample, drawings, photographs, and ware descriptions appear on pages 247-257 of this volume. Each sherd is referred to in the text by the number that identifies its drawing on the plates (pages 259-267). The periodization and associated chronology cited in this text (see page 27) are based on Sauer's model (Sauer 1973: 3-4, and pers. comm.).

James A. Sauer, then director of the American Center of Oriental Research in Amman, examined the pottery collected during the initial 1978 survey season. The writer joined the project for the subsequent 1979 and 1982 seasons and prepared preliminary chronological classifications of sherds gathered during these campaigns. During the 1979 season Sauer served the project in an advisory capacity and I am grateful for this valuable assistance.

Over 50,000 sherds were collected during the survey. In selecting sherds from this corpus for publication several subjective criteria were applied. First, it was determined that the most widely useful samples of pottery would be those that most typically represent the assemblage from each period, in terms of forms, ware characteristics, or both. Second, sherds that appear less typical of the Kerak region, but are attested in other parts of the southern Levant, were included. Third, a few apparently unusual or problematic sherds, whose classifications may be considered tentative, were selected with the intention of generating discussion and ideas among a broader audience. Generally, the number of sherds presented for a period bears no correlation to the proportion of sherds from that period within the total corpus. There are however, some exceptions. There were greater constraints on selection of sherds from the Chalcolithic, Early Bronze IVB, Persian, Early Islamic (Umayyad, Abbasid, and Fatimid), and Ottoman assemblages, which are relatively small and contain fewer sherds suitable for illustration. However, it is anticipated that future research with the survey collection will further clarify the density of ceramics from these periods, which may be under-represented in our present statistics. The entire corpus of sherds from the survey is permanently housed at the Emory University Museum of Art and Archaeology, Atlanta, Georgia and is available to the public for educational and research purposes.

In this review, the later ceramic groups are presented in a series of chronological frameworks defined by specific political superstructures, from the Persian through the Ottoman periods, in accordance with the field classifications of the Kerak plateau survey ceramics and the vast majority of classifications prepared by other regional surveys of Transjordan. While this particular chronological reference scheme is useful in many respects, the problems and potential misconceptions that it embodies are well recognized on theoretical and practical grounds. In recent years these issues have been raised by several historical archaeologists, particularly with regard to the classification of ceramic sequences from the Islamic periods (e.g., Pringle 1981: 46-47; Gawlikowski 1986: 118; Whitcomb 1989a, 1989b, forthcoming a, b). Yet, as all chronological reference schemes are to some extent arbitrary, each retains various disadvantages as well as advantages. A growing awareness among archaeologists as to the potential pitfalls in the indiscriminate reliance on political history as a framework for organizing material culture can only be applauded. While these observations do not necessitate a rejection of political chronology, they do encourage explicit qualification of the ways in which history may, or may not, interact with ceramic distributions. Therefore, political chronology is retained in this discussion as a general organizing principle, but with the following caveats. This framework does not represent implicit theoretical postulates predicting: (1) a direct relationship between a governing body and the nature of the contemporary ceramic assemblage, or (2) that specific ceramic forms are necessarily temporally confined to the duration of a governing body. This does not, however, deny the fact that circumstances exist in which either, or both, may occur.

The presentation of vessel forms and comparative chronological typology in this review draw largely on published data from southern Levantine sites. And, in some instances it has been possible to offer preliminary interpretations regarding the extent to which forms or assemblages of a given period represent either localized styles or broader regional trends in ceramic production and distribution. However, the references to comparative forms from southern Levantine sites do not purport to be exhaustive. As can be expected, the form comparisons often demonstrate affinities with ceramics from stratified deposits excavated at sites in Transjordan and particularly those in the central and southern highlands and the Dead Sea region. Furthermore, it could be assumed that stratified deposits from sites on the Kerak plateau would be the most valuable in the chronological assessment of the survey assemblage. Yet published excavations of sites on the Kerak plateau have been relatively few: Khirbet Baluᶜ (Crowfoot 1934); Ader (Albright 1934; Cleveland 1960); Mdeinet el-Muᶜrrajeh (Olávarri 1977-78, 1983); Lejjūn and Khirbet el-Fityan (Parker 1981, 1982, 1983); and Shqeirah (Zayadine 1970). However, data from these sites have been considered wherever possible. In recent years additional works on Kerak plateau sites have appeared, including reports on: continuing excavation at Lejjun and other *limes Arabicus* Project sites (Parker 1985, 1986a, 1987a and b, 1988a and b, 1990b, and Parker [ed.] 1987); renewed research at Khirbet Baluᶜ (Worschech et al. 1986); excavations at Khirbet Faris/Tedun (Johns et al. 1989; Johns and McQuitty 1989); and a brief investigation at Kerak Castle (Brown 1989). However, this review of the Kerak plateau survey pottery was completed during the spring of 1985, and it has not been feasible to consider data from these recent reports fully, or the many other pertinent new publications dealing with archaeological excavations and surveys in other areas of Transjordan. Thus the comparative references cited in the text are largely limited to materials available at the time of manuscript preparation. The primary exceptions to this are the sections on Early Islamic and Ayyubid-Mamluk ceramics, which were revised in order to introduce at least some of the vast quantity of new material on these periods.

With respect to methods, this study offers a few general observations regarding the interpretation of ceramic distributions for each period based on a preliminary review of the corpus. It does not seek to critically evaluate or explain either the distortions that are inherent in virtually any survey collection, or the interpretive problems posed by such distorions. Thus, the tentative conclusions presented in the discussions that follow each descriptive section below are to be viewed as wholly impressionistic. Furthermore, specialists in various archaeological periods, historians, historical geographers, and scholars of other disciplines are encouraged to develop and pursue, or challenge and refute, the questions and issues raised herein, for a detailed consideration of the vast wealth of contextual data is beyond the scope of this presentation.

While assuming full responsibility for the contents of this review, I am very pleased to acknowledge the enthusiastic and essential contributions of many friends and colleagues who freely shared their professional expertise. Pointed and indispensable criticisms of earlier drafts were offered by: Michael D. Coogan, E. Axel Knauf, S. Thomas Parker, Suzanne R. Richard, James A. Sauer, and R. Thomas Schaub. Copies of ceramic drawings and/or manuscripts (either unpublished or in press) were generously provided by Jeremy Johns and Alison McQuitty (Khirbet Faris), Nancy L. Lapp (Araq el-Emir), Cherie J. Lenzen (er-Risha), Patrick E. McGovern (Baqᵓah Valley), S. Thomas Parker (Umm el-Jimal, Lejjun, Fityan, and Rujm Beni Yasser), and Donald S. Whitcomb (ᶜAqabah, Khirbet el-Mefjer, and the southern Ghor). For the opportunity to examine and discuss other unpublished ceramic assemblages, I wish to thank: Khairieh ᶜAmr, Edward B. Banning, Alison Betts, Christa Clammer, Michael D. Coogan, Colin Gillette, David F. Graf, Joseph A. Greene, Larry G. Herr, Linda K. Jacobs, Geoffrey R. King, Øystein S. LaBianca, Nancy L. Lapp, Cherie J. Lenzen, Jonathan Mabry, Burton MacDonald, David W. McCreery, Mohammed Najjar, Emilio Olávarri, John P. Oleson, Gaetano Palumbo, S. Thomas Parker, Konstantinos D. Politis, Sami Rabadi, Walter E. Rast, Essa al-Sadi, James A. Sauer, R. Thomas Schaub, Emsaytif Suleiman, Alan D. Walmsley, Donald S. Whitcomb, and Donald H. Wimmer. Over the years during which this manuscript was in preparation, I sought the expertise of many other colleagues whose suggestions have been invaluable. In addition to those mentioned above, I am especially grateful to Nancy L. Benco, Colin Brooker, Steve E. Falconer, Albert Leonard Jr., Janet MacLennan, Amy W. Newhall, and Carol Redmount. I also wish to express my tremendous debt to the late Jennifer C. Groot for many years of consultation and consistent support for this endeavor. In addition, I take this opportunity to extend my deep appreciation to the members of the Moab Survey staff for their generous assistance with the many, and often unglamorous, chores involving the management of a colossal amount of pottery.

This study is dedicated to James A. Sauer, an exceptionally gifted teacher.

Chalcolithic

Description: Chalcolithic. The small assemblage of Chalcolithic sherds presented here reflects some of the diversity of ware types and manufacturing techniques that characterizes ceramics of this period (Balfet 1965: 172-7; Elliott 1978). Grey wares are represented (Nos. 1, 7), yet the dominant fabric colors range from pink-orange and buff to brown, comparable to Chalcolithic wares at Pella (Smith 1973: pl. 87). In the majority of the sherds the inclusions consist of large to medium sized mineral grits. Organic material was also used as temper, as demonstrated by Nos. 1 and 2, both of which contain a large percentage of organic inclusions. Similarly, Hennessy has noted the occasional use of straw temper at Ghassul (1969: 7). Hand coiling was the principal, if not the exclusive, method of manufacture, and firing was highly variable.

Several different decorative techniques were employed. Slips appear on a few sherds and these include shades of grey (No. 5), brown (No. 8), reddish brown (No. 4) and pale brown (Nos. 10, 14). Less frequent is the pale red paint found upon the rims of hole-mouth jar No. 3 and body sherd No. 13. In contrast, plastic decoration is well represented, particularly finger impressing, which was practiced upon both vessel rims (Nos. 2, 6, 13) and raised bands of clay (Nos. 6, 11, 12). Scalloping also appears (Nos. 13, 14). Other techniques include modeling (No. 15) and simple parallel grooving (No. 10), although these decorative elements are not found frequently among published Chalcolithic assemblages.

Forms: Chalcolithic. The flattened rim sherd shown in No. 1 represents a large bowl or small basin that is paralleled at **Ḥorvat Usa** (Ben-Tor 1966: fig. 4: 7). Another large bowl or small basin form, sherd No. 2, has a thickened rim, flattened along the top. The distinctive aspect of this sherd is the exterior "wheel ribbing," a common characteristic of Chalcolithic pottery from **Beersheba, Ḥorvat Beter** (Dothan 1959a). At this site, wheel ribbing appears on several open forms including bowls and basins from Stratum I (ibid.: figs. 7: 14, 20; 8: 7-8) as well as large bowls and basins from Strata II-III (ibid.: fig. 13: 1). While this exterior finish may have been executed with a rotational device, the vessel represented in No. 2 was clearly manufactured by hand.

The hole-mouth jar is an ubiquitous component of Chalcolithic assemblages, and rim forms of these vessels show a great deal of variability. The hole-mouth jar shown in No. 3 has a thin band of red paint along the rim. Other examples of hole-mouth vessels painted in this manner are found at **Beersheba, Ḥorvat Beter**, Strata II-III (Dothan 1959a: fig. 14: 2, 16) and **Jericho** (Garstang 1935: pl. XL: 27-28).

Jar rims are pictured in Nos. 4-7. Of the high necked jars Nos. 4 and 5, the former, with a slightly splayed rim, may be compared with an example from **Tell el-Far^cah** (north), Chalcolithique Moyen (de Vaux 1961: fig. 1: 27). The out-turned rim of jar No. 5 is paralleled in the assemblages from two **Judean Desert** sites, including **Naḥal Ḥever** (Aharoni 1961: fig. 10: 4; Aharoni 1962: fig. 1: 15) and **Beersheba, Ḥorvat Beter**, Stratum I (Dothan 1959a: fig. 9: 25). A larger form may be noted from **Ghassul** (Koeppel et al. 1940: pl. 77: 7). Rim sherd No. 6 belongs to a large neckless jar. The peaked, flared rim is thumb impressed in the "pie crust" style. The vessel shoulder is decorated with a thin raised band of clay, which is also marked with thumb impressions. Other examples have appeared at: **Beisan**, Level XVIII (Fitzgerald 1935: pl. I: 20); **Jericho** (Garstang 1935: pl. XL: 8); and **Tell Sahl es-Sarabet** (Suleiman and Betts 1981: pl. LVIII: 1, lower left). On a parallel form from **Beersheba, Ḥorvat Beter**, Stratum I (Dothan 1959a: fig. 9: 14) thumb impressing is absent and paint has been applied to the rim. Sherd No. 7, a short necked jar with flaring rim, is attested at **Ghassul**, Phase A (Hennessy 1969: fig. 5: 8) and **Beersheba, Abu Matar** (Perrot 1957: fig. 19: 12).

Thick flat bases, shown in Nos. 8 and 9, are common to a variety of Chalcolithic forms including bowls, jars, and hole-mouth vessels. The heel on base No. 9, which superficially resembles a disc base, is a frequent feature among bases of this period, and parallels are found at several sites: **Arad**, Stratum V (Amiran 1978: pls. 1: 16; 6: 7); **Beersheba, Ḥorvat Beter**, Stratum I (Dothan 1959a: fig. 7: 4, 9, 11); the **Judean Desert, Um Qatafa** (Neuville and Mallon 1931: pl. XIX: 15, 17); and may be likened to a sherd from **Tell Iktanu** (Mallon et al. 1934: pl. 62: 8).

Sherds Nos. 11 and 12 are decorated with thumb impressions. Sherd No. 11 has a distinctive raised band appliqué, while the thumb impressions on the clay band of sherd No. 12 are deeper, larger, and more closely spaced. On this sherd, apparently from a pithos or large jar, the decoration was applied to the zone where the vessel shoulder and neck were joined. Finger-molded clay bands, comparable to No. 11, are found at a number of sites: **Beisan**, Level XVIII (Fitzgerald 1935: pl. I: 24); **Tell Abu Habil** (de Contenson 1960: fig. 23: 8); **Beersheba** (de Contenson 1956: fig. 12: 8-9); and the **Judean Desert**, **Um Qatafa** (Neuville and Mallon 1931: fig. 9). The more emphatic impressing displayed by sherd No. 12 is characteristic of a variety of large forms manufactured during the Chalcolithic period. On pithoi, basins, and hole-mouth jars these impressed bands often appear below the vessel rim: **Wadi Rabah** (Kaplan 1958: fig. 5: 1); **Ghassul** (Hennessy 1969: 9; fig. 9b: 1); **Tell el-Far^cah** (north) (de Vaux 1961: fig. 1: 9, 12); and **Neve Ur** (Perrot et al. 1967: fig. 17: 6). Direct parallels to sherd No. 12 include large jars from several sites: **Munḥatta**, Level I (Perrot 1964: fig. 6: 6); **Ghassul**, Level IV (Mallon et al. 1934: fig. 52: 8); **Megiddo**, Stratum XIX (Shipton 1939: pl. 20: 18, 20); and **Beisan**, Stratum XVII (Fitzgerald 1935: pl. I: 16) and Stratum XVIII (ibid.: pl. I: 20-21, 23).

Scalloped, decorative bands are illustrated in Nos. 13 and 14. The former is a fragment of a basin with a flattened, red-painted rim (profile not illustrated). This wide, deeply scalloped band is paralleled at **Tell esh-Shuneh**, Level I (de Contenson 1960: fig. 4: 13). The less prominent scalloped band shown in No. 14 marks the juncture of the shoulder and neck of what was probably a jar. Comparable sherds are noted from: **Ghassul** (Mallon et al. 1934: fig. 60: 17); **Tell Umm Hamad esh-Sherqi** (Glueck 1945: pls. 7: 4; 9: 15); **Tell Abu Habil**, Level III (de Contenson 1960: fig. 26: 18); and Chalcolithic sites in the **Golan** (Epstein 1978: figs. 9a: top row; 10b: lower right).

The two decorative nodules of clay that distinguish sherd No. 15 are similar to examples from **Ghassul**

(Mallon 1932: fig. 5: E) and **Tell Gat**, Stratum IX (Yeivin 1961: pl. VIII: lower right).

Discussion: Chalcolithic. The Chalcolithic pottery from the Kerak plateau is utilitarian and domestic in function and consists of a narrow repertoire of types. Notably absent are several diagnostic forms that are among the hallmarks of Chalcolithic ceramics, figuring frequently in assemblages of the Ghassul-Beersheba tradition as well as elsewhere. Among these unrepresented elements are the churn and coronet forms, but more conspicuously lacking are the V-shaped bowl and triangular lug handles, which are associated with a variety of forms. With regard to decorative techniques, there are no examples of the more complex painted designs that are present in the Ghassulian and Beersheba ceramic groups. Also absent are the Ghassulian punctured and incised decorations (Mallon et al. 1934: fig. 60).

The plastic decorative techniques that are manifest in the Chalcolithic assemblage from the Kerak plateau are common throughout the southern Levant. Finger-impressed rims and raised bands as well as other forms of rope molding are attested at northern and southern sites, including those of the Jordan Valley. It is not surprising however, that the more regionally circumscribed northern styles of decorative impressing and incising, as found at Tell Turmus (Dayan 1969: figs. 4: 6-8; 7) and Ain el-Jarba (Kaplan 1969: fig. 8), are not represented in the Kerak plateau group.

In summary, the Chalcolithic pottery from the Kerak plateau includes some attributes that are characteristic of the Ghassul-Beersheba tradition and likewise shows affinity with ceramics from the northern sites of Beisan, Tell esh-Shuna, and Tell el-Far^cah (north). Yet, despite these apparent correlations, the limited amount of Chalcolithic pottery from the survey precludes more specific chronological interpretations.

Early Bronze I

Description: EB I. The EB I ceramic types described below show some continuity with Chalcolithic forms and attributes, such as bowls (Nos. 16-18), hole-mouth vessels (No. 32), and flat bases (Nos. 37-38). More significantly, the EB I ceramic repertoire reflects the development of new forms and decorative styles such as shallow, hemispherical bowls (Nos. 20-26), amphoriskoi (Nos. 27-31), and line group painting (Nos. 39-41), in addition to changes in paste preparation and manufacturing techniques.

The ware colors of the EB I sherds in this sample are consistently within pink and tan ranges, and fabric textures tend to be soft. The majority of these handmade wares are marked by finger impressions that were left on both the interior and exterior of the vessels during the forming process. The size and amount of the mineral tempering inclusions is variable, but notably finer than among the Chalcolithic sherds. Well levigated clays with medium to fine mineral components are present (Nos. 26, 30). The fabrics of bulky ledge handles (Nos. 34-36) and thick, flat bases (Nos. 37-38) associated with large domestic forms are coarser and contain both higher percentages of inclusions and larger mineral grits. With few exceptions, the fabrics are well fired.

Red painting and slipping are common EB I decorative techniques, though self-slipped surface finishes are also evident. Red slips are found on sherds Nos. 17 (mottled), 20, 29-30, 37. Handles Nos. 34-36 are slipped in tones of pink and white. Red paint is preserved on sherds Nos. 19, 22, 25-28, 33. Less common are the red painted designs of the EB IB line-group style (Nos. 39-41). Bowl No. 25 provides an example of burnishing, an EB I decorative technique well attested from many sites but not common among the EB I wares of the Kerak plateau. Plastic decoration in the form of thumb or finger impressing distinguishes ledge handle No. 35.

Forms: EB I. Medium to large-sized, deep bowls are shown in Nos. 16-18. The peaked, slightly everted rim style that distinguishes this group from other deep bowl forms is known from several sites. At **Bab edh-Dhra^c** these vessels are well represented in the EB IA Tomb A 78 NW (Schaub 1981), and among them several specific parallels may be cited (ibid.: figs. 3:8-9, 11; 4:3). Additional **Bab edh-Dhra^c** parallels have been published from Tomb A 76 (P. W. Lapp 1968b: fig. 10: 1, 5-6). It should be noted, however, that the decorative incising that is common among the deep bowls from the Bab edh-Dhra^c cemetery is not found among the Kerak plateau bowls. Other parallel bowls are attested in the predominantly EB IB assemblages from Tomb C at **ᶜAi** (Marquet-Krause 1949: pl. LXVII: 25) and the cave site at **ᶜArqub edh-Dhahr** (Parr 1956: fig. 13: 50). In addition to these examples, variations may be cited from **Tell esh-Shuneh**, Level II (de Contenson 1960: fig. 10: 10) and **Kataret es-Samra** (Leonard 1983: fig. 9: 22). The Chalcolithic prototype for this form is known from Ghassul-Beersheba assemblages, as well as being found at a number of other sites including: **Meṣer** (Dothan 1959b: fig. 6: 11); Tell esh-**Shuna** (de Contenson 1960: fig. 3: 4); **Tell es-Saᶜidiyyeh** (ibid.: fig. 32: 14).

The medium-sized, thin-walled, deep bowl pictured in No. 19 displays a simple, vertically-tapered rim and retains traces of red slip on both the interior and exterior. Similar forms appear at **Bab edh-Dhraᶜ** in the EB IA Tomb A 78 NW (Schaub 1981: fig. 4: 9) and **Tell el-Farᶜah** (north), Tomb 2 (de Vaux and Stève 1949: fig. 6: 10).

Medium-sized, shallow hemispherical bowls with peaked rims are presented in Nos. 20-22. These hemispherical bowls are a common feature in EB I assemblages, both funerary and occupational, and display considerable variety. The slightly carinated form, illustrated in Nos. 20-22, is represented at numerous sites, but the best parallels are found among the assemblages from Bab edh-Dhraᶜ, Jericho, ᶜArqub edh-Dhahr and ᶜAi. Parallels from **Bab edh-Dhraᶜ** include vessels from two EB IB tombs: Tomb A 100 N (Schaub 1981: fig. 7: 12) and Tomb A 88 L (ibid.: fig. 16: 2, 5). A similar form comes from the EB IA Tomb A 78 SW (ibid.: fig. 2: 9). At **ᶜAi** these vessels occur in EB IB contexts: Tomb C (Marquet-Krause 1949: pl. LXX: 686) and Tomb G (ibid.: pl. LXXIV: 1012). These bowls are also present in two of Kenyon's Proto-Urban A deposits at **Jericho**: Tomb A 114(A) (Kenyon 1960: fig. 17: 8) and Tomb A 124 (Kenyon 1965: fig. 13: 3), although the latter is a smaller version. Also from **Jericho** is a variation of this form published by Garstang (1936: pl. XXVI: 10). Another example is included in the EB IB assemblage from **ᶜArqub edh-Dhahr** (Parr 1956: fig. 14: 87). Finally, variations may be found at **Tell el-Farᶜah** (north) (de Vaux 1952: fig. 10: 5) and **Arad**, Stratum IV (Amiran 1978: pl. 7: 4-5), an apparent EB IB occupation. This distribution indicates that the carinated hemispherical bowl shown in Nos. 20-22 is most frequently associated with EB IB assemblages.

Uncarinated hemispherical bowls with peaked rims are pictured in Nos. 23-26. These simple curved, open bowls belong to a widely attested genre, which is associated with both flat and low ring bases. Omphalos bases also occur, although these tend to characterize burnished bowls of this class (Amiran 1963: 43). Rim forms similar to No. 23 are attested in several EB IA and EB IB contexts. Examples include: **Bab edh-Dhraᶜ**, Tomb A 78 NW (Schaub 1981: fig. 4:7); **Jericho**, excavations (Garstang 1936: pl. XXXVI:8) and Tombs A 114, A 94, and K2(II) (Kenyon 1960: figs. 17:5; 11:13; Kenyon 1965: fig. 8:2); **Tell el-Farᶜah** (north), Tomb 3 (de Vaux and Stève 1949: fig. 1:2) and **ᶜArqub edh-Dhahr** (Parr 1956: fig. 13:56). A similar form may be noted from **ᶜAi**, Tomb C (Marquet-Krause 1949: pl. LXX:524). Rim forms specifically similar to Nos. 24 and 25 are known from **Bab edh-Dhraᶜ** where they occur in both EB IA contexts: Tomb A 78 NW (Schaub 1981: fig. 4:6), Tomb A 76 (P. W. Lapp 1968b: fig. 8:2); and EB IB contexts: Tomb A 100 N (Schaub 1981: fig. 7:8), Tomb A 88 L (ibid.: fig. 15:4). This particular bowl form is also well represented at **Jericho** in the Proto-Urban A burials, Tomb A 94 and Tomb A 114(A) (Kenyon 1960: figs. 10:15; 17:8).

Variations of this form are documented at several other sites: **ᶜAi**, Tomb G (Marquet-Krause 1949: pls. LXXII: 902; LXXIII: 919); **Tulul Abu el-ᶜAlayiq** (Pritchard 1958: pl. 57: 19); **Tell el-Farᶜah** (north), Tomb 3 (de Vaux and Stève 1949: fig. 1: 3); **ᶜArqub edh-Dhahr** (Parr 1956: fig. 13: 4, 17); and **Gibeon**, Tomb 3 (Pritchard 1963: fig. 6: 5, 10). Smaller versions of this bowl are found at **Arad**, Stratum IV (Amiran 1978: pl. 7: 2) and **Kataret es-Samra** (Leonard 1983: fig. 8: 12).

The thin walled bowl with peaked incurved rim shown in No. 26 is paralleled at **Bab edh-Dhraᶜ**, Tomb A 88 L (Schaub 1981: fig. 16: 13) where it occurs with a ring base.

Sherds Nos. 27-31 are small juglet rims representing amphoriskoi, a form particularly characteristic of EB I tomb deposits and often decorated in the EB IB line-group painted style (see body sherds Nos. 39-41 below). These small juglets have rounded bases, and pierced lug handles are attached to the vessel shoulders. Amphoriskoi are common to EB IB tomb groups including those from: **Jericho**, Tomb A 13 and Tomb K2(I) (Kenyon 1960: fig. 22:11-13; Kenyon 1965: fig. 4: 26-31); **Bab edh-Dhraᶜ**, Tomb A 88 L and Tomb A 100 N (Schaub 1981:

figs. 6:2; 11:10); **Tell el-Far^cah** (north), Tomb 2, Tomb 5, and Tomb 13 (de Vaux and Stève 1949: figs. 6: 27-30; 8: 27-28); **ᶜArqub edh-Dhahr** (Parr 1956: figs. 15: 169-80; 16: 187-89, 197); **ᶜAi**, Tomb B, Tomb C, and Tomb G (Marquet-Krause 1949: numerous examples); and **Azor**, Tomb 1 and Tomb 4 (Ben-Tor 1975a: figs. 7; 11:16-29). The amphoriskos also appears, although less frequently, in non-funerary occupation contexts. Examples include: **Jericho**, Layers IV-VII (Garstang 1936: pls. XXXV: 11; XXXVI: 12, 16; XXXIX: 6) and **Arad**, Stratum IV (Amiran 1978: pl. 10: 1-5).

Temporal longevity of the amphoriskos form is demonstrated by its presence in EB II assemblages from: **Jericho**, Tomb A 108, Tomb A 127, Tomb D 12, and Tomb A 114 (B) (Kenyon 1960: figs. 23: 12-18; 25: 23-31; 37: 20-25; 68: 7); **Bab edh-Dhraᶜ**, charnal house Tomb A 55 and charnal house Tomb A 56 (Johnston and Schaub 1978: fig. 1: 1; Schaub 1981: fig. 19: 9-17); and **Lachish**, Cave 1535 (Tufnell 1958: pl. 58: 110-17).

Each of the amphoriskos rims shown in Nos. 27-31 belongs to short necked vessels, and Nos. 30-31 are squatter than the others. Nos. 28-30 are thickened at the junction of the neck and shoulder. Broadly similar types are known from **ᶜArqub edh-Dhahr** (Parr 1956: fig. 14: 131); **Tell el-Farᶜah** (north), Tomb 14 (de Vaux 1952: fig. 11: 12); **ᶜAi**, Tomb G (Marquet-Krause 1949: pl. LXXI: 818); and **Azor** (Ben-Tor 1975a: figs. 7: 18; 11: 24).

No. 32 is a hole-mouth vessel with a plainly rounded rim. The hole-mouth jar or cooking pot is a consistent aspect of EB I domestic assemblages and, while a variety of different styles occur, the simple rounded rim of No. 32 is well documented. Examples are found at the following sites: **Tell esh-Shuna**, Level II (de Contenson 1960: fig. 11: 5); **Jericho**, Site AI (Kenyon 1952: fig. 5: 26); **Tulul Abu el-ᶜAlayiq** (Pritchard 1958: pl. 56: 3); **Ras Abu Lofeh** (Glueck 1951: pl. 128: 14); and **Kataret es-Samra** (Leonard 1983: fig. 9: 6).

The red slipped loop handle, shown in cross-section in No. 33, is a typical feature of EB I pottery and can be documented at most EB I sites. In Transjordan, examples may be noted from **Kataret es-Samra** (Leonard 1983: fig. 12). This handle is a distinctive attribute of the frequently attested EB I "high loop handled cup" form, as demonstrated at **Jericho**, Tomb A 94 (Kenyon 1960: figs. 12, 13). It is also associated with jugs: **Tell el-Farᶜah** (north), Tomb 8 (de Vaux and Stève 1949: fig. 13: 11-12) and spouted jars: **Azor**, Tomb 4 (Ben-Tor 1975a: fig. 8: 14).

A group of three rather coarse utilitarian handles is presented in Nos. 34-36. Of horizontal ledge handles Nos. 34 and 35, the former has a rounded crescent shape and the latter is thicker and slightly squared. These handles are commonly attached to the sides of jars, either perpendicular to the vessel or pushed upward. Among the sites with handles comparable to No. 34 are: **Megiddo**, Stratum XIX, (Shipton 1939: pl. 17: 9); **ᶜAfula** (Sukenik 1948: pl. VII: 16); **Tell ed-Dhiyabeh** (Glueck 1946: pl. 20: 4); and **Tell Deir Saᶜaneh Mekhlediyeh** (Glueck 1951: pl. 135: 10). Handle No. 35 has a slightly arched, horizontal profile, a shallow thumb impression at its distal end, and additional thumb impressions upon each lateral where the handle joined the body of the vessel. The shape of No. 35 is similar to a handle from **Feifeh** (Rast and Schaub 1974: fig. 7: 197). Other related forms from Transjordan are attested at **Tell Deir Saᶜaneh Mekhlediyeh** (Glueck 1946: pl. 26: 1-2) and **Tell esh-Shuneh**, Level II (de Contenson 1960: fig. 12: 9). The pointed, elongated, and sharply angled handle shown in No. 36 appears to have pointed upward from its base of attachment on the vessel surface. This is not a common form but a parallel may be cited from **Tell el-Farᶜah** (north), Tomb 5 (de Vaux and Stève 1949: fig. 8: 23), and a similar, though smaller, version is attested at **Jawa** (Helms 1976: fig. 8: 2).

Flat bases, shown in Nos. 37 and 38, are common to several EB I vessel forms and show strong affinity with earlier Chalcolithic bases, such as those found on V-shaped bowls. During the EB I period these bases are especially typical of large jars, spouted vessels, bowls, and hole-mouth forms. An indentation just above the heel, as pictured in No. 38, is not uncommon and may be compared with a base from **Ras Abu Lofeh** (Glueck 1951: pl. 128: 15).

The line-group painting style that is the hallmark of the EB IB ceramic tradition is illustrated in sherds Nos. 39-41. On the exterior surfaces of these sherds are groups of parallel red lines painted at oblique and right angles to one another. EB IB funerary assemblages provide many examples of line-group painted vessels, and these assemblages have been found at a number of sites, many of which are located in southern Palestine and Transjordan. Among these sites with EB IB line-group painting are:

ᶜArqub edh-Dhahr (Parr 1956); **Bab edh-Dhraᶜ**, Tomb A 88 L (Schaub 1981); **Jericho**, Tomb A 13, Tomb K 2 (Kenyon 1960, 1965); **Jerusalem, Ophel**, Tomb 3 (Vincent 1911); **ᶜAi**, Tomb B, Tomb C, Tomb G (Marquet-Krause 1949); and **Tell en-Naṣbeh**, Cave 5, Cave 6 (Badé 1928: pl. XX). Among the sites where line-group painted wares have been found in domestic contexts are: **Megiddo**, Stratum XX (Shipton 1939); **Arad**, Stratum IV (Amiran 1978); and **Jericho**, Layer VII (Garstang 1936). The continuation of this decorative style into the EB II period is demonstrated at **Jericho**, Tomb A 108 (Kenyon 1960) and **Bab edh-Dhraᶜ**, charnal house Tomb A 56 (Schaub 1981).

Discussion: EB I. Early Bronze I culture in the southern Levant is distinguished from Chalcolithic culture on the basis of changes in social organization and material culture. The EB I period has been interpreted as sharply contrasting with the preceding Chalcolithic period (e.g. P. W. Lapp 1970a). In terms of ceramics, continuities have been noted (Leonard 1983; P. W. Lapp 1970a; Hennessy 1967) and the above discussion of vessel forms has referred to aspects of continuity between the Chalcolithic and EB I assemblages. But these similarities are relatively minimal, possibly best illustrated in the utilitarian assemblages from rural settlements. When the range of EB I ceramics and their attributes are taken into consideration, it is evident that the EB I ceramic repertoire is more elaborate and marked by a proliferation of new and diverse forms. Not all of this diversity is represented in the survey collection, yet the forms from the Kerak plateau are well attested in the contexts of large, more diverse, excavated assemblages.

As indicated above, there is a marked contrast within EB I ceramic groups between assemblages from funerary deposits and those from domestic occupations. This contrast is reflected in the quality of paste preparation and in the quantity of decorated and specialized forms. In general, domestic assemblages contain higher proportions of vessels that functioned in activities linked to food preparation and storage. Conversely, funerary deposits contain more of the finer, special purpose and serving vessels. The discussion of forms has shown that some, but not all, of the vessel types represented by the sherds from the Kerak plateau are found in funerary assemblages. Parallels between EB I ceramics from the Kerak region and EB I pottery from small, rural occupations, such as at Kataret es-Samra and Glueck's Jordan Valley sites, demonstrate anticipated affinities in ceramic styles, for there are no EB I urban centers or recognized burial sites on the Kerak plateau.

The parameters of the EB IA, IB, and IC stylistic typologies have been defined on the basis of temporal sequencing, as documented in the EB IA-EB IB transitions at Bab edh-Dhraᶜ and Jericho, and an overlap of EB IB-EB IC has been suggested for the latter site by P. W. Lapp (1970a). Furthermore, a degree of regional differentiation has long been proposed on the basis of concentrations of EB IB material in southern Palestine and Transjordan, and EB IA and IC in the north (Amiran 1969). With regard to the EB I Kerak plateau survey wares, a direct link is established with the EB IB ceramic tradition that is manifest in the presence of the amphoriskos form and in the decorative line-group painting. However, these EB IB wares comprise only a small percentage of the total EB I assemblage from the Kerak plateau. Furthermore, it appears that the EB I sherds from the survey cannot be linked exclusively to either the EB IA or EB IC traditions. With the possible exception of sherd No. 25, the characteristic red burnished EB IA ware is absent, as are the northern band slip or grain wash wares and EB IC grey burnished wares. The Kerak plateau wares are thus best summarized as constituting a functional domestic assemblage with some EB IB elements.

Early Bronze II-III

Description: EB II-III. The Early Bronze II-III wares from the Kerak plateau are numerous, uniform in fabric, and stylistically repetitive. This sample presents some of the diversity of EB II-III forms as well as demonstrating homogeneity in aspects of manufacture. Some forms, such as hole-mouth vessels, and some attributes, such as flat bases and raised band decorations, have clear antecedents in the Chalcolithic and EB I periods. In addition, some characteristics of EB II-III fabrics are specifically associated with the preceding EB IB tradition. As outlined below, other aspects of EB II-III assemblages, including the development of the platter bowl, specific rim forms on hole-mouth vessels, and the extensive use of red slip and burnish techniques, are among the principal components of EB II-III assemblages that continue into the following EB IV A period.

The manufacturing methods of the EB II-III period are related to earlier hand-production processes, but these ceramics show increasing sophistication due to the partial use of rotational and other techniques that resulted in vessels that were better finished. Improved techniques combined with extensive use of covering slips and decorative surface finishes have left fewer obvious traces of the production process on the vessel surfaces in comparison with the EB I assemblage.

EB II-III fabrics are harder and, in a number of instances, thicker than in the preceding period. Differential use of temper is also evident. Serving vessels, including bowls and platter bowls, and the smaller jar forms, generally contain high proportions of small mineral inclusions, whereas hole-mouth cooking vessels contain white, calcite inclusions. As in the EB I period, firing is generally good, though there are a few exceptions. Ware color is nearly exclusively confined to pink, tan, and pale orange, colors that also occur among the slips. The common red slip surface treatment is frequent among platter bowls (Nos. 44-48) and incurved bowls (Nos. 49-51). Jar forms in this sample tend to be self-slipped or slipped in pale buff colors. The majority of the hole-mouth vessels show no indication of having been slipped.

Line, radial, and overall-covering burnish patterns that often occur in conjunction with red slip are particularly frequent among serving vessels, though the range of care exercised in the application of the burnish varied greatly. The surface combing that is widely indicative of EB II-III forms is represented in sherds Nos. 69 and 70. Finger impressing, though less common, is illustrated by sherd No. 71; in this case the decoration was applied to the zone where the neck and the vessel shoulder met. Various styles of raised band impressing are found on large jar or vat forms, such as No. 74, but occur on platter bowls as well (e.g. No. 47).

Forms: EB II-III. The incurved platter bowls shown in Nos. 42-48 are widely represented in Early Bronze Age deposits of the southern Levant, though they are particularly prevalent in EB III assemblages. The example shown in No. 42 is a simple, rounded and unprofiled rim. A pale brown exterior slip overlaps the rim, and the interior surface is marked with a broadly stroked radial burnish. **Jericho**, Tomb A 127 (Kenyon 1960: fig. 25: 7) and **ᶜAi**, Phase III (Wagner 1972: fig. 15: 11) provide analogous forms.

Platter bowl rim No. 43 has a gently rounded inverted-knob profile and an unusual dark grey-brown, burnished slip. Comparable illustrations are published from: **Jericho**, Tomb 351 (Garstang 1935: pl. XXXIV: 37), Tomb D 12 (Kenyon 1960: fig. 38: 22), and Tomb F (ibid.: fig. 57: 32); **ᶜAi**, Sanctuary A (Marquet-Krause 1949: pl. LXXVIII: 2394); **Tell el-Farᶜah** (north) (de Vaux and Stève 1947: fig. 5: 5); and the **Bab edh-Dhraᶜ** survey (Rast and Schaub 1974: fig. 2: 55). Related forms are found in late EB III strata at **Tell Beit Mirsim**, Stratum J (Dever and Richard 1977: fig. 1: 1) and **Bab edh-Dhraᶜ**, Field X, Phase 1 (Johnston and Schaub 1976: fig. 3: 11).

Nos. 44 and 45 are similar to No. 43, but are distinguished by thickened inverted-knob rims that are flattened on top. Both retain vestiges of a dark red-burnished slip on the interior and exterior surfaces. Among the numerous parallels to this form from EB II-III deposits are examples from **Megiddo**, Stratum XVIII (Shipton 1939: pl. 14: 9; Loud et al. 1948: pl. 102: 31) and Stratum XVI (ibid.: pl. 6: 13); **Lachish**, Locus 1535 (Tufnell 1958: pl. 58: 91); **Beisan**, Level XIV (Fitzgerald 1935: pl. VI: 2) and Level XII (ibid.: pl. VIII: 23); **ᶜAi**, Phase III (Callaway 1972: fig. 26: 21); **Tell Beit Mirsim**, Stratum J (Dever and Richard 1977: fig. 1: 8); and **Arad**, Stratum II (Amiran 1978: pl. 23: 20). Additional examples include **Bab edh-Dhraᶜ** (Albright et al. 1944: pl. 1: 30; Rast and Schaub 1974: fig. 1: 4); **Tell el-Farᶜah** (north) (de Vaux and Stève 1947: fig. 6: 1); and **Jericho** (Garstang 1935: pl. XXVIII: 34).

The exaggerated profile shown in No. 46 is a development of the EB III "hammer rim" (see Tell Beit Mirsim, Dever and Richard 1977: fig. 1: 5) that appears in both EB III and EB IV contexts at **Lachish**, Caves 6005 and 6013 respectively (Tufnell 1958: pls. 63:308; pl. 64:348). The flattened hammer rim No. 47 is a subtler form. This sherd has exterior traces of an unpolished red slip. A raised band of impressed clay was molded to the exterior just below the vessel rim. An example of this rim style is known from ᶜ**Ai**, Phase V (Callaway 1980: fig. 92: 15).

Platter bowl No. 48 has a sharp, angular profile and a flattened, everted rim that is thicker than the other platter bowl rims. The red slipped surface is marked with broad, haphazard burnish lines. The predominantly late EB III Stratum J at **Tell Beit Mirsim** (Dever and Richard 1977) features a similar form (Albright 1932b: fig. 1: 3). Other examples are from **Bab edh-Dhra**ᶜ (Albright et al. 1944: pl. 1: 3) and **Tell el-Ḥesi** (Petrie 1891: pl. VI: 58).

Simple, rounded bowl rims are shown in Nos. 49-51, each of which displays a burnished red slip on both the interior and exterior. At **Jericho**, Tomb A (Garstang 1932: fig. 4: 14) and Tomb F 4 (Kenyon 1960: fig. 43: 16) small hemispherical bowls similar to No. 49 are associated with both rounded and flat bases. Bowls Nos. 50 and 51 are incurved. Examples of the former appear at **Jericho**, Tomb F 4 (ibid.: fig. 47: 8-14) and Tomb 3 (ibid.: fig. 53: 5), in Kenyon's class of "small globular jars." These are also noted at **Tell el-Far**ᶜ**ah** (north) (Huot 1967: fig. 1: II) and **Khanazir** (Rast and Schaub 1974: fig. 11: 300). An example from **Bab edh-Dhra**ᶜ, Field X, Phase 1 (Johnston and Schaub 1978: fig. 4: 36) occurred in a late EB III context. The concave profile of No. 51 compares with examples from **Jericho**, Tomb F 2 (Kenyon 1960: fig. 57: 20) and ᶜ**Ai**, Phase III (Callaway 1980: fig. 61: 30).

The short necked "cup-bowl" form pictured in No. 52 is well represented at **Arad**, where a close parallel is found in Stratum II (Amiran 1978: pl. 24: 30).

Hole-mouth vessels are as frequent a component of EB II-III assemblages as the platter bowls and, in both cases, the range of variation in rim styles is considerable, though hole-mouth forms are more difficult to fix chronologically. Examples of EB II-III hole-mouth vessels are represented in Nos. 53-58. The simple bulbous rims of Nos. 53 and 54 are rounded on the exterior, and the interior surfaces are flattened. The rounded rim of No. 53 is paralleled at **Bab edh-Dhra**ᶜ, Field X, Phase 1 (Johnston and Schaub 1978: fig. 3:19) and ᶜ**Ai**, Phase IV (Callaway 1972: fig. 88: 16) and Phase III (ibid.: fig. 28:23). The tapered rim of No. 54 appears in deposits at **Megiddo**, Stratum XVIII (Shipton 1939: pl. 14: 39) and **Beisan**, Level XI (Fitzgerald 1935: pl. IX: 8) and has been noted at **Feifeh** as well (Rast and Schaub 1974: fig. 7: 180).

Nos. 55 and 56 are probably cooking pots, for both have reddish fabrics containing numerous calcite grits, and the former is fire blackened. The beveled rim of No. 55 is similar to rims from **Tell el-Far**ᶜ**ah** (north) (Huot 1967: fig. 2: BIe) and ᶜ**Ai** (Marquet-Krause 1949: pl. LXXXIV: 1210). The exterior of No. 56 is marked with shallow vertical slashes. This hatching also occurs on a hole-mouth jar from **Megiddo**, Stratum XVI (Loud et al. 1948: pl. 6: 9), where it is apparently a decorative technique. But the irregular pattern of the hatching on sherd No. 56 is more directly paralleled at **Tell el-Far**ᶜ**ah** (north) (de Vaux and Stève 1947: fig. 5: 15). Similar examples from **Tell el-Ḥesi**, Phase 4b have been interpreted as potters' marks (Fargo 1979: fig. 5: a, f, h).

The angular and thickened profile shown in No. 57 is a form that is prevalent in EB III assemblages, yet stylistically variable. Sites with comparable hole-mouth rims include: **Arad**, Stratum II (Amiran 1978: pl. 48: 35) and Stratum III (ibid.: pls. 18: 15; 19: 7); ᶜ**Ai**, Phase VI (Callaway 1980: fig. 113: 1, 35); and **Khirbet el-**ᶜ**Auja el-Foqa** (Glueck 1951: pl. 124: 4).

The thick, squared hole-mouth rim shown in No. 58 is attested at several sites, among them: ᶜ**Ai**, Phase III (Callaway 1972: fig. 30: 7; see also Marquet-Krause 1949: pl. LXXXIV: 2568); **Beisan**, Level XII (Fitzgerald 1935: pl. IX: 7); **Tell el-Far**ᶜ**ah** (north) (Huot 1967: fig. 2: BIc); and **Bab edh-Dhra**ᶜ, Field X, Phase 1 (Johnston and Schaub 1978: fig. 3: 20).

Sherds 59-64 designate various necked jar rims. These fairly simple forms are not widely documented, thus comparisons with excavated sherds are limited. Nos. 59-61 are associated with medium-sized jars. This vessel form is typically characterized by a flat base and a splayed rim, and it is often accompanied by pierced lug handles and/or horizontal ledge handles that are attached to the body at or below the point of the vessel's maximum circumference. Examples of this form with a lightly splayed rim are noted from **Bab edh-Dhra**ᶜ, Tomb A 56 (Schaub 1981: fig. 18: 2); **Beit Sahur** (Hennessy 1966a: fig. 3: 114), and **Tell el-Far**ᶜ**ah** (north) (Huot 1967: fig. 2: AIIa). The peaked, upright rim No. 59 is not as common as the rounded, splayed rims Nos. 60-61. The latter are similar to several pieces from ᶜ**Ai**, Phase III (Callaway 1972: fig. 27: 14; Callaway 1980: fig. 69: 2) and Phase V (Callaway 1972: fig. 46: 9).

The splayed, tapered jar rim No. 62 belongs to a tall-necked jar of the type from **Bab edh-Dhra^c**, Tomb A 56 (Schaub 1981: fig. 18: 3). Other comparable rims are published from **Tell Beit Mirsim**, Stratum J (Dever and Richard 1977: fig. 2: 11) and **Arad**, Stratum III (Amiran 1978: pl. 15: 26). The gently rolled rim of No. 63 is not frequent in the literature, although one example can be cited from **cAi**, Phase V (Callaway 1980: fig. 92: 25). A heavy jar with tall neck and everted rim is represented by sherd No. 64. The entire vessel form with an identical rim is found at **Arad**, Stratum III (Amiran 1978: pl. 17: 13). A schematic design (not illustrated) was impressed on the neck of No. 64 with a stamp or, more likely, a cylinder seal. Ben-Tor (1978) discusses similar seal-impressed ceramics of this period in the southern Levant, yet his thorough study does not contain a parallel design.

Flat bases are common to a large percentage of EB II-III forms. The combed exterior surface of base No. 65 suggests that it belonged to a jar or jug, for the popular body combing of this period is most common among these vessels (see Nos. 69-70 below).

Examples of EB II-III burnishing are presented in Nos. 66-68. No. 66, a platter bowl sherd (profile not illustrated) displays an interior radial burnish. In this instance, the burnish and red slip were applied to the top of the rim and overlap the upper exterior surface. As a widely employed technique, burnish patterns, particularly radial burnish, are common at numerous EB II-III sites, though the strokes were often thinner and more delicately executed than shown in No. 66. Illustrations may be cited from **Tell Beit Mirsim**, Stratum J (Dever and Richard 1977: pl. 1: 1-3); **Megiddo**, Stratum XVIII (Shipton 1939: pl. 14: 12, 14; Loud et al. 1948: pl. 104: 7-13); **Tell el-Ḥesi**, Phase 4b (Fargo 1979: fig. 7: 3-5, 7-9); **Beisan**, Level XI (Fitzgerald 1939: pl. VIII: 22) and Level XII (ibid.: pl. VIII: 20, 23, 25); **Tell el-Far^cah** (north) (de Vaux and Stève 1947: fig. 4: 8); **Jericho**, Tomb D 12 (Kenyon 1960: fig. 38: 12, 21); and **Tell Yarmuth** (Ben-Tor 1975b: fig. 6: 22-26). A radially burnished platter bowl from **Ader**, Phase C (Cleveland 1960: pl. 19: C[1]) indicates the continuation of this style into EB IV. Exterior surface burnishing is shown in Nos. 67 and 68. Sherd No. 67 is from a closed vessel, and No. 68 belonged to an open vessel that was line burnished with horizontal strokes on the exterior and vertical strokes on the interior.

Body combing in broad sets of oblique lines, as pictured in Nos. 69 and 70, is clearly illustrated in photographs of sherds from **Tell Beit Mirsim**, Stratum J (Albright 1932b: pl. 1: 14-15; Dever and Richard 1977: pl. 1: 5-6). This surface treatment also continued into EB IV, as noted at cAro^cer, Levels VIa and VIb (Olávarri 1969: pl. IV:1-6).

Plastic decorations are illustrated in Nos. 71-74. Finger impressing is well attested among EB II-III ceramics, but it was usually performed on raised bands of clay. The portion of a jar neck, shown in No. 71, is uncommon in this respect, for this row of finger indented marks was pressed directly into the body of the vessel. A similar technique is found at **cAi** (Marquet-Krause 1949: pl. LXV: 1476).

The scalloped ridge shown in No. 72 was formed by deep finger impressing on a raised band and is best paralleled at **Bab edh-Dhra^c** (Rast and Schaub 1974: fig. 2: 47). Sherds Nos. 73 and 74 both show low-relief raised bands that have been flattened in segments. The curvature of sherd No. 74 implies that it represents a pithos or similar large form. This decorative appliqué is found on a number of vessel forms including: (a) jars (usually a band that encircles the vessel body in any one of a number of places), **Arad**, Stratum II (Amiran 1978: pl. 41: 19-22, 28) and **Sinai** (Beit-Arieh 1983: pl. IVB); (b) hole-mouth vessels, **cAi**, Phase V (Callaway 1980: fig. 91: 10-12); (c) bowls, **cAi**, Phase V (ibid.: fig. 91: 16); and (d) spouted bowls, **cAi**, Phase V (ibid.: fig. 91: 15). Platter bowls may also have impressed bands adhering on the exterior beneath the rim, as in No. 47 above. This and similar forms of relief decoration occur in later Early Bronze Age phases also, as exemplified by a large EB IV bowl or vat from **Ader**, Phase B (Cleveland 1960: fig. 13: 18).

Discussion: EB II-III. The Early Bronze Age ceramic repertoire is marked by strong continuities and developmental trends that endure from EB I through EB IVA. Two general observations can be noted in characterizing the EB II-III pottery from the Kerak plateau. First, many of the same vessel types are found throughout the EB II-III phases. Second, within these persisting vessel classes, there is a wide diversity among specific stylistic attributes, e.g., rim forms, as is particularly evident among the platter bowls and hole-mouth pots. This consistency of vessel form and diversity of diagnostic attributes, plus the demonstrable linkages between both the preceding EB I and later EB IV periods, are factors that encourage chronological generalization when dealing with an unstratified survey corpus. While stratified deposits at some excavated sites may be distinguished as either EB II or EB III, most of the assemblages, like those of the EB II-III Kerak plateau sites, contain forms that are associated with both phases, and critical chronological indicators are not always present. Thus in a number of instances, parallels to the sherds presented above are cited from both EB II and EB III contexts. Some of the Kerak sherds (Nos. 61, 63, 65, 67, 71-72) exhibit a distinctive orange-pink slip (Munsell: 2.5YR 6/6 and 5YR 6/6) that can be tenuously considered EB II. Yet, because a consistent criterion for differentiation is lacking, EB II and III wares have been treated together in this review.

The association of some EB IB forms and decorative styles with EB II deposits has been noted in the previous section. Transitions within the ceramic repertoire are manifest in the EB II-III development of a number of pre-existing forms and, although burnish supersedes the earlier painting tradition, there is a lack of radical or abrupt change. However, EB II-III ceramics represent a more standardized repertoire in comparison with the EB I assemblages. EB II-III ceramics show a less clear-cut dichotomy between the kinds of vessels found in burial deposits and those associated with occupational contexts, although the utilitarian domestic wares, such as cooking vessels, continue to be represented largely in occupational strata. EB II-III wares also display greater regional homogeneity, and the selected examples from the Kerak survey that are illustrated here show that this corpus is well within the mainstream of EB II-III southern Levantine ceramics.

Early Bronze IVA and B

Several important synthetic works dealing with the problematics of the EB IV period have emerged over the last two decades (Dever 1980; Richard 1980; Prag 1974; Dever 1973; Oren 1973a). Most importantly, Dever (1973, 1980) has developed a regional and chronological typology of EB IV pottery, and Richard (1980) has demonstrated continuity of ceramic forms between EB IVA and EB IVB, in contrast to earlier research that emphasized the distinctiveness of EB IVB pottery and its possible external origins (Prag 1974). As a result, there has been a growing tendency to accept "EB IVB" as a replacement term for Amiran's (1969) "MB I" (see Dever 1973: 38), a scheme that is followed in this presentation.

Description: EB IVA. The EB IVA pottery from the Kerak plateau is a direct outgrowth from the EB II-III tradition in many aspects of vessel form, fabric, and decorative techniques. In addition, there is strong regional continuity among the wares of the EB IVA survey corpus and EB IVA assemblages from excavated sites in Transjordan. Two prominent features of EB II-III ceramics, platter bowls and hole-mouth vessels, continue to develop through EB IVA. Yet, while some of these EB IVA forms may be distinguished from earlier vessels by exaggerated rim styles, many rims from these vessels are similar, if not identical, to those of the preceding period, making specific periodization conjectural. Ceramic innovations and developments during the EB IVA period include the increasing occurrence of the "teapot," a spouted hole-mouth form, and the appearance of rilled or ridged rims on both bowls and hole-mouth jars, features that became significant components within the EB IVA assemblage.

There are no major developments in either fabric composition or manufacturing techniques that distinguish EB IVA pottery from EB II-III wares. The majority of the wares in this assemblage are pink, fairly well fired, and mixed with medium to small tempering agents. Red slip, often carelessly applied, is prominent especially among rilled-rim and platter bowl forms (Nos. 75-77, 79-81) but is also apparent on hole-mouth jars (e.g. No. 85) and other forms. Burnishing continues to be commonly applied to red slipped vessels (Nos. 75, 80, 91), but the poor state of preservation of many of the sherds in this sample makes it impossible to determine the presence or absence of burnishing. Other slip colors include pink, buff, and beige. Among the other decorative and surface treatments, light body combing (No. 93) and grooving (Nos. 85, 87) are evident. Plastic decorations include scalloping or finger impressing on rims (No. 82) and raised-band impressing on necks of large jars (Nos. 92-93). EB IVA witnesses the introduction and widespread use of "pie-crust" decorations that are particularly characteristic of vestigial ledge handles, and the thin thumb-impressed bands of clay that are affixed to jars, teapots, and other hole-mouth vessels, as well as to large bowl forms (No.75). The tiny pierced lug handles that occur at this time are associated with the rilled-rim hole-mouth forms. The incising that is so characteristic of the subsequent EB IVB period is rare, but one example (No. 91) has been included in the discussion below.

Forms: EB IVA. Large bowl forms are illustrated in Nos. 75 and 76. The thickened rim and sharply inverted lip of the former is paralleled at **Bab edh-Dhra^c**, Field X, Phase 1 (Johnston and Schaub 1978: fig. 3: 4), a late EB III context. However, the presence of a vestigial ledge handle in the form of a "pie-crust" indented band on the exterior of No. 75 indicates that this form continued into EB IVA, for these vestigial handles are more common in that phase. An illustration is provided from **Ader**, Phase B (Cleveland 1960: pl. 24A: 11). The deep bowl or vat shown in No. 76 has a similar profile with a thickened rim, but the inverted lip is more rounded and knob-like. This form is found at the EB IV sites of **Ader**, unprovenienced (ibid.: fig. 15: 19) and **^{c}Aro^{c}er**, Level VIb (Olávarri 1969: fig. 3: 6). A horizontal, raised, and impressed band is attached to the exterior surface. Examples of this decorative element that display higher and more distinctive relief occur on vats from **Ader**, Phase B (Cleveland 1960: fig. 13: 18) and **Khirbet Iskander** (Richard and Boraas 1984: fig. 18: 20). As in the case of No. 75, this example cannot be associated exclusively with the EB IV period. As discussed in the preceding section, sherd No. 47 of the EB II-III sample has an identical raised band.

The two rolled-rim platter bowl fragments, Nos. 77 and 78, are similar to a late EB III form from **Bab edh-Dhra^c**, Field X, Phase 1 (Johnston and Schaub 1978: fig. 3: 12), but the later development of this rounded, hooked rim is clear from its presence in EB IV deposits. No. 77 is paralleled at **Bab edh-Dhra^c**, Field X, Phase 2 (ibid.: fig. 4: 45) and **Ader**, unprovenienced (Cleveland 1960: fig. 15: 10, 12), and a similar form may be noted from **Khirbet Iskander** (Parr 1960: fig. 1: 9). Specific parallels to No. 78 are also found at **Bab edh-Dhra^c** (Albright et al. 1944: pl. 1: 29) and **Ader**, Phase A (Cleveland 1960: fig. 13: 6).

The widespread EB IV rilled-rim platter bowl, No. 79, is distinguished by a sloping, inverted rim and gentle grooves or rills on the exterior. This vessel type is well documented in both EB IVA and B contexts in southern Transjordan, though the later EB IVB profiles tend to be more exaggerated: **Ader**, Phase B (Cleveland 1960: fig. 14: 5, 15-17) and Phase A (ibid.: fig. 13: 4, 7-9), **^{c}Aro^{c}er**, Level VIb (Olávarri 1969: fig. 1) and Level VIa (ibid.: fig. 4: 4-12), and probably **Bab edh-Dhra^c**, Field X, Phase 3 (Johnston and Schaub 1978: fig. 5: 62-65, 67-70) and Field X, Phase 4 (ibid.: fig. 5: 73, 75-76, 78-79). The most directly comparable examples to No. 79, however, are found in EB IVA levels at **Ader**, Phase B (Cleveland 1960: fig. 14: 5) and **Tell Iktanu**, Phase 1 (Prag 1974: fig. 3: 22). Yet another example can be cited from an EB IVB context at **Tell Beit Mirsim**, Strata H/I (Albright 1932b: pl. 4: 10). This form is also attested at **Khirbet Iskander** (Parr 1960: fig. 1: 10).

No. 80 represents another style of inverted bowl rim, yet it lacks the characteristic rilling of No. 79 and is not easily paralleled in the literature. The plain, peaked rim of a deep bowl, pictured in No. 81, has a slight indentation on the inner surface but is simple in all other respects. As is the case with No. 80, this form is not readily documented among stratified assemblages.

A group of hole-mouth vessels is shown in Nos. 82-87. The upper edge of the thick, squared rim of No. 82 is scalloped with finger indentations. The paste and red slip indicate that this vessel was a jar rather than a cooking pot. Related forms are found at **Ader**, Phase B (Cleveland 1960: fig. 14: 7) and **el-Fakhat** (Glueck 1951: pl. 119: 11). As Richard and Boraas have noted (1984: 81), hole-mouth vessels with a beveled lip include both storage jar and cooking pot forms. The profiles shown in Nos. 83 and 84 appear to belong to storage jars. These pieces generally compare with forms from **Ader**, Phase B (Cleveland 1960: fig. 14: 19); **Tell Iktanu**, Phase 1 (Prag 1974: fig. 3: 18); **el-Fakhat** (Glueck 1951: pl. 119: 14); and **Khirbet ^{c}Ayn Riyashi** (ibid.: pl. 123: 14). The deeply grooved hole-mouth pot rim illustrated in No. 85 is paralleled at **^{c}Aro^{c}er**, Level VIb (Olávarri 1969: fig. 2: 4).

Rilled-rim hole-mouth vessels are well represented among EB IVA sites of the southern Levant and of

Transjordan in particular. Although this form is often spouted, and hence the term "teapot," the example shown in No. 86 is too fragmentary to determine whether or not a spout had been attached. The widespread presence of this form is demonstrated at **Bab edh-Dhra^c**, Tomb A 54 (Schaub 1973: figs. 6: 5, 8, 14; 7: 17; 8: 23), an EB IVA context, and **Ader**, Phase A (Cleveland 1960: pl. 24B: 6), where it was found with EB IVB sherds. Specific parallels occur at **Tell Iktanu**, Phase 1 (Prag 1974: fig. 4: 11); **^{c}Aro^{c}er**, Level VIb (Olávarri 1969: fig. 2: 2; pl. IV: 15); **Khirbet Iskander** (Richard and Boraas 1984: fig. 18: 29); and in the **Negev**, **Beer Resisim** (Cohen and Dever 1979: fig. 18: 15).

No. 87, representing another neckless teapot, has an upturned rim and the shoulder bears shallow incising. An excellent example of this form was recovered from an EB IVA tomb at **Bab edh-Dhra^c** (Rast and Schaub 1980: fig. 11: 7).

The jug or jar rim No. 88, with a concave profile, probably belonged to a form similar to a vessel from **Tell Iktanu**, Phase 1 (Prag 1974: fig. 5: 22).

The ovoid loop handle, shown in section in No. 89, is a common attribute of EB IVA jugs and jars, and comparisons are found at **Bab edh-Dhra^c**, Tomb A 54 (Schaub 1973: figs. 6: 11, 15; 7: 21; 8: 22, 24-25). The small pierced lug handle presented in No. 90 is attached to the shoulder of a rilled-rim hole-mouth vessel just beneath the rilling (profile not illustrated). An example of this handle appears on a teapot from **Bab edh-Dhra^c**, Tomb A 54 (Schaub 1973: fig. 6: 14).

Sherd No. 91 appears to be from the shoulder of a jar or jug. Its surface displays an unusual combination of two EB IV decorative treatments that typically occur independently. The horizontal bands of parallel and wavy incised combing are highly characteristic of EB IVB ceramics. Yet heavily stroked radial burnish lines were applied to this surface prior to the incising. In Transjordan this style of burnishing dates back to EB III, becomes prominent during EB IVA, and is found among sherds from some EB IVB deposits as well. One instance of the co-occurrence of incising and burnishing may be cited from **Ader**, Phase B (Cleveland 1960: pl. 24: 6).

Sherds Nos. 92 and 93 belong to necks of large jars and illustrate a technique of raised band impressing in which a small flat paddle or stamp was used to press the band. This style of relief molding is present at **Ader**, Phase B (Cleveland 1960: pl. 23B:8). Light body combing (not illustrated) is preserved on No. 93 beneath, and perpendicular to, the impressed band. This combination of molding and body combing is also documented at **Ader** (ibid.: pl. 23A: 4).

Description: EB IVB. EB IVB wares from the Kerak plateau are very few in comparison with the relatively broadly distributed EB II-III and EB IVA wares from the region, and in some respects, this sample from the survey diverges from other EB IVB collections of southern Transjordan.

Richard (1980) has demonstrated that interpretations of EB IVB ceramics that emphasize a radical break from forms of the EB IVA ceramic tradition are not wholly consistent with the data. Her comparative analysis of vessel morphology (ibid.) indicates that there is demonstrable continuity between some of the principal EB IVA and EB IVB forms. These apparent continuities imply that some of the EB IV sherds from the Kerak plateau could date to either EB IVA or EB IVB. The sherds discussed in this section, however, represent either forms or wares that appear to be distinctly EB IVB.

Though limited, the EB IVB corpus from the survey reflects some of the ceramic innovations and changes, in terms of ware characteristics and general forms, that characterize assemblages from this period. Fragments of simple cups and shallow bowls (Nos. 94-97), and one sherd from a jar with a short but sharply splayed neck (No. 98), are the most chronologically diagnostic sherds with respect to form. The fact that these vessels are not easily paralleled in terms of stylistic details may indicate locally diverse trends in ceramic manufacture.

The EB IVB sample largely consists of hard, thin fabrics, yet these are not always well fired, and paste preparation in some instances is inferior to that of EB IVA. Pale brown and light buff slips dominate, though in one or two cases a dull red slip has been applied (Nos. 95, 107). Surface treatments concentrate upon grooving and incising. The former is often subtle (Nos. 95, 97-98), marking the exterior of bowls or jar shoulders. Incising is highly typical among EB IVB assemblages, and in the Kerak plateau corpus it occurs both as bands of slash marks (Nos. 101-104) and as bands of parallel horizontal and/or wavy lines (Nos. 105-7).

Forms: EB IVB. The simple rounded rim of No. 94 represents a cup that compares with an example from ᶜAroᶜer, Level VIA (Olávarri 1969: fig. 4: 15). The same vessel occurs with incising at **Tell el-ᶜAjjul**, Tomb A 244 (Kenyon 1956: fig. 7: 4). A group of shallow bowls with simple rims is presented in Nos. 95-97, and these forms are generally similar to rims from **ᶜAroᶜer**, Level VIa (Olávarri 1969: fig. 4: 13). They are distinct, however, from the common EB IVB bowl profiles that include the cyma of **Khirbet Iskander** (Richard and Boraas 1984: fig. 18:14) and **ᶜAroᶜer**, Level VIa (Olávarri 1969: fig. 4: 19), and carinated forms of **ᶜAroᶜer**, Level VIa (ibid.: fig. 4: 16). In terms of surface decoration, the outer vessel wall of No. 96 is marked with broad grooves, and No. 95 is lightly incised on the exterior of the rim in a similar manner as found at ᶜAroᶜer, Level VIa (ibid.: fig. 4: 13).

Similarly, the jar rim shown in No. 98 is not well attested among EB IVB assemblages of Transjordan. The rounded rim is splayed and the shoulder is marked by two wide, shallow grooves. Broadly similar forms occur in the Negev, **Beer Resisim** (Cohen and Dever 1979: fig. 17: 11) and at **Wadi ed-Daliyeh**, Cave II (Lapp and Lapp 1974: pl. 5: 3), but for the most part, EB IVB splayed neck jars are taller than sherd No. 98. From the Kerak plateau another comparable form can be noted from a largely EB IVA context at **Ader**, Phase B (Cleveland 1960: fig. 14: 18). The fabric of this sherd from Ader is typical of EB IVA pottery.

Flat bases are difficult to type chronologically as they remain relatively uniform throughout the Early Bronze Age. However, the light cream slip and hard fabric of Nos. 99 and 100 indicate that they most likely date to EB IVB occupations. The interior bulge of No. 99 and the thick heel and tapered bottom of No. 100 are evident on bases in the **Negev**, **Beer Resisim** (Cohen and Dever 1978: fig. 10: 19, 18).

The sherd shown in No. 101 is an unusual and enigmatic form. The pierced hole indicates that it could be a strainer fragment, yet the presence of only one puncture is puzzling. The finished, curved inner edge of the sherd suggests that the vessel mouth may have been ringed with a strainer while the orifice was either open or fitted with a stopper. Traces of decorative incising are preserved on the exterior.

Hatched and incised decorations are especially popular during EB IVB, and several examples of these surface treatments are shown in Nos. 102-7. Although necks of vessels are frequently decorated in this fashion, No. 102 is not a typical example. In this case the vertical incising was applied to a thick raised band. A similar instance of a raised band applied to the base of a jar neck is found at **Jericho**, Tomb P 24 (Kenyon 1965: fig. 68: 1).

Incising directly into a vessel wall at or near the juncture of the neck and shoulder of closed vessels is more common, and Nos. 103 and 104 show simple and direct hatching of this style. Among the numerous examples of this characteristic EB IVB decoration, a few are selected for comparison: **ᶜAroᶜer**, Level VIa (Olávarri 1969: pl. V: 10); **Amman**, tomb (Zayadine 1978: pl. X: 4); **Tell el-Hayyat** (Falconer and Magness-Gardiner 1984: fig. 12: 6); **Ḥusn** (Harding 1953a; Isserlin 1953a: figs. 2: 26, 42, 43; 3: 48, 50, 54); **Jericho**, Trench I (Kenyon 1952: fig. 6: 39); and **Silwan** (Saᶜad 1964: pl. XXXV: 5).

Incising in bands of parallel, horizontal and wavy lines is a principal EB IVB decorative treatment. As in the case of the incised hatch marks mentioned above, this incising was often applied to the zone where a jug or jar neck joined the vessel shoulder. Multiple incised bands occur on cups and hole-mouth vessels as well, as illustrated by forms from **Jericho**, Trench I (Kenyon 1952: fig. 6: 42) and in the **Negev**, **Beer Resisim** (Cohen and Dever 1981: fig. 10: 25). This incising, illustrated in Nos. 105-7, is well documented at EB IVB sites in Transjordan: **ᶜAroᶜer**, Level VIa (Olávarri 1969: pl. III: 10-11, 13-14, 16); **Khirbet Iskander** (Parr 1960: fig. 1: 17, 20-21; Richard and Boraas 1984: fig. 18: 25-26); and **Tell Iktanu**, Phase 2 (Prag 1974: fig. 8: 7, 9). At **Ader** this treatment is associated with EB IVA remains in Phase B (Cleveland 1960: pl. 24A: 6-7). Two tomb groups from sites farther north, **Amman** (Zayadine 1978) and **Ḥusn** (Harding 1953a; Isserlin 1953a), do not contain vessels incised in this manner, whereas comparisons to Nos. 105-7 are widespread in Palestine.

The shallow fork impressing seen in No. 105 is paralleled at a number of sites: **ᶜAroᶜer**, Level VIa (Olávarri 1969: pls. III: 11, 16; V: 2); **ᶜAin es-Samiya** (Dever 1972: fig. 2: 1); **Tell Beit Mirsim**, Strata H/I

(Albright 1932b: pl. 4: 41); **Wadi ed-Daliyeh** (Lapp and Lapp 1974: pl. 6: 3); **Jericho** (Garstang 1932: pl. XII: 10), and in the **Negev, Beer Resisim** (Cohen and Dever 1979: fig. 17: 7-8 and 1981: fig. 11: 5, 9).

Discussion: EB IVA and EB IVB. The EB IVA assemblage from the Kerak plateau shows particularly strong affinity with pottery from other EB IVA ceramic groups in Transjordan. Yet the widespread diagnostic attributes of EB IVA ceramics, such as the inverted rill-rimmed vessels and liberal use of red slip and burnish that distinguish these deposits from EB II-III assemblages, are not wholly restricted to EB IVA assemblages. Richard (1980) has demonstrated that these features can occur in EB IVB contexts, as is particularly clear in a comparison of the EB IVA and EB IVB strata at either ᶜAroer or Ader. Nevertheless, these essentially EB IVA elements do not figure prominently in the EB IVB strata of Transjordan, and their presence in the Kerak plateau survey collection probably can be treated, for the most part, as indicative of EV IVA settlement.

The EB IVB assemblage, being significantly smaller, is more difficult to characterize, particularly with respect to vessel forms. However, despite this ambiguity, the decorative incising observed in this assemblage is consistent with EB IVB pottery on a very broad geographic scale and demonstrates, in this respect, thematic homogeneity with EB IVB assemblages throughout the southern Levant.

The presence of both EB IVA and EB IVB occupation on the Kerak plateau accords well with data from excavated EB IV sites in central and southern Transjordan. EB IVA is particularly well-represented, and as Dever (1980) has noted, this ceramic group may, in part, reflect a higher density of sedentary population in Transjordan than in Palestine, where presently this pottery is rarely attested. However, the apparently low proportion of EB IVB pottery in the Kerak plateau survey collection begs explanation, particularly when viewed in terms of Dever's (1980) analysis. In this work Dever suggested that fairly widespread EB IVB occupation in both Palestine and Transjordan is characterized by ceramic assemblages that constitute geographically circumcised and regionally distinct "families," including "Family TR," a Transjordanian group constituting the EB IVB assemblages from Ader, ᶜAroᶜer, Khirbet Iskander, and Tell Iktanu. In addition, there are a few apparent EB IVB features at Bab edh-Dhraᶜ (ibid.). While the presence of at least some EB IVA and EB IVB occupation at each of these sites indicates continuity of settlement occupation in central /southern Transjordan during the EB IVA-B transition, the dearth of evidence for EB IVB occupation in the survey collection may indicate that the sedentary population on the Kerak plateau during this latter stage of EB IV occupation was actually fairly restricted, perhaps concentrated at Ader and possibly a few other sites as yet to be identified.

Middle Bronze I-II

The Middle Bronze Age ceramic tradition represents a clear divergence from the preceding Early Bronze IV period. Recently this divergence has been recognized as sufficient justification for adopting terminology that reflects the stylistic contrast between the often termed "MB IIA" ceramic group and the later assemblages traditionally referred to as "MB IIB-C." Hence, these traditional terms "MB IIA" and "MB IIB-C" (Amiran 1969) have been replaced, in this text, with the terms "MB I" and "MB II," in accordance with the terminology proposed by Dever (1973, 1980) and Gerstenblith (1980, 1983); the term "MB I" replaces the MB IIA designation, and "MB II" is substituted for the MB IIB-C designation.

Middle Bronze Age pottery from central and southern Transjordan is still relatively unknown. Few settlements have been identified and, accordingly, there are few published MB assemblages. In southern Transjordan a shift in settlement pattern is evident with the onset of the Middle Bronze Age. None of the excavated EB IVB sites in or near the Kerak region—Bab edh-Dhraᶜ, Ader, ᶜAroᶜer, and Khirbet Iskander—was occupied during the Middle Bronze Age. Glueck recognized only a few MB sherds on the Kerak plateau (1934: 82), and the recent Wadi el-Ḥasa survey has recorded only two potential MB sites from a total of 214 (MacDonald 1982: 45, 49). However, it appears that the Middle Bronze Age is represented on the Kerak plateau to a greater extent than anticipated by Glueck's earlier research, for 15 sites with 5 or more sherds have now been identified. While this tentative evaluation does not indicate widespread settlement, it does open avenues for future research concerning the nature of MB occupation in the region.

Because of this apparent low density of occupation and the corresponding lack of local ceramic sequences in the region, it is necessary to assess the MB assemblage from the Kerak plateau almost solely in terms of the ceramics found at large urban sites and in tomb groups from the more populated regions of the southern Levant. In this respect the excavation of Tell el-Hayyat (Falconer and Magness-Gardiner 1983, 1984; Falconer 1987), a rural Middle Bronze Age settlement in the east Jordan Valley, has made a valuable contribution to an understanding of village occupation in Transjordan during this period. Typological relationships are suggested below in the discussion of forms, but the proposed periodizations and associations should be treated as preliminary.

Description: MB I-II. The major development in Middle Bronze Age ceramics is the introduction of the potter's wheel on a broad scale. The ceramics described in this section are nearly all wheel thrown, with the exception of the cooking pot (No. 121) and possibly one or two other pieces. The MB assemblage from the Kerak plateau is fairly limited, and the most representative sherds are largely from bowls, jugs, and jars. Some of these forms are attested at other MB sites, but a number of them may be local variations that are specific to the Kerak region.

The assemblage presented in this section consists of several different ware types and surface treatments that contrast with the EB IVB pottery. Given that our perception of how the particular forms illustrated here relate to MB material culture from other regions of Palestine and Transjordan is tentative, the ware characteristics are sometimes a major factor in evaluating the approximate chronology.

Soft, pale-brown fabrics and a few harder grey wares dominate this corpus. The brown wares, highly characteristic of MB pottery in general and of MB I in particular (see Smith 1973: pl. 88A: 924), are noted among bowl forms (especially Nos. 108-9, 119-20); jars (Nos. 128, 131, 133-34); jugs (Nos. 135-37); a juglet (No. 140); bases (Nos. 147-51, 154-55); and a painted body sherd (No. 157). Grey wares (see Smith 1973: pl. 88A: 919) from the Kerak plateau are represented by sherds from some closed vessels (Nos. 123-25, 130, 138). Red wares also occur, though less frequently, as attested by juglet handle No. 141 and bowl rim No. 112. A comparison between MB wares from Pella (ibid.: pls. 88A; 88D; 89B; 89C) and those of the Kerak region shows that there are many similarities. In addition to this apparent regional continuity, Smith has observed (ibid.: 197) that MB I and MB II wares at Pella are similar to one another, demonstrating temporal homogeneity.

Red and cream colored slips are present as well as brown and self-slipped finishes. The red slip that is so consistent among MB wares in the southern Levant is common among bowl fragments in the Kerak collection (Nos. 108-10, 112, 116-18) but is also found on a juglet handle (No. 141) and a composite braided handle (No. 143). Cream slips occasionally occur on the exterior of bowls that have an interior red slip (Nos. 112, 116, 118), but both cream and buff slips are more frequent among jars. One open bowl (No. 114) is distinguished by a thick cream slip that was particularly heavily applied to the vessel interior.

Painted rim bands and designs in red and dark reddish brown are found on several pieces including the rim and interior of a bowl (No. 119); the rim and exterior surface of another bowl (No. 120); and on the interior rims of jars (No. 122) and jugs (No. 135). Red painted body design is also attested (No. 157), but this piece should not be mistaken for the glossy, burnished, chocolate-on-cream wares. Many of the sherds are poorly preserved, and it is often difficult to detect the presence or absence of burnishing. There is, however, one very clear instance in which the interior surface of a base (No. 146) was comprehensively burnished, partially over a bright red slip and partially over a brown slip. Red burnished MB wares have been extremely rare in Jordan, yet other examples on body sherds (not illustrated) are included in the survey collection.

The quality of paste preparation and the nature of tempering agents are highly variable. The large proportion of poorly prepared fabrics contrasts with the sophistication of techniques that developed during the Early Bronze Age. Many of the sherds are coarse and contain large amounts of mineral inclusions that sometimes mar the surfaces, despite slipping. In some instances, chaff, dung, or other organic inclusions were well ground and thoroughly mixed with the clay. Yet frequently these tempering agents were not well integrated and, consequently, have left pock marks in the fabrics. It is noteworthy that the use of organic temper has not been described at Pella (see Smith 1973). The thick, grey-blue cores which are found at Pella (ibid.: pl. 88D: 706, 669) are numerous among the Kerak sherds, indicating that relatively little attention was devoted to the firing process in a number of instances. Brown wares, however, tend to be well prepared and exhibit excellent firing.

Only a few examples of plastic decoration are represented in this corpus. One open bowl (No. 111) has an exterior knob of clay affixed, while another (No. 115) has a longer, pointed and curved knob that may have served as a handle. Modeling occurs on two loop handles, one with a strip of clay attached to the upper surface (No. 142) and the other with elaborately intertwined strips of clay bonded to its surface (No. 143). The only examples of thumb impressing and raised band decoration are both found on cooking pot No. 121.

Forms: MB I-II. Several different types of bowls are presented in Nos. 108-20 including: a straight-sided bowl (No. 108); open bowls (Nos. 109-18); an incurved bowl (No. 119); and a carinated bowl (No. 120). The straight-sided bowl No. 108 with a rounded rim and an exterior red slip is not a common form; it is paralleled in two MB I strata of the "Palace" Phase at **Ras el-ᶜAyn**, Stratum A, IVb (Beck 1975: fig. 6: 7) and Stratum A, IVa (ibid.: fig. 8: 7). A less flared vessel of this type occurs at **Tell el-Hayyat**, Phase 5 (Falconer and Magness-Gardiner 1984: fig. 13: 5).

Open bowls that are reminiscent of the Early Bronze Age platter bowls figure prominently in MB I and II assemblages, but the specific rim styles associated with these forms are not apparent in the literature from sites in other regions and, therefore, may be local developments. As in the case of earlier platter bowls, these forms persist and can be found throughout MB I and II deposits with a wide range of diverse rim styles.

Various rim forms occur among the open bowls. Nos. 109-11 are flattened rims. No. 109 is distinguished by a thickened, squared rim and a heavy red slip. In Transjordan, bowls of this profile with a ring base are noted from a late MB tomb in **Amman** (Harding 1953b; Isserlin 1953b: fig. 6:3-4, 6, 9). In contrast to No. 109, two of these examples are cream slipped. At **Megiddo**, other squared, upright bowl rims are found in MB II contexts (Kenyon 1969: fig. 8: 2, 4) and are accompanied by either a raised disc base or a flat disc base. Of the shallower bowls with flattened rims, No. 110 has a tapered rim and red slip, while No. 111 is self-slipped, pale brown, and compares with a bowl from **Ras el-ᶜAyn** that has a disc base: "Palace" Phase, Stratum A, IVa (Beck 1975: fig. 8: 9). A rounded knob of clay is attached to the exterior of No. 111, and a similar knob was broken from the exterior surface of No. 110. These decorative knobs are well known from MB I deposits at **Tell el-Hayyat**, Phase 4 (Falconer and Magness-Gardiner 1984: 61; fig. 14: 11); **Megiddo**, T. 911D (Guy 1938: pl. 31: 13), and **Ras el-ᶜAyn**, "Palace" Phase, Stratum A, IVb (Beck 1975: fig. 4: 17).

Open bowls with simple rounded rims are illustrated in Nos. 112-14. No. 112 is comparable, in both form and reddish ware, to a vessel from an MB I deposit at **ᶜAfula**, Pit F, Tomb 19 (Sukenik 1948: pl. XV: 13) which shows this form with a ring base. No. 112 also bears a close resemblance to a bowl from **Gibeon**, Tomb 42 (Pritchard 1963: fig. 46: 1), in an assemblage that may date to early MB II (Dever 1976). The brown slipped sherd shown in No. 113, which belongs to a shallower bowl, may be a later, MB II type. Its form is similar to a cream slipped dish from **Pella**, Stratum IIA (Smith 1973: pl. 35: 556) and a red slipped dish from **Shechem** (Seger 1974: fig. 3: 20), though the ware and surface treatment of No. 113 are inferior to these examples.

The plainly rounded and faintly everted rim of No. 114 is not easily documented at other sites, and it may be noted that inverted rims are more widespread during the Middle Bronze Age. However, simple, unthickened bowl rims are frequent in a late MB II tomb at **Amman** (Harding 1953b; Isserlin 1953b: fig. 6) where cream slip is common among these vessels (as noted above, No. 109). Although the fabric and firing of No. 114 are exceptionally poor, the slip and form imply a very late MB II or possibly LB I date. It can be observed that sherds Nos. 113 and 114 are alike with respect to form and appear best paralleled in these late MB contexts. Both show some affinity, however, with an MB I form from **Jericho**, Tomb K3 (Kenyon 1965: fig. 93:3).

The beveled rim and everted lip of bowl No. 115 are paralleled by a vessel of similar ware from an MB I layer at **Ras el-ᶜAyn**, Stratum A, IVa (Beck 1975: fig. 8: 14). No. 115 has an exterior white slip, and a small pointed handle or decorative knob joins the rim. Another vessel of comparable form with knob handles and a ring base may be cited from **ᶜAin es-Samiyeh** (Dever 1975: fig. 3: 4).

The flattened, elongated bowl rim pictured in No. 116 compares with an example from **Jericho**, the MB II Phase 1 (Kenyon 1966: fig. 30: 1), which has a disc base. At **Tell el-Farᶜah** (south) a more exaggerated form, dated late MB II, appears: Tomb F559 (Williams 1977: fig. 35: 9). Two gently curved bowls with thickened rims and red slip are shown in Nos. 117 and 118. An MB I date may be suggested for No. 117, for this everted rim is found at **Lachish**, MB Fill (Tufnell 1958: fig. 57: 201) and **ᶜAfula**, Pit F, Tomb 19 (Sukenik 1948: pl. XV: 7). This form persists into the Late Bronze Age, as demonstrated at **Baqᶜah**, Cave A2 (McGovern 1986: fig. 17:7); **Queen Alia Airport** (Kafafi 1983: fig. 22: 149); and **Gibeon**, Tomb 10B (Pritchard 1963: fig. 9: 5). The fabric of No. 118 is identical to that of No. 117, but the rim form is not clearly paralleled in the literature.

Incurved bowls, such as No. 119, appear in MB assemblages but are far less common than the open and carinated bowl forms. Approximate MB I forms appear at **Ras el-ᶜAyn** (Iliffe 1936: 122, no. 15); **ᶜAfula**, Pit F, Tomb 19 (Sukenik 1948: pl. XV: 15-16); and **Megiddo** (Kenyon 1966: fig. 27: 4). Some of these examples are of brown fabric with red painted rims, but none precisely replicates the curved profile of No. 119, nor is the dripped red interior paint attested. This genre of bowls continues into MB II. It appears occasionally with a ring base and white slip as at **Pella**, Tomb 1 (Smith 1973: pl. 48: 135), and variations are found at **Dhahrat el-Humraiya**, Grave 5 (Ory 1948: fig. 10) and **Tell el-Farᶜah** (south), Tomb F596 (Williams 1977: fig. 106: 1). A comparable bowl from **Beisan**, Tomb 59 (Oren 1973b: fig. 26: 4) indicates that this form continued into the Late Bronze Age.

The rim shown in No. 120 represents a carinated bowl with a gentle, rounded profile. The soft, brown fabric has a horizontal band of dark red-brown paint that covers the rim and a portion of the exterior. The carinated bowl, in a variety of forms, is a consistent feature of MB assemblages. In MB I Transjordan it occurs at **Pella**, Area I (Smith 1973: pl. 27: 924); **Jawa** (Helms 1975: fig. 5: 5); and **Tell el-Hayyat**, Phases 5 and 4 (Falconer and Magness-Gardiner 1984: figs. 13: 2; 15: 12). No. 120 is best paralleled, however, by a vessel with a flat base and painted band from **Ras el-ᶜAyn**, "Palace" Phase, Stratum A, IVb (Beck 1975: fig. 6: 6; see also Iliffe 1936: 122, no. 7) and at **Tell Beit Mirsim**, Strata G-F (Albright 1933: pl. 4: 8).

The straight-sided, hand-made cooking pot, No. 121, is virtually an ubiquitous component of MB I domestic assemblages. Its prototype, a broad based form, dates to the EB IVB period as demonstrated at **ᶜAroᶜer**, Level VIa (Olávarri 1969: fig. 5: 12). The coarse ware of No. 121 contains numerous dark mineral inclusions and some organic material and displays a substantial core. A thick, impressed band of clay was applied directly beneath the rim, and above this raised band are deep, though not fully penetrating, thumb indentations. The slightly splayed rim is best paralleled at **Megiddo**, Stratum XV (Loud et al. 1948: pl. 9: 19) and at **ᶜAfula**, Pit F, Tomb 19 (Sukenik 1948: pl. XV: 20). The same pattern of impressed decoration is also well illustrated at **ᶜAfula**, Pit F, Tomb 19 (ibid.: pl. XV: 19). Numerous other examples which show the wide distribution of this vessel type may be cited from **Tell el-Hayyat**, Phase 5 (Falconer and Magness-Gardiner 1984: fig. 13: 3), Phase 4 (ibid.: fig. 14: 5) and Phase 3, (ibid.: fig. 18: 6-9); **Ras el-ᶜAyn**, "Pre-Palace" Phase, Strata A, VII and A, VI (Beck 1975: figs. 1: 2; 2: 15-16) and "Palace" Phase, Strata A, IVb and A, IVa (ibid.: figs. 5: 1-2; 8: 19); **Wadi ed-Daliyeh**, Cave II (Lapp and Lapp 1974: pl. 15: 6); **Tell el-Farᶜah** (north) (de Vaux and Stève 1947: fig. 8: 9-10); **Hazor**, Stratum XVII (Yadin et al. 1961: pl. CLVI: 24-25); and **Lachish**, MB Fill (Tufnell 1958: fig. 3: 176). Later versions with thumb-impressed bands at the rim of the cooking pot are found at **Tell Beit Mirsim**, Stratum D (Albright 1933: pl. 13: 3-5) and **Shechem**, Strata XX, XIX, XVIII (Cole 1984: pls. 23; 24a).

Jar rims are pictured in Nos. 122-34. The simple, rounded rim of No. 122 retains traces of red paint on the interior. This form is paralleled at **Tell Beit Mirsim**, Stratum E (Albright 1933: pl. 7: 10). **Shechem**, Stratum XVIII (Cole 1984: pl. 48: g) provides a rim variation that is more widely flared. Nos. 123-29 show a range of variations among thickened and profiled storage jar rims.

The basic everted style of Nos. 123-25 is exemplified in an MB I context at **Ras el-ᶜAyn** (Iliffe 1936: 124, no. 68), but closer parallels emerge from MB II strata. A sherd from **Tell el-Farᶜah** (north) (de Vaux and Stève 1947: fig. 8: 6) may be compared with No. 123. No. 124 is paralleled at **Nahariya** (Ben-Dor 1950: fig. 19: i), and similar jars occur at **Achzib** (Oren 1975: fig. 3: 68) and **Shechem**, Strata XIX and XVIII (Cole 1984: pl. 33: b, i). No. 125 is paralleled at **Shechem** (Seger 1974: fig. 4: 18). Jars 126-28 with thickened, everted rims, shallowly grooved across the top, may be local developments, for they are not clearly attested within published Middle Bronze Age assemblages. Similarly, the peaked and exterior grooved profile of No. 129 is not a typical form.

The slightly thickened and indented rim No. 130 appears to have a broad chronological history, for similar forms are noted at **Tell el-Hayyat**, Phase 5 (Falconer and Magness-Gardiner 1984: fig. 3: 8); **Ras el-ᶜAyn**, "Pre-Palace" Phase, Stratum A, IVa (Beck 1975: fig. 10: 6); **Shechem** (Wright 1965: fig. 111: p); and **Nahariya** (Ben-Dor 1950: fig. 21a). The hooked rim of jar No. 131 is broadly comparable to sherds from two MB I sites: **Tell el-Hayyat**, Phase 4 (Falconer and Magness-Gardiner 1984: fig. 16: 1-6) and **Ras el-ᶜAyn**, "Pre-Palace" Phase, Strata A, VII and A, VI (Beck 1975: figs. 1: 5; 3: 3). The out-turned and flattened profile of No. 132 is paralleled at **Ras el-ᶜAyn**, "Post-Palace" Phase, Stratum A, II (ibid.: fig. 13: 11). Related sherds from **Shechem**, Stratum XX (Cole 1984: fig. 33: g; see also Seger 1974: fig. 3: 8) indicate that this form developed during the MB II period as well.

Neither the large storage jar rim, No. 133, nor the pithos rim, No. 134, is a common form, yet this genre of thickened, bulbous rims is represented at **Tell el-Hayyat**, Phase 5 (Falconer and Magness-Gardiner 1984: fig.13:13).

Of the jug forms that are presented in Nos. 135-39, Nos. 135-37 are buff wares. Hooked rims that resemble No. 135 are noted at **Tell el-Hayyat**, Phase 4 (Falconer and Magness-Gardiner 1984: fig. 16: 1-6) and **Shechem**, Strata XX, XVIII (Cole 1984: pl. 40: i, j). Nos. 136 and 137 are quite similar to one another, though the neck of No. 137 is distinguished by a light exterior groove. These rims compare with a jug from **Megiddo** (Kenyon 1969: fig. 13: 14) and probably date to MB II. Of the splayed, bulbous rims of taller necked jugs, Nos. 138 and 139, the former is represented at **Tell el-Farᶜah** (north), Tomb A (Mallet 1974: fig. 2: 1) and **Megiddo** (Kenyon 1969: fig. 7: 16), and the latter is also found at **Megiddo**, Tomb 24 (Guy 1938: pl. 23: 21). The plain, thickened rim of a brown ware juglet or small jug is shown in No. 140.

Several distinctive handles are shown in Nos. 141-44. The handle of a small juglet, shown in section in No. 141, has many parallels in MB strata; a few examples include red slipped juglet handles from **Khirbet Minḥa** (Ferembach et al. 1975: fig. 5: 10) and **ᶜAin es-Samiyeh** (Dever 1975: fig. 3: 6). Loop handles are typical of Middle Bronze Age jugs and juglets, but the example shown in No. 142 is distinguished by an applied band of clay with a punctured design. Similar jug handles from a number of sites show that this attached band was often modeled in the image of a snake: **Gibeon**, Tomb 22 (Pritchard 1963: fig. 30: 9); **ᶜAin Shems** (Grant 1929: figs. 6-8); **Amman**, **Citadel** (Bennett 1978: fig. 7); **Shechem**, Strata XX, XVIII (Cole 1984: pl. 29: h, i); and **Megiddo** (Kenyon 1969: figs. 2: 14-15; 10: 1).

The braided handle shown in No. 143 may be unique, for it consists of a clay trough in which rests a band of carefully braided strands of clay. There are no apparant parallels to this handle from excavated sites, but an MB origin is strongly suggested by the brown ware and red slip. A similar concept, that of "twisted" handles employing two strands of clay, is evidenced in MB deposits at **Tell el-Farᶜah** (north) (Mallet 1974: fig. 2: 3) and **Megiddo**, Stratum XI (Loud et al. 1948: pl. 34: 11).

Simple double handles such as No. 144 are very common in Middle Bronze Age ceramic repertoires and are particularly frequent on jugs and juglets. These handles are well attested in MB II contexts, but some MB I examples are noted from: **Ras el-ᶜAyn**, "Palace" Phase, Stratum A, IVa (Beck 1975: fig. 9: 2, 5); **ᶜAfula**, Pit F, Tomb 19 (Sukenik 1948: pl. XV: 1-3); and **Tell el-Hayyat**, Phase 4 (Falconer and Magness-Gardiner 1984: fig. 15: 3).

The development of vessel bases during the Middle Bronze Age can be distinguished from that of the preceding EB IVB period by criteria of form and fabric. Though flat bases are common to EB IVB vessels, those shown in Nos. 145-48 consist of pale brown and pinkish wares that are characteristic of the MB ceramic tradition. The red and brown burnished interior of No. 146 indicates that it belonged to an open bowl. An MB I example of this form with a flat base and interior burnish is found at

Megiddo, Stratum XIV, Tomb 3148 (Loud et al. 1948: pl. 14: 17). This flat base, often associated with both open and closed MB I vessels, is less common in later phases but does occur occasionally, most often on closed forms including jugs, juglets and storage jars, as at **Tell el-Far^cah** (south), Tomb F555, Tomb F578 (Williams 1977: figs. 22: 6-10, 14; 75: 3); **Shechem** (Seger 1974: fig. 5: 22); **Pella**, Tomb 22 (Smith et al. 1981: fig. 25: 3).

The disc base is highly typical of Middle Bronze Age vessels and appears on much the same range of forms as the flat base, including bowls, jugs, jars, as well as kraters and juglets. Low disc bases are shown in Nos. 149-50, and higher, thicker bases are shown in Nos. 151-53. Disc bases (as well as flat bases) are common throughout the MB I phases at **Tell el-Hayyat** (Falconer and Magness-Gardiner 1984: 58) and are easily documented at numerous MB II sites, among them **Tananir** (Boling 1975: pl. 1: 21-22); **Tell el-Far^cah** (south), Tomb F557 (Williams 1977: fig. 29: 4); **Shechem** (Seger 1974: fig. 5: 19-20); and **Amman**, tomb (Harding 1953b; Isserlin 1953b: fig. 8: 90).

The Middle Bronze Age is noted for the development of the ring base, and the examples presented in Nos. 154-56 have typical MB fabrics. The ring base is an attribute that became increasingly popular on open vessels throughout this period and the succeeding Late Bronze Age.

Body sherd No. 157 illustrates a style of red-brown painted decoration, which in this instance has been applied to the exterior of a closed vessel. This piece is easily differentiated from MB II chocolate-on-cream ware by a relatively dull pink slipped fabric and lack of burnish. A similar sherd appears at **Tananir** (Boling 1975: pls. 4: 85; 6: 7). This type of painting is also a feature of Late Bronze Age pottery, as noted at **Shechem** (Toombs and Wright 1963: fig. 23: 23), and an example from **Pella** may be Late Bronze in date also (Smith 1973: pl. 38: 701).

Discussion: MB I-II. The Middle Bronze Age pottery from the Kerak plateau can be summarized as utilitarian, consisting of domestic wares with little decoration, in contrast to the rich, almost ornamental vessels that occur among the MB assemblages of Palestine. The forms are repetitive to some degree, showing variations of basic bowl, jug, and jar forms. A number of the parallels in the text are cited from Tell el-Hayyat, a village settlement in the Jordan Valley that has a similar repertoire of functional forms, yet several of the MB I sherds presented above are not represented in the publication of ceramics from this site and, therefore, may reflect styles that were produced in the south-central Transjordanian highland plateau region. The more exotic and novel aspects of the ceramic assemblage of the later Middle Bronze phases, such as the chalice, trumpet-base vase, and sharply carinated bowl and goblet are not found in the Kerak plateau assemblage. Nor is there evidence of elaborate decorative techniques, such as the painted and burnished chocolate-on-cream ware, bichrome painting, or body combing. These finer wares may have been produced at a few centers (Smith 1973: 203) whose distribution spheres would appear not to have encompassed south-central Transjordan. However, the presence of MB I burnished red slip sherds (see No. 146 above), indicates that MB I pottery on the Kerak plateau is not wholly provincial.

This review of forms and their relationships to stratified Middle Bronze pottery indicates that both the MB I (previously "MB IIA") and MB II (previously "MB II B-C") periods are represented on the Kerak plateau. In some instances it appears that specific period designations can be assigned, but in other cases it has been demonstrated that forms or attributes of style are not restricted to a single sub-phase, an observation that is anticipated by the strong continuities and developmental trends that characterize Middle Bronze Age pottery.

Late Bronze I-II

Description: LB I-II. A number of sherds were collected on the survey that have been provisionally assigned to the Late Bronze Age, but, as in the case of the preceding period, there are relatively few clearly diagnostic sherds that are well documented among the assemblages from stratified deposits or tomb groups. This sample illustrates some well-known forms as well as presenting forms that appear to be less common outside of the Kerak region. Only a portion of the wide range of diverse LB forms is represented on the plateau. These types include bowls, kraters, jugs, and jars that, in contrast to ceramics from LB tomb deposits and urban sites, comprise a narrow, utilitarian repertoire. Neither imported wares nor foreign-influenced local products, such as Levanto-Mycenaean wares, are present.

The ware types show considerable variability. Well prepared pale brown clays that are similar to the finer MB wares are present (Nos. 159, 161, 176, 183). Orange fabrics, usually with a core, are also attested (Nos. 158, 165-67, 171-72, 175). One example, No. 173, has a very pale green fabric that is not typical of LB wares in this assemblage. The quality of paste preparation is inconsistent, but there is a notable trend towards the use of fine-grained mineral temper. A number of different slips occur, though most are white, cream, or beige colored. A thick, yellowish cream slip is found on two bowl fragments, Nos. 158 and 160. The uneven slip application of No. 158 is particularly characteristic of later LB pottery and contrasts with the general evenness of MB slips. Lighter cream slips are observed on bowl No. 162, kraters Nos. 164-65, as well as on jugs Nos. 175 and 177 and a few jar forms. White slipped sherds include bowl rim No. 161 and painted body sherd No. 184. A pink slip is found on the decorated krater No. 163. Of the remaining vessel fragments that retain traces of surface finish, most are shades of pale brown.

Other than slipping, surface decoration is rare among the sherds of this assemblage. No traces of burnishing are evident, although bowls, such as No. 161, are found burnished at Baqᶜah and other sites. Nor is LB bichrome painting evident in the Kerak corpus. Four examples of monochrome red painting occur: kraters Nos. 163 and 164; handle No. 178; and body sherd No. 184. In each instance, linear designs are painted in dark reddish hues. Both kraters have vertical strokes of paint that extend down from the rim, though no coherent designs can be identified.

Forms: LB I-II. Bowls are shown in Nos. 158-62. Rim No. 158 belongs to a type of rounded bowl that was particularly prevalent during the LB IB and LB II periods. The simple rounded rim, wheel-ribbed exterior, and unevenly applied cream slip indicate that an LB II date is highly probable for this sherd. However, a series of parallels demonstrates the longevity of this basic form. **Pella**, Tomb 20 (Smith et al. 1981: fig. 24: 19), provides an example from an LB I context. Other occurrences are noted at **Tell Gezer**, Field I, Stratum 6 (Dever et al. 1970: pl. 29: 17, 19), in a deposit that has been dated LB II by the excavators, though it may well be LB IB, as Sauer has suggested (1979a: 71). Among the numerous LB II examples, this form may be compared with vessels from three Transjordanian sites: **Amman**, **Jebel Nuzha**, tomb (Dajani 1966b: pl. XVII: 5); **Queen Alia Airport** (Kafafi 1983: fig. 20: 28); and **Baqᶜah**, Cave B3 (McGovern 1985: fig. 28:13). The latter is painted on the interior. Among the Palestinian LB II sites, **Hazor** provides many forms some of which are wheel-ribbed in a similar manner as No. 158 (Area A, Stratum XIV and Area H, Stratum 1b [Yadin et al. 1961]). Examples of whole vessels with this rim most typically show this bowl with a disc or concave disc base.

The rim style of sherd No. 159 from a bowl with widely flaring sides is not frequently attested. The beveled, inverted profile does, however, appear in LB IIB deposits from two sites: **Shechem**, Field IX, Phase 12 (Bull et al. 1965: fig. 3: 12) and **Tell Gezer**, Field II, Stratum 12 (Dever et al. 1974: pl. 25: 17). It may also be compared with a chalice from **Jericho**, Tomb 4 (Garstang 1933: pl. XV: 10).

The beveled rim of an open bowl is shown in No. 160, a sherd that displays the same cream slip as No. 158. **Beisan**, Tomb 42 (Oren 1973b: fig. 27: 14) and Tomb 29 A-C (ibid.: fig. 39: 3) show this form in LB I and II contexts respectively. Another example is found at **Baqᶜah**, Cave A2 (McGovern 1986: fig. 17: 5).

The sharp carination so characteristic of MB II bowls became much more subtle during the Late Bronze Age. The gentle fold that is commonplace during this period is shown in the white-slipped rim No. 161. The fabric of this sherd, however, is identical to that of late MB bowl wares from **Pella** (Smith 1973: pl. 89B: 867, 883, 703). This softly ridged bowl is a nearly omnipresent feature of LB assemblages, particularly those dated to LB II. In Transjordan this form is known from several sites: the predominantly LB II **Sahab**, tomb (Dajani 1970: pl. XIV: SA.69, SA.216); **Queen Alia Airport** (Kafafi 1983: fig. 21: 56); **Baqᶜah**, Cave B3 (McGovern 1986: fig. 25: 19); **Kataret es-Samra** (Leonard 1979: fig. 9: 8); and **Irbid**, tomb (Dajani 1964: pl. XXXVIII: 1). At **Megiddo** a similar form is found in the LB IA Tomb 77 (Guy 1938: pl. 42: 11). Both LB IB/LB II and LB IIB strata at **Tell Gezer** contain this form; Field I, Stratum 6 (Dever et al. 1970: pl. 29: 3) and Field II,

Stratum 13 (Dever et al. 1974: pl. 22: 5), respectively. Other sources attributed to LB II include: **Hazor**, Area A, L. 280a (Yadin et al. 1961: pl. CLXI: 15); **Tell Abu Hawam**, Phase V (Hamilton 1935a: 48: 291); and **Beisan**, Tomb 29 A-C (Oren 1973b: fig. 39: 7).

The rounded everted rim of bowl No. 162 is similar to forms from an LB I assemblage at **Beisan**, Tomb 42 (ibid.: fig. 28: 27), and deposits that indicate an LB II date: **Amman, Jebel Nuzha**, tomb (Dajani 1966b: pl. XVII: 26); **Queen Alia Airport** (Kafafi 1983: figs. 20: 3; 21: 44); and **Megiddo**, Tomb 912D (Guy 1938: pl. 36: 6). An MB II prototype of this form is found at **Shechem**, Stratum XVIII (Cole 1984: pl. 19: 1).

The pink-slipped krater rim, No. 163, has a small pointed handle attached to the exterior. Part of a red-painted linear design is preserved on the exterior, and a thin band of red paint was applied to the rim. The ware and designs of this sherd are also found at **Lachish**, Temple II (Tufnell et al. 1940: pl. XLVIII: 251). This rim style is documented at **Khirbet el-Baluᶜ** (Glueck 1934: pl. 20: 24) and **Hazor**, Area A, L. 254b (Yadin et al. 1961: pl. CLX: 14) and Area C, Stratum 1b (Yadin et al. 1958: pl. LXXXV: 17). Both Hazor vessels are painted and associated with LB II deposits. A related form occurs at **Sahab**, tomb (Dajani 1970: pl. VIII: SA.3). This form of krater is not restricted to LB assemblages, however, for related forms are found in the transitional LB-Iron Stratum VIIB-VIIA at **Megiddo** (Loud et al. 1948: pl. 67: 18) and in an Iron I layer at **Tel Yinᶜam**, Stratum VIA (Liebowitz 1981: fig. 7: 6).

Cream-slipped krater No. 164 has an upright, everted rim and is painted in the same manner as No. 163. In Transjordan this form is found in a late LB-Iron Age tomb at **Madaba** (Harding 1953c, Isserlin 1953c: fig. 14: 57). In Palestine a parallel occurs in a LB IB context at **Hazor**, Area H, Stratum 2 (Yadin et al. 1961: pl. CCLXIV: 9). Several other examples from **Hazor** may date to LB II: Area A, L. 256b (ibid.: pl. XLXI: 19); Area C, Stratum 1b (Yadin et al. 1958: pl. LXXXV: 18); and Area D, L. 9017 (ibid.: pl. CVIII: 2). Other comparable forms are found at **Megiddo**, Tomb 73 (Guy 1938: pl. 64: 34) and **Tell Qaimun** (Ben-Tor and Rosenthal 1978: fig. 13: 6). In several instances these vessels are accompanied by painted decoration, vertical loop handles, or both.

The same cream slip as noted on No. 164 also appears on the exterior of sherd No. 165. The distinctive squared rim of this krater is not typical but does occur on a larger vessel from **Hazor**, Area H, Stratum 1a (Yadin et al 1961: pl. CCLXXX: 10). Nor is the splayed, everted rim of krater No. 166 widely attested, though **Ashdod**, Stratum 2 (Dothan and Freedman 1967: fig. 19: 7) provides one illustration.

Of the jar rims shown in Nos. 167-73, Nos. 167-69 display the basic "collar" style of rim associated with domestic storage vessels, and Nos. 170-72 present a sequence of variations of this style. Specific parallels to Nos. 167-69 are not common, but as a group they generally compare with jars from several sites, including **Beisan**, Tomb 27 (Oren 1973b: fig. 38: 7). At **Tell Gezer** this form dates to LB I: Field I, L. 9011 (Dever et al. 1970: pl. 22: 4, 16), and Field I, Stratum 6 (ibid: pl. 29: 7) as well as LB II contexts: Field II, Stratum 13 (Dever et al. 1974: pl. 24: 15), and Field VII, Stratum sub-XII (Gitin 1979: pl. 1: 2). Other LB II parallels include examples from **Madaba**, tomb (Harding 1953c; Isserlin 1953c: fig. 15: 65); **Tell es-Saᶜidiyyeh**, Tomb 109 (Pritchard 1980: fig. 12: 4); and **Hazor**, Area D, Stratum 1 (Yadin et al. 1958: pl. CXXVIII: 10). This form continues into Iron I, as indicated by a jar from **Tell Gezer**, Field VII (Gitin 1979: pl. 4: 21). Jar rim No. 168 compares with an LB I example from **Megiddo**, Tomb 77 (Guy 1938: pl. 41: 26).

Variations of this jar rim style include a peaked rim, flattened on the exterior, as seen in Nos. 170-71, and a bulb rim, shown in No. 172. Each of these profiles compares with vessels from **Hazor** that probably date to LB II: No. 170, Area D, L. 7017 (Yadin et al. 1958: pls. CIX: 1; CXXXIV: 7); No. 171, Area F, Stratum 1 (Yadin et al. 1960: pl. CXLIV: 2); and No. 172, Area E, L. 7013 (Yadin et al. 1958: pl. CXLVI: 1). No. 170 may also be compared with a form from **Akko** (Ben-Arieh and Edelstein 1977: fig. 10: 6).

The rounded, outturned rim of No. 173 belongs to a LB II storage jar. This form is found at several sites: **Tell Gezer**, Field I, Stratum 5 and L. 9011 (Dever et al. 1970: pl. 28: 2; Dever et al. 1974: pl. 22: 14-15); **Hazor**, Area K, Stratum 1b (Yadin 1961: pl. CCXCIII: 2); **Gibeon**, Tomb 10A (Pritchard 1963: fig. 8: 29); and **Shechem**, Field IX, Phase 12 (Bull et al. 1965: fig. 3: 3). A related form occurs at **Tell es-Saᶜidiyyeh** (Pritchard 1980: fig. 3: 2). The pale greenish paste of No. 173 is also noted for the example cited above from Hazor.

The jug rims pictured in Nos. 174-77 display some affinity with forms from the Late Bronze Age urban centers of Palestine but are less common in Transjordan. The flared, cut-away rim of No. 174 is paralleled at **Queen Alia Airport** (Kafafi 1983: fig. 21: 71). A similar profile from **Megiddo**, Tomb 989 A1 (Guy 1938: pl. 16: 14) occurs on a globular jug with a thick ring base. A related MB II form from **Shechem**, Stratum XIX (Cole 1984: pl. 40: g) may be considered a prototype. The taller straight-necked jug No. 175 with an everted rim appears at **Megiddo**, Tomb 989 A1 (Guy 1938: pl. 17: 4) where the vessel has a narrowed and rounded base. Other parallels may be cited from two LB II deposits at **Hazor**, Area K, Stratum 1a (Yadin et al. 1961: pl. CCXCV: 10) and Area K, Stratum 1b (ibid: pl. CCXCII: 14); the latter vessel is a smaller version. The smaller, narrower necked jug rim of No. 176 may be likened to a form from **Megiddo**, Tomb 73 (Guy 1938: fig. 66: 6). The bulbous, everted rim of No. 177 is identical to that of a jug from an LB I context at **Megiddo**, Tomb 1100 A (ibid.: pl. 46: 8).

Jug handle No. 178 is ovoid in section and may be compared with a handle from **Queen Alia Airport** (Kafafi 1983: fig. 21: 87). The surface of this loop handle is decorated with three narrow parallel lines of red paint. Horizontally painted handles are common to numerous small closed forms including jugs and jars, and they appear on kraters as well. Stratified examples from **Megiddo** illustrate long-term popularity of this style during the Late Bronze Age: Tomb 1100 A (Guy 1938: pls. 45: 18; 46: 14) and Tomb 877 A1 (ibid.: pls. 12: 21; 13: 24). In Transjordan these decorated handles are attested at **Tell es-Saᶜidiyyeh**, Tomb 110 (Pritchard 1980: fig. 14: 3) and Tomb 141 (ibid.: fig. 41: 3), and at **Amman, Jebel Nuzha**, tomb (Dajani 1966b: pl. XVII: 32).

Late Bronze Age bases include low ring bases Nos. 179-81 and high ring bases Nos. 182-83. Although disc, concave disc, and flat bases are prevalent, especially during LB II, the ring base occurs as well on bowls and a number of other forms. The very low ring base, No. 179, is the least common, but one parallel example is noted at **Shechem**, Field IX, Phase 12 (Bull et al. 1965: fig. 3: 36). No. 180 may belong to a biconical amphoriskos form, such as at **Kataret es-Samra** (Leonard 1979: fig. 8: 4). Another low ring base, No. 181, could belong to one of several vessel types including bowls: **Ashdod**, Stratum 2 (Dothan and Freedman 1967: fig. 19: 1) and **Baqᶜah**, Cave A2 (McGovern 1986: fig. 17: 4); jars: **Kataret es-Samra** (Leonard 1979: fig. 8: 2); and kraters: **Amman, Jebel Nuzha**, tomb (Dajani 1966b: pl. XVII: 7, 8). Numerous other examples are known from **Queen Alia Airport** (Kafafi 1983: figs. 21-22). The steep walls adjoining the higher ring bases, illustrated in Nos. 182 and 183, suggest a deep V-shaped bowl form as at **Hazor**, Cistern 9024 (Yadin et al. 1958: pl. CXXII: 18, 20).

Sherd No. 184 is decorated with an unburnished, chalky-white slip and a band of red paint. A similar white-slipped and red-painted sherd has been found at **Queen Alia Airport** (Kafafi 1983: fig. 22: 161).

Discussion: LB I-II. Late Bronze Age pottery in Transjordan is best known from burial sites. Among these funerary groups, LB I material is found at Pella, Tomb 20 (Smith et al. 1980); Baqᶜah, Cave A2 (McGovern 1986); and Kataret es-Samra (Leonard 1979). Later tombs containing LB II pottery include Madaba (Harding 1953c; Isserlin 1953c); Sahab (Dajani 1970); Amman, Jebel Nuzha (Dajani 1966b); Baqᶜah, Cave B3 (McGovern 1986); Tell es-Saᶜidiyyeh (Pritchard 1980); and Irbid (Dajani 1964). Non-funerary strata have been excavated at the LB II Queen Alia Airport site (Hennessy 1966b, Hankey 1974, Herr 1983). Farther south, the Wadi el-Ḥasa survey (MacDonald 1982, 1988) has found possible LB occupation at 19 sites, yet most of these readings are tentative, a situation similar to that of the LB readings from the Kerak plateau survey.

This section has shown that there are demonstrable similarities between: (1) the ceramics from the Kerak plateau, where LB sites appear to be occupational, and (2) ceramics from the tomb groups of Transjordan, particularly the LB II burials. However, many of the specialized and decorated forms, both Levantine and foreign, that figure largely in the published tomb groups are not found on the Kerak plateau, nor are LB IA forms distinctly represented. Dipper juglets, chalices, goblets, bichrome vessels, amphoriskoi, pilgrim's flasks, and imported Cypriot and Mycenaean wares are absent. Furthermore, common attributes of LB vessels, such as the trumpet base and painted horizontal loop handles, are also not in evidence. Among the utilitarian wares, cooking pot forms and the widely distributed Canaanite jars are not as yet apparent in the Kerak survey collection.

The Late Bronze Age pottery from the Kerak region is utilitarian and domestic in nature, as in earlier periods. Some of these types, i.e. bowls and kraters, share characteristics of form with vessels from Transjordanian or urban Palestinian sites while other forms, i.e., jugs and jars, appear more locally popular. A similar situation is presented in the assemblage from the most recent excavations at the Queen Alia Airport site (Kafafi 1983). It can be suggested that the more elaborate Late Bronze Age forms were apt to experience change more rapidly while domestic, provincial wares, such as those of the Kerak plateau corpus, may demonstrate more stability of form and, hence, tend to appear in more than one cultural phase. The archaeological evidence from the Kerak plateau and southern Transjordan suggests that these regions were culturally peripheral and less populated than northern Transjordan during the Late Bronze Age. For these reasons localized production may be expected to account for the majority of ceramic remains from the Kerak region.

The close relationship between MB II and LB I pottery has been problematic for archaeologists, though the presence of imported wares can provide criteria for distinguishing between the two (Guy 1938: 151). Furthermore, as Sauer has observed (pers. comm.), the ceramic transition within the Late Bronze Age is seen more sharply in the divergence between LB IA and LB IB assemblages rather than between those of LB I and LB II. LB IB marks the beginning of the ceramic trend that has often been referred to as a "degeneration" of the Middle Bronze Age ceramic tradition in which forms became less elaborately stylized and more standardized, and manufacturing techniques show a decreasing quality of production. Many of the forms that are presented above appear in different sub-phases of the Late Bronze Age at various sites indicating the persistence of these vessel types throughout much of the period. However, the majority of stratified comparisons are with ceramics from LB IB and, even more frequently, LB II strata. This apparent pattern may be due, in part, to the problem of differentiating MB II from LB IA in surface collections or to the fact that there is a higher percentage of excavated LB II deposits within the relatively small number of excavated LB sites in Transjordan, which could introduce an element of bias. However, the possibility that Late Bronze Age occupation on the Kerak plateau was predominantly LB II should not be discounted.

Iron I

Description: Iron I. The sample of Iron I wares presented in this section represents characteristics of Iron I pottery that are noted throughout Transjordan. Forms, particularly kraters and jars, tend to be thick and heavy as a result of the use of a slow wheel and large amounts of mineral temper. Aside from tomb groups, most Iron I assemblages in Transjordan are dominated by plain, utilitarian forms. Bowls, kraters, and jars, including both medium-sized and larger storage jars, are the most numerous Iron I forms found on the Kerak plateau. The elaborately stylized jar and cooking pot rims that are so prevalent at Tell Deir ᶜAlla (Franken 1969) are not common in the Kerak region. Iron I pottery in Transjordan is generally plain, and the great majority of these sherds in the survey corpus are decorated only with a surface slip.

As is typical of southern Levantine Iron I pottery, particularly of the Iron IA period, the quality of manufacture declined with the adoption of a slower turning device and the use of finishing techniques during the manufacturing process that sometimes left traces of uneven hand smoothing and wiping on the vessel surfaces. The wares are generally coarse and tend to contain high percentages of mineral inclusions that add weight to the fabrics. Organic temper was occasionally added to the paste, and dense calcite inclusions are present in some sherds, notably jars Nos. 220 and 221.

The surfaces of the Iron I sherds are more spalled and pitted than those of sherds from the earlier periods, and firing can be thorough but frequently is poor. Exception may be taken for bowl No. 186 which is of excellent quality in terms of both paste preparation and manufacture. Thick, grey-black cores occur among a number of the jars, particularly Nos. 208-13 and 220-21. The rim styles of these jars are frequent in the Kerak plateau corpus but not well documented outside of this region and, therefore, may have been local products. Fabric colors are fairly restricted to shades of pink, orange, and brown. White slips are common, though reds and browns are also attested. Surface decoration is minimal. The red paint that appears occasionally among Iron I wares is found on two bowl fragments, Nos. 188 and 190. The former shows only faint traces of paint on the rim; the latter, being better preserved, has a deep red-painted rim and dripped red paint on the interior.

Burnishing occurs but is relatively rare. Bowls 195 and 196 are red-slipped and wheel burnished, and bowl No. 197 and krater No. 200 are brown-slipped and hand burnished. On the basis of form and surface treatment, these may be interpreted as Iron IC, though wheel burnishing is more frequent in the Iron II rather than the Iron IC period. Iron IB Philistine painted decoration is absent. Except for handle No. 222, plastic decoration is also lacking.

Forms: Iron I. A thick platter with a peaked, upright rim is shown in No. 185. 12th century parallels are found at **Pella**, Area IIIC (Hennessy et al. 1981: fig. 14: 11), and in the later, 11th-10th century, Phase G at **Tell Deir ᶜAlla** (Franken 1969: fig. 64: 101).

The open, flaring bowl No. 186 has a deep pink-orange fabric and exterior white slip. This form is present in the transitional Late Bronze-Iron I **Madaba**, tomb (Harding 1953c; Isserlin 1953c: fig. 12: 17) and in 12th century strata at **Tell Deir ᶜAlla**, Phase A (Franken 1969: fig. 46: 23) and **Taanach**, Period IA (Rast 1978: fig. 1: 15). It is also included among 11th to 10th century assemblages from **Tell Deir ᶜAlla**, Phase G (Franken 1969: fig. 64: 83) and **Jericho**, Tomb A85 (Tushingham 1965: fig. 253: 2). The Jericho example pictures this vessel with a low ring base.

Bowls Nos. 187 and 188 have simple, rounded rims that are slightly thickened. An early Iron I date is indicated for No. 187 by the occurrence of this form at **Mdeinet el-Muᶜrrajeh** (Olávarri, 1977-78: fig. 2: 16); **Pella**, Area IIIC (Hennessy et al. 1981: fig. 14: 7); and **Taanach**, Period IA (Rast 1978: fig. 8: 6) and Period IB (ibid.: fig. 13: 9). Other Iron I sites with this form include **Mafraq**, tomb (Piccirillo 1976: fig. 4: 14), where this vessel has a low disc base, and **Hazor**, Area A, Strata IX-X (Yadin et al. 1958: pl. XLV: 6), which shows a painted rim. This Hazor vessel is assigned to a transitional Iron I-II phase. Another example dates to Iron II A at **Dhiban**, Tomb J 7 (Tushingham 1972: fig. 24: 13). The very similar bowl No. 188 with a rounded, slightly inverted rim is distinguished by faint traces of red paint on the rim. It is best paralleled by 12th century bowls from **Taanach**, Period IA (Rast 1978: fig. 8: 2) and Period IB (ibid.: fig. 13: 6). The squared rim of a shallow bowl, shown in No. 189, may be dated to the 12th century, Iron IA, on the basis of sherds from: **Madaba**, tomb (Harding 1953c; Isserlin 1953c: fig. 12: 18); **ᶜAroᶜer** (Olávarri 1965: fig. 1: 10); and **Tell Gezer**, Field VII, Stratum XII (Gitin 1979: pl. 2: 15).

Everted bowl rim No. 190 is decorated with red paint that dripped into the vessel interior in a similar manner as that shown on a 12th century bowl from **Pella**, Area IIIC (Hennessy et al. 1981: fig. 14: 2). The vessel form is attested in late-12th century strata at **Tell Deir ᶜAlla**, Phase C (Franken 1969: fig. 54: 44) and **Tell Gezer**, Field II, Stratum 10 (Dever et al. 1974: pl. 28: 33). This rim style is also found within an Iron II assemblage at **Dhiban**, Tomb J 5 (Tushingham 1972: fig. 18: 8).

The deep bowl pictured in No. 191 appears to have a broad chronological distribution. A close parallel may be cited from **Taanach**, Period IB (Rast 1978: fig. 13: 7-8) where it is dated to the 12th century. A larger vessel with this profile at **Tell Deir ᶜAlla**, Phase F (Franken 1969: fig. 61: 69), is also attributed to the Iron I period. Related forms include: a 10th century vessel from **Taanach**, Period IIB (Rast 1978: fig. 45: 5); a bowl from transitional Iron I-II strata at **Hazor**, Area B, Strata IX-X (Yadin et al. 1961: pl. CCX: 4); and an Iron II form from **Hazor**, Area B, Stratum V (ibid.: pl. CCXXII: 8). Bowl No. 192 has an everted rim with a shallow groove on top and may be compared with a mid-10th century form at **Ain Gev**, Stratum V (Mazar et al. 1964: fig. 4: 10).

The everted, peaked rim of a large bowl is shown in No. 193. This sherd is characterized by inferior fabric and poor firing. A parallel bowl is noted in an Iron IC context at **Taanach**, Period IIB (Rast 1978: fig. 65: 5), though this example is burnished. A second comparable form, with handles attached to the rim, probably dates to Iron IIA, **Dhiban** (Tushingham 1972: fig. 1: 57). Presented in No. 194 is another wide bowl form distinguished by a rounded, bulbous rim that compares with a sherd from the Philistine occupation at **Tell Gezer**, Field I, Stratum 3 (Dever et al. 1970: pl. 26: 27). In southern Transjordan a similar bowl occurs at the Iron Age site of **Khirbet Abu Banna** (Weippert 1982b: fig. 7: 8).

Three burnished bowls are presented in Nos. 195-97. No. 195 has a flattened, unprofiled rim, well prepared fabric, and a wheel burnished red slip in the interior and over the rim. This sherd generally compares with 11th century bowls at **Tell Deir ᶜAlla**, Phase C (Franken 1969: fig. 54: 22) and **Hazor**, Area B, Stratum XI (Yadin et al. 1961: pl. CCIII: 5); the latter example is wheel burnished. A parallel form at **Tell Gezer**, Field VII, Stratum VIII (Gitin 1979: pl. 7: 9) is associated with an Iron IC layer. The inverted bowl shown in No. 196 is also red-slipped and burnished on the rim and interior. An identical burnished bowl from **Taanach**, Period IIB (Rast 1978: fig. 47: 1) dating to Iron IC shows this vessel with handles and a ring base. The development of this form into the 9th century is indicated by a similar example from **Hazor**, Area A, Stratum VIII (Yadin et al. 1960: pl. LIII: 33).

The sharply incurved deep bowl profile of No. 197 is brown-slipped and hand burnished on both the interior and exterior. Sites with comparable bowls from Iron I contexts include **Bethel** (Kelso 1968: pl. 60: 1) and **Tel Mevorakh**, Stratum VII (Stern 1978: fig. 12: 6), and a smaller burnished bowl is noted from **Irbid**, Tomb B (Dajani 1966a: pl. XXXIV: 8). The best parallels to No. 197 in terms of both form and surface treatment are found among a group of 11th century bowls at **Tell Gezer**, Field VII, Stratum IXA (Gitin 1979: pl. 6: 3-9), one of which is identical to No. 197 (ibid.: pl. 6: 8), and in a 10th century layer at **Taanach**, Period IIA (Rast 1978: fig. 24: 7). Yet this bowl type, both burnished and unburnished, has also appeared during Iron IIA, as exemplified at **Tell Gezer**, Field VII, Stratum VIIA (Gitin 1979: pl. 10: 3) and **Beisan**, Level IV (James 1966: fig. 67: 22-23).

A variety of different Iron I kraters is shown in Nos. 198-205. No. 198, a thick, rounded and upright rim, is well documented in Transjordan at **Dhiban** (Winnett and Reed 1964: pl. 73: 4) and **Khirbet Abu Banna** (Weippert 1982b: fig. 8: 1), as well as in 12th and 11th century deposits from **Madaba**, tomb (Harding 1953c; Isserlin 1953c: fig. 14: 5), where it features two vertical loop handles and a low ring base; **Baqᶜah**, Cave A4 (McGovern 1986: fig. 55: 63); and a related form is noted at **Tell Deir ᶜAlla**, Phase A (Franken 1969: fig. 46: 11). In Palestine this krater occurs at **Megiddo**, Stratum VIIA (Loud et al. 1948: pl. 70: 2) and in the **Negev**, **Horvat Ritma**, Period III (Meshel 1977: fig. 6: 11). The tapered profile of krater No. 199 compares with a vessel from **ᶜAroᶜer** (Olávarri 1965: fig. 2: 1).

In contrast to the other kraters in this group, sherd No. 200 is decorated. Wide, hand-burnished lines are evident on the rim and exterior. Identical vessels with burnishing appear in late-10th and 9th century contexts at **Hazor**, Area A, Stratum X (Yadin et al. 1960: pl. LI: 10) and **Tell Gezer**, Field II, Stratum 6A (Dever et al. 1974: pl. 33: 6).

The rounded rim of No. 201 represents a krater or possibly a deep bowl that may date to the 12th century, as indicated at **Tell Deir ᶜAlla**, Phase B (Franken 1969: fig. 49: 55). The thickened and splayed rim shown in No. 202 is attested at several Transjordanian Iron IA sites: **Dhiban** (Winnett and Reed 1964: pl. 75: 19); **Mdeinet el-Muᶜrrajeh** (Olávarri 1977-78: fig. 2: 19); and **Pella**, Area IIIC (Hennessy et al. 1981: fig. 16: 11); as well as in a survey corpus from **Museitiba** (Parker 1986b: 191: No. 172). The krater shown in No. 203 is similar to No. 198 in fabric and thickness but has a distinctly notched and profiled rim. Comparable forms may date to the 10th century at **Tel ᶜAmal** (Levy and Edelstein 1972: fig. 15: 20) and **Beth Zur** (Sellers et al. 1968: fig. 14: 16) and the 9th or even 8th century at **Dhiban** (Tushingham 1972: fig. 2: 4). The off-set and out-turned rim of No. 204 forms a "canal" that is characteristic of Iron I deep bowl profiles. A similar rim is found at **Pella**, Area IIIC (Hennessy et al. 1981: fig. 14: 10) in a 12th century deposit. Though a less substantial form, **Tell Gezer**, Field I, Stratum 4 (Dever et al. 1970: pl. 27: 9) provides another 12th century example. The large hooked-rim krater No. 205 appears in the late 11th to 12th century Phase G at **Tell Deir ᶜAlla** (Franken 1969: fig. 64: 22).

The cooking pot rim shown in No. 206 is somewhat unusual, for the majority of Iron Age cooking vessels are characterized by sloping rims that are more distinctly profiled, as illustrated by numerous examples from **Tell Deir ᶜAlla** (Franken 1969) and **Dhiban** (Tushingham 1972). No. 206 is most similar to two vessels from 10th century occupations: **Tell Gezer**, Field II, Stratum 6 (Dever et al. 1970: pl. 34: 27) and **Tell Abu Hawam**, Stratum III (Hamilton 1935a: pl. 23: 90).

Jar forms are pictured in Nos. 207-21. The peaked, everted jar rim No. 207 is paralleled in the terminal Late Bronze-early Iron Age stratum III at **Tel Masos**

(Kempinski and Fritz 1977: fig. 4: 11), and similar forms appear in later Iron I strata at **Tell Gezer**, Field VII, Stratum XI (Gitin 1979: pl. 3: 2) and in the **Negev, Ramat Matred** (Aharoni et al. 1960: fig. 11: 3). The neckless jar with a sharply hooked rim shown in No. 208 was found at **Khirbet el-Baluᶜ** (J. W. Crowfoot 1934: pl. II: fig. 2: 7).

Nos. 209-12 constitute a group of closely related jar rims that were found at several Iron Age sites on the Kerak plateau. The rim style of these medium-sized jars is characterized by an everted, lightly peaked profile. Although these rims do not figure in the literature from Iron Age tombs and settlements of Transjordan, they are noted in a few Iron I contexts in Palestine: **Taanach**, Period IIA (Rast 1978: fig. 25: 3) and **Bethel** (Kelso 1968: pl. 56: 4). No. 213 is similar to this group in paste and form but is distinguished by a splayed rim that may belong to a jug rather than a jar. At **Taanach** this form dates to Iron IC, Period IIB (Rast 1978: fig. 58: 3). Other examples occur at **Dhiban** (Winnett and Reed 1964: pl. 73: 2) and in southern Transjordan, **Khirbet Mashmil** (Weippert 1982b: fig. 6: 7).

Elongated, rounded jars are represented in Nos. 214 and 215. No. 214 can be dated from the 12th through 10th centuries: **Tell el-Ful**, Period I (Sinclair 1960: pl. 20: 9); **Megiddo**, Stratum VIIB (Loud et al. 1948: pl. 64: 8); and **Tell Gezer**, Field II, Stratum 7 (Dever et al. 1970: pl. 35: 17). **Bethel** (Kelso 1968: pl. 56: 23) provides another Iron I example. The profile shown in No. 215 is attested in late 11th and 10th century occupations in Palestine: **Tel Mevorakh**, Stratum VIII (Stern 1978: fig. 19: 1) and **Tell el-Ful**, Stratum II (N. Lapp 1981: pl. 48: 1).

Rounded rolled-rim jars are illustrated in Nos. 216-18. A wide range of rolled-rim styles is common on jars throughout this period, but for each of these examples from the Kerak plateau parallel or similar forms are apparent from Palestine. No. 216 is attested in an Iron IC phase at **Tell Gezer**, Field VII, Stratum VIII (Gitin 1979: pl. 7: 1). The neckless, more distinctly rounded No. 217 is noted in Iron I deposits from **Bethel** (Kelso 1968: pl. 57: 1) and **Megiddo**, Strata VIIB-VI (Loud et al. 1948: pl. 83: 1), and in an Iron IIA assemblage from **Dhiban** (Tushingham 1972: fig. 1: 3). The more heavily molded rim No. 218 is attested at **Bethel** (Kelso 1968: pl. 56: 36); **Taanach**, Period IB (Rast 1978: fig. 9: 1); and **Megiddo**, Stratum VIIB (Loud et al. 1948: pl. 64: 8).

The heavy collar rim jar pictured in sherd No. 219 is represented at **Bethel** (Kelso 1968: pl. 56: 13) and **Khirbet Kefire** (Vriezen 1975: fig. 3: 2). A related form is found at **Tell el-Ful**, Stratum pre-IIIA (N. Lapp 1981: pl. 48: 2). The hooked-rim jars Nos. 220 and 221 are similar to one another in paste and, as the jar group shown in Nos. 209-12, may reflect vessels manufactured in a local style. No. 220 is paralleled at **Khirbet el-Baluᶜ** (J. W. Crowfoot 1934: pl. II: fig. 2: 6), and a similar form is noted at **Bethel** (Kelso 1968: pl. 56: 20). The more angular and exaggerated form shown in No. 221 is also present in an Iron I assemblage of collar rim jars from **Bethel** (ibid.: pl. 56: 19).

The handle pictured in No. 222 is broken on one side and badly eroded. However, this sherd appears to have been a short triangular lug handle, vertically affixed to a vessel wall or rim. The thumb impression on the upper surface is featured on loop and lug handles in both Iron I and Iron II, though it is more frequent in Iron I, and usually associated with storage jar forms. Among the numerous examples of Iron I thumb-impressed handles are 12th century handles from **Taanach**, Period IA (Rast 1978: figs. 4: 5; 6: 2), and Period IB (ibid.: fig. 10: 12-14); 11th century handles from **Hazor**, Area B, Stratum XI (Yadin et al. 1961: pl. CCIII: 22) and **Tel Mevorakh**, Stratum VIII (Stern 1978: fig. 20: 10); and a 10th century impressed handle from **Taanach**, Period IIIB (Rast 1978: fig. 32: 4).

Among the bases shown in Nos. 223-26, a flat base is pictured in No. 223, low ring bases are shown in Nos. 224 and 225, and a ring base of medium height is seen in No. 226. Flat and ring bases, both occurring in a wide variety of styles, are well documented throughout the Iron Age and appear interchangeably upon otherwise identical vessel forms. The flat base, No. 223, was white slipped on both the interior and exterior and across the bottom. The interior slip suggests that it may have belonged to a bowl or other open form, although similar bases are found on jars as well. In Transjordan these bases are found at virtually every Iron Age site. Among the numerous occurrences are examples from **ᶜAroᶜer** (Olávarri 1965: fig. 1: 13) and **Mdeinet el-Muᶜrrajeh** (Olávarri 1977-78: fig. 2: 11-12). A burnished base is recorded from **Pella**, Area IIIC (Hennessy et al. 1981: fig. 15: 2).

The low ring base No. 224 compares with bases from **Khirbet el-Baluᶜ** (J. W. Crowfoot 1934: pl. II: fig. 2: 9, 15);

Dhiban (Winnett and Reed 1964: pl. 75: 9); **Madaba**, Tomb B (Piccirillo 1975: fig. II: 4); and **Tell Deir ᶜAlla**, Phase C (Franken 1969: fig. 53: 25). Examples of No. 225 are found at **Madaba**, Tomb B (Piccirillo 1975: fig. IX: 4) and **Amman, Citadel** (Hadidi 1970: pl. I: 28). The higher ring base No. 226 is similarly well documented at a number of sites, among them **Tell Deir ᶜAlla**, Phase B (Franken 1969: fig. 48: 47).

Discussion: Iron I. This sample, representing the Iron I corpus from the Kerak plateau, consists of a few basic forms that are associated with domestic activities. Lamps and chalices are among the common Iron Age forms that are not accounted for within the Kerak material, and few cooking pots or jugs have been identified. Of the forms that are presented here a number of different rim styles occur within the categories of bowls, kraters, and jars, though a few of the bowls (Nos. 187-88) and jars (Nos. 209-12, 214-15) are stylistically redundant.

Many of the sherds discussed above are paralleled at Iron I occupation sites in Transjordan, such as Khirbet el-Baluᶜ (J. W. Crowfoot 1934), ᶜAroᶜer (Olávarri 1965), Mdeinet el-Muᶜrrajeh (Olávarri 1977-78), Tell Deir ᶜAlla (Franken 1979), and Pella (Hennessy et al. 1981). Additional Iron I material has been excavated at Dhiban (Winnett and Reed 1964) and Amman, Citadel (Hadidi 1970). Sites in Palestine also provide a number of related or identical forms, and it appears that most of the Iron I pottery from the Kerak region shares attributes found among Iron I ceramics throughout the southern Levant.

In addition to settlement remains, a number of Iron I tomb groups have been excavated in Transjordan: Madaba (Harding 1953c; Isserlin 1953c); Madaba, Tomb B (Piccirillo 1975); Mafraq (Piccirillo 1976); Irbid (Dajani 1966a); Sahab (Albright 1932a); Baqᶜah, Cave A4 (McGovern 1986); and Tell es-Saᶜidiyyeh, Tomb 101 (Pritchard 1968). However, the mixture of Late Bronze and Iron IA materials in some of these tombs has obfuscated an understanding of the transition from Late Bronze to Iron I ceramics in Transjordan. Despite stratigraphic uncertainties and the tendency of burial sites to contain higher percentages of specialized forms, continuities among bowl and krater forms are apparent when these assemblages are compared with the material from the Kerak plateau survey collection.

A number of the sherds presented in this discussion occur in strata at various sites that date to different phases of the Iron I period, and some are clearly related to forms in Iron II contexts as well, demonstrating longevity of a number of forms and rim styles. Yet there is sufficient representation of 12th through 10th century pottery to indicate with certainty that the Kerak plateau was inhabited throughout the Iron I period. Iron IB painted Philistine pottery is not present. This absence is anticipated on the basis of the geo-political make-up of the southern Levant during the Iron I period as well as the current archaeological record of Iron I ceramic distributions. However, some of the Kerak plateau sherds show morphological affinity with forms in Philistine strata at Tell Gezer and Tell Deir ᶜAlla. Iron IC occupation in the Kerak region is indicated by the burnished wares and other 10th century forms. The Iron IC mensif plate is not attested, yet as Franken has pointed out (1982: 142), this form was probably a regionally circumscribed product of the north Jordan Valley.

In summary, the Kerak plateau corpus presents a number of forms that have demonstrable temporal continuity through the Iron I period as well as spatial distributional continuity with assemblages from Transjordan and Palestine. In addition to the absence of Philistine wares, imports are unattested, as is generally the case during Iron I. The ceramic evidence suggests that the occupation, or at least the sedentary occupation, of the plateau increased significantly from that of the Middle and Late Bronze Ages, for Iron I wares are both numerous and widely distributed across the landscape.

Iron II

Description: Iron II. As in the case of the preceding Iron I period, the corpus of Iron II pottery from the Kerak region is fairly substantial. The Iron II assemblage, however, shows greater diversity both of vessel types and of specific forms within these types. A wide variety of open and hole-mouth bowls and necked and hole-mouth jars are represented as well as krater, jug, amphoriskos, and cooking pot forms. Cooking pots and necked jars continue to be of simpler styles than their more sharply profiled contemporaries at Tell Deir ᶜAlla (Franken 1969).

Some of the sherds in this corpus show evidence of manufacturing techniques that were prevalent during the Iron I period, yet the use of a faster wheel clearly effected a general improvement in vessel quality. There is also a marked proliferation of decorative treatments. Whereas the Iron I assemblage from the Kerak plateau corpus only minimally represented the surface treatment styles of that period, Iron II burnish, paint, and plastic decorations are fairly well documented in the survey assemblage.

There is little consistency of fabric or surface treatment within vessel classes, though there are specific trends that generally characterize this sample. Ware colors include buff, brown, pink, red and to a lesser extent orange and grey. Slip colors include red, white, pink, beige, and buff. A distinctive white slip, similar to the Iron I white slip, is found on a few bowls (Nos. 237, 240, 243) and jars (Nos. 257-58) as well as a jug form (No. 270). Shades of pale red slip are noted on several bowls and a few jars and cooking pots. A more distinctive red slip is found on jug No. 273 and a modeled body sherd, No. 279. Burnished slip decoration occurs among bowls Nos. 229, 235, 238, 241-43 and base No. 275. With the exception of the grey painted and burnished rim of bowl No. 242, the slips on these vessels are red and orange-brown and cover either the rim and interior of the vessel (No. 243), the rim and exterior (No. 241) or, more commonly, the entire surface (Nos. 229, 235, 238).

One decorated body sherd, No. 280, has a polished white slip painted over with parallel lines of black. Other examples of paint are found on hole-mouth bowl No. 248 and body sherds Nos. 281-87, all of which are painted in the multi-colored Moabite style that consists of alternating horizontal parallel bands or zones of red and white set off by thin black lines.

Ridging became more frequent during the Iron II period as demonstrated by bowls Nos. 237 and 239 and jars 264-66. Similarly, shallow incised lines appear on several forms including the shoulders of krater No. 250, cooking pot No. 252, and jar No. 268. In addition, two styles of plastic decoration are evident. Krater No. 249 has thickly molded vertical knobs attached to the rim, a style that J. W. Crowfoot (1934) had recognized at Khirbet el-Baluᶜ, though the extent to which this was intended as a functional rather than a decorative attribute is uncertain.

The quality of paste preparation varies considerably, and while some sherds are very well fired, others show a range of thick to faint cores. The interior fabric color of several pieces, among them some of the painted Moabite sherds, is black, a typical result of firing techniques during the Iron II period in Transjordan. Similarly, the size and quantity of mineral inclusions varies greatly, yet there is no straightforward correlation between firing quality and fineness or coarseness of the paste. Cooking pots are coarse, and Nos. 253 and 254 contain notable amounts of white calcite inclusions.

Forms: Iron II. Three different types of open bowls are pictured in Nos. 227-29. The squared, upright rim shown in No. 227 belongs to an 8th-7th century bowl that occurs at **Pella**, Area VIII (Smith et al. 1983: fig. 18: left, second from bottom); **Hazor**, Area B, Stratum V (Yadin et al. 1958: pl. LVXVII: 8) and Stratum Va (Yadin et al. 1961: pl. CCXXVI: 3); and the Edomite site of **Tawilan** (Glueck 1935: pl. 23: 13-16).

The buff-slipped, hammer-head bowl rim No. 228 is thickened to form a narrow, gracefully curved ledge handle (not illustrated). J. W. Crowfoot (1934: 79) noted the frequent occurrence of these grip handles on vessel fragments from **Khirbet el-Baluᶜ**, and he presents two examples (ibid.: pl. II: fig. 2: 11, 14) of which the latter most closely resembles the style of the rim-thickened handle on No. 228. A similar handle is also found at **Dhiban** (Winnett and Reed 1964: pl. 76: 16). The profile of rim No. 228 has a long history of development dating from late Iron I through the 8th century, at which time it became a common feature in the ceramic repertoire. A decorated 10th century bowl from **Megiddo**, Stratum Va (Loud et al. 1948: pl. 89: 9) shows this form in an early context. Examples from the 8th century, both decorated and undecorated, occur at **Hazor** in several contexts: Area B, Stratum V (Yadin et al. 1958: pl. LXVII: 23), Area B, Stratum Va (Yadin et al. 1960: pl. XCII: 12) and Area A, Stratum IV (Yadin et al. 1958: pl. LI: 17). Also from the Iron IIA period is a parallel bowl fragment from **Dhiban** (Tushingham 1972: fig. 1: 57) with a knob handle attached to the rim.

An Iron IC date might be suggested for No. 229 on the basis of the wheel-burnished, pale brown slip that covers the interior of the sherd. Although the thickened and flattened profile is not well attested in the literature, a similar form from **Hazor**, Area A, Stratum IX (Yadin et al. 1961: pl. CLXXV: 6) indicates a later, 9th century date.

The group of bowls with notched and everted rims presented in Nos. 230-33 illustrates an Iron II open bowl form that is common on the Kerak plateau. In Transjordan similar vessels are known from Edomite sites: **Tawilan** (Glueck 1935: pl. 23: 4); **Khirbet Hamr Ifdan** (ibid.: pl. 23: 5); **Umm el-Biyara** (Bennett 1966: fig. 3: 2); and **Buseirah** (Bennett 1975: fig. 6: 3). Morphologically, these compare with No. 232, though unlike the bowls from Tawilan and Buseireh the bowls in the Kerak survey corpus are unpainted. In Palestine this form is very common in the 8th century strata at Hazor where several of these vessels are decorated with red slip or paint. Among the many comparisons that may be cited from **Hazor**, No. 230 occurs in Area B, Stratum Va (Yadin et al. 1961: pl. CCXXX: 1); No. 231 is similar to a vessel from Area A, Stratum V (Yadin et al. 1958: 2); No. 232 is present in Stratum V, Area B (Yadin et al. 1958: pl. LXXIII: 21; ibid.: 1960: pl. LXXXII: 3) and is also a form that appears among the "Samarian" bowls of Area B, Stratum V (ibid.: pl. LXXXII: 12); and No. 233 is paralleled in Area B, Stratum IV (Yadin et al. 1960: pl. XCVIII: 29).

The beveled, profiled rim of bowl No. 234 belongs to a large utilitarian vessel that is documented in the Iron IIA corpus from **Dhiban** (Tushingham 1972: fig. 3: 51) and in two later contexts: a burial assemblage from **Amman**, Tomb C (Harding 1951a: fig. 1: 39) and **Hazor**, Area B, Stratum IV (Yadin et al. 1960: pl. XCVIII: 13). The latter illustration shows this bowl with two vertical loop handles.

The deep open bowl No. 235, with a rounded, everted knob rim, is red-slipped, and widely spaced wheel burnish lines are preserved on the interior and rim. The form, though not the decoration, is paralleled at **Hazor** in a late 8th century stratum, Area G, Stratum IV (Yadin et al. 1969: pl. CCLIV: 12) and also resembles a larger bowl from **Tell el-Ful**, Period III (Sinclair 1960: pl. 22: 2). This genre of bowls is well attested at **Tell Beit Mirsim**, Stratum A. The numerous illustrations from this site show similar burnished kraters and bowls with thickened rims and both flat and ring bases (Albright 1932b: pls. 60-62).

Bowl No. 236, characterized by a thickened rim, rounded on the exterior, is found in Iron II levels at **Beth-Zur** (Sellers 1933: pl. IX: 21) and **Bethel** (Kelso 1968: pl. 62: 11). Rim No. 237, displaying a sharply everted profile and deep body ridging, is not a common form, though similar flanged bowls are attested at **Tawilan** (Glueck 1935: pl. 23: 3) and in 9th-8th century strata at **Hazor**: Area A, Stratum VIII (Yadin et al. 1960: pl. LIV: 13-14); Area A, Stratum VI (ibid.: pl. LXVI: 28); and Area B, Stratum V (Yadin et al. 1961: pl. CCXXII: 10).

Bowl No. 238 has a graceful flaring profile, and the red-slipped surfaces are comprehensively burnished to a polish. This form compares with several 9th and 8th century forms including "Samarian" bowls from **Samaria**, Period III (Crowfoot et al. 1957: fig. 4: 17) and **Hazor**, Area A, Stratum VIII (Yadin et al. 1958: pl. XLVII: 20), and related forms from **Tell el-Ful**, Stratum pre-IIIA (N. L. Lapp 1981: pl. 62: 26) and **Dhiban** (Winnett and Reed 1964: pl. 75: 3). The Samaria and Dhiban vessels show this form with low and high ring bases respectively.

The beige-slipped bowl shown in No. 239 has a simple rounded rim that is grooved on the exterior. This form occurs in 8th century strata at **Hazor**, Area B, Stratum VI (Yadin et al. 1961: pl. CCXIX: 1) and Area A, Stratum V (Yadin et al. 1958: pl. LXIII: 9), but strong comparisons also appear in Iron IIC and Persian strata at **Tell Keisan**, Level 5 (Briend and Humbert 1980: pl. 41: 12) and **Tell Gezer**, Field VII, Stratum IV (Gitin 1979: pl. 31: 6), which suggest a broad chronological range.

A straight sided bowl with abrupt carination and unprofiled rim is shown in No. 240. This form occurs at **Tell Deir ʿAlla**, Phase L (Franken 1969: fig. 75: 4), a 9th century layer, and is also found at **Tell Jemmeh**, GV 186 (Duncan 1930: 18 L 1). The deep, sharply carinated bowl with simple rim and splayed neck pictured in No. 241 has an exterior brown slip with distinct broad horizontal burnish lines. The form is duplicated in a 9th century layer at **Tell Deir ʿAlla**, Phase L (Franken 1969: fig. 74: 71).

Hole-mouth bowls are shown in Nos. 242-48. A small globular bowl is represented by the simple incurved and black burnished rim No. 242. This form occurs with a red burnished slip and disc base at **Tell Beit Mirsim**, Stratum A (Albright 1943: pl. 15: 13); an Iron IIC assemblage. A similar form, without burnish, is found at **Taanach** in a mid-5th century Persian pit (P. W. Lapp 1970b: fig. 5: 11). It should be noted, however, that red-burnished incurved bowls of a similar style are present in earlier, 8th century deposits at **Hazor**, Area B, Strata IV-V (Yadin et al. 1958: pl. LXXI: 15), and Area G, Stratum IV (ibid.: 1961: pl. CCLIV: 11).

A white exterior slip and red-burnished interior and over-the-rim slip distinguish the incurved and thickened rim of hole-mouth bowl No. 243. This decorative style occurs among Iron IIA sherds from **Dhiban**, but the form is most generally comparable to a group of white-slipped, unburnished vessels from that site (Tushingham 1972: fig. 1: 62-65), though none of these bowls displays an identical profile. The thicker, knob-rimmed hole-mouth bowl No. 244 shows uneven firing that is characteristic of kiln-stacked vessels. This large bowl form occurs at two Transjordanian sites: **Pella**, in an 8th-7th century stratum, Area VIII (Smith et al. 1983: fig. 18: left, third from bottom), and **Dhiban**, in an Iron IIA corpus (Winnett and Reed 1964: pl. 75: 18).

A group of hole-mouth deep bowls with thickened and everted rims is shown in Nos. 245-48. Nos. 245-47 are decorated with a pale-red slip, and No. 248 is decorated in the Iron II band-painted style of Ammonite and Moabite pottery. The form of No. 246 is illustrated at **Beisan**, Level IV (James 1966: fig. 38: 9) where it is accompanied by two vertical loop handles and a rounded base. On this basis, a late 9th-8th century date may be postulated. Parker has also suggested an Iron II date for this form at **Qasr Saliya** (1986b: 189: No. 146). However, this genre of hole-mouth bowls continues into the early Persian period, as indicated at **Shechem**, Stratum V (P. W. Lapp 1970b: fig. 3: 11). Lapp has dated this Shechem vessel with its highly characteristic Persian decoration to ca. 500 B.C.E., but the comparison drawn here applies only to the general form.

The thicker, more squared profile of the deep bowl represented in No. 247 compares with a vessel from **Jericho**, Phase 22 (Franken 1974: fig. 8: 20). No. 248 is decorated with a dripped band of red paint on the interior of the rim. On the exterior, the white-slipped surface is red-painted beneath the rim, and two thin bands of black paint follow. A vertical handle joined to the vessel shoulder has been broken off. In Transjordan this bowl occurs at **Dhiban** (Winnett and Reed 1964: pl. 76: 10), yet Iron IIA hole-mouth deep bowls from the site are generally larger and usually have vertical loop handles attached to the rim rather than the vessel shoulder: **Dhiban**, Tomb J 5 (Tushingham 1972: fig. 17: 12-14). In Palestine this rim style is also noted at **Jericho**, Phase 5 (Franken 1974: fig. 19: 12). The best example of this form, accompanied by shoulder handles, is found in an Iron IIC corpus from **Tell Beit Mirsim**, Stratum A (Albright 1943: pl. 13: 1).

Krater forms are shown in Nos. 249 and 250. The exterior rim of No. 249 is decorated with a thick band of clay molded into three consecutive vertical knobs that either constituted a ledge handle or completely encompassed the circumference of the rim. Vertical knobs are found on finer, slipped and burnished bowls at sites such as Hazor during the Iron II period, yet this particular molding technique is also paralleled on a utilitarian hole-mouth form at **Khirbet el-Balu^c** (J. W. Crowfoot 1934: pl. II: fig. 2: 12). The hole-mouth krater No. 250 is distinguished by a band of grooved lines across the vessel shoulder. The flattened knob rim and incised decoration are paralleled in an Iron IIA assemblage from **Dhiban** (Tushingham 1972: fig. 1: 42, see also 43-44).

Iron II cooking pots are represented by the straight-necked rim No. 251 and hole-mouth rims Nos. 252-54. The upright, faintly ridged cooking pot rim No. 251 is associated with a vessel group whose form and rim style were widespread in Palestine and Transjordan throughout the Iron Age. The upright stance and lightly profiled rim of this piece, however, occur less frequently than the more profiled and exaggerated sloping rims that are so versatile and widely documented. Among the sites where this particular form appears are **Khirbet el-Balu^c** (Glueck 1934: pl. 20: 22); **Tell Deir ^cAlla**, Phase K (Franken 1969: fig. 71: 60), a late 9th century context; and **Tell Gezer**, Field VII, Stratum V-sub-IV (Gitin 1979: pl. 27: 18), an Iron IIC context. Similar cooking pots are observed at **Tawilan** (Glueck 1935: pl. 24: 21), and in 9th century strata at **Tell Deir ^cAlla**, Phase L (Franken 1969: fig. 74: 53) and **Hazor**, Area B, Stratum VII (Yadin et al. 1961: pl. CCXVIII: 8).

Of the hole-mouth cooking pot rims, the interior of No. 252 is crazed and stained, and Nos. 253-254 consist of coarse red-slipped fabrics that contain numerous calcite inclusions. No. 252 may be compared with a 7th-6th century rim from **Tell Ḥesban** (Lugenbeal and Sauer 1972: pl. VI: 317), as well as a form from **Tell en-Naṣbeh**,

Cistern 325 (McCown 1947: fig. 27: 28X7). A similar, though larger, vessel is noted at **Tell Keisan**, Level 5 (Briend and Humbert 1980: pl. 46: 6). Nos. 253 and 254 are not frequently found in the literature, though one excellent Iron IIA parallel is found at **Dhiban** (Tushingham 1972: fig. 1: 36). That these sherds may represent a form native to south-central Transjordan is apparent from observing later 7th-6th century variants at **Tell Ḥesban** (Lugenbeal and Sauer 1972: pl. V: 306-9); **Sahab**, tomb (Harding 1948: fig. 7: 67); and **Amman, Jebel Jofeh**, tomb (Dajani 1966c: pl. V: 59).

Jar forms are presented in Nos. 255-59. The simple wedge-thickened profile and drip ring of the small jar shown in No. 255 are paralleled in a 9th century layer at **Hazor**, Area A, Stratum VIII (Yadin et al. 1960: pl. LXI: 4) and at **Jericho**, Phase 19 (Franken 1974: fig. 9: 20). Comparable sherds from Transjordan are not apparent. The plain buff jar with everted rim, No. 256, is found in Palestine at **Tell Beit Mirsim**, Stratum A (Albright 1943: pl. 13: 3), an Iron IIC assemblage.

Ridged-neck storage jars are shown in Nos. 257 and 258. No. 257, a thicker, gently ridged form with a hooked rim, appears to be a transitional late Iron I-early Iron II form. At **Tell Deir ᶜAlla** it occurs in an Iron I C level, Phase F (Franken 1969: fig. 62: 30), and at **Hazor** it is documented in Strata IX-X, Area A (Yadin et al. 1960: pl. LII: 23-24) and Area B (Yadin et al. 1961: pl. CCXI: 10) and in the early 9th century Stratum IXa (ibid.: pl. CLXXIX: 15). This specific form is interpreted as a variation within a broad category of storage jar rims that typically have a thicker hooked profile and more deeply grooved neck. These more exaggerated jar rims are found in all Iron I and Iron II phases at **Tell Deir ᶜAlla** (Franken 1969). The sharply ridged jar rim No. 258 is white-slipped in the same manner as No. 257. With regard to form, it represents a variant of the general class of ridged, necked jars. This rim compares with **Beisan**, Level V, upper (James 1966: fig. 64: 1). The sloping neck and hooked rim of jar No. 259 represent a form that is not well attested. Only the 7th-6th century **Tell Ḥesban** corpus provides parallels (Lugenbeal and Sauer 1972: pl. VIII: 403-48, see especially 424).

Large storage jars are shown in Nos. 260-68. No. 260 represents a cylindrical hole-mouth jar that was in common use in Palestine from the 7th to the 5th centuries. Typically these jars have a broad flanged rim and rounded base. The profile of No. 260 is paralleled at **Tell Beit Mirsim**, Stratum A (Albright 1932b: pl. 52: 3); **Khirbet Rabud**, Stratum B1 (Kochavi 1974: fig. 8: 15); and **Gibeon** (Pritchard 1961: fig. 48: P737). Similar forms are found at **Shechem**, Stratum VI (Toombs and Wright 1963: fig. 22: 7), **Tell Gezer**, Field VII, Stratum VIa (Gitin 1979: pl. 18: 1); and **Lachish** (Tufnell 1953: fig.22: 7).

The thick, rounded bulb-rims Nos. 261-267 belong to large neckless storage vessels, a genre that is well illustrated in the **Tell Ḥesban** corpus (Lugenbeal and Sauer 1972: pl. VII: 376-87). The upturned rim No. 261 compares to jar rims dated to the 7th-8th centuries at **Kadesh-Barnea** (Dothan 1965: fig. 6: 14) and to the 7th-6th centuries at **Tell Ḥesban** (Lugenbeal and Sauer 1972: pl. VII: 376). A similar, though thicker and taller, rim is pictured in No. 262, and the rim of No. 263 is rounded and marked by a single groove. An Iron IIC date seems likely for both, though neither is clearly paralleled in the literature. Nos. 264 and 265 are both marked by three grooves across the thickened rim. The form of No. 265 is found at **Tell Ḥesban** (ibid.: pl. VII: 385), though this example is grooved on the shoulder and has fewer grooves on the rim. The shoulder ridging or deep grooving that occurs on several of these large jars from the **Tell Ḥesban** assemblage (ibid.: pl. VII: 377, 383, 385-86) is shown in No. 266. The horizontal rim of a neckless jar that was notched at the shoulder is illustrated in No. 267. Similar profiles are noted from **Tell el-Ful**, Period III (Sinclair 1960: pl. 23: 15) and Stratum IIIA (N. L. Lapp 1981: pl. 49: 23), forms which have been dated by Lapp to the 7th-6th centuries (ibid.: 89). The elongated rim No. 268 is red slipped, and two shallow grooves mark the upper surface. This form generally compares with a 7th-6th century jar from **Tell Ḥesban** (Lugenbeal and Sauer 1972: pl. VII: 361). The squared hole-mouth jar rim pictured in No. 269 appears, with a number of variations, at many sites. This example is paralleled at **Lachish** (Tufnell 1953: pl. 97: 543), and a close comparison may be drawn with a form from **Beth-Zur**, Stratum III (Sellers et al. 1968: fig. 15: 7).

Iron II jug rims are shown in Nos. 271 and 272. The decanter jug, with a neck that is tall and narrow in proportion to the ovoid or, later, squared vessel body, occurs in both Iron I and Iron II assemblages. The simple, unprofiled decanter rim shown in No. 270 is present in Iron IC contexts: **Irbid**, Tomb C (Dajani 1966a: pl. XXXII: 4) and **Taanach**, Period IIB (Rast 1978: fig. 62: 8). It also occurs among Iron II assemblages: **Sahab**, tomb (Harding 1948: fig. 6: 56) and **Tell Beit Mirsim**, Stratum A (Albright 1932b: pls. 58: 2; 59: 8; and 1943: pl. 16: 7).

The simple, thickened and rounded rims shown in Nos. 271 and 272 belong to small jugs and may be compared with a jug in the Iron IIA corpus from **Dhiban** (Winnett and Reed 1964: pl. 74: 2). The offset rim No. 273 represents a squat, globular jug with a tall neck. Traces of red slip adhere to the exterior, though this surface is not sufficiently preserved to detect the presence or absence of burnishing. **Amman, Jebel Jofeh**, tomb (Dajani 1966c: pl. VI: 5a) provides an identical rim.

Rim No. 274 may belong to the Iron IIC genre of Assyrian-influenced handleless bottle-amphoriskoi known from the 7th-6th century tombs at **Amman, Adoni Nur Tomb** (Harding 1953d: fig. 22: 89-90) and **Meqabelein**, tomb (Harding 1950a: pl. XVI: 4-5). However, the example shown in No. 274 is less elaborately profiled and clearly a local product. The light buff ware and hooked rim may be compared with the indigenous bottle-amphoriskoi of the 6th-5th century burials at **Tell el-Mazar**, Cemetery A (Yassine 1984: fig. 5: 2-3).

String-cut disc bases are shown in Nos. 275-76. The concentric lines left by this finishing process are illustrated on an Iron IIC vessel from **Hazor** (Yadin et al. 1958: pl. CXLVII). The bright red slip on the interior of No. 275 is wheel-burnished. Two other bases show characteristics of Iron II, particularly Iron IIC, manufacturing techniques. No. 277 is a very low step-cut base, a type that appears in the 7th-6th century **Tell Ḥesban** corpus (Lugenbeal and Sauer 1972: pl. XI: 555-57). Ring base No. 278 is blackened on the interior from kiln stacking, a technique that is often associated with Iron IIC ceramics. However, an Iron IIA-B date should also be considered, for Lugenbeal and Sauer (ibid.: 61) observe that the ring base is not clearly attested in the Iron IIC assemblages of Transjordan.

A small, globular, red-slipped body sherd with two sharply pointed knobs or rivets on the exterior is shown in No. 279. Rivets are a practiced form of decoration during the Iron II period, though they are not as common as other forms of plastic decoration. They are usually applied to the exterior of vessels on, or immediately beneath, the rim, as is evident on a number of vessel types such as: late 10th century jugs from **Taanach**, Cultic Structure (P. W. Lapp 1964: fig. 20: 1) and Period IIB (Rast 1978: fig. 39: 4); Iron IIA and 7th century bowl rims, **Lachish**, Stratum III (Tufnell et al. 1953: pl. 81: 100); **Sahab**, tomb (Harding 1948: fig. 3: 10-11); Iron IIA kraters, **Dhiban** (Tushingham 1972: fig. 24: 25); and cult vessels, **Ashdod**, Area D (Dothan 1964: fig. 3: 10). Perhaps more directly relevant to the interpretation of sherd No. 279 is a strainer jug from **Buseirah** (Bennett 1975: fig. 6: 2) with three rivets on the vessel body below the handle. Similarly, two rivets appear beneath the handle of a trefoil-mouth jug at **Tel Ḥalif** (Biran and Gophna 1970: fig. 6: 8).

Decorated sherds are shown in Nos. 280-87. No. 280, although of a poor fabric, has a white exterior slip that was highly polished and painted over with bands of black, a surface treatment characteristic of the Iron IIA and B periods.

Band-painted sherds in the Ammonite and Moabite style are shown in Nos. 281-87 (see also No. 248 above). The precisely drawn horizontal bands of alternating black and white paint or wash appear to have been applied over a red slip, though with the exception of No. 281, these sherds are so faded as to preclude detailed observations of the surface finishes. First noted at **Kerak** by Albright (1924: 10-11), the painted wares of Moab and their distribution were later investigated by Glueck who recorded their presence at **Khirbet el-Medeiyineh** (=**Mdeinet el-Muᶜrrajeh**), **Qasr Saliyeh**, **Qasr Zaᶜferan I**, **Khirbet el-Baluᶜ**, **Khirbet el-Jemeil**, and **Zobayir el-Qastal** (1934: 14-22, pls. 22-23). Parker's more recent survey also found painted Moabite sherds at **Qasr Saliyeh** (1986b: Nos. 152-54).

Discussion: Iron II. On the basis of the comparative discussion above, it is clear that all phases of the Iron II period are represented in the pottery from the Kerak plateau. Parallels cited from Palestine indicate that a number of the forms from the Kerak region relate to aspects of the southern Levantine Iron II ceramic traditions and are thus not strictly regional developments.

In Transjordan the most comprehensively published Iron IIA ceramic groups are from Dhiban and Tell Deir ᶜAlla. Of these, a much stronger correlation with the Kerak plateau material emerges from Dhiban. Styles of basic forms, such as cooking pots, jars, and bowls at Tell Deir ᶜAlla where the long history of intra-site ceramic development has been analyzed by Franken (1969), share little with the Iron II wares in the Kerak plateau survey collection. Of the 7th-6th century sites in Transjordan, the Tell Ḥesban wares can be linked with those of the Kerak region, particularly some of the cooking pot and large jar forms. Similarly the late Iron II Ammonite tombs of Amman, Meqabelein, and Sahab also exhibit parallel forms, although some of the forms that occur frequently in these mortuary assemblages (e.g., off-set rim bowls, tripod cups, lamps, globular-amphoriskoi, etc.) do not figure in the Kerak plateau corpus. It may also be noted that common characteristics are observed with Iron IIC pottery from Tell Ṣafuṭ (pers. comm., D. Wimmer), situated just north of Amman. Less affinity is apparent with the largely 7th-6th century wares of the Edomite sites of southern Transjordan: Tawilan, Buseirah, Umm el-Biyara, and Tell el-Kheleifeh. Several comparisons of form are cited above, but Edomite painting styles and other decorative features are absent from the Kerak plateau survey collection.

Assyrian ceramics or Assyrian influenced ceramic forms and decorations are found at several excavated sites in Transjordan including tombs in the Amman region, Edomite sites (Bennett 1982), and Tell el-Mazar (Yassine 1984), but these wares are not evident in the Kerak plateau corpus, with the possible exception of bottle amphoriskos No. 274. Although the form of this vessel type ultimately derives from the Assyrian tradition, it is most probable that this particular sherd represents a local product.

Persian

Description: Persian. There appears to be very little pottery from the Persian period on the Kerak plateau. Of the forms that are present, jars are the most prevalent and these are well attested at Persian sites in Palestine. It has been observed that Persian wares from Tell en-Naṣbeh and Beth-Zur tend to display hard, chalky fabrics of various shades of orange (Wampler 1940: 15; Lapp and Lapp 1968: 70). The fabrics of the sherds presented here are generally quite hard, yet the wares exhibit a range of orange, brown, and grey colors and do not match the descriptions of Palestinian fabrics cited above. Plastic decoration is best represented by the triangular or chevron stamping on jar rims Nos. 290-92 that is so well known from Palestinian assemblages of this period.

The use of medium and small mineral grits for temper continued in the same manner as during the Iron II period, and firing ranges from excellent (Nos. 288-89, 297) to very poor (Nos. 290-91). A few instances of surface spalling occur (Nos. 292, 297). For the most part the wares are quite similar, if not identical, to those of the Iron II period. Jars No. 290 and 291 however, are exceptions, for the quality of these pieces is much poorer than that of the rest of the corpus.

Forms: Persian. A Persian mortarium, a shallow bowl with a footed base and thickened everted rim, is represented in No. 288. This example has a more rounded, less sharply defined rim than most mortaria. The fabric of this sherd is pale pink, and both the interior and exterior surfaces retain a cream slip. The lightly grooved wavy line decoration beneath the rim exterior (not illustrated) appears to have been impressed by movement of the potter's finger tip across the wet clay surface. P. W. Lapp, in his definitive discussion of Persian ceramic typology and chronology, suggested a mid-5th through 3rd century time span for this vessel (1970b: 184) on the basis of the stratification at **Taanach** (ibid.: fig. 7: 12-13). However, excavations at **Tell Keisan**, where occupation from the late Iron II through the Persian periods is continuous, indicate that this form may appear as early as Iron IIC, Level 5 (Briend and Humbert 1980: pl. 45: 5). Mortaria are also noted at **Tell Keisan** in the transitional Iron IIC-Persian, Level 4 (ibid.: pls. 28: 1; 31: 5-6), as well as in the Persian Level 3 (ibid.: pl. 20: 17-19, 21).

The late 5th century *terminus a quo* suggested for this form at **Taanach** by P. W. Lapp is supported by Rast's analysis of Period VIA (1978: fig. 77: 7-8) and Period VIB (ibid.: figs. 84: 2; 85:9), which date to 450-400 B.C.E. Later, 4th century, examples are known from **Hazor**, Area B, Stratum II (Yadin et al. 1958: pl. LXXIX: 17-18, 20, 24) and Area G, Stratum II (Yadin et al. 1961: pl. CCLVII: 1-10). Mortaria occur in Persian strata at a number of other sites, though these are less specifically dated: **Tell Gezer**, Field VII, Stratum IV (Gitin 1979: pl. 30: 1-16) and Field II, Stratum 3 (Dever et al. 1974: pl. 37: 3); **Ramat Raḥel**, Pit 484 (Aharoni et al. 1964: fig. 12: 19, 22); **Qadum** (Stern and Magen 1984: fig. 5: 13-15); and **Tell en-Naṣbeh**, Cistern 361 (Wampler 1941: fig. 12: X74).

The open, curved bowl shown in No. 289 with an indented and rounded rim has a dark pink fabric and exterior cream slip. This may be tentatively assigned to the Persian period. An identical sherd is noted at Tell Gezer, Field II, Stratum 3 (Dever et al. 1974: pl. 37: 10).

Necked jars or jugs with deeply stamped triangular impressions on the rim are shown in Nos. 290-92. All three have coarse utilitarian fabrics, and Nos. 291 and 292 are very poorly fired. The profile of No. 292 is paralleled by a **Taanach** form published by both P. W. Lapp (1970b: fig. 6: 7) and Rast (1978: fig. 85: 1). Lapp originally proposed a late 5th century date for this vessel, and Rast similarly assigned it to Period VIB, dating to the second half of the 5th century. Related profiles are found at **Tell en-Naṣbeh**, Cistern 370 (Wampler 1941: fig. 2: X7) and Cistern 304 (ibid.: fig. 7: X27), though the stratification of these cisterns is uncertain.

The essential criterion for including sherds Nos. 290-92 in this discussion of Persian pottery is the presence of the triangular impressing on the rims. The chronology of this decoration among Palestinian wares has been addressed in several studies. Wampler (1940) suggested a late 6th through 5th century date for triangular impressed sherds from the Tell en-Naṣbeh cisterns on the basis of synchronisms with imported Aegean wares. Lapp and Lapp (1968: 68-69) initially interpreted their distribution as ranging from the late 7th to early 5th centuries in accordance with stratification at Beth-Zur, Lachish, Tell en-Naṣbeh, and Ramat Raḥel. P. W. Lapp later narrowed the date to the second half of the 6th century through the early 5th century (1970b: 185) and asserted that the disappearance of this decorative motif was contemporary with the introduction of the mortaria bowls. Stern, in his recent summary discussion of triangular stamped designs and associated vessel types (1982: 133-36), concluded that a chronology from the end of the 6th through the end of the 5th century best correlates with the archaeological record.

Stern provides a catalogue of triangular stamped vessels from Palestine and neighboring regions (ibid.: 133), to which additional published occurrences may be added: **Jerusalem** (Lux 1972: fig. 5: 1); **Qadum** (Stern and Magen 1984: figs. 4; 9: 1); **Tell Anafa** (Weinberg 1971: pl. 20A); **Khirbet Kefire** (Vriezen 1975: fig. 4: 24); **Tell Gezer**, Field VII, Stratum IV (Gitin 1979: pl. 28B: 29); and **Tell el-Ful**, Period III (N. L. Lapp 1981: pl. 65: 5-6). The Tell el-Ful vessels with this design may actually pre-date the Persian period or closely coincide with its beginning.

The triangular stamped jar or jug rims pictured in Nos. 290-92 appear to be the first occurrences of this design in Transjordan and can be contrasted with examples from Palestine in two respects. First, chevron stamping is rarely attested on jar and jug forms in Palestine, but occurs largely on open vessels including deep bowls, kraters, and hole-mouth jars (Stern 1982: 133). Second, the deep impressing which characterizes Nos. 290-92 is much coarser than the delicate styles of shallow impressing that are found among the majority of triangle-stamped vessels (e.g., **Tell el-Ful**, Stratum IIIA-B, N. L. Lapp 1981: pl. 39: 1-3) published from Palestinian sites.

Hole-mouth jars from the Persian period are shown in Nos. 293-97. No. 293 pictures a thick, upturned rim from a neckless storage jar, a form derived from the angular, Iron II "sausage jar." Related jars are found at **Shechem**, Stratum V (P. W. Lapp 1970b: fig. 3: 4); **Tell Gezer**, Field II, Stratum 3 (Dever et al. 1974: pl. 37: 12); **Mugharet Abu Shinjeh** (Lapp and Lapp 1974: pl. 18: 5); **Tell el-Hesi** (Coogan 1975: fig. 8: 12); **Tell Qasile** (Maisler 1951: fig. 13: e); **Shavei Zion** (Prausnitz et al. 1967: fig. 11: 2); and at the pre-Persian site of **Meṣad Ḥashavyahu** (Naveh 1962: fig. 6: 15). The peaked rim of No. 294 is associated with the same vessel form as No. 293. A parallel rim from Taanach was originally dated to the mid-5th century by P. W. Lapp (1970b: fig. 4: 4) and later published in the Period VIA corpus (Rast 1978: fig. 80: 5). Another example may be cited from **Tell Keisan**, Level 3 (Briend and Humbert 1980: pl. 18: 1).

The thick, rounded rim of No. 295 occurs at **Tell Gezer**, Field VII, Stratum VIA (Gitin 1979: pl. 17: 1) and at **Taanach** in a stratum dated to the second half of the 5th century, Period VIA (Rast 1978: fig. 81: 3). Sloping, horizontal bulb rims of hole-mouth jars are pictured in Nos. 296 and 297. The simple bulbous rim of No. 296

compares with rims from **Tell Gezer**, Field II, Stratum 3 (Dever et al. 1974: pl. 37: 25) and **Hazor**, Area G, Stratum II (Yadin et al. 1961: pl. CCLVII: 30). An earlier variant may be noted at **Tell Keisan**, Level 4 (Briend and Humbert 1980: pl. 25: 7), a transitional Iron IIC-Persian layer. Another rim style that is associated with the cylindrical storage jar and has origins in the Iron II period is shown in No. 297. At **Tell Keisan** similar forms occur in both Level 5 (Briend and Humbert 1980: pl. 47: 1), dated Iron IIC, and Level 4 (ibid.: pls. 25: 8; 27: 2-3). At **Taanach** this rim has been attributed to the second half of the 5th century (Rast 1978: fig. 81: 1; see also P. W. Lapp 1970b: fig. 4: 5), and P. W. Lapp dated a parallel form from **Shechem**, Stratum V (ibid.: fig. 3: 5) to ca. 525-475 B.C.E.

Discussion: Persian. Aside from vessels recovered during the excavation of the 6th-5th century cemetery at Tell el-Mazar (Yassine 1984), stratified Persian pottery is not well-attested in Transjordan and, as a result, this discussion has relied on comparisons with ceramic groups from Palestine. This lack of comparative material from excavated sites in Transjordan is reflected in data from site surveys as well, for Persian pottery is conspicuously lacking, or only minimally represented, in survey documentation. A few examples of survey reports that record virtually no Persian pottery include: north Jordan (Mittmann 1970), the *limes Arabicus* (Parker 1976, 1986b, see also Clark 1987), Wadi ʿIsal (Jacobs 1983), and Wadi el-Ḥasa (MacDonald 1982, 1988). A survey of the Tell Ḥesban region identified one site bearing pottery from the Persian period (Ibach 1987). An east Jordan Valley survey encountered 16 sites (of a total 224 sites) that appear to have been occupied at this time (Ibrahim et al. 1976; Yassine et al. 1988). The Kerak plateau survey recorded 20 sites (of a total of 443 sites) with Iron IIC/Persian and/or Persian period ceramics. As in the case of the east Jordan Valley, these sites on the Kerak plateau generally yielded very few sherds. Without larger samples, attempts to distinguish Iron IIC/Persian ceramics (from the end of the Iron Age and the beginning of the Persian period) and ceramics that are more specifically characteristic of the Persian period may be premature in the context of the Kerak plateau survey collection. Nevertheless, the survey findings from the Kerak plateau accord well with the data from other regional surveys in Transjordan and contribute to the preliminary conclusion that southern Transjordan was largely unsedentarized during Persian rule.

The few Persian wares from the Kerak region that are presented in the text above are neither homogenous nor particularly distinctive. Yet the assemblage shows some association with the established Persian ceramic typology of Palestine, for the triangular-stamped decorations and most of the forms are attested among Palestinian sites with Persian occupation. However, the fact that jars appear relatively heavily represented in this corpus, and ware types still lack a comprehensive description (in comparison with the assemblages from most other periods), could reflect a gap in our understanding of the Persian pottery of Transjordan. While the jar forms are clearly related to those of Palestine, these forms represent only a portion of the broader contemporaneous ceramic repertoire in Palestine. It is probable, therefore, that in Transjordan other vessel types of this period may have been more provincial, sharing fewer characteristics of form and ware types with the Palestinian assemblages, and remain as yet unidentified in the survey assemblage. However, if this is indeed the case, the question remains as to whether the identification of a fuller range of forms from within the survey corpus would actually alter, in a significant manner, our present perspective on settlement density on the Kerak plateau during the Persian period.

Hellenistic

Description: Hellenistic. Hellenistic pottery is found at a number of sites on the Kerak plateau but seldom occurs in significant quantity at any one location. However, the distinctive Hellenistic ceramics generally can be differentiated from fabrics of Nabataean and Roman pottery. With the introduction of Hellenism, Hellenistic ceramic forms exercised substantial influence upon the pottery of the southern Levant. Transjordanian pottery underwent radical changes that are evident in several respects. Principally, indigenous ceramic producers imitated the forms and fabrics of Hellenistic pottery exported to the Levant at this time.

Among the local wares of this assemblage, pink-orange fabrics are predominant (Nos. 298-300, 303, 308-9). A bricky red ware is noted for base No. 305, and cooking pot No. 301 is similar. Fish-plate base No. 307 consists of a coarse beige ware, and the characteristic Hellenistic grey ware is noted in base No. 306. All of the bowl and jug forms (Nos. 298-300, 303) are dark red-brown slipped on the exterior and mottled red-orange-brown slipped on the interior. The careless application of this finish is particularly illustrated in No. 298 in which the dark exterior slip is broadly dripped over the vessel rim and interior slip. The semi-glossy, streaked deep reddish slip that is so typical of Hellenistic surface finish is evident on base No. 305. Bases Nos. 308-9 belong to closed forms such as jars or jugs and have a bright orange exterior slip. No. 308 is stained on the exterior with smudges of a darker brown slip, again showing a lack of attention to the application of surface treatments. The grey slip of base No. 306 is the same color as the fabric. Cooking pot No. 301 has a dark reddish-grey slip and a coarse fabric mixed with white calcite inclusions. The pink-slipped fish-plate base No. 307 has a dull red interior slip that does not appear on any of the other sherds in this sample.

Generally, the Hellenistic wares are very well prepared with fine temper, and firing tends to be very good to excellent, with a few pieces showing a faint core, though the cooking pot illustrated as No. 301 has a thick core. Painting, rouletting, stamping and other characteristic Hellenistic decorative features are not reflected in this assemblage, though finger modeling distinguishes handle No. 304.

The two sherds in this sample that represent vessels of non-local origin are the Rhodian jar rim No. 302 and the Megarian bowl fragment No. 310. The Rhodian jar rim is of exceptional ware with a finely prepared and evenly fired buff paste. The Megarian bowl sherd has an orange-pink paste and deep bright red varnish covering both surfaces. The variation on the "egg-and-dart" theme, and the palmettes shown in No. 310 are both characteristic of the decorative motifs found on the mold-made Megarian bowls. Representing the only apparent imported Hellenistic material in the Kerak plateau corpus, No. 302 may be of Aegean origin, while it is likely that No. 310 is a Syrian product.

Forms: Hellenistic. Small incurved deep bowls are a well known component of Hellenistic assemblages of the southern Levant. This form is presented in Nos. 298-300. Nos. 298 and 299 are quite similar, both having simple rounded rims with gently incurved profiles. These sherds are dark slipped on the exterior with mottled orange interior finishes. As demonstrated by P. W. Lapp (1961: 172) this genre of bowls (Lapp's Type 51:1), which is associated with both flat and ring bases, dates from the Late Hellenistic (ca. 200 B.C.E.) through the first century of the Roman period (ca. 50 C.E.).

The incurved bowl is quite common in the Hellenistic repertoire and appears both in the local fabrics and, less commonly, among the imported wares. Several specific examples that are similar to Nos. 298 and 299 and illustrate a broad chronological duration of this form are noted. At **Shechem** the incurved bowl is first documented in Stratum III, and a parallel is cited from Stratum IIIb (N. L. Lapp 1964: fig. 1b: 35) dated ca. 250-225 B.C.E. At **Tell Gezer** comparable incurved bowls are attested in Field VII, Stratum III (Gitin 1979: pl. 33: 15), an Early Hellenistic deposit dated from the late 3rd to early 2nd century B.C.E. The later Stratum IIC at **Tell Gezer**, dating from the early to the mid-2nd century, contains several examples with red slip, Field VII (Gitin 1979: pl. 35: 1-2, 5). In Transjordan the locally produced incurved bowl with mottled red and black ware occurs at **Pella**, Area VIII (Smith et al. 1981: fig. 14: 5) in a clear Late Hellenistic stratum dated 145-82 B.C.E. A later, Early Roman, incurved bowl from **Qumran** (P. W. Lapp 1961: 172: K) dated 50-68 C.E. may also be compared with Nos. 298 and 299.

Less specifically dated occurrences may be noted at the following sites: **Pella**, a mixed Late Hellenistic fill (Smith et al. 1980: pl. XIX: 8); **Tell Gezer**, Field II, Stratum 2 (Dever et al. 1970: pl. 33: 28); **Beth-Zur**, Stratum II (Sellers et al. 1968: fig. 24: 11); and **Akko**, Area A, Strata 3-2 (Dothan 1976: fig. 30: 5). Other Hellenistic incurved bowls from Transjordan have been published from **ᶜAroᶜer** (Olávarri 1965: fig. 3: 1-2) and **Amman, Citadel** (Zayadine 1977-78: see fig. 13), but these are more sharply incurved, or display other rim styles that do not compare with the examples presented here. No bowls of this type have as yet been published from Dhiban or Tell Ḥesban.

The small hemispherical deep bowl No. 300, with mottled orange-brown exterior slip and orange interior slip, is distinguished by a tapered and peaked upright rim. This form corresponds with P. W. Lapp's Type 51.2 (1961: 73). As in the case of Nos. 298 and 299, this incurved bowl occurs with either a flat or a ring base and spans the Late Hellenistic period through the first century of the Early Roman period (ca. 200 B.C.E.-68 C.E.). The rim style of No. 300 is not as prevalent in the published literature as the simple rounded rims discussed above. It occurs at **Amman, Forum** (Hadidi 1970: pl. III: 4), and at **Tell Gezer** the peaked rim bowl is evident in Field VII, Stratum IIB (Gitin 1979: pl. 40: 4), dated to the mid-2nd century. A thicker, heavier, variant from **Shechem** has been attributed to a 150-100 B.C.E. context (P. W. Lapp 1961: 173: C). Among other sites where this form is noted are: **Beth-Zur**, Stratum II-I (Sellers et al. 1968: fig. 28: 5); and **Amman, Citadel** (Zayadine 1977-78: fig. 13: 342). Another example, with a red "glaze," is attested in **Caesarea** (Roller 1980: fig. 2: 24).

The unprofiled cooking pot rim is typical of Hellenistic assemblages, though most often the neck and rim are splayed, as at **Tell el-Ful**, Stratum IV (N. L. Lapp 1981: pl. 78: 3-9). While characteristically Hellenistic in fabric and finish the cooking pot fragment shown in No. 301 has an upright, unprofiled rim that is not frequently found. However, excellent parallels from stratified deposits occur at **Tell Gezer**, Field VII, Stratum IIC (Gitin 1979: pl. 35: 14) from the early to mid-2nd century B.C.E., and **Tulul Abu el-ᶜAlayiq**, Area E3 (Netzer and Meyers 1977: fig. 6: 14), which dates from very Late Hellenistic through the beginning of the Early Roman period. Both examples show this form with flattened strap handles. In Transjordan similar, though not identical, vessel fragments are found in mixed fills at **Dhiban** (Tushingham 1972: fig. 3: 17) and **Araq el-Emir** (N. L. Lapp 1983: fig. 32: 58). The latter is dated Early Hellenistic.

The tall, straight-necked Rhodian jar fragment shown in No. 302 has a highly distinctive, finely levigated, pink ware that is common among these amphorae: **Beth-Zur** (Sellers et al. 1968: fig. 28: 15) and **Araq el-Emir** (N. L. Lapp 1983: 68). A portion of the join between one of the handles and the vessel body is present just beneath the rounded, everted rim. An identical form is found at **Tell Keisan**, Level 2 (Briend and Humbert 1980: pl. 15: 11) for which the excavators suggest a 280-180 B.C.E. dating range (ibid: 112). A similar amphora is noted at **Tell Qaimun** (Ben-Tor and Rosenthal 1978: fig. 9: 9).

The flaring, everted jug rim seen in No. 303 is of identical ware and finish as Nos. 298 and 299. This jug appears at **Beth-Zur** in the 2nd century B.C.E. (P. W. Lapp 1961: 157: C) as well as at **Shechem** and **Samaria** (ibid.). P. W. Lapp assigned this form to Type 21.1, among the large wide-neck jugs, and suggested a chronological framework of 175-100 B.C.E. At **Tell el-Ful** a parallel form is associated with Stratum IVA (N. L. Lapp 1981: pl. 75: 21). This vessel, dated ca. 175-135 B.C.E., shows the jug with an omphalos base. A parallel from **Bethel** exhibits a footed ring base (Kelso 1968: pl. 70: 25).

Handle No. 304, illustrated in section, consists of a light beige ware that was well prepared and fired, yet no trace of slip survives. Attached to the handle is a fragment of a tall-necked jar. The handle joins the jar neck at right angles that imply a very wide loop handle or a sharply angled handle. Although these features are reminiscent of the Rhodian jar, the ware is clearly not of the same quality as the Rhodian jar fragment No. 302, and the join between the handle and vessel wall is crudely executed. The deep finger impressions that extend along the handle from its stump are suggestive of Hellenistic twisted handles, but these are prevalent on smaller closed vessels such as flasks, amphoriskoi, and juglets: **Tell Gezer**, Strata IIA, IIC (Gitin 1979: pls. 41: 25; 34: 28; 44: 2).

The bases that appear in Nos. 305-9 are common throughout the Hellenistic period and are differentiated from Roman and Nabataean bases by their proportions as well as by ware and decorative attributes. The low flattened ring bases pictured in Nos. 305-6 occur both on open vessels, such as the incurved bowls whose rims are shown in Nos. 298-300, and on closed forms including jugs and jars of various sizes (P. W. Lapp 1961: 173: G, Type 51.2; 165: A, Type 33; 160: A, Type 21.2). No. 305, the higher of the flattened ring bases, is paralleled in the Late Hellenistic assemblage from **Tell Ḥesban** (Sauer 1973: fig. 1: 4-5), and the lower base, No. 306, may be compared with **Tulul Abu al-ᶜAlayiq** (P. W. Lapp 1961: 165: A, Type 251.2). The more conventional tapered ring base is shown in No. 308.

No. 309 illustrates a higher ring base than those described above. The ware and workmanship displayed by this sherd are crude in comparison with the rest of the corpus. The scooped depression in the center of the vessel interior denotes the Hellenistic fish-plate. The fish-plate form, replicating imported Greek fish-plates, usually shows a finer quality of manufacture than that of No. 309. Examples of Early Hellenistic Palestinian fish-plates are found at **Tell Gezer**, Field VII, Stratum III (Gitin 1979: pl. 33: 12); **Shechem**, Stratum IIIb (N. L. Lapp 1964: fig. 1b: 38); and **Akko**, Area A, Stratum 3 (Dothan 1976: fig. 30: 1-3). P. W. Lapp's study demonstrates that indigenous Levantine fish-plates (1961: 206: B, Type 153.1) of the fine "Hellenistic decorated ware" are frequent throughout the 2nd century. An Eastern Sigilatta A fish-plate at **Tell Gezer**, Field VII, Stratum IIB (Gitin 1979: pl. 38: 22) is also dated to the late 2nd century.

In Transjordan fish-plates are included in the Late Hellenistic layers at **Pella**. Two of these are associated with mid-2nd century to ca. 82 B.C.E. deposits (Smith et al. 1980: pl. XVIII: 7) and Area VIII (Smith et al. 1981: fig. 14: 1). A third example from **Pella** has been associated with the 83/82 B.C.E. destruction debris, Area III (McNicoll and Smith 1980: fig. 9: bottom row, right). **Amman, Citadel** (Zayadine 1977-78: fig. 14: 146, 346) and **ᶜAroᶜer** (Olávarri 1965: fig. 3: 3) provide additional instances of this form in Transjordan.

The Megarian bowl fragment illustrated in No. 310 appears to represent the only piece of Hellenistic fine ware from the Kerak plateau survey collection, and the possibility that it may actually be Late Hellenistic Eastern Sigillata A of Syrian provenience cannot be ruled out. The fabric is of finely levigated pink-orange clay, covered with a deep red varnish. The molded exterior decoration consists of a variation on the popular "egg-and-dart" motif in which the dart element has been omitted. This pattern, which typically fills the upper zones of Megarian bowls, is found among bowls from a cistern deposit in the **Athenian Agora** (Thompson 1934: fig. 48: c: 30), which is dated from the beginning of the 3rd century to the beginning of the 2nd century B.C.E. In Palestine this motif appears at **Samaria** (Crowfoot et al. 1957: fig. 64: 1, 1a) and **Tell Gezer**, Field VII, Stratum II A (Gitin 1979: pl. 44: 15). Kenyon asserted a 150 B.C.E. *terminus a quo* for the appearance of the Megarian bowls at **Samaria** and, although there has been a lack of consensus regarding this date (Crowfoot et al. 1957: 218, 220, 273-74), P. W. Lapp (1961: 66) accepted Kenyon's analysis. In his study, Lapp concluded that the chronology of the Samaria bowls extended from the mid-2nd century B.C.E. through to the Early Roman period (ibid.: 209, Type 158).

Discussion: Hellenistic. The technological changes in ceramic production that are manifest in southern Levantine Hellenistic pottery demonstrate the impact of Greek manufacturing techniques upon indigenous ceramic producers. Vessel form was also influenced by Aegean products, and imported Greek wares became part of the Levantine ceramic repertoire. As shown in the discussion of vessel forms above, the use of a faster wheel, the production of new and thinner vessel forms, and the introduction of orange and red-brown mottled slips combined to transform aspects of the ceramic assemblage in sharp contrast to the attributes of the Iron II and Persian repertoires. Table wares, such as the hemispherical and incurved bowls, show two trends. First is an emphasis on fabric preparation and firing practices that effected a qualitative improvement. Second is a distinct lack of attention to the application of surface finish. These factors, plus the sheer quantity of hemispherical and incurved bowls that appear in Palestine and Transjordan, indicate that this form may have been mass-produced.

Among the forms discussed above, both the bowls and the fish-plate were first introduced in this period. By virtue of their stratigraphic contexts and spatial distributions, these vessels illustrate the temporal duration and wide geographic scope of Hellenistic culture and its influence upon local craft production. The infusion of this influence in the Kerak region is demonstrated by the attributes of locally produced pottery as well as by the presence of non-local vessels, the Rhodian jar and Megarian bowl. Hellenistic imports were apparently infrequent here, but their presence demonstrates the far reaching network through which Hellenistic products of the Aegean and Syria circulated.

Nabataean and Early Roman

During the 1st century B.C.E. and the 1st century C.E., the Kerak plateau was an integral part of the Nabataean cultural sphere. Yet the ceramic assemblage of this period shows two patterns of material culture association. The patterns are clearly differentiated in some respects and inextricably blended in others, though they share a heritage within the Hellenistic tradition. First, there are the numerous sherds that are demonstrably similar and sometimes identical to the wares of Petra, some of which are discussed below under the rubric of "Nabataean." Second, there are contemporary wares whose attributes of form, fabric, and decoration show strong affinity with Early Roman pottery and are paralleled at sites more closely interactive with the Roman geo-political sphere, such as those of the Judaean Desert. However, there is a great deal of ambiguity in the Kerak plateau assemblage of this period, for the distinction between Nabataean and Early Roman pottery cannot be consistently applied to all of the sherds that date between the 1st century B.C.E. and the 1st century C.E.

Description: Nabataean. Nabataean pottery is well documented at numerous sites throughout the Kerak plateau, and the substantial corpus from this survey accords well with the level of Nabataean occupation recorded in the adjacent Wadi el-Ḥasa region to the south (MacDonald 1982; 1988). The forms and fabrics of the Nabataean corpus are very much like those of Petra and other sites in southern Transjordan and include a range of coarse wares as well as fine wares. This section reviews a small group of Nabataean sherds. Among them are some of the principal egg-shell ware forms, heavily profiled rims, and two types of handles that are particularly frequent in the plateau region. Despite the prevalence of Nabataean pottery in south-central and southern Transjordan, publications of stratified deposits are few. Some progress has been made in attempting to define temporal horizons within the Nabataean ceramic traditions on the basis of stratified assemblages, but chronological subdivisions are still tenuous. Citations, wherever possible, refer to sherds and vessels with known provenience, yet in some instances comparisons are drawn with vessels whose provenience is unconfirmed or unstratified.

The wares of this assemblage are nearly all orange or red; exceptions include: brown (No. 314), buff (No. 328), and beige (No. 330). Overall, the fabrics show less variation in color than in any of the preceding periods and may indicate the development of standardized pastes. A preliminary study by Hammond (1962) suggests that Nabataean potters may also have attempted to standardize vessel sizes. The two principal surface treatments in this assemblage are white slip (Nos. 311, 313, 315, 317-21, 323, 326, 329) and, to a lesser extent, red slip (Nos. 316, 322, 324-25). Bowl No. 315 is white-slipped on the exterior and red-slipped on the interior. Another white-slipped bowl, No. 313, is covered with a red wash or thin red paint on the interior. An example of the common Nabataean painted style, consisting of dark reddish painted motifs upon the interior of open bowls, is found on body sherd No. 331. Stamping and rouletting, including rouletted bases, are attested among the Nabataean wares of the Kerak plateau, though none is represented in this sample (see Khairy 1983 for a discussion of these techniques).

Several modeling techniques are represented in the Nabataean corpus. Body grooving or ribbing is well articulated on the shoulder of cooking pot No. 318 and appears faintly on the shoulder of cooking pot No. 319. Multiple strands of clay pressed together form handles; examples are shown in section in Nos. 323-26. The upper surface of the pithos handle No. 322 is lightly grooved with wide, very shallow lateral depressions that result from a potter having drawn his or her fingers across the wet clay surface. This finger-grooving is frequently attested among pithos handles, though it is often deeper and more distinctive than that of No. 322.

The quality of paste preparation among the Nabataean fine wares probably is technologically the finest ever achieved in Transjordan. Few visible inclusions occur and these are generally barely perceptible. For the most part firing is excellent, and cores tend to be light rather than dark. Some sandwich firing occurs; see for instance sherd No. 331 in this assemblage. Surface spalling is rare but can be noted on cooking pot No. 318. Nabataean vessels are generally thin, the most delicate of which are the "egg-shell wares" illustrated in Nos. 312-14, 317, 321, 327, and 331.

Forms: Nabataean. A deep plate or flared open bowl with a horizontally splayed rim is shown in No. 311. This vessel is paralleled at **Dhiban** (Winnett and Reed 1964: pl. 70: 13) and is of the same general form as a *terra sigillata* bowl from **ᶜAroᶜer** (Olávarri 1965: fig. 3: 5).

The egg-shell ware bowl with carinated and inverted rim, No. 312, is a form that occurs in abundance and with a wide range of subtle stylistic variations. It occurs with painted floral designs or florally derived geometric motifs as well as without decoration, as in this instance. Hammond illustrates this form in his type-classification of Nabataean bowls from **Petra**, Class I (1962: 176: I1[b]: 3). In Parr's ceramic sequence from **Petra**, this bowl and its variations occur in 1st century B.C.E. deposits, Phases V, VII, VIII (1970: figs. 2: 10; 3: 36; 4: 42-43) and in the post C.E. 76 Phase XIII (ibid.: fig. 7: 109). Numerous examples are also known from **Dhiban**, one of which shows this form with a painted interior design motif similar to that of No. 331 (Tushingham 1972: fig. 2: 60). **Rujm Beni Yasser** (Parker 1987b: fig. 92:18), **ᶜAroᶜer** (Olávarri 1965: fig. 3: 7), and **Sbaita** (G. M. Crowfoot 1936: pl. 4: 6) provide additional examples.

The carinated egg-shell ware bowl with an elongated rim, illustrated in No. 313, compares with a vessel from **Petra**, Hammond's Class I (1962: 176: I2[b]: 6), which shows this form with a ring base. The exterior cream slip and interior red paint or wash of No. 313 is a standard Nabataean style of surface treatment. Inspiration for this form may, however, have origins in Eastern Sigillata A ceramics, as seen at **Dhiban** (Tushingham 1972: fig. 3: 31) and 1st century B.C.E. **Samaria** (Crowfoot et al. 1957: figs. 17-19, 21). Early Roman examples, probably also derived from the *terra sigillata* form, may be cited as well: **Qumran**, Level II (de Vaux 1954: figs. 4: 2; 5: 6).

The slender cup or hemispherical bowl No. 314 is also treated in Hammond's classification of fine wares from **Petra**, Class II (1962: 178: II2[c]: 12), and this vessel, as well as additional examples from **Petra** (Hammond 1973: 45: 69-70), shows this form with a ring base. A stratified parallel from **Petra**, Phase VIII (Parr 1973: fig. 4: 45) is dated to the 1st century B.C.E., and it appears that in the subsequent century the form is essentially still present, though considerably thicker, e.g., **Petra**, Phases X/XII, XIII (ibid.: figs. 6: 97; 7: 110). Comparisons also occur at **Dhiban** (Tushingham 1972: figs. 3: 3-4; 4: 4).

Hemispherical bowl No. 315 is gently carinated with a delicately rolled and everted rim. As No. 313, the interior is decorated with a red surface treatment while the exterior is white-slipped. A similar, thicker, version appears at **Petra**, Phase IX (Parr 1973: fig. 5: 63) and probably dates to the 1st century C.E. The best parallel to No. 315 is from Parker's survey at **Khirbet el-Qirana**, southwest of Maᶜan (Parker 1986b: 213: No. 514).

The distinctively flared and grooved profiled rim of sherd No. 316 probably represents a krater. A prototype of this form may occur at **Araq el-Emir**, Gateway, Stratum 3 (Dentzer et al. 1983: fig. 64: 4), but the ware of this sherd is very different, and the authors have suggested that it is a 2nd century B.C.E. cooking pot.

The necked globular cooking vessels which are represented by sherds Nos. 317-19 are forms that are most often characterized by rounded bases, vertical loop or strap handles, and body ribbing. The wares of Nos. 317 and 318, which both belong to unusually small vessels, are exceptionally fine while the fabric of No. 319 is coarser and more typical of Nabataean cooking wares. The profile of No. 317, showing a peaked rim and sharp concave join between the neck and shoulder, compares with a cooking pot from **Nessana** (Baly 1962: pl. LVI: 5). This general form is well documented at **Petra** in the 1st century B.C.E., Phases VI and VIII (Parr 1973: figs. 3: 32-33; 4: 50) and in the 1st century C.E., Phases X/XII (ibid: fig. 7: 104-5). Other examples from **Petra** are noted as well (Cleveland 1960: fig. 6: 2; Zayadine 1974: pl. LXIII: 18). More elaborately profiled cooking pot rims, as illustrated in the heavily ridged neck of No. 319, are also frequent in the Kerak region. Precise parallels are not evident, but similar forms occur at **Petra** (Zayadine 1974: pl. LXIII: 2, 17, 19, 33).

The jar or jug rim No. 320 with a swollen and offset junction between the neck and shoulder is not typical but does illustrate the kinds of elaborate vessel profiles of Nabataean manufacture that occur in forms other than the cooking pot. The inverted off-set rim of a fine ware jug shown in No. 321 has appeared in a largely 1st century C.E. context at **Petra**, Phase IX (Parr 1973: fig. 5: 60), and two unstratified parallels from that site are also attested (Hammond 1973: No. 12; Sivan 1977: fig. 1: 9).

The large pithos strap handle pictured in No. 322 is very common in the Kerak region, and this example, like most of the others in the assemblage, is white-slipped and ridged on the exterior surface, though in this instance the ridging is extremely faint. A published parallel may be cited from **Petra**, Period V (Hammond 1965: pl. 54: [2]: 13), and a second example from the Kerak plateau was collected during a survey at **Muḥaṭṭet el-Ḥajj** (upper) (Parker 1986b: 187: No. 108).

A series of handles consisting of multiple rolls of clay pressed together is presented in section in Nos. 323-26. No. 323 displays two rolls of clay and Nos. 324-25 show the same technique with three rolls of clay. The tapered section of No. 326 shows four joined sections of clay. These handles are numerous in the Kerak plateau survey corpus and compare with handles from **Petra**, Period IC and Period V (Hammond 1965: pls. 52: [1]: 11; 54: [2]: 13); **Dhiban** (Tushingham 1972: figs. 3: 28; 4: 42); and **Sbaita** (G. M. Crowfoot 1936: pl. 4: 4). Handles of two pressed coils are also known from an Early Roman context at **Jerusalem** (Bagatti and Milik 1958: fig. 27: 7-8).

Nabataean ring bases Nos. 327-30 appear as the standard type of base for many Nabataean forms, which occasionally even include cooking pots (Horsfield and Horsfield 1941: pl. 20). Of the bowl bases Nos. 327-28, the latter is paralleled at **Petra**, Phase V (Parr 1973: fig. 2: 17) where it dates to the 1st century B.C.E. A higher ring base with a deeply sloping center is seen in No. 329. This base is also associated with a number of vessel forms; examples include a necked, globular pot (Weippert 1979a: fig. 4: 15) and a jug (Sivan 1977: fig. 1: 4). A similar base, though with a less sloping center, is associated with a carinated cup (ibid.: fig. 1: 1). A narrower, low ring base with depressed center is shown in No. 330 and most closely compares with bases of tall V-shaped chalices as noted at **Petra** (Hammond 1973: No. 91) and **Shqeirah** (Zayadine 1970: fig. 11: 220) on the southern edge of the Kerak plateau.

Body sherd No. 331 is one of many painted Nabataean sherds in the Kerak plateau survey corpus. This painting is especially common on the interiors of open bowls, such as the one pictured in No. 312. The design, executed in dark red-brown paint, consists of bands of parallel and sloping parallel lines interspersed with solid circles. Both elements appear in Hammond's classification of Nabataean painted designs (1959: 375: A7; D9c). Schmitt-Korte illustrates one example of this motif in which repetitions of the design are arranged in a concentric pattern that covers the entire inner surface of a bowl (1970: fig. 183: 26). Other instances of this motif are found at **Petra**, Phase X/XII (Parr 1973: fig. 6: 95), dated to the 1st century C.E., and Phase XIII (ibid.: fig. 7: 106), dated post-C.E. 76; **Dhiban** (Tushingham 1972: fig. 4: 56); and **Sbaita** (G. M. Crowfoot 1936: pl. 2: [5]: 1, 4).

Discussion: Nabataean. Hammond (1959, 1962) has noted that, despite the obscurity of the origins of the uniquely thin and often delicately painted ceramic tradition of Nabataean fine ware with its excellent fabric quality, it is clear that Hellenistic influence provided some measure of impetus for what became a highly sophisticated and individualistic ceramic culture. At Petra, Nabataean pottery first appears in basal strata concomitant with Late Hellenistic wares. Parr's excavations (1973) have shown that the earliest 1st century B.C.E. phases at Petra contained coarse, undecorated wares, yet it is within this century that the fine wares emerge.

Nabataean pottery reached its zenith of technical quality and artistic expression in the 1st century C.E. Although this ceramic tradition did not vanish in C.E. 106 with the Roman annexation of Nabataea, its development in the 2nd century C.E. is problematic. On the basis of limited stratified parallels it appears that most, if not all, of the corpus discussed above can be dated within this 1st century B.C.E. to 1st century C.E. time frame, a period during which Nabataean culture was dominant in Moab (Negev 1977).

Description: Early Roman. Early Roman pottery on the Kerak plateau is distinctive in a number of respects, yet a merging of Nabataean and Roman ceramic styles is also evident. This blending of ceramic attributes in the Kerak region would appear to mirror the cultural and political geography of the Roman and Nabataean spheres and their interactions. However, the material presented in this section is intended to represent wares and forms that are specifically characteristic of Early Roman pottery in Nabataean Moab. Where relevant, correlations with contemporary ceramics that are distinctly Nabataean in style are also observed.

Following the Hellenistic tradition, Early Roman ceramics tend to be small and delicate. Wares are often thin, having been turned on a fast wheel; examples include bowls Nos. 333, 335; cooking pots Nos. 336-37; and juglet No. 345. Few Early Roman sherds, however, approach the thinness of the Nabataean egg-shell wares. Paste preparation is generally very good, though few sherds are of the same fabric quality as Nabataean fine wares. Firing is usually thorough, although dark cores are found in jar No. 340 and jar stand No. 348.

Ware color is less consistent than that of Nabataean fabrics; pink, buff, red, orange, pale brown, and occasional greyish wares are all represented. Surface treatments show diversity as well. Red or reddish-brown slips are present as noted among cooking pots Nos. 336-37, cooking pot lid No. 338, jar No. 340, juglet No. 346, and on the interior of bowl No. 334. A band of brown slip marks the exterior of bowl No. 335 and is also found on base No. 347. Tones of white slip are usually quite worn, yet traces remain on jars Nos. 341-42, jug No. 343, and jar stand No. 348, as well as on the exterior of bowls Nos. 333-34 and the interior of jar No. 339. In this sample, red paint occurs on a jar and two bowl forms. Bowls Nos. 333 and 335 are both painted on the interior. On the former, the design consists of irregular tear drops of paint dripped down from the rim, and the latter has a simple interior band of red paint below its rim. A wide, irregular blotch of red paint covers much of the exterior of jar No. 342.

The forms of Early Roman pottery include tall necked jars (Nos. 339-41), thin walled, incurved bowls (No. 333), and globular juglets with origins in the Hellenistic ceramic tradition. Bowl and juglet forms of *terra sigillata* occur as well. Two examples of Eastern Sigillata A, bowl No. 332 and juglet No. 344, are presented in this sample. Both are finely turned pieces with glossy red slips and light colored fabrics, yet there are clear differences between the two. The juglet sherd has a deeper red, less orange-toned, slip than the bowl, and its paste is a light cream color with less of the pinkish tone exhibited in the bowl. The exterior of the bowl is rouletted beneath the rim but with less care and precision than is often found on these vessels.

Forms: Early Roman. The sherd pictured in No. 332 is a flaring *terra sigillata* bowl rim. The underside of the rim is rouletted with delicate oblique strokes and, as is characteristic of Eastern Sigillata A pottery, the glossy red-orange surface slip is mottled. Parallel forms occur at **ᶜAroᶜer** (Olávarri 1965: fig. 3: 5); **Sbaita** (G. M. Crowfoot 1936: pl. 4: 2); and **Samaria** (Crowfoot et al. 1957: pl. 77: 8). P. W. Lapp's study proposes a 1st century B.C.E. time frame for the introduction of Eastern Sigillata A in Palestine (1961: 210-18), and this chronological interpretation is probably relevant to Eastern Sigillata A in Transjordan as well. While the duration of these wares on the East Bank is not certain, there does not appear to be evidence for Eastern Sigillata A in Transjordan after the end of the 1st century C.E.

Open bowl No. 333 closely approaches the Nabataean open bowl with up-turned rim and well exemplifies the closeness of Nabataean and Early Roman forms. The red-painted exterior rim and dripped red paint on the interior are a common mode of decoration in this period. Flaring bowls with incurved rims, a development from the rounded Hellenistic incurved bowls, are present at the settlements of Qumran, ᶜAin Feshka, and other Judean Desert sites. The upright stance of No. 333 specifically corresponds with a vessel from **Qumran** (de Vaux 1953: fig. 4: 20) that P. W. Lapp classified as Type 51:1 (1961: 172: K) and dated to C.E. 50-68. An earlier example from **Qumran**, dating to the beginning of the Early Roman period, was found in Trench A (de Vaux 1954: fig. 2: 10). Of the several instances of small incurved bowls at the **Judean Desert** site of **ᶜEn el-Ghuweir**, one provides a particularly apt comparison (Bar-Adon 1977: fig. 15: 7). A similar bowl from **ᶜAin Feshka** is shown with a red-painted decoration on the interior (de Vaux 1959: fig. 2: 7).

Two less common bowl forms are shown in Nos. 334 and 335, though by virtue of their wares and decorative treatments they can be considered provincial Early Roman forms. No. 334 is distinguished by its S-shaped profile. No. 335 appears to belong to a deep bowl or krater similar to a handleless krater with a ring base, Lapp's Type 45.2, **Qumran** (1961: 170: B), which has been dated C.E. 50-68.

The two rims from closed cooking pots presented in Nos. 336 and 337 have upright, simple, rounded rims that appear to have been derived from the simple splayed-rim Hellenistic cooking pot. No. 336 has a short neck and No. 337 is elongated and thinner. Both have a bright orange ware and exterior red or red-brown slip. No. 336 is paralleled at **Caesarea** (Riley 1975: 49: 110) and **Dhiban** (Winnett and Reed 1964: pl. 69: 9). A similar cooking pot is associated with Level II at **Qumran** (de Vaux 1954: fig. 4: 15) and is included in Lapp's Type 71.1 (1961: 188: N2), which he dated C.E. 50-68. It should be noted that this rim style is also similar to that of a small, squat globular vessel from **Petra**, Tomb B1.1 (Zayadine 1979: pl. LXXXVII: 2). No. 337, which has a taller neck, compares with a single-handled globular cooking vessel from **Qumran**, Trench A (de Vaux 1954: fig. 2: 2) and is also found in Lapp's Type 71.1 (1961: 187: L), dated 50-31 B.C.E. However, these forms are distinct from the typical grooved rim or sharply carinated Early Roman cooking pots as illustrated at **Jerusalem, Jason's Tomb** (Rahmani 1967: fig. 16: 1, 7), and **Tell Ḥesban** (Sauer 1973: fig. 1: 6-9). Other styles, such as the bowed rim Early Roman cooking pots of the **Judaean Desert, Naḥal Ḥever** (Aharoni 1961: fig. 7: 6, 8; see also **Qumran**, Level I, de Vaux 1954: fig. 3: 22) and the profiled Nabataean rims of **Petra** (Zayadine 1974: pl. LXIII: 2, 17-19, 33), are equally remote in form.

The straight-edged, beveled cooking pan lid pictured in No. 338 has its origins in the Early Roman period as the open cooking pan form developed concurrently with the closed cooking pot (Nos. 336 and 337). Other Early Roman lids are noted from the **Judaean Desert** (Aharoni 1962: fig. 2: 9-10); **Qumran**, Level III (de Vaux 1954: fig. 6: 5); **Jericho** (Bennett 1965: fig. 268: 17); and in Transjordan, **Tell Ḥesban** (Sauer 1973: fig. 1: 10). A similar lid is cited from the Nabataean occupation at **Rujm Beni Yasser** (Parker 1987b: fig. 90: No. 5). This form continued to develop and is well documented in Transjordan in Late Roman strata at **Tell Ḥesban** (Sauer 1973: fig. 2: 51-53) and **Umm el-Jimal** (Parker forthcoming d: No. 3). An Early Byzantine example with an upturned lip is noted at **Araq el-Emir**, Stratum I (Brown 1983: fig. 56: 116).

Tall-necked storage jar rims are pictured in Nos. 339-41. The groove or ridge at the juncture of the neck and shoulder dates, initially, to the beginning of the 1st century C.E. (P. W. Lapp 1961: 15; Type 12). The plainly rounded and upright rims Nos. 339 and 340 appear at **Tell Ḥesban** (Sauer 1973: fig. 1: 17-18); **Tell el-Ful**, Period V (N. L. Lapp 1981: pl. 81: 4); **Ramat Raḥel**, Stratum IVA (Aharoni 1964: fig. 27: 9); **Jericho** (Bennett 1965: fig. 276: 3); and two **Judaean Desert** sites (Bar-Adon 1961: fig. 1: 5 and 1977: fig. 10: 4, 10). A number of examples are known from **Jerusalem** as well: **Tyropoeon Valley** (Hamilton 1931: 109: 9); **Bishop Gobat School** (Hamilton 1935b: pl. 6: 11); **Jason's Tomb** (Rahmani 1967: fig. 17: 1); and **French Hill** (Strange 1975: fig. 15: 11). At **Pella** it appears that this form continues into the Late Roman period (Smith et al. 1980: pl. XXIV: 7).

Jar rim No. 341 features a rounded and everted rim. Sites with comparable forms include **Tell Ḥesban** (Sauer 1973: fig. 1: 15-16) and **Araq en-Naʾsaneh** (Lapp and Lapp 1974: pl. 25: 2-3, 5-6, 8-9, 11). A similar vessel is published from the **Judaean Desert, Naḥal Ḥever** (Aharoni 1961: fig. 7: 29).

The thickened, offset, and grooved rim No. 342 may belong to a jug. This particular rim style, however, is generally associated with a smaller form, as demonstrated by juglets from **Araq en-Naʾsaneh** (Lapp and Lapp 1974: pl. 28: 5); **Jerusalem, French Hill** (Strange 1975: fig. 15: 23); and the **Judaean** Desert, **Naḥal Ḥever** (Aharoni 1961: fig. 7: 12). The fabric and surface treatment of No. 342 share characteristics of Nabatean utilitarian wares, yet the profile is not evident among the Petra assemblages, and the splashed exterior red paint is more common among Early Roman rather than Nabataean pottery.

A small *terra sigillata* jug with a simple rounded and out-turned rim is illustrated in No. 343. Although closed forms of *terra sigillata* are not as common as plates, bowls, and other open vessels, this Eastern Sigillata A jug is documented at **Samaria** (Crowfoot et al. 1957: fig. 82: 2) with an inferred chronological range from the 1st century B.C.E. to the 1st century C.E.

Juglets are shown in Nos. 344 and 345. No. 344 illustrates the rim profile of a small globular juglet, a form with antecedents in the Hellenistic period. This frequently attested Early Roman juglet occurs with a number of variations in rim style. P. W. Lapp's Type 31.1 shows a similar rim (1961: 163: E), though it is tilted inward. This piece from **Tulul Abu el-ᶜAlayiq** is dated to the first half of the 1st century C.E. (ibid). Among the examples from **Qumran**, this juglet compares with vessels from Level II (de Vaux 1954: fig. 4: 9) and Level III (ibid.: fig. 6: 2). Parallels are found at a number of sites, including: **Jerusalem, Jason's Tomb** (Rahmani 1967: fig. 11: 12) and **French Hill** (Strange 1975: fig. 15: 27, 30); **Ramat Raḥel**, Stratum IVA (Aharoni et al. 1964: fig. 28: 4); **Bethany**, Tomb 1 (Loffreda 1969: fig. 2: 23); **Jericho**, Tomb G66

(Bennett 1965: fig. 274: 6); **Tell Ḥesban** (Sauer 1973: fig. 1: 24); and two **Judaean Desert** sites (Aharoni 1961: fig. 7: 10 and Aharoni 1962: fig. 2: 13).

The side view of a similar globular juglet, No. 345, shows a portion of the vessel neck and shoulder with a small flattened handle that joins the broken rim. This vessel was not skillfully manufactured, and the coarse brick red ware mixed with small white inclusions is more typical of Early Roman cooking pot than juglet fabrics. Unfortunately, the broken upper edge of the rim precludes specific comparisons, but a few general observations may be noted. Handles on this common juglet form are usually attached at the top of the rim, in contrast to No. 345 where the handle joins the base of the rim. Similar handle attachments are infrequent but comparisons are found in assemblages from **Jerusalem, Tyropoeon Valley** (Crowfoot and Fitzgerald 1929: pl. XII: 25; Hamilton 1931: 109: 7). As with No. 344 above, P. W. Lapp classified these vessels as Type 31.1 (1961: 163: D4-5) and dated them to 37-4 B.C.E. The **Amman, Forum** provides examples from Transjordan (Hadidi 1970: pl. II: 10-11).

No. 346 is a common string-cut base from a bowl or other open vessel and occurs at many sites including the **Judaean Desert, ᶜEn el-Ghuweir** (Bar-Adon 1977: fig. 12: 10-11, 18), and **Tell Ḥesban** (Sauer 1973: fig. 1: 42). Ring bases are also frequent, and No. 347, probably from a bowl, occurs at **Qumran**, Period Ib (de Vaux 1956: fig. 2: 6-7); **ᶜAin Feshka** (de Vaux 1959: fig. 2: 14); and **Amman, Forum** (Hadidi 1970: pl. IV: 16).

Jar stands similar to the one shown in No. 348 are well attested at Qumran and other Early Roman sites. The example presented here is thinner and less sharply angled than most, but an approximate comparison is found at **Qumran**, trench A (de Vaux 1954: fig. 2: 17), which dates to the 1st century B.C.E.

Discussion: Early Roman. The Early Roman and Nabataean assemblages both show the continued development of forms and wares derived from Hellenistic pottery. The presence of Early Roman pottery in the Kerak region is indicative of the fluidity of material culture, particularly ceramic products and styles, between these two geographically defined polities. Excavations at Rujm Beni Yasser, near Lejjun on the eastern fringe of the Kerak plateau, have also demonstrated the occurrence of both Early Roman and Nabataean forms (Parker 1987b). The references to comparative chronology of some of the sherds presented above indicate that this cultural interaction began prior to the official Roman annexation of Nabataea in 106 C.E.. This is particularly evident in the presence of the tall-necked jar, a Roman form that dates, initially, to the beginning of the 1st century C.E. (P. W. Lapp 1961: 15). Other evidence is found in the strong links between the pottery from Qumran and other Judaean Desert sites, some of which has been dated by Lapp (1961). The presence of Eastern Sigillata A forms is also significant. These wares probably date to the 1st century C.E., and may, therefore, demonstrate that non-locally produced Roman wares were available to Nabataean consumers.

Late Roman

Description: Late Roman. Late Roman pottery is directly related to the Early Roman ceramic tradition in two principal respects. First, there is continuity of vessel forms, and second, the vessels of these two periods represent very similar ceramic technologies. In other respects, however, Late Roman pottery is highly individualistic. Ware colors, thickness, and surface treatments contrast with those of Early Roman pottery. Other specifically Late Roman developments include stylistic attributes such as notching on bowl rims, grooving on cooking pot rims, and pinched handles. These attributes serve to distinguish Late Roman pottery in Transjordan from the Early Roman assemblages, despite the similarities noted above.

Three ware types characterize Late Roman pottery in the Kerak region, and each of these has recently been attested during excavations at the sites of Lejjun, Khirbet el-Fityan, and Qasr Bshir (Parker pers. comm.). Most frequent are wares in various shades of pink, red, or orange that occasionally match the color of surface slips. Less widely attested, but highly contrastive, are the cream wares (Munsell: 7.5YR 8/4 pink, 10YR 8/3 very pale brown) that tend to occur among cooking pots (Nos. 358-59, 364) and some bowls (No. 355). These wares are also found at Araq el-Emir (unpublished). Similar, though slightly darker, wares are attested at Tell Ḥesban (Sauer 1973). The third category of Late Roman fabrics in the Kerak plateau corpus consists of grey wares, represented in this sample by base No. 367. Late Roman grey wares are also found at Tell Ḥesban, notably among jars (Sauer 1973), and Tulul Abu el-ᶜAlayiq (Kelso and Baramki 1955).

Red and red-orange slips are the principal surface treatments. Often unevenly applied and mottled in appearance, these finishes range from glossy (bowl No. 349) to duller matt tones (bowl No. 351, bases Nos. 365-66). A homogeneous bright orange slip is found on bowl No. 356. The cream-colored wares usually exhibit a very bright orange slip that is mottled in tones of burnt orange and brown. This uniquely variable blend of colors is highly indicative of Transjordanian Late Roman ceramics. In this selection, cooking pot No. 358 provides the best example of mottled-orange surface tones. Although no instances of painting are present, band-slipping on the exterior of bowl rims is noted for Nos. 351 and 352.

Rouletting occurs on the exterior of open forms, particularly bowls (Nos. 349, 353-54). In Transjordan, Late Roman rouletted sherds are documented at Amman, Rujm el-Malfuf (north) (Boraas 1971: figs. 30: 6013; 32: 5591, 6195, 5952). In Palestine clear illustrations of this decorative style are published from Jerusalem, North Wall (Hamilton 1944: pl. XI: 5, 8) and Khirbet el-Karak (Delougaz and Haines 1960: pl. 32: 1-9).

Late Roman ceramic manufacturing techniques do not represent a technological improvement over those of the Early Roman period, though they are closely related in some respects. Late Roman pottery, however, is notably thicker and, in many instances, the quality of paste preparation is slightly coarser. Handles, such as those of cooking pots, are roughly joined to the pot wall, and deep finger impressions often mark the bases of these handles.

Forms: Late Roman. Pictured in No. 349 are the rim and rouletted exterior of a splayed, flaring bowl or deep plate. This combination of form and decoration occurs among *terra sigillata* wares, but in this instance the resemblance is superficial for the fabric and finish of bowl No. 349 indicate that it was locally produced. The exterior is covered with a glossy red-orange slip, and the interior has a darker, mottled matt finish. This form, with rouletted decoration, is found at **Amman, Rujm el-Malfuf** (north) (Boraas 1971: fig. 30: 6013). A similar pattern of rouletting consisting of rows of short parallel incisions occurs at **Khirbet al-Karak** (Delougaz and Haines 1960: pl. 32: 1- 2). It should be noted that this bowl fragment is among the finest of the Late Roman sherds in the Kerak plateau collection.

Two frequently occurring types of Late Roman bowls include incurved bowls Nos. 350-52 and straight-sided bowls with notched rims Nos. 353-56. Sherd No. 350 illustrates the incurved rim of a deep, V-shaped bowl with a wide mouth. This fragment displays a thicker profile than its Early Roman predecessors, as seen at **Tulul Abu el-ᶜAlayiq** (Pritchard 1958: pl. 59: 37), yet clearly illustrates the continuation of the Late Hellenistic incurved bowl form through the Late Roman period. Incurved bowls with less sharply inverted rims such as Nos. 351 and 352 also continued to develop from the Early Roman period. These rim sherds are distinguished by fabrics and surface finishes that are characteristically Late Roman. Yet the pointed rim of No. 351 is best paralleled in an assemblage from the **Judaean Desert** (Avigad 1962: fig. 5: 14) which dates to C.E. 135, exactly at the transition between the Early and Late Roman eras. The thicker bowl rim No. 352 is rounded and only slightly incurved, and a band of red-orange slip overlaps from the interior onto the exterior surface. This form is paralleled at **Amman, Rujm el-Malfuf** (north) (Boraas 1971: fig. 37: 6752) but is also very similar to a pseudo-*terra sigillata* vessel from an Early Roman deposit at **Capernaum** (Loffreda 1974: fig. 17: 2).

Among the straight-sided bowls, the squared rim profile shown in No. 353 is highly diagnostic of Late Roman bowls in Transjordan. The pattern of exterior rouletting consists of long curved vertical ridges. This form appears both with and without rouletting, as demonstrated by examples from **Tell Ḥesban** (Sauer 1973: fig. 2: 67); **Amman, Rujm el-Malfuf** (north) (Boraas 1971: fig. 32: 6195); and **Jerash**, Tomb 4 (Kraeling 1938: fig. 36: x9). The sherds shown in Nos. 354 and 355 are also typical of Late Roman bowls in Transjordan. Both are distinguished by squared rims, thinner than that of No. 353, and exterior notches. Comparable bowls are known from **Tell Ḥesban** (Sauer 1973: fig. 2: 64-66). Despite their similarity of form, Nos. 354 and 355 exemplify different Late Roman fabrics and finishing techniques. The former consists of an orange ware with a red slip and is rouletted with irregular horizontal bands of short wedge-shaped incisions. The latter is a cream-ware sherd with a dark orange-brown exterior slip.

The bowl rim shown in No. 356 also illustrates the concept of the side-notched rim, but the offset and inverted angular profile is more unusual. Similar Late Roman bowl rims with deep notching may be cited from **Rujm Beni Yasser** (Parker forthcoming b: Reg. Nos. 1034, 1680). Shallow, exterior grooving such as that seen in the profile of No. 356 is also found on notched bowls at **Tell Ḥesban** (Sauer 1973: fig. 2: 63, 66).

As in the case of the notched-rim bowls, the grooved-rim cooking pots shown in Nos. 357 and 358 are specifically Late Roman forms without clear prototypes among the Early Roman assemblages of Transjordan. These sherds represent a globular closed cooking pot form that is generally comparable to Nabataean and Early Roman cooking pots. Yet in addition to the grooved rim, these vessels are consistently characterized by shallow, gentle body ribbing and two loop handles with pinched profiles. A good illustration of the entire vessel form is noted from **Amman, Citadel** (Zayadine 1973: fig. 4), and examples of pinched cooking pot handles are discussed below (see Nos. 362 and 363).

No. 357 shows this grooved-rim cooking pot with an upright, slightly thickened neck. No. 358, of cream-colored ware with a mottled burnt-orange exterior slip, has a slightly splayed neck. This form is well attested in Transjordan, and parallels are found at a number of sites: **Amman, Rujm el-Malfuf** (north) (Boraas 1971: fig. 25) **Amman, Jebel Jofeh**, tomb (Harding 1950b: pl. XXVI: 12, 105); **Tell Ḥesban** (Sauer 1973: fig. 2: 45-50); **Jerash** (Fisher and McCown 1931: pl. 2); **Umm el-Jimal** (Parker forthcoming d: Nos. 1-2); and **Araq el-Emir** (N. Lapp 1983). Grooved-rim cooking pot fragments are also well attested at **Lejjun** (Parker 1987b: fig. 100: Nos. 82-3; fig. 101: Nos. 96-8; and unpublished). Largely from 4th century contexts, these examples from Lejjun generally display more elaborate rim and neck profiles than Nos. 357-58 in this sample. Late Roman cooking pots of this style also appear at sites in Palestine, including **Jerusalem, Tyropoeon Valley** (Crowfoot and Fitzgerald 1929: pl. XIII: 34) and **Capernaum** (Loffreda 1974: fig. 10: 4).

The open cooking pan or casserole was in use during the Early Roman period (see sherd No. 338 above), though not as commonly as the globular closed cooking pot. Open cooking vessels became more frequent during the Late Roman and Byzantine periods. Presented in Nos. 359 and 360 are fragments of Late Roman casserole lids. Lid rim No. 359 is a cream ware sherd with a bright orange slip. No. 360 is distinguished by a darker red-orange mottled slip and a pinched horizontal band of clay that served as a handle.

Lids similar to No. 359 have occurred in Late Roman deposits at **Tell Ḥesban** (Sauer 1973: fig. 2: 51, 53), **Khirbet el-Fityan** (Parker 1987b: fig. 97: No. 62) and **Umm el-Jimal** (Parker forthcoming d: No. 3), and in Palestine at **Capernaum** (Loffreda 1974: fig. 33: 13). A casserole lid with a pinched clay handle similar to No. 360 is attested at **Amman, Forum** (Hadidi 1970: pl. 5: 16).

The everted rim and ridged neck of juglet No. 361 may be compared with a group of vessels from **Amman, Jebel Jofeh**, tomb (Harding 1950b: pl. XXVI: 7, 22, 150, 200) in which both flat and stump bases are found. This form is also known from the Early Roman period, as demonstrated by a sherd from **Magdala** (Loffreda 1976: fig. 10: 12). An example from **Dhiban** (Winnett and Reed 1964: pl. 69: 13) may also be Early Roman in date.

The rounded handles with grooved and pinched profiles, Nos. 362-63, are associated with the globular closed cooking pots described above in Nos. 357-58. These handles are found at a number of Transjordanian sites with Late Roman occupation, including: **Amman, Rujm el-Malfuf** (north) (Boraas 1971: figs. 24: 5864; 25: 6001; 26: 6894, 6006); **Amman, Citadel** (Zayadine 1977-78: fig. 4, pl. 15: 2); **Amman, Forum** (Hadidi 1970: pl. 6: 8); **Tell Ḥesban** (Sauer 1973: fig. 2: 83); **Umm el-Jimal** (Parker forthcoming d: No. 5); and **Araq el-Emir** (unpublished). Pinched handles are predominantly associated with cooking vessels. Less common are larger pinched handles, such as No. 364 which is elliptical in section. This handle was clearly attached to the rim of a closed vessel, probably a jug. At Lejjun such pinched handles are known to be associated with jug forms (Parker: pers. comm.). Comparative examples include a pinched handle found on a "Byzantine" tall-necked jar from **Ramat Raḥel**, Cave 800 (Aharoni et al. 1964: fig. 34: 4) and another associated with a jar from **Jerusalem, North Wall** (Hamilton 1944: fig. 21: 1).

String-cut bases are shown in Nos. 365-67. These bases contrast with those of the Early Roman period (see sherd No. 346 above) in that they tend to be higher and can often be distinguished by their ware characteristics. No. 365, with an interior red slip and flaring side walls, probably represents the lower portion of a bowl. No. 366 is ribbed and red-slipped only on the exterior and, thus, appears to belong to a jug or other closed vessel. Similar Late Roman string-cut bases are known from **Tell Ḥesban** (Sauer 1973: fig. 2: 77-78). The thicker grey ware string-cut base No. 367 may have been associated with a juglet.

Discussion: Late Roman. Late Roman pottery displays attributes that, ultimately, can be traced to the Hellenistic and Nabataean manufacturing styles. More directly manifested are the influences of Early Roman ceramics, which are particularly evident in the temporal duration of forms. Yet the unique stylistic attributes of Late Roman pottery delineate an individualistic repertoire, as noted in the application of different finishing techniques, details of vessel form, and the influence of *terra sigillata* decorative styles. These combined traits form a distinctive blend that characterizes Late Roman pottery throughout Transjordan.

Strong homogeneity is expressed in the comparison of the survey corpus with ceramics from *limes Arabicus* sites on the eastern fringes of the Kerak Plateau, particularly the Roman legionary fortress at Lejjun. Yet in addition to this regional homogeneity within the Kerak plateau, a broad geographic consistency is apparent among Late Roman ceramics of Transjordan, as expressed in the strong continuities between the Kerak plateau assemblages and those from sites farther north, including: Tell Ḥesban; Amman, Rujm el-Malfuf (north); Amman, Jebel Jofeh, tomb; Araq el-Emir; Jerash; and Umm el-Jimal, all of which share a common Late Roman ceramic tradition. Similarly, Roman *limes* sites as far south as Aqaba also exhibit the same ceramic continuity as noted among the northern sites (Parker pers. comm.). However, attributes of Late Roman pottery in Transjordan, such as the grooved-rim cooking pot, notched-rim bowls, and pinched handles, are not as common among Late Roman sites in Palestine. These factors could indicate that the dominant Late Roman ceramic tradition of Transjordan experienced indigenous stylistic development within East Bank production centers, and that the products of these centers circulated largely within Transjordan.

The technical qualities of Nabataean and Early Roman pottery demonstrate that highly developed skills were necessary to produce these vessels, and it could be inferred that ceramic production in these societies was both specialized and centralized. However, the clearest indications of mass-production in Transjordan during the Classical periods are perhaps to be found among Late Roman assemblages. Three trends emerge from this brief review of Late Roman pottery that may have implications for the organization of ceramic production. First, Late Roman forms, such as bowls and cooking pots, are repetitive and occur frequently at Late Roman sites throughout Transjordan. Second, some variability is noted in stylistic details, but vessel morphology is consistent. Third, finishing details, such as individual vessel surface-slip applications and handle attachments, show a lack of attention. Together, these observations could be interpreted as indicators of centralized ceramic production at a few specific locations in which some vessel classes were mass-produced.

Political developments may also have played a role in the patterns of ceramic production and distribution during the Late Roman period. With the annexation of Nabataea as a province of the Roman Empire and the quelling of the Second Jewish Revolt, the Romans fully consolidated the various territories of Palestine and Transjordan. The lack of political obstacles and the continued development of avenues of commerce and communication, such as the completion of the *via nova Traiana* between C.E. 111 and 114, may have facilitated centralization of ceramic production and systematic exchange of ceramic products resulting in a geographically homogeneous ceramic repertoire in Transjordan.

Early and Late Byzantine

Description: Early Byzantine. Early Byzantine pottery embodies a number of traits from the preceding Late Roman period, but developments in fabric and surface finish as well as certain elements of form serve to differentiate the Early Byzantine corpus. Generally, Early Byzantine wares tend to be thicker, darker-slipped, and display more diverse fabric colors. The most typical Early Byzantine fabrics include buff, pink, beige, and orange wares, but these specific fabric types are not consistently associated with particular forms. In this sample, however, bright orange wares, which are reminiscent of Late Roman pottery, are best represented by bowl rims (Nos. 369-71). Similar shades of orange are found in cooking pots Nos. 376, 378, handle No. 387, and body sherd No. 391. The buff ware of cooking pot No. 377 is also similar to wares from the Late Roman period. Grey wares occur in the Early Byzantine repertoire but are more frequent in Late Byzantine assemblages. In this selection, forms that are predominantly associated with Early Byzantine grey wares include cooking pot handles Nos. 384-385 and jug base No. 389. Fine red wares occur in both Early and Late Byzantine contexts. Three of the four examples included in this study are virtually identical in both ware and slip tone. The two African Red Slip ware bowls presented in the Early Byzantine corpus, Nos. 372 and 373, are chronologically differentiated from a Late Byzantine African Red Slip sherd (No. 395) on the basis of form alone.

Some Early Byzantine slips show similarity with the preceding Late Roman slips, although the bright orange and mottled orange-brown tones that are especially indicative of Late Roman pottery were largely replaced with a darker and more consistently applied brown slip that has fewer orange tones (cooking pot No. 377, jug handle No. 388). Charcoal-grey and red-brown slips are noted on two other cooking pots, Nos. 378 and 379. Grey slips occur with grey wares, as on cooking pot handles Nos. 384 and 385, but not exclusively, as demonstrated by No. 368. A reddish slip, darker than Late Roman red slips, is found on bowl rims Nos. 369-70. Lighter treatments appear on two krater rims, Nos. 374 and 375. The former has a white-cream slip, while the latter has a white slip with an unusual pale-greenish tone. As in the case of the fabric colors, the diversity among Early Byzantine slips contrasts with Late Roman pottery, which shows less variability in surface treatment colors.

Tempering practices and firing techniques show diversity as well. Some wares (No. 370) have fine inclusions with very few visible particles. Yet for the most part, visible mineral inclusions were added to the fabrics. Examples of excellent firing are present (e.g., bowl No. 371, cooking pot No. 377), but both light and dark cores are frequent (e.g., bowl No. 369 and jar No. 381). The fine red wares such as bowls Nos. 372-73 are fine tempered and thoroughly fired. With regard to manufacturing techniques, two examples of non-wheel produced pottery are included. Lamp fragment No. 383 was pressed in a mold, and body sherd No. 391 represents a handmade vessel.

Other han slipping, surface decoration in this sample consists of incising; three examples are included: jar No. 381 and body sherds Nos. 391-92. The jar sherd is incised with a wavy band-combed decoration (not illustrated) on the flattened upper surface of the rim, and larger designs of straight and wavy incised lines are found on the body sherds. These styles of incising are also frequent in Late Byzantine assemblages.

Forms: Early Byzantine. Bowl rim No. 368 is distinguished by a flaring everted lip and peaked interior ridge. This form is well documented in Transjordan and occurs on bowls of various sizes. This example, a small bowl, has a typical Early Byzantine surface treatment that consists of a dark grey-brown exterior slip and dull red-brown interior slip. Stratified occurrences of this bowl date to the 4th century at **Araq el-Emir** (unpublished: Reg. Nos. 556, 257) and the late 5th century at **Amman, Citadel** (Zayadine 1977-78: fig. 17: 329). Other examples, dated to the Early Byzantine period are found at **Lejjun** (Parker forthcoming b: Reg. Nos. 8601, 4645), and similar sherds are attested at **Dhiban** (Tushingham 1972: fig. 10: 40-41).

Another open bowl form is represented by sherds Nos. 369-70, which have thickened rims, flattened on top with a distinctive exterior ridge. These sherds are typical of Early Byzantine pottery in Transjordan and illustrate the continuation of Late Roman buff and pink-orange wares with a red-orange slip. Precise parallels are lacking, but similar forms, sometimes rouletted on the exterior in the Late Roman style, are noted in Palestine: **Jerusalem, North Wall** (Hamilton 1944: fig. 22: 3) and **Tyropoeon Valley** (Crowfoot and Fitzgerald 1929: pl. XIII: 18); **Khirbet Siyar el-Ghanam** (Corbo 1955: fig. 21: 4); and **Bethany** (Saller 1957: fig. 50: 1574).

The bowl rim pictured in No. 371 also has a familiar red-orange fabric, and traces of a cream slip are preserved on the exterior. This rim has two grooves on the upper surface and an everted lip. Comparable vessels, such as from **Bethany** (Saller 1957: fig. 50: 2341), are rouletted. More heavily profiled rims of this style are dated to the end of the 5th century at **Capernaum** (Loffreda 1979: fig. 2: 30-31), and a superficial resemblance can be noted between these ridged-rim bowls and the Cypriot Red Slip bowls of **Capernaum** that are also dated to the end of the Early Byzantine period (ibid.: fig. 1: 15-20).

Fine red ware rims from open bowls Nos. 372-73 have red fabrics and bright red exterior slips. These squared, thickened rims belong to shallow bowls with widely flaring sides. In Hayes' typology of African Red Slip wares, both are classified as Form 67 (1972: fig. 19), and Hayes notes that rim shapes of this form occur in a variety of styles (ibid.: 116). On the basis of unpublished material from Araq el-Emir he suggests a C.E. 360-470 range for these vessels (ibid.). No. 372 compares with Early Byzantine vessels from **Beit Sahur** (Tzaferis 1975: pl. 11: 8) and **Lejjun** (Parker 1987b: fig. 111: No. 172). Other parallels may be cited from **Bethany** (Saller 1957: fig. 49: 3486) and **Ramat Raḥel**, Stratum IIA (Aharoni et al. 1964: fig. 7: 11). No. 373 is documented at **Meiron** in Early Byzantine surface debris that included late 4th century coins (Meyers et al. 1981: pl. 8.31, nos. 29-30).

A thickly profiled, everted krater rim is shown in No. 374. The pink ware and cream colored slip of this sherd are not particularly common among Early Byzantine ceramics. This style of krater rim may derive from Roman prototypes, an example of which is found at **Tell Ḥesban** (Sauer 1973: 26). No. 374 is paralleled by a 4th century sherd from **Hebron** (M. A. Bennett 1972: pl. III: II.A.4). Probably also dating to the Early Byzantine period is a parallel from **Jerusalem, North Wall** (Hamilton 1944: fig. 22: 47). Variants are noted at **Abu Gosh** (de Vaux and Stève 1950: fig. 4: 27, 29) and **Khirbet Siyar el-Ghanam** (Corbo 1955: fig. 19: 11).

An Early Byzantine date is suggested for the krater shown in No. 375. As in the case of krater No. 374, the fabric of this sherd is not well attested. In this instance, the ware is pale brown, the slip is white with a very pale greenish tone, and the surface texture is unusually smooth. The angular, flared rim is grooved and thickened in a style that is morphologically similar to African Red Slip Form 52, Type B (Hayes 1972: fig. 13: 22), which Hayes dates to the late 5th century. The best comparisons with this form are from **Jerusalem, North Wall** (Hamilton 1944: fig. 22: 37, 46). A number of kraters are published from this excavation (ibid.: fig. 22: 33-49) some of which have wares and surface slips that are similar to No. 375. Other sites where this form is documented include **Abu Gosh** (de Vaux and Stève 1950: fig. 4: 31-33) and **Bethany** (Saller 1957: fig. 52: 1803).

Early Byzantine cooking pot rims are presented in Nos. 376-80. The deep orange fabric of cooking pot No. 376 is coarse textured, and a loop handle (not illustrated) joins the vessel rim and shoulder. This cooking pot, a neckless vessel with a simple rounded rim, appears related to Late Roman cooking pots, for a shallow groove is present along the top of the rim. At **Meiron** this vessel occurs in a late 4th to early 5th century context, Stratum V (Meyers et al. 1981: pl. 8.14, no. 15), and a similar vessel occurs at **Khirbet Shema^{c}**, Stratum IV (Meyers et al. 1976: pl. 7.19, no. 17). This profile is also paralleled at **Beisan** (Tzori 1973: fig. 5: 12) and possibly **Nessana** (Baly 1962: pl. LV: 130: 6). A vessel from **Tell Ḥesban** (Sauer 1973: fig. 2: 89) with a more sharply angled shoulder may represent a later version of this form.

Necked Early Byzantine cooking pots Nos. 377-79 are more common, and the body ribbing on these sherds is sharper than that of No. 376. No. 377 has a rounded rim and a tall, unprofiled, vertical neck that is indented on the interior. This sherd illustrates the development of the ridge or drip ring at the junction of the neck and shoulder, a frequent feature among Early Byzantine cooking pot rims. The buff ware and dark orange-brown mottled surface of this sherd demonstrate direct continuity with Late Roman fabrics. The form is paralleled in Early Byzantine contexts at several sites, including: **Araq el-Emir** (Brown 1983: fig. 56: 99, 101; unpublished: Reg. No. 537); **Amman, Citadel** (Zayadine 1977-78: fig. 22: 312); and **Tell er-Ras** (Bull and Campbell 1968: fig. 11: 2). An additional example is found at **Dhiban** (Tushingham 1972: fig. 9: 1).

The offset-rim cooking pot profiles illustrated in Nos. 378-79 also occur at **Tell Ḥesban** (Sauer 1973: fig. 2: 85-86). No. 378 has an unthickened, squared profile, orange fabric, and charcoal slip. This form compares with sherds from **Araq el-Emir** (unpublished: Reg. No. 585) and

Amman, Citadel (Zayadine 1977-78: fig. 21: 334). Similar sherds are also noted at **Lejjun** (Parker forthcoming b: Reg. Nos. 3559, 5056). Resembling No. 378 in many respects, cooking pot rim No. 379 has a shorter, slightly splayed neck. The physical attributes of this sherd are among those most characteristic of Early Byzantine pottery. Yet a very shallow groove along the rim that was pinched, then for the most part resealed, shares the Late Roman style of cooking pot rim formation. No. 380 is a hooked-rim cooking pot fragment with a tall, bowed neck, thickened at the shoulder join. This form is paralleled at **Tell er-Ras** (Bull and Campbell 1968: fig. 11: 6) in a deposit dated from the second half of the 3rd century through the first half of the 4th century.

The pale-orange-slipped jar rim No. 381 has a rounded and thickened everted lip and the broad, flattened upper surface is decorated with a band of incised wavy lines. Rim incising typically occurs among the larger basin forms, as at **Pella** (Smith 1973: pl. 44: 1301, 1243, 1268) and among later, 9th century basins at **Jerash** (Schaefer and Falkner 1986: fig. 10:1-4). No. 382 is a fragment of an Early Byzantine jug with an everted rim and ridged neck. The handle is attached to the upper portion of the rim and neck. In section, the ovoid handle shows three flattened surfaces, a shape that is quite common among handles of this period. The red fabric, however, contains a number of white inclusions, which is not typical among Early Byzantine assemblages. Juglets of this form occur with a variety of rim styles. A parallel jug from **Araq el-Emir** (unpublished: Reg. No. 264) is associated with an Early Byzantine stratum, and a similar vessel is found at **Lejjun** (Parker forthcoming b: Reg. No. 7800).

A fragment from a mold-made lamp is presented in No. 383. This sherd shows a portion of the upper half of the lamp; the nozzle has been completely broken away. A simple linear pattern of ridges radiates from the filling-hole area to the edge of the lamp. This decorative style is found on lamps from **Amman, Jebel Jofeh**, tomb (Bisheh 1972: fig. 2); and **ʿAin Yabrud** (Husseini 1937: pls. 7: 11; 8: 5, 7). At **Capernaum** a similar example is dated to the end of the 5th century (Loffreda 1979: fig. 2: 38). Additional lamps with this motif may be cited from **Jerusalem, Dominus Flevit** (Bagatti and Milik 1958: fig. 26: 2-5); **Bethany** (Saller 1957: fig. 34: 4-6); and **Dhiban** (Tushingham 1972: fig. 11: 45-46, 49).

A number of different Early Byzantine handles are shown in Nos. 384-88. The horizontal handle of grey ware shown in section in No. 384 is associated with the open cooking casserole or pan that appeared in the Roman period and became increasingly frequent during the Byzantine era. This rolled and folded-over loop handle is particularly common among Early Byzantine deposits. In Transjordan comparable casserole handles are found at **Lejjun** (Parker forthcoming b: Reg. No. 4555) and **Araq el-Emir** (Brown 1983: fig. 56: 135-36; unpublished: Reg. Nos. 576, 221, 207).

The ovoid handle No. 385 is probably from a closed globular cooking pot. A dark grey slip was applied to the pale metallic grey fabric of this sherd, and the upper surface is grooved. A similar grooved cooking pot handle is found at **Tell er-Ras** (Bull and Campbell 1968: fig. 11: 12).

Elliptical or ovoid jar handles with grooved surfaces appear in a wide variety of styles. The example presented in No. 386 shows an irregular outline that is the result of alternating grooving and flattening of the surface along the length of the handle. Another style of loop handle from a jar is shown in No. 387. This sherd is thicker with a more sharply modeled outline that shows three clearly distinct flattened and grooved faces across the upper surface. Similar handles are found at **Araq el-Emir** (unpublished: Reg. Nos. 210, 206). This style of handle, however, is not restricted to the Early Byzantine period. A similar, though more clearly delineated, profile occurs at **Hebron** (M. A. Bennett 1972: pl. VIII: IV.13) in both Late Byzantine and Early Islamic deposits.

A broader handle, No. 388, is joined to a portion of a jug rim. The beige ware and dark red-brown mottled slip are characteristically Early Byzantine, and shallow grooves mark the upper and lower faces of the profile.

Two bases are shown in Nos. 389 and 390. No. 389 is a low ring base of grey ware that probably belonged to a jug. No. 390 shows a higher ring base with a low, sloping center that is common among jars.

Body sherds decorated with band-combed patterns are presented in Nos. 391 and 392. No. 391 is a very thick fragment of a large handmade vessel, probably a deep basin. The decoration consists of a band of incised grooves and several rows of incised wavy bands. No. 392 may be a portion of a neck from a large jar, a vessel that was at least partially turned on a wheel. The deeply incised decoration consists of horizontal wavy bands and vertical straight parallel bands. This mode of surface treatment is found throughout the Byzantine period. Examples from Early Byzantine contexts are found at sites in Transjordan and Palestine, including: **Araq el-Emir** (unpublished: Reg. Nos. 204, 705); **Beit Sahur** (Tzaferis 1975: pl. 16: 2, 4); and **Capernaum** (Loffreda 1979: fig. 2: 36). Band-incised basin sherds from **Mt. Nebo** are associated with a Late Byzantine deposit (Schneider 1950: 77: 307, 309 and Saller 1941: pl. 152: 27, 32). Additional instances from probable Late Byzantine contexts are found at **Maᶜon** (Levy 1960: fig. 5: 2, 4) and **Ramat Raḥel**, Stratum IIA (Aharoni et al. 1964: fig. 22: 22).

Description: Late Byzantine. The Late Byzantine assemblage from the survey collection is characterized by an increase in the number of grey wares. In this sample grey wares are represented by kraters Nos. 397-98, jars Nos. 403-4, and pithos handles Nos. 411-12. Brick red and orange-red wares are also numerous and occur on a variety of forms, among them: bowls Nos. 393 and 396; pithos No. 399; jars Nos. 402, 405-7; and pithos handle No. 410. Lid No. 401 and handle No. 408, both from open cooking casseroles, share a gritty deep-red fabric typical of Late Byzantine cooking wares. Other red fabrics in this assemblage include fine red ware bowl rims Nos. 394-95. Of these, the fabric of No. 395 is identical to the African Red Slip fabrics discussed above (Nos. 372-73), while No. 394, representing a Late Roman C vessel, has a more orange tone. The fine red wares and most of the other sherds in the Late Byzantine assemblage are well fired, although dark cores do occur.

White, red, and grey slips are attested in this corpus. White slips tend to be associated with red fabrics: bowls Nos. 393 and 396, pithos No. 399, jar No. 402, and handle No. 410. Cooking casserole handle No. 408, which is characterized by a coarse red fabric, provides an example of the less common red slip. Sherds with grey or darker charcoal slips include krater No. 398 and jars Nos. 404-5, 407.

Some Late Byzantine pottery is characterized by coarse sandy-textured surfaces. Examples found in this group include: pithos No. 399; jars Nos. 402-3, 407; cooking pot lid No. 401; handle No. 408; and pithos handle No. 410.

Decorative incising is a feature of Late Byzantine as well as of Early Byzantine pottery, as exemplified by krater No. 397. This sherd is decorated with three horizontal bands of simple parallel and wavy incised bands. Two types of Late Byzantine plastic decoration are also included in this sample. The bowl rim shown in No. 393 has an indented "pie-crust" rim (not illustrated), and jar rim No. 407 retains a fragment of a decorative appliqué.

Forms: Late Byzantine. Sherd No. 393 belongs to an open bowl with an everted rim marked with "pie-crust" indentations. Although clearly stratified comparisons of this profile are few, "pie-crust" decorations are noted among several Late Byzantine assemblages in Palestine: **Ramat Raḥel**, Stratum IIA (Aharoni et al. 1964: fig. 7: 15); **Jerusalem, North Wall** (Hamilton 1944: fig. 8: 10); **Beit Sahur** (Tzaferis 1975: pl. 17: 2); and **Maᶜon** (Levy 1960: fig. 5: 8). However, the presence of "pie-crust" decoration on the shoulder of a 4th-5th century jar from **Araq el-Emir** (unpublished: Reg. No. 222), indicates that this technique was not restricted to bowls of the Late Byzantine period.

The fine red wares that gained popularity in the Levant during the Early Byzantine period became more prevalent in Transjordan during the Late Byzantine period. Bowl rim No. 394 is among the most widespread and frequently occurring Levantine fine red ware forms. This squared, up-turned rim style occurs with many variations and is often accompanied by exterior rouletting. While No. 394 appears to be a local product, its shape and fabric are clearly derived from imported fine red wares. Hayes classified this profile as Late Roman C, Form 3 (1972: figs. 67-68), which he dated from the 5th through 7th centuries in the eastern Mediterranean, noting that it was particularly widespread from the second half of the 5th through the first half of the 6th centuries (ibid.: 323, 337; see also Meyers et al. 1978: 22, no. 2)). Sauer has observed that in Transjordan Late Roman C pottery is more frequent in Late Byzantine than Early Byzantine strata (Meyers et al. 1978: 22, no. 2). He has also noted its presence, though rare, in 6th century contexts at Tell Ḥesban (ibid.).

Bowls similar to No. 394, including Late Roman C imports as well as their imitations, were especially common in Palestine where this form experienced a long history of use, as indicated by its presence in a range of contexts: 4th to 5th centuries, **Capernaum** (Loffreda 1974: fig. 44: 3; Loffreda 1979: fig. 1: 1-14) and **Beit Sahur** (Tzaferis 1975: pl. 12: 3); 5th to 6th centuries, **Capernaum** (Loffreda 1974: fig. 41: 16); 6th century, **Caesarea** (Wiemken and Holum 1981: figs. 15: 29; 14: 20); mid-6th to mid-7th centuries, **Beisan** (Fitzgerald 1931: pl. XXXI: 16). Other instances from less clearly stratified contexts among Palestinian sites include: **Silet edh-Dhahr** (Sellers and Baramki 1953: fig. 30: 1, 3); **Khirbet al-Karak** (Delougaz and Haines 1960: pl. 52: 10-12); **Magdala** (Loffreda 1976: fig. 10: 18); **Bethany** (Saller 1957: fig. 49: 1, 3330); **Khirbet Shema^c** (Meyers et al. 1976: pl. 7.23, no. 2); **Ramat Raḥel** (Aharoni et al. 1964: fig. 22: 25); and **Khirbet Siyar el-Ghanam** (Corbo 1955: fig. 22). Archaeological survey has documented the prevalence of this bowl, and other Late Roman C forms, in the Galilee, leading investigators to suggest the possibility that a manufacturing center for production of imitation fine red wares had been located in this region (Meyers et al. 1978: 20; fig. 14: 8-12).

In Transjordan examples of bowl No. 394 are found at: **Umm el-Jimal** (Parker forthcoming d: No. 23); **Lejjun** (Parker forthcoming b: Reg. No. 7383); **Dhiban** (Tushingham 1972: figs. 4: 83; 11: 1-9); **Araq el-Emir** (unpublished: Reg. No. 511); **Mt. Nebo** (Schneider 1950: fig. 12: 3); and **Khirbet** es-**Samra** (Desreumaux and Humbert 1981: fig. 2: 29).

The rim shown in No. 395 is associated with African Red Slip bowls Form 99, for which a 6th century date has been proposed (Hayes 1972: 155; fig. 28). No. 395 is paralleled at **Caesarea** in an early 6th century deposit (Riley 1975: pl. 38: 50). This form may be rare in Transjordan, though one instance is included among the pottery retrieved from a survey at **Deir al-Kahf** (Parker 1986b: No. 364).

The large deep bowl shown in No. 396 has an everted lip marked by grooves on both the interior and exterior. Similar bowls have been published from **Jerusalem, North Wall** (Hamilton 1944: fig. 9: 7) and **Ramat Raḥel**, Stratum IIA (Aharoni et al. 1964: pl. 22: 16).

Rims of grey ware kraters are presented in Nos. 397-98. No. 397 has a dark charcoal slip, a high carination, and a simple peaked rim of a style that is not easily paralleled in the literature. Krater No. 398 has a flattened, everted rim and distinct carination. Wavy band combing (not illustrated) marks the top surface of the rim and the vessel wall above the carination, and a third incised band, consisting of straight lines, is found below the carination. This style of band combing is illustrated on a krater, although of a different form, from **Jerusalem, North Wall** (Hamilton 1944: fig. 9: 4). Such decoration may also be compared with sherds from **Khirbet al-Karak** (Delougaz and Haines 1960: pl. 33: 17-18). The form of krater No. 398 is paralleled in Late Byzantine assemblages at **Lejjun** (Parker 1987b: fig. 121: 228) and **Mt. Nebo** (Schneider 1950: fig. 8: 2).

The pithos rim shown in No. 399 is well known in Transjordan where it has occurred throughout the Roman, Byzantine, and Umayyad periods. This neckless jar has a thick rolled rim that is usually peaked and the outer face is often indented above the lip. An earlier version of the pithos rim is found at Tell Ḥesban in an Early Roman context (Sauer 1973: fig. 1: 25). Early Byzantine occurrences include examples from **Amman, Citadel** (Zayadine 1977-78: fig. 16: 249) and **Araq el-Emir** (unpublished: Reg. No. 728). Late Byzantine variations are attested at **Lejjun** (Parker 1987b: figs. 119: 219; 120: 220-22). A Late Byzantine date is suggested for No. 399 by its coarse red ware and thick cream slip. A sherd of similar ware and form is noted from **Jerusalem, North Wall** (Hamilton 1944: fig. 23: 5) and in Transjordan a number of white-slipped pithos rims are published from **Dhiban** (Tushingham 1972: fig. 12: 46-58). For discussion of this form in Umayyad contexts see sherd No. 415 below.

Neckless globular cooking pots are featured in a number of Late Byzantine assemblages, but the example presented by sherd No. 400 is fairly unusual. This sherd is distinguished by a profiled rim and thick shoulder wall. The rim is peaked, indented on the interior, and forms a short lip on the exterior. A similar cooking vessel rim appears in a Late Byzantine context at **Lejjun** (Parker 1987b: fig. 113: 180).

Knob-handled casserole cooking pot lids of the type shown in No. 401 are a fairly consistent feature of Byzantine and Early Islamic assemblages in the southern Levant. In Transjordan examples occur at **Lejjun** (Parker 1987b: fig. 100: 86), 4th century; **Araq el-Emir** (unpublished: Reg. Nos. 450, 563), 4th-5th century; and **Tell Ḥesban** (Sauer 1973: fig. 2: 91), post 4th century. Late Byzantine occurrences include: **Mt. Nebo** (Schneider 1950: fig. 14: 2); **Jerusalem, Tyropoeon Valley** (Crowfoot and Fitzgerald 1929: pl. XV: 22); and **Beisan** (Fitzgerald 1931: pl. XXXI: 12). For notes on Early Islamic versions see the discussion of sherd No. 416 below.

A variety of jar forms is presented in Nos. 402-7. No. 402 shows the flattened and grooved rim of a splayed-neck jar with a ridge at the base of the neck. The hard red fabric of this sherd is coated with a thick white slip on the exterior. Although the form is not apparent among stratified deposits, a parallel sherd is noted at **Khirbet es-Samra** (Desreumaux and Humbert 1981: fig. 2: 4) and a similar vessel is found at **Pella** (Smith 1973: pl. 44: 1257).

Jar No. 403 is distinguished by a short, bowed neck that forms a right angle with the vessel shoulder. The friable ware is extremely coarse, consisting of a brown fabric mixed with numerous mineral inclusions of various colors. This matrix and the pitted rough-textured surface are suggestive of Late Byzantine cooking pot wares, and the vessel form is best paralleled by a jar from **Silet edh-Dhahr** (Sellers and Baramki 1953: fig. 32: 8).

The metallic grey-ware jar No. 404 has a slightly thickened elongated rim with an exterior indentation. The neck is decorated with band combing. A parallel sherd from a Late Byzantine context at **Lejjun** (Parker 1987b: fig. 115: 191) shows this rim style associated with tall necked jars characterized by a drip ring at the shoulder. Earlier versions of this form, with thicker rims, are documented in an Early Byzantine deposit at **Lejjun** (ibid.: fig. 109: 154, 156).

Two heavily profiled jar rims are shown in Nos. 405-6. Both illustrations show complex modeling of the peaked rim with a sharply notched exterior. A similar sherd is associated with a Late Byzantine context at **Lejjun** (Parker 1987b: fig. 116: 194).

Another sharply distinctive jar rim is shown in No. 407. This flattened and down-turned rim is not apparent in the literature, though the coarse red-orange fabric and dark grey slip are typical of this period. A fragment of an incised clay nodule adheres to the upper surface of the rim. This relief appliqué appears to have been a purely decorative element.

A horizontal loop handle from an open casserole is shown in No. 408. In contrast to the folded-over casserole handles that are prevalent during the Early Byzantine period, this handle is squared and pinched toward the top, with a flattened upper face marked by ridges. The granular red ware is mixed with numerous calcite inclusions and covered with a matt red slip. Handle No. 409, probably belonging to a large jar, is broad, deeply grooved, and displays an elliptical profile. The exaggerated modeling and pale buff-orange slip indicate a possible Late Byzantine date, yet this piece is singular, without apparent parallels in the literature.

A thick ovoid handle from a large jar is shown in No. 410. Such rounded handles, with varying degrees of grooving along the upper surface, appear to have persisted throughout the Byzantine period. This particular sherd was formed of coarse red ware and covered with a cream slip, and thus probably belongs to the later phases of the Byzantine period. Comparisons illustrate the duration of this form. An Early Byzantine example is found at **Araq el-Emir** (unpublished: Reg. No. 193). A similar handle from **Maᶜon** may date to the 6th century (Levy 1960: fig. 6: 1). At **Hebron** these handles occur in the Late Byzantine and Early Islamic periods (M.A. Bennett 1972: pl. VIII: IV.3), and a similar distribution is noted at **Tell Ḥesban** (Sauer 1973: fig. 3: 102, 130).

Spherical handle sections are shown in Nos. 411-12. These grey ware handles are associated with large jars, but they also occur on basins: **Nazareth** (Bagatti 1969: fig. 17: 22). No. 411 is paralleled by a jar handle from a 7th century deposit at **Caesarea** (Wiemken and Holum 1981: fig. 13: 7). An additional example of identical ware appears at **Dhiban** (Tushingham 1972: fig. 12: 62). The deeply ridged handle No. 412 may be a product of the Kerak region for it is not common in the literature.

Discussion: Early and Late Byzantine. Elements of Early Byzantine pottery in Transjordan have been interpreted as direct stylistic developments from the Late Roman repertoire; a relationship that is manifest in aspects of vessel form and surface treatments. However, attributes without strongly established precedence in indigenous or imported Late Roman ceramics are also prominent in Byzantine assemblages. Furthermore, throughout the duration of the Byzantine era in Transjordan the ceramic assemblage became increasingly divergent from the characteristically Late Roman repertoire. The rising popularity of grey wares, incised and "pie-crust" decorations, more sharply defined body ribbing on jars and cooking pots, and a growing preference for both light and dark slips, among other traits, became definitive in the characterization of Byzantine pottery. During the Late Byzantine period many Early Byzantine attributes, including some with Late Roman origins, remained an integral part of the assemblage, but new trends emerged as well, such as the production of coarse textured dark red and grey wares.

Aside from these and other specific developments that distinguish Byzantine from Late Roman pottery, there are notable differences in several aspects of ceramic manufacture. In contrast with Late Roman pottery of Transjordan, the Byzantine repertoire represents a wide proliferation of fabric types (illustrated in Smith 1973: pl. 90), surface treatments, and forms. If this is a legitimate generalization, it may indicate reduced standardization in Byzantine ceramic production. Specifically, the diversity among Byzantine forms and fabrics suggests that production may have been less centralized, and correspondingly, there may have been an increase in the number of producers.

This interpretation draws not only upon the diversity of Byzantine pottery within the Kerak region, but also upon apparent regional patterns of Byzantine ceramic manufacture. The discussion of forms has shown that parallels for a number of the sherds presented here can be found in Transjordan, Palestine, or both. However, a review of the pottery from Umm el-Jimal, Araq el-Emir, Lejjun, Mt. Nebo, Tell Ḥesban, and other East Bank sites indicates that regional practices of paste preparation and details of vessel morphology were stronger during the Byzantine period than in the Late Roman period.

The problem of determining the extent to which the Byzantine potters of Transjordan were engaged in local versus regional manufacturing and marketing of their products is not readily solved, for the issue is obscured to some extent by ambiguities between the Early and Late Byzantine assemblages. A number of forms, including many of those presented here, can be differentiated as specifically Early or Late Byzantine. Yet in many instances the assignment of sherds to these sub-periods is tenuous. There are two factors that limit the chronological evaluation of Byzantine assemblages. First, it appears that some forms and wares are common to both sub-periods, and second, there are forms that are not sufficiently understood stratigraphically to enable more precise chronological interpretation. Ibrahim, Sauer, and Yassine have noted this problem in Byzantine ceramic chronology in their report on the East Jordan Valley Survey (1976: 59). These investigators determined that 40 of the 67 Byzantine sites from the valley could not be assigned sub-period designations with certainty. Similarly, MacDonald's report of the Wadi el-Ḥasa Survey does not differentiate between Early and Late Byzantine sites (1988: 232-49). This ambiguity may owe less, however, to the nature and quantity of documented Early and Late Byzantine strata and their assemblages in Transjordan and more to the temporal duration of elements within the ceramic repertoire, as well as an increasing diversity. This diversity may be related to a growth in localized patterns of production and distribution in addition to, or at the expense of, broader, regional production and distribution networks.

Early Islamic

The small sample of Early Islamic sherds presented in this section reflects a few of the many trends in ceramic development that took place during the Umayyad, Abbasid, and Fatimid periods. In addition to fragments of widely recognized forms, sherds that may represent locally circumscribed products of the Early Islamic period are also included, although discussion of these pieces should be considered preliminary.

Description: Umayyad. Umayyad assemblages include a number of domestic forms (e.g. cooking pots, casseroles, and large handmade basins) that are attested in the Byzantine period and remain essentially unchanged through much of the Early Islamic period. Yet the hallmarks of Umayyad assemblages are found in an array of ceramic innovations that constitute a repertoire of "fine wares." These vessels demonstrate sophisticated production technologies as well as the emergence of a new ceramic aesthetic. Generally, the development of the Early Islamic fine wares appears to date to the 8th century, thus encompassing the late Umayyad and early Abbasid periods. Given the problems of interpreting unstratified remains of the more static cooking vessels and domestic wares within their long duration of use, the sample presented in this section emphasizes some of the more distinctive and innovative features of the Umayyad assemblage as represented in the Kerak plateau survey corpus.

Among the sherds presented here are wares that range among buff, pink, orange-pink, and grey tones. Handles Nos. 417-19 are pink to orange-pink, whereas handle No. 420 is buff. Fabrics of pink and orange are represented by painted body sherds Nos. 422-24 and knob handle No. 416. The fabric of small bowl No. 413 is pale grayish white. The deep grey fabric of pithos rim No. 415 is identical to the grey wares of the Late Byzantine period. Cut-ware bowl No. 414 has a distinctive dark metallic- grey fabric.

White and cream-colored slips of various shades are present among the following: bowl No. 413, knob handle No. 416, handle No. 417, and painted body sherd No. 422. Handles Nos. 418 and 420, and painted body sherd No. 423, have pale-pink surface finishes. A deeper pink-orange slip is noted on handle No. 419 and on the interior of incised body sherd No. 421. Decorative techniques include band combing on No. 421 and painting in both red, as shown by Nos. 417-18, 422-24, and white, as on No. 419. The well-worn paint on the surface of No. 413 appears to have been grey-green, which is unusual in this period. Deep surface cutting in an elaborate design is noted on the rim and body of bowl No. 414. Umayyad pottery is usually well fired and in this sample only handles Nos. 417 and 419 have cores. Inclusions are particularly visible in the sections of pithos rim No. 415 and handle No. 420, but well-levigated pastes are more common especially among the fine wares.

Forms: Umayyad. The small bowl pictured in No. 413 is a common 8th century form belonging to a class of vessels generally characterized by straight sides, beveled or squared rims, pink or buff ware, and exterior painted designs. These bowls are usually decorated with the red, red-brown, or purple-brown paints that also characterize some of the jugs and jars of this period. While the grey-green exterior paint of bowl No. 413 is anomalous, in every other respect (including attributes of form, ware, and painted design) this piece can be treated within the well attested genre of 8th century painted bowls. The painted design, consisting of interlocking elements, is attested at **Khirbet el-Mefjer** (Baramki 1940-42: fig. 9: 2) and several East Bank sites, including: **Amman, Citadel** (Olávarri-Goicoechea 1985: fig. 15: 13); **Tell Abu Qaᶜdan** (Franken and Kalsbeek 1975: figs. 21: 19, 22: 31); el-Bassa (Safar 1974: pl. 6: top and center rows); and **Dhiban** (Winnett and Reed 1964: pl. 13: 14). The rim form shown in No. 413 may be compared with several variations from **Khirbet el-Mefjer** (Baramki 1944: fig. 6: 1-5, 7).

The dating of these bowls, which can be treated as a subset of a broader category of vessels characterized by buff fabric and red, tends to focus on the 8th century, though with some variation. Sauer has suggested a late Umayyad date (first half of the 8th century) for these vessels (1982: 332) on the basis of occurrences at several sites. Among those sites with examples of this particular bowl are: **Tell Ḥesban** (Sauer 1973: 41; fig. 3: 123); **Mt. Nebo** (Schneider 1950: fig. 13: 5-6); **Dhiban** (Tushingham 1972: fig. 6: 36-37; Winnett and Reed 1964: pl. 67: 7; see also Sauer 1975: 107); **Amman, Citadel** (Bennett and Northedge 1977-78: pl. CI, 1: 4; Olávarri-Goicoechea 1985: fig. 15); and **Tell Abu Qaᶜdan**, Phases B-F (Franken and Kalsbeek 1975: 93; fig. 22; see also Sauer 1976: 93). For discussion of Umayyad red-painted bowls of a different form see ᶜAmr (1988).

Examples from **Khirbet el-Mefjer** were associated with debris dated by Baramki to the second quarter of the 8th century (1944: 65; fig. 6: 1-7). Whitcomb's recent review of the **Khirbet el-Mefjer** sequence ascribes these bowls to the second half of the 8th century, Period 1 (1988a: 56; fig. 1: 1H). These bowls are also dated to the second half of the 8th century at **Pella** (Walmsley 1982: 152; pl. 147: 2). Similarly, red-painted bowls from **Jerash** are interpreted as products of the second half of the 8th century through the 9th century (Gawlikowski 1986: 117-18; pls. XII, XIIIB). Another example associated with a 9th century context is found at **Amman, Citadel** (Northedge 1984: fig. 74: 7).

In Palestine, red-painted bowls from less certain contexts are found at a number of sites, e.g.: **Tulul Abu** ᶜ**Alayiq** (Kelso and Baramki 1955: pl. 30: A24); **Khirbet Siyar el-Ghanam** (Corbo 1955: fig. 41: 13); **Beisan** (Fitzgerald 1931: pl. XXXIII: 20, 27, 31), and **Capernaum** (Peleg 1989: fig. 45: 1-6).

Handmade cut-ware bowls are also a feature of 8th century assemblages. The example shown in No. 414 has a thin metallic-grey ware and a deeply incised design consisting of rim-notching and triangular-wedge cuts enclosed by crescent shaped grooves. As in the case of bowl No. 413 discussed above, this genre may best be described as 8th century, for it has been attributed to late Umayyad as well as early Abbasid contexts (Sauer 1982: 332-33). Cut-ware bowl fragments cited from Umayyad deposits include examples from: **Tell Ḥesban** (Sauer 1973: 43); **Mt. Nebo** (Saller 1941: pl. 158B: 22); **Amman, Citadel** (Olávarri-Goicoechea 1985: 27; fig. 17: 13-15); **Amman, Forum** (Hadidi 1970: pl. VIB: 12); and possibly **Tell Abu Qaᶜdan**, Phase E (Franken and Kalsbeek 1975: fig. 25: 15; see also Sauer 1976: 93). Currently, no clearly stratified cut-ware bowls have been published from **Pella** (Walmsley 1982: 152). However, they are reported in two late Umayyad contexts at **Jerash** (Walmsley, in Ball et al. 1986: 355; Gawlikowski 1986: 117-18), where they may continue into the 9th century (Gawlikowski 1986: 117). Cut-ware vessels at **Khirbet el-Mefjer** (Baramki 1944: fig. 6: 16, 20-25) are included in Whitcomb's Period 2 (with a single exception from Period 1), which he dates to the second half of the 8th century (1988a: 56; fig. 1: 2D). Cut-ware may have continued in use as late as the 11th century, as indicated by a bowl or basin fragment from **Amman Citadel** (Northedge 1984: fig. 76: 4).

In Palestine, these bowls have been dated from the mid-7th to the mid-8th centuries at **Capernaum**, Stratum IV (Peleg 1989: fig. 46: 1-6). Sites with other examples, whose provenience is less certain, include: **Caesarea** (Brosh 1986: fig. 1: 9); **Ramat Raḥel** (Aharoni 1956: fig. 6); **Beisan** (Fitzgerald 1931: pls. XXVI: 3; XXVII: 1); **Samaria** (Crowfoot et al. 1957: fig. 84A: 4-5); **Tell Qaimun** (Ben-Tor and Rosenthal 1978: fig. 8: 3); and in Transjordan, **Umm er-Rasas** (Glueck 1970: fig. 79: fourth row, left).

The pithos form, which was discussed in the Late Byzantine section (see No. 399, above), continued into the Umayyad period, as demonstrated at **Tell Ḥesban** (Sauer 1973: fig. 3: 117) and **Mt. Nebo** (Saller 1941: pl. 144: 4-6). Sherd No. 415 represents a variation of the Byzantine pithos rim distinguished by a rounded, less sharply modeled profile. An excellent parallel to this sherd, with regard to the profile and grey fabric, is found at **Dhiban** (Tushingham 1972: fig. 7: 10). This form of grey ware pithos does not appear to be represented among the grey wares published from Jerash or Pella, and thus it may not have been among the repertoire of grey wares produced in the Jerash kilns. However, the large utilitarian grey ware basins with rim and body combing that were produced at Jerash during the Umayyad period (Schaefer and Falkner 1986) are represented in the Kerak plateau survey corpus, although none is illustrated here.

A knob handle from a lid is shown in No. 416. The exceptionally finely prepared pink fabric and cream slip are characteristic of Transjordanian Umayyad fine wares. However, the majority of Umayyad knob handles belong to cooking casserole lids that, in contrast to No. 416, are of coarse dark fabrics similar to those of the Late Byzantine casseroles. Furthermore, the Umayyad casserole lid handles tend to be taller than No. 416, as demonstrated among the following: **Tell Ḥesban** (Sauer 1973: fig. 3: 110); **Mt. Nebo** (Schneider 1950: fig. 14: 1); **Pella** (Smith 1973: pl. 30: 1185); **Amman, Citadel** (Bennett 1978: fig. 6: 718b; 717b; Bennett and Northedge 1977-78: pl. CI, 1: 3). Other examples of tall lid handles of red and pink-orange wares occur with red or white-painted swirls, e.g. **Amman, Citadel** (Harding 1951b: fig. 2: 51) and **Jerash** (Pierobon 1983-84: fig. C: 1), decorations that are typical of bowls, jugs, and jars of this period. While No. 416 is too fragmentary to determine the presence or absence of paint, the low profile of the knob handle is clearly not typical, though it may be surmised that it represents a lidded fine ware dish, probably of 8th century origin.

The handle pictured in No. 417 probably joined the neck and shoulder of a wide-mouthed jug or jar, as at **Tell Abu Qaᶜdan**, Phase B (Franken and Kalsbeek 1975: fig. 9: 14). The red-painted triangle on the upper surface is similar to that shown on a handle from **Pella** (Smith 1973: pl. 30: 492), which belonged to a wide-mouthed tall-necked jar. The sides of handle No. 417 are pinched at the base, a feature associated with both Umayyad and Abbasid handles at **Tell Ḥesban** (Sauer 1982: fig. 4: third row from top, third from left; fig. 5: bottom row, second from right). The ovoid section of No. 417 compares with an Umayyad handle from **Umm el-Jimal** (Parker forthcoming d: No. 50).

The handle shown in No. 418 has a pale pink slip and a band of red paint that covers a portion of the upper surface. This small handle, elliptical in section, is attached to a fragment of the vessel rim and compares with rim-attached handles of red-painted jugs and tall-necked jars from **Pella** (Smith 1973: pl. 30: 492; Smith et al. 1980: pl. XX: 7; Smith et al. 1983: fig. 10: 1) and **Amman, Citadel** (Harding 1951b: fig. 3: 39, 61-62). No. 418 may also be compared with a sherd from **Dhiban** (Tushingham 1972: fig. 5: 19).

Handle No. 419 is distinguished by an orange-slipped and white-painted surface. The use of white paint emerges during the Late Byzantine period (see Sauer 1973: 37-38; 1982: 330 for a review) in conjunction with ribbed bag-shaped jars, and continues through the Umayyad period, and perhaps into the late 8th century as well. Although rarely attested on the Kerak plateau, examples of white-painted bag-jars from contexts dated to after the mid-7th century are noted from a number of sites to the north, including: **Pella** (Smith 1973: pls. 31: 495; 92a: 1139, 1156; Walmsley 1988: ill. 7: 7); **Tell Ḥesban** (Sauer 1973: 43); **Umm el-Jimal** (Parker forthcoming d: No. 54); **Amman, Citadel** (Harding 1951b: fig. 4: 41, see also fig. 4: 66); and **Qasr Hallabat** (Bisheh 1980: pl. XLIX: 4). These jars also occur at **Khirbet el-Mefjer** (Baramki 1944: fig. 3: 1-3) in Whitcomb's Period 1, for which a second half of the 8th century date is suggested (1988a: 56; fig. 1: 1A). However, white paint was also applied to a range of reddish wares, as in the case of No. 419. These attributes are documented at a number of sites, including: **Tell Abu Qaᶜdan**, Phase E (Franken and Kalsbeek 1975: fig. 16: 5); **Amman, Citadel** (Olávarri-Goicoechea 1985: fig. 16: 13); **Umm el-Jimal** (Parker forthcoming d: No. 41); **Qasr Hallabat** (Bisheh 1980: pl. L: 3, upper left); **Mt. Nebo** (Saller 1941: pl. 149: 25; Schneider 1950: 42); **Khirbet el-Mefjer** (Baramki 1944: figs. 4: 16-17; 15: 1; Whitcomb 1988a: 56, Period 1); and **Jerash** (Gawlikowski 1986: 118; Schaefer and Falkner 1986: 429, 431; fig. 11: 9-12; Kraeling 1938: 282). Examples from **Pella** (Smith 1973: pls. 30: 86; 92a: 1156; Walmsley 1988: ill. 7: 2-3) have been attributed to the **Jerash** kilns (Walmsley 1988: 152). A white-painted red-ware jug from **Pella** (Smith et al. 1980: pl. XXX) with a handle attached to the rim may approximate the original form of No. 419. It may also be noted that research at **Umm el-Jimal** (Parker forthcoming d) and **Jerash** (Gawlikowski 1986: 118) indicates that at these sites red-painted vessels occur stratigraphically later than white-painted vessels, suggesting that white paint may have been an early Umayyad feature, while the red paint may represent a late Umayyad development (see also Sauer 1973: 48-49).

The large pithos handle pictured in section in No. 420 is best paralleled in an Umayyad context at **Tell Ḥesban** (Sauer 1973: fig. 3: 130).

Band combing on cream ware is illustrated by body sherd No. 421. In terms of ware and combing style, this fragment best compares with a jar from **Amman, Citadel** (Harding 1951b: fig. 4: 38), which has been attributed to an Umayyad context. A fragment of a white ware jar with an incised neck is found at **Tell Abu Qaᶜdan**, Phase B (Franken and Kalsbeek 1975: fig. 23: 10), which may also be assigned to the Umayyad period (see Sauer 1976: 93). This incising also occurs on a grey-green jar from **Khirbet el-Mefjer** (Baramki 1944: fig. 3: 4). This jar, essentially the same form as documented at **Amman, Citadel**, belongs to Whitcomb's Period 2, which he dates to the 9th century (1988a: 56; fig. 1: 2A), thus placing it in the Abbasid period. Incised white-ware basins at **Khirbet el-Mefjer** (Baramki 1944: fig. 10: 2, 6) are associated with Whitcomb's 10th century Period 3 (1988a: 57).

However, incising is overwhelmingly associated with large handmade basins during the 7th through 9th centuries. While these occur in a variety of fabrics, grey ware basins, many of which were produced at **Jerash** (Schaefer and Falkner 1986), dominate the repertoire of incised forms. Such basins and large bowls are attested at numerous sites in addition to **Jerash** (Schaefer and Falkner 1986: 425, 427; figs. 8-9; Gawlikowski 1986: 118), among them: **Qasr Hallabat** (Bisheh 1980: pl. XLIX: 1, 3); **Amman, Citadel** (Harding 1951b: figs. 2: 57; 3: 50; Bennett and Northedge 1977-78: Pl. CI, 1: 6; Zayadine 1977-78: fig. 26: 508); **Pella** (Smith 1973: pl. 33: 504; pl. 92C: 1142, 1148, 1161; Walmsley 1982: pls. 139: 2; 145: 6; 148: 3; Walmsley 1988: ill. 8: 5-6); **Tell Abu Qaᶜdan**, Phases A-E (Franken and Kalsbeek 1975: fig. 46: 1-7); and **Mt. Nebo** (Saller 1941: pl. 152: 22, 26; Schneider 1950: 72-78).

Three body sherds with exterior red painted designs are illustrated in Nos. 422-24. The painted designs presented here include a florally derived motif (No. 422), simple linear bands (No. 423), and an ambiguous group of vertical and dripped horizontal lines (No. 424). The design on No. 422 is commonly found on small bowls and cups (e.g. No. 413). No. 424 is a lightly carinated jar or jug fragment. On this sherd the horizontal, painted and dripped bands of paint delineate the carination between the shoulder and body of the original vessel. For consideration of red paint in 8th century contexts see the discussion of sherd No. 413 above.

Specific parallels to the designs on sherds Nos. 422 and 424 may be cited. The red-painted floral pattern of No. 422 compares with sherds from **Amman, Forum** (Hadidi 1970: pl. VI: 6) and **Khirbet el-Mefjer** (Baramki 1944: fig. 9:3). Painting along the carination of closed, unribbed forms, as illustrated in No. 424, is attested at **Pella** (Smith 1973: pl. 30: 492) and **Mt. Nebo** (Saller 1941: 31; Schneider 1950: 40). It is not possible to associate the pattern on No. 423 with a particular motif, but it is similar to painted vessel fragments from **Tell Abu Qaᶜdan** (Franken and Kalsbeek 1975: fig. 22: 2-3, 9).

Description: Abbasid. Of the few sherds in the Kerak plateau assemblage that, at the time of the survey, could be dated at least tentatively to the second half of the 8th through the 9th centuries, those most appropriate for illustration are included in this review. Some of these sherds have traits that are highly diagnostic of Abbasid pottery in Transjordan; others are not as well attested and therefore may be more problematic for interpretation. This sample consists of bowl and lamp fragments (Nos. 425-26), a handle (No. 427), a base (No. 428), three incised body sherds (Nos. 429-31), and two glazed sherds (Nos. 432-33).

While a range of fabric colors occurs among 8th to 9th century assemblages, the sherds presented in this sample are either pink, including Nos. 425 and 427, or white to greenish-white, as represented by Nos. 426, 428-33. Nos. 425 and 427 are characterized by exceptionally fine quality paste, excellent firing, and smooth textures. Similarly, the smooth white wares of Nos. 428 and 430 also demonstrate a high level of technical skill, including accomplished firing techniques. Surface treatments include molded decorative relief on lamp fragment No. 426 and incising on sherds Nos. 429-31. The two glazed sherds, Nos. 432 and 433, are nearly identical to one another with respect to decoration. The buff-white fabrics of these pieces are more friable than those of the unglazed sherds, and both exhibit polychrome underglaze surfaces with lines of green and brown paint on a yellow-green background.

Until recently the only pottery published from Abbasid contexts in Transjordan included pieces from: Tell Abu Qaᶜdan (Franken and Kalsbeek 1975; see also Sauer 1976: 93); Tell Ḥesban (Sauer 1982); and possibly Dhiban (Winnett and Reed 1964; Tushingham 1972). Observations on these ceramic groups as well as unpublished assemblages are included in Sauer's review of Abbasid pottery (1982: 332). Another small, but very important, assemblage from the 9th and 10th centuries occupation at Amman, Citadel was studied by Northedge (1984: fig. 74). However, recent excavations at several sites in Transjordan have added significantly to the corpus of stratified Abbasid pottery, including: ᶜAqaba (Whitcomb 1987: fig. 8: d, h, i; Whitcomb 1989a); Pella (Walmsley 1988: ill. 9: 7-18; 10: 1-15); Amman, Citadel (Olávarri-Goicoechea 1985: fig. 52); Jerash (Gawlikowski 1986: 114-118, 120); and probably Khirbet Faris (R. Falkner, J. Johns, A. McQuitty, pers. comm.; see also Johns et al. 1989).

Forms: Abbasid. The offset rim of a small bowl or cup pictured in No. 425 is similar to two rim sherds from **Tell Ḥesban** (Sauer 1982: fig. 5: 2nd row, 2nd and 3rd from left; and Sauer, pers. comm.). A later, more exaggerated, offset bowl rim is noted at **Abu Gosh** in a 10th-11th century context (de Vaux and Stève 1950: pl. B: 10).

A small fragment of the upper portion of a mold-cast slipper lamp is shown in No. 426. The vine scroll and grape cluster motif found on this sherd is a common theme among assemblages dating to the second half of the 8th century and onwards in Transjordan, e.g., **Tell Ḥesban** (Sauer 1982: fig. 5: third row from top, fifth from left); **Amman, Citadel** (Olávarri-Goicoechea 1985: figs. 24: 3-5; 52: 15-16; Northedge 1984: fig. 76: 5, 9); **Jerash** (Gawlikowski 1986: 117, 120; pl. XIVB: center). In Palestine, several examples are found at **Khirbet el-Mefjer** (Baramki 1944: pl. XVII: 4) and **Abu Gosh** (de Vaux and Stève 1950: fig. 33: 4-5, 12). Less clearly stratified occurrences include: **Dhiban** (Winnett and Reed 1964: pl.

66: 7; Tushingham 1972: figs. 5: 18; 7: 6); **el-Hammam** (Parker 1986b: 211: 492); **Caesarea** (Brosh 1986: fig. 5: 11); **Tulul Abu ᶜAlayiq** (Kelso and Baramki 1955: pl. 14: 7); **Jerusalem, Tyropoeon Valley** (Crowfoot and Fitzgerald 1929: pl. XVII: 38); and **Khirbet Siyar al-Ghanum** (Corbo 1955: fig. 40: 11). A much more unusual occurrence of the vine scroll and grape cluster motif from the **Amman, Citadel** (Olávarri-Goicoechea 1985: fig. 16: 7) shows this design executed in red paint on a bowl of the type described above in the discussion of No. 413. However, it appears that painted renderings of this design were relatively few.

The handle shown in No. 427 consists of two rolls of clay that were pressed together and smoothed on the underside. This type of handle, probably belonging to a water jug or jar, is not clearly attested in published assemblages, though a handle formed of three clay strands and smoothed on the underside is noted from **Tell Abu Qaᶜdan**, Phase K (Franken and Kalsbeek 1975: fig. 9: 10). Handles formed with double and triple rolls of clay and without smoothed undersides are better attested, e.g.: **Tell Abu Qaᶜdan** (Franken and Kalsbeek 1975: fig. 9: 2); **Ramla** (Kaplan 1959: fig. 3A: 3); **Abu Gosh** (de Vaux and Stève 1950: pl. C: 13, 20).

No. 428 represents the flat base of a thin-walled fine white ware vessel, probably a jar. The fabric and form of this piece correspond with a class of post A.D. 747 cream ware vessels from **Pella** (Walmsley 1988: 156; e.g. ill. 9: 10). Similar vessels from **Abu Gosh** (de Vaux and Stève 1950: pl. C: 16, 19, 21-24) have been associated with 10th-11th century contexts. Another parallel may be cited from **Caesarea** (Brosh 1986: 12).

Early Islamic incising has already been introduced (see discussion of No. 421, above), however a few more notes may be added with respect to Nos. 429-31. Incising, other than in the context of the deep basins that were prevalent during the 7th to the 9th centuries, is relatively rare during the 8th century. Whitcomb associates incising at **Khirbet el-Mefjer** with 9th and 10th century occupation, Periods 2 and 3 (1988a: 53). Numerous examples of 10th-11th century incising associated with several vessel forms and wares occur at **Abu Gosh** (de Vaux and Stève 1950: pls. B: 29; C: 10; E: 1-7, 14). In the sample presented from the Kerak plateau survey, No. 429 bears vertical and oblique combed bands (see Abu Gosh, de Vaux and Stève 1950: pl. E: 1), while distinct patterns are more difficult to reconstruct from the fragments shown in Nos. 430-31. Perhaps most germane to Nos. 429-31 are the incising on the light colored wares of a jar fragment from **Tell Abu Qaᶜdan**, Phase N (Franken and Kalsbeek 1975: fig. 36: 4) and a bowl from **Pella** (Walmsley 1988: ill. 9: 13). The latter is dated to the second half of the 8th century, though earlier examples are attested as well (Walmsley 1982: pl. 147: 5).

Polychrome glazed wares, featuring color schemes of yellow, green, and purple or brown, first emerge in Transjordan during the Abbasid period (Sauer 1982: 333). These wares, illustrated by fragments pictured in Nos. 432 and 433, are very rare in the Kerak plateau survey corpus. Both body sherd No. 432 and rim sherd No. 433 (profile not illustrated) belong to an open bowl form. The design colors are identical; thick green and brown lines highlighted against a yellow-green background. A close parallel for this decorative treatment is found at **Dhiban** (Winnett and Reed 1964: pl. 13: 18). At **Pella** (Walmsley 1988: ill. 9: 18) this style of glazing is associated with 9th century occupation. Similar glaze is documented at **Khirbet el-Mefjer** (Baramki 1944; fig. 11: 2). Whitcomb assigns this, and other glazed vessels at **Khirbet el-Mefjer** to the 10th century Period 3 (1988a: 53). A comparable example from **Amman, Citadel** (Northedge 1984: fig. 74: 8) is also dated to the 10th century, while another similarly glazed vessel from that site is assigned to a less specific post-Umayyad context (Olávarri-Goicoechea 1985: fig. 22: 15). Later material from 10th-11th century **Abu Gosh** (de Vaux and Stève 1950: pl. A: 1-5) may also be related.

Description: Fatimid. Archaeologically, the Fatimid period is little known in Transjordan, and, at present, published ceramics from the mid-10th to 12th centuries are few. Nevertheless, important information is available from: 11th century deposits at Amman, Citadel (Northedge 1984) and mid-8th to early 12th century ("medieval antiqua") occupation at that site Olávarri-Goicoechea 1985: 36-39; figs. 22-23; see also Sauer 1982: fig. 6); 11th century occupation at ᶜAqaba (Whitcomb 1988b); and possibly some of the material from Tell Abu Qaᶜdan, Phases F-G (Franken and Kalsbeek 1975; Sauer 1976: 93; Sauer 1982: 333). 12th century Transjordan, which witnessed the demise of Fatimid rule, the invasion of forces led by Nur al-Din Zengi of Damascus, the entrenchment of Crusader armies, and the establishment of Ayyubid hegemony, remains perhaps even more obscure. Published materials include an assemblage from el-Wuᶜeira (Brown 1987) and possibly some sherds from Dhiban (Tushingham 1972; see also Brown 1987: 284).

With respect to the Fatimid assemblage in the Kerak plateau survey corpus, it appears that the latter 10th through the 12th centuries are poorly represented. Certainly the imported wares attested at ᶜAqaba (Whitcomb 1988b) are virtually absent from the collection, yet locally produced wares also appear relatively sparse. While it is apparent that a reexamination of the corpus may yield new insights, at present all of the interpretations of Fatimid pottery in the collection must be regarded as preliminary. The sample presented here includes a few cooking pot fragments that are clearly documented, as well as sherds that are not easily paralleled, though with ware characteristics that indicate a possible 10th to 11th century context. The corpus of 12th century wares from el-Wuᶜeira (Brown 1987) may find parallels within the Kerak plateau survey assemblage, however, these are not evident at the present.

Three fabric colors are represented in this sample (see Sauer 1982: 334 for fuller description). Orange-pink wares characterize bowl rim No. 434 and jar rim No. 436, while a buff-brown ware is attested by base No. 439. Of these, orange-pink slips are found on the exterior of bowl No. 434 and the interior of base No. 439. Traces of a reddish surface treatment are noted for No. 436. The third fabric type is a deep orange-red ware represented by Nos. 437 and 438 and typical of cooking vessels of the Fatimid period. Of these cooking pot handle fragments, No. 437 is red-brown slipped on one side and white slipped on the other, while a dark charcoal slip was applied to No. 438. This ware is also noted for the thin-walled rim sherd No. 435, which probably also represents a cooking pot. The coarse gritty fabric of this sherd is mixed with white calcite inclusions, and a clear interior glaze overlaps the rim and upper portion of the neck. Interior glazing of cooking pots is common during this period.

Forms: Fatimid. A portion of a substantial bowl or basin is illustrated in No. 434. A thick vertical strap handle was attached below the simple rounded, and slightly thickened, rim. As noted above, a coarse red ware with interior glaze distinguishes sherd No. 435. These attributes strongly suggest some type of cook-ware, although this profile is not found among the popular cooking pot forms of the Fatimid period. The profile shown in No. 436 probably belongs to a jug or jar.

Two forms of cooking vessels, characterized by brick red or red-orange ware and occasionally an interior glaze, occur during the Fatimid period. These include globular neckless cooking pots with in-turned or short upright rims, and flat-bottomed cooking casseroles (Sauer 1982: 334; Northedge 1984: 279-80). Both forms are accompanied by horizontal handles, many of which have a lenticular section as shown in Nos. 437-38. Examples of such cooking vessels, or their handles, are found at **Tell Abu Qaᶜdan**, Phase G (Franken and Kalsbeek 1975: fig. 9: 26), and in an 11th century context at **Amman**, **Citadel**, Stratum III (Northedge 1984: figs. 75: 5-6; 76: 2; 77: 1; 78: 1-2; see also Olávarri-Goicoechea 1985: fig. 23: 10). The long history of these vessels is indicated by an assemblage dated from the 12th through the 13th or 14th centuries at **al-Burj al-Ahmar**, Phases B-D (Pringle 1986: 146: fig. 48: 36-46). Other occurrences from sites in Palestine and Lebanon that are ascribed to Crusader assemblages (12th to 13th centuries) include: **Caesarea** (Pringle 1985: figs. 2: 3-8; 3: 9-10; Brosh 1986: fig. 4: 1-10, 14-17); **Tell Qaimun** (Ben-Tor and Rosenthal 1978: fig. 6: 9-13); **Abu Gosh** (de Vaux and Stève 1950: pl. G: 38); and **Tell ᶜArqa** (Thalmann 1978: figs. 31: 2-6; 32: 1-7). However, it seems clear that these researchers do not intend to imply that these forms were in any way a specific product of the Crusader presence, but merely that they were in common circulation during the period of Crusader occupation in Palestine. In Transjordan, these vessels are conspicuously absent from the 12th century Crusader deposits at **el-Wuᶜeira** (Brown 1987), although **Dhiban** (Tushingham 1972: fig. 7: 25) provides an example that could be associated with Ayyubid occupation from the late 12th to the mid-13th centuries.

The flat base shown in No. 439 is probably associated with an open, hemispherical bowl.

Discussion: Early Islamic. Two preliminary observations regarding the nature of the Early Islamic corpus could be drawn from a review of the Kerak plateau survey statistics. First, the total number of Early Islamic sherds is noticeably small, and second, the sherds are dispersed across the landscape with no single site providing a significant concentration of Early Islamic pottery. These apparent trends stand in contrast to ceramic data from the preceding Byzantine period and subsequent Ayyubid-/Mamluk period. But these factors alone should not be accepted as justification for concluding that settlement on the Kerak plateau declined during the Early Islamic period, for the nature of the survey assemblage betrays specific biases. With respect to the Umayyad and Abbasid pottery, the majority of the Kerak plateau survey statistics refer to highly diagnostic fine ware sherds, whereas the Fatimid corpus consists largely of cooking pot fragments that in many cases could be placed in a later context with equal justification. Thus as compared with excavated assemblages, significant aspects of the Early Islamic ceramic repertoire are either not represented or only minimally attested in this collection.

At the time that the survey was carried out, comparative material from Transjordan was limited, particularly with respect to assemblages from the mid-8th to 12th centuries. Since that time, a number of important Early Islamic excavations have been published, some of which have added to the ceramic corpus, e.g. Amman, Citadel (Northedge 1984; Olávarri-Goicoechea 1985), ᶜAqaba (Whitcomb 1987, 1988b, 1989a, 1989b), Jerash (Pierobon 1983-84; Gawlikowski 1986; Schaefer and Falkner 1986; Walmsley, in Ball et al. 1986); Pella (Walmsley 1982, 1988), and Khirbet Faris (Johns et al. 1989). Whitcomb's reevaluation of Khirbet el-Mefjer (1988a) represents another important contribution. In addition, new survey data from er-Risha (Lenzen 1989) and the southern ghors (Whitcomb forthcoming a), as well as synthetic and bibliographic works (Pringle 1981; Sauer 1982; Johns forthcoming; Whitcomb forthcoming b) have appeared. The ceramic sequences found among these works have added valuable dimensions to the essential and pioneering ceramic studies of Harding (1951b), Sauer (1973, 1976), Smith (1973), and Franken and Kalsbeek (1975).

Whitcomb has suggested that "there are more than enough ceramics published as Umayyad and Ayyubid /Mamluk to fill in the Abbasid/Fatimid period and make it quite a respectable occupation in Jordan's history" (forthcoming b). The extent to which this statement may be relevant to the Early Islamic assemblage from the Kerak plateau survey can be ascertained only by an extensive reexamination of the data from the Byzantine through the Mamluk periods. However, specific observations may be put forward with respect to the limitations of the statistics representing the Early Islamic corpus from the survey. First, the presentations from Pella and Jerash have lent further credence to the long-standing observation regarding the endurance of many 5th-6th century domestic forms through much of the Early Islamic period (Sauer, pers. comm.), while also expanding our understanding of specific 8th-9th century grey ware products. It is clear that Early Islamic (particularly Umayyad and Abbasid) domestic wares stemming from the Byzantine tradition are under-represented in the survey statistics, and are likely to be found within the Byzantine assemblage. Second, the 11th-12th century handmade wares documented at: Amman, Citadel (Northedge 1984: fig. 75: 2); ᶜAqaba (Whitcomb 1988b: fig. 5); and el-Wuᶜeira (Brown 1987: figs. 8-10) present another potential interpretative problem, for in the absence of stratification it may be difficult to isolate these wares from the numerous Late Islamic handmade vessel fragments. Hence, it is assumed that some of this material is erroneously classified within the Late Islamic assemblages.

Another issue involves the interpretation of the 8th-9th century fine wares that account for most of the survey pottery assigned to the Umayyad and Abbasid periods. In terms of actual numbers of sherds, the fine ware corpus is very small. This fact raises a critical question that may be pertinent to the interpretation of Early Islamic survey data across the landscape of southern Transjordan. Is the amount of fine ware represented in the survey corpus the result of: (1) relatively low-level sedentary occupation that signals a decline from the Byzantine settlement pattern; (2) constraints on the distribution of fine ware vessels; or (3) both? If assumptions that all ceramic products of a given period were equally distributed throughout Transjordan, without consideration of product cost or transportation distance from product source, are rejected as simply unrealistic, then a simple correlation between the relative abundance of fine ware sherds and relative assessment of population cannot be accepted. In other words, if the fine ware vessels were produced in central and/or north Transjordan, their apparent minimal representation in the southern regions may express limitations of the geographic spheres in which these products were distributed through institutions of marketing of exchange. This dismissal of superficial treatment of the data may complicate the issue, but it also advocates in favor of new avenues of research, for the question of Early Islamic occupation on the Kerak plateau as represented by archaeological survey data remains a challenging and, hopefully, provocative issue.

Ayyubid-Mamluk

Ceramics from the 13th through the 15th centuries in Transjordan include handmade wares (of a wide variety of vessel types), often painted with distinct geometric patterns, and wheel-thrown wares including both industrial and domestic pots, of which some of the latter are glazed. In addition, there are occasional mold-cast pieces, and a few imported wares, generally from Syria, although Egyptian and Southeast Asian examples are also known. Of these trends in Ayyubid-Mamluk ceramic production, the large corpus from the rural Kerak plateau represents the following specific characteristics: (1) painted and unpainted handmade vessels dominate the assemblage, and (2) wheel-thrown wares, consisting mostly of bowl fragments decorated with monochrome glazes, constitute a much smaller proportion of the corpus. Vessel types that are rarely represented in the Kerak plateau assemblage include: unglazed wheel-thrown vessels (both industrial and domestic); wheel-thrown glazed bowls with sgraffito decoration; mold-cast wares, sphero-conic vessels; and fragments of imported glazed vessels.

Several aspects of 13th to 15th century assemblages, including the vast quantities of handmade wares, the widespread use of geometric painted decorations, and the lesser, but consistent, presence of wheel-thrown plain, and monochrome glazed, wares stand in sharp contrast to the ceramic history of the region during the Umayyad and Abbasid periods. However, the process of describing the nature of the relationship between the Early Islamic and Late Islamic assemblages has been greatly hindered by a poverty of data from the 11th to 12th centuries. Nevertheless, there is enough current evidence to at least suggest that some of the apparent radical changes that characterize Ayyubid-Mamluk assemblages can in fact be traced to developments within the Early Islamic period. The evidence for this conclusion is found largely in the 11th century data from ^{c}Aqaba (Whitcomb 1988b) and Amman, Citadel (Northedge 1984), and the 12th century material from el-Wu^{c}eira (Brown 1987). Unfortunately, neither ^{c}Aqaba nor el-Wu^{c}eira can be considered a typical late Fatimid site. As a port city geographically removed from historic areas of sedentary occupation, ^{c}Aqaba was exposed to foreign influences and goods (Whitcomb 1988b), while perhaps at the same time developing an indigenous ceramic repertoire that may or may not be characteristic of Transjordan in general. El-Wu^{c}eira, on the other hand, was a Crusader-occupied site. The stratified pottery from this military fortress bears little resemblance to assemblages from Crusader coastal Palestine. Thus, while it may be assumed that the material from el-Wu^{c}eira is typical of 12th century southern Transjordan, the question remains to be further investigated. Nevertheless, the 11th-12th century evidence from ^{c}Aqaba and el-Wu^{c}eira indicates that, with particular respect to the handmade painted wares, these features were neither inspired by external "alien" influences (cf. Franken and Kalsbeek 1975), nor *sui generis* products of a shift to Ayyubid administration at the end of the 12th century.

Aside from the apparent developments towards the end of the Early Islamic period that led to the growth of a highly distinctive ceramic repertoire in the 13th-15th centuries, the Ayyubid-Mamluk corpus stands among the most dominant and widespread of all the ceramic groups on the Kerak plateau, ranking approximately with the ceramic densities documented for the Nabataean and Classical periods. As such, this distribution provides a sharp contrast to the current evaluation of the Early Islamic corpus. This apparent abundance of Late Islamic pottery across the landscape may, in part, result from some Early Islamic material, particularly from the Fatimid period, having been subsumed within the 13th-15th century assemblage. There is also the possibility that 16th century, and later, wares exist within the assemblage catalogued as Ayyubid-Mamluk. However, the consistent association of glazed bowl fragments with many assemblages suggests that the bulk of the material assigned to the Ayyubid-Mamluk period is in fact correctly placed.

In 1955 Dothan published drawings of wheel-thrown and handmade Ayyubid-Mamluk pottery from ᶜAfula, Stratum I (1955: 25-27; figs. 5-8), as well as some summary remarks regarding their chronology as currently understood from excavations at several sites in Palestine (ibid.: 25-27). Thus, while the essential aspects of the Late Islamic repertoire have long been established in Palestine, it was not until the publications of: Dhiban (Tushingham 1972); Pella (Smith 1973; Sauer 1974); Tell Ḥesban (Sauer 1973); and Tell Abu Qaᶜdan (Franken and Kalsbeek 1975; Sauer 1976) that a solid body of comparative material began to develop in Transjordan.

Description: Ayyubid-Mamluk. Three types of wheel-thrown wares are included in this sample: (1) glazed bowls (Nos. 440-44, 449-51), (2) plain wares that may belong to jugs, jars, or pitchers (Nos. 445, 448), and (3) plain industrial wares commonly known as "sugar pots" (Nos. 446-47). Fabrics among the sample of wheel-thrown pottery consist of both light-colored wares, of mostly buff or pink tones, and red wares. The buff and pink-colored fabrics (Nos. 440-44, 447-49) are generally well prepared and well fired (see Smith 1973: pl. 93c: 964, 967). Hard, thin, dark red fabrics (Nos. 445, 450-51) are also well levigated, as is the paste of a softer lighter red ware (No. 446) that also occurs. Of these wheel-thrown pieces, only the bowl fragments display glaze treatments. Monochrome glazes of yellow (No. 440) and green (Nos. 441-43) cover the interior surfaces and exterior rims of these sherds. The quality and consistency of these glazes is relatively poor. Carelessly dripped glaze on the exterior of some of these sherds indicates that only brief attention was paid to the decorative process. Exterior glazing of bowl bases (No. 449) is less common. Bichrome glazing is represented by one bowl fragment (No. 444) with a brown interior and green exterior. White underglaze slip is noted on some examples (Nos. 441-43; see also Smith 1973: pl. 93c: 996, 967). Two bowl fragments are decorated with the sgraffito technique of underglaze incising (Nos. 450-51). The thin linear pattern engraved on No. 450 is coated with a yellow glaze. The more widespread sgraffito technique illustrated by No. 451 consists of a much broader pattern cut through a white-slipped surface and covered with a mottled yellow and green glaze. Burnishing is another decorative technique found among the wheel-thrown wares, though it is less common. Jar neck No. 445 was burnished with multiple horizonal lines (not illustrated).

Mold-cast wares also exhibit several fabric hues. Most common are: pink (Nos. 452-56); white (No. 457); and red (No. 458). In this sample, all of the glazed molded pieces (Nos. 452-57) belong to bowls. Yellow monochrome glaze, with white underglaze slip, covers the interior and exterior surfaces of Nos. 453-56. These pieces show portions of relief designs or inscriptions on the exterior. No. 457 bears a monochrome green glaze. Bichrome glazing is represented by bowl rim No. 452, where the interior green glaze was dripped over the rim and covers part of the exterior yellow glaze. Lamp fragment No. 458 provides an example of unglazed mold-cast ware. In addition to these typical examples of molded wares, the sample includes two pieces of sphero-conic vessels, Nos. 459-60, which are rare in Transjordan. The physical characteristics of these sherds are highly distinctive and unlike those of any other category of Ayyubid-Mamluk pottery. The metallic grey fabric is unusually heavy and extremely hard, possibly due to scoria inclusions.

Sherds from handmade vessels (Nos. 461-77) illustrate rudimentary construction techniques. While coiling and the partial use of rotational devices occur, it seems that modeling with clay slabs was a more common technique, especially in the manufacture of the painted closed forms, such as jugs and jars. The occasional presence of textile impressions on the interior of these vessels suggests that techniques such as wrapping clay around a sand-filled cloth sack (Smith 1973: 240) or use of cloth in conjunction with shaping dishes (Franken and Kalsbeek 1975: figs. 50-51) were employed, although actual traces of cloth were often obliterated by final smoothing of the vessel walls.

Of the unpainted wares, fabrics include shades of brown (Nos. 461-62, 476), a less typical orange (No. 463), and buff (No. 477). Among the painted sherds in this sample (Nos. 464-75), light-colored fabrics range among various tones of white, cream, buff, and pink. Exterior surface colors associated with the painted wares are typically either white-cream-slipped (Nos. 465-471) or pink-slipped (Nos. 464, 472-75), although light-fired surfaces without slips are also common (see also Smith

1973: pl. 94b). Firing among handmade pottery of this period varies widely, and while poor examples are frequent, excellent examples are also attested. In this sample, cores are evident in a number of the sherds, but the majority may be considered well fired. Organic and mineral inclusions are dominant, and they often appear in combination. Grog temper was used during this period as well, though in the Kerak region it was not as commonly used as other tempers. Generally, the density of visible tempering agents is unusually high, often constituting between ten and thirty percent of the fabric. A number of factors contribute to the general coarseness that characterizes the Ayyubid-Mamluk handmade wares. Among these are: irregular thickness of vessel walls; finger impressions resulting from the manufacturing process; the frequent use of large quantities of coarse, poorly integrated organic and mineral tempers; surface crackling; and occasional surface spalling.

Painted wares are decorated with geometric designs in monochrome black (Nos. 464, 466-67, 469, 471, 474-75) and bichrome red and black (Nos. 465, 468, 470, 472-73). Dark paints may fire either black or brown depending on the density of paint application and the conditions of firing. Monochrome red paint also occurs, though no instances are included in this sample. The quality and precision of design execution, as well as the combination and coherence of design elements varies considerably.

Forms: Ayyubid-Mamluk. Wheel-thrown, unglazed, domestic pottery from the 13th to 15th centuries in Transjordan consists of a variety of forms, both open and closed, as documented at: **Tell Abu Qaᶜdan**, Phases H-T (Franken and Kalsbeek 1975: 107-130); **Shobak Castle** (Brown 1988: 237); and **Kerak Castle** (Brown 1989: 296-297; and unpublished). This material is also known in Palestine, e.g. **al-Burj al-Ahmar**, Phase D1 (Pringle 1986: 137, 145). However, the distribution of these wares appears to have been limited, for they constitute an extremely small proportion of the Ayyubid-Mamluk assemblage from the rural sites surveyed on the Kerak plateau. Similarly, only a few examples are illustrated among the pottery published from **Tell Ḥesban** (Sauer 1973: fig. 4: 162-63) and the "post-12th century" corpus from **Khirbet Faris** (Johns et al. 1989: figs. 26: 46; 27: 50).

In contrast, glazed wheel-thrown vessels, mostly bowls, are found in many of the Ayyubid-Mamluk assemblages from the Kerak plateau, and a small selection of rims is presented in Nos. 440-44. These monochrome, and occasionally bichrome, glazed vessels that were a hallmark of the Ayyubid-Mamluk period have appeared in earlier archaeological contexts as well, e.g. the 11th century at **Amman, Citadel** (Northedge 1984: fig. 76: 6), and the 12th century at **el-Wuᶜeira** (Brown 1987: fig. 10: 28), and **al-Burj al-Ahmar**, Phase B (Pringle 1986: 147). However, these vessels are standard components among assemblages attributed to 13th century, and later, contexts, as at: **Tell Abu Qaᶜdan** (Franken and Kalsbeek 1975: 131-141; Sauer 1976: 94); **Tell Ḥesban** (Sauer 1973: 52); **Pella** (Smith 1973: 239), **Khirbet Faris** (Falkner, in Johns et al. 1989: 89); **Shobak Castle** (Brown 1988: 237); and **Kerak Castle** (Brown 1989: 296). A few of the numerous sites in Palestine where these wares are present include: **al-Burj al-Ahmar**, Phases C and D (Pringle 1986: 137, 147-48); **Abu Gosh** (de Vaux and Stève 1950: 137); **ᶜAfula** (Dothan 1955: 26); and **Tell Jemmeh** (Schaefer 1989: 48). In south Syria examples are found at **Bosra** (Berthier 1985: 14).

The rims of both carinated and uncarinated glazed bowls display a wide range of styles (e.g. Franken and Kalsbeek 1975: fig. 37), and for this reason few precise parallels are cited for the profiles presented in this discussion. The dark yellow-brown glazed sherd shown in No. 440 is a common form that occurs with a wide range of variation. The simple rounded rim and high carination compare with pieces from **Khirbet Shemaᶜ**, Stratum VII (Meyers et al. 1976: pl. 7.18, no. 11); **Pella** (Smith 1973: pl. 72: 494/1019); and **Khirbet el-Mefjer**, Period 4 (Baramki 1944: fig. 11: 8; see also Whitcomb 1988a: 271). Of these citations, the latter two examples show more complex decoration on the vessel interior. Similar forms are also noted at **Tell Abu Qaᶜdan**, Phase R (Franken and Kalsbeek 1975: fig. 37: 26), **al-Burj al-Ahmar**, Phase E (Pringle 1986: fig. 49: 54), and **Qubeibeh** (Bagatti 1947: fig. 31: 12).

Profiled bowl rims decorated with green glaze over white slip are presented in Nos. 441-43. The hammerhead rims Nos. 441-42 may be compared with **Abu Gosh** (de Vaux and Stève 1950: fig. 32: 6) and **Pella** (Smith 1973: pl. 72: 967). More exaggerated versions of No. 442 are found at **Khirbet Faris** (Johns et al. 1989: fig. 26: 44) and ᶜ**Ain as-Siyah** (Pringle 1984: fig. 7: 41). The in-curved rim shown in No. 443 is attested at **Tell Ḥesban** (Sauer 1973: fig. 4: 137), as well as at **Tell Abu Qaᶜdan**, Phase L (Franken and Kalsbeek 1975: fig. 37: 34) and **Pella** (Smith 1973: pl. 72: 843). No. 444, probably belonging to a carinated bowl, has a thickened rim style that is not clearly attested in the literature, although a similar rim is documented at **Tell Abu Qaᶜdan**, Phase K (Franken and Kalsbeek 1975: fig. 37: 50).

Among the unglazed wheel-thrown wares is a fragment of a tall-neck jug with tapered rim shown in No. 445. The strainer, once lodged in the neck interior, has broken away. The red-orange fabric of this sherd was covered by a brick-red slip, and the exterior surface was hand burnished in widely spaced horizontal lines, attributes that are generally more characteristic of contemporary cooking wares (Sauer 1982: 335). Burnishing is not attested among the buff and white ware water jugs from the region (Kerak Castle, unpublished). Wheel-thrown red wares are attested at **Tell Abu Qaᶜdan**, Phase H (Franken and Kalsbeek 1975: fig. 34: 6-26). Yet the only evident parallels for this form are found among handmade, rather than wheel-thrown, assemblages. A particularly apt comparison is offered by a geometric painted jug neck from **Tell Ḥesban** (Sauer 1973: 157).

Unglazed, wheel-thrown, industrial vessels associated with the prosperous Mamluk sugar refineries of the Jordan Valley and southern *ghors* are shown in Nos. 446-47. These sugar pots are heavily represented at a number of sites surveyed in the Jordan Valley (Ibrahim et al. 1976: 63; Yassine et al. 1988: 203), and have also emerged from excavations at **Pella** (Smith 1973: pl. 70) and **Tell Abu Qaᶜdan**, Phases H-T (Franken and Kalsbeek 1975: figs. 42-45). MacDonald's survey of the southern *ghors* region also documents sugar pots at: **Tawahin al-Sukkar** (Whitcomb forthcoming a: fig. 1: J-M), **Feifa** (ibid., not illustrated); **Khirbet Sheikh ᶜIsa** (ibid.: fig. 3: A-F, V); and **al-Rujoum** (ibid.: fig. 5: A-B, I-K). Although seldom encountered on the Transjordan highland plateau, a few fragments have been recovered from **Wardeh** (Coughenour 1976: pl. XXXII.1: lower left), and **Kerak Castle** (Brown 1989: fig. 6: 15).

Sugar pots are generally of two types, (1) a vat with wide mouth, flaring sides, and splayed rim (Smith 1973: pl. 70: 930; Franken and Kalsbeek 1975: fig. 40: 11), and (2) a deep, bag-shaped jar that was often ribbed and accompanied by an omphalos base (Smith 1973: pl. 70; Franken and Kalsbeek 1975: fig. 40: 11). Nos. 446 and 447 show rims from bag-shaped sugar pots. The many profiles of these vessels from **Tell Abu Qaᶜdan**, Phases H-T (Franken and Kalsbeek 1975: figs. 42-45) show a wide range of stylistic variation, though a few may be compared with No. 446: **Tell Abu Qaᶜdan**, Phases P and R (Franken and Kalsbeek 1975: figs. 44: 43; 45: 35). No. 447 is similar to a jar from **al-Rujoum** (Whitcomb forthcoming a: fig. 5: A).

Wheel-thrown ring bases are illustrated in Nos. 448 and 449. The low ring base No. 448 consists of a buff ware without trace of slip or glaze. This sherd represents a water jar, or a similar closed form, as illustrated at **Abu Gosh** (de Vaux and Stève 1950: pl. G: 23-33). Comparable bases from stratified contexts in the Kerak region include **Khirbet Faris** (Johns et al. 1989: fig. 26: 46; post-12th century) and **Kerak Castle** (Brown 1989: fig. 6: 16-19; 14th century). However, as noted above, these wheel-thrown plain wares are relatively rare in the survey corpus. The higher ring base shown in No. 449 is from a bowl with green glaze on both the interior and exterior surfaces. This base belongs to the same genre of bowls represented by rims Nos. 440-44. While this manner of exterior glazing is not common among these bowls, a comparable bowl base with exterior glaze extending to the foot ring is found at **Tell Abu Qaᶜdan**, Phase R (Franken and Kalsbeek 1975: fig. 38: 29).

Sgraffito bowl fragments of hard thin red ware are shown in Nos. 450 (rim profile not illustrated) and No. 451. These vessels were decorated by, (1) carving designs through a light slip that exposed the contrasting dark clay surface below, then (2) the application of a covering glaze. Sgraffito wares of many types and origins are common among a number of Crusader and medieval assemblages in Palestine and Syria. While a broad range of dates and influences is suggested for these pieces, their height of popularity appears to have been during the 13th century. Among the numerous sites where these wares have been attested are: ᶜ**Atlit** (Johns 1934); **Abu Gosh** (de Vaux and Stève 1950); ᶜ**Afula** (Dothan 1955); **al-Burj al-Ahmar** (Pringle 1986); **Caesarea** (Brosh 1986; Pringle 1985); ᶜ**Ain as-Siyah** (Pringle 1984); **Jerusalem, Damascus Gate** (Wightman 1989: pls. 67: 5-8; 68: 1, 3, 5-8; 225-26); **Mt. Tabor** (Battista and Bagatti 1976: pl. 28.2-3: bottom row);

Tell Qaimun (Ben-Tor and Rosenthal 1978); **Hama** (Riis and Poulsen 1957); **al-Mina** (Lane 1937); and **Qasr al-Hayr ash-Sharqi** (Grabar et al. 1978). These examples demonstrate a broad scope of artistic variations that characterize both local and imported sgraffito wares of the Levant. In Transjordan, however, local and imported sgraffito wares rarely appear in the literature. Among the few published examples are sherds from: **ᶜAqaba** (Whitcomb 1988b: fig. 7: Q-R); **Tell Abu Qaᶜdan**, Phases H-S (Franken and Kalsbeek 1975: 137); **Shunat Nimrin** (Piccirillo 1982: pl. CX.2: bottom row, center); and from survey at **al-Rujoum** (Whitcomb forthcoming a: fig. 7: K, O-R). Additional instances from **Amman, Citadel** (Northedge 1984: fig. 76: 8; Olávarri-Goicoechea 1985: fig. 52: 12-13) may predate the 12th century.

In this sample, the thinly engraved lines of No. 450 (under yellow glaze) and the broadly cut pattern of No. 451 (under yellow and green glaze) are both represented at **Tell Abu Qaᶜdan**, Phases K-L (Franken and Kalsbeek 1975: fig. 38: 21-23). These simple and aesthetically undistinguished pieces share only basic technical similarities with the majority of sgraffito wares of the coastal Levant and probably represent local products. In contrast with the rare appearance of sgraffito fragments from the survey assemblages from the rural Kerak plateau, the higher density of these wares observed on the surface at Um Qais and in the region east of Salt suggests that sgraffito vessels were more widely circulated, and perhaps manufactured, in the northern highlands of Transjordan. Yet these specific types of local sgraffito ware are not restricted to Transjordan, for examples are also know from northern Palestine, as at ᶜAin as-Siyah (Pringle 1984: 106; fig. 8: 70-71).

Fragments of mold-cast vessels are shown in Nos. 452-60. Glazed bowls with exterior relief decorations are represented by Nos. 452-57, of which Nos. 452-54 are rim fragments (Nos. 453-54, profiles not illustrated). Yellow (exterior) and green (interior) bichrome glaze distinguishes No. 452, and monochrome green is found on No. 457. The remainder of these pieces have monochrome yellow glazes. Portions of inscriptions, or possibly pseudo-calligraphic designs, are preserved on Nos. 452-54, and may be compared with **Tell Ḥesban** (Sauer 1973: fig. 4: 140). No. 455 bears a lattice pattern, No. 456 may represent a floral design, and No. 457 has a dot and triangle motif similar to examples from **Tell Ḥesban** (Sauer 1973: fig. 4: 139) and **Beisan** (Zori 1966: pl. 10E). Fragments of mold-cast glazed bowls do not appear to have been very common in Palestine, though there are published fragments from **Jersualem, Damascus Gate** (Wightman 1989: pls. 64: 9-13; 65: 1-2; 220-22). Similarly, they are seldom attested in Transjordan, although a few published examples may be cited from **Tell Abu Qaᶜdan**, Phases L, M, T (Franken and Kalsbeek 1975: fig. 38: 31-33) and **Khirbet Faris** (Johns et al. 1989: fig. 27: 59), as well as the pieces from **Tell Ḥesban** (Sauer 1973: fig. 4: 138-140). The specialized skills required to produce the decorative molds may have been a factor in limiting the production and availability of these vessels.

Sherd No. 458 shows a portion of a mold-pressed lamp with relief decoration consisting of medallions and smaller filler elements. Many of these lamps are characterized by schematic designs of various types and occasionally Arabic inscriptions. Found in both Transjordan and Palestine, this ovoid slipper lamp may be accompanied by a channel nozzle. Handles are usually either low knobs of clay or higher attachments with pointed and curved profiles. No specific parallels to the fragmentary design of No. 458 are evident in a brief review of the literature, yet similar lamps occur at: **Kerak Castle** (Brown 1989: fig. 6: 25); **Pella** (Smith 1973: pl. 58: 57); and **Tell Sahl es-Sarabet** (Suleiman and Betts 1981: pl. LXIII: 1). In Palestine, further examples may be cited from **Abu Gosh** (de Vaux and Stève 1950: fig. 33: 1, 6); **al-Burj al-Ahmar**, Phase D (Pringle 1986: fig. 47: 34); **ᶜAin as-Siyah** (Pringle 1984: fig. 5: 9); **Beit Sahur** (Tzaferis 1975: pl. 20: 6-9); **La Fève** (Kedar and Pringle 1985: fig. 4: 3); **Jerusalem, Damascus Gate** (Wightman 1989: pls. 62: 2-5, 7-8; 217-18); and **Qubeibeh** (Bagatti 1947: fig. 34: 1-9).

The fragments of sphero-conic vessels shown in Nos. 459-60 belong to a specific genre of vessels whose function has been debated vigorously for over a century (Ettinghausen 1965). These small, hand-sized conical vessels are characterized by a distinct pyriform body shape, short neck, tiny orifice, and pointed base. As in the case of many sphero-conic vessels, the mold-cast fragments shown in Nos. 459-60 share a hard, dense, metallic fabric and have thick heavy vessel walls and metallic grey exterior surfaces. The exterior surface treatments exhibited by these fragments are also typical, for both the stamped designs (Nos. 459) and crudely carved initials or other graffiti (No. 460) are highly characteristic, as demonstrated by numerous examples from **Mt. Tabor** (Battista and Bagatti 1976: figs. 7-10; pls. 21-23). Sphero-conic vessels of a wide variety of types have appeared in Egypt, the Levant, Asia Minor, Iraq, Iran, Afghanistan, Central Asia, and Russia. Specific instances are far too numerous to recount, although a few examples are noted from such widely dispersed sites as: **Quseir al-Qadim** in Egypt (Whitcomb and Johnson 1979: 37: K); **Khirbet al-Karak** in Palestine (Delougaz and Haines 1960: pls. 34: 13; 56: 2); and **Nishapur** in Persia (Wilkinson 1973: 109-17). The presence of a kiln and waster dump demonstrates that Nishapur was a manufacturer of these vessels (ibid.: 293). Among the occurrences in Syria are pieces from **Hama** (Riis and Poulsen 1957: 277: Nos. 1047-55; 279: Nos. 1056-57) and **Apamea** (Rogers 1984: pl. LXIX: 5). In addition to Khirbet al-Karak, Palestinian examples include: **Khirbet el-Mefjer** (Baramki 1944: fig. 5: 1); **Jerusalem, Damascus Gate** (Wightman 1989: pls. 62: 9-11; 219); and **Jerusalem, Zion Gate** (Broshi and Tsafrir 1977: fig. 5: 1). Yet the largest collection of sphero-conic vessels in the southern Levant is found at **Mt. Tabor** (Battista and Bagatti 1976: figs. 8-10; pls. 21-23), where they are identified as "bombe a fucco greco." In Transjordan they are almost unknown aside from a small but significant collection of complete vessels from the town of **Ajlun** (S. Rabadi, pers. comm.).

With respect to dating sphero-conic vessels, Ettinghausen offers evidence for a *terminus a quo* within the Early Islamic period, possibly as early as the Umayyad caliphate (1965: 224). These vessels clearly endured for some time and may in fact have reached the height of their circulation in the southern Levant during the 13th century, for the large collection from Mt. Tabor is associated with the 13th century fortress (Battista and Bagatti 1976), and the smaller corpus from Ajlun was retrieved in conjunction with Ayyubid-Mamluk pottery (S. Rabadi, pers. comm.).

Of the many functional interpretations that have been presented, Ettinghausen discusses four possibilities, for which there is least some evidence, (1965; see also Wilkinson 1973: 293-294). Ettinghausen listed the following in rank order from highest to lowest credibility: (1) containers for mercury, which was a widely traded and apparently precious commodity; (2) containers for perfumes or other luxury liquid substances; (3) aeopiles or "fire-blowers;" and (4) grenades, either as molotov cocktails or mechanically launched by devices of warfare. Chemical analyses have proven that some of the vessels contained mercury, however, it is also clear that no one explanation can be applied consistently to all instances included within the rubric of "sphero-conic" vessels (Ettinghausen 1965: 223).

Sherds from handmade vessels are presented in Nos. 461-77. These consist of both plain wares (Nos. 461-63, 476-77) and painted pieces (Nos. 464-75). As noted above, assemblages from Ayyubid-Mamluk contexts are distinguished by (1) a prevalence of handmade wares representing a wide range of vessel types many of which had formerly been produced by the wheel, and (2) the widespread application of painted geometric designs among these handmade wares. While this combination of features is not found in Umayyad and Abbasid assemblages, their development appears to emerge in 11th and 12th century contexts. At **ᶜAqaba** handmade wares appear from the late 10th century through the abandonment of the site early in the 12th century (Whitcomb 1988b: fig. 5: A-I). Among these are a few vessels painted with linear designs including one instance with geometric motifs (ibid.: fig. 5: E). A handmade jug from **Amman, Citadel** (Northedge 1984: fig. 75: 2) illustrates an 11th century form that became the single most commonly produced form among the handmade repertoire by the 13th century. Sherds from handmade vessels painted in a linear style, and to a lesser extent geometric painted sherds, also appear in 12th century contexts at **el-Wuᶜeira** (Brown 1987: figs. 8: 8: 9: 20-25; 10: 29- 35, 38-39) and **Shobak Castle** (Brown 1988: figs. 11: 2-7, 10-15; 12: 16-26). It also seems pertinent to note that the assemblage from el-Wuᶜeira consisted almost exclusively of handmade products, with only a half dozen or so sherds of wheel-turned vessels represented. These observations indicate that the proportional increase in production of handmade wares, the increasing diversity of handmade vessel forms, and the development of geometric painting may be found in Fatimid and Crusader contexts, prior to the 13th century.

Of the unpainted handmade vessels represented by Nos. 461-63, bowl rims are shown in Nos. 461-62. No. 461

has a simple thickened rim, and a raised band with thumb impressions is attached to the exterior surface. Other bowls with this plastic treatment are known from: **Tell Abu Qaᶜdan**, Phase L (Franken and Kalsbeek 1975: fig. 74: 24); **Dhiban** (Tushingham 1972: fig. 8: 6, 8); **Abu Thawab** (Coughenour 1976: pl. XXXII, 2: top row, left; fourth row, left and center); and **Jerusalem, Damascus Gate** (Wightman 1989: pl. 50: 9-10). A painted example is found at **Tell Ḥesban** (Sauer 1973: fig. 4: 150) and variations of this form are documented at **Khirbet Faris** (Johns et al. 1989: fig. 25: 27) and **Amman, Citadel** (Northedge 1984: fig. 79: 7). The heavy, crudely made bowl represented by sherd No. 462 is not specifically paralleled, as is often the case with handmade vessels of this period. However, the thick everted rim and sloping vessel walls are similar to large basin forms at **Qubeibeh** (Bagatti 1947: fig. 30: 8-9).

The distinctly squared jar or jug rim shown in No. 463 has a well fired fabric containing dense mineral inclusions, and a light red exterior slip. Although parallels are not evident in the literature, a number of identical or very similar rims were collected from several sites on the Kerak plateau with heavy concentrations of Ayyubid-Mamluk pottery. Additional instances are observed in the assemblage from Kerak Castle (unpublished), which consisted of a large cache of ceramics dating from the 13th to the 15th centuries. A rectangular impression stamped on the rim of No. 463 (not illustrated) consists of six tiny squares arranged in two rows of three each. Most of the other rim fragments of this type in the survey assemblage bear insignia as well, either stamped or incised, though as yet no two rims share the same markings. While these jars may have had an industrial function, it is also possible that they were used for transport and storage of a particular commodity. Thus, the insignia could refer to the nature of the contents, a volume, or a weight. Yet perhaps more plausible is the notion that the markings identified individual consumers. In this case, the supplier could ensure that the jar was filled with the desired quantity of the product (perhaps honey, sugar, or olive oil) and returned to the right customer, as indicated on the vessel rim.

Handmade painted wares of the 13th to 15th centuries are illustrated in Nos. 464-75. These wares are widely attested throughout Transjordan and, although published studies are still relatively few, there are several important contributions, e.g., **Tell Ḥesban** (Sauer 1973), **Pella** (Smith 1973), **Tell Abu Qaᶜdan** (Franken and Kalsbeek 1975), and **Khirbet Faris** (Johns et al. 1989), as well as numerous smaller presentations. Similarly, these vessels are well known from many contexts in Palestine, among them: **Abu Gosh** (de Vaux and Stève 1950); **ᶜAfula** (Dothan 1955); **ᶜAtlit** (Johns 1936); **ᶜAin as-Siyah** (Pringle 1984); **al-Burj al-Ahmar**, Phases C-F (Pringle 1986); **Jerusalem, Damascus Gate** (Wightman 1989); and **Tell Jemmeh** (Schaefer 1989). These vessels are also known from sites in central and south Syria: **Bosra** (Berthier 1985); **Hama** (Riis and Poulsen 1957); and **Qasr al-Hayr ash-Sharqi** (Grabar et al. 1978).

The painted patterns illustrated in Nos. 464-75 show a few of the design elements and motifs that typically occur on handmade wares, some of which are recorded in the large corpus from **Tell Abu Qaᶜdan** (Franken and Kalsbeek 1975: figs. 51-73). The elements and their various combinations are numerous, and a comparative discussion of each design set noted among the sherds in this sample is beyond the scope of the present review. Thus, with respect to the painted body sherds, only a few general observations are offered. Fuller discussions of decorative styles have been provided by Sauer (1973: 55-56) and Franken and Kalsbeek (1975: 168-75).

Nos. 464-65 show profiles of common tall-necked jars or jugs. Linear and geometric painted designs usually cover the entire exterior surface of these vessels, including the handle. This form is quite well documented and occurs in various sizes, either as a single handle jug or a two handle jar, and normally accompanied by a flat or concave disc base (see No. 477, below). Examples of whole jars and jugs of this type have appeared at many sites. In Palestine these include: **Abu Gosh** (de Vaux and Stève 1950: pl. F: 1-2); **al-Burj al-Ahmar**, Phase C (Pringle 1986: fig. 42: 7); **Samaria** (Crowfoot et al. 1957: fig. 84a: 9); **Beisan** (Fitzgerald 1931: pl. XXV: 2), and **Mt. Tabor** (Battista and Bagatti 1976: pl. 28: 1, top row, center). Syrian examples are found at **Hama** (Riis and Poulsen 1957: 273) and **Qasr al-Hayr ash-Sharqi** (Grabar et al. 1978: D: 1a). In Transjordan complete examples of these vessels have been published from **el-ᶜAl** (Reed 1972: fig. 5: center), **Dhiban** (Winnett and Reed 1964: pls. 54: 1; 64: 10), and **Pella** (Smith 1973: pl. 73: 24). Fragments are attested at: **Tell Abu Qaᶜdan** (Franken and Kalsbeek 1975: fig. 51 ff.); **Amman, Citadel** (Northedge 1984: fig. 79: 5; Olávarri-Goicoechea 1985: fig. 54: 10, 13); **Dhiban** (Tushingham 1972: figs. 7: 33; 8: 18); **Tell Ḥesban** (Sauer 1973: fig. 4: 153-157); **Khirbet Ain Jenin** (Hart 1987: fig. 17: 1-2); **Khirbet Faris** (Johns et al. 1989: fig. 25: 28, 31-32, 34); **Shobak Castle** (Brown 1988: fig. 14: 47-48); and **el-Wuᶜeira** (Brown 1987: fig. 10: 31). The general chronological parameters set by these examples span from the 12th century to probable post-15th century contexts. No. 464 has a splayed neck, and a strap handle with a common rectangular section joins the shoulder and neck, as illustrated from **Jersualem**, **Damascus Gate** (Wightman 1989: pl. 53: 12). The specific rim style of No. 464 may be paralleled in many contexts, including **Tell Ḥesban** (Sauer 1973: fig. 4: 153-156) and **Dhiban** (Tushingham 1972: fig. 7: 33). Decoration extending to the handle of the vessel is also common, e.g. **Amman, Citadel** (Olávarri-Goicoechea 1985: fig. 54: 10) and **Jerusalem, Damascus Gate** (Wightman 1989: pl. 53: 9-14). The more sharply splayed rim of No. 465 may be compared with **Tell Ḥesban** (Sauer 1973: fig. 4: 153).

Body sherds from handmade painted wares are presented in Nos. 466-75. Sherd No. 466 has the stump of a decorated horizontal loop handle. This style of handle occurs on unpainted kraters at **Dhiban** (Tushingham 1972: fig. 7: 35, 52), while painted examples have been observed at **ᶜAyn el-Basha** (unpublished). No. 467 shows an oblique band of enclosed and opposing scrolls, while No. 468 displays a common series of wavy lines, as also found at **Tell Abu Qaᶜdan** (Franken and Kalsbeek 1975: fig. 58: 21). Checkerboard patterns are frequent, and No. 469 shows a variation of this pattern with enclosed scrolls. The dot-and-net pattern of No. 470 may be compared with examples from **Khirbet el-Minyeh** (Grabar et al. 1960: pl. 30: 6), **ᶜAfula** (Dothan 1955: fig. 5: 11), and **Pella** (Smith 1973: pl. 73: 24). The dot- in-checkerboard pattern of No. 471 is found at: **Khirbet el-Mefjer** (Baramki 1944: fig. 14: 1); **el-Wuᶜeira** (Brown 1987: fig. 10: 31); and **Shunat Nimrin** (Piccirillo 1982: pl. CX: 2, bottom row, right). No. 472, a bichrome painted sherd, is exceptional for the precision of design execution and the closeness of the elements. The scroll, or sequence of spirals, is one of the most common and enduring elements in the repertoire; among innumerable examples are pieces from **Tell Ḥesban** (Sauer 1973: fig. 4: 149, 153, 158) and **Tell Abu Qaᶜdan**, Phases H-O and Q-T (Franken and Kalsbeek 1975). The diamond-net pattern in the lower portion of No. 472 is also found at **Tell Ḥesban** (Sauer 1973: fig. 4: 151, 160) and **Tell Abu Qaᶜdan**, Phases H, J-L, O, Q (Franken and Kalsbeek 1975: numerous examples). No. 473 shows a simple checkerboard within a feathered triangle. The large diamond spiral shown on No. 474 is noted at **Dhiban** (Winnett and Reed 1964: pl. 64: 9) and **Tell Abu Qaᶜdan**, Phases H, K, S (Franken and Kalsbeek 1975: numerous examples). The star element on No. 475 is not particularly common, but a parallel example occurs at **Abu Gosh** (de Vaux and Stève 1950: fig. F: 19).

The fragmentary nature of these designs as they are found on sherds, and the repetition of a broad range of elements within a vast set of possible design combinations, pose difficulties in analytical attempts to determine whether the use of specific elements and designs can be monitored chronologically. Nevertheless, Franken and Kalsbeek have observed that the painted wares at Tell Abu Qaᶜdan show a clear degeneration in the quality of design execution during the later phases of occupation (1975: 199). The large corpus of Ayyubid-Mamluk painted pottery from the Kerak plateau sites also shows a broad qualitative spectrum with regard to design execution. Yet the extent to which these observations can be linked to temporal trends remains to be systematically investigated.

Of the remaining unpainted handmade wares (Nos. 476-77), the large elephant-eared handle No. 476 is of a coarse poorly fired fabric that contains numerous mineral inclusions. These handles were primarily associated with globular closed cooking pots of the Ayyubid-Mamluk period and have been found with many stylistic variations at **Tell Ḥesban** (Sauer 1973: 56), **Pella** (Smith 1973: pls. 76: 917, 905,; 77: 821, 483), and a number of sites in Palestine (Sauer 1973: 56; Crowfoot 1932). These handles are not, however, confined to Ayyubid-Mamluk sequences, and examples such as No. 476 could post-date the 15th century. Crowfoot's comparative study (1932) of medieval cooking pots and cooking pots manufactured in Palestine during the early 20th century demonstrates that the same styles have persisted through the Ottoman centuries and into the Modern Era. However, recent study of handmade 20th century cooking pots from northern Transjordan indicates that the elephant-ear handle is not common among these vessels (Mershen 1985: 77; fig. 10).

The concave disc base pictured in No. 477 is a common feature of Ayyubid-Mamluk handmade vessels, e.g. **Tell Ḥesban** (Sauer 1973: fig. 4: 159), although flat bases occur frequently as well. The diameter of base No. 477 indicates that it belonged to a large vessel, possibly a bowl or basin, although this style of base is particularly common among jugs and jars. A variety of these bases have occurred throughout the medieval layers at **Tell Abu Qaᶜdan**, Phases H/J-O, Q-T (Franken and Kalsbeek 1975: numerous examples).

Discussion: Ayyubid-Mamluk. From the time of the widespread adoption of the potter's wheel in the Levant there has always remained some percentage of vessels that were made by hand. From the Hellenistic through the Early Islamic periods the dichotomy between wheel-thrown vessels, which constituted the majority of ceramics, and handmade vessels was primarily functional. Large vats, basins, and pithoi tended to be hand-constructed, while virtually all other household ceramics were wheel-thrown. During the Ayyubid-Mamluk period this coexistence of wheel-thrown and hand-constructed ceramics continued, yet there were major changes in both the proportions and kinds of vessels manufactured with these techniques. In contrast to the previously established trend, handmade pottery heavily dominates Ayyubid-Mamluk assemblages, while wheel-thrown wares play a much lesser role. Further contrast is emphasized by the fact that the same general repertoire of forms was produced by both technologies. Although this is not apparent among the rural plateau assemblages, excavations and survey collection at Kerak Castle (Brown 1989; and unpublished) show that a full range of wheel-thrown plain wares was produced, in addition to the common wheel-thrown glazed wares that are represented in the assemblages from the sites documented on the Kerak plateau. Thus, by the inception of the 13th century, the association between (1) manufacturing techniques, and (2) specific vessel forms, which had long characterized ceramic manufacture in the southern Levant, is no longer evident.

There is a sharp qualitative distinction between the assemblages that represent these two principal technologies. The distinct contrasts in the quality of fabric preparation, firing, and technology employed in surface decoration reflect not only disparate levels of expertise, but different commitments to investment in raw materials and equipment. Thus, the predominant handmade wares appear to represent a low-cost consumer option, for these vessels were produced with fewer capital investments than required for the manufacture of wheel-thrown glazed wares. The vast quantity of handmade wares and the diversity of fabrics and firing techniques that they reflect indicate that numerous different clay resources as well as different clay preparation and firing practices were employed by many potters. It may also be inferred that these vessels were easily obtained from village or household producers, or through local marketing and exchange systems. In contrast, the wheel-thrown and molded wares required higher levels of skill, capital investment, and access to specific raw materials; and these products are less frequently encountered in archaeological surveys of rural sites in many regions, including the Kerak plateau. Regardless as to whether these, possibly mass-produced, wheel-thrown wares were manufactured in the immediate vicinity, the lower density of sherds and the higher production costs associated with wheel-throwing and glazing technologies, in addition to likely costs of transportation, indicate that wheel-thrown wares were less readily available to the population than the handmade wares.

It would appear, therefore, that qualitative distinctions between handmade and wheel-thrown ceramic vessels, and the replication of forms within the assemblages of these two very different production technologies, underscore socio-economic distinctions. It may be hypothesized that wheel-turned and handmade vessels were distributed in different social and economic spheres, and functioned in different social contexts within the household. Low household purchasing power, either based on currency or in the form of reciprocal exchange, may have restricted access to glazed serving vessels or other luxury ceramic items with high social visibility and, consequently, personal status value. At the same time, the archaeological record suggests that handmade pottery was available in abundance.

Most of the Ayyubid-Mamluk sherds presented in this section are either handmade or wheel-thrown wares that are commonly found throughout the Kerak plateau region. However, the preliminary observations under discussion are also based on a highly distinct 13th-15th century assemblage recovered during the 1982 surface survey within Kerak Castle (unpublished). Comparisons between this corpus and the more typical assemblages on the plateau may further illustrate the relationship between ceramics and patterns of consumption pertaining to socio-economic status during this period. The proportions of ceramic types within the Kerak Castle corpus represent the inverse of the proportions of types described for the rural sites on the Kerak plateau. Of the over 2,000 13th-15th century sherds collected during the survey of the castle, wheel-thrown glazed bowls, and plain wares of a wide variety of forms constitute the great majority of the assemblage, while handmade wares are relatively few. The assemblage also displays a complete repertoire of vessel forms among the wheel-thrown wares, rather than the more typical presence of only glazed bowl fragments, as observed among the rural plateau sites.

In addition to these southern Levantine wares, the Kerak Castle assemblage contains dozens of fragments of imported wares of at least six distinct types dated to the Mamluk period. Among these are fragments of: (1) Lu'ang Ch'uan celadons from China, comparable to Fustat (Scanlon 1971: 228; Scanlon 1984: pl. 2); (2) imitation celadons, of at least two categories, comparable to Fustat (Scanlon 1971: 230; Scanlon 1984: pls. 3, 4); (3) white slip-trailed under green glaze, comparable to Fustat (Scanlon 1971: 229; Scanlon 1984: 118-119); (4) polychrome underglaze sgraffito, comparable to Fustat (Scanlon 1984: pl. 16: center row, left); (5) blue and black painted on white, of Egyptian and Syrian manufacture, comparable to Fustat (Scanlon 1984: pls. 10-12; see also Jenkins 1984), Qasr al-Hayr ash-Sharqi (Grabar et al. 1978: G7: 5b-14), and Hama (Riis and Poulsen 1957: nos. 417, 475-477); and (6) "Rusafa" ware, comparable to Hama (Riis and Poulsen 1957: 614). Aside from perhaps a dozen fragments in total, these wares are not represented in the survey assemblages from other sites on the Kerak plateau.

The Kerak Castle material constitutes a distinctly elite and cosmopolitan corpus that directly pertains to the role of this site as a periodic residence for self-exiled and deposed Mamluk sultans, as well as heirs to the sultanate (Gaudefroy-Demombynes 1923; Peake 1958; Shäfer 1971; see also Brown 1989). Clearly these royal inhabitants and their entourages maintained a life-style that included consumption of both local and foreign luxury ceramics that are either virtually unattested in the assemblages from other sites on the Kerak plateau, or are represented in very low proportions.

The complex diversity within the Ayyubid-Mamluk corpus from the Kerak region and the relationship of this diversity to production technologies are by no means fully understood. Yet preliminary inferences suggest a correlation between these technologies and the socio-economic patterns of consumption that influenced the distribution of ceramics across the landscape during the late medieval period. The wealth of data from Kerak Castle adds to the perspective gained from the rural Kerak plateau assemblages by providing valuable insights into the distribution of ceramics in different social and economic contexts within this society.

Ottoman-Early Modern and Modern

This section treats a few examples of pottery from the Ottoman and Early Modern periods as well as fragments of distinctly Modern products. The handmade wares that characterize assemblages from the 16th to the early 20th centuries are still manufactured in a few villages today, though production has been rapidly decreasing. This genre of ceramics is discussed in a sub-section on Ottoman-Early Modern pottery, whereas other ceramic types that are more specifically associated with the second half of the 20th century are presented in a sub-section of Modern pottery.

A review of Modern pottery holds obvious advantages, for the role of these vessels in contemporary Jordan may be observed directly, and examples recovered in archaeological survey very seldom present ambiguities in identification. However, the ceramic tradition from the 16th to the early 20th century is more difficult to assess. In this respect, unresolved issues stem from a lack of controlled data from Ottoman period sites and give rise to questions regarding the eventual discontinuation of ceramic types that were prevalent from the 13th to the 15th centuries.

A paucity of controlled data has constrained typological analyses of pottery from the 16th century to the Modern Era. Not a single one-period site within this time frame has been the object of controlled archaeological excavation in Transjordan. Of the excavated multi-period sites that include occupations within the scope of Ottoman hegemony, the results of investigations of these latter occupations have, unfortunately, been limited, e.g. Umm el-Jimal (Parker forthcoming d); Khirbet Faris (Johns et al. 1989); Kerak Castle (Brown n.d.a.; Brown 1989); and Shobak Castle (Brown 1988). Similar ambiguities have been encountered in Palestine as well, e.g. al-Burj al-Ahmar (Pringle 1986). Despite the frequent availability of historical, ethno-historical, and architectural data, the problems of characterizing 16th to early 20th century occupations stem from interrelated factors, including: (1) a general lack of absolute dating that may be due to low levels of hard currency circulation in rural Transjordan during this period; (2) the absence of clear criteria with which to differentiate residual sherds from those contemporary with their stratigraphic context; and (3) difficulties in establishing consistently reliable diagnostic traits within the variable and enduring handmade assemblage that, ultimately, traces its origins to the 11th century.

At present there is little data with which to describe the decline of the 13th to 15th centuries' wheel-thrown ceramic industry, other than in very general terms. During the 15th century Syria ceased to produce luxury wheel-thrown glazed wares (Lapidus 1984: 33), which had been exported to Transjordan and other regions. Aside from these fine wares, it appears that all other wheel-thrown ceramics also dropped out of the ceramic repertoire in Transjordan sometime after the 15th century. Among the handmade vessels, the geometric painting style was also discontinued, probably through gradual and subtle changes that constituted a long term trend toward simpler, less labor-intensive designs. Franken and Kalsbeek (1975) observed a qualitative degeneration of handmade painted wares, including a diminished coherence among geometric patterns and an increasing application of more schematic and cursory painted decorations, during the last occupation phases at Tell Abu Qa[c]dan. However, Falkner has suggested (in Johns et al. 1989: 89) that the Khirbet Faris sequence may demonstrate the continuation of "Ayyubid-Mamluk" handmade painted wares during the Ottoman period. Similarly, handmade geometric painted wares also occur in strata that appear to date to the Ottoman period at: Umm el-Jimal (Parker forthcoming d); Shobak Castle (Brown 1988: 240); and Kerak Castle (Brown 1989: table 2; Brown n.d.a.: 25-26). Yet clear chronological documentation for the dissolution of the geometric painted style has yet to emerge. Later studies of 20th century handmade village pottery indicate that, in cases where paint has been applied (e.g. Mershen 1985: fig. 2), the design styles are not comparable with the geometric patterns well attested during the 13th to 15th centuries, except in a very broad generic sense. Therefore, while conclusions remain tenuous, it appears that handmade pottery continued to be produced from the 16th century on and that at some point the painting styles shifted away from the elaborate geometric frameworks that had previously dominated this repertoire.

Despite the relative obscurity that veils the history of ceramics in their archaeological contexts from the 15th century through the early 20th century, several important ethnographic works have provided a basic framework for investigating late 19th to 20th century assemblages. Among these are: Gatt's notes on the ceramic industry of Gaza (1885); G. M. Crowfoot's ethno-archaeological pottery study (1932); Dalman's well illustrated descriptive ethnographies of the 1930s and 1940s (1964, 1971); and Mershen's recent ethnographic studies of contemporary ceramic production in villages of north Jordan (1985, 1987). Additional resources are cited in the bibliographies of these works.

The developmental history of Modern pottery in Transjordan differs from that of Palestine. While handmade production continued into the 20th century in both regions, the production of Modern wheel-thrown wares began earlier in Palestine. By the late 19th century, several Palestinian towns were producing wheel-thrown pottery of a variety of forms (Gatt 1885), and among these the products of Gaza are particularly distinctive for their dark grey ware and black surfaces. While some of these vessels appeared on the East Bank, the development of a Transjordanian wheel-thrown industry did not take place until after 1948-49, when Palestinian refugee potters established small workshops (Sauer pers. comm.; see also Homes-Fredericq and Franken 1986: 244-48). At the same time there was a rapid increase in the availability of inexpensive imported coffee cups and table wares without functional equivalents among the products of the local wheel-thrown repertoire.

Description and Forms: Ottoman-Early Modern. Aside from the problems posed by the apparent high diversity among these handmade assemblages and the lack of comparative corpora, tentative identifications may be offered on the basis of vessel shapes, handles and other attributes, and to some extent aspects of manufacture. This sample includes a few pieces from handmade vessels and one sherd belonging to a wheel-turned vessel.

In general, handmade pottery from this period is technologically poor, and, while painted and molded decorations do occur, no examples are included here. Cooking pot No. 478 and handles Nos. 479-80 exhibit rudimentary technological skills and very basic resources of manufacture. Minimal vessel surface finishing is demonstrated by the deep finger impressions left on the neck and interior surface of cooking pot No. 478, and the crude formation of handles Nos. 479-80. Thick black cores and coarse fabrics characterize each of these pieces. Mineral tempers and often large quantities of organic temper are typical. Chaff-pocked surfaces, as exhibited by Nos. 478 and 480, are also common. Nos. 478 and 479 retain traces of a light slip.

The neck and shoulder profile of the globular cooking pot illustrated in No. 478 represent a form that can be traced to cooking pots associated with the Mamluk period, **Pella** (Smith 1973: pls. 76-77; see also Sauer 1974: 172). A similar cooking pot, attributed to Ottoman occupation, is noted at **Dhiban** (Tushingham 1972: fig. 8: 4), and Crowfoot's study of Early Modern village cooking pots (1932) indicates that this vessel continued into the 20th century as well. Cooking pot handles are shown in Nos. 479-80. The triangular-shaped handle No. 479 was horizontally attached to the vessel wall, and tilted upward to facilitate lifting. Similar cooking pot handles, pierced through the center, are found among early 20th century village assemblages of Palestine (Crowfoot 1932: pl. III: fig. 10; Dalman 1971: pl. 98). The cone-shaped handle No. 480 may also belong to a cooking pot, though this style may be less common than the triangular handle.

An example of wheel-thrown pottery of the type produced in **Gaza** during the late 19th century and into the Modern period (Gatt 1885; see also Rye 1981: fig. 2) is shown in rim No. 481. This grey-ware sherd represents a tall-necked, bag-shaped water jar that is documented among household ceramic assemblages in Palestinian villages during the early 20th century (Dalman 1964: pl. 49), and occasionally in Transjordan (Mershen 1985: fig. 1). Very few fragments of Gaza-ware vessels are represented in the Kerak plateau survey corpus. Other Palestinian wares that appear in Transjordan include the highly distinctive handmade vessels from Sinjil, which were decorated with white slip and red-painted designs consisting of a specific set of motifs. Thus far, no sherds of Sinjil-ware have been identified in the survey collection. It seems, therefore, that the Kerak region was not a beneficiary of the exchange spheres in which these Palestinian commodities were distributed.

Discussion: Ottoman-Early Modern. The most pivotal change in the ceramics of rural Transjordan during this period is the disappearance of wheel-thrown products some time after the 15th century and prior to the availability of late 19th to 20th century wheel-thrown wares from Gaza or other Palestinian towns. The corollary to this development was the emergence of what appear to have been exclusively local handmade assemblages. This transition to fully handmade ceramics, which reflect only very basic manufacturing skills, appears anomalous given the long developmental history of wheel-thrown ceramics in Transjordan, and in particular the high levels of expertise that characterized the wheel-thrown industries of the 13th through 15th centuries. The implications of this transition are many and cannot be fully explored in this context, although preliminary observations suggest a few socio-economic factors that may have encouraged this trend, including: (1) constraints on the production of wheel-thrown vessels; (2) a decrease in consumer demand; and (3) a breakdown of distribution and or marketing institutions.

Although a number of circumstances could have discouraged production of wheel-thrown vessels during this period, the decline in production may have been influenced, although perhaps only partially, by imperial taxation of potters' wheels or ceramic products throughout the Ottoman provinces, as suggested by Adams (1979: 732) whose studies of pottery in the Nubian province show a trend similar to that of Transjordan. But the potential impact of local socio-economic conditions in rural Transjordan may be considered as well. Specifically, the Kerak region experienced a decrease in sedentary occupation, as well as economic isolation, during the Ottoman centuries, and these factors probably encouraged greater household self-sufficiency with respect to subsistence and production of basic material items.

16th century Ottoman fiscal records (Hütteroth 1975; Hütteroth and Abdulfattah 1977) show a smaller number of settlements and lower population statistics for the Kerak region than might be anticipated. It could be argued that these figures probably under-represent the actual extent of 16th century settlement in the Kerak area. Nevertheless, even if taken at face value, it is apparent from Burckhardt's (1822) accounts that by the early 19th century there were so few settlements in the region as to represent a significant decline in comparison with the 16th century data.

Local political conditions in Transjordan during this period also may have played a role, for regional trade and communications appear to have been severely restricted during the late Ottoman period. Travelers and tribal historians portray the Kerak plateau as an isolated region whose natural geographic barriers became even more intimidating as local political and economic competition erupted giving rise to opposing coalitions of powerful tribes battling for supremacy over the town of Kerak and its hinterland (Forder 1902; Peake 1958; Gubser 1973). These historical events, and the accounts of witnesses, indicate that inter-regional trade was frequently disrupted and communications were so poor that messages between Kerak and Jerusalem could take months (Hill 1891). In this context, the shipment of bulky and fragile ceramics to Kerak on animal backs certainly would have been a high-risk and low-profit venture, and therefore it is not surprising that very few pieces of Gaza-ware are attested in the survey assemblage.

In summary, it appears that demand for wheel-thrown products was sharply curtailed by a decrease in sedentary population and internal political circumstances that would discourage overland transport of ceramics. These conditions probably fostered household production of ceramics and other items, for self-reliance must have been essential to much of the population of the Kerak region, at least during the 19th century.

Description and Forms: Modern. Modern Jordanian pottery consists of wheel-thrown wares produced by specialized workshops, such as those found in Karameh, Marsa, Zarka, Zizia, and Rusafa, and imported wares from Southeast Asia that can be purchased in urban centers as well as village shops. The handmade pottery tradition of the Ottoman period has endured in a few villages (Mershen 1985; Mershen 1987), but these vessels constitute a very small proportion of the Modern assemblage.

The small, saucerless cup pictured in No. 482 is a typical import. These inexpensive cups, which are mass-produced by slip-molded or similar modern techniques, are common household items in Jordan and used for serving unsweetened Arabian coffee.

Sherds Nos. 483-84 represent vessels that are mass-produced in modern Jordanian workshops. Rim No. 483 belongs to a painted flowerpot or large vase. The fabric of this sherd is gritty and the coarse paste contains small and medium-sized inclusions. The surface is spalled, and small mineral inclusions protrude through the paint, leaving a rough surface. The process of decorating this vessel was undertaken in four steps: (1) white enamel was painted over the exterior body; (2) the enamel was covered with a thin layer of brown paint; (3) the painted surface was varied by hand prints, particularly of the palm and fingers; and (4) once dried, the painted surface was then coated with a clear lacquer. An elongated collar rim from a deep vase without painted decoration is shown in No. 484. This wheel-thrown vessel is commonly used as a flowerpot and is particularly frequent in households of urban centers and small towns. The pink fabric is rough-textured but better prepared and fired than that of No. 483.

The paste of painted body sherd No. 485 is among the better quality Modern fabrics found in Jordan. It is similar to that of No. 484, but the surface is spalled. The decoration on this sherd consists of a bright canary yellow exterior surface with thin overlying stripes of green, blue, and white. The thinness of the stripes and blending of colors across the surface were achieved by adding powdered paint to a bucket of water and spinning the vessel in the bucket. Only a few examples of this particular decoration were found among the survey corpus. Observations, and conversations with merchants marketing wheel-thrown pottery in road-side stands, indicate that this painting technique is applied only to simple bi-conical musical drums.

The painted and unpainted vases shown in Nos. 483-84, and the unusual painted decoration of No. 485, can be put into broader perspective with a brief review of recent developments in the Modern industry of wheel-thrown ceramic manufacture and marketing in Jordan (Brown n.d.b.). Vases, as well as *zirs*, *ibriks*, and a few other basic utilitarian forms have been available in Jordan since the development of local workshops specializing in wheel-thrown pottery. Painted vases, however, were not common until the late 1970s, and at that time the painted repertoire consisted almost exclusively of either plain monochrome decorated vessels or monochrome painted vessels with hand prints, often of one or two colors that contrasted with the overall surface paint. During the following decade the popularity of painted wares increased dramatically. At the same time the range of vessel forms increased manifold to include even miniature replications of the larger traditional forms, which are highly portable and can be sold to tourists or as children's toys. Paint is now applied to all of these forms, although unpainted pieces of a wide range of types are also available. The 1980s also brought a tremendous expansion in painted designs, the repertoire of colors applied, and the combinations of colors used on a single vessel. These vary from subtle artistic scenes combining a few delicate motifs such as hearts, flowers, birds, palm trees, and bands of simple geometric-designed panel borders to more schematic experiments employing bold combinations of primary colors, in addition to the, now traditional, vessels decorated only with hand-print patterns.

These developments show that ceramic items, previously of purely functional intent, now offer decorative value as well, and with the expansion of painted styles and vessel repertoire the consumer base within which to market these vessels has broadened considerably. Thus, from the cautious experiments of a few among a handful of roadside ceramic merchants there developed an entirely new genre of ceramic folk art that is now displayed at a growing number of roadside stands, particularly in the more heavily populated and trafficked areas of central Jordan. While during the previous decades one may have reasonably predicted a decline in the wheel-thrown industry due to the increasing availability of piped water and inexpensive containers of plastic and metal, in fact the industry has diversified to create a new market for ceramics as decorative items, and hence unleashed a strong competition among roadside merchants seeking to provide fresh and appealing color schemes, while the potters continue to supply new and innovative forms.

Discussion: Modern. There are approximately sixty modern villages and settlements on the Kerak plateau, all of which were included in the survey. Yet the proportion of Modern sherds within the Kerak corpus is smaller than might be expected given the contemporary population. The majority of these sherds from wheel-thrown vessels produced in Jordan represent a narrow range of vessel types. Observations of rural households indicate that several factors may pertain to this distribution. Prior to the developments of the 1980s, locally manufactured wheel-thrown pottery had a very specific and limited role within household assemblages. The most common vessels included *ibriks*, large *zirs* for water storage, and large vases and flower pots that accommodated household plants. Open bowls and cooking pots constituted a much smaller proportion of the contemporary wares and were seldom observed in domestic contexts. Of these vessel types, the *zirs* and vases have relatively low mobility, compared with serving vessels, and may have low breakage rates as well. Thus, the limited functions of these ceramic vessels, and possibly low replacement rates, may influence the patterns that emerge in the archaeological record. This limited repertoire of locally produced containers is enhanced by imported ceramics that fill a range of functions for which local products are not intended. In village households these socially visible items include coffee cups, tea cups with saucers, bowls of various sizes, and small plates for serving fruit and sweets to guests.

The limited functions of ceramics in the Modern Era is also linked to the use of non-ceramic containers that are either locally produced or have otherwise been available in Jordan for many years, and household assemblages tend to be complex mixtures of items manufactured from a variety of materials. These include highly mobile, but durable, vessels such as: thick pyrex tea glasses; trays and bowls of metal, wood, or plastic; metal tea pots; and woven baskets. Many rural households, especially those of tent dwellers, rely on plastics, some of which have replaced ceramic containers. Most notably, the plastic *ibrik* is often substituted for the heavier, more fragile, ceramic prototype, and plastic jerry cans may be found instead of the large *zirs*. Therefore, the circumscribed role of modern ceramics within contemporary rural households compares well with the representation of these sherds in the survey corpus.

The dynamic nature of pottery is reflected in its shifting role within the material culture repertoire, as is well illustrated by Jordanian patterns of usage that have developed over the last half century. The functional differentiation between imported wares and locally manufactured wares, the rapid incorporation of innovations, the diversity of ratios between ceramic and non-ceramic containers within household assemblages, and the changes in these ratios through time, are all trends that are linked to the local and regional economic structures of contemporary Jordan. Yet these patterns and the processes that motivate them are by no means purely Modern phenomena.

Ware Descriptions

Column 1 indicates the sherd number as presented in the plates on pages 271-79; column 2 indicates the site number (if applicable) and field number for the pottery sampling; column 3 indicates the sherd's registration number. There is no site number corresponding to the following field numbers, since the samplings are from places not treated in the numbered site descriptions.

Field no. 2124 = Um el-Khanazir on a shelf of the north bank of Wadi el-Ḥesa (sherd no. 481).

Field no. 9280 = Khaif in Wadi Ibn-Hammad (sherd no. 10)

Field no. 9282 = Krashea in Wadi Ibn-Hammad (sherd no. 400)

Field no. 9287 = An unnamed site in Wadi Ibn-Hammad. PG: 11.1/77.6; UTMG: 51.0/65.2 (sherd nos. 311, 313, 316, 317, 319, 322, 328, 341, 348, 380, 388, 403, 410)

Field no. 9029 = Sherds collected along a roadway bed. From PG: 22.1/78.0 to PG: 22.6/79.5; UTMG: 63.0/67.0 to 62.5/65.5. (sherd nos. 247, 304, 415)

The ware descriptions include observations arranged in the following sequence: ware color; surface treatment color, including slip, paint, and glaze; inclusion size and type; and core presence or absence. Color descriptions are based on the Munsell Color Charts (Munsell 1975), with the exception of the glazes and some of the paints. The inclusion-size category expresses the predominate size of inclusions. Where more than one size is listed, the first size reflects a higher percentage of inclusions than the second. Inclusion size was measured in accordance with the scale cited in Glock (1975: 18). The following abbreviations appear in the ware descriptions: ext = exterior; incl = inclusions; int = interior; lg = large; med = medium; min = mineral; org = organic; sm = small. The majority of the sherd drawings were provided by Abed Raziq Yousef, and additional drawings were contributed by Thomas C. Webster, Carol Powers, and Lynn Ploss.

CHALCOLITHIC: Plate 1 (sherds 1-15)

Sh.#	Site/field#	Reg.#	Form	Diameter	Description
1	210/2303	597	bowl	27	5YR 6/1 grey; incl. med., min., org.; no core
2	294/2028	2187	bowl	30	5YR 7/4 pink; incl. lg., min.; core
3	294/2028	2189	hole-mouth vessel	14	7.5 YR 7/4 pink; paint 10R 6/4 pale red; incl. lg., min.; no core
4	210/2303	598	jar	15	5YR 6/1 grey; slip 5YR 6/4 light reddish brown; incl. med., min., org.; core
5	73/9072	5147	jar	12	7.5 YR 7/4 pink; slip 5YR 6/1 grey; incl. lg., min.; core
6	227/9060	4797	jar	25	5YR 6/4 light reddish brown; incl. med., min.; core
7	227/9065	4923	jar	10	7.5YR 7/4 pink; incl. med., min.; no core
8	71/9112	5823	base sherd		10YR 5/1 grey; slip 10YR 6/3 pale brown; incl. med., min.; no core
9	132/9160	7179	base sherd		5YR 7/4 pink; incl. lg., min.; no core
10	9280	8179	body sherd		5YR 6/4 light reddish brown; slip 7.5YR 7/2 pinkish grey; incl. med., min.; core

11	349/2358	1065	body sherd		7.5YR 6/4 light brown; incl. med., min., org.; core
12	294/2028	2176	body sherd		5YR 7/4 pink; incl. med., min.; no core
13	294/2028	2184	body sherd		5YR 7/2 pinkish grey; paint 10R 6/6 light red; incl. med., min.; core
14	294/2028	2167	body sherd		5YR 6/4 light reddish brown; slip 7.5YR 6/4 light brown; incl. med., min; core
15	101/9049	4505	body sherd		10YR 8/2 white; incl. med., min.; no core

EARLY BRONZE I: Plate 1 (sherds 16-41)

Sh.#	Site/field#	Reg.#	Form	Diameter	Description
16	73/9072	5138	bowl	24	5YR 7/4 pink; incl. med., lg., min.; no core
17	132/9160	8762	bowl	?	5YR 7/4 pink; slip 10R 6/6 light red; incl. med., min.; no core
18	73/9072	5144	bowl	18	5YR 7/6 reddish yellow; incl. med., min.; no core
19	132/9160	8764	bowl	19	7.5YR 8/4 pink; paint 2.5YR 6/4 light reddish brown; incl. med., min.; no core
20	132/9160	8763	bowl	15	5YR 7/4 pink; slip 10R 6/6 light red; incl. med., min.; no core
21	132/9160	8771	bowl	11	5YR 7/4 pink; incl. med., min.; no core
22	132/9160	7182	bowl	16	5YR 7/4 pink; paint 10R 6/4 pale red; incl. med., lg., min.; no core
23	132/9160	7183	bowl	15	5YR 7/4 pink; paint 10R 6/6; light red; incl. med., lg., min.; no core
24	132/9160	8766	bowl	16	5YR 7/4 pink; incl. med., min.; no core
25	239/9066	4974	bowl	18	2.5YR 6/6 light red; paint 2.5YR 6/6 light red; burnish; incl. med., sm., min.; core
26	132/9160	7180	bowl	11	5YR 7/4 pink; paint 2.5YR 6/4 light reddish brown; incl. med., sm., min.; no core
27	132/9160	8768	amphoriskos	5	5YR 8/3 pink; paint 10R 6/6 light red; incl. med., min.; no core
28	132/9160	8767	amphoriskos	5	7.5YR 8/4 pink; paint 10R 6/6 light red; incl. med., min.; no core
29	132/9160	8765	amphoriskos	4	5YR 7/4 pink; slip 2.5YR 6/6 light red; incl. med., min.; no core
30	132/9160	8769	amphoriskos	4	5YR 7/4 pink; slip 2.5YR 6/6 light red; incl. med., sm., min.; no core
31	132/9160	7184	amphoriskos	5	5YR 7/4 pink; incl. med., min.; no core
32	40/9272	7792	hole-mouth vessel	?	5YR 7/4 pink; incl. med., lg., min.; no core
33	132/9160	8770	handle section		5YR 7/4 pink; paint 10R 5/6 red; incl. med., min.; no core

34	40/9272	7794	handle		5YR 7/4 pink; slip 7.5YR 8/2 pinkish white; incl. lg., med., min.; core
35	73/9072	5136	handle		7.5YR 7/4 pink; slip 10YR 8/3 very pale brown; incl. med., min.; core
36	289/2021	1862	handle		7.5YR pink; slip 5YR 8/4 pink; incl. lg., med., min.; no core
37	73/9072	5069	base sherd		5YR 7/3 pink; slip 2.5YR 6/6 light red; incl. lg., min., org.; no core
38	73/9072	5170	base sherd		5YR 7/4 pink; incl. lg., med., min.; no core
39	73/9047	4257	body sherd		5YR 7/4 pink; paint 10R 5/6 red; incl. med., sm., min.; no core
40	73/9072	5172	body sherd		5YR 7/4 pink; paint 10R 5/6 red; incl. med., min.; no core
41	132/9160	8773	body sherd		7.5YR 7/6 reddish yellow; paint 10R 5/6 red; incl. med., min.; no core

EARLY BRONZE II-III: Plate 1 (sherds 42-50) and Plate 2 (sherds 51-74)

Sh.#	Site/field#	Reg.#	Form	Diameter	Description
42	78/9041	4087	platter bowl	23	5YR 7/4 pink; slip 5YR 6/4 light reddish brown; int. burnish; incl. sm., med., min.; no core
43	101/9049	8123	platter bowl	22	5YR 7/4 pink; slip 5YR 4/1 dark grey; burnish; incl. sm., med., min.; no core
44	88/9016	3625	platter bowl	19	5YR 7/4 pink; slip 10R 5/6 red; burnish; incl. med., sm., min.; no core
45	73/9047	4269	platter bowl	24	2.5YR 6/6 light red; slip 10R 5/6 red; burnish; incl. sm., min.; core
46	73/9047	4263	platter bowl	15	2.5YR 6/6 light red; slip 10R 5/6 red; burnish; incl. med., sm., min.; no core
47	101/9049	4487	platter bowl	23	5YR 7/4 pink; slip 10R 6/6 light red; incl. med., sm., min.; no core
48	239/9066	4982	platter bowl	25	10R 6/6 light red; slip ext. 10YR 8/3 very pale brown, int. 10R 6/6 light red; int. burnish; incl. sm., med., min.; core
49	73/9047	4319	bowl	12	5YR 7/4 pink; slip 10R 5/6 red; burnish; incl. med., sm., min.; no core
50	101/9049	8130	bowl	14	5YR 7/4 pink; slip 10R 5/6 red; burnish; incl. sm., med., min.; no core
51	73/9047	4310	bowl	8	5YR 7/4 pink; slip 10R 5/6 red; burnish; incl. med., sm., min.; no core
52	101/9049	4534	cup/bowl	13	5YR 7/4 pink; incl. med., min.; no core
53	88/9016	3639	hole-mouth vessel	17	5YR 6/3 light reddish brown; incl. lg., min.; no core
54	89/9004	2869	hole-mouth vessel	22	5YR 7/4 pink; incl. lg., min.; no core

55	101/9049	4485	hole-mouth vessel	21	5YR 6/4 light reddish brown; incl. lg., min.; no core
56	101/9049	4491	hole-mouth vessel	18	2.5YR 5/4 reddish brown; incl. lg., min; no core
57	333/2307	2855	hole-mouth vessel	17	5YR 6/4 light reddish brown; slip 5YR 7/3 pink; incl. med., min.; no core
58	90/9005	3022	hole-mouth vessel	19	5YR 7/1 light grey; slip 5YR 7/4 pink; incl. med., min.; no core
59	73/9072	5160	jar	17	5YR 7/3 pink; incl. med., sm., min.; no core
60	89/9004	2907	jar	14	5YR 7/4 pink; slip 7.5YR 6/4 light brown; ext. burnish; incl. med., min.; no core
61	88/9016	3591	jar	17	5YR 7/4 pink; slip 2.5YR 6/6 light red; incl. sm., med., min.; no core
62	101/9049	4535	jar	9	5YR 7/3 pink; incl. med., sm., min.; no core
63	88/9016	3595	jar	20	5YR 7/4 pink; slip 5YR 6/6 light reddish brown; incl. med., min.; no core
64	88/9016	3590	jar	15	5YR 7/4 pink; slip 2.5YR 6/4 light reddish brown; incl. med., min.; no core
65	73/9047	4255	base sherd		5YR 7/4 pink; slip 2.5YR 6/6 light red; incl. med., lg., min.; no core
66	101/9049	4542	platter bowl		5YR 7/4 pink; slip 2.5YR 6/4 light reddish brown; burnish; incl. sm., med., min.; no core
67	227/9060	4778	body sherd		5YR 7/4 pink; slip 2.5YR 6/6 light red; ext. burnish; incl. med., min.; no core
68	227/9065	4904	body sherd		2.5YR 6/4 light reddish brown; slip 2.5YR 5/4-5/6 reddish brown; burnish; incl. med., min.; no core
69	40/9272	7791	body sherd		5YR 7/4 pink; slip 5YR 7/6 reddish yellow; incl. med., min.; no core
70	88/9016	3619	body sherd		5YR 7/4 pink; slip 5YR 7/6 reddish yellow; incl. med., min.; no core
71	73/9047	4311	body sherd		5YR 7/6 reddish yellow; slip 2.5YR 6/6 light red; incl. lg., min.; no core
72	239/9066	4998	body sherd		5YR 7/3 pink; slip 5YR 6/6 light reddish brown; incl. sm., min.; no core
73	101/9049	4571	body sherd		5YR 7/3 pink; incl. med., sm., min.; no core
74	88/9016	3630	body sherd		5YR 7/4 pink; incl. lg., min.; core

EARLY BRONZE IV: Plate 2 (sherds 75-102) and Plate 3 (sherds 103-7)

Sh.#	Site/field#	Reg.#	Form	Diameter	Description
75	294/2028	2185	bowl	20	5YR 7/4 pink; slip 2.5YR 6/4 light reddish brown; burnish; incl. med., min.; core

76	73/9072	5140	bowl	45	5YR 7/4 pink; slip 10R 6/4 pale red; incl. med., lg., min.; core
77	294/2028	2186	platter bowl	26	5YR 7/3 pink; slip 10R 5/6 red; incl. sm., med., min.; no core
78	40/9272	7798	platter bowl	18	5YR 7/4 pink; incl. sm., min.; no core
79	88/9016	3638	platter bowl	32	5YR 7/4 pink; slip 10R 5/6 red; incl., sm., min.; no core
80	89/9004	2910	bowl	22	5YR 7/4 pink; slip 10R 6/6 light red; burnish; incl. sm., min.; no core
81	73/9047	4267	bowl	22	5YR 6/4 light reddish brown; slip 10R 5/6 red; incl., sm., med., min.; no core
82	73/9047	4341	jar	?	5YR 7/4 pink; slip 2.5YR 6/6 light red; incl. lg., med., min.; core
83	40/9272	7785	jar	18	5YR 7/4 pink; slip 5YR 6/4 light reddish brown; incl. sm., min.; no core
84	89/9004	2904	jar	18	5YR 7/4 pink; slip 5YR 7/4 pink; incl. sm., med., min.; no core
85	88/9016	3616	hole-mouth vessel	9	5YR 7/4 pink; slip 10R 5/6 red; incl. sm., med., min.; no core
86	227/9060	4798	hole-mouth vessel	8	5YR 7/4 pink; slip 10R 6/6 light red; incl. sm., min.; no core
87	73/9047	4256	hole-mouth vessel	16	5YR 7/4 pink; slip 5YR 6/6 reddish yellow; incl. sm., min.; no core
88	294/2028	2168	jar/jug	13	5YR 7/4 pink; incl. sm., min.; no core
89	88/9016	3649	handle section		5YR 7/4 pink; slip 10R 5/6 red; incl. sm., min; no core
90	88/9016	3656	handle		5YR 7/4 pink; slip 10R 6/6 red; incl. sm., min.; no core
91	227/9065	4929	body sherd		5YR 7/4 pink; slip 5YR 6/6 reddish yellow; burnish; incl. sm., med., min.; core
92	294/2028	2109	body sherd		2.5YR 6/6 light red; slip 7.5YR 7/4 pink; incl. lg., med., min.; no core
93	294/2028	2154	body sherd		5YR 6/6 reddish yellow; slip 2.5YR 6/6 light red; incl. med., min.; no core
94	210/2303	568	cup	14	7.5YR 6/6 reddish yellow; incl. sm., min.; no core
95	294/2028	2137	bowl	17	5YR 6/4 light reddish brown; slip 2.5YR 6/6 light red; incl. sm., min.; no core
96	294/2028	2147	bowl	17	5YR 6/4 light reddish brown; slip 5YR 7/4 pink; incl. med., min.; core
97	294/2028	2139	bowl	17	5YR 6/4 light reddish brown; slip 5YR 6/6 reddish yellow; incl. med., min.; core
98	88/9016	3589	jar	18	5YR 7/4 pink; slip 7.5YR 8/2 pinkish white; incl. sm., med., min.; no core
99	294/2028	2145	base sherd		2.5YR 6/4 light reddish brown; slip 7.5YR 8/2 pinkish white; incl. sm., med., min.; core

100	294/2028	2144	base sherd		5YR 7/4 pink; slip 7.5YR 8/2 pinkish white; incl. med., lg., min.; core
101	294/2028	2136	strainer (?)		5YR 7/4 pink; slip 7.5YR 8/2 pinkish white; incl. med., min.; no core
102	294/2028	2140	body sherd		5YR 7/4 pink; slip 5YR 6/4 light reddish brown; incl. med., min.; no core
103	73/9047	4321	body sherd		5YR 7/4 pink; slip 7.5YR 8/4 pink; incl. sm., min.; no core
104	60/9027	3789	body sherd		5YR 6/6 reddish yellow; slip 7.5YR 8/4 pink; incl. sm., min.; core
105	294/2028	2141	body sherd		7.5YR 6/4 light brown; incl. sm., min.; core
106	294/2028	2135	body sherd		5YR 6/6 reddish yellow; incl. med., min.; core
107	294/2028	2146	body sherd		5YR 7/6 reddish yellow; slip 2.5YR 6/6 light red; incl. sm., med., min.; core

MIDDLE BRONZE I-II: Plate 3 (sherds 108-57)

Sh.#	Site/field#	Reg.#	Form	Diameter	Description
108	399/2049	3237	bowl	14	5YR 7/3 pink; slip 10R 5/6 red; incl. sm., min.; no core
109	399/2049	3240	bowl	?	7.5YR 7/4 pink; slip 10R 5/6 red; incl. sm., min.; no core
110	429/2402	7915	bowl	14	5YR 7/4 pink; slip 2.5YR 6/4 light reddish yellow; incl. sm., med., min., org.; core
111	210/2303	593	bowl	16	7.5YR 8/4 pink-8/6 reddish yellow; incl. sm., med., min., org.; core
112	294/2028	2132	bowl	17	10R 6/6 light red; slip ext. 10YR 8/2 white, int. 2.5YR 6/4 light reddish brown; incl. sm., min., org.; no core
113	294/2028	2133	bowl	20	7.5YR 8/4 pink-8/6 reddish yellow; slip 5YR 6/4 light reddish brown; incl. med., org.; core
114	294/2028	2128	bowl	19	5YR 6/4 light reddish brown; slip 10YR 8/2 white; incl. med., sm., min., org.; core
115	399/2049	3215	bowl	?	5YR 7/3 pink; slip 7.5YR 8/4 pink; incl. sm., med., min., org.; no core
116	294/2028	2129	bowl	13	slip ext. 7.5YR 8/2 pinkish white, int. 5YR 6/6 reddish yellow; incl. sm., lg., min., org.; core
117	255/2103	7845	bowl	16	5YR 7/4 pink; slip 2.5YR 6/6 light red; incl. sm., min., org.; no core
118	294/2028	2131	bowl	?	5YR 7/4 pink; slip ext. 7.5YR 8/2 pinkish white, int. 10R 6/6 light red; incl. sm., min., org.; core
119	399/2049	3136	bowl	14	7.5YR 7/4 pink; paint int. 2.5YR 5/4 reddish brown; incl. sm., min.; no core

120	399/2049	3216	bowl	20	7.5YR 8/4-7/4 pink; paint 2.5YR 5/6 red; incl. med., sm., min., org.; no core
121	21/8008	601	cooking pot	?	5YR 6/6 reddish yellow; incl. med., min., org.; core
122	399/2049	3202	jar	12	7.5YR 7/4 pink; slip 5YR 8/3 pink; paint 10R 5/6 red; incl. sm., min.; no core
123	366/2375	6733	jar	12	7.5YR 6/2 pinkish grey; slip 10YR 8/3 very pale brown; incl. sm., min.; no core
124	366/2375	3105	jar	12	7.5YR 6/2 pinkish grey; slip 10YR 8/2 white; incl. sm., min.; no core
125	366/2375	6873	jar	14	7.5YR 6/2 pinkish grey; slip 10YR 8/2 white; incl. sm., min.; no core
126	366/2375	6898	jar	?	5YR 7/4 pink; slip 10YR 8/2 white; incl. sm., min., org.; core
127	366/2375	3097	jar	10	5YR 7/4 pink; slip 10YR 8/4 very pale brown; incl. sm., min., org.; core
128	366/2375	6872	jar	11	5YR 7/4 pink; slip 10YR 8/4 very pale brown; incl. sm., min.; no core
129	211/2304	1312	jar	12	5YR 7/6 reddish yellow; slip 7.5YR 8/2 pinkish white; incl. sm., min., org.; core
130	40/9272	7773	jar	13	7.5YR 6/2 pinkish grey; incl. sm., min.; no core
131	333/2307	2866	jar	?	5YR 7/4 pink; slip 10YR 8/2 white; incl. med., sm., min., org; no core
132	429/2402	7921	jar	10	10YR 6/2 light brownish grey; slip 10YR 7/3 very pale brown; incl. med., sm., min.; core
133	211/2304	1450	jar	16	7.5YR 7/4 pink; incl. sm., min., org.; no core
134	366/2375	6869	jar	17	7.5YR 7/4 pink; incl. sm., min., org.; core
135	366/2375	3102	jug	11	10YR 7/3 very pale brown; paint 2.5YR 4/2 weak red; incl. sm., min., org.; no core
136	255/2103	7833	jug	12	5YR 7/3 pink; slip 10YR 8/3 very pale brown; incl. sm., min., org.; no core
137	255/2103	7841	jug	9	5YR 7/3 pink; slip 10YR 8/3 very pale brown; incl. sm., min., org.; no core
138	211/2304	1449	jug	?	7.5YR 6/2 pinkish grey; incl. sm., min., org.; no core
139	88/9016	3650	jug	12	2.5YR 6/4 light reddish brown; slip 10YR 8/2 white; incl. sm., min.; no core
140	210/2303	595	juglet	7	10YR 8/3 very pale brown; incl. sm., min.; no core
141	390/2048	6994	handle section		2.5YR 6/6 light red; slip 10YR 5/6 red; incl. sm., min.; no core
142	73/9072	5165	handle		5YR 7/4 pink; incl. med., sm., min., org.; core
143	266/2005	316	handle		2.5YR 6/6 light red; paint 10R 5/4 weak red; incl. sm., min.; core

144	390/2048	6993	handle section		2.5YR 6/6 light red; incl. med., sm., min., org.; core
145	40/9272	7777	base sherd		5YR 7/6 reddish yellow; 5YR 7/4 pink; incl. med., min.; core
146	399/2049	3234	base sherd		5YR 7/4 pink-6/4 light reddish brown; slip 10YR 5/6 red; burnish; incl. med., min.; core
147	211/2304	1452	base sherd		5YR 7/3 pink; incl. sm., min., org.; core
148	349/2358	2358	base sherd		5YR 7/3 pink; incl. sm., min.; no core
149	399/2049	3242	base sherd		5YR 7/3 pink; incl. sm., min.; no core
150	399/2049	3233	base sherd		5YR 7/3 pink; incl. sm., min., org.; no core
151	349/2358	1059	base sherd		7.5YR 8/4 pink-8/6 reddish yellow; slip 7.5YR 8/4 pink; incl. med., sm., min.; no core
152	211/2304	1454	base sherd		5YR 7/3 pink; slip 10YR 8/2 white; incl. med., sm., min., org.; no core
153	210/2303	579	base sherd		5YR 7/4 pink; incl. sm., min., org.; core
154	399/2049	3231	base sherd		5YR 7/2 pinkish grey; slip 7.5YR 8/2-7/2 pink; incl. med., sm., min., org.; core
155	255/2103	7834	base sherd		7.5YR 7/4 pink; incl. sm., min., org.; core
156	429/2402	7918	base sherd		7.5YR 7/2 pinkish grey; slip 7.5YR 8/2 pinkish white; incl. sm., min.; no core
157	391/2101	7837	body sherd		10YR 8/3 very pale brown; slip 7.5YR 8/4 pink; paint 5YR 5/4 yellowish red; incl. sm., min.; no core

LATE BRONZE I-II: Plate 3 (sherds 158-71) and Plate 4 (sherds 172-84)

Sh.#	Site/field#	Reg.#	Form	Diameter	Description
158	210/2303	585	bowl	?	10YR 6/6 light red; slip 7.5YR 8/4 pink; incl. sm., med., min.; core
159	108/9127	6308	bowl	14	7.5YR 7/2 pinkish grey; slip 5YR 7/4 pink; incl. sm., min.; no core
160	211/2304	1311	bowl	17	5YR 6/4 light reddish brown; slip 7.5YR 8/4 pink; incl. sm., min.; core
161	333/2307	3889	bowl	?	5YR 7/3 pink; slip 5YR 8/2 pinkish white; incl. sm., min., org.; no core
162	71/9112	5611	bowl	20	5YR 6/3 light reddish brown; slip 7.5YR 8/4 pink; incl. sm., min.; core
163	211/2304	1307	krater	20	2.5YR 6/6 light red; slip ext. 5YR 8/3 pink; paint 10YR 5/4 weak red; incl. sm., med., min.; core
164	162/9062	4840	krater	20	5YR 7/3 pink; slip 7.5YR 8/2 pinkish white; paint 2.5YR 6/4 light reddish brown; incl. sm., min.; no core
165	114/9115	5980	krater	13	5YR 7/4 pink; slip 7.5YR 8/4 pink; incl. sm., med., min.; no core

166	55/9024	3770	krater	16	2.5YR 6/6 light red; incl. sm., med., min.; core
167	399/2049	3210	jar	10	2.5YR 6/4 light reddish brown; slip 7.5YR pink; incl. sm., min.; core
168	211/2304	1318	jar	10	7.5YR 7/4 pink; slip 10YR 8/3 very pale brown; incl. sm., min.; no core
169	219/9043	4102	jar	9	7.5YR 7/4 pink; slip 7.5YR 8/4 pink; incl. sm., med., min.; no core
170	15/9015	3580	jar	10	7.5YR N6/ grey; slip 2.5YR 6/6 light red; incl. sm., min.; no core
171	15/9017	8607	jar	12	2.5YR 6/4 light reddish brown; slip 7.5YR 8/4 pink; incl. sm., min.; no core
172	108/9129	6563	jar	12	2.5YR 6/6 light red; slip 7.5YR 7/4 pink; incl. sm., med., min.; core
173	108/9130	6710	jar	12	2.5Y 8/2 white; incl. sm., min.; no core
174	9311b	8734	jug	9	5YR 6/4 light reddish brown; incl. sm., min.; core
175	114/9115	5931	jug	16	2.5YR 6/6 light red; slip 7.5YR 8/4 pink; incl. sm., min.; core
176	71/9112	5612	jug	8	7.5YR 6/2 pinkish grey; slip 10YR 8/2 white; incl. sm., min.; no core
177	216/9048	4362	jug	9	7.5YR 7/4 pink; incl. sm., min.; core
178	60/9027	3773	handle section		5YR 7/3 pink; slip 10YR 8/3 very pale brown; paint 2.5YR 5/4 reddish brown; incl. sm., min., org.; core
179	399/2049	3207	base sherd		5YR 7/4 pink; slip 7.5YR 8/4 pink; incl. sm., med., min., org.; no core
180	108/9130	6715	base sherd		7.5YR 7/2 pinkish grey; sm., min.; no core
181	211/2304	1317	base sherd		5YR 7/4 pink; slip 10YR 8/2 white; incl. sm., med., min.; no core
182	108/9130	6831	base sherd		7.5YR 8/2 pinkish white; incl. sm., med., min., org.; no core
183	215/9030	3834	base sherd		7.5YR 7/2 pinkish grey; slip 7.5YR 7/4 pink; sm., min.; no core
184	55/9024	3751	body sherd		2.5YR 6/6 light red; paint 10YR 8/1 white, 10R 5/4 weak red; incl. sm., med., min.; core

IRON I: Plate 4 (sherds 185-226)

Sh.#	Site/field#	Reg.#	Form	Diameter	Description
185	108/9130	6707	platter	28	5YR 7/4 pink; slip ext. 10YR 8/2 white; incl. med., min.; core
186	108/9127	6345	bowl	24	2.5YR light reddish brown; slip ext. 10YR 8/2 white; incl. fine, min.; no core

187	333/2307	2879	bowl	24	7.5YR 7/4 pink; slip 10YR 8/3 very pale brown; incl. sm., min.; no core
188	333/2307	2880	bowl	18	7.5YR 7/4 pink; slip 7.5YR 7/4 pink; paint 5YR 6/4 light reddish brown; incl. med., sm., min., org.; no core
189	108/9130	6704	bowl	?	5YR 6/4 light reddish brown; slip ext. 7.5YR 8/2 pinkish white; incl. sm., min.; core
190	211/2304	1410	bowl	21	7.5YR 7/4 pink; slip 5YR 7/4 pink; paint 10R 5/6 red; incl. sm., min.; no core
191	40/9272	7808	bowl	?	5YR 7/4 pink; incl. sm., min.; no core
192	60/9027	3776	bowl	22	2.5YR 6/6 light red; slip 7.5YR 8/2 pinkish white; incl. med., sm., min.; no core
193	391/2101	7838	bowl	25	7.5YR 7/4 pink; slip 7.5YR 7/4-8/4 pink; incl. sm., min., org.; core
194	71/9112	5562	bowl	24	7.5YR 7/2 pinkish grey; slip 10YR 8/2 white; incl. sm., min.; core
195	333/2307	2860	bowl	16	5YR 7/4 pink; slip int. 10R 5/8 red; burnish; incl. fine min.; no core
196	399/2049	3298	bowl	20	5YR 7/4 pink; slip int. 10YR 5/8 red; burnish; incl. sm., min.; core
197	211/2304	1390	bowl	18	5YR 7/4 pink; slip 5YR 6/4 light reddish brown; burnish; incl. sm., min.; no core
198	161/9044	4168	krater	34	7.5YR 7/4 pink; incl. med., min.; no core
199	211/2304	1368	krater	27	2.5YR 6/6 light red; slip 7.5YR 7/4 pink; incl. med., sm., min.; core
200	211/2304	1388	krater	19	5YR 6/4 light reddish brown; slip 5YR 6/4 light reddish brown; burnish; incl. sm., med., min.; no core
201	366/2375	6731	krater	19	5YR 7/4 pink; slip 10YR 8/3 very pale brown; incl. sm., med., min.; no core
202	211/2304	1369	krater	27	2.5YR 6/6 light red; slip 7.5YR 7/2 pinkish grey; incl. med., sm., min.; no core
203	211/2304	1378	krater	27	7.5YR 7/2 pinkish grey; slip 7.5YR 7/2 pinkish grey; incl. med., sm., min.; no core
204	15/9017	8615	krater	24	5YR 7/3 pink; slip 5YR 7/3 pink; incl. sm., med., min.; no core
205	399/2049	3328	krater	?	10R 6/6 light red; slip 7.5YR 8/4 pink; incl. med., sm., min., org.; core
206	88/9016	3633	cooking pot	12	5YR 7/6 reddish yellow; slip 5YR 5/2 reddish grey; incl. sm., fine., min.; no core
207	15/9017	8614	jar	12	2.5YR 6/4 light reddish brown; slip 7.5YR 8/4 pink; incl. sm., min.; no core
208	399/2049	3201	jar	12	5YR 6/1 grey; slip 7.5YR 7/4 pink; incl. sm., min., org.; core
209	52/9022	3747	jar	16	5YR 6/1 grey; slip 5YR 6/3 light reddish brown; incl. sm., min.; core

210	289/2021	1871	jar	13	5YR 6/2 pinkish grey; slip 7.5YR 8/4 pink; incl. sm., min., org.; core
211	289/2021	1875	jar	?	5YR 7/4 pink; slip 7.5YR 7/6 reddish yellow; incl. sm., min., org.; core
212	108/9129	5099	jar	14	5YR 7/6 reddish yellow; slip ext. 2.5YR 6/4 light reddish brown; slip int. 5YR 6/4 light reddish brown; incl. sm., min.; core
213	108/9128	6388	jar	14	5YR 7/4 pink; slip ext. 10YR 8/1 white, int. 10R 6/4 pale red; incl. sm., min.; core
214	211/2304	1364	jar	12	10YR 8/3 very pale brown; slip 10YR 8/3 very pale brown; incl. med., min.; no core
215	35/8014	956	jar	14	2.5YR 6/6 light red; slip 10YR 8/3 very pale brown; incl. med., min.; core
216	108/9127	6305	jar	14	7.5YR 7/2 pinkish grey; slip 7.5YR 7/2 pinkish grey; incl. med., min.; no core
217	108/9123	5996	jar	13	2.5YR 6/6 light red; slip 10YR 8/2 white; incl. med., min.; no core
218	211/2304	1366	jar	?	7.5YR 7/4 pink; slip 10YR 8/3 very pale brown; incl. med., sm., min.; no core
219	35/8014	953	jar	16	7.5YR 7/4 pink; slip 10YR 8/3 very pale brown; incl. med., min.; core
220	108/9123	6000	jar	15	2.5YR 6/6 light red; slip 10R 6/4 pale red; incl. med., lg., min.; core
221	108/9123	6006	jar	17	5YR 7/4 pink; slip 5YR 7/4 pink; incl. sm., min.; core
222	54/9026	3766	handle		2.5YR 6/4; slip 5YR 8/3 pink; incl. sm., min.; core
223	219/9043	4121	base sherd		5YR 7/4 pink; slip 10YR 8/2 white; incl. sm., med., min.; no core
224	227/9065	4955	base sherd		7.5YR 7/2 pinkish grey; slip 7.5YR 7/2 pinkish grey; incl. sm., med., min.; no core
225	108/9131	6832	base sherd		5YR 7/3 pink; slip 2.5YR 6/4 light reddish brown; incl. sm., min.; core
226	16/9046	4197	base sherd		7.5YR 7/4 pink; incl. med., sm., min.; no core

IRON II: Plate 4 (sherds 227-34) and Plate 5 (sherds 235-87)

Sh.#	Site/field#	Reg.#	Form	Diameter	Description
227	227/9065	4944	bowl	18	5YR 7/4 pink; slip 7.5YR 7/4 pink; incl. med., min.; core
228	88/9016	3606	bowl	23	7.5YR 7/4 pink; slip 7.5YR 7/4 pink; incl. sm., min.; no core
229	211/2304	1391	bowl	16	slip 7.5YR 6/4 light brown-6/6 reddish yellow; burnish; incl. sm., min., org.; core

230	71/9112	5584	bowl	?	7.5YR 7/4 pink; slip 7.5YR pink; incl. sm., min.; no core
231	399/2049	3334	bowl	19	7.5YR 7/4 pink; slip 10R 6/6 light red; incl. sm., min.; no core
232	399/2049	3323	bowl	16	5YR 7/4 pink; slip 10R 6/6 light red; incl., sm., min., org.; core
233	2013	3033	bowl	16	7.5YR 7/2 pinkish grey; slip 5YR 7/4 pink; incl. sm., min.; no core
234	399/2049	3225	bowl	?	7.5YR 6/4 light brown; incl. sm., min., org.; core
235	399/2049	3304	bowl	26	5YR 7/6 reddish yellow; slip 10R 5/6 red; burnish; incl. sm., med., min.; core
236	40/9272	7810	bowl	?	5YR 7/4 pink; incl. sm., min., no core
237	73/9072	5168	bowl	15	5YR 7/4 pink; slip 7.5YR 7/2 pinkish grey - 8/2 pinkish white; incl. fine; core
238	262/2013	3030	bowl	16	5YR 7/4 pink; slip 2.5YR 6/6 light red; burnish; incl. sm., med., min.; core
239	211/2304	1442	bowl	11	7.5YR 7/4 pink; incl. fine, min.; no core
240	108/9123	6128	bowl	15	7.5YR 7/2 pinkish grey; slip ext. 10YR 8/3 very pale brown; incl. fine; core
241	211/2304	1393	bowl	16	5YR 7/4 pink; slip 5YR 6/6 reddish yellow; burnish; incl. sm., min.; no core
242	211/2304	1441	bowl	14	5YR 6/1 grey; slip 10YR 8/2 white - 7/2 light grey; paint 10YR 4/1 dark grey; incl. fine; no core
243	399/2049	3332	bowl	13	7.5YR 7/4 pink; slip ext. 10YR 8/2 white, slip int. 5YR 5/4 reddish brown; incl. sm., med., min.; no core
244	211/2304	1438	bowl	22	7.5YR 6/2 pinkish grey; slip 2.5YR 6/4 light reddish brown; incl. sm. min.; core
245	211/2304	1418	bowl	24	7.5YR 7/2 pinkish grey; slip 2.5YR 6/4 light reddish brown; incl. sm., min.; core
246	71/9112	5569	bowl	16	7.5YR 7/2 pinkish grey; slip 10R 6/6 light red; incl. sm., min.; no core
247	9029	3796	bowl	18	5YR 7/4 pink; slip 2.5YR 6/6 light red; incl. sm., min.; core
248	399/2049	3330	bowl	13	7.5YR 7/2 pinkish grey; slip 7.5YR 7/2 pinkish grey-8/2 pinkish white; paint 10R 6/6 light red, 5YR 3/1 very dark grey; incl. sm., min.; core
249	161/9044	4181	krater	20	5YR 7/4 pink; incl. sm., med., min.; core
250	399/2049	3212	krater	18	5YR 6/6 reddish yellow; slip 7.5YR pink; incl. sm., min.; core
251	16/9058	4677	cooking pot	12	5YR 6/2 pinkish grey; slip 5YR 6/4 light reddish brown; incl. sm., min.; core
252	90/9005	3177	cooking pot	12	7.5YR 7/4 pink; 5YR 6/4 light reddish brown; incl. sm., min.; no core
253	211/2304	1371	cooking pot	12	2.5YR 6/6 light red; slip 10R 6/6 light red; incl. sm., med., min.; core

254	399/2049	3297	cooking pot	15	7.5YR 6/2 pinkish grey; slip 2.5YR 5/6 red; incl. sm., med., min.; no core
255	436/2328	1824	jar	8	5YR 7/4 pink; slip 5YR 7/4 pink; incl. sm., min.; core
256	366/2375	3096	jar	12	7.5YR 6/4 light brown; slip 7.5YR 8/2 pinkish white; incl. sm., min.; core
257	108/9130	6708	jar	10	5YR 7/3 pink; 10YR 8/3 very pale brown; incl. fine, min.; no core
258	15/9015	3575	jar	12	2.5YR 6/6 light red; slip 10YR 8/3 very pale brown; incl. sm., min.; no core
259	15/9017	8623	jar	8	5YR 7/3 pink; slip 5YR 7/3 pink; incl. sm., min.; no core
260	211/2304	1405	jar	22	2.5YR 6/4 light reddish brown; slip 2.5YR 6/4 light reddish brown; incl. sm., min.; core
261	15/9015	3561	jar	11	5YR 7/3 pink; incl. sm., min.; no core
262	63/9002	2757	jar	16	7.5YR 7/2 pinkish grey; slip 2.5YR 6/4 light reddish brown; incl. sm., med., min.; core
263	108/9123	6009	jar	15	5YR 7/4 pink; incl. sm., min.; core
264	262/2013	3039	jar	14	2.5YR 6/4 light reddish brown; incl. sm., min.; core
265	266/2005	297	jar	?	5YR 6/4 light reddish brown; incl. sm., min., org.; no core
266	399/2049	3318	jar	16	7.5YR 7/2 pinkish grey; slip 5YR 7/3 pink - 6/3 light reddish brown; incl. sm., min.; core
267	76/9068	5004	jar	14	2.5YR 6/4 light reddish brown; slip 10YR 8/3 - 7/3 very pale brown; incl. sm., min.; core
268	211/2304	1439	jar	36	5YR 6/6 reddish yellow; slip 2.5YR 6/4 light reddish brown; incl. sm., min.; core
269	90/9005	3032	jar	18	5YR 7/4 pink; slip 7.5YR 8/4 pink; incl. med., sm., min.; core
270	108/9132	6928	jug	5	2.5YR 6/4 light reddish brown; slip 10YR 8/2 white; incl. fine, min.; no core
271	399/2049	3308	jug	5	7.5YR 7/2 pinkish grey; slip 7.5YR 8/2 pinkish white; incl. sm., med., min.; no core
272	3/9070	5067	jug	5	7.5YR 7/2 pinkish grey; incl. sm., med., min.; no core
273	399/2049	3331	jug	9	2.5YR 6/4 light reddish brown; slip 10R 5/6 red; incl. fine, min., org.; core
274	108/9123	6012	amphoriskos	11	5YR 7/3 pink; slip 10YR 7/3 very pale brown; incl. sm., med., min.; no core
275	211/2304	1407	base sherd		2.5YR 6/4 light reddish brown; slip 10R 5/6 red; burnish; incl. sm., med., min.; core
276	108/9126	6266	base sherd		5YR 7/3 pink; slip 2.5YR 6/4 light reddish brown; sm., min.; no core

277	399/2049	3342	base sherd		2.5YR 6/4 light reddish brown; incl. sm., min.; core
278	399/2049	3337	base sherd		2.5YR 6/6 light red; slip 7.5YR 8/4 pink; incl. sm., min.; core
279	399/2049	3336	body sherd		2.5YR 6/4 light reddish brown; slip ext. 10R 6/8 red; incl. fine, min.; no core
280	273/2017	1178	body sherd		7.5YR 7/2 pinkish grey; slip 10YR 8/1 white - 7/1 light grey; paint 10YR 3/1 very dark grey; burnish; incl. sm., min.; no core
281	35/8014	959	body sherd		5YR pink; slip 10R 5/6 red; paint 5YR 4/1 dark grey; incl. sm., min.; no core
282	71/9112	5598	body sherd		5YR 7/3 pink; slip 2.5YR 6/4 light reddish brown; paint 10YR 8/2 white, 5YR 4/1 dark grey; incl. sm., min.; no core
283	71/9112	5593	body sherd		5YR 7/3 pink; slip 2.5YR 6/4 light reddish brown; paint 10YR 8/2 white, 5YR 4/1 dark grey; incl. sm., min.; core
284	71/9112	5589	body sherd		5YR 7/4 pink; slip 2.5YR 6/4 light reddish brown; paint 10YR 8/2 white, 5YR 4/1 dark grey; incl. sm., min.; core
285	211/2304	1132	body sherd		2.5YR light reddish brown; slip 2.5YR 6/4 light reddish brown; incl. sm., min.; core
286	35/8014	968	body sherd		7.5YR 7/4 pink; slip 2.5YR 6/4 light reddish brown; paint 10YR 8/2 white, 5YR 4/1 dark grey; incl. sm., min.; core
287	399/2049	3335	body sherd		2.5YR 6/4 light reddish brown; slip 2.5YR 6/4 light reddish brown; paint 10YR 8/2 white, 5YR 4/1 dark grey; incl. sm., min.; core

PERSIAN: Plate 5 (sherds 288-97)

Sh.#	Site/field#	Reg.#	Form	Diameter	Description
288	108/9123	6849	bowl	27	5YR 7/3 pink; slip 10YR 8/3 very pale brown; incl. med., sm., min.; no core
289	294/2028	2130	bowl	?	2.5YR 6/4 light reddish brown; slip ext. 10YR 8/2 white; incl. sm., med., min.; no core
290	86/9273	7839	jar/jug	14	2.5YR 6/6 light red; slip 2.5YR 6/6 light red; incl. sm., min.; core
291	64/9017	3677	jar/jug	13	5YR 6/4 light reddish brown; slip 5YR 6/4 light reddish brown; incl. sm., min.; core
292	63/9002	2755	jar/jug	14	5YR 7/3 pink; slip ext. 10YR 8/2 white; incl. sm., med., min.; core
293	64/9017c	8625	jar	16	10YR 7/3 very pale brown; slip 10YR 8/3-7/3 very pale brown; incl. sm., min.; core
294	211/2304	1444	jar	?	5YR 7/4 pink; incl. med., sm., min.; no core
295	63/9002	2754	jar	15	5YR 7/4 pink; incl. med., sm., min.; no core

296	162/9062	4843	jar	13	2.5YR 6/4 light reddish brown; slip ext. 10YR 8/3 very pale brown; incl. sm., med., min.; core
297	108/9125	6251	jar	15	10YR 7/2 light grey; slip ext. 2.5YR 6/4 light reddish brown; incl. sm., min.; no core

HELLENISTIC: Plate 5 (sherds 298-306) and Plate 6 (sherds 307-10)

Sh.#	Site/field#	Reg.#	Form	Diameter	Description
298	399/2049	3250	bowl	11	5YR 7/4 pink; slip ext. 5YR 5/3 reddish brown; int. 2.5YR 5/4 reddish brown - 5/6 red; incl. fine; core
299	366/2375	3093	bowl	15	5YR 7/4 pink - 7/6 reddish yellow; slip ext. 5YR 5/3 reddish brown; int. 5YR 6/6 reddish yellow; incl. fine; no core
300	366/2375	3095	bowl	15	5YR 7/4 pink; slip 2.5YR 6/6 light red; incl. fine; no core
301	436/2328	1729	cooking pot	11	2.5YR 6/4 light reddish brown; slip 2.5YR 5/2 weak red; incl. sm., min.; core
302	108/9123	6110	jar	10	5YR 7/3 - 8/3 pink; incl. fine; no core
303	366/2375	3088	jug	11	7.5YR 8/4 pink - 8/6 reddish yellow; incl. fine; no core
304	9029	3791	handle section		7.5YR 7/4 pink; incl. sm., med.; no core
305	366/2375	6856	base sherd		2.5YR 6/4 light reddish brown; slip 10R 5/6 red; incl. fine; no core
306	399/2049	3251	base sherd		10YR 5/1 grey; slip 10YR 5/1 grey; incl. fine; no core
307	333/2307	2808	base sherd		2.5YR 6/2 pale red - 6/4 light reddish brown; slip 2.5YR 6/6 light red; incl. fine; no core
308	177/2211	7963	base sherd		5YR 7/4 pink - 6/4 light reddish brown; slip 2.5YR 6/6 light red; incl. fine; no core
309	405/2052	6837	base sherd		7.5YR 7/4 - 8/4 pink; slip ext. 5YR 8/3 pink - 7.5YR 8/4 pink; int. 10R 6/3 pale red; incl. sm., min.; no core
310	418/2363	8667	body sherd		5YR 7/4 pink; varnish 2.5YR 4/6 red; incl. fine; no core

NABATAEAN: Plate 6 (sherds 311-31)

Sh.#	Site/field#	Reg.#	Form	Diameter	Description
311	9287	8342	bowl	27	10R 6/6 light red; slip ext. 10YR 8/2 white; int. 10R 6/6 light red; incl. fine; core
312	108/9124	6228	bowl	20	5YR 6/3 light reddish brown; incl. fine; core
313	9287	8389	bowl	14	5YR 6/3 light reddish brown; slip ext. 7.5YR 8/2 pinkish white; paint int. 10R 6/4 pale red; incl. fine; no core

314	108/9130	6732	bowl/cup	12	7.5YR 6/4 light brown; incl. fine; no core
315	108/9130	6727	bowl	9	2.5YR 6/6 light red; slip ext. 7.5YR 8/2 pinkish white; int. 10R 4/6 red; incl. fine; core
316	9287	8365	krater	12	2.5YR 6/6 light red; slip ext. 2.5YR 6/4 light reddish brown; incl. fine; no core
317	9287	8339	cooking pot	7	2.5YR 6/6 light red; slip ext. 7.5YR 8/4 pink; incl. fine; no core
318	90/9005	3042	cooking pot	8	2.5YR 6/6 light red; slip ext. 7.5YR 8/4 pink; incl. fine; no core
319	9287	8349	cooking pot	11	2.5YR 6/6 light red; slip 7.5YR 8/2 pinkish white; incl. fine; no core
320	108/9124	6209	jar/jug	8	10R 6/6 light red; slip 7.5YR pinkish white; incl. fine; no core
321	108/9124	6208	jug	4	2.5YR 6/6 light red; slip 10YR 8/2 white; incl. fine; no core
322	9287	8386	handle section		10R 6/6 light red; slip 7.5YR 8/2 pinkish white; incl. sm., min.; no core
323	217/9051	4612	handle section		2.5YR 6/6 light red; slip 2.5YR 6/4 light reddish brown; incl. fine; no core
324	63/9002	2770	handle section		2.5YR 6/6 light red; slip 7.5YR 8/2 pinkish white; incl. fine; core
325	71/9112	5631	handle section		2.5YR 6/6 light red; slip 10R 5/6 red; incl. fine; no core
326	71/9112	5626	handle section		2.5YR 6/6 light red; slip 10R 5/6 red; incl. fine; no core
327	108/9123	6017	base sherd		2.5YR 6/4 light reddish brown; slip 10YR 4/1 dark grey; incl. fine; no core
328	9287	8394	base sherd		5YR 6/2 pinkish grey; incl. fine; no core
329	108/9123	6086	base sherd		5YR 6/4 light reddish brown; slip ext. 7.5YR 8/2 pinkish white; incl. fine; core
330	108/9130	6715	base sherd		5YR 7/2 pinkish grey; incl. fine; no core
331	108/9126	6270	body sherd		2.5YR 6/6 light red; paint 2.5YR 5/4 reddish brown; incl. fine; core

EARLY ROMAN: Plate 6 (sherds 332-48)

Sh.#	Site/field#	Reg.#	Form	Diameter	Description
332	108/9138	7026	bowl	27	5YR 7/4 pink; slip 10R 6/8 light red; incl. fine; no core
333	108/9140	7075	bowl	18	5YR 7/4 pink; slip 7.5YR 8/2 pinkish white; paint 2.5YR 6/6 light red; incl. fine; no core
334	108/9129	6567	bowl	16	10YR 8/3 very pale brown; slip ext. 7.5YR 6/6 reddish yellow; paint 10R 5/6 red; incl. fine; no core

335	71/9112	5668	bowl/krater	18	2.5YR 6/6 light red; slip ext. 10YR 8/3 very pale brown; int. 2.5YR 6/6 light red; incl. fine; no core
336	108/9140	7094	cooking pot	9	2.5YR 6/6 light red; slip ext. 10R 5/6 red; incl. fine; no core
337	108/9140	7090	cooking pot	9	10R 6/6 light red; slip ext. 2.5YR 6/4 light reddish brown; incl. fine; no core
338	9086	5301	lid	15	2.5YR 6/6 light red; slip 2.5YR 6/4 light reddish brown; incl. fine; no core
339	71/9112	5676	jar	7	5YR 7/4 pink; slip 7.5YR 8/2 pinkish white; incl. fine; no core
340	108/9127	6318	jar	10	2.5YR 6/4 light reddish brown; slip 7.5YR 7/6 reddish yellow; incl. fine; core
341	9287	8396	jar	7	10YR 7/3 very pale brown; slip 10YR 8/2 white; incl. fine; no core
342	108/9124	6203	jug	9	10R 6/6 light red; slip 7.5YR 8/2 pinkish white; paint 10R 5/6 red; incl. sm., fine; no core
343	108/9130	6729	jug	4	7.5YR 8/4 pink; slip 10R 5/8 red; incl. fine; no core
344	90/9005	3045	juglet	4	5YR 6/4 light reddish brown; incl. sm., fine, min.; no core
345	108/9132	6864	juglet	?	2.5YR 6/6 light red; slip 10R 5/6 red; incl. fine; no core
346	101/9049	4513	base sherd		5YR 6/3 light reddish brown; slip 7.5YR 6/4 light brown; incl. sm., fine, min.; no core
347	108/9123	6033	base sherd		5YR 6/3 light reddish brown; slip 5YR 6/3 light reddish brown; incl. fine; core
348	9287	8376	stand		5YR 7/4 pink; slip 7.5YR 8/4 pink; incl. sm., min., fine; core

LATE ROMAN: Plate 6 (sherds 349-61) and Plate 7 (sherds 362-67)

Sh.#	Site/field#	Reg.#	Form	Diameter	Description
349	100/9020	3702	bowl	22	5YR 7/4 pink; slip 2.5YR 6/8 light red; incl. sm., min., fine; core
350	52/9059	4697	bowl	17	5YR 7/4 pink; slip 2.5YR 6/6 light red; incl. sm., min., fine; no core
351	3/9070	5066	bowl	18	5YR 7/4 pink; slip 10R 6/4 pale red; incl. sm., min.; core
352	3/9070	5065	bowl	15	5YR 7/3 pink; slip 10R 6/6 light red; incl. fine; no core
353	108/9130	6753	bowl	17	2.5YR 6/6 light red; slip 2.5YR 5/6 red; incl. fine; core
354	71/9112	5687	bowl	11	2.5YR 6/6 light red; slip 10R 6/6 light red; incl. fine; no core

355	108/9130	6748	bowl	14	10YR 8/3 very pale brown; slip 5YR 6/4 light reddish brown; incl. fine; no core
356	108/9130	6746	bowl	22	2.5YR 6/6 light red; slip 2.5YR 6/6 light red; incl. sm., min., fine; core
357	88/9016	3609	cooking pot	11	7.5YR 7/4 pink; incl. fine; no core
358	108/9132	6873	cooking pot	11	10YR 8/3 very pale brown; slip ext. 5YR 7/6 - 6/6 reddish yellow; incl. sm., min.; no core
359	71/9112	5681	lid	13	7.5YR 8/4 pink; slip ext. 5YR 7/6 reddish yellow; incl. fine; no core
360	108/9130	6754	lid	11	5YR 7/4 pink; slip ext. 2.5YR 6/4 light reddish brown; incl. fine; no core
361	108/9123	6046	juglet	?	5YR 7/6 reddish yellow; slip ext. 2.5YR 6/6 light red; incl. fine; no core
362	108/9123	6056	handle section		2.5YR 6/6 light red; slip 10R 5/4 weak red; incl. fine; no core
363	90/9005	3106	handle section		10YR 8/3 very pale brown; slip 2.5YR 6/4 light reddish brown - 6/6 light red; incl. fine; no core
364	104/9021	3732	handle section		5YR 7/4 pink; incl. fine, sm., min.; core
365	108/9132	6871	base sherd		5YR 7/4 pink; slip int. 10R 6/6 light red; incl. sm., min.; core
366	89/9004	2924	base sherd		5YR 6/3 light reddish brown; slip 2.5YR 6/6 light red; incl. fine; core
367	108/9123	6037	base sherd		5YR 6/1 grey; incl. sm., min.; no core

EARLY AND LATE BYZANTINE: Plate 7 (sherds 368-412)

Sh.#	Site/field#	Reg.#	Form	Diameter	Description
368	108/9129	6582	bowl	18	5YR 7/4 pink; slip ext. 5YR 5/1 grey; slip int. 7.5YR 6/4 light brown; incl. sm., min.; core
369	3/9070	5086	bowl	19	2.5YR 6/6 light red; slip 10R 6/6 light red; incl. fine, sm., min.; core
370	15/9015	3584	bowl	?	2.5YR 6/6 light red; slip 2.5YR 6/4 light reddish brown; incl. fine; no core
371	108/9123	6092	bowl	14	2.5YR 6/6 light red; slip 7.5YR 8/4 pink; incl. fine, sm., min.; no core
372	87/9001	2692	bowl	24	10R 6/8 light red; slip 10R 6/8 light red; incl. fine; no core
373	108/9123	6090	bowl	22	10R 6/8 light red; slip 10R 6/8 light red; incl. fine; no core
374	108/9132	6939	krater	24	5YR 7/4 pink; slip 7.5YR 8/4 pink; incl. sm., min.; no core
375	108/9130	6768	krater	27	7.5YR 7/2 pinkish grey; slip 2.5Y 8/2 white; incl. sm., min.; core

376	108/9135	7004	cooking pot	8	2.5YR 6/6 light red; slip 5YR 6/4 light reddish brown; incl. fine; no core
377	108/9132	7002	cooking pot	13	5YR 7/4 pink; slip ext. 2.5YR 5/4 reddish brown; incl. fine, sm., min.; no core
378	108/9132	6893	cooking pot	12	2.5YR 6/6 light red; slip ext. 5YR 4/1 dark grey; int. 10R 5/3 weak red; incl. fine, sm., min.; no core
379	108/9132	6879	cooking pot	10	2.5YR 6/4 light reddish brown; slip ext. 10R 5/1 reddish grey; incl. sm., min.; no core
380	9287	8450	cooking pot	13	2.5YR 6/4 light reddish brown; slip 7.5YR 6/2 pinkish grey; incl. sm., min.; core
381	216/9048	4395	jar	16	5YR 7/4 pink; slip 5YR 7/4 pink; incl. sm., min.; core
382	52/9059	4730	jug	3	2.5YR 5/2 weak red; slip 2.5YR 6/4 light reddish brown; incl. sm., min.; no core
383	216/9048	4447	lamp		2.5YR 6/4 light reddish brown; slip 7.5YR 8/2 pinkish white; incl. fine; core
384	304/2023	7636	handle section		5YR 6/1 grey; incl. sm., min.; no core
385	216/9048	4433	handle section		5YR 7/1 light grey; slip 5YR 5/1 grey; incl. fine; no core
386	108/9130	6775	handle section		10R 6/6 light red; slip 5YR 7/3 pink; incl. sm., min.; no core
387	15/9015	3579	handle section		2.5YR 6/6 light red; slip 2.5YR 6/6 light red; incl. fine; core
388	9287	8448	handle section		7.5YR 7/4 pink; slip 5YR 6/3 light reddish brown; incl. fine; no core
389	108/9124	6250	base sherd		5YR 6/1 grey; slip 7.5YR 8/2 pinkish white; incl. sm., min.; no core
390	52/9059	4699	base sherd		5YR 7/4 pink; slip 5YR 6/1 grey; incl. sm., min.; core
391	9071	5131	body sherd		10R 6/6 light red; incl. sm., min.; no core
392	108/9132	6918	body sherd		5YR 7/4 pink - 6/4 light reddish brown; incl. sm., min.; no core
393	52/9059	4701	bowl	22	2.5YR 6/4 light reddish brown; slip 10YR 8/2 white; incl. sm., min.; no core
394	166/9031	3850	bowl	15	2.5YR 6/8 light red; slip 10R 6/8 light red; incl. fine; no core
395	52/9022	3745	bowl	10	10R 6/8 light red; slip 10R 6/8 light red; incl. fine; no core
396	108/9135	7003	bowl	26	2.5YR 6/6 light red; slip 10YR 8/3 very pale brown; incl. sm., min.; core
397	108/9137	7019	krater	23	7.5YR 6/2 pinkish grey; slip 10YR 7/2 light grey; incl. sm., min.; no core
398	71/9112	5731	krater	?	10YR 6/1 grey; slip 10YR 4/1 dark grey; incl. fine, sm., min.; core

399	76/9068	5022	pithos	28	2.5YR 6/6 light red; slip ext. 10R 8/3 very pale brown; incl. sm., min.; no core
400	9282	8294	cooking pot	15	7.5YR 6/2 pinkish grey; incl. fine, sm., min.; core
401	108/9130	6679	lid handle		2.5YR 5/4 reddish brown; slip 10YR 8/2 white; incl. sm., min.; core
402	108/9132	6900	jar	14	2.5YR 6/6 light red; slip ext. 10YR 8/2 white; incl. sm., min.; no core
403	9287	8444	jar	10	10R 5/1 reddish grey; incl. sm., min.; no core
404	109/9113	5872	jar	7	5YR 6/1 grey; slip 10YR 5/1 grey; incl. sm., min.; no core
405	88/9012	3535	jar	8	2.5YR 6/4 light reddish brown; slip 5YR 5/1 grey; incl. fine; core
406	16/9046	4247	jar	9	2.5YR 6/4 light reddish brown; slip 7.5YR 7/2 pinkish grey; incl. sm., min.; core
407	420/2320	1921	jar	11	2.5YR 6/6 light red; slip 7.5YR 5/2 brown; incl. sm., min.; core
408	108/9128	6462	handle section		10R 6/6 light red; slip 10R 5/4 weak red; incl. sm., min.; no core
409	76/9068	5037	handle section		5YR 7/4 pink; slip 7.5YR 6/4 light brown; incl. sm., min.; no core
410	9287	8440	handle section		2.5YR 6/4 light reddish brown; slip 7.5YR 8/4 pink; incl. sm., min.; no core
411	76/9068	5021	handle section		5YR 6/1 grey; slip 5YR 6/1 grey; incl. sm., min.; no core
412	87/9001	2700	handle section		5YR 6/1 grey; slip 5YR 6/1 grey; incl. sm., min.; no core

EARLY ISLAMIC: Plate 7 (sherds 413-24) and Plate 8 (sherds 425-39)

Sh.#	Site/field#	Reg.#	Form	Diameter	Description
413	92/9006	3269	bowl	11	10YR 8/1 white - 7/1 light grey; slip 10YR 8/2 white; paint 10YR 6/2 light brownish grey; incl. fine; no core
414	71/9112	5752	bowl	?	10YR 5/1 grey; slip 5YR 6/3 light reddish brown; incl. fine; no core
415	9029	3817	pithos	13	10YR 6/1 grey; incl. sm., min.; no core
416	108/9132	6948	lid handle		5YR 8/4 pink; slip ext. 10YR 8/3 very pale brown; incl. fine; no core
417	52/9059	4737	handle		7.5YR 8/2 pinkish white; slip 10YR 8/2 white; paint 2.5YR 6/2 pale red; incl. fine; core
418	436/2328	1735	handle		5YR 7/4 pink; slip 7.5YR 8/4 pink; paint 10R 5/4 weak red; incl. fine, sm., min.; no core

419	436/2328	1734	handle		2.5YR 6/6 light red; slip 2.5YR 6/6 light red; paint 10YR 8/1 white; incl. fine; core
420	108/9126	6285	handle section		7.5YR 7/2 pinkish grey; slip 7.5YR 7/4 pink; incl. sm., min.; no core
421	273/2017	1154	body sherd		10YR 8/3 - 7/3 very pale brown; slip 5YR 7/4 pink; incl. sm., min.; no core
422	91/9008	3427	body sherd		5YR 7/4 pink; slip ext. 5YR 8/2 pinkish white; int. 10YR 8/3 very pale brown; paint 10R 5/4 weak red; incl. fine, sm., min.; no core
423	92/9006	3277	body sherd		5YR 7/4 pink; slip 7.5YR 8/2 pinkish white; paint 10R 5/4 weak red; incl. fine; no core
424	108/9131	6844	body sherd		5YR 7/6 reddish yellow; slip 10YR 7/3 very pale brown; paint 2.5YR 5/4 reddish brown; incl. fine, sm., min.; no core
425	91/9008	3432	cup	9	2.5YR 6/6 light red; incl. fine; no core
426	91/9008	3435	lamp		10YR 8/2 pinkish grey; incl. fine; no core
427	91/9008	3511	handle		5YR 7/4 pink; slip 5YR 7/4 pink; incl. fine; no core
428	91/9008	3434	base sherd		10YR 8/2 white; slip 10YR 8/3 very pale brown; incl. fine; no core
429	91/9008	3433	body sherd		10YR 8/1 white; incl. fine; no core
430	57/9014	3552	body sherd		10YR 8/2 white; slip 2.5Y 8/2 white; incl. fine; no core
431	91/9008	3431	body sherd		10YR 8/2 white; slip 7.5YR 8/2 pinkish white; incl. fine; no core
432	108/9128	6527	body sherd		7.5YR 8/2 pinkish white; paint: green, brown; glaze: greenish-yellow; incl. fine; no core
433	108/9127	6369	decorated		10YR 8/3 very pale brown; paint: green, brown; glaze: greenish-yellow; incl. fine; no core
434	211/2304	1352	bowl/basin	34	5YR 7/4 pink; slip ext. 7/5YR 8/4 pink - 7/6 reddish yellow; incl. sm., med., min.; core
435	211/2304	1357	cooking pot	15	2.5YR 6/6 light red; slip ext. 10R 6/4 pale red; glaze: clear; incl. sm., min.; core
436	211/2304	1354	jar/jug	11	5YR 7/4 pink; slip 2.5YR 6/4 light reddish brown; incl. fine, sm., min.; core
437	92/9006	3270	handle section		2.5YR 6/4 light reddish brown; slip ext. 7.5YR 8/2 pinkish white; int. 2.5YR 5/2 weak red; incl. fine; no core
438	91/9008	3441	handle		10R 6/6 light red; slip 10R 4/1 dark reddish grey; incl. fine; no core
439	211/2304	1351	base sherd		10YR 7/3 very pale brown; slip int. 5YR 7/4 pink; incl. med., sm., min.; no core

AYYUBID-MAMLUK: Plate 8 (sherds 440-69) and Plate 9 (sherds 420-77)

Sh.#	Site/field#	Reg.#	Form	Diameter	Description
440	108/9126	6299	bowl	17	2.5YR 8/2 white; glaze: int. dark yellow; incl. fine, sm., min.; no core
441	108/9129	6624	bowl	24	5YR 8/2 pinkish white; glaze: green; incl. sm., min.; no core
442	166/9031	3866	bowl	?	7.5YR 7/2 pinkish grey; glaze: int. green; incl. sm., min.; no core
443	166/9031	3863	bowl	21	5YR 8/3 pink; glaze: int. green; incl. fine, sm., min.; no core
444	108/9127	6208	bowl	16	7.5YR 8/2 pinkish white; glaze: ext. dark green, int. brown; incl. fine; no core
445	108/9132	6853	jug	15	10R 6/6 light red; slip 10R 5/4 weak red; incl. fine, sm., min.; no core
446	215/9030	3829	sugar pot	?	2.5YR 6/6 light red; incl. sm., min.; no core
447	108/9124	6239	sugar pot	11	7.5YR 8/2 pinkish white; incl. sm., min.; no core
448	71/9112	5769	base sherd		5YR 7/3 pink; incl. sm., med.; no core
449	108/9139	6847	base sherd		7.5YR 8/2 pinkish white; glaze: green; incl. fine, sm., min.; no core
450	108/9123	6115	decorated		2.5YR 6/6 light red; glaze: yellow; incl. fine; no core
451	108/9128	6525	body sherd		2.5YR 6/6 light red; glaze: yellow, green; incl. fine, sm., min.; no core
452	16/8022	1925	bowl		5YR 7/4 pink; glaze: ext. yellow, int. dark green; incl. fine, sm., min.; no core
453	108/9126	6293	decorated		5YR 7/4 pink; glaze: yellow; incl. fine, sm., min.; no core
454	215/9030	3819	decorated		5YR 7/3 pink; glaze: yellow; incl. fine, sm., min.; no core
455	233/9111	5527	body sherd		5YR 7/4 pink; glaze: yellow; incl. sm., min.; no core
456	16/8022	1924	body sherd		5YR 7/4 pink; glaze: yellow; incl. sm., min.; no core
457	108/9124	6244	body sherd		10YR 8/2 white; glaze: dark green; incl. fine, sm., min.; no core
458	86/9273	7920	lamp		2.5YR 6/4 light reddish brown; slip 10YR 8/2 white; incl. sm., min.; no core
459	204/2599	3962	body sherd		2.5YR N4/ dark grey; slip 2.5YR N4/ dark grey; incl. fine; no core
460	204/2599	3945	body sherd		2.5YR N4/ dark grey; slip 2.5YR N4/ dark grey; incl. fine; no core
461	57/9014	3546	bowl	27	5YR 6/4 light reddish brown; slip ext. 5YR 8/2 pinkish white - 7/3 pink; incl. sm., min.; no core

462	108/9132	6958	bowl	22	5YR 4/3 reddish brown; incl. med., min.; no core
463	211/2304	1486	jar/jug	16	5YR 7/6 reddish yellow; slip 2.5YR 6/6 light red; incl. med., min.; no core
464	108/9129	6620	jar/jug	?	7.5YR 8/2 pinkish white; slip 7.5YR 7/4 pink - 2.5YR 6/4 light reddish brown; paint 2.5YR 3/2 dusky red; incl. sm., min., org.; core
465	356/2387	2489	jar/jug	16	5YR 7/3 pink; slip 7.5YR 8/2 pinkish white - 7/2 pinkish grey; paint, 5YR 3/1 very dark grey; 10R 5/4 weak red; incl. sm., min.; core
466	427/2327	2362	body sherd		5YR 7/4 pink; slip 7.5YR 8/2 pinkish white; paint 5YR 4/1 dark grey; incl. sm., min.; no core
467	427/2327	2661	body sherd		5YR 7/4 pink; slip 7.5YR 8/2 pinkish white; paint 5YR 4/1 dark grey; incl. sm., med., min.; no core
468	108/9127	6367	body sherd		10YR 8/2 white; paint 7.5YR N4/ very dark grey, 10R 5/4 weak red; incl, sm., min.; no core
469	427/2327	2421	body sherd		2.5YR 6/4 light reddish brown; slip 7.5YR 8/2 pinkish white; paint 5YR 4/1 dark grey; incl. sm., min.; no core
470	427/2327	2540	body sherd		5YR 7/3 pink; slip 7.5YR 8/2 pinkish white; paint 5YR 4/1 dark grey; 10R 4/2 weak red; incl. sm., min.; no core
471	81/9090	5355	body sherd		5YR 7/4 pink; slip 7.5YR 8/2 pinkish white; paint 5YR 4/1 dark grey; incl. sm., min., org.; no core
472	235/9082	5251	body sherd		5YR 7/4 pink; slip 5YR 7/4 pink- 2.5YR 6/4 light reddish brown; paint 5YR 4/1 dark grey; paint 10R 5/4 weak red; incl. sm., min.; no core
473	108/9128	6512	body sherd		5YR 7/4 pink; slip 7.5YR 8/2 pinkish white - 5YR 8/4 pink; paint 5YR 4/1 dark grey; 10R 5/4 weak red; incl. sm., min., org.; core
474	81/9090	5348	body sherd		7.5YR 8/2 pinkish white; slip 5YR 8/4 pink; paint 5YR 4/1 dark grey; incl. sm., min., org.; core
475	92/9006	3363	body sherd		5YR 7/4 pink; slip 2.5YR 6/4 light reddish brown; paint 5YR 4/1 dark grey; incl. sm., min., org.; core
476	108/9128	6502	handle		5YR 7/3 pink; slip 5YR 6/3 light reddish brown; incl. sm., med., min.; core
477	91/9008	3449	base sherd		7.5YR 8/2 pinkish white - 7/2 pinkish grey; slip 7.5YR 8/2 pinkish white; incl. sm., min.; no core

OTTOMAN AND MODERN: Plate 9 (sherds 478-85)

Sh.#	Site/field#	Reg.#	Form	Diameter	Description
478	108/9127	6353	cooking pot	20	5YR 7/3 pink; slip 7.5YR 8/2 pinkish white; incl. sm., med., min., org.; core
479	108/9128	6499	handle		5YR 7/4 pink; slip 7.5YR 8/2 pinkish white; incl. sm., min.; core
480	108/9128	6535	handle		5YR 7/3 pink; incl. sm., med., min., org.; core

481	2124	8013	jar	9	10YR 5/1 grey; slip 2.5YR N3/ very dark grey; incl. sm., min.; no core
482	211/2304	1326	cup	7	white; glaze: clear; paint ext.: red, green, gold; no core
483	333/2307	2967	vase	?	5YR 7/4 pink; glaze: red-brown; incl. sm., med., min.; core
484	333/2307	2964	vase	21	5YR 7/4 pink; incl. sm., min.; core
485	333/2307	2972	body sherd		5YR 7/4 pink - 5YR 6/4 light reddish brown; paint: yellow, blue, green, white; incl. sm., min.; no core

CHALCOLITHIC

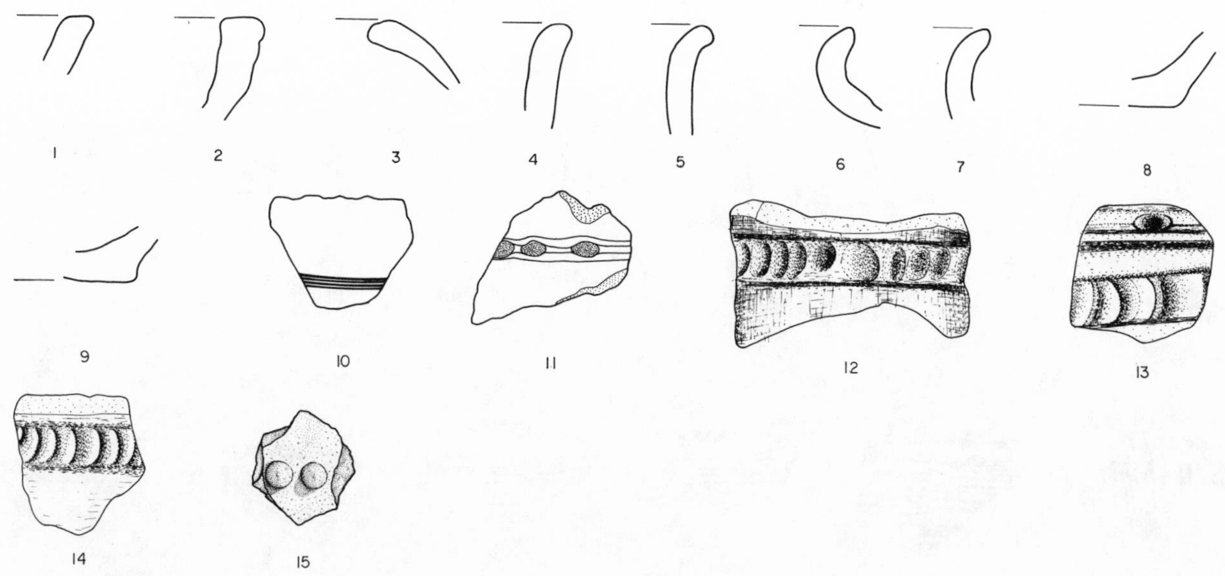

EARLY BRONZE I

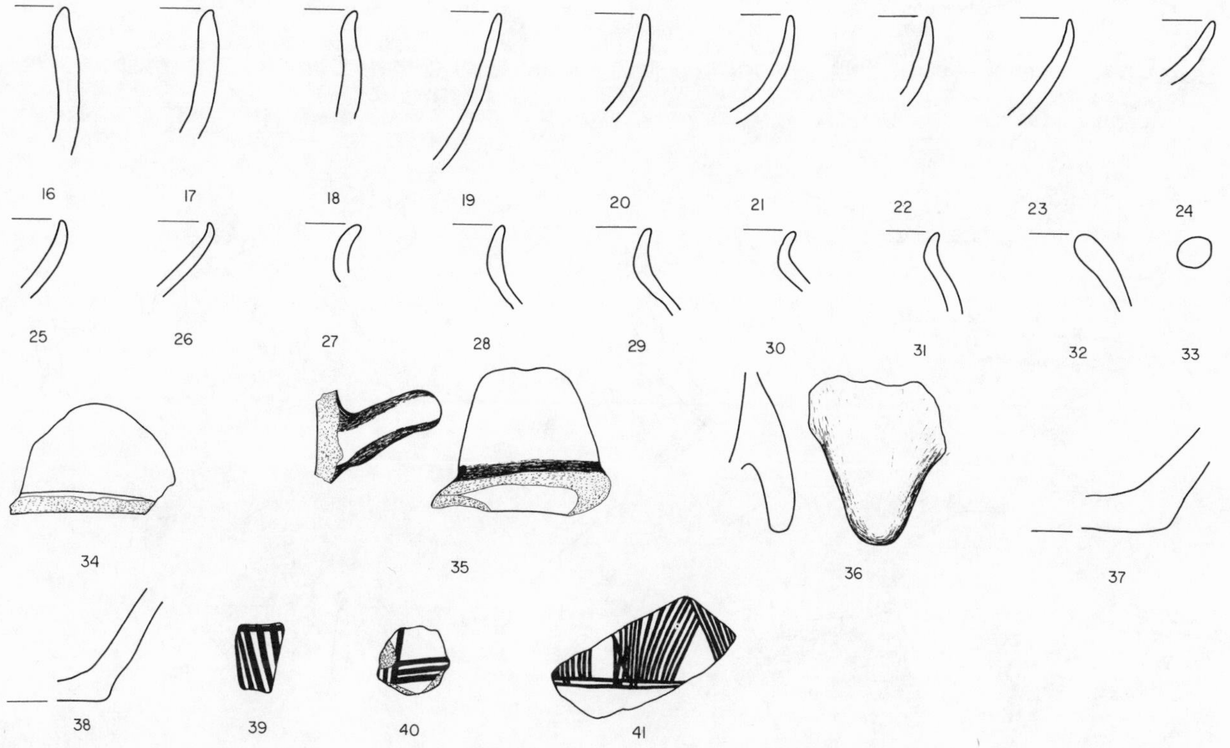

EARLY BRONZE II-III

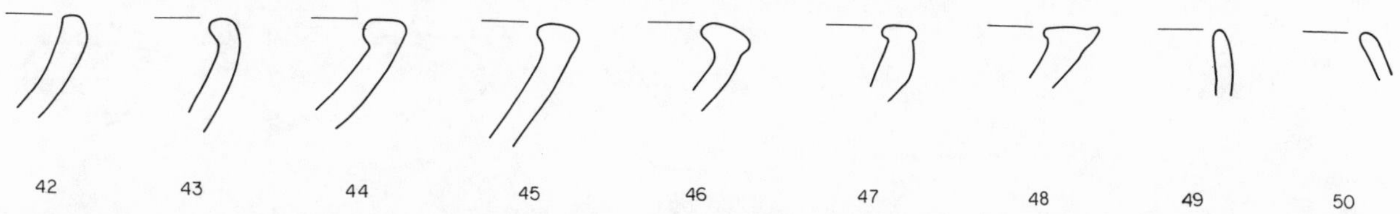

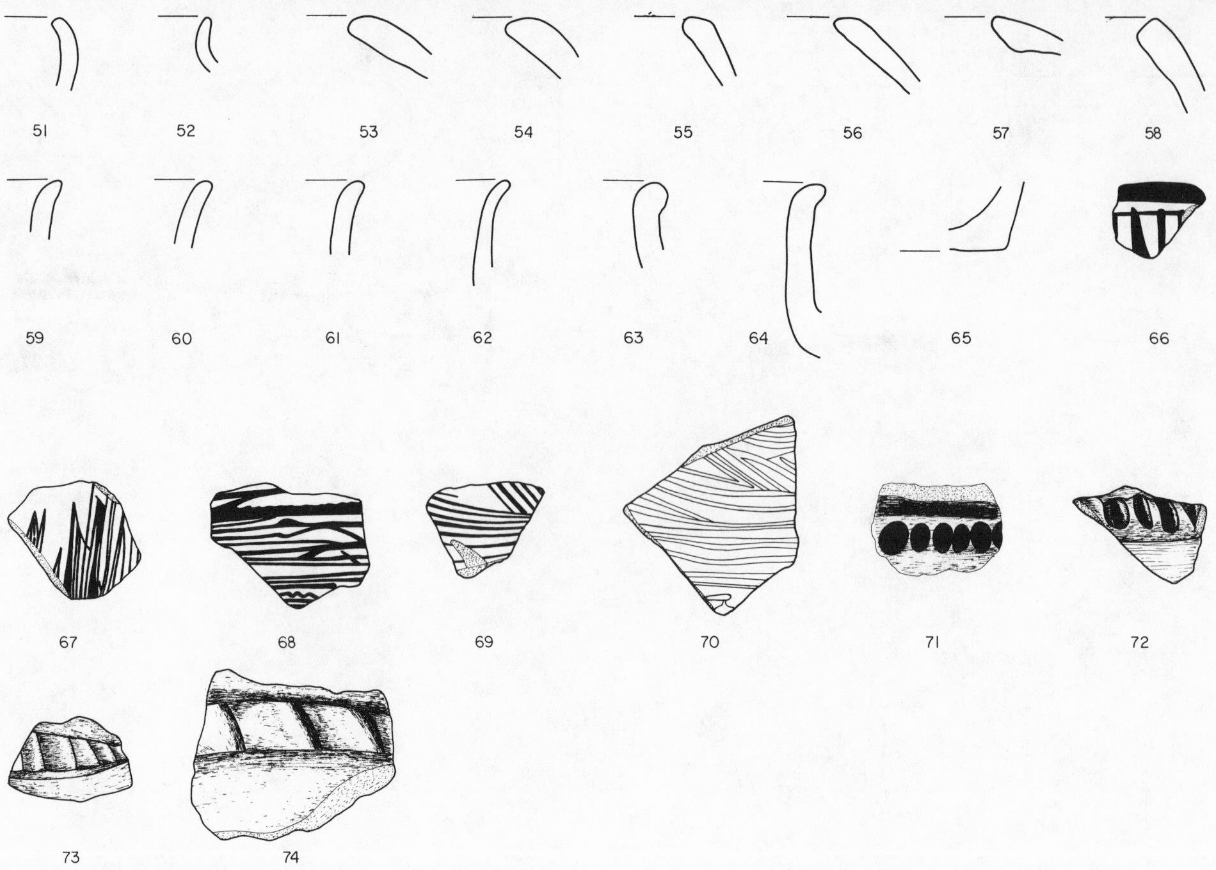

EARLY BRONZE IV

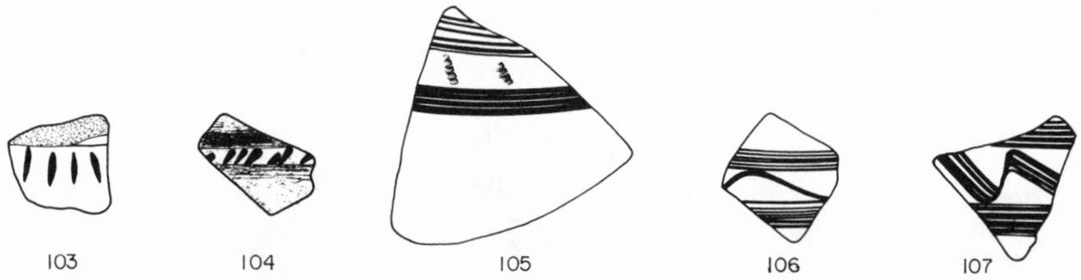

MIDDLE BRONZE I-II

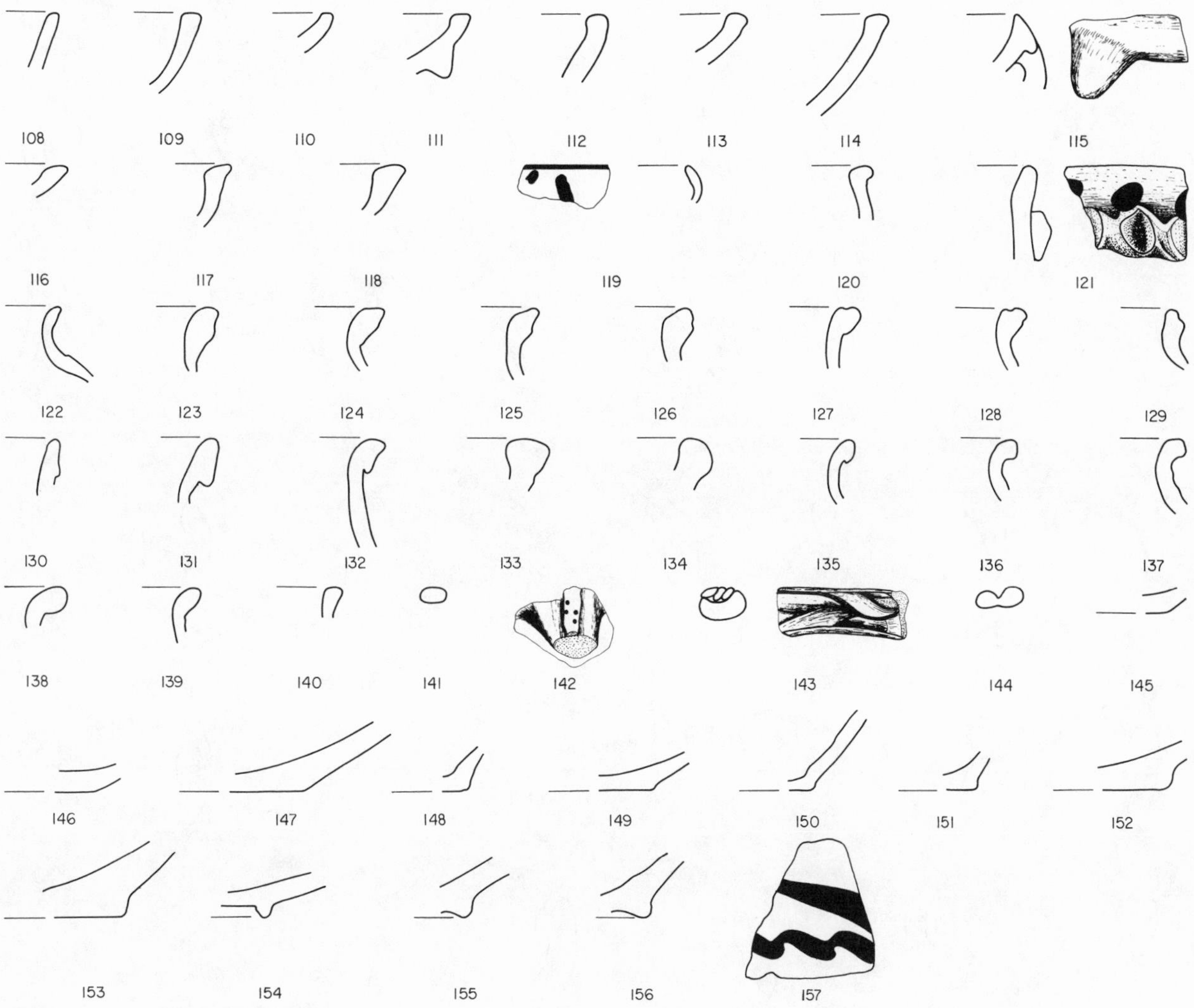

LATE BRONZE I-II

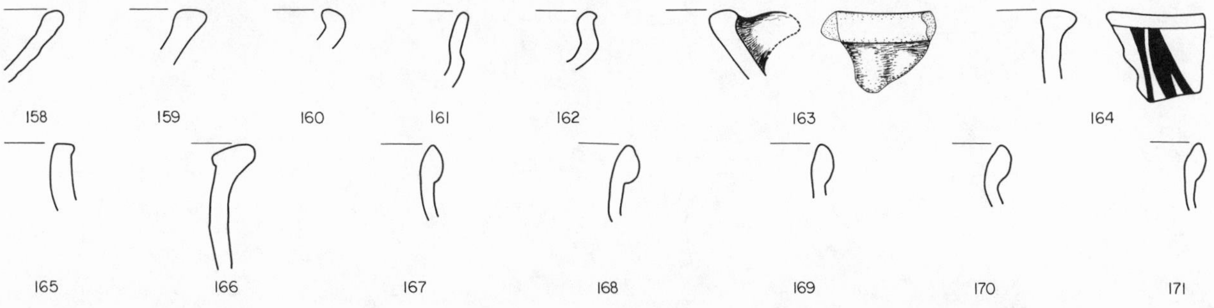

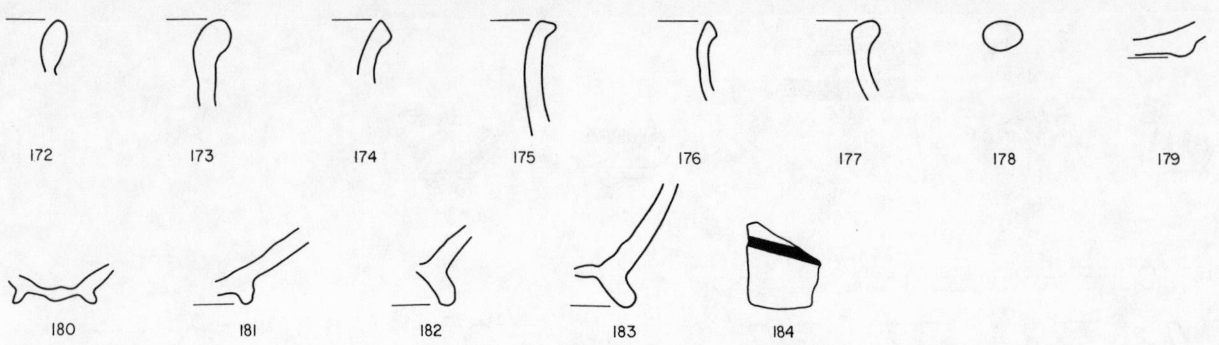

IRON I

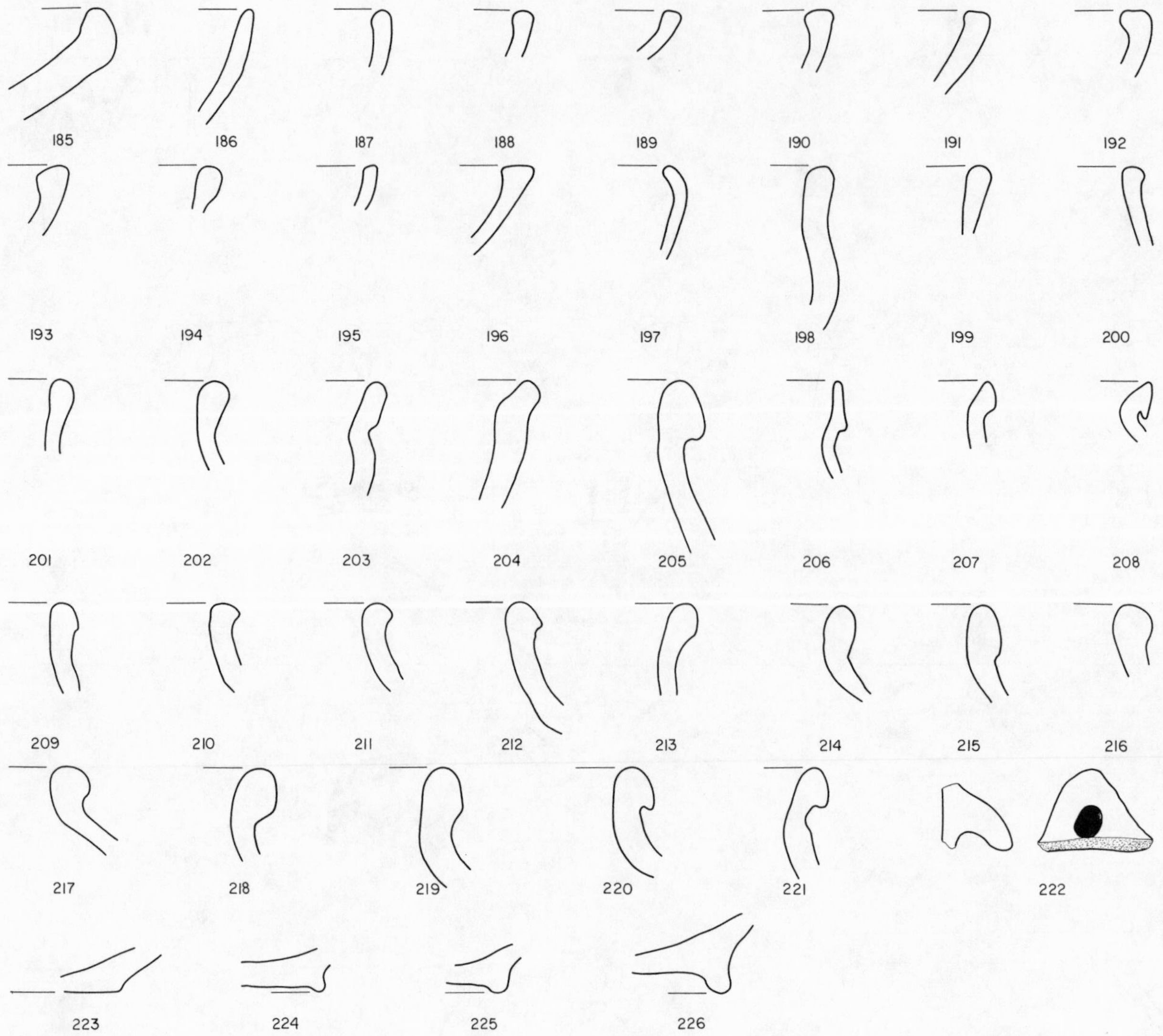

IRON II

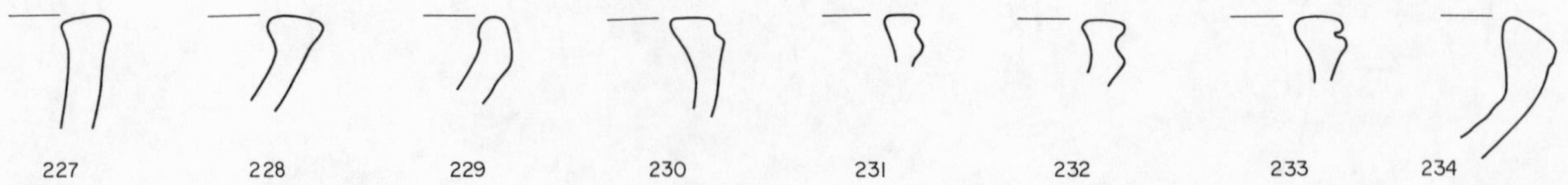

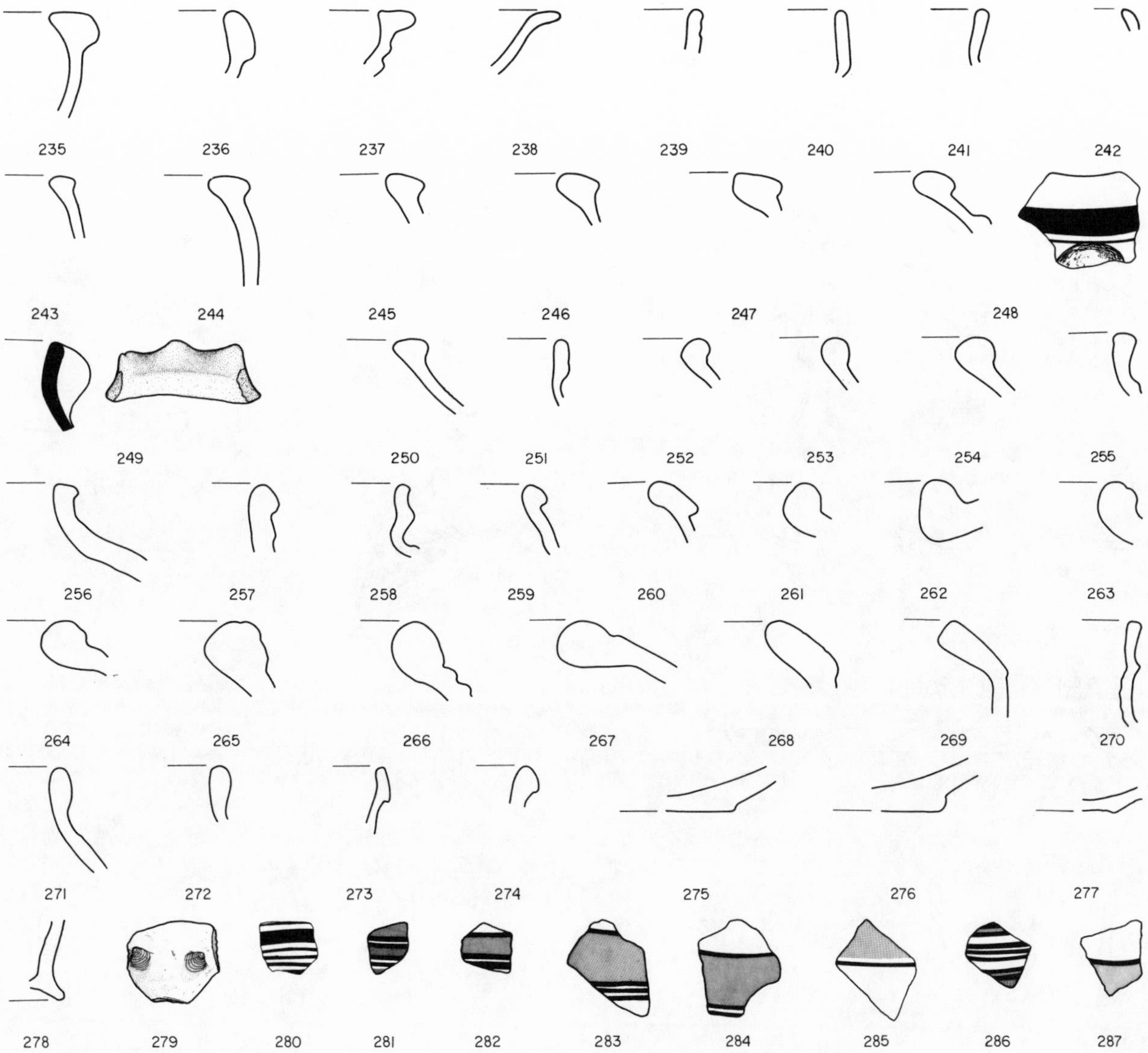

PERSIAN

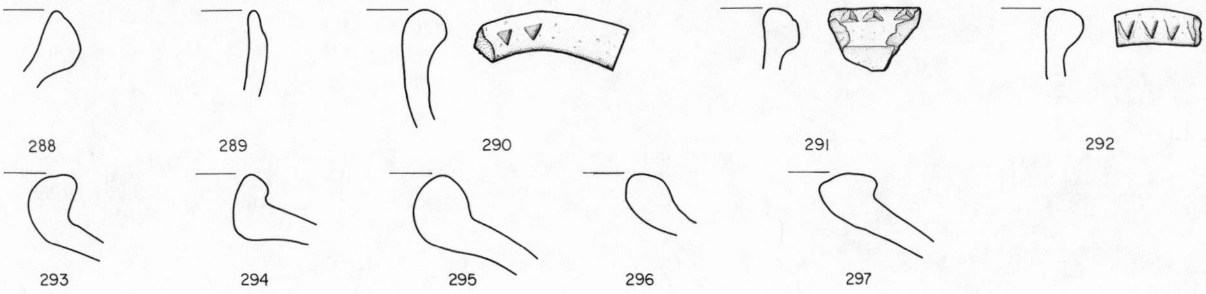

HELLENISTIC

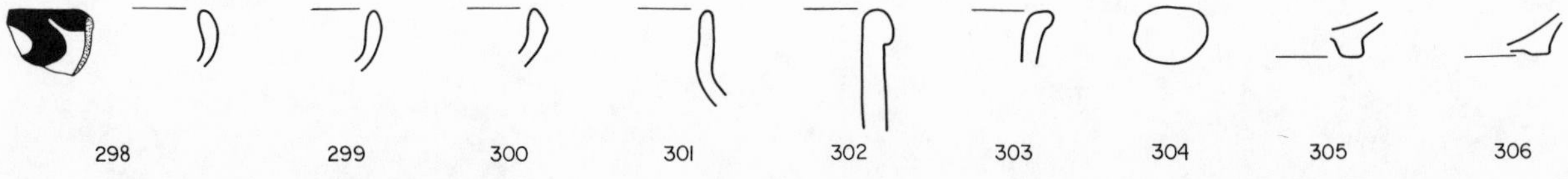

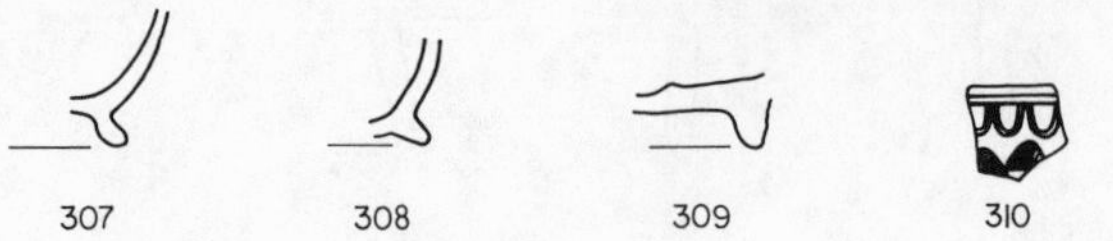

NABATAEAN

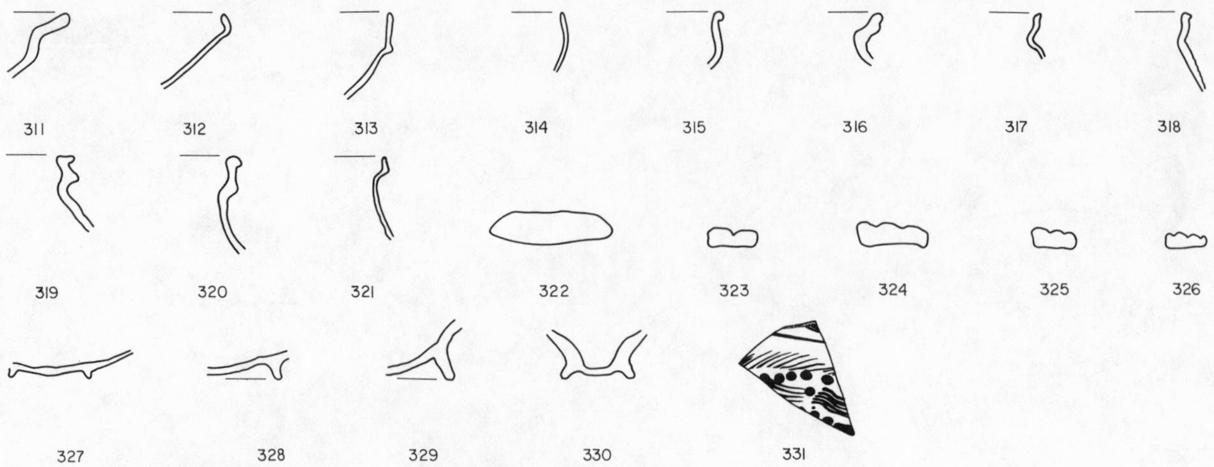

EARLY ROMAN

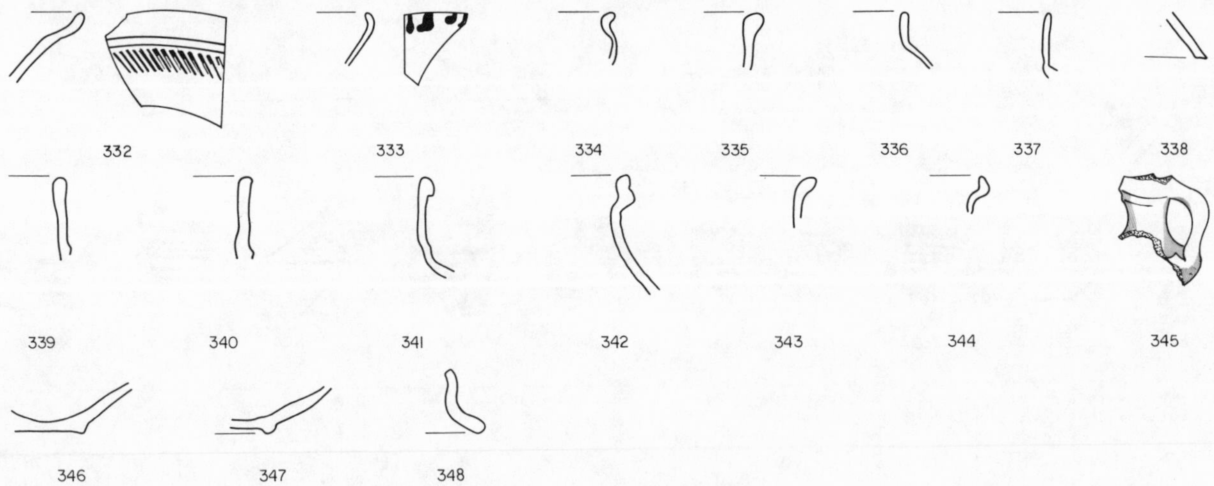

LATE ROMAN

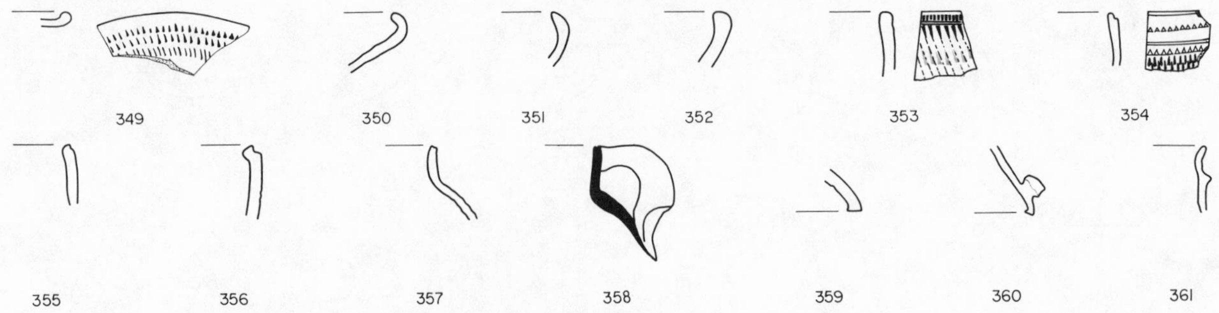

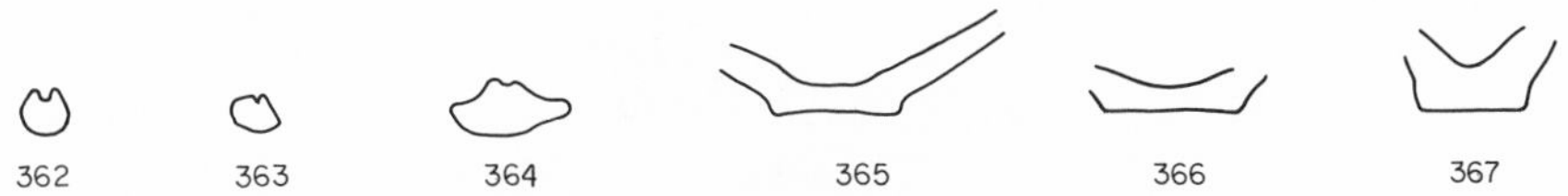

EARLY AND LATE BYZANTINE

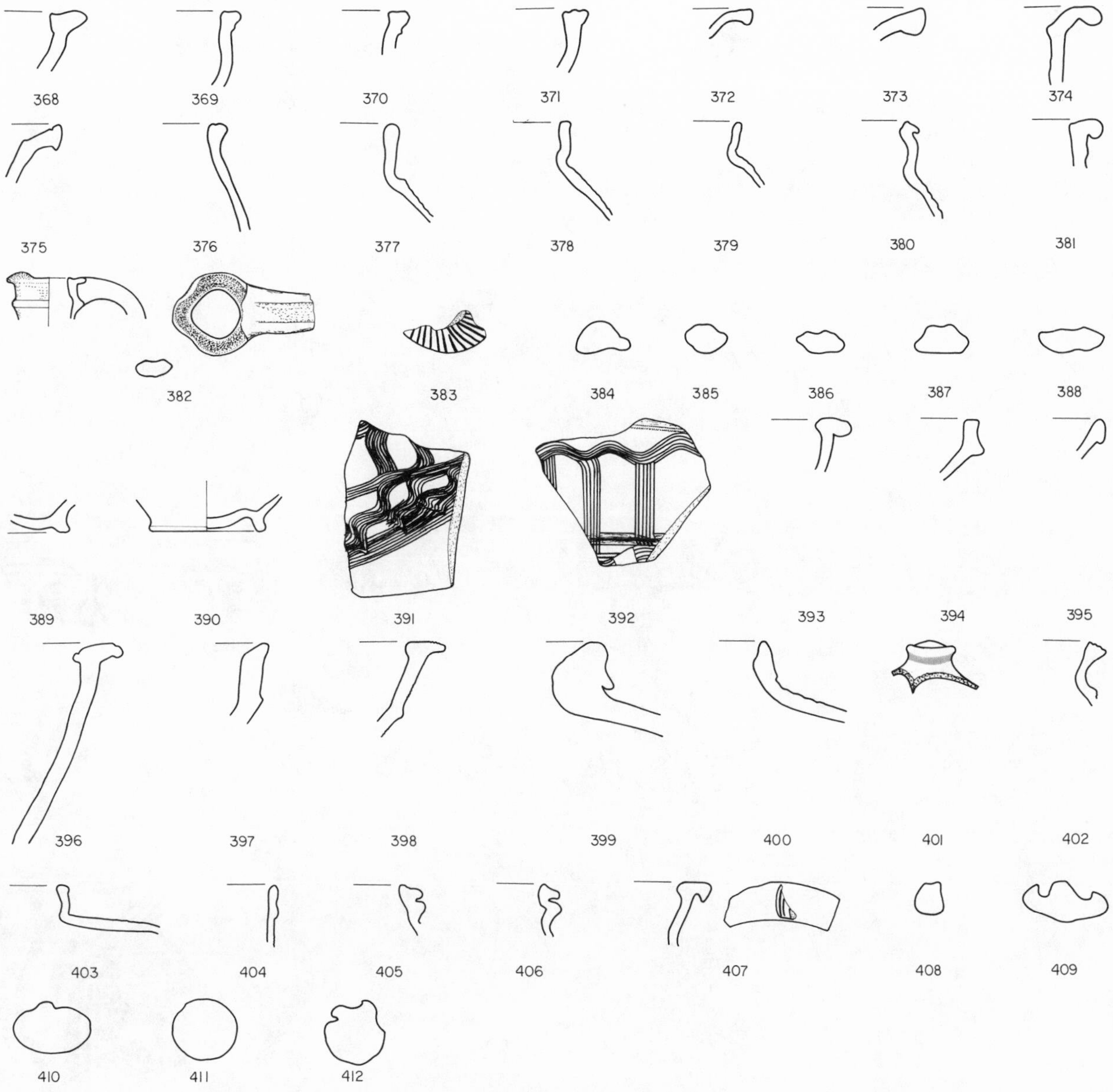

EARLY ISLAMIC

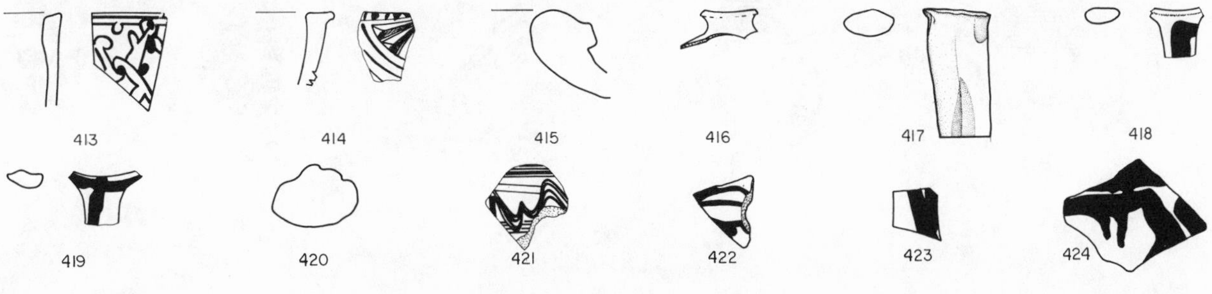

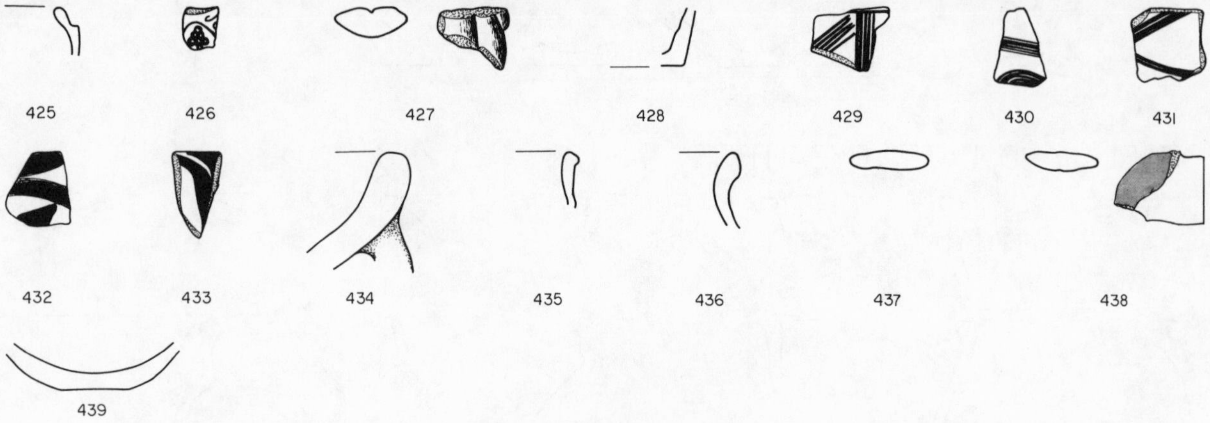

AYYUBID - MAMLUK

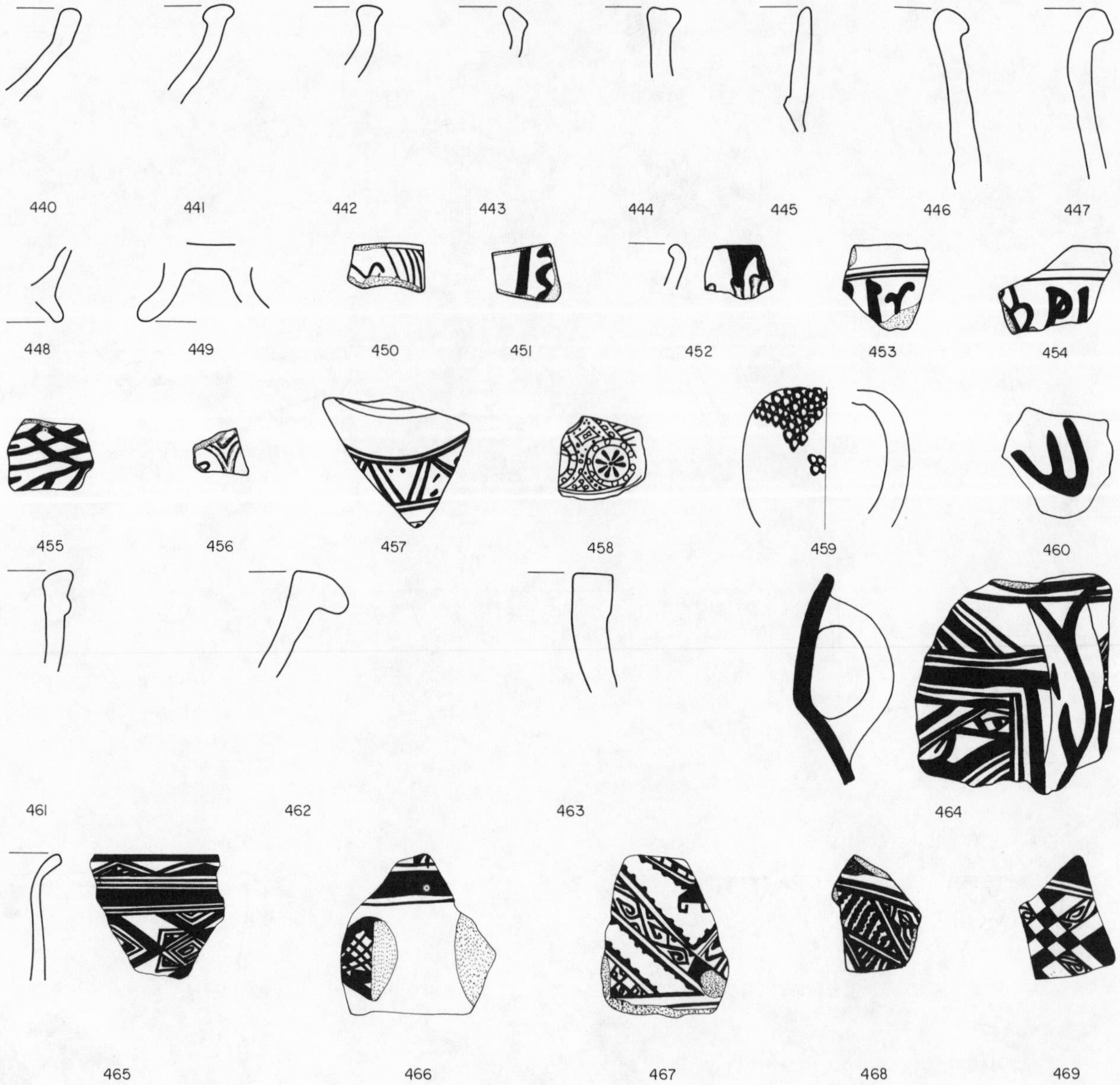

470

471

472

473

474

475

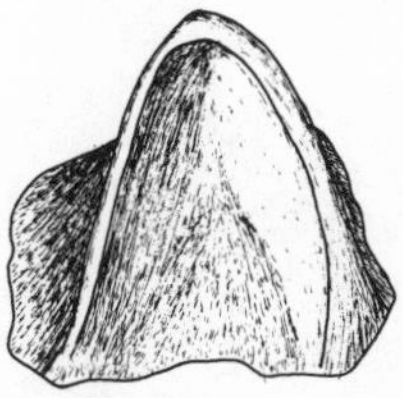
476

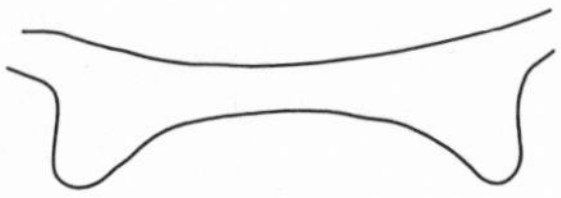
477

OTTOMAN AND MODERN

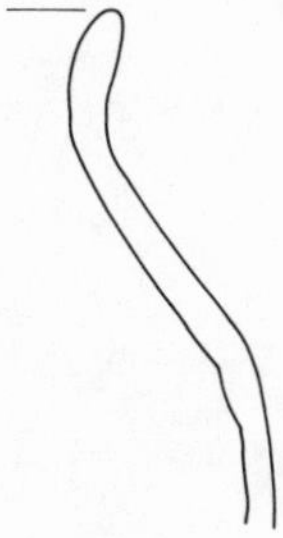
478

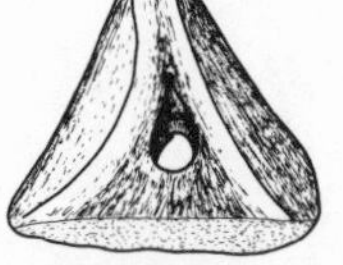
479

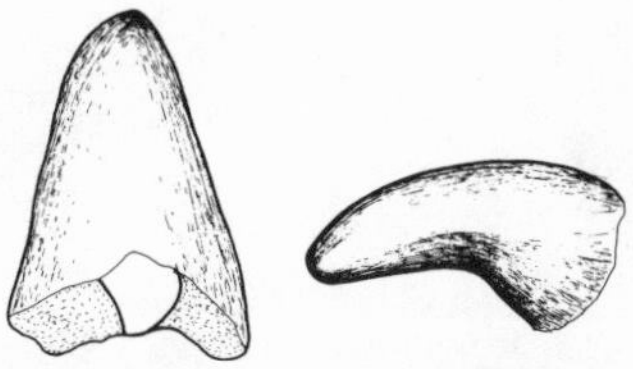
480

481

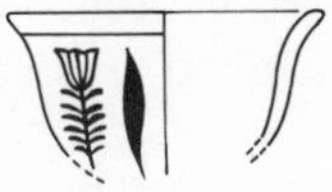
482

483

484

485

Chapter IV

TOPONYMY OF THE KERAK PLATEAU

by

Ernst Axel Knauf

It is generally acknowledged that toponyms survive more than one change in the political, economic, social, ethnic, or linguistic conditions within the society, or the succession of societies, which first coined and later transmitted them. Gubla, for example, first attested in the 3rd millennium B.C.E., is, after 5000 years, still Jbeil (Wild 1973: 249-51; Knauf 1984a: 120). The place names "Paris" and "London" are pre-Roman, pre-Germanic, pre-French and pre-English. Places tend to keep the names attributed to them by their original settlers unless a major event in the history of the particular place causes a change in its name. Adir was the political center of the Moabite plateau in the EB II-III period and the site has preserved a Canaanite name: "Glory," or "the Glorious" (Steele 1983: 51f). Lejjūn, near Adir, was also an important center during the 3rd millennium B.C.E., but its Canaanite name was lost because the Romans established a legionary camp, a "castra legionis," in its immediate vicinity and obliterated the linguistic remnants of earlier occupation (Steele 1983: 53). Both names, Adir and Lejjūn, are opaque to the present inhabitants of the region, yet they are still preserved. A systematic study of toponymy, therefore, may help to elucidate periods in the history of the Near East for which no written documentation exists (Knauf 1987a; 1988).

Historical Studies of Toponymy

Although toponymical studies play an important role in European pre-history (Borée 1968: 1-3; Wagner 1967), they figure rather marginally in ancient Near Eastern studies. Moreover, scholars dealing with the toponymy of the ancient Near East have tended to focus on site identification. The intellectual movement usually begins with the ancient sources and proceeds--sometimes jumps—to the present. The process tends to be unsystematic, and is characterized by remarkable pitfalls (Miller 1983; Lenzen and Knauf 1987). However, studies of place names which amply demonstrate the breadth of linguistical, historical, geographical, ecological, and anthropological knowledge to be retrieved from toponymy do exist (Kampffmeyer 1892; Borée 1968; Rainey 1978; Bailey 1984; Kislev 1985).

In the realm of Semitic studies, toponymical interest was first directed to the survival of Biblical names in the contemporary Near East (Kampffmeyer 1892). The extent of Phoenician/Punic colonialization in the West became, then, another focus of toponymical studies (Degen 1977; Huss 1985: 24-36). A series of seminal articles by B. S. J. Isserlin encompasses the whole Semitic world and has yet to be fully appreciated by fellow researchers. Isserlin collected material decisive for understanding the spread of the Semites in the Near East (1956), the stratigraphy of Arabic toponymy (1986a), and the periods in which certain place-name types were productive (1956; 1986b).

The study of Semitic toponyms reached a new standard with S. Wild's *Libanesische Ortsnamen* (1973). Wild established a sound stratigraphy for Syrian and Palestinian place names, based on typological screening of a complete corpus from a geographically well-defined sub-region of Greater Syria--i.e. Lebanon. His stratigraphy, which distinguishes a Canaanite, an Aramaic, and an Arabic stratum, can be refined—e.g. by introducing sub-strata such as "pre-standard Arabic" (Knauf 1984a)—but cannot be basically altered. Wild studied a contemporary corpus without consistent attention to earlier names and without regard to the location of his toponyms. Thus he left some work for others. A. Kuschke (1977) plotted Wild's Canaanite toponyms on a map, which resulted in clusters of places surrounding the major Phoenician port cities such as Tyre, Sidon, Beirut, Byblos, and Tripoli (Kuschke 1977: 80 Abb.1). This may help to establish the immediate agricultural *hinterland* of each of these cities.

The present contribution derives from the preparatory stage of a monograph which aims to establish the linguistic stratigraphy of the toponyms on the Kerak Plateau, and to correlate the various linguistic strata to the topography, ecology, and known cultural history of the Kerak plateau (Brown and Knauf, in preparation). The intention is to begin with the current place names on the plateau, but to make full use of earlier name forms. Hopefully some conclusions can be reached, on a statistically sound basis, regarding the transmission of place names and the conditions that shape this transmission (cf. preliminarily Thilo 1958: 20-21; Wild 1973: 5-11; 14-17; Miller and Hayes 1986: 29-30). Semantic analysis of the various place name corpora, present and ancient, is also intended. The Kerak Plateau is ideal for this study since it is geographically well-defined, was covered extensively by late 19th and early 20th century travellers, and now has been subjected to a systematic archaeological survey. A. Musil (1907-8) figures foremost among the travellers, having recorded contemporary toponymy painstakingly and with sufficient competence.

The Present Toponymy of the Kerak Plateau

The data base for the following discussion is defined by the sign-posts along the asphalted roads of the Kerak Plateau as they were photographed by the present author and C. H. Brooker in August 1987. This is the most recent and most "official" collection of toponyms available for the area. Naturally this data base is not fully comprehensive, since some of the settlements on the plateau do not have sign posts. Neither are the earlier corpora of toponyms for the region fully comprehensive—i.e., the official maps, the collections of A. Musil, the Early Ottoman tax records (Hütteroth and Abdulfattah 1977; Hütteroth 1978), the list of pilgrimage sites by al-Harawī (1957), the Madaba mosaic map, and the references to Moab in Isaiah 15-16 and Jeremiah 48. Incompleteness itself constitutes a peculiar kind of consistency between the 1987 road signs and the earlier corpora. However, each of these various corpora provides a collection of toponyms from one and the same time, recorded in a consistent way. In spite of their incompleteness, it was decided to base the present study on these corpora (secondarily amplified by isolated references in other written sources), rather than to attempt to develop a data base of current place names from oral sources. Important as a data base derived from oral sources may have been (Degen 1977: 228), it would have required an enormous amount of cross-checking along with the collection of primary dialectological data, which the author regarded as beyond his competence. Moreover, the dialectological data are missing for most of the tribes and villages of the Kerak Plateau.

The data base contains 57 toponyms. References to sites outside the plateau (Qaṭranah, Wadi el-Mujib, Wadi Ibn Ḥammad) are disregarded. The transcription of these names follows a modified "Syrian Koine" form, modified insofar as orthographical features are indicated which are not distinctive in the spoken language (such as the difference between *-ah*, *ā*ʾ, *ā* and *-a*). Since the population of the Kerak Plateau in August 1987 can be regarded as basically literate, the written form of a place name is as much part of the common linguistic consciousness as is the spoken form (cf. also Chafe and Tannen 1987).

Starting from the present, the following seven strata can be separated: (1) *Hashemite*—place names which originated within the past two decades and are not attested previously. (2) *Post-Standard Arabic*—place names which originated among the illiterate local population after the decline of an effective imperial administration in this area in the 16th/17th centuries C.E. Some Post-Standard Arabic names may antedate this time. (3) *Standard (Classical) Arabic*—names restricted to places which figure in the geographical and historiographical literature of medieval Islam, based no doubt on official administrative documents, and which have been reintroduced by the Hashemite administration to the detriment of the orally transmitted form. (4) *Pre-Standard Arabic*—names which originated from the pre-Islamic

Arab population of this area, such as the Nabataeans, Safaites, and the various "Thamudic" tribes. (5) *Greek and Roman*—names introduced to the area following Trajan's annexation of the Nabataean realm in 106 C.E., and remaining in official use until the Sasanid (614 C.E.) and Muslim (634 C.E.) conquests. (6) *Aramaic*—names originating from a language which invaded the Kerak Plateau in the 6th century B.C.E., when Aramaic became the language of administration in the course of the region's take-over by the Neo-Babylonians and Achaemenid Persians. In the course of time, Aramaic became a spoken language among the agricultural population of Transjordan and thrived well into the 12th century C.E. when, as a result of the military and administrative actions of the Crusaders and their adversaries, the Christian rural population on the periphery of Palestine became virtually extinct (Brooker and Knauf 1988). (7) *Canaanite and/or Aramaic*—names which may belong to either of the two pre-Arab strata but, in most cases, are Canaanite names in Aramaic transmission. These names were coined from the 4th/3rd millennia B.C.E., if not earlier, to the first half of the 1st millennium B.C.E.. There are no pre-Canaanite place names in this area, nor are there any in Palestine or Lebanon (Wild 1973: 61-65). This observation agrees well with the assumption that Greater Syria is the homeland of the Semites, from where they spread to other regions of the Near East (Knauf 1988).

Three minor linguistic strata known from Palestine do not occur on the road sign-posts of the Kerak Plateau: British, Ottoman Turkish, and Crusader place names. This fact relates to the marginality of the region, which gave foreign occupants little opportunity to establish permanent settlement. British place names are attested in northern Jordan: el-Jfūr (= H4) and el-Jfāyif (= H5). One Turkish name occurs among the presently unsettled archaeological sites on the Kerak plateau: Karakūn (from *Karakol*, "police station"; the word has been borrowed into Syrian colloquial Arabic). No Crusader names (as Sinjil < St. Giles, Laṭrūn < La Toron in Palestine) exist throughout Jordan, although el-Franj near Kerak and Kufrinjī (< Kufr el-Franjī, "the village of the Franks") clearly relate to the presence of this foreign population group.

Discussion

Hashemite. 18 out of 57 toponyms (31.58%) derive from the past two decades. Two of these are restored Classical Arabic names to the detriment of post-classical names: Muʾta for Mautah, and el-Mazār for el-Jaᶜfariyyah. Seven names relate to new settlements, for which no predecessor can be identified: el-ᶜĀlyah, az-Zahrāʾ, el-Manshiyyah, er-Rāshdiyyah, el-Wasiyyah, Zaḥūm, el-Feiṣaliyyah. This does not imply that these eight places have never been settled before. Two of these were recorded as regional designations by A. Musil: el-Wasiyyah ("the clean-shaven," i.e. treeless, plain; Musil 1907-8: 86, 369) and Zaḥūm ("the pushed," i.e., wadi; Musil 1907-8: 369). Two of the remaining names also refer to land-formation: el-ᶜĀlyah ("the high") and az-Zahrāʾ ("the shining," by antinomy from the local basalt-dominated landscape; cf. the case of Khirbet el-Beiḍāʾ in Syria: Gaube 1974). The remaining nine names from this stratum derive from renaming settlements or unsettled places which had proper names previously: esh-Shihābiyyah (< el-Franj), eṣ-Ṣālḥiyyah (< Khirbat aẓ-Ẓuṭṭ), el-Ḥawiyyah (< en-Naqqāz), el-ᶜAdnāniyyah (< Miḥnā), el-ᶜUmariyyah (< Dleiqa), el-Khāldiyyah (< Um Zabāyir), el-Hāshmiyyah (< Majrā and Jweir), el-Ḥseiniyyah (< Rujm eṣ-Ṣakharī), el-Maʾmūniyyah (< Abū esh-Shaḥm). All of these names consist of a personal or clan/family name and the feminine *nisbah*-ending. In two cases, the names are drawn from those of the presently ruling family of the country. This toponymic class could easily be interpreted as a typical case of "toponymics of resettlement," or the settlement of "nomads" or "bedouin," were there no earlier names recorded for these settlements. This could indicate that the socio-politics of "bedouinization" are more complicated than could be described as a simple process of settlement. As for the earlier names which seem to be condemned to oblivion (although future centuries will reveal which names survive; cf. the discussion of Greek-Latin toponymy below), el-Franj ("the Frank's [settlement]," possibly a suburb of Crusader Kerak), Khirbat aẓ-Ẓuṭṭ ("the ruin of the gypsies"), en-Naqqāz ("the frightener"), Um Zabāyir ("the mother of the peaks [literally, pricks]"), Rujm eṣ-Ṣakharī ("the rocky heap of stones" or "the stone-heap of the Ibn Ṣakhr") all derive from the immediately preceding toponymical stratum (post-standard Arabic), but have connotations that the inhabitants of the new or old settlements may have regarded as detrimental to their reputation. This is clearly the case with Miḥnā, a Canaanite name meaning "camp," but re-etymologized in Arabic as "strife, infliction." The name Miḥnā is already attested for the pre-Islamic period, which lends support to the stratigraphic interpretation offered here. The same holds true for Majrā (Majra, Majrah), a Canaanite name (cf. Hebr. *Migrōn*, 1 Sam 14:2; Is 10:28), but reminding one of *majr* ("watercourse, sewage system") in Arabic. Jweir ("little hole" or "pit") is not a very favorable designation for one's home village either. In other cases, the re-naming of one's settlement may be due to adherence to a fashion and/or a similar action by one's neighbours. There is nothing detrimental in Abū esh-Shaḥm ("Father of Fat," as a designation for one's fields and pasturages), a typical post-standard Arabic name. The translations of Arabic names indicated in this section and below are based on Denizeau (1960) and Wehr and Cowan (1976).

Post-Standard Arabic. 13 out of 57 toponyms belong to this stratum (22.80%). Its characteristics are: formations with *abū/umm*, preceding a topographical feature and replacing *dhū/dhāt* of Standard Arabic, as in Abū Trābah ("Father of Dust"), Kh. Um Rummānah ("Mother of a Pomegranate Tree"), Um Ḥamāṭ ("Mother of the Pseudo-Sycamores"; cf. Bailey 1984: 52). The diminutive *fuᶜail*-form became predominant, a feature well attested in colloquial Arabic as opposed to Standard Arabic: Mgheir ("the little cave"), Ghuweir ("the very small depression"), Jdeiyidah ("the little [new-founded] settlement"), Mḥai ("the little obliterated [ruin]"), Msheirfah ("the little elevated one"; attested in the Arabic conquest narratives as Mashārif; see al-Ṭabarī 1879-1901: I, 1614; 1960-79: 3, 39 and parallels). The formation Personal/Clan Name with *-iyyah* ending originated in this period, replacing the same formation with *-ah* in Classical Arabic (Isserlin 1986a): Smākiyyah (cf. Simāk in Caskel 1966: 512f). This formation is still productive, whereas the *umm*- and *abū* names of this period are gradually being replaced. In one case, an unaltered personal name became a place name: Ḥmūd (which, as a personal name, is post-standard Arabic as well; cf. the el-Ḥamūd among the ᶜAdwān; Oppenheim 1943: 215, and the el-Ḥamāydah, ibid. 251-54, 268). The name el-ᶜIrāq ("the cliff, cave") is derived from a noun which does not belong to Standard Arabic.

Place names which refer to individual trees attest widespread deforestation within this period (Um Ḥamāṭ, Kh. Um Rummānah). Mḥai and el-Jdeiyidah refer to the presence of ruins, and a certain amount of resettlement, sometime between the 13th and the 19th centuries C.E.

Standard Arabic. All names that can be explained by the lexicographical stock of Standard Arabic have been included in this category. Since Standard Arabic overlaps with Pre-Standard and Post-Standard Arabic chronologically, and, at least as far as the vast majority of the population of the Kerak plateau is concerned, was never a spoken language, the category has little chronological significance. Five out of 57 toponyms belong to this stratum (8.77%). These are: eth-Thaniyyah ("the narrow pass"), a road-station in the 13th and 14th centuries C.E. and still a resting place on the Jerusalem pilgrim's caravan on its way to Mecca (Musil 1907-8: 26, 77, 85); el-Qaṣr ("the castle"; i.e., the impressive ruin of a Roman-Nabataean temple); ed-Dimnah ("dung-heap"; actually a Canaanite toponym re-etymologized); Mazār ("the tomb which is a center of pilgrimage," i.e., that of Jaᶜfar b. Abī Ṭālib. The Hashemite administration has superimposed this Standard Arabic form on the site which was known colloquially as Jaᶜfariyyah in the 19th century, the latter being a typical Post-Standard Arabic formation [cf. Musil 1907-8: 152; 361]); Muᵓta ("the uninstigated, fervent attack," according to the lexicographical tradition [cf. Yāqūt 1957: V, 219], and clearly a hypercorrection of the colloquial form, Mautah, which is still preserved in the English transcription of the road signs. Mautah derives from Canaanite *Mōtō* and is avoided because of its obvious meaning, "place of death").

Pre-Standard Arabic. There is only one example (1.75 %) of this class: Dhāt Rās ("The One on/of the Hilltop"). Because of the *dhāt*- formation, the name can be neither Post-Standard Arabic nor non-Arabic. Standard Arabic, on the other hand, would require the definite article in front of Rās (cf. Knauf 1984b: 21 and n. 14). In short, the name Dhāt Rās represents a linguistic survival of the 1000 years which Arab tribes (among other population groups) spent on the Kerak Plateau before the coming of Islam (M. Weippert 1987: 99).

Arabic toponymy derives, roughly speaking, from the last 2000 years of the Kerak Plateau's linguistic history. All four strata together represent 35 of the 57 names in the data base (61.40%). Not unexpectedly, the frequency of names from each stratum decreases steadily from the present to the more remote past. The more time passed, in other words, the higher the chances that a place would be renamed. The pre-Arabic strata—Greek-Latin, Aramaic, and Canaanite—comprise 21 of the 57 names (36.84%). These strata represent a linguistic history which began at the end of the 4th millennium B.C.E. (if not with the beginning of the 6th) and ended with the Crusades (when Aramaic disappeared as a spoken language on the Kerak Plateau). Thus the pre-Arabic linguistic history of the region covered some 5000 years. One name, Sūl, has not yet been classified.

Greek-Latin. There is only one example for this class: el-Lajjūn (from "castra legionis" i.e., IV Martiae; cf. Parker 1986b). Interestingly enough, this was not the official name of the site in the Roman period, which was Betthoro /Batora (Canaanite, Aramaic, or Pre-Standard Arabic: Knauf 1985a). The name "legion" obviously was given by the local population during Roman times, using the Latin for a military installation which had no counterpart in the ancient Semitic world. The doubling of the "*j*" adapted the name to the triliteral pattern of Semitic "roots."

Hellenization was never deep-rooted on the Kerak Plateau. One of the two major cities, el-Kerak, never adopted a Greek name; the other, er-Rabbah, supposedly did (Areopolis), but never used this Hellenistic name on its coins, which were its most official documents (Spijkerman 1978: 262-77; Spijkerman 1984). Specifically, the coins were minted either in the name of Rabbathmoba (an Aramized Canaanite name) or Arsapolis (a Pre-Standard Arabic/Greek mixture: Knauf 1984c). There is, however, one archaeological site with a Greek name: Tadūn, derived from "St. Theodoros" via Tadūr and Tadhūr (Weippert and Knauf 1988: 150). As the site shows traces of a Byzantine church, the name probably refers to its patron saint.

Aramaic. Only 3 toponyms are Aramaic (5.26%): el-Kerak ("the Fortress City"), previously Karakmōbā ("the Fortress City of Moab"); Kathrabbā (< Kafr Rabbā, Megalokōmē), attested previously as Kufrabbah (Musil 1907: 68, 73, 77) and as Kafr Rabbā (in the 16th century C.E. Ottoman tax records, Hütteroth 1978: 79 M10); and Rākīn ("the sloping [settlement]"). Two of these names, el-Kerak and Kathrabbā, imply the significance of the two sites for their larger or more restricted environment. This agrees with the fact that Aramaic was introduced to the Kerak Plateau as the language of administration when the region fell to the Neo-Babylonian and Persian empires. Kerak rose to prominence during the 5th/4th centuries B.C.E., although a city or town existed on the spot before. Names like Kathrabbā, which is a non-urban name by definition, and Rākīn ("the sloping [settlement]") attest that Aramaic was a spoken language on at least part of the Plateau. As indicated above, Aramaic died out in central and southern Transjordan in the course of the Crusades. After the depopulation of Jerusalem following its initial conquest, the city was repopulated by *Suriani* from Transjordan (Prawer 1980: 92-93). By this term, the Crusader sources refer to the Aramaic speaking Christian peasant population as opposed to *Saraceni* "bedouin." The concentration of this population in Crusader towns on both sides of the Jordan—e.g. at Kerak and Shaubak—led, in the course of political and military events, to their actual expulsion from the countryside.

Under the impact of Aramaic, Canaanite names in *ō(n)* may have shifted the *-ō* to *-ā*; some may have adopted the *-ā* locative ending in this period (ed-Dimnah < Dīmōn), which in the spoken language coincided with the ending of the Aramaic determined state. In Arabic, this ending indiscriminately appears as *-ā* (Jadᶜā, Arīḥā) or *-ah* (Mautah, ed-Dimnah).

Canaanite and Canaanite/Aramaic. There are ten Canaanite and seven Canaanite and/or Aramaic place names among those attested on the road signs. Together they constitute 29.82% of the data base. The Canaanite /Aramaic names are included in the present category, since it can be reasonably assumed that most of them were originally Canaanite, especially given the temporally and socio-linguistically restricted distribution of Aramaic on the Kerak plateau. This stratum includes names in *-ā(n)* < *-ōn*: Arīḥā, another Jericho, a site of the Moongod; Jadᶜā, a site either named after a person (cf. Gideon) or after the wood-cutting that preceded its foundation (cf. *Gidᶜōm* in Judah; but cf. also Meyer and Donner 1987: 203); Shīḥān, named either after its vegetation of shrubs (Hebrew, Aramaic and Arabic *š₂yh*, "wormwood," "artemisia," "shrubs in the desert," cp. Gen 2:5; 21:15; Job 30:4, 7) or, more likely, after its dominating position used as a look-out post (cf. Akkadian *šiāḫum*, "grow high" [of gods, men; eagles, lions; trees, grain; mountains]; von Soden 1965-81: 1224). Although the noun *shīḥ* is Arabic as well as Canaanite, the *-ān* ending was no longer productive when Arabic invaded the Kerak plateau. Further names in *-ā(n)* include ᶜIzra, either after a personal name or from Late Hebrew *ᶜezrah* "courtyard," and ᶜAinūn, which did not change the "ō" to "ā". In some cases, present *-ah* derives from the Canaanite "feminine"-ending: er-Rabbah ("the capital") from Rabbath-Mōᵓab (Rabbath-Mōbā in Aramaic transmission, Maᵓāb in early Standard Arabic, later er-Rabbah); Ṣirfa (cf. Phoenician *ṣrpt*/Sarepta); and el-ᶜAmaqah ("the little plain").

A second type is constituted by names with *m-* prefix: Misᶜar, either from Late Hebrew *miṣᶜar* ("storm"), or, if Musil who recorded the name with "ṣ" was accurate (1907-8: 138), from Hebrew *misᶜar* ("small;" the root has a *ghain* in Arabic). Note however Musil's tendency to "phonemicize" *tafkhīm* (Knauf 1983: 154 n. 8). In the latter case, the modern form would be due to recent re-etymologizing, either according to Modern Standard Arabic ("fire iron") or according to a non-standard meaning ("crazy dog with rabies," as reported by one informant). Neither, of course, can be the correct etymology of the place name. For Mirwid, cf. Phoenician Arwad.

According to their vowel pattern, the following names are Canaanite and/or Aramaic: Faqūᶜ (var. Fāqūᶜ), the root corresponding to the Aramaic counterpart of Hebrew and Arabic *bqᶜ*; Imraᶜ ("pasturage"), the lexeme being Canaanite and Arabic, the vowel pattern Aramaic; Yārūt, which illustrates a very archaic place name formation consisting of the simple imperfect (Isserlin 1956; Knauf 1988). Most probably, the latter name was originally connected with Wadi Yarut (cp. Tigre *rotä* "to remain," of water after the rain; Müller 1977: 127).

According to parallels and/or roots, the following names are Canaanite: Batīr, 13th century B.C.E. Canaanite in Egyptian transmission *Bōtart (Knauf 1984c), Hebrew Bether; Adir ("Glory, the Glorious"; note however that Arabic *adir* does not have this meaning [Nöldeke 1952-54: 13b]; ᶜAi ("ruin"); Middīn (cp. Middīn in Jos. 15:61).

Shīḥān (as a name in *-ān*) and Yārūt (a name consisting of a simple imperfect) derive from the most ancient stratum of Semitic toponymy, going back to the 3rd millennium B.C.E. if not to an even earlier period (Isserlin 1956; Knauf 1987a; 1988). In the case of Yārūt, its South Semitic etymon provides further proof for the antiquity of the name. Since the forefathers of the South Semites left Syria-Palestine before 2000 B.C.E. (Knauf 1987a; 1988), the lexical stock and the toponyms common to those two branches of Semitic should antedate the beginning of the 2nd millenium B.C.E. By the same argument, the name Miṣnaᶜ ("fortification," as in Sabaic) can confidently be dated back to the 3rd or early 2nd millennia B.C.E. It is difficult to tell when the *-ān* type and the *yfᶜl*-type ceased to be productive in Palestine; the writer has the impression that no names belonging to these types (as opposed to sentence-names like Yokteel) were formed in 1st millennium B.C.E. Palestine (although in South Arabia and North Arabia both types remained productive until the beginning of the 1st millennium C.E.). This view presupposes that Shomron and Heshbon, two foundations of the 9th/8th centuries B.C.E., inherited their names from the hills on which they were constructed.

Canaanite toponymy falls within the same semantic classes encountered in the more recent strata: land formation (Faqūᶜ, Shīḥān?, Batīr), vegetation (Jadᶜā?, Imraᶜ), the availability of water (ᶜAinūn, Yārūt), destruction and resettlement (ᶜAi, Jadᶜā?), personal and/or tribal/clan names (ᶜIzra, Jadᶜā?), and the sociopolitical significance of a settlement (er-Rabbah, Adir).

Ancient Corpora of Place-Names

Whereas the preceding section traced the survivals of pre-modern toponymy in the data base derived from 1987 road signs, this section will discuss three ancient corpora and investigate their relationship to the data base.

Ottoman tax registers of the late 16th century C.E. These, as published by Hütteroth and Abdulfattah (1977: 171-72) and Hütteroth (1978: 79), list nine places on the plateau, two in the Ghor (Ṣāfīya, Mazraᶜa), and two which cannot be identified with known sites and may have been situated either on the plateau or in the Ghor (ᶜAin Musa, Ṭaiyiba; possibly Wadi Musa and aṭ-Ṭeiyibah south of Petra which, as Ṭafīleh which appears on the same list, may have come under the administration of Kerak at that time). Of the nine sites listed in the tax register for the plateau, six are attested in the 1987 sign-post corpus: Kerak, Ṣarmā (read Ṣarfā, present Ṣirfa), Mazār, Kafr Rabbā (Kathrabba), Mūtah (Mōta), ᶜIrāq. The three remaining sites all appear in the 1979 edition of the "Archaeological Map of Jordan, Sheet 2" (originally compiled in 1949/1952 on the basis of Glueck 1934-1939, who in turn relied on Musil for his toponym forms). These are: Mazāriᶜ (ez-Zarrāᶜah), Shajara ("Sajara" near el-Qaṣr, originally Shajarat Beit Allāh, "The Tree of the House of God"), and Rās (er-Rās west of Faqūᶜ; less likely, Dhāt Rās). The survival of this 16th century C.E. corpus of toponyms into present toponymy, therefore, rates at 100% (note that some of the identifications differ from those proposed by Hütteroth and Abdulfattah). One name out of the nine is Post-Standard Arabic: ᶜIrāq; four are Standard Arabic: Mazāriᶜ, Mazār, Rās, Shajarah (since the list was compiled by Turkish officials with a limited command of Arabic, the definite article is missing throughout); four names are pre-Arabic: Kerak, Ṣarfā, Kafr Rabbā, Mūtah. The pre-Arabic forms represent 44.44% of the total nine, equally distributed between Canaanite and Aramaic.

The Madaba map. The Madaba Mosaic Map, most probably compiled and executed during the reign of Justinian (Donner and Cüppers 1977), contains three toponyms from the Kerak Plateau: Charachmōba, Ai and Tharais. Kerak and ᶜAi figure in the 1987 sign-post corpus; and the name Tharais is preserved in that of a ruin, Tarᶜīn, covered by the present-day village of ᶜIrāq (Donner 1982: 185-87). Tarᶜīn (*tarᶜ* + locative *-īn* < *ain) corresponds to the original Aramaic form which means "gate" and refers to the location of the village on the outlet of Seil el-Ḥudeirah/Seil en-Numeirah, which itself is still a major footpath connecting the Plateau to the Ghor. Tharais, on the other hand, is a slightly Hellenized form. The survival of the Madaba Map names also scores at 100%. One name is Canaanite (ᶜAi); the other two are Aramaic.

Since the Madaba map provides such a small corpus, one will not attribute too much significance to the 100% survival. On the other hand, the same statistics hold true for the two sites attested in the Roman provincial coinage: Charachmōba (Aramaic) and Rabbathmōba (Aramaized Canaanite; *-mōba* is Aramaic). Of course, both the Ottoman tax registers and the sources from Greek-Roman-Byzantine antiquity represent a selection of major sites in the most favorable environments and, therefore, thriving through the ages.

The Hebrew Bible. Isa 15-16 and Jer 48 present a corpus of Moabite toponyms out of which the following refer to the region between Wadi el-Mujib and Wadi el-Ḥesa: Ar (possibly a regional name, M. Weippert 1979b: 18 and n. 7); Qir Moab; Zoar; Luhit; Horonaim; the waters of Nimrin; Eglaim/Eglath Shelisha; Beer Elim; Dimon; and Qir Heres. It is impossible to define the period of this list's origin more closely than to the 6th through the 3rd centuries B.C.E. (Worschech and Knauf 1986: 83). In order to achieve a broader basis for statistics, sites in the Ghor are included in the following discussion.

Of these ten toponyms, the writer regards the following identifications as probable: Qir Moab = Rabbathmoba = er-Rabbah; Zoar = Ṭawāḥīn as-Sukkar near eṣ-Ṣāfī (Rast and Schaub 1974); Luhit = Kathrabbā (Mittmann 1982); Horonaim = ed-Deir (Worschech and Knauf 1986: 80-85); waters of Nimrin = Seil and Ghor en-Numeirah (ibid.: 82); Eglaim/Eglath Shelisha = el-Bleidah (ibid.: 81); Dimon = ed-Dimnah (ibid.: 70-75). Two of the ten toponyms from the Isaiah-Jeremiah corpus have survived, regardless of whether the identifications affirmed above are correct: Dimon/ed-Dimnah and Nimrin /Numeirah. Formally, both Numeirah and ed-Dimnah are Standard Arabic names, and only in the case of ed-Dimnah do the semantics of the name raise the suspicion that it is an Arabicized pre-Arabic name (see supra). Were there no biblical reference to the "waters of Nimrin" somewhere along the shore of the Dead Sea between Zoar and Eglaim, in other words, there would be no reason to question that the name Numeirah derived from the Banu Numeir who are attested in this region by a

14th century Arab geographer, al-Dimishqī (cf. Musil 1907-8: 74; Worschech and Knauf 1986: 82).

"The city of GN" as an expression for the capital city of the land GN seems to reflect Assyrian usage (cf. M. Weippert 1982b: 296), and if one agrees that *Rabbath Moab (> er-Rabbah) is a translation of Moabite Qir Moab into "Standard Canaanite" the survival rate of the toponyms from the Isaiah-Jeremiah corpus is 20-30%. Of the identifications proposed, one is Canaanite (er-Rabbah), two are Aramaic (Kerak [=Qir Hereś?] and Kathrabbā), the remaining are Standard and post-Standard Arabic. Although the Isaiah-Jeremiah corpus and the road-sign corpus have only half a name in common—i.e., Qir Moab=er-Rabbah, linked by a chain of transmission without any logical or temporal gap: Qir Moab/Rabbath Moab/Rabbathmōba/Areopolis/ Maʾāb/ er-Rabbah)—this corresponds roughly to the percentage of typologically Canaanite names attested in the road sign corpus.

One is inclined to attribute the lower rate of survival from the Isaiah-Jeremiah corpus vis-a-vis the more recent corpora to the former's being more remote. This is undoubtedly one of the main contributing factors. However, the Hebrew Bible is concerned with only the western and northern peripheries of Moab, the area within the horizon of a Jerusalem-based author (Worschech and Knauf 1986: 83). Only one site out of the ten refers indisputably to the Plateau—namely, Qir Moab. This site is the only one whose name, in transformation, is still contained in the 1987 road-sign corpus. It is the present writer's impression (which will be tested in a forthcoming publication) that a relatively small degree of Pre- and Post-Standard Arabic toponyms have survived in "peripheral Moab"—i.e. in the Ghor and the Wadis leading down to it. As opposed to the "random-centered" selection of Moabite sites in the Hebrew Bible, the Madaba Mosaic Map and the Ottoman tax registers provide a much more balanced and consistent selection of sites. In the case of the tax registers, one would assume that they tend to be exhaustive. Still the impression remains that, if there was a major break in the transmission of toponyms on the Moabite plateau, the break has to be sought between the Iron Age and the Persian/Hellenistic period rather than later.

Three out of the ten names are decisively Moabite: Qir Moab; Qir Hereś (because of Moabite *qīr* instead of standard Canaanite *ᶜīr*, *qiryah* "town, city"); and Nimrin (because of Moabite *-īn*, *-ain* instead of common Canaanite *-īm*, *-aim*; but cf. Borée 1968: 64 for *-īn* in non-Moabite Canaanite toponyms). Horonaim is pre-Moabite Canaanite or, like *Rabbat Mōʾab, post-Moabite Canaanite (in Moabite *ḥwrnn* *Ḥawrōnēn). Qīr Ḥereś ("the town of the woodland") and Beer Ēlīm ("the spring of the terebinths") refer to vegetation; Lūḥīt ("the tabular one") to land formation; Nimrīn and ᶜEglaim to local animal life (panthers and cattle, if these names do not refer to a panther-shaped ridge or a calf-shaped hill); Qir Moab ("the capital of Moab") and Zoar ("the small one") to the socio-economic importance of the settlement, or the lack thereof; Dīmōn to the character of the place as a settled one, or one suitable for a stay (Worschech and Knauf 1986: 74); and Horonaim to the chief deity of this place (cf. Arīḥā in the 1987 corpus). Basically, the semantics of late 1st millennium B.C.E. toponymy (represented by the Isaiah-Jeremiah corpus) coincide with the semantics of the Canaanite stratum in the 1987 road sign corpus and exhibit a profile not significantly different from the Hashemite stratum (disregarding its high amount of "socio-political" names). This observation forms a strong argument for the assumption that there has been more continuity than discontinuity in the social organization, the modes of production, and the perception of the world among the rural population of Palestine and Jordan during the last 3000 years.

Conclusions

This study leads to two main conclusions. First, it is clear that discontinuity of toponyms does not necessarily testify to a discontinuity of population. It does, however, testify to socio-economic and ideological changes which may affect a pre-existing population. Toponymical discontinuity within a persisting population and administration is primarily evidenced by the "Hashemite" stratum of the 1987 corpus. Second, it is evident that continuity of toponyms does not necessarily testify to a continuity of population or administration. Continuity does, however, presuppose a certain amount of interaction between the pre-existing population and any newcomers, and their co-existence over some time. A citizen of Charachmōba in the 1st century C.E., and an inhabitant of

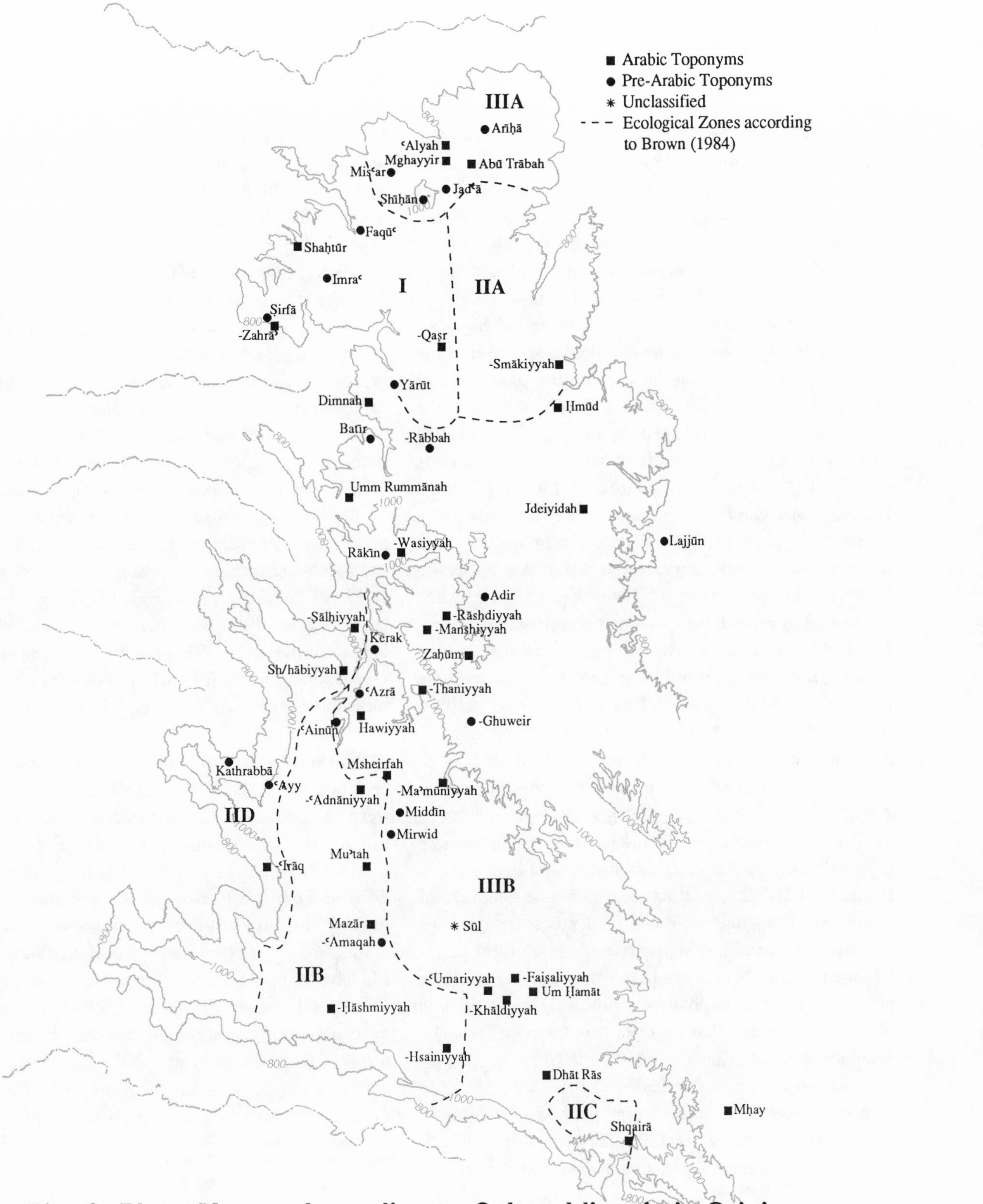

Fig. 8: Place Names According to Cultural-linguistic Origin

today's el-Kerak, would not be able to talk to each other if they were ever to meet; they would, however, be able to recognize the name of their town in the other's writing, given a chance to learn the script.

An argument for a basic degree of continuity among the population of the Kerak Plateau can be drawn from the distribution of the pre-Arabic toponyms. The assumption of such a continuity would not exclude the possibility that newcomers continuously have been absorbed into pre-existing tribes, or that pre-existing tribes and villages repeatedly have been integrated into political structures, both administrative and tribal, imposed by newcomers.

If we disregard the most recent toponymic changes for the purpose of this evaluation and define as "present" the toponymy represented on the 1979 reprint of the "Archaeological Map" of Jordan (Sheet 2: Kerak), then 27 of the investigated sites are situated west of the "Kings' Highway." Among those, 19 still have pre-Arabic names (70.37%). 26 sites are situated east of the "Kings' Highway," on the other hand, with only 5 or 6 pre-Arabic names represented (23.08% or less). Undoubtedly a more refined analysis will increase the difference in profile between those areas most favorable to agriculture (according to rainfall, soil, and protection against intruders) and those areas which have been cultivated only in periods of a strong central government and/or a strong economic climate (which in turn enhanced agricultural surplus production). The latter would have reverted to pastoralism in periods of political instability and insecurity. The observation that pre-Arabic toponyms are preserved predominantly in the agricultural core areas of the Kerak plateau, in spite of the fact that Arabic became the prevailing spoken language of this area between 500 B.C.E. and 500 C.E. and has served as the language of administration since ca. 700 C.E., lends support to the view that the area has supported an agricultural population continuously over the past 5000 years and has been affected only marginally by the political, linguistic, and ideological changes that took place in Greater Syria (H. Weippert 1985: 26; Knauf 1985b: 129; 1987b: 34).

Whereas a general conclusion like this seems feasible with reference to the whole Kerak plateau area, less can be said with certainty regarding the occupation of individual sites. Basically, this author would regard the survival of a Canaanite name at a site as more meaningful for verifying its ancient occupation than the presence, or absence, of a handful of pre-500 B.C.E. sherds collected during a survey or by a casual visitor. It goes without saying that this statement does not apply to sites where large quantities of sherds are found, especially if linked with architectural features, or to excavated sites. On the other hand, the fact that its current name is of Canaanite origin does not suggest anything more than that the site was of importance to a Canaanite group sometime between ca. 6000 and 500 B.C.E. It may not have been occupied during much of that time, especially if the name does not belong to a type with a known period of productivity (as is the case with the *abil-*, *bēt-*, and *gat-* names; Isserlin 1956: 84-87); or it may never have been an occupied site at all. The name Imra^c means "Pasturage." ^{c}Ai was destroyed and most probably resettled during this time-span, but neither the time of destruction nor the time of re-settlement can be determined toponymically.

More information can be retrieved as far as the ancient environment of the Kerak Plateau is concerned. Jad^{c}ā, a "woodcutting" site, seems to have originated in a process of agricultural colonialization of former woodland. Again, the name does not indicate whether this happened during the EB period or the Iron Age, the two periods most likely for this kind of process, but it does indicate that the area between Jebel Shīḥān and Wadi Bālū^c was once forested.

Not only must the available place name corpora be regarded as too small for valid statistical analysis, but they were compiled from specific points of view which did not provide the kind of objectivity and coverage a modern researcher would want (especially the case with corpora derived from the Hebrew Bible and the Arab geographers), and they suffered tremendous losses of information during transmission (especially the case with the Madaba Map and other epigraphical sources). It can be observed, however, that the rate of survival of the toponyms of a given corpus tends to decrease with this corpus' distance from the present. One would expect this from common sense. This observation also agrees with the quantitative of the Kerak plateau's toponymic strata presented above.

Chapter V

SITE LISTS

Sites According to Site Numbers and Map Sections

Map Section 1

Site#	Name	field#	PG	UTMG
1		9161	20.6/92.0	60.8/79.5
2		9122	18.3/91.3	58.4/78.6
3	ᶜAwarwareh	8013	19.0/91.4	59.2/78.6
4	Um eṭ-Ṭawābīn	9117	18.6/90.3	58.8/77.7
5	Freiwān	8012	20.7/90.1	60.8/77.6
6		9119	15.7/89.5	56.2/76.9
7		9120	17.6/89.6	57.8/76.9
8		9121	20.4/89.3	60.5/76.8
9		9118	15.4/88.3	55.4/75.6
10		9095	17.6/88.3	57.8/75.7
11	Abū Ḥalīb	9116	17.7/88.4	58.0/75.9
12	Kh. Shīḥān	8020	20.1/87.7	60.4/75.2
13	Rujm Um Ḥlāl	8015	16.4/86.9	56.7/74.3
14	Faqūᶜ	8016	16.5/86.5	56.8/73.8
15	Imraᶜ	8017	15.3/84.5	55.6/71.7
16	Majdalein	8022	18.1/82.6	58.5/70.0

Map Section 2

Site#	Name	field#	PG	UTMG
17		9144	22.3/93.6	62.5/81.0
18	Mḥaṭṭat el-Ḥājj	8001	25.7/93.7	65.8/81.2
19		9165	21.9/92.8	62.0/80.3
20		9162	21.9/91.7	62.0/79.0
21	Um el-Qleib	8008	23.3/92.0	63.6/79.7
22	Arīḥa	8007	24.8/92.0	65.0/79.5
23	Abū Trābah	8009	25.1/90.8	65.2/78.5
24		9216	26.5/91.4	66.5/78.9
25	Misᶜar	8011	21.5/90.0	61.8/77.5
26		9243	25.7/89.3	66.1/77.0
27	el-Harbaj	9244	25.9/89.3	66.2/77.1
28		9267	29.0/89.9	69.1/77.4
29		9265	29.3/88.8	69.4/76.5
30	Kh. el-Jadᶜa	9214	22.0/87.8	62.2/75.3
31		8010	25.5/87.9	65.7/75.6
32		9241	25.1/86.8	65.3/74.5
33		9266	28.2/87.4	68.4/75.0
34	Jadᶜa el-Jbur	8028	21.3/86.0	61.5/73.5
35	Kh. el-Bālūᶜ	8014	24.4/85.5	64.5/72.9
36	ed-Denn wa-l-Baradān	8025	21.4/85.1	61.9/72.4
37	er-Ribᶜī	8026	21.5/84.8	61.9/72.2
38	Kh. es-Saᶜadūnī	8027	21.4/84.0	61.8/71.4
39	Naṣīb	8032	22.4/83.1	62.7/70.6
40		9272	25.7/84.3	65.9/71.4
41		9269	26.3/83.9	66.7/71.4
42		9271	27.7/84.3	68.0/71.9
43	ᶜAzzūr	8029	28.1/84.3	68.4/71.9
44		9194	31.0/84.2	71.3/71.9
45		9195	31.3/84.2	71.5/71.9
46		9196	31.1/84.0	71.4/71.7
47	Kh. es-Sanīnah	8030	29.6/83.4	69.8/70.8
48		9197	30.8/82.7	71.2/70.8
49		9198	31.2/83.1	71.4/70.8
50		9203	30.8/82.7	71.1/70.3
51		9191	31.2/82.6	71.5/70.4

Map Section 3

Site#	Name	field#	PG	UTMG
52	Ṣirfa	9059	12.4/81.8	52.4/69.3
53	Ḥimmeh	9035	14.5/82.0	54.8/69.6
54	Shaḥtūr	9026	17.5/81.7	57.7/69.3
55	Qaṣr el-Ḥimmeh	9023	18.2/82.0	58.6/69.4
56	Tadūn	8033	19.2/81.2	59.5/68.6
57	Beit Lajjah	9014	19.0/79.8	59.4/67.3
58	Abū el-Wsheish	9313	16.4/79.9	56.7/67.4
59		9007	16.7/79.4	57.1/66.6
60	Kh. el-Kharziyyah	9027	18.0/79.2	58.2/66.7
61	Um Sidreh	9013	16.8/78.6	57.2/66.1
62		9009	18.4/78.8	58.7/66.3
63	el-Yārūt	9002	18.8/78.7	59.0/66.1

64	ed-Dimnah	9017	17.1/77.9	57.4/65.3
65		9256	18.3/76.2	58.7/63.6
66	Batīr	9073	17.2/74.8	57.5/62.3
67	Kh. el-Ḥdeib	2588	12.5/75.3	52.9/62.6
68		2589	12.9/75.0	53.3/62.3
69		2590	13.6/73.2	54.2/60.4
70	Kh. Zabūbah	2593	13.1/72.7	53.6/60.0
71	ed-Deir	9070	14.8/73.3	55.3/60.6
72	el-Qabū	9098	16.0/74.0	56.5/61.5
73	Rujm Birjis	9047	17.2/73.9	57.7/61.2
74	Kh. Zughriyyeh	9074	16.0/73.2	56.6/60.6
75		9067	16.8/73.2	57.6/60.6
76	Bteiyir	9068	18.3/73.5	58.7/61.0

Map Section 4

Site#	Name	field#	PG	UTMG
77	Rujm Abū Zaᶜrūrah	8031	23.9/82.2	64.3/69.5
78	el-Kharīᶜ	9041	26.5/81.5	66.7/69.2
79	Rujm Ghneim	9033	27.3/81.2	67.6/68.8
80		9263	28.0/82.0	68.3/69.7
81	Dalāleḥ	9084	28.0/81.5	68.3/69.2
82		9262	29.6/81.4	69.9/69.1
83		9184	29.5/81.1	69.9/68.6
84		9182	29.4/80.5	69.8/68.1
85	Shajarah	8034	19.8/80.5	60.1/67.9
86	el-Qaṣr	9273	21.2/80.5	61.3/67.9
87	el-Misdāḥ	9001	20.9/79.4	61.2/66.8
88	Um el-Habāj	9012	23.0/81.0	63.4/68.4
89	Ḥmeimāt (NW)	9004	22.6/80.3	63.0/67.8
90	Ḥmeimāt (SW)	9005	25.7/79.8	63.1/67.4
91	Ḥmeimāt (NE)	9008	23.5/79.9	63.9/67.4
92	Ḥmeimāt (SE)	9006	23.2/79.0	63.6/66.4
93		9018	23.3/78.2	63.8/65.7
94	es-Smākiyyah	9037	26.5/79.6	66.9/67.2
95		9226	26.9/79.4	67.4/66.8
96	Kh. ᶜAleiyān	9218	25.6/78.7	66.0/66.2
97	Kh. Mḥeisin	9225	28.1/78.7	68.5/66.3
98	Rujm Qneiṭrah	9223	28.3/79.2	68.8/66.8
99	Kh. el-Makhārīm	8035	28.9/78.9	69.7/66.5
100	Ḥmūd	9020	26.2/77.8	66.5/65.4
101	Kh. el-Minsaḥlāt	9049	25.8/77.3	66.0/64.6
102	Kh. el-Ḥinū	9025	25.1/76.8	65.7/64.3
103		9309	25.8/77.3	66.2/64.9
104	Qaṣr Ḥamdān	9021	26.1/77.2	66.5/64.5
105	el-Jilimeh	9003	21.1/77.0	61.6/64.5
106	Miṣnaᶜ	8024	22.3/76.7	62.8/64.2
107	[el-Miyāl]	9143	20.4/76.5	60.7/64.0
108	er-Rabbah	9123	20.3/75.5	60.8/63.0
109	Kh. Um Kharīᶜah	9113	23.7/74.9	64.0/62.4
110		9221	28.4/76.4	68.9/63.9
111		9091	29.2/76.3	69.7/63.8
112		9307	28.0/75.8	69.0/63.5
113	Rujm et-Teis	9089	28.0/75.0	68.5/62.6
114	Mḥarraqāt (N)	9115	21.6/73.3	62.1/61.2
115	Mḥarraqāt (S)	9114	21.6/73.3	62.1/60.9
116		9185	22.2/73.9	62.6/61.4
117		9176	22.3/73.8	62.8/61.2
118		9177	22.2/73.7	62.8/61.1
119	Jdeiyidah	9045	27.3/73.6	67.8/61.3

Map Section 5

Site#	Name	field#	PG	UTMG
120		9186	29.9/81.6	70.3/69.3
121		9188	30.0/81.5	70.4/69.2
122		9189	30.1/81.4	70.4/69.0
123		9187	29.8/81.3	70.1/68.9
124		9183	29.9/81.0	70.2/68.2
125		9205	31.2/82.1	71.5/69.7
126		9210	31.0/81.7	71.4/69.4
127		9211	31.8/82.0	72.0/69.7
128		9212	32.0/81.9	72.3/69.6
129	Kh. Mdeinet el-Muᶜrrajeh	8018	32.2/81.3	72.5/69.0
130		9207	31.1/81.0	71.5/68.7
131		9220	31.5/80.9	71.9/68.6
132		9160	31.5/80.3	71.9/68.0
133		9213	29.9/79.6	70.2/67.2
134		9159	30.7/79.4	71.0/67.0
135		9158	29.8/77.8	70.3/65.5
136		9147	30.6/77.6	70.9/65.3
137		9148	30.5/78.0	71.0/65.9
138		9145	31.2/77.6	71.5/65.3
139		9157	29.6/77.2	70.0/64.9
140		9156	29.8/76.8	70.3/64.6
141		9155	30.4/76.3	70.9/63.9
142		9305	30.3/76.0	70.8/63.7
143	Kh. Mdeinet ᶜAliyā	8019	33.0/76.8	73.4/64.5
144		9166	32.2/76.3	72.6/64.0
145		9168	32.2/75.7	72.7/63.4
146		9304	29.8/74.5	70.2/62.0
147		9310	30.0/74.7	70.6/62.4
148		9169	31.5/74.7	72.1/62.5
149		9170	32.4/74.5	72.8/62.3
150		9171	31.2/74.3	71.7/62.0
151		9167	31.8/74.3	72.2/61.9
152		9245	31.6/73.3	72.4/61.4
153	Rujm el-Qanāṭir	9052	30.3/72.8	70.9/60.5
154	Fityān	9317	31.6/72.6	72.1/60.2

Map Section 6

Site#	Name	field#	PG	UTMG
155		2217	10.5/72.1	51.3/59.5
156		2592	14.4/72.6	54.9/59.9
157		9076	15.4/72.4	55.8/59.7
158	Kh. Um Rummānah	9069	15.6/72.4	56.1/59.9
159		2594	13.9/71.3	54.4/58.6
160	el-Minqaṭʿah	9107	19.2/72.6	59.8/60.0
161	Um Najīl	9044	17.2/71.1	57.8/58.4
162	Rākīn	9062	17.3/70.4	57.8/57.8
163		9103	18.2/71.0	58.5/58.5
164		9099	18.7/70.9	59.1/58.4
165	Kh. el-Minḥār	9063	19.5/70.5	59.9/58.0
166	Qreifilla	9031	19.4/69.4	60.0/56.8
167	Ḥabāsh/Ḥabāj	2595	14.9/69.9	55.5/57.3
168		9105	15.9/69.8	56.7/57.3
169	Badhdhān	9277	12.1/71.5	54.2/57.4
170	Kh. el-Mrabbaʿah	9275	13.9/68.7	54.6/56.4
171	Kh. Ṭrunjeh	9276	13.7/68.6	54.2/56.3
172	Um ed-Dajāj	2218	11.9/70.2	53.5/56.7
173	ʿAin Um Jamʿān	2219	12.0/69.5	52.7/56.6
174	Kh. Sakka	2204	12.5/69.0	53.2/56.0
175	Samrāʾ	2205	12.2/67.5	52.7/54.8
176	Zeita	2221	11.4/66.8	51.9/54.1
177		2211	09.8/65.9	50.5/53.3
178		2068	08.8/66.1	49.9/53.3
179	Kh. el-Qashab	2212	09.9/66.7	50.3/53.9
180	el-ʿĀrūḍ	2213	09.0/67.3	49.8/54.5
181		2214	08.5/68.2	49.2/55.4
182	Kh. Btheinah	2215	08.9/68.4	49.7/55.5
183	Rujm esh-Shmūs	2216	09.1/69.0	49.9/56.2
184	Kh. ʿAizār	2002	12.9/66.9	53.8/54.1
185	Um Kharūf	2001	14.3/67.3	54.9/54.7
186		9258	15.7/67.8	56.3/55.1
187	Kh. Sārah	2003	16.3/67.3	57.0/54.6
188		9108	17.7/67.2	58.4/54.7
189		9110	18.4/67.0	59.1/54.3
190	Ẓweihirah	9109	18.9/67.1	59.7/54.5
191	Kh. er-Rṣeifah	2209	11.4/65.4	52.2/52.6
192	Qaṣr er-Rṣeifah	2210	11.9/64.8	52.7/51.9
193	el-ʿUmyān	2108	11.0/63.7	51.8/51.0
194	Kh. el-ʿOkbar	2004	13.2/64.3	53.8/51.6
195	Mseimṭah (S)	2207	13.5/64.7	54.3/52.0
196	Mseimṭah (N)	2208	13.6/65.1	54.3/52.5
197	Mgheir	2202	14.1/65.9	54.7/53.1
198	Ibn Ayyūb	2201	14.8/66.2	55.6/53.4
199	Kh. es-Samrāʾ	2203	14.7/65.3	55.2/52.5
200	Kaminna	2206	15.2/64.2	55.8/51.5
201	el-Franj	2220	15.6/64.5	56.1/52.0
202	eth-Thallājah	2122	16.8/65.2	57.5/52.7
203		2302	17.9/65.6	58.5/53.0
204	Kerak	2599	17.0/66.0	58.0/53.5
205	ʿIzra	2090	16.0/63.2	56.7/50.5
206	Kh. ʿIzra	2083	16.3/63.1	57.1/50.3
207	Kh. en-Neqqāz	2305	17.1/62.7	57.8/50.0
208		2301	17.3/64.3	58.0/51.6
209		2364	17.6/63.4	58.3/51.0
210	Kh. el-Qaryatein	2303	17.7/64.5	58.4/51.8
211	eth-Thaniyyah	2304	18.8/64.1	59.5/51.4

Map Section 7

Site#	Name	field#	PG	UTMG
212	Kh. ed-Dāwūdiyyah	9061	19.3/71.8	60.1/59.2
213	Kh. ed-Dāwūdiyyah	9064	19.4/71.6	60.2/58.9
214	ez-Zarrāʿah	9040	23.0/72.0	63.4/59.6
215	Qmeir	9030	22.0/71.4	62.5/58.8
216	Abū er-Ruzz	9048	20.0/69.8	60.5/57.3
217	Kh. Qamarein	9051	21.3/70.7	61.7/58.0
218		9173	22.2/70.7	62.9/58.2
219	Ḥujfah	9043	24.4/71.0	65.0/58.4
220		9088	28.3/72.4	68.8/60.0
221		9279	27.9/70.9	68.5/58.6
222		9290	27.6/70.9	68.2/58.5
223		9295	27.1/70.3	67.8/57.7
224	Rujm el-ʿAbsī	9092	26.2/69.6	66.9/57.2
225		2634	28.8/69.6	69.5/57.2
226		9294	27.7/68.6	68.3/56.2
227	Adir	9060	22.5/68.5	63.1/55.7
228	Rujm el-Jazūr	2638	26.4/67.3	67.0/54.8
229		9080	27.5/67.3	68.2/57.0
230	Kh. ʿArbīd	2635	29.2/67.4	69.8/55.0
231		2641	28.9/65.9	69.5/53.5
232		2642	29.2/65.6	69.7/53.3
233	Kinnār	9111	19.3/66.7	60.0/54.3
234		9079	20.9/65.7	61.6/53.1
235	el-Ḥaddādah	9082	21.3/65.5	62.0/53.0
236		9078	20.4/64.3	60.9/51.7
237	Rujm esh-Sharīf	2639	26.7/64.3	67.3/51.8
238	esh-Sharīf	2643	27.6/63.2	68.3/50.8

Map Section 8

Site#	Name	field#	PG	UTMG
239	Lejjūn (Bronze)	9066	31.7/71.9	72.3/59.6
240	Lejjūn (Roman)	9316	32.7/72.0	73.1/59.7
241		2685	31.7/68.2	72.1/56.0
242	el-Bṭeimah	9255	30.7/69.9	71.2/57.5

243		2632	31.8/68.0	72.4/55.6
244		2629	32.1/67.8	72.7/55.5
245		2628	32.3/67.3	72.9/54.9
246		2631	31.1/66.8	71.9/54.4
247		2627	32.4/66.7	72.7/54.5
248	Kh. Thamāyil	2630	31.5/66.3	72.1/53.9
249		2637	30.9/66.0	71.5/53.6
250		2626	31.8/66.4	72.5/54.2
251	Rujm el-Merīḥ	2625	33.1/66.1	73.8/53.8
252		2640	29.7/64.8	70.3/52.4
253		2633	31.2/64.2	72.4/51.9
254		2676	33.4/64.1	74.1/51.9

Map Section 9

Site#	Name	field#	PG	UTMG
255	Kh. eḍ-Ḍweibi^{c}	2103	10.1/62.2	50.9/49.4
256	Jauza	2006	11.4/62.8	52.1/49.9
257	^{c}Alaqān	2102	11.7/61.4	52.5/48.6
258		2107	12.3/61.6	53.1/48.9
259	Kh. el-Meidān	2012	07.7/60.8	48.6/47.8
260	Meidān (SE)	2092	07.9/60.5	48.8/47.6
261	Kathrabba	2010	09.3/60.8	50.2/48.0
262	^{c}Ai	2013	11.0/60.4	51.8/47.5
263	Kh. el-Meiseh	2014	13.1/60.2	53.8/47.5
264	^{c}Ainūn	2085	15.2/62.7	55.9/49.8
265		2091	16.0/62.7	56.8/49.8
266	Kh. eṭ-Ṭalīsah	2005	16.1/62.0	57.2/49.5
267	Kh. el-Labūn	2008	15.3/62.0	56.5/49.3
268		2084	15.8/61.6	56.6/49.2
269	Kh. el-Mṣāṭeb	2007	16.1/61.7	57.0/49.0
270	Kh. el-Ḥawiyyah	2306	15.2/62.7	58.0/48.6
271	el-Msheirfah	2361	18.7/60.3	59.4/47.7
272	Kh. el-Jūbah	2015	16.7/59.6	57.5/46.9
273	Miḥna	2017	16.0/59.0	56.8/46.4
274	Kh. el-Jeljūl	2016	14.6/59.7	55.3/47.0
275		2088	14.1/58.7	54.9/46.4
276		2089	14.8/58.6	55.8/45.7
277		2087	14.5/58.0	55.1/45.1
278	Kfeirāz	2020	13.3/57.6	54.1/44.8
279		2109	11.7/58.2	52.6/45.4
280		2128	09.7/58.4	50.6/45.6
281	Kh. el-Ḥwāleh	2104	09.0/58.8	49.9/45.9
282		2086	15.1/57.3	56.2/44.5
283		2394	17.1/57.2	57.9/44.6
284		2393	18.5/57.1	59.3/44.5
285	Mirwid	2309	19.1/57.1	59.9/44.5
286	Um Naṣr	2129	10.7/56.7	51.6/43.9
287	Rujm el-Ḥleileh	2024	10.9/56.9	51.8/43.9
288		2119	11.0/56.6	51.9/43.8
289	Kh. Um el-Qṣeir	2021	11.7/56.1	52.6/43.5
290	Kh. Zabdah	2022	12.8/56.2	53.7/43.5
291	Kh. Ghifrah	2120	10.6/55.1	51.4/42.6
292	el-^{c}Irāq	2029	11.2/55.5	52.1/42.8
293		2121	11.0/55.2	51.9/42.5
294	Fqeiqes	2028	11.3/54.9	52.3/42.3
295	Kh. Mishrāqah	2025	13.1/55.4	54.0/42.7
296		2093	14.0/55.6	54.8/42.8
297	Rujm Mes^{c}īd	2026	13.0/54.8	53.8/42.2
298	Rujm Um el-^{c}Aṭāṭ	2027	13.5/54.5	54.5/41.9
299	Rujm el-Baqr	2033	13.8/54.0	54.6/41.5
300	el-Bqei^{c}	2032	12.6/53.7	53.4/41.0
301	Kh. Fqeiqes	2030	11.5/53.8	52.4/40.8
302	Kh. el-Beiḍā	2034	11.5/53.4	52.0/41.1
303	Beit Sahm	2031	08.9/53.9	49.8/41.2
304	Mauta	2023	16.7/55.8	57.1/43.2
305	el-Mashhad	2312	17.5/55.5	58.4/42.9
306		2395	18.5/55.4	59.4/42.8
307	Kh. el-^{c}Edūl	2396	18.8/55.5	59.7/42.9
308		2359	17.4/54.8	58.3/42.2
309		2355	17.3/54.3	58.1/41.8
310		2365	17.0/53.7	57.9/41.2
311	el-Mazār	2019	16.4/52.8	57.3/40.3
312	Kh. eṭ-Ṭūr	2316	17.8/53.7	58.7/41.0

Map Section 10

Site#	Name	field#	PG	UTMG
313	Ghuweir	2360	22.1/61.1	62.9/48.6
314		2677	23.4/61.5	64.2/49.0
315		2678	24.9/60.7	65.8/48.2
316	el-Mreigha	2602	26.2/60.8	67.0/48.4
317		2654	27.8/60.8	68.6/48.4
318		2653	28.2/60.8	68.9/48.5
319		2644	28.4/62.4	69.4/49.9
320		2646	28.3/61.6	69.4/49.0
321		2648	29.2/61.4	70.1/48.8
322		2650	29.6/60.9	70.4/48.4
323		2651	29.7/61.2	70.5/48.8
324		2656	28.2/60.1	69.0/47.7
325		2661	27.2/59.8	67.9/47.5
326		2657	28.5/59.6	69.4/47.3
327		2658	29.0/59.8	69.8/47.4
328		2663	27.7/59.3	68.5/46.9
329		2659	28.2/59.5	69.0/46.9
330		2669	28.7/58.4	69.5/46.0
331		2660	29.5/57.5	70.8/44.8
332	Kh. el-Weibdeh	2405	22.2/59.9	62.9/47.3
333	Middīn	2307	19.7/58.7	60.5/46.2
334		2416	21.6/58.1	62.4/45.5
335		2417	23.4/59.3	64.2/46.8
336		2391	20.1/56.7	60.9/44.2

337		2392	20.8/57.1	61.6/44.5
338		2366	19.6/65.3	60.4/43.7
339		2390	20.4/56.2	61.2/43.7
340		2413	22.5/57.9	63.3/45.5
341		2412	22.4/57.6	63.2/45.1
342		2411	22.4/57.3	63.2/44.8
343		2410	22.5/56.9	63.4/44.5
344		2409	22.5/56.5	63.4/44.0
345	Um Zebel	2397	19.1/55.4	60.0/42.8
346		2400	19.3/55.2	60.2/42.7
347		2367	19.7/55.5	60.6/42.9
348		2399	19.2/54.6	60.0/42.1
349	Kh. Um ᶜAlanda	2358	20.1/55.1	61.0/42.6
350	Rujm Rafīyeh	2357	21.3/55.0	62.2/42.5
351		2407	21.5/54.5	62.4/42.0
352		2356	22.5/55.1	63.4/42.6
353	Kh. en-Nsheinish	2314	22.3/55.2	63.1/42.7
354		2418	24.1/56.2	64.9/43.7
355	Kh. el-Baṭrāᵓ	2308	25.4/58.3	66.2/45.9
356		2387	26.2/57.1	67.0/44.6
357		2377	26.9/57.0	67.6/44.7
358		2386	26.0/55.5	66.9/43.0
359	Nāṣir	2385	26.3/56.2	67.2/43.8
360		2384	26.9/55.8	67.7/43.4
361		2371	26.3/57.6	69.7/42.7
362		2372	28.7/55.4	69.5/43.0
363		2369	29.0/54.7	69.7/42.4
364		2370	29.0/54.9	69.9/42.5
365		2374	29.4/54.0	70.3/41.7
366	el-Māhrī	2375	29.5/53.7	70.4/41.5
367		2376	29.7/53.6	70.6/41.2
368		2378	30.2/53.2	71.3/40.8
369		2381	30.4/53.0	71.4/40.5
370	Rujm Khashm eṣ-Ṣīrah	2382	30.9/52.9	71.8/40.3

Map Section 11

Site#	Name	field#	PG	UTMG
371		2675	33.7/61.6	74.6/49.6
372		2681	33.1/61.5	73.8/48.8
373		2682	33.4/60.2	74.2/47.6
374		2674	34.8/59.5	75.6/47.2
375		2683	32.8/59.3	73.5/46.9
376		2684	33.2/59.0	73.9/46.7
377	Kh. Abū Rukbah	2603	33.5/58.9	74.3/46.6
378	Qaṣr Abū Rukbah	2604	33.9/58.0	74.7/45.7
379	Qaṣr et-Tamrah	2605	33.0/57.0	73.9/44.7
380		2607	32.2/56.8	73.0/44.4
381	Bīr Bashbash	2608	32.0/56.2	72.8/43.9
382		2383	31.2/52.5	72.1/40.1

Map Section 12

Site#	Name	field#	PG	UTMG
383	ed-Dabbākah	2036	12.3/52.4	53.3/39.6
384	el-Jauza	2038	13.8/51.9	54.7/39.2
385	Kh. el-Bāsiliyyah	2037	14.5/52.0	55.4/39.4
386		2096	13.8/51.1	54.8/38.5
387	Rujm Um Ṣuwwānah	2047	13.5/50.3	54.5/37.7
388	Rujm el-Ḥleileh	2044	13.1/50.8	54.2/37.8
389		2125	12.3/50.8	53.3/38.1
390	Kh. el-Mudawwarah	2048	12.7/50.2	53.6/37.4
391	Juḥra	2101	12.3/49.9	53.3/37.2
392		2126	11.7/51.1	52.7/38.4
393		2127	11.2/51.1	52.2/38.5
394	Sdeir (E)	2097	10.5/50.6	52.1/37.8
395	Khāneq en-Naṣāra	2042	10.8/50.8	51.8/38.1
396	Kh. eṭ-Ṭayyibeh	2043	09.8/50.7	50.8/38.0
397	Kh. es-Sdeir (W)	2046	10.2/50.5	52.0/37.7
398		2110	10.3/49.9	51.3/37.2
399	Kh. Ḍubāb	2049	10.5/49.4	51.4/36.7
400	Merzab Mezraᶜah	2050	08.8/49.2	49.8/36.4
401	Khanzīrah	2040	07.3/51.6	48.3/38.8
402	Kh. Medīnet er-Rās	2041	05.9/51.1	46.9/38.3
403	Rujm er-Rās	2113	06.3/50.1	47.4/37.3
404	Kh. Um Rummānah	2051	07.0/49.0	48.1/36.3
405	el-Mjeidel	2052	12.9/48.7	53.9/35.9
406		2114	13.2/48.7	54.2/36.1
407		2116	14.4/48.3	55.4/35.8
408		2117	13.9/48.5	54.9/35.7

Map Section 13

Site#	Name	field#	PG	UTMG
409		2098	15.4/52.4	56.4/39.6
410	el-ᶜAmaqa	2039	16.8/51.7	57.8/39.1
411	Sūl	2319	19.7/52.4	60.7/39.7
412	Rujm Um ᶜAlanda	2045	15.7/50.6	56.6/38.0
413		2095	15.7/50.7	57.0/38.2
414	Rujm Eshqāḥ	2094	16.5/50.5	57.7/37.8
415	Rujm el-Awsaj	2425	16.6/50.4	57.5/37.8
416	Dleiqa	2324	19.1/49.5	60.1/36.9
417	el-Ḥseiniyyah	2326	19.1/48.6	60.1/36.0
418	Um Zabāyir	2363	20.3/48.8	61.3/36.4
419	Um Ḥamāṭ	2323	22.8/49.8	63.8/37.3
420	Nakhl	2320	24.5/52.3	65.4/39.8
421	Rujm al-Mismar	2433	26.8/47.9	67.8/35.5
422		2427	18.5/45.8	59.6/33.3
423	Majra	2053	15.1/48.3	56.1/35.6

424	Jweir	2054	15.9/48.1	56.9/35.5
425		2426	16.2/48.0	57.2/35.3
426	el-Hāshimiyyah	2059	18.0/46.7	59.1/34.1
427	Dhāt Rās	2327	22.8/46.0	63.8/33.6
428	Kh. el-ᶜAkūzeh	2331	18.6/45.2	59.6/32.6
429		2402	19.2/46.0	60.4/33.4
430	Rujm ᶜAbdeh	2404	19.7/45.3	60.7/32.7
431	Kfeir/Kh. el-ᶜAbdeh	2403	19.3/45.2	60.4/32.6
432	Kh. el-Quṣūbah	2332	24.6/43.5	65.7/31.0
433	Kh. esh-Shqeirah	2362	25.0/43.4	66.1/30.9
434	Shqeirah	2424	26.3/43.2	67.4/30.8

Map Section 14

Site#	Name	field#	PG	UTMG
435	Mḍeibiᶜ	2322	30.6/50.3	71.6/38.0
436	Mḥai	2328	31.9/44.9	73.0/32.6
437		2431	29.6/45.1	70.7/32.7
438		2432	29.3/45.2	70.4/32.8
439		2429	29.7/44.5	70.8/32.1
440		2430	30.0/44.4	71.1/32.1
441	Qfeiqef	2428	29.2/44.4	70.3/32.0
442		2389	30.3/43.3	71.4/30.9
443		2388	30.4/43.1	71.5/30.7

Sites According to Names

Name	Site#/Section		PG	UTMG
Abū Ḥalīb	11	1	17.7/88.4	58.0/75.9
Abū er-Ruzz	216	7	20.0/69.8	60.5/57.3
Abū Trābah	23	2	25.1/90.8	65.2/78.5
Abū el-Wsheish	58	3	16.4/79.9	56.7/67.4
Adir	227	7	22.5/68.5	63.1/55.7
^{c}Ain Um Jam^{c}ān	173	6	12.0/69.5	52.7/56.6
^{c}Ainūn	264	9	15.2/62.7	55.9/49.8
^{c}Ai	262	9	11.0/60.4	51.8/47.5
^{c}Alaqān	257	9	11.7/61.4	52.5/48.6
el-^{c}Amaqa	410	13	16.8/51.7	57.8/39.1
Arīḫa	22	2	24.8/92.0	65.0/79.5
el-^{c}Ārūḍ	180	6	09.0/67.3	49.8/54.5
^{c}Awarwareh	3	1	19.0/91.4	59.2/78.6
^{c}Azzūr	43	2	28.1/84.3	68.4/71.9
Badhdhān	169	6	12.1/71.5	54.2/57.4
el-Bqei^{c}	300	9	12.6/53.7	53.4/41.0
Batīr	66	3	17.2/74.8	57.5/62.3
Beit Lajjah	57	3	19.0/79.8	59.4/67.3
Beit Sahm	303	9	08.9/53.9	49.8/41.2
Bīr Bashbash	381	11	32.0/56.2	72.8/43.9
Bteiyir	76	3	18.3/73.5	58.7/61.0
el-Bṭeimah	242	8	30.7/69.9	71.2/57.5
ed-Dabbākah	383	12	12.3/52.4	53.3/39.6
Dalāleḥ	81	4	28.0/81.5	68.3/69.2
ed-Denn wa-l-Baradāṇ	36	2	21.4/85.1	61.9/72.4
ed-Deir	71	3	14.8/73.3	55.3/60.6
Dhāt Rās	427	13	22.8/46.0	63.8/33.6
ed-Dimnah	64	3	17.1/77.9	57.4/65.3
Dleiqa	416	13	19.1/49.5	60.1/36.9
Faqū^{c}	14	1	16.5/86.5	56.8/73.8
Fityān	154	5	31.6/72.6	72.1/60.2
Fqeiqes	294	9	11.3/54.9	52.3/42.3
el-Franj	201	6	15.6/64.5	56.1/52.0
Freiwān	5	1	20.7/90.1	60.8/77.6
Ghuweir	313	10	22.1/61.1	62.9/48.6
el-Harbaj	27	2	25.9/89.3	66.2/77.1
Ḥabāsh/Ḥabāj	167	6	14.9/69.9	55.5/57.3
el-Ḥaddādah	235	7	21.3/65.5	62.0/53.0
el-Ḥāshimiyyah	426	13	18.0/46.7	59.1/34.1
Ḥimmeh	53	3	14.5/82.0	54.8/69.6
Ḥmeimāt (NE)	91	4	23.5/79.9	63.9/67.4
Ḥmeimāt (NW)	89	4	22.6/80.3	63.0/67.8
Ḥmeimāt (SE)	92	4	23.2/79.0	63.6/66.4
Ḥmeimāt (SW)	90	4	25.7/79.8	63.1/67.4
Ḥmūd	100	4	26.2/77.8	66.5/65.4
Ḥujfah	219	7	24.4/71.0	65.0/58.4
el-Ḥseiniyyah	417	13	19.1/48.6	60.1/36.0
Ibn Ayyūb	198	6	14.8/66.2	55.6/53.4
Imra^{c}	15	1	15.3/84.5	55.6/71.7
el-^{c}Irāq	292	9	11.2/55.5	52.1/42.8
^{c}Izra	205	6	16.0/63.2	56.7/50.5
Jad^{c}a el-Jbur	34	2	21.3/86.0	61.5/73.5
el-Jauza	384	12	13.8/51.9	54.7/39.2
Jauza	256	9	11.4/62.8	52.1/49.9
Jdeiyidah	119	4	27.3/73.6	67.8/61.3
el-Jilimeh	105	4	21.1/77.0	61.6/64.5
Juḥra	391	12	12.3/49.9	53.3/37.2
Jweir	424	13	15.9/48.1	56.9/35.5
Kaminna	200	6	15.2/64.2	55.8/51.5
Karakūn	18	2	25.7/93.7	65.8/81.2
Kathrabba	261	9	09.3/60.8	50.2/48.0
Kerak	204	6	17.0/66.0	58.0/53.5
Kfeir	431	13	19.3/45.2	60.4/32.6
Kfeirāz	278	9	13.3/57.6	54.1/44.8
Kh. el-^{c}Abdeh	431	14	19.3/45.2	60.4/32.6
Kh. Abū Rukbah	377	11	33.5/58.9	74.3/46.6
Kh. ^{c}Aizār	184	6	12.9/66.9	53.8/54.1
Kh. el-^{c}Akūzeh	428	13	18.6/45.2	59.6/32.6
Kh. ^{c}Aleiyān	96	4	25.6/78.7	66.0/66.2
Kh. ^{c}Arbīd	230	7	29.2/67.4	69.8/55.0
Kh. el-Bālū^{c}	35	2	24.4/85.5	64.5/72.9
Kh. el-Bāsiliyyah	385	12	14.5/52.0	55.4/39.4
Kh. el-Baṭrāʾ	355	10	25.4/58.3	66.2/45.9
Kh. el-Beiḍā	302	9	11.5/53.4	52.0/41.1
Kh. Btheinah	182	6	08.9/68.4	49.7/55.5
Kh. ed-Dāwūdiyyah	213	7	19.4/71.6	60.2/58.9
Kh. ed-Dāwūdiyyah	212	7	19.3/71.8	60.1/59.2
Kh. ed-Dweikhleh	426	13	18.0/46.7	59.1/34.1
Kh. eḍ-Ḍribbān	30	2	22.0/87.8	62.2/75.3
Kh. Ḍubāb	399	12	10.5/49.4	51.4/36.7
Kh. eḍ-Ḍweibi^{c}	255	9	10.1/62.2	50.9/49.4
Kh. el-^{c}Edūl	307	9	18.8/55.5	59.7/42.9
Kh. Eshjar	281	9	09.0/58.8	49.9/45.9
Kh. Fqeiqes	301	9	11.5/53.8	52.4/40.8
Kh. Ghifrah	291	9	10.6/55.1	51.4/42.6
Kh. el-Ḥawiyyah	270	9	15.2/62.7	58.0/48.6
Kh. el-Ḥdeib	67	3	12.5/75.3	52.9/62.6
Kh. el-Ḥinū	102	4	25.1/76.8	65.7/64.3
Kh. el-Ḥwāleh	281	9	09.0/58.8	49.9/45.9
Kh. ^{c}Izra	206	6	16.3/63.1	57.1/50.3
Kh. el-Jad^{c}a	30	2	22.0/87.8	62.2/75.3
Kh. el-Jeljūl	274	9	14.6/59.7	55.3/47.0
Kh. el-Jūbah	272	9	16.7/59.6	57.5/46.9
Kh. el-Kharziyyah	60	3	18.0/79.2	58.2/66.7
Kh. el-Labūn	267	9	15.3/62.0	56.5/49.3
Kh. el-Makhārīm	99	4	28.9/78.9	69.7/66.5
Kh. Mdeinet el-Mu^{c}rrajeh	129	5	32.2/81.3	72.5/69.0
Kh. Mdeinet ^{c}Aliyā	143	5	33.0/76.8	73.4/64.5
Kh. Medīnet er-Rās	402	12	05.9/51.1	46.9/38.3
Kh. el-Meidān	259	9	07.7/60.8	48.6/47.8
Kh. el-Meiseh	263	9	13.1/60.2	53.8/47.5
Kh. Mḥeisin	97	4	28.1/78.7	68.5/66.3

Kh. el-Minḥār	165	6	19.5/70.5	59.9/58.0
Kh. el-Minsaḥlāt	101	4	25.8/77.3	66.0/64.6
Kh. Mishrāqah	295	9	13.1/55.4	54.0/42.7
Kh. el-Mrabbaᶜah	170	6	13.9/68.7	54.6/56.4
Kh. el-Mudawwarah	390	12	12.7/50.2	53.6/37.4
Kh. el-Mṣāṭeb	269	9	16.1/61.7	57.0/49.0
Kh. en-Neqqāz	207	6	17.1/62.7	57.8/50.0
Kh. en-Nsheinish	353	10	22.3/55.2	63.1/42.7
Kh. el-ᶜOkbar	194	6	13.2/64.3	53.8/51.6
Kh. Qamarein	217	7	21.3/70.7	61.7/58.0
Kh. el-Qaryatein	210	6	17.7/64.5	58.4/51.8
Kh. el-Qashab	179	6	09.9/66.7	50.3/53.9
Kh. el-Quṣūbah	432	13	24.6/43.5	65.7/31.0
Kh. er-Rṣeifah	191	6	11.4/65.4	52.2/52.6
Kh. es-Saᶜadūnī	38	2	21.4/84.0	61.8/71.4
Kh. Sakka	174	6	12.5/69.0	53.2/56.0
Kh. es-Samrāᵓ(N)	34	2	21.3/86.0	61.5/73.5
Kh. es-Samrāᵓ(S)	199	6	14.7/65.3	55.2/52.5
Kh. es-Sanīnah	47	2	29.6/83.4	69.8/70.8
Kh. Sārah	187	6	16.3/67.3	57.0/54.6
Kh. es-Sdeir	397	12	10.2/50.5	52.0/37.7
Kh. Shīḥān	12	1	20.1/87.7	60.4/75.2
Kh. esh-Shqeirah	433	13	25.0/43.4	66.1/30.9
Kh. Thamāyil	248	8	31.5/66.3	72.1/53.9
Kh. Ṭrunjeh	171	6	13.7/68.6	54.2/56.3
Kh. eṭ-Ṭayyibeh	396	12	09.8/50.7	50.8/38.0
Kh. eṭ-Ṭalīsah	266	9	16.1/62.0	57.2/49.5
Kh. eṭ-Ṭūr	312	9	17.8/53.7	58.7/41.0
Kh. Um ᶜAlanda	349	10	20.1/55.1	61.0/42.6
Kh. Um Kharīᶜah	109	4	23.7/74.9	64.0/62.4
Kh. Um el-Qṣeir	289	9	11.7/56.1	52.6/43.5
Kh. Um Rummānah	158	6	15.6/72.4	56.1/59.9
Kh. Um Rummānah	404	12	07.0/49.0	48.1/36.3
Kh. el-Weibdeh	332	10	22.2/59.9	62.9/47.3
Kh. Zabdah	290	9	12.8/56.2	53.7/43.5
Kh. Zabūbah	70	3	13.1/72.7	53.6/60.0
Kh. Zughriyyeh	74	3	16.0/73.2	56.6/60.6
Khāneq en-Naṣāra	395	12	10.8/50.8	51.8/38.1
Khanzīrah	401	12	07.3/51.6	48.3/38.8
el-Kharīᶜ	78	4	26.5/81.5	66.7/69.2
Kinnār	233	7	19.3/66.7	60.0/54.3
Lejjūn (Bronze)	239	8	31.7/71.9	72.3/59.6
Lejjūn (Roman)	240	8	32.7/72.0	73.1/59.7
el-Māhrī	366	10	29.5/53.7	70.4/41.5
Majdalein	16	1	18.1/82.6	58.5/70.0
Majra	423	13	15.1/48.3	56.1/35.6
Maᶜmūdiyyeh	185	6	14.3/67.3	54.9/54.7
el-Mashhad	305	9	17.5/55.5	58.4/42.9
el-Mazār	311	9	16.4/52.8	57.3/40.3
Mḍeibiᶜ	435	14	30.6/50.3	71.6/38.0
Meidān (SE)	260	9	07.9/60.5	48.8/47.6
Merzab Mezraᶜah	400	12	08.8/49.2	49.8/36.4
Mgheir	197	6	14.1/65.9	54.7/53.1
Mḥai	436	14	31.9/44.9	73.0/32.6
Mḥaṭṭat el-Ḥājj	18	2	25.7/93.7	65.8/81.2
Mḥarraqāt	115	4	21.6/73.3	62.1/60.9
Mḥarraqāt (N)	114	4	21.6/73.3	62.1/61.2
Middīn	333	10	19.7/58.7	60.5/46.2
Miḥna	273	9	16.0/59.0	56.8/46.4
el-Minqaṭᶜah	160	6	19.2/72.6	59.8/60.0
Mirwid	285	9	19.1/57.1	59.9/44.5
Misᶜar	25	2	21.5/90.0	61.8/77.5
el-Misdāḥ	87	4	20.9/79.4	61.2/66.8
Miṣnaᶜ	106	4	22.3/76.7	62.8/64.2
[el-Miyāl]	107	4	20.4/76.5	60.7/64.0
el-Mjeidel	405	12	12.9/48.7	53.9/35.9
Mauta	304	9	16.7/55.8	57.1/43.2
el-Mreigha	316	10	26.2/60.8	67.0/48.4
Mseimṭah (N)	196	6	13.6/65.1	54.3/52.5
Mseimṭah (S)	195	6	13.5/64.7	54.3/52.0
el-Msheirfah	271	9	18.7/60.3	59.4/47.7
Nakhl	420	13	24.5/52.3	65.4/39.8
Naṣīb	39	2	22.4/83.1	62.7/70.6
Nāṣir	359	10	26.3/56.2	67.2/43.8
el-Qabū	72	3	16.0/74.0	56.5/61.5
el-Qaṣr	86	4	21.2/80.5	61.3/67.9
Qaṣr Abū Rukbah	378	11	33.9/58.0	74.7/45.7
Qaṣr Ḥamdān	104	4	26.1/77.2	66.5/64.5
Qaṣr el-Ḥimmeh	55	3	18.2/82.0	58.6/69.4
Qaṣr er-Rṣeifah	192	6	11.9/64.8	52.7/51.9
Qaṣr et-Tamrah	379	11	33.0/57.0	73.9/44.7
Qfeiqef	441	14	29.2/44.4	70.3/32.0
Qmeir	215	7	22.0/71.4	62.5/58.8
Qreifilla	166	6	19.4/69.4	60.0/56.8
er-Rabbah	108	4	20.3/75.5	60.8/63.0
Rākīn	162	6	17.3/70.4	57.8/57.8
er-Ribᶜī (es-Samrāᵓ)	37	2	21.5/84.8	61.9/72.2
Rujm ᶜAbdeh	430	13	19.7/45.3	60.7/32.7
Rujm el-ᶜAbsī	224	7	26.2/69.6	66.9/57.2
Rujm Abū Zaᶜrūrah	77	4	23.9/82.2	64.3/69.5
Rujm el-Awsaj (?)	415	13	16.6/50.4	57.5/37.8
Rujm el-Baqr	299	9	13.8/54.0	54.6/41.5
Rujm Birjis	73	3	17.2/73.9	57.7/61.2
Rujm Eshqāḥ	414	13	16.5/50.5	57.7/37.8
Rujm Ghneim	79	4	27.3/81.2	67.6/68.8
Rujm el-Ḥleileh	388	12	13.1/50.8	54.2/37.8
Rujm el-Ḥleileh	287	9	10.9/56.9	51.8/43.9
Rujm el-Jazūr	228	7	26.4/67.3	67.0/54.8
Rujm Khashm eṣ-Ṣīrah	370	10	30.9/52.9	71.8/40.3
Rujm el-Merīḥ	251	8	33.1/66.1	73.8/53.8
Rujm Mesᶜīd	297	9	13.0/54.8	53.8/42.2
Rujm el-Mismar	421	13	26.8/47.9	67.8/35.5
Rujm el-Qanāṭir	153	5	30.3/72.8	70.9/60.5
Rujm Qneiṭrah	98	4	28.3/79.2	68.8/66.8
Rujm Rafīyeh	350	10	21.3/55.0	62.2/42.5
Rujm er-Rās	403	12	06.3/50.1	47.4/37.3
Rujm eṣ-Ṣakharī	417	13	19.1/48.6	60.1/36.0

Rujm esh-Sharīf	237	7	26.7/64.3	67.3/51.8
Rujm esh-Shmūs	183	6	09.1/69.0	49.9/56.2
Rujm et-Teis	113	4	28.0/75.0	68.5/62.6
Rujm Um ᶜAlanda	412	13	15.7/50.6	56.6/38.0
Rujm Um el-ᶜAṭāṭ	298	9	13.5/54.5	54.5/41.9
Rujm Um Ḥlāl	13	1	16.4/86.9	56.7/74.3
Rujm Um Ṣuwwānah	387	12	13.5/50.3	54.5/37.7
Samrāᵓ	175	6	12.2/67.5	52.7/54.8
Sdeir	394	12	10.5/50.6	52.1/37.8
Shaḥtūr	54	3	17.5/81.7	57.7/69.3
Shajarah	85	4	19.8/80.5	60.1/67.9
esh-Sharīf	238	7	27.6/63.2	68.3/50.8
esh-Shihābiyyah	201	6	15.6/64.5	56.1/52.0
Shqeirah	434	13	26.3/43.2	67.4/30.8
es-Smākiyyah	94	4	26.5/79.6	66.9/67.2
Sūl	411	13	19.7/52.4	60.7/39.7
Ṣirfa	52	3	12.4/81.8	52.4/69.3
Tadūn	56	3	19.2/81.2	59.5/68.6
eth-Thallājah	202	6	16.8/65.2	57.5/52.7
eth-Thaniyyah	211	6	18.8/64.1	59.5/51.4
eṭ-Ṭayyibeh	401	12	07.3/51.6	48.3/38.8
el-Umariyyah	416	13	19.1/49.5	60.1/36.9
Um ed-Dajāj	172	6	11.9/70.2	53.5/56.7
Um Dimis	38	2	21.4/84.0	61.8/71.4
Um el-Habāj	88	4	23.0/81.0	63.4/68.4
Um Ḥamāṭ	419	13	22.8/49.8	63.8/37.3
Um Kharūf	185	6	14.3/67.3	54.9/54.7
Um Najīl	161	6	17.2/71.1	57.8/58.4
Um Naṣr	286	9	10.7/56.7	51.6/43.9
Um el-Qleib	21	2	23.3/92.0	63.6/79.7
Um Sidreh	61	3	16.8/78.6	57.2/66.1
Um eṭ-Ṭawābīn	4	1	18.6/90.3	58.8/77.7
Um Zabāyir	418	13	20.3/48.8	61.3/36.4
Um Zebel	345	10	19.1/55.4	60.0/42.8
el-ᶜUmyān	193	6	11.0/63.7	51.8/51.0
el-Yārūt	63	3	18.8/78.7	59.0/66.1
ez-Zarrāᶜah	214	7	23.0/72.0	63.4/59.6
Zeita	176	6	11.4/66.8	51.9/54.1
eẓ-Ẓheiriyyeh	190	6	18.9/67.1	59.7/54.5

Sites According to Field Numbers

Field#	Name	Site#	PG	UTMG
2001	Um Kharūf	185	14.3/67.3	54.9/54.7
2002	Kh. ᶜAizār	184	12.9/66.9	53.8/54.1
2003	Kh. Sārah	187	16.3/67.3	57.0/54.6
2004	Kh. el-ᶜOkbar	194	13.2/64.3	53.8/51.6
2005	Kh. eṭ-Ṭalīsah	266	16.1/62.0	57.2/49.5
2006	Jauza	256	11.4/62.8	52.1/49.9
2007	Kh. el-Mṣāṭeb	269	16.1/61.7	57.0/49.0
2008	Kh. el-Labūn	267	15.3/62.0	56.5/49.3
2010	Kathrabba	261	09.3/60.8	50.2/48.0
2012	Kh. el-Meidān	259	07.7/60.8	48.6/47.8
2013	ᶜAi	262	11.0/60.4	51.8/47.5
2014	Kh. el-Meiseh	263	13.1/60.2	53.8/47.5
2015	Kh. el-Jūbah	272	16.7/59.6	57.5/46.9
2016	Kh. el-Jeljūl	274	14.6/59.7	55.3/47.0
2017	Miḥna	273	16.0/59.0	56.8/46.4
2019	el-Mazār	311	16.4/52.8	57.3/40.3
2020	Kfeirāz	278	13.3/57.6	54.1/44.8
2021	Kh. Um el-Qṣeir	289	11.7/56.1	52.6/43.5
2022	Kh. Zabdah	290	12.8/56.2	53.7/43.5
2023	Mōta	304	16.7/55.8	57.1/43.2
2024	Rujm el-Ḥleileh	287	10.9/56.9	51.8/43.9
2025	Kh. Mishrāqā	295	13.1/55.4	54.0/42.7
2026	Rujm Mesᶜīd	297	13.0/54.8	53.8/42.2
2027	Rujm Um el-ᶜAṭāṭ	298	13.5/54.5	54.5/41.9
2028	Fqeiqes	294	11.3/54.9	52.3/42.3
2029	el-ᶜIrāq	292	11.2/55.5	52.1/42.8
2030	Kh. Fqeiqes	301	11.5/53.8	52.4/40.8
2031	Beit Sahm	303	08.9/53.9	49.8/41.2
2032	el-Bqeiᶜ	300	12.6/53.7	53.4/41.0
2033	Rujm el-Baqr	299	13.8/54.0	54.6/41.5
2034	Kh. el-Beiḍā	302	11.5/53.4	52.0/41.1
2036	ed-Dabbākah	383	12.3/52.4	53.3/39.6
2037	Kh. el-Bāsiliyyah	385	14.5/52.0	55.4/39.4
2038	el-Jauza	384	13.8/51.9	54.7/39.2
2039	el-ᶜAmaqa	410	16.8/51.7	57.8/39.1
2040	Khanzīrah	401	07.3/51.6	48.3/38.8
2041	Kh. Medīnet er-Rās	402	05.9/51.1	46.9/38.3
2042	Khāneq en-Naṣāra	395	10.8/50.8	51.8/38.1
2043	Kh. eṭ-Ṭayyibeh	396	09.8/50.7	50.8/38.0
2044	Rujm el-Ḥleileh	388	13.1/50.8	54.2/37.8
2045	Rujm Um ᶜAlanda	412	15.7/50.6	56.6/38.0
2046	Kh. es-Sdeir	397	10.2/50.5	52.0/37.7
2047	Rujm Um Ṣuwwānah	387	13.5/50.3	54.5/37.7
2048	Kh. el-Mudawwarah	390	12.7/50.2	53.6/37.4
2049	Kh. Ḍubāb	399	10.5/49.4	51.4/36.7
2050	Merzab Mezraᶜah	400	08.8/49.2	49.8/36.4
2052	el-Mjeidel	405	12.9/48.7	53.9/35.9
2053	Majra	423	15.1/48.3	56.1/35.6
2054	Jweir	424	15.9/48.1	56.9/35.5
2059	el-Hāshimiyyah	426	18.0/46.7	59.1/34.1
2068		178	08.8/66.1	49.9/53.3
2083	Kh. ᶜIzra	206	16.3/63.1	57.1/50.3
2084		268	15.8/61.6	56.6/49.2
2085	ᶜAinūn	264	15.2/62.7	55.9/49.8
2086		282	15.1/57.3	56.2/44.5
2087		277	14.5/58.0	55.1/45.1
2088		275	14.1/58.7	54.9/46.4
2089		276	14.8/58.6	55.8/45.7
2090	ᶜIzra	205	16.0/63.2	56.7/50.5
2091		265	16.0/62.7	56.8/49.8
2092	Meidān (SE)	260	07.9/60.5	48.8/47.6
2093		296	14.0/55.6	54.8/42.8
2094	Rujm Eshqāḥ	414	16.5/50.5	57.7/37.8
2095		413	15.7/50.7	57.0/38.2
2096		386	13.8/51.1	54.8/38.5
2097	Sdeir	394	10.5/50.6	52.1/37.8
2098		409	15.4/52.4	56.2/38.5
2101	Juḥra	391	12.3/49.9	53.3/37.2
2102	ᶜAlaqān	257	11.7/61.4	52.5/48.6
2103	Kh. eḍ-Ḍweibiᶜ	255	10.1/62.2	50.9/49.4
2104	Kh. el-Ḥwālehh	281	09.0/58.8	49.9/45.9
2107		258	12.3/61.6	53.1/48.9
2108	el-ᶜUmyān	193	11.0/63.7	51.8/51.0
2109		279	11.7/58.2	52.6/45.4
2110		398	10.3/49.9	51.3/37.2
2113	Rujm er-Rās	403	06.3/50.1	47.4/37.3
2114		406	13.2/48.7	54.2/36.1
2116		407	14.4/48.3	55.4/35.8
2117		408	13.9/48.5	54.9/35.7
2119		288	11.0/56.6	51.9/43.8
2120	Kh. Ghifrah	291	10.6/55.1	51.4/42.6
2121		293	11.0/55.2	51.9/42.5
2122	eth-Thallājah	202	16.8/65.2	57.5/52.7
2125		389	12.3/50.8	53.3/38.1
2126		392	11.7/51.1	52.7/38.4
2127		393	11.2/51.1	52.2/38.5
2128		280	09.7/58.4	50.6/45.6
2129	Um Naṣr	286	10.7/56.7	51.6/43.9
2201	Ibn ᶜAyyūb	198	14.8/66.2	55.6/53.4
2202	Mgheir	197	14.1/65.9	54.7/53.1
2203	Kh. Samrāᵓ	199	14.7/65.3	55.2/52.5
2204	Kh. Sakka	174	12.5/69.0	53.2/56.0
2205	Samrāᵓ	175	12.2/67.5	52.7/54.8
2206	Kaminna	200	15.2/64.2	55.8/51.5
2207	Mseimṭah (S)	195	13.5/64.7	54.3/52.0
2208	Mseimṭah (N)	196	13.6/65.1	54.3/52.5
2209	Kh. er-Rṣeifah	191	11.4/65.4	52.2/52.6
2210	Qaṣr er-Rṣeifah	192	11.9/64.8	52.7/51.9
2211		177	09.8/65.9	50.5/53.3
2212	Kh. el-Qashab	179	09.9/66.7	50.3/53.9
2213	el-ᶜĀrūḍ	180	09.0/67.3	49.8/54.5

2214		181	85.0/68.2	49.2/55.4
2215	Kh. Btheinah	182	08.9/68.4	49.7/55.5
2216	Rujm esh-Shmūs	183	09.1/69.0	49.9/56.2
2217		155	10.5/72.1	51.3/59.5
2218	Um ed-Dajāj	172	11.9/70.2	53.5/56.7
2219	ᶜAin Um Jamᶜān	173	12.0/69.5	52.7/56.6
2220	el-Franj	201	15.6/64.5	56.1/52.0
2221	Zeita	176	11.4/66.8	51.9/54.1
2301		208	17.3/64.3	58.0/51.6
2302		203	17.9/65.6	58.5/53.0
2303	Kh. el-Qaryatein	210	17.7/64.5	58.4/51.8
2304	eth-Thaniyyah	211	18.8/64.1	59.5/51.4
2305	Kh. en-Neqqāz	207	17.1/62.7	57.8/50.0
2306	Kh. el-Ḥawiyyah	270	15.2/62.7	58.0/48.6
2307	Middīn	333	19.7/58.7	60.5/46.2
2308	Kh. el-Baṭrāʾ	355	25.4/58.3	66.2/45.9
2309	Mirwid	285	19.1/57.1	59.9/44.5
2312	el-Mashhad	305	17.5/55.5	58.4/42.9
2314	Kh. en-Nsheinish	353	22.3/55.2	63.1/42.7
2316	Kh. eṭ-Ṭūr	312	17.8/53.7	58.7/41.0
2319	Sūl	411	19.7/52.4	60.7/39.7
2320	Nakhl	420	24.5/52.3	65.4/39.8
2322	Mḍeibiᶜ	435	30.6/50.3	71.6/38.0
2323	Um Ḥamāṭ	419	22.8/49.8	63.8/37.3
2324	Dleiqa	416	19.1/49.5	60.1/36.9
2326	el-Ḥseiniyyah	417	19.1/48.6	60.1/36.0
2327	Dhāt Rās	427	22.8/46.0	63.8/33.6
2328	Mḥai	436	31.9/44.9	73.0/32.6
2331	Kh. el-ᶜAkūzeh	428	18.6/45.2	59.6/32.6
2332	Kh. el-Quṣūbah	432	24.6/43.5	65.7/31.0
2355		309	17.3/54.3	58.1/41.8
2356		352	22.5/55.1	63.4/42.6
2357	Rujm Rafīyeh	350	21.3/55.0	62.2/42.5
2358	Kh. Um ᶜAlanda	349	20.1/55.1	61.0/42.6
2359		308	17.4/54.8	58.3/42.2
2360	Ghuweir (N)	313	22.1/61.1	62.9/48.6
2361	el-Msheirfah	271	18.7/60.3	59.4/47.7
2362	Kh. esh-Shqeirah	433	25.0/43.4	66.1/30.9
2363	Um Zabāyir	418	20.3/48.8	61.3/36.4
2364		209	17.6/63.4	58.3/51.0
2365		310	17.0/53.7	57.9/41.2
2366		338	19.6/65.3	60.4/43.7
2367		347	19.7/55.5	60.6/42.9
2369		363	29.0/54.7	69.7/42.4
2370		364	29.0/54.9	69.9/42.5
2371		361	26.3/57.6	69.7/42.7
2372		362	28.7/55.4	69.5/43.0
2374		365	29.4/54.0	70.3/41.7
2375	el-Māhrī	366	29.5/53.7	70.4/41.5
2376		367	29.7/53.6	70.6/41.2
2377		357	26.9/57.0	67.6/44.7
2378		368	30.2/53.2	71.3/40.8
2381		369	30.4/53.0	71.4/40.5
2382	Rujm Khashm eṣ-Ṣīrah	370	30.9/52.9	71.8/40.3
2383		382	31.2/52.5	72.1/40.1
2384		360	26.9/55.8	67.7/43.4
2385	Nāṣir	359	26.3/56.2	67.2/43.8
2386		358	26.0/55.5	66.9/43.0
2387		356	26.2/57.1	67.0/44.6
2388		443	30.4/43.1	71.5/30.7
2389		442	30.3/43.3	71.4/30.9
2390		339	20.4/56.2	61.2/43.7
2391		336	20.1/56.7	60.9/44.2
2392		337	20.8/57.1	61.6/44.5
2393		284	18.5/57.1	59.3/44.5
2394		283	17.1/57.2	57.9/44.6
2395		306	18.5/55.4	59.4/42.8
2396	Kh. el-ᶜEdūl	307	18.8/55.5	59.7/42.9
2397	Um Zebel	345	19.1/55.4	60.0/42.8
2399		348	19.2/54.6	60.0/42.1
2400		346	19.3/55.2	60.2/42.7
2402		429	19.2/46.0	60.4/33.4
2403	Kfeir/Kh. el-ᶜAbdeh	431	19.3/45.2	60.4/32.6
2404	Rujm ᶜAbdeh	430	19.7/45.3	60.7/32.7
2405	Kh. el-Weibdeh	332	22.2/59.9	62.9/47.3
2407		351	21.5/54.5	62.4/42.0
2409		344	22.5/56.5	63.4/44.0
2410		343	22.5/56.9	63.4/44.5
2411		342	22.4/57.3	63.2/44.8
2412		341	22.4/57.6	63.2/45.1
2413		340	22.5/57.9	63.3/45.5
2416		334	21.6/58.1	62.4/45.5
2417		335	23.4/59.3	64.2/46.8
2418		354	24.1/56.2	64.9/43.7
2424	Shqeira	434	26.3/43.2	67.4/30.8
2425	Rujm el-Awsaj	415	16.6/50.4	57.5/37.8
2426		425	16.2/48.0	57.2/35.3
2427		422	18.5/45.8	59.6/33.3
2428	Qfeiqef	441	29.2/44.4	70.3/32.0
2429		439	29.7/44.5	70.8/32.1
2430		440	30.0/44.4	71.1/32.1
2431		437	29.6/45.1	70.7/32.7
2432		438	29.3/45.2	70.4/32.8
2433	Rujm al-Mismar	421	26.8/47.9	67.8/35.5
2588	Kh. el-Ḥdeib	67	12.5/75.3	52.9/62.6
2589		68	12.9/75.0	53.3/62.3
2590		69	13.6/73.2	54.2/60.4
2592		156	14.4/72.6	54.9/59.9
2593	Kh. Zabūbah	70	13.1/72.7	53.6/60.0
2594		159	13.9/71.3	54.4/58.6
2595	Ḥabāsh/Ḥabāj	167	14.9/69.9	55.5/57.3
2599	Kerak	204	17.0/66.0	58.0/53.5
2602	el-Mreigha	316	26.2/60.8	67.0/48.4
2603	Kh. Abū Rukbah	377	33.5/58.9	74.3/46.6
2604	Qaṣr Abū Rukbah	378	33.9/58.0	74.7/45.7

2605	Qaṣr et-Tamrah	379	33.0/57.0	73.9/44.7
2607		380	32.2/56.8	73.0/44.4
2608	Bīr Bashbash	381	32.0/56.2	72.8/43.9
2625	Rujm el-Merīḥ	251	33.1/66.1	73.8/53.8
2626		250	31.8/66.4	72.5/54.2
2627		247	32.4/66.7	72.7/54.5
2628		245	32.3/67.3	72.9/54.9
2629		244	32.1/67.8	72.7/55.5
2630	Kh. Thamāyil	248	31.5/66.3	72.1/53.9
2631		246	31.1/66.8	71.9/54.4
2632		243	31.8/68.0	72.4/55.6
2633		253	31.2/64.2	72.4/51.9
2634		225	28.8/69.6	69.5/57.2
2635	Kh. ^{c}Arbīd	230	29.2/67.4	69.8/55.0
2637		249	30.9/66.0	71.5/53.6
2638	Rujm el-Jazūr	228	26.4/67.3	67.0/54.8
2639	Rujm esh-Sharīf	237	26.7/64.3	67.3/51.8
2640		252	29.7/64.8	70.3/52.4
2641		231	28.9/65.9	69.5/53.5
2642		232	29.2/65.6	69.7/53.3
2643	esh-Sharīf	238	27.6/63.2	68.3/50.8
2644		319	28.4/62.4	69.4/49.9
2646		320	28.3/61.6	69.4/49.0
2648		321	29.2/61.4	70.1/48.8
2650		322	29.6/60.9	70.4/48.4
2651		323	29.7/61.2	70.5/48.8
2653		318	28.2/60.8	68.9/48.5
2654		317	27.8/60.8	68.6/48.4
2656		324	28.2/60.1	69.0/47.7
2657		326	28.5/59.6	69.4/47.3
2658		327	29.0/59.8	69.8/47.4
2659		329	28.2/59.5	69.0/46.9
2660		331	29.5/57.5	70.8/44.8
2661		325	27.2/59.8	67.9/47.5
2663		328	27.7/59.3	68.5/46.9
2669		330	28.7/58.4	69.5/46.0
2674		374	34.8/59.5	75.6/47.2
2675		371	33.7/61.6	74.6/49.6
2676		254	33.4/64.1	74.1/51.9
2677		314	23.4/61.5	64.2/49.0
2678		315	24.9/60.7	65.8/48.2
2681		372	33.1/61.5	73.8/48.8
2682		373	33.4/60.2	74.2/47.6
2683		375	32.8/59.3	73.5/46.9
2684		376	33.2/59.0	73.9/46.7
2685		241	31.7/68.2	72.1/56.0
8001	Mḥaṭṭat el-Ḥājj	18	25.7/93.7	65.8/81.2
8007	Arīḥa	22	24.8/92.0	65.0/79.5
8008	Um el-Qleib	21	23.3/92.0	63.6/79.7
8009	Abū Trābah	23	25.1/90.8	65.2/78.5
8010		31	25.5/87.9	65.7/75.6
8011	Mis^{c}ar	25	21.5/90.0	61.8/77.5
8012	Freiwān	5	20.7/90.1	60.8/77.6
8013	^{c}Awarwareh	3	19.0/91.4	59.2/78.6
8014	Kh. el-Bālū^{c}	35	24.4/85.5	64.5/72.9
8015	Rujm Um Ḥlāl	13	16.4/86.9	56.7/74.3
8016	Faqū^{c}	14	16.5/86.5	56.8/73.8
8017	Imra^{c}	15	15.3/84.5	55.6/71.7
8018	Kh. Mdeinet el-Mu^{c}rrajeh	129	32.2/81.3	72.5/69.0
8019	Kh. Mdeinet ^{c}Aliyā	143	33.0/76.8	73.4/64.5
8020	Kh. Shīḥān	12	20.1/87.7	60.4/75.2
8022	Majdalein	16	18.1/82.6	58.5/70.0
8024	Miṣna^{c}	106	22.3/76.7	62.8/64.2
8025	ed-Denn wa-l-Baradān	36	21.4/85.1	61.9/72.4
8026	er-Rib^{c}ī (es-Samrāʾ)	37	21.5/84.8	61.9/72.2
8027	Kh. es-Sa^{c}adūnī	38	21.4/84.0	61.8/71.4
8028	Jad^{c}at el-Jubur	34	21.3/86.0	61.5/73.5
8029	^{c}Azzūr	43	28.1/84.3	68.4/71.9
8030	Kh. es-Sanīnah	47	29.6/83.4	69.8/70.8
8031	Rujm Abū Za^{c}rūrah	77	23.9/82.2	64.3/69.5
8032	Naṣīb	39	22.4/83.1	62.7/70.6
8033	Tadūn	56	19.2/81.2	59.5/68.6
8034	Shajarah	85	19.8/80.5	60.1/67.9
8035	Kh. el-Makhārīm	99	28.9/78.9	69.7/66.5
9001	el-Misdāḥ	87	20.9/79.4	61.2/66.8
9002	el-Yārūt	63	18.8/78.7	59.0/66.1
9003	el-Jilimeh	105	21.1/77.0	61.6/64.5
9004	Ḥmeimāt (NW)	89	22.6/80.3	63.0/67.8
9005	Ḥmeimāt (SW)	90	25.7/79.8	63.1/67.4
9006	Ḥmeimāt (SE)	92	23.2/79.0	63.6/66.4
9007		59	16.7/79.4	57.1/66.6
9008	Ḥmeimāt (NE)	91	23.5/79.9	63.9/67.4
9009		62	18.4/78.8	58.7/66.3
9012	Um el-Habāj	88	23.0/81.0	63.4/68.4
9013	Um Sidreh	61	16.8/78.6	57.2/66.1
9014	Beit Lajjah	57	19.0/79.8	59.4/67.3
9017	ed-Dimnah	64	17.1/77.9	57.4/65.3
9018		93	23.3/78.2	63.8/65.7
9020	Ḥmūd	100	26.2/77.8	66.5/65.4
9021	Qaṣr Ḥamdān	104	26.1/77.2	66.5/64.5
9023	Qaṣr el-Ḥimmeh	55	18.2/82.0	58.6/69.4
9025	Kh. el-Ḥinū	102	25.1/76.8	65.7/64.3
9026	Shaḥtūr	54	17.5/81.7	57.7/69.3
9027	Kh. el-Kharziyyah	60	18.0/79.2	58.2/66.7
9030	Qmeir	215	22.0/71.4	62.5/58.8
9031	Qreifilla	166	19.4/69.4	60.0/56.8
9033	Rujm Ghneim	79	27.3/81.2	67.6/68.8
9035	Ḥimmeh	53	14.5/82.0	54.8/69.6
9037	es-Smākiyyah	94	26.5/79.6	66.9/67.2
9040	ez-Zarrā^{c}ah	214	23.0/72.0	63.4/59.6
9041	el-Kharī^{c}	78	26.5/81.5	66.7/69.2
9043	Ḥujfah	219	24.4/71.0	65.0/58.4
9044	Um Najīl	161	17.2/71.1	57.8/58.4
9045	Jdeiyidah	119	27.3/73.6	67.8/61.3
9047	Rujm Birjis	73	17.2/73.9	57.7/61.2
9048	Abū er-Ruzz	216	20.0/69.8	60.5/57.3

9049	Kh. el-Minsaḥlāt	101	25.8/77.3	66.0/64.6	9157		139	29.6/77.2	70.0/64.9
9051	Kh. Qamarein	217	21.3/70.7	61.7/58.0	9158		135	29.8/77.8	70.3/65.5
9052	Rujm el-Qanāṭir	153	30.3/72.8	70.9/60.5	9159		134	30.7/79.4	71.0/67.0
9059	Ṣirfa	52	12.4/81.8	52.4/69.3	9160		132	31.5/80.3	71.9/68.0
9060	Adir	227	22.5/68.5	63.1/55.7	9161		1	20.6/92.0	60.8/79.5
9061	Kh. ed-Dāwūdiyyah	212	19.3/71.8	60.1/59.2	9162		20	21.9/91.7	62.0/79.0
9062	Rākīn	162	17.3/70.4	57.8/57.8	9165		19	21.9/92.8	62.0/80.3
9063	Kh. el-Minḥār	165	19.5/70.5	59.9/58.0	9166		144	32.2/76.3	72.6/64.0
9064	Kh. ed-Dāwūdiyyah	213	19.4/71.6	60.2/58.9	9167		151	31.8/74.3	72.2/61.9
9066	Lejjūn (Bronze)	239	31.7/71.9	72.3/59.6	9168		145	32.2/75.7	72.7/63.4
9067		75	16.8/73.2	57.6/60.6	9169		148	31.5/74.7	72.1/62.5
9068	Bteiyir	76	18.3/73.5	58.7/61.0	9170		149	32.4/74.5	72.8/62.3
9069	Kh. Um Rummānah	158	15.6/72.4	56.1/59.9	9171		150	31.2/74.3	71.7/62.0
9070	ed-Deir	71	14.8/73.3	55.3/60.6	9173		218	22.2/70.7	62.9/58.2
9073	Batīr	66	17.2/74.8	57.5/62.3	9176		117	22.3/73.8	62.8/61.2
9074	Kh. Zughriyyeh	74	16.0/73.2	56.6/60.6	9177		118	22.2/73.7	62.8/61.1
9076		157	15.4/72.4	55.8/59.7	9182		84	29.4/80.5	69.8/68.1
9078		236	20.4/64.3	60.9/51.7	9183		124	29.9/81.0	70.2/68.2
9079		234	20.9/65.7	61.6/53.1	9184		83	29.5/81.1	69.9/68.6
9080		229	27.5/67.3	68.2/57.0	9185		116	22.2/73.9	62.6/61.4
9082	el-Ḥaddādah	235	21.3/65.5	62.0/53.0	9186		120	29.9/81.6	70.3/69.3
9084	Dalāleḥ	81	28.0/81.5	68.3/69.2	9187		123	29.8/81.3	70.1/68.9
9088		220	28.3/72.4	68.8/60.0	9189		122	30.1/81.4	70.4/69.0
9089	Rujm et-Teis	113	28.0/75.0	68.5/62.6	9191		51	31.2/82.6	71.5/70.4
9091		111	29.2/76.3	69.7/63.8	9194		44	31.0/84.2	71.3/71.9
9092	Rujm el-ᶜAbsī	224	26.2/69.6	66.9/57.2	9195		45	31.3/84.2	71.5/71.9
9095		10	17.6/88.3	57.8/75.7	9196		46	31.1/84.0	71.4/71.7
9098	el-Qabū	72	16.0/74.0	56.5/61.5	9197		48	30.8/82.7	71.2/70.8
9099		164	18.7/70.9	59.1/58.4	9198		49	31.2/83.1	71.4/70.8
9103		163	18.2/71.0	58.5/58.5	9203		50	30.8/82.7	71.1/70.3
9105		168	15.9/69.8	56.7/57.3	9205		125	31.2/82.1	71.5/69.7
9107	el-Minqaṭᶜah	160	19.2/72.6	59.8/60.0	9207		130	31.1/81.0	71.5/68.7
9108		188	17.7/67.2	58.4/54.7	9210		126	31.0/81.7	71.4/69.4
9109	eẓ-Ẓheiriyyeh	190	18.9/67.1	59.7/54.5	9211		127	31.8/82.0	72.0/69.7
9110		189	18.4/67.0	59.1/54.3	9212		128	32.0/81.9	72.3/69.6
9111	Kinnār	233	19.3/66.7	60.0/54.3	9213		133	29.9/79.6	70.2/67.2
9113	Kh. Um Kharīᶜah	109	23.7/74.9	64.0/62.4	9214	Kh. el-Jadᶜa	30	22.0/87.8	62.2/75.3
9114	Mḥarraqāt	115	21.6/73.3	62.1/60.9	9216		24	26.5/91.4	66.5/78.9
9115	Mḥarraqāt (N)	114	21.6/73.3	62.1/61.2	9218	Kh. ᶜAleiyān	96	25.6/78.7	66.0/66.2
9116	Abū Ḥalīb	11	17.7/88.4	58.0/75.9	9220		131	31.5/80.9	71.9/68.6
9117	Um eṭ-Ṭawābīn	4	18.6/90.3	58.8/77.7	9221		110	28.4/76.4	68.9/63.9
9118		9	15.4/88.3	55.4/75.6	9223	Rujm Qneiṭrah	98	28.3/79.2	68.8/66.8
9119		6	15.7/89.5	56.2/76.9	9225	Kh. Mḥeisin	97	28.1/78.7	68.5/66.3
9120		7	17.6/89.6	57.8/76.9	9226		95	26.9/79.4	67.4/66.8
9121		8	20.4/89.3	60.5/76.8	9241		32	25.1/86.8	65.3/74.5
9122		2	18.3/91.3	58.4/78.6	9243		26	25.7/89.3	66.1/77.0
9123	er-Rabbah	108	20.3/75.5	60.8/63.0	9244	el-Harbaj	27	25.9/89.3	66.2/77.1
9143	[el-Miyāl]	107	20.4/76.5	60.7/64.0	9245		152	31.6/73.3	72.4/61.4
9144		17	22.3/93.6	62.5/81.0	9255	el-Bṭeimah	242	30.7/69.9	71.2/57.5
9145		138	31.2/77.6	71.5/65.3	9256		65	18.3/76.2	58.7/63.6
9147		136	30.6/77.6	70.9/65.3	9258		186	15.7/67.8	56.3/55.1
9148		137	30.5/78.0	71.0/65.9	9262		82	29.6/81.4	69.9/69.1
9155		141	30.4/76.3	70.9/63.9	9263		80	28.0/82.0	68.3/69.7
9156		140	29.8/76.8	70.3/64.6	9265		29	29.3/88.8	69.4/76.5

9266	Jadᶜa el-Jbur	33	28.2/87.4	68.4/75.0	9294		226	27.7/68.6	68.3/56.2
9267		28	29.0/89.9	69.1/77.4	9295		223	27.1/70.3	67.8/57.7
9269		41	26.3/83.9	66.7/71.4	9304		146	29.8/74.5	70.2/62.0
9271		42	27.7/84.3	68.0/71.9	9305		142	30.3/76.0	70.8/63.7
9272		40	25.7/84.3	65.9/71.4	9307		112	28.0/75.8	69.0/63.5
9273	el-Qaṣr	86	21.2/80.5	61.3/67.9	9309		103	25.8/77.3	66.2/64.9
9275	Kh. el-Mrabbaᶜah	170	13.9/68.7	54.6/56.4	9310		147	30.0/74.7	70.6/62.4
9276	Kh. Ṭrunjeh	171	13.7/68.6	54.2/56.3	9313	Abū el-Wsheish	58	16.4/79.9	56.7/67.4
9277	Badhdhān	169	12.1/71.5	54.2/57.4	9316	Lejjūn (Roman)	240	32.7/72.0	73.1/59.7
9279		221	27.9/70.9	68.5/58.6	9317	Fityān	154	31.6/72.6	72.1/60.2
9290		222	27.6/70.9	68.2/58.5					

Sites According to Periods Represented

Sites with five or more sherds from the period indicated are marked with an asterisk (*); sites with only questionable sherds from the period are marked with a question mark (?).

Chalcolithic

59	
66	Batīr
71	ed-Deir
73	Rujm Birjis
101	Kh. el-Minsaḥlāt
114	Mḥarraqāt (N)
204 *	Kerak
207 ?	Kh. en-Neqqāz
210	Kh. el-Qaryatein
227	Adir
231 ?	
270 *	Kh. el-Ḥawiyyah
315 ?	
337 *	
347	
349 *	Kh. Um ^{c}Alanda
362	

Early Bronze I

21 *	Um el-Qleib
35	Kh. el-Bālū^{c}
40	
71	ed-Deir
73 *	Rujm Birjis
88	Um el-Habāj
101	Kh. el-Minsaḥlāt
132 *	
187	Kh. Sārah
219	Ḥujfah
239	Lejjūn (Bronze)
264	^{c}Ainūn
289 *	Kh. Um el-Qṣeir
303 *	Beit Sahm
315	
337 *	
349	Kh. Um ^{c}Alanda
353	Kh. en-Nsheinish
361 *	
390	Kh. el-Mudawwarah
402 *	Kh. Medīnet er-Rās
420	Nakhl

Early Bronze II-III

3 *	^{c}Awarwareh
15 *	Imra^{c}
21 *	Um el-Qleib
25 *	Mis^{c}ar
31	
35	Kh. el-Bālū^{c}
40 *	
43	^{c}Azzūr
57	Beit Lajjah
59 *	
60	Kh. el-Kharziyyah
63	el-Yārūt
73 *	Rujm Birjis
78 *	el-Kharī^{c}
79	Rujm Ghneim
81	Dalāleḥ
88 *	Um el-Habāj
89 *	Ḥmeimāt (NW)
90 *	Ḥmeimāt (SW)
101 *	Kh. el-Minsaḥlāt
106 *	Miṣna^{c}
114 *	Mḥarraqāt (N)
115 *	Mḥarraqāt
174 *	Kh. Sakka
178	
201	el-Franj
204	Kerak
207	Kh. en-Neqqāz
210 *	Kh. el-Qaryatein
211	eth-Thaniyyah
219 *	Ḥujfah
227 *	Adir
230	Kh. ^{c}Arbīd
239 *	Lejjūn (Bronze)
247	
262 *	^{c}Ai
264 *	^{c}Ainūn
268	
270 *	Kh. el-Ḥawiyyah
274	Kh. el-Jeljūl
278	Kfeirāz
288	
294 *	Fqeiqes
313	Ghuweir (N)
316	el-Mreigha
333 *	Middīn
336	
337 *	
347	
349 *	Kh. Um ^{c}Alanda
390 *	Kh. el-Mudawwarah
411 ?	Sūl
420	Nakhl
427	Dhāt Rās
429 *	

Early Bronze IV

15 *	Imra^{c}
21 *	Um el-Qleib
25 *	Mis^{c}ar
35	Kh. el-Bālū^{c}
40 *	
59 *	
60 *	Kh. el-Kharziyyah
73 *	Rujm Birjis
78 *	el-Kharī^{c}
88 *	Um el-Habāj
89 *	Ḥmeimāt (NW)
90	Ḥmeimāt (SW)
101 *	Kh. el-Minsaḥlāt
106 *	Miṣna^{c}
114 *	Mḥarraqāt (N)
115 *	Mḥarraqāt
129	Kh. Mdeinet el-Mu^{c}rrajeh
132	
210 ?	Kh. el-Qaryatein
211	eth-Thaniyyah
227 *	Adir

239 * Lejjūn (Bronze)
264 * ᶜAinūn
294 * Fqeiqes
333 Middīn
337
424 ? Jweir
427 Dhāt Rās

Sites with undifferentiated Early Bronze Sherds

61 Um Sidreh
62
75
108 er-Rabbah
197 Mgheir
231 ?
233 Kinnār
244
298 Rujm Um el-ᶜAṭāṭ
300 el-Bqeiᶜ
304 Mauta
308
312 Kh. eṭ-Ṭūr
319
404 Kh. Um Rummānah
423 Majra
426 el-Hāshimiyyah
435 Mḍeibiᶜ

Middle Bronze

3 * ᶜAwarwareh
5 ? Freiwān
12 ? Kh. Shīḥān
25 ? Misᶜar
31
35 Kh. el-Bālūᶜ
40
56 Tadūn
63 el-Yārūt
66 ? Batīr
86 ? el-Qaṣr
88 ? Um el-Habāj
89 Ḥmeimāt (NW)
97 Kh. Mḥeisin
101 Kh. el-Minsaḥlāt
106 * Miṣnaᶜ
108 ? er-Rabbah
143 Kh. Mdeinet ᶜAliyā
155
175 Samrāᵓ
177
198 Ibn Ayyūb
204 Kerak
210 * Kh. el-Qaryatein
211 eth-Thaniyyah
216 Abū er-Ruzz
230 ? Kh. ᶜArbīd
255 * Kh. eḍ-Ḍweibiᶜ
266 Kh. eṭ-Ṭalīsah
270 * Kh. el-Ḥawiyyah
283
289 Kh. Um el-Qṣeir
294 * Fqeiqes
303 ? Beit Sahm
304 Mauta
313 Ghuweir (N)
316 el-Mreigha
333 Middīn
337 *
347
349 * Kh. Um ᶜAlanda
351
355 Kh. el-Baṭrāᵓ
359 Nāṣir
360 *
362
366 * el-Māhrī
390 Kh. el-Mudawwarah
393
399 * Kh. Ḍubāb
411 * Sūl
419 * Um Ḥamāṭ
424 Jweir
429 *
433 *

Late Bronze

3 * ᶜAwarwareh
5 ? Freiwān
15 Imraᶜ
21 Um el-Qleib
25 * Misᶜar
32
35 * Kh. el-Bālūᶜ
40
42
53 ? Ḥimmeh
55 Qaṣr el-Kheimeh
56 Tadūn
60 * Kh. el-Kharziyyah
64 ed-Dimnah
71 * ed-Deir
73 Rujm Birjis
76 Bteiyir
86 el-Qaṣr
88 Um el-Habāj
102 Kh. el-Ḥinū
106 * Miṣnaᶜ
114 Mḥarraqāt (N)
155 *
160 el-Minqaṭᶜah
162 Rākīn
166 Qreifilla
167 Ḥabāsh/Ḥabāj
174 Kh. Sakka
175 Samrāᵓ
176 Zeita
177 *
190 eẓ-Ẓheiriyyeh
193 el-ᶜUmyān
196 Mseimṭah (N)
201 el-Franj
204 * Kerak
206 * Kh. ᶜIzra
207 * Kh. en-Neqqāz
210 * Kh. el-Qaryatein
211 eth-Thaniyyah
215 Qmeir
216 Abū er-Ruzz
217 Kh. Qamarein
219 Ḥujfah
227 Adir
230 ? Kh. ᶜArbīd
235 el-Ḥaddādah
255 * Kh. eḍ-Ḍweibiᶜ
257 ᶜAlaqān
262 * ᶜAi
264 ᶜAinūn
266 Kh. eṭ-Ṭalīsah
270 * Kh. el-Ḥawiyyah
273 Miḥna
275
277 *
278 Kfeirāz
285 Mirwid
289 * Kh. Um el-Qṣeir
290 Kh. Zabdah
294 Fqeiqes
296
297 Rujm Mesᶜīd

298 Rujm Um el-^{c}Aṭāṭ
299 Rujm el-Baqr
301 Kh. Fqeiqes
303 ? Beit Sahm
304 Mauta
306
309
312 Kh. eṭ-Ṭūr
313 Ghuweir (N)
333 * Middīn
337 *
338
347
349 Kh. Um ^{c}Alanda
353 Kh. en-Nsheinish
359 Nāṣir
360 *
362 *
365
366 el-Māhrī
383 ed-Dabbākah
384 * el-Jauza
388 Rujm el-Ḥleileh
395 * Khāneq en-Naṣāra
398
399 * Kh. Ḍubāb
402 Kh. Medīnet er-Rās
411 * Sūl
412 Rujm Um ^{c}Alanda
413 *
414 Rujm Eshqāḥ
415 * Rujm el-Awsaj
416 Dleiqa
419 * Um Ḥamāṭ
420 Nakhl
421 Rujm al-Mismar
424 Jweir
425
427 Dhāt Rās
428 Kh. el-^{c}Akūzeh
429 ?
431 * Kfeir/Kh. el-^{c}Abdeh
433
435 Mḍeibi^{c}
436 Mḥai
441 Qfeiqef

Iron I

15 Imra^{c}
16 * Majdalein
35 * Kh. el-Bālū^{c}
38 Kh. es-Sa^{c}adūnī
39 * Naṣīb
40
53 Ḥimmeh
54 Shaḥtūr
56 * Tadūn
71 * ed-Deir
72 el-Qabū
73 Rujm Birjis
77 * Rujm Abū Za^{c}rūrah
86 el-Qaṣr
87 el-Misdāḥ
89 Ḥmeimāt (NW)
90 Ḥmeimāt (SW)
92 Ḥmeimāt (SE)
94 es-Smākiyyah
106 * Miṣna^{c}
108 * er-Rabbah
114 Mḥarraqāt (N)
115 * Mḥarraqāt
120
129 * Kh. Mdeinet el-Mu^{c}rrajeh
143 * Kh. Mdeinet ^{c}Aliyā
155 *
161 * Um Niqil
162 Rākīn
168
174 * Kh. Sakka
187 Kh. Sārah
193 el-^{c}Umyān
197 Mgheir
198 Ibn Ayyūb
204 * Kerak
206 Kh. ^{c}Izra
207 * Kh. en-Neqqāz
208
210 * Kh. el-Qaryatein
211 * eth-Thaniyyah
214 ez-Zarrā^{c}ah
216 Abū er-Ruzz
219 Ḥujfah
227 Adir
238 esh-Sharīf
255 ? Kh. eḍ-Ḍweibi^{c}
257 ^{c}Alaqān
258
259 Kh. el-Meidān (NW)
260 Meidān (SE)
262 * ^{c}Ai
264 ^{c}Ainūn
266 Kh. eṭ-Ṭalīsah
267 Kh. el-Labūn
270 * Kh. el-Ḥawiyyah
273 Miḥna
290 Kh. Zabdah
293 *
299 Rujm el-Baqr
304 Mauta
333 * Middīn
349 Kh. Um ^{c}Alanda
359 Nāṣir
399 * Kh. Ḍubāb
411 * Sūl
415 Rujm el-Awsaj
419 * Um Ḥamāṭ
423 Majra
427 Dhāt Rās
433
436 Mḥai

Iron II

14 Faqū^{c}
15 * Imra^{c}
16 * Majdalein
25 Mis^{c}ar
34 Jad^{c}at el-Jbūr
35 * Kh. el-Bālū^{c}
40
56 Tadūn
57 Beit Lajjah
63 el-Yārūt
71 * ed-Deir
73 Rujm Birjis
76 Bteiyir
77 * Rujm Abū Za^{c}rūrah
86 el-Qaṣr
88 Um el-Habāj
90 Ḥmeimāt (SW)
94 es-Smākiyyah
106 * Miṣna^{c}
108 * er-Rabbah
110
114 Mḥarraqāt (N)
144
161 * Um Niqil
162 Rākīn
174 Kh. Sakka
177 *
182 * Kh. Btheinah
184 Kh. ^{c}Aizār
187 Kh. Sārah
190 eẓ-Ẓheiriyyeh

193	el-ᶜUmyān
196	Mseimṭah (N)
197	Mgheir
198	Ibn Ayyūb
199	Kh. es-Samrāᵓ
200	Kaminna
204 *	Kerak
206	Kh. ᶜIzra
207 *	Kh. en-Neqqāz
210	Kh. el-Qaryatein
211 *	eth-Thaniyyah
227	Adir
228	Rujm el-Jazūr
230	Kh. ᶜArbīd
233	Kinnār
235 *	el-Ḥaddādah
238	esh-Sharīf
248 *	Kh. Thamāyil
255	Kh. eḍ-Ḍweibiᶜ
256	Jauza
257 *	ᶜAlaqān
261	Kathrabba
262 *	ᶜAi
263	Kh. el-Meiseh
264 *	ᶜAinūn
265	
266	Kh. eṭ-Ṭalīsah
268	
269	Kh. el-Mṣāṭeb
270 *	Kh. el-Ḥawiyyah
272	Kh. el-Jūbah
273	Miḥna
274	Kh. el-Jeljūl
283	
290	Kh. Zabdah
293	
299	Rujm el-Baqr
300	el-Bqeiᶜ
304 *	Mauta
307	Kh. el-ᶜEdūl
316 *	el-Mreigha
330	
333 *	Middīn
344	
349	Kh. Um ᶜAlanda
355 *	Kh. el-Baṭrāᵓ
359	Nāṣir
363	
364 *	
370	Rujm Khashm eṣ-Ṣīrah
372	
383	ed-Dabbākah
384	el-Jauza
392	
399 *	Kh. Ḍubāb
401	Khanzīrah
402	Kh. Medīnet er-Rās
411 *	Sūl
416	Dleiqa
419 *	Um Ḥamāṭ
420	Nakhl
426	el-Hāshimiyyah (el-Hāshimiyyah)
427	Dhāt Rās
428 *	Kh. el-ᶜAkūzeh
435	Mḍeibiᶜ
436	Mḥai
441	Qfeiqef

Iron IIC/Persian

15	Imraᶜ
35	Kh. el-Bālūᶜ
63	el-Yārūt
64 ?	ed-Dimnah
90	Ḥmeimāt (SW)
108	er-Rabbah
193	el-ᶜUmyān
197	Mgheir
198	Ibn Ayyūb
204	Kerak
207	Kh. en-Neqqāz
211 *	eth-Thaniyyah
233	Kinnār
238	esh-Sharīf
262	ᶜAi
264	ᶜAinūn
307	Kh. el-ᶜEdūl
363	
399	Kh. Ḍubāb
419	Um Ḥamāṭ

Sites with undifferentiated Iron Age Pottery

12	Kh. Shīḥān
28	
42	
60	Kh. el-Kharziyyah
66	Batīr
68	
82	
95	
98	Rujm Qneiṭrah
102	Kh. el-Ḥinū
105	el-Jilimeh
109	Kh. Um Kharīᶜah
121	
136	
146	
165	Kh. el-Minḥār
167	Ḥabāsh/Ḥabāj
170	Kh. el-Mrabbaᶜah
205	ᶜIzra
212	Kh. ed-Dāwūdiyyah
215	Qmeir
225	
237	Rujm esh-Sharīf
242	el-Bṭeimah
278	Kfeirāz
287	Rujm el-Ḥleileh
297	Rujm Mesᶜīd
298	Rujm Um el-ᶜAṭāṭ
306	
313	Ghuweir
314	
324	
343	
358 *	
360 *	
362 *	
365	
373	
377	Kh. Abū Rukbah
378	Qaṣr Abū Rukbah
390 *	Kh. el-Mudawwarah
403	Rujm er-Rās
410	el-ᶜAmaqa
431	Kfeir/Kh. el-ᶜAbdeh

Hellenistic

15 *	Imraᶜ
16 *	Majdalein
35 *	Kh. el-Bālūᶜ
37	er-Ribᶜī (es-Samrāᵓ)
40	
52	Ṣirfa
53	Ḥimmeh
71	ed-Deir
73	Rujm Birjis
86	el-Qaṣr
88	Um el-Habāj

89 Ḥmeimāt (NW)
91 Ḥmeimāt (NE)
92 Ḥmeimāt (SE)
94 ? es-Smākiyyah
108 * er-Rabbah
155
160 el-Minqaṭʿah
177
182 Kh. Btheinah
185 Um Kharūf
190 eẓ-Ẓheiriyyeh
196 Mseimṭah (N)
199 Kh. es-Samrāʾ
204 Kerak
206 Kh. ʿIzra
207 Kh. en-Neqqāz
211 eth-Thaniyyah
214 ez-Zarrāʿah
217 Kh. Qamarein
224 Rujm el-ʿAbsī
259 Kh. el-Meidān (NW)
264 ʿAinūn
270 * Kh. el-Ḥawiyyah
273 Miḥna
274 Kh. el-Jeljūl
278 Kfeirāz
289 Kh. Um el-Qṣeir
295 Kh. Mishrāqah
299 Rujm el-Baqr
304 Mauta
306
316 el-Mreigha
333 Middīn
349 Kh. Um ʿAlanda
351
353 Kh. en-Nsheinish
355 * Kh. el-Baṭrāʾ
359 Nāṣir
366 * el-Māhrī
368
383 ed-Dabbākah
395 * Khāneq en-Naṣāra
399 * Kh. Ḍubāb
401 Khanzīrah
405 * el-Mjeidel
411 Sūl
417 el-Ḥseiniyyah
418 Um Zabāyir
419 * Um Ḥamāṭ
420 Nakhl
423 Majra
424 Jweir
426 el-Hāshimiyyah (el-Hāshimiyyah)
427 * Dhāt Rās
431 Kfeir/Kh. el-ʿAbdeh
435 Mḍeibiʿ
436 * Mḥai

Nabataean

2
3 * ʿAwarwareh
4 * Um eṭ-Ṭawābīn
5 Freiwān
8
12 * Kh. Shīḥān
14 * Faqūʿ
15 * Imraʿ
16 * Majdalein
17 ?
18 * Mḥaṭṭat el-Ḥājj
21 * Um el-Qleib
22 * Arīḥa
23 * Abū Trābah
24
25 Misʿar
26
27 * el-Harbaj
29
30 * Kh. el-Jadʿa
31
33
34 Jadʿat el-Jbūr
35 * Kh. el-Bālūʿ
36 * ed-Denn wa-l-Baradān
37 * er-Ribʿī (es-Samrāʾ)
38 Kh. es-Saʿadūnī
39 * Naṣīb
41
42 *
43 * ʿAzzūr
47 * Kh. es-Sanīnah
52 * Ṣirfa
53 * Ḥimmeh
56 * Tadūn
57 * Beit Lajjah
59
61 Um Sidreh
62
63 * el-Yārūt
64 * ed-Dimnah
66 * Batīr
68 *
70 * Kh. Zabūbah
71 * ed-Deir
73 * Rujm Birjis
74 * Kh. Zughriyyeh
76 * Bteiyir
77 * Rujm Abū Zaʿrūrah
78 * el-Kharīʿ
79 Rujm Ghneim
81 Dalāleḥ
86 * el-Qaṣr
87 * el-Misdāḥ
88 * Um el-Habāj
89 * Ḥmeimāt (NW)
90 * Ḥmeimāt (SW)
91 * Ḥmeimāt (NE)
92 * Ḥmeimāt (SE)
93
94 * es-Smākiyyah
95 *
96 * Kh. ʿAleiyān
97 Kh. Mḥeisin
98 Rujm Qneiṭrah
100 * Ḥmūd
101 * Kh. el-Minsaḥlāt
102 Kh. el-Ḥinū
104 Qaṣr Ḥamdān
105 * el-Jilimeh
106 * Miṣnaʿ
108 * er-Rabbah
109 * Kh. Um Kharīʿah
110 ?
111
114 * Mḥarraqāt (N)
115 * Mḥarraqāt
116
118
119 * Jdeiyidah
133
146
155
156
158 Kh. Um Rummānah
159 *
160 * el-Minqaṭʿah
161 Um Niqil
162 ? Rākīn
163
164
165 * Kh. el-Minḥār
168 ?
170 * Kh. el-Mrabbaʿah
174 Kh. Sakka
175 * Samrāʾ
176 * Zeita
177 *

178
179 Kh. el-Qashab
180 el-ᶜĀrūḍ
181
182 Kh. Btheinah
184 * Kh. ᶜAizār
187 ? Kh. Sārah
188 *
189 *
190 * eẓ-Ẓheiriyyeh
192 Qaṣr er-Rṣeifah
193 * el-ᶜUmyān
194 * Kh. el-ᶜOkbar
195 * Mseimṭah (S)
196 * Mseimṭah (N)
197 Mgheir
198 Ibn Ayyūb
199 * Kh. Samrāᵓ
200 Kaminna
201 el-Franj
202 eth-Thallājah
204 * Kerak
205 * ᶜIzra
206 * Kh. ᶜIzra
207 * Kh. en-Neqqāz
208
210 * Kh. el-Qaryatein
211 * eth-Thaniyyah
212 * Kh. ed-Dāwūdiyyah
213 Kh. ed-Dāwūdiyyah
214 ez-Zarrāᶜah
216 * Abū er-Ruzz
217 * Kh. Qamarein
219 Ḥujfah
225
227 * Adir
228 Rujm el-Jazūr
229 *
230 Kh. ᶜArbīd
231
233 * Kinnār
234
235 * el-Ḥaddādah
236 *
238 * esh-Sharīf
247
248 Kh. Thamāyil
251 * Rujm el-Merīḥ
252
255 * Kh. eḍ-Ḍweibi
256 Jauza
257 ᶜAlaqān
258
259 * Kh. el-Meidān (NW)
260 * Meidān (SE)
261 Kathrabba
262 * ᶜAi
263 * Kh. el-Meiseh
264 * ᶜAinūn
265
266 * Kh. eṭ-Ṭalīsah
267 * Kh. el-Labūn
268 *
269 * Kh. el-Mṣāṭeb
270 * Kh. el-Ḥawiyyah
271 * el-Msheirfah
272 * Kh. el-Jūbah
273 * Miḥna
274 * Kh. el-Jeljūl
275 *
276
277 *
278 * Kfeirāz
279 *
280
281 Kh. el-Ḥwāleh
282
283 *
284 *
285 * Mirwid
286 Um Naṣr
287 Rujm el-Ḥleileh
288
290 * Kh. Zabdah
291 * Kh. Ghifrah
292 el-ᶜIrāq
293
295 * Kh. Mishrāqah
297 * Rujm Mesᶜīd
298 * Rujm Um el-ᶜAṭāṭ
299 * Rujm el-Baqr
300 * el-Bqeiᶜ
301 * Kh. Fqeiqes
302 * Kh. el-Beiḍā
303 * Beit Sahm
304 * Mauta
305 el-Mashhad
306 *
307 * Kh. el-ᶜEdūl
308
309 *
310
312 * Kh. eṭ-Ṭūr
314
315
316 * el-Mreigha
319
324
328
330
333 * Middīn
337 *
338 *
339
341
343
344
345 * Um Zebel
347 *
348 *
349 * Kh. Um ᶜAlanda
350 * Rujm Rafīyeh
351 *
353 * Kh. en-Nsheinish
354
355 * Kh. el-Baṭrāᵓ
356 *
359 Nāṣir
360
362 *
364 *
369
372
373
374 ?
375
376 ?
377 * Kh. Abū Rukbah
378 Qaṣr Abū Rukbah
379 Qaṣr et-Tamrah
380
381 * Bīr Bashbash
383 * ed-Dabbākah
384 * el-Jauza
385 Kh. el-Bāsiliyyah
386
388 * Rujm el-Ḥleileh
389 *
391 Juḥra
392 *
393 *
394 Sdeir
395 Khāneq en-Naṣāra
396 Kh. eṭ-Ṭayyibeh
397 Kh. es-Sdeir
398
399 * Kh. Ḍubāb
400 Merzab Mezraᶜah
401 Khanzīrah
402 Kh. Medīnet er-Rās
403 Rujm er-Rās
404 * Kh. Um Rummānah

405 * el-Mjeidel
406 *
407
408
410 * el-ᶜAmaqa
411 * Sūl
412 Rujm Um ᶜAlanda
414 Rujm Eshqāḥ
415 * Rujm el-Awsaj
416 * Dleiqa
417 * el-Ḥseiniyyah
418 * Um Zabāyir
419 * Um Ḥamāṭ
420 * Nakhl
421 Rujm al-Mismar
423 * Majra
424 * Jweir
425 *
426 * Kh. ed-Dweikhleh (el-Hāshimiyyah)
427 * Dhāt Rās
429
430 * Rujm ᶜAbdeh
431 * Kfeir/Kh. el-ᶜAbdeh
433 *
434 * Shqeira
435 Mḍeibiᶜ
436 * Mḥai
441 * Qfeiqef
442 *
443 *

Early Roman

4 Um eṭ-Ṭawābīn
5 Freiwān
11 Abū Ḥalīb
12 Kh. Shīḥān
14 Faqūᶜ
15 * Imraᶜ
16 Majdalein
17 ?
18 * Mḥaṭṭat el-Ḥājj
21 * Um el-Qleib
27 el-Harbaj
33
35 * Kh. el-Bālūᶜ
39 Naṣīb
40
41
42 *
43 ᶜAzzūr
47 * Kh. es-Sanīnah
52 * Ṣirfa
55 Qaṣr el-Kheimeh
60 Kh. el-Kharziyyah
63 el-Yārūt
66 Batīr
68
71 * ed-Deir
72 el-Qabū
74 Kh. Zughriyyeh
75
76 * Bteiyir
77 Rujm Abū Zaᶜrūrah
78 el-Kharīᶜ
81 Dalāleḥ
86 * el-Qaṣr
87 el-Misdāḥ
88 * Um el-Habāj
89 Ḥmeimāt (NW)
90 * Ḥmeimāt (SW)
91 * Ḥmeimāt (NE)
92 Ḥmeimāt (SE)
93
94 es-Smākiyyah
99 Kh. el-Makhārīm
100 Ḥmūd
101 Kh. el-Minsaḥlāt
108 * er-Rabbah
110 ?
111
115 Mḥarraqāt
117
119 Jdeiyidah
122
131
135 *
143 Kh. Mdeinet ᶜAliyā
159
162 Rākīn
168
176 Zeita
177
179 Kh. el-Qashab
184 Kh. ᶜAizār
185 Um Kharūf
187 ? Kh. Sārah
188
190 eẓ-Ẓheiriyyeh
192 Qaṣr er-Rṣeifah
194 Kh. el-ᶜOkbar
196 Mseimṭah (N)
200 Kaminna
204 * Kerak
206 * Kh. ᶜIzra
207 * Kh. en-Neqqāz
210 Kh. el-Qaryatein
211 * eth-Thaniyyah
216 * Abū er-Ruzz
217 Kh. Qamarein
219 Ḥujfah
225
227 Adir
229
233 Kinnār
238 * esh-Sharīf
255 Kh. eḍ-Ḍweibiᶜ
262 * ᶜAi
264 ᶜAinūn
265
266 Kh. eṭ-Ṭalīsah
268
270 * Kh. el-Ḥawiyyah
274 Kh. el-Jeljūl
275
277
285 Mirwid
295 Kh. Mishrāqah
298 Rujm Um el-ᶜAṭāṭ
299 Rujm el-Baqr
300 * el-Bqeiᶜ
301 Kh. Fqeiqes
304 Mauta
306 *
307 Kh. el-ᶜEdūl
309
312 Kh. eṭ-Ṭūr
314
316 * el-Mreigha
328
333 Middīn
340
347
349 * Kh. Um ᶜAlanda
350 Rujm Rafīyeh
351
353 * Kh. en-Nsheinish
355 * Kh. el-Baṭrāᵓ
362
364 *
372
374
376 ?
377 * Kh. Abū Rukbah
389
392
395 Khāneq en-Naṣāra
399 * Kh. Ḍubāb

401		Khanzīrah
404		Kh. Um Rummānah
405		el-Mjeidel
413		
416		Dleiqa
417		el-Ḥseiniyyah
418		Um Zabāyir
419	*	Um Ḥamāṭ
420	*	Nakhl
424		Jweir
426	*	Kh. ed-Dweikhleh (el-Hāshimiyyah)
427	*	Dhāt Rās
431	*	Kfeir/Kh. el-ʿAbdeh
433	*	
435	*	Mḍeibiʿ
436	*	Mḥai
441		Qfeiqef

Late Roman

4		Um eṭ-Ṭawābīn
12		Kh. Shīḥān
15	*	Imraʿ
16		Majdalein
18	*	Mḥaṭṭat el-Ḥājj
21		Um el-Qleib
22	*	Arīḥa
25	*	Misʿar
26		
30		Kh. el-Jadʿa
33		
36	*	ed-Denn wa-l-Baradān
37		er-Ribʿī (es-Samrāʾ)
38		Kh. es-Saʿadūnī
42		
43		ʿAzzūr
47		Kh. es-Sanīnah
53		Ḥimmeh
56		Tadūn
61		Um Sidreh
64		ed-Dimnah
68		
71	*	ed-Deir
72		el-Qabū
74		Kh. Zughriyyeh
78		el-Kharīʿ
86		el-Qaṣr
87		el-Misdāḥ
88	*	Um el-Habāj
89	*	Ḥmeimāt (NW)
90	*	Ḥmeimāt (SW)
91		Ḥmeimāt (NE)
92	*	Ḥmeimāt (SE)
93		
94		es-Smākiyyah
96		Kh. ʿAleiyān
104	*	Qaṣr Ḥamdān
108	*	er-Rabbah
109		Kh. Um Kharīʿah
116		
117		
146		
160		el-Minqaṭʿah
162		Rākīn
163		
165		Kh. el-Minḥār
170	*	Kh. el-Mrabbaʿah
176		Zeita
194	*	Kh. el-ʿOkbar
195		Mseimṭah (S)
196		Mseimṭah (N)
198		Ibn Ayyūb
199		Kh. es-Samrāʾ
200		Kaminna
206		Kh. ʿIzra
207		Kh. en-Neqqāz
210		Kh. el-Qaryatein
211		eth-Thaniyyah
212		Kh. ed-Dāwūdiyyah
214		ez-Zarrāʿah
216		Abū er-Ruzz
217		Kh. Qamarein
224	*	Rujm el-ʿAbsī
227		Adir
233		Kinnār
234		
235		el-Ḥaddādah
238		esh-Sharīf
248		Kh. Thamāyil
251		Rujm el-Merīḥ
259		Kh. el-Meidān (NW)
261		Kathrabba
262	*	ʿAi
266		Kh. eṭ-Ṭalīsah
270	*	Kh. el-Ḥawiyyah
273	?	Miḥna
274		Kh. el-Jeljūl
278		Kfeirāz
298		Rujm Um el-ʿAṭāṭ
300	*	el-Bqeiʿ
303		Beit Sahm
304	*	Mauta
306		
312		Kh. eṭ-Ṭūr
314		
316	*	el-Mreigha
333	*	Middīn
338		
349		Kh. Um ʿAlanda
350	*	Rujm Rafīyeh
351		
355	*	Kh. el-Baṭrāʾ
360		
362	*	
364		
370		Rujm Khashm eṣ-Ṣīrah
371		
376	?	
377	*	Kh. Abū Rukbah
378		Qaṣr Abū Rukbah
390		Kh. el-Mudawwarah
399		Kh. Ḍubāb
405		el-Mjeidel
416		Dleiqa
419	*	Um Ḥamāṭ
420	*	Nakhl
424		Jweir
426	*	Kh. ed-Dweikhleh (el-Hāshimiyyah)
427		Dhāt Rās
431		Kfeir/Kh. el-ʿAbdeh
433	*	
434		Shqeira
435		Mḍeibiʿ
436	*	Mḥai
441		Qfeiqef

Early Byzantine

14		Faqūʿ
15	*	Imraʿ
18	*	Mḥaṭṭat el-Ḥājj
21		Um el-Qleib
22	*	Arīḥa
23	*	Abū Trābah
27		el-Harbaj
34		Jadʿat el-Jbūr
35		Kh. el-Bālūʿ
36	*	ed-Denn wa-l-Baradān
38		Kh. es-Saʿadūnī
40	*	
43	*	ʿAzzūr
52	*	Ṣirfa
53		Ḥimmeh
56		Tadūn
57		Beit Lajjah

61 Um Sidreh
63 el-Yārūt
64 ed-Dimnah
67 Kh. el-Ḥdeib
71 * ed-Deir
72 el-Qabū
76 Bteiyir
86 * el-Qaṣr
87 * el-Misdāḥ
88 * Um el-Habāj
89 * Ḥmeimāt (NW)
90 * Ḥmeimāt (SW)
92 * Ḥmeimāt (SE)
94 * es-Smākiyyah
97 Kh. Mḥeisin
100 Ḥmūd
106 Miṣnaᶜ
108 * er-Rabbah
109 Kh. Um Kharīᶜah
162 Rākīn
165 Kh. el-Minḥār
166 Qreifilla
170 Kh. el-Mrabbaᶜah
175 Samrāᵓ
181
182 Kh. Btheinah
184 Kh. ᶜAizār
190 ? eẓ-Ẓheiriyyeh
194 Kh. el-ᶜOkbar
196 Mseimṭah (N)
199 Kh. es-Samrāᵓ
200 Kaminna
204 * Kerak
206 Kh. ᶜIzra
207 * Kh. en-Neqqāz
210 * Kh. el-Qaryatein
211 eth-Thaniyyah
212 Kh. ed-Dāwūdiyyah
216 * Abū er-Ruzz
227 * Adir
238 esh-Sharīf
251 Rujm el-Merīḥ
255 Kh. eḍ-Ḍweibiᶜ
261 * Kathrabba
262 * ᶜAi
264 * ᶜAinūn
267 Kh. el-Labūn
270 Kh. el-Ḥawiyyah
274 * Kh. el-Jeljūl
283
289 Kh. Um el-Qṣeir
295 Kh. Mishrāqah
296
298 * Rujm Um el-ᶜAṭāṭ
299 Rujm el-Baqr
304 * Mauta
307 Kh. el-ᶜEdūl
312 Kh. eṭ-Ṭūr
315
316 * el-Mreigha
333 * Middīn
341
355 Kh. el-Baṭrāᵓ
361
362 *
364 *
366 el-Māhrī
376 ?
377 * Kh. Abū Rukbah
383 ed-Dabbākah
394 Sdeir
398
401 Khanzīrah
404 Kh. Um Rummānah
405 * el-Mjeidel
410 el-ᶜAmaqa
411 Sūl
416 Dleiqa
417 el-Ḥseiniyyah
418 Um Zabāyir
419 Um Ḥamāṭ
420 * Nakhl
424 Jweir
427 * Dhāt Rās
431 Kfeir/Kh. el-ᶜAbdeh
432 Kh. el-Quṣūbah
433 *
435 * Mḍeibiᶜ
436 * Mḥai
442

Late Byzantine

---

12 * Kh. Shīḥān
13 * Rujm Um Ḥlāl
14 * Faqūᶜ
15 * Imraᶜ
18 * Mḥaṭṭat el-Ḥājj
21 Um el-Qleib
22 Arīḥa
23 * Abū Trābah
26
27 el-Harbaj
30 Kh. el-Jadᶜa
32
33
34 Jadᶜat el-Jbūr
36 ed-Denn wa-l-Baradān
37 er-Ribᶜī (es-Samrāᵓ)
38 Kh. es-Saᶜadūnī
40 *
41
43 * ᶜAzzūr
52 * Ṣirfa
56 * Tadūn
57 * Beit Lajjah
63 el-Yārūt
66 * Batīr
70 Kh. Zabūbah
71 * ed-Deir
72 el-Qabū
74 * Kh. Zughriyyeh
76 Bteiyir
86 el-Qaṣr
87 * el-Misdāḥ
88 Um el-Habāj
89 * Ḥmeimāt (NW)
90 * Ḥmeimāt (SW)
91 Ḥmeimāt (NE)
92 Ḥmeimāt (SE)
94 es-Smākiyyah
95
97 Kh. Mḥeisin
100 * Ḥmūd
101 Kh. el-Minsaḥlāt
104 * Qaṣr Ḥamdān
105 el-Jilimeh
106 Miṣnaᶜ
108 * er-Rabbah
109 . Kh. Um Kharīᶜah

111
114 Mḥarraqāt (N)
116
118
119 Jdeiyidah
160 el-Minqaṭᶜah
163
165 Kh. el-Minḥār
166 * Qreifilla
170 * Kh. el-Mrabbaᶜah
175 * Samrāᵓ
184 * Kh. ᶜAizār
185 * Um Kharūf
187 Kh. Sārah
190 eẓ-Ẓheiriyyeh
191 * Kh. er-Rṣeifah
192 Qaṣr er-Rṣeifah
193 el-ᶜUmyān
194 * Kh. el-ᶜOkbar
197 Mgheir

198 * Ibn Ayyūb
199 Kh. es-Samrāʾ
200 * Kaminna
206 Kh. ʿIzra
210 * Kh. el-Qaryatein
211 eth-Thaniyyah
214 ez-Zarrāʿah
216 * Abū er-Ruzz
217 Kh. Qamarein
219 Ḥujfah
225
227 * Adir
233 * Kinnār
238 esh-Sharīf
247
259 Kh. el-Meidān (NW)
261 * Kathrabba
262 * ʿAi
264 * ʿAinūn
267 Kh. el-Labūn
270 Kh. el-Ḥawiyyah
273 * Miḥna
274 * Kh. el-Jeljūl
286 Um Naṣr
291 Kh. Ghifrah
295 * Kh. Mishrāqah
298 * Rujm Um el-ʿAṭāṭ
299 Rujm el-Baqr
300 * el-Bqeiʿ
301 Kh. Fqeiqes

302 Kh. el-Beiḍā
304 * Mauta
306
307 Kh. el-ʿEdūl
316 * el-Mreigha
333 * Middīn
354
355 Kh. el-Baṭrāʾ
366 el-Māhrī
373
383 * ed-Dabbākah
390 Kh. el-Mudawwarah
392
397 * Kh. es-Sdeir
398
403 Rujm er-Rās
404 Kh. Um Rummānah
405 * el-Mjeidel
410 el-ʿAmaqa
411 Sūl
416 Dleiqa
417 el-Ḥseiniyyah
418 Um Zabāyir
419 * Um Ḥamāṭ
420 * Nakhl
424 Jweir
426 * Kh. ed-Dweikhleh (el-Hāshimiyyah)
427 * Dhāt Rās
430 Rujm ʿAbdeh
431 * Kfeir/Kh. el-ʿAbdeh
433 *
434 Shqeira
435 Mḍeibiʿ
436 * Mḥai
441 Qfeiqef

Sites with undifferentiated Byzantine Sherds

16 Majdalein
25 Misʿar
28
29
31
39 Naṣīb
42

47 Kh. es-Sanīnah
54 Shaḥṭūr
55 Qaṣr el-Kheimeh
65
68
75
77 Rujm Abū Zaʿrūrah
78 el-Kharīʿ
79 Rujm Ghneim
80
85 Shajarah
96 Kh. *Aleiyan
99 Kh. el-Makhārīm
110
115 ? Mḥarraqāt
123
158 Kh. Um Rummānah
164
167 Ḥabāsh/Ḥabāj
174 Kh. Sakka
179 Kh. el-Qashab
201 el-Franj
205 ʿIzra
208
213 Kh. ed-Dāwūdiyyah
234
239 Lejjūn (Bronze)
260 Meidān (SE)
268
275
276
278 Kfeirāz
281 Kh. el-Ḥwāleh
292 el-ʿIrāq
293
303 Beit Sahm
308
338
349 Kh. Um ʿAlanda
353 Kh. en-Nsheinish
365
388 Rujm el-Ḥleileh
391 Juḥra
400 Merzab Mezraʿah
423 Majra

Umayyad

15 Imraʿ

34 Jadʿat el-Jbūr
36 ed-Denn wa-l-Baradān
37 er-Ribʿī (es-Samrāʾ)
39 Naṣīb
56 Tadūn
71 ed-Deir
74 ? Kh. Zughriyyeh
91 Ḥmeimāt (NE)
92 Ḥmeimāt (SE)
97 Kh. Mḥeisin
108 * er-Rabbah
162 Rākīn
182 Kh. Btheinah
190 ? eẓ-Ẓheiriyyeh
198 Ibn Ayyūb
210 Kh. el-Qaryatein
211 eth-Thaniyyah
216 Abū er-Ruzz
262 * ʿAi
267 Kh. el-Labūn
273 Miḥna
292 el-ʿIrāq
295 Kh. Mishrāqah
298 Rujm Um el-ʿAṭāṭ

300 el-Bqeiᶜ
304 Mauta
307 Kh. el-ᶜEdūl
349 Kh. Um ᶜAlanda
353 Kh. en-Nsheinish
355 Kh. el-Baṭrāᵓ
360
405 el-Mjeidel
418 Um Zabāyir
427 Dhāt Rās
432 Kh. el-Quṣūbah
436 * Mḥai

Abbasid

12 Kh. Shīḥān
57 Beit Lajjah
108 er-Rabbah

207 Kh. en-Neqqāz
273 * Miḥna
312 Kh. eṭ-Ṭūr

Fatimid (Possibly)

12 Kh. Shīḥān
14 Faqūᶜ
18 Mḥaṭṭat el-Ḥājj
22 Arīḥa
38 Kh. es-Saᶜadūnī
56 Tadūn
92 Ḥmeimāt (SE)
108 er-Rabbah
166 Qreifilla
184 Kh. ᶜAizār
204 * Kerak
210 Kh. el-Qaryatein
211 * eth-Thaniyyah
238 esh-Sharīf
264 * ᶜAinūn
270 Kh. el-Ḥawiyyah
273 Miḥna
278 Kfeirāz
290 Kh. Zabdah
292 el-ᶜIrāq
312 Kh. eṭ-Ṭūr
316 * el-Mreigha
349 Kh. Um ᶜAlanda

353 * Kh. en-Nsheinish
384 el-Jauza
400 Merzab Mezraᶜah
411 Sūl
416 Dleiqa
420 Nakhl
423 * Majra
427 * Dhāt Rās
431 Kfeir/Kh. el-ᶜAbdeh
432 * Kh. el-Quṣūbah
436 * Mḥai

Ayyubid/Mamluk

3 ᶜAwarwareh

5 Freiwān
12 * Kh. Shīḥān
14 Faqūᶜ
15 Imraᶜ
16 * Majdalein
18 * Mḥaṭṭat el-Ḥājj
22 Arīḥa
25 Misᶜar
27 el-Harbaj
30 Kh. el-Jadᶜa
32
35* Kh. el-Bālūᶜ
36 * ed-Denn wa-l-Baradān
37 er-Ribᶜī
38 * Kh. es-Saᶜadūnī
39 Naṣīb
47 Kh. es-Sanīnah
52 Ṣirfa
53 Ḥimmeh
54 Shaḥṭūr
56 Tadūn
57 * Beit Lajjah
59
63 el-Yārūt
64 ed-Dimnah
66 * Batīr
67 Kh. el-Ḥdeib
70 * Kh. Zabūbah
71 * ed-Deir
76 Bteiyir
78 el-Kharīᶜ
81 Dalāleḥ
86 * el-Qaṣr
87 el-Misdāḥ
88 Um el-Habāj
89 Ḥmeimāt (NW)
91 * Ḥmeimāt (NE)
92 * Ḥmeimāt (SE)
94 * es-Smākiyyah
95
96 * Kh. ᶜAleiyān
97 * Kh. Mḥeisin
100 * Ḥmūd
101 Kh. el-Minsaḥlāt
102 Kh. el-Ḥinū
106 Miṣnaᶜ
108 * er-Rabbah
141
160 el-Minqaṭᶜah
161 Um Niqil
162 Rākīn
166 * Qreifilla
167 * Ḥabāsh/Ḥabāj
179 Kh. el-Qashab
182 * Kh. Btheinah
184 * Kh. ᶜAizār
187 Kh. Sārah
188
190 eẓ-Ẓheiriyyeh
191 Kh. er-Rṣeifah
194 * Kh. el-ᶜOkbar
197 * Mgheir
198 * Ibn Ayyūb
200 Kaminna
202 eth-Thallājah
204 * Kerak
205 * ᶜIzra
206 Kh. ᶜIzra
207 * Kh. en-Neqqāz
208 *
210 * Kh. el-Qaryatein
211 * eth-Thaniyyah
212 Kh. ed-Dāwūdiyyah
214 * ez-Zarrāᶜah
215 * Qmeir
221
227 Adir
230 Kh. ᶜArbīd
233 * Kinnār
235 * el-Ḥaddādah
236 *
237 Rujm esh-Sharīf
238 * esh-Sharīf
239 Lejjūn (Bronze)
260 Meidān (SE)
261 * Kathrabba
262 ᶜAi
264 * ᶜAinūn
265

267	*	Kh. el-Labūn
268		
269		Kh. el-Mṣāṭeb
270	*	Kh. el-Ḥawiyyah
273	*	Miḥna
274	*	Kh. el-Jeljūl
278	*	Kfeirāz
281		Kh. el-Ḥwāleh
285		Mirwid
289	*	Kh. Um el-Qṣeir
290	*	Kh. Zabdah
294	*	Fqeiqes
295	*	Kh. Mishrāqah
298	*	Rujm Um el-^{c}Aṭāṭ
299		Rujm el-Baqr
300		el-Bqei^c
303		Beit Sahm
304	*	Mauta
305	*	el-Mashhad
307	*	Kh. el-^{c}Edūl
308		
311	*	el-Mazār
312		Kh. eṭ-Ṭūr
313	*	Ghuweir (N)
315		
316	*	el-Mreigha
332	*	el-Weibdeh
333	*	Middīn
345		Um Zebel
349	*	Kh. Um ^{c}Alanda
353	*	Kh. en-Nsheinish
355		Kh. el-Baṭrāʾ
358		
359		Nāṣir
362		
366	*	el-Māhrī
369	*	
370		Rujm Khashm eṣ-Ṣīrah
372		
383		ed-Dabbākah
384		el-Jauza
385		Kh. el-Bāsiliyyah
400		Merzab Mezra^{c}ah
401	*	Khanzīrah
402		Kh. Medīnet er-Rās
404		Kh. Um Rummānah
405		el-Mjeidel
410	*	el-^{c}Amaqa
411	*	Sūl
416	*	Dleiqa
417		el-Ḥseiniyyah
418	*	Um Zabāyir
419	*	Um Ḥamāṭ
420	*	Nakhl
423	*	Majra
427	*	Dhāt Rās
430	*	Rujm ^{c}Abdeh
431		Kfeir/Kh. el-^{c}Abdeh
432	*	Kh. el-Quṣūbah
434	*	Shqeira
435	*	Mḍeibi^c
436	*	Mḥai

Ottoman

12		Kh. Shīḥān
16		Majdalein
19	*	
25	*	Mis^{c}ar
26		
36		ed-Denn wa-l-Baradān
52		Ṣirfa
97		Kh. Mḥeisin
108		er-Rabbah
197		Mgheir
202	?	eth-Thallājah
210		Kh. el-Qaryatein
211	*	eth-Thaniyyah
212		Kh. ed-Dāwūdiyyah
219		Ḥujfah
256		Jauza
273		Miḥna
304		Mauta
311		el-Mazār
369		
372		
376		
401	?	Khanzīrah
427	*	Dhāt Rās
429		
432		Kh. el-Quṣūbah
441		Qfeiqef

Sites with undifferentiated Late Islamic Sherds

7	*	
8		
10		
11		Abū Ḥalīb
13		Rujm Um Ḥlāl
23		Abū Trābah
29		
33		
34	*	Jad^{c}a el-Jbur
42		
43	*	^{c}Azzūr
61		Um Sidreh
68		
72		el-Qabū
74		Kh. Zughriyyeh
77	*	Rujm Abū Za^{c}rūrah
80		
85	*	Shajarah
90	*	Ḥmeimāt (SW)
98	*	Rujm Qneiṭrah
104		Qaṣr Ḥamdān
105		el-Jilimeh
109	*	Kh. Um Kharī^{c}ah
113		Rujm et-Teis
115		Mḥarraqāt
119	*	Jdeiyidah
120		
124	*	
133	*	
151		
155	*	
157		
158		Kh. Um Rummānah
172	*	Um ed-Dajāj
173		^{c}Ain Um Jam^{c}ān
174		Kh. Sakka
175	*	Samrāʾ
176		Zeita
178		
189		
192	*	Qaṣr er-Rṣeifah
193	*	el-^{c}Umyān
195		Mseimṭah (S)
196		Mseimṭah (N)
201		el-Franj
217	*	Kh. Qamarein
222	*	
224		Rujm el-^{c}Absī
252		
255		Kh. eḍ-Ḍweibi^c
257		^{c}Alaqān
259		Kh. el-Meidān
266		Kh. eṭ-Ṭalīsah
271		el-Msheirfah
276		
277		
281	*	Kh. el-Ḥwāleh
282		
283		
286		Um Naṣr

288	
291	Kh. Ghifrah
292 *	el-ᶜIrāq
297	Rujm Mesᶜīd
301	Kh. Fqeiqes
309	
330	
332 *	Kh. el-Weibdeh
350	Rujm Rafīyeh
360 *	
365	
373	
386	
388	Rujm el-Ḥleileh
389 *	
391	Juḥra
396 *	Kh. eṭ-Ṭayyibeh
399	Kh. Ḍubāb
407	
412	Rujm Um ᶜAlanda
415	Rujm el-Awsaj
421	Rujm al-Mismar
424	Jweir
425	
426 *	Kh. ed-Dweikhleh (el-Hāshimiyya)
428	Kh. el-ᶜAkūzeh
433*	

BIBLIOGRAPHY

Adams, W. Y.
1979 On the Argument from Ceramics to History: A Challenge Based on Evidence from Medieval Nubia. *Current Anthropology* 20: 727-44.

Aharoni, Y.
1956 Excavations at Ramath Raḥel, 1954: Preliminary Report. *IEJ* 6: 102-11.
1961 The Caves of Naḥal Ḥever. *'Atiqot* 3: 148-62.
1962 The Expedition to the Judean Desert, 1961: Expedition B —the Cave of Horror. *IEJ* 12: 186-99.

Aharoni, Y., et al.
1960 The Ancient Desert Agriculture of the Negev, V: An Israelite Agricultural Settlement at Ramat Maṭred. *IEJ* 10: 97-111.
1964 *Excavations at Ramat Raḥel II: Seasons 1961 and 1962*. Rome: Centro di Studi Semitici.

Aḥituv, S.
1972 Did Ramesses II Conquer Dibon? *IEJ* 22: 141-42.

Albright, W. F.
1924 The Archaeological Results of an Expedition to Moab and the Dead Sea. *BASOR* 14: 1-12.
1932a An Anthropoid Clay Coffin from Sahab in Transjordan. *AJA* 36: 259-306.
1932b *The Excavation of Tell Beit Mirsim I: The Pottery of the First Three Campaigns*. *AASOR* 12.
1933 The Excavation of Tell Beit Mirsim, I: The Bronze Age Pottery of the Fourth Campaign. *AASOR* 13: 55-127.
1934 Soundings at Ader, A Bronze Age City in Moab. *BASOR* 53: 13-18.
1943 *The Excavation of Tell Beit Mirsim III: The Iron Age*. *AASOR* 21-22.

Albright, W. F.; Kelso, J. L.; and Thorley, J. P.
1944 Early Bronze Age Pottery from Bāb edh-Dhrā[c] in Moab. *BASOR* 95: 3-18.

Alt, A.
1928 Zwölf christliche Grabsteine aus Moab. *ZDPV* 51: 218-33.

Amiran, R.
1963 *The Ancient Pottery of Eretz Yisrael. From its Beginnings in the Neolithic Period to the end of the First Temple*. Jerusalem: Israel Exploration Society.
1969 *Ancient Pottery of the Holy Land. From its Beginnings in the Neolithic Period to the End of the Iron Age*. Jerusalem: Masada Press.
1978 *Early Arad: The Chalcolithic Settlement and Early Bronze Age City*. Jerusalem: Israel Exploration Society.

[c]Amr, A-J.
1988 Shallow Umayyed Painted Pottery Bowls from Rujm el-Kursi. *ADAJ* 32: 247-54.

Armstrong, G.
1890 *Palestine From the Surveys Conducted for the Committee of the Palestine Exploration Fund and Other Sources*. Compiled by G. Armstrong, Revised by C. W. Wilson and C. R. Conder. London: Palestine Exploration Society.

Avigad, N.
1962 Expedition A —Naḥal David. *IEJ* 12: 169-83.

Avi-Yonah, M.
1954 *The Madaba Mosaic Map: With Introduction and Commentary*. Jerusalem: Israel Exploration Society.
1976 *Gazetteer of Roman Palestine*. *QMIA* 5. Jerusalem: Institute of Archaeology of the Hebrew University of Jerusalem.

Bacher, J.
1901 Von Jerusalem über Karak nach Petra und Safieh (im Chor). *Die Warte des Temples* 57: 109-11, 115-18, 123-4.

Badé, W. F.
1928 *Excavations at Tell en-Naöbeh 1926 and 1927: A Preliminary Report*. *Palestine Institute Publication* 1. Berkeley: Palestine Institute.

Bagatti, B.
1947 *I Monumenti di Emmaus el Qubeibeh e dei Dintorni*. *SBF* 4. Jerusalem: Franciscan Printing Press.

1969 *Excavations in Nazareth*, Vol. 1. *SBF* 17. Jerusalem: Franciscan Printing Press.

Bagatti, B., and Milik, J.

1958 *La Necropoli del Periodo Romano, Part I: Gli Scavi del "Dominus Flevit." SBF* 13. Jerusalem: Franciscan Printing Press.

Bailey, C.

1984 Bedouin Place-Names in Sinai: Towards Understanding a Desert Map. *PEQ* 116: 42-57.

Bakhit, M. A.

1982 Jordan in Perspective: The Mamluk-Ottoman Period. Pp. 361-62 in *Studies in the History and Archaeology of Jordan I*, ed. A. Hadidi. Amman: Department of Antiquities of Jordan.

Balfet, H.

1965 Ethnographic Observations in North Africa and Archaeological Interpretation. Pp. 161-77 in *Ceramics and Man*, ed. F. Matson. New York: Wenner Gren Foundation.

Ball, W., et al.

1986 The North Decumanus and North Tetrapyon at Jerash: an Archaeological and Architectural Report. Pp. 351-94 in *Jerash Archaeological Project 1981-1983, I*, ed. F. Zayadine. Amman: Department of Antiquities.

Baly, C. T. J.

1962 Pottery. Pp. 270-303 in Vol. 1 of *Excavations at Nessana*, ed. H. D. Colt. London: British School of Archaeology in Jerusalem.

Bar-Adon, P.

1961 The Expedition to the Judean Desert, 1960: Expedition C. *IEJ* 11: 25-35.

1977 Another Settlement of the Judean Desert Sect at ᶜEn el-Ghuweir on the Shores of the Dead Sea. *BASOR* 227: 1-25.

Baramki, D. C.

1940-42 The Pottery from Kh. el Mefjer. *QDAP* 10: 65-103.

Baratto, C., ed.

1978 *Guide to Jordan*. Jerusalem: Franciscan Printing Press.

Bartlett, J. R.

1973 The Moabites and Edomites. Pp. 229-58 in *Peoples of Old Testament Times*, ed. D. J. Wiseman. Oxford: Clarendon.

1983 The "United" Campaign against Moab in 2 Kings 3:4-27. Pp. 135-46 in *Midian, Moab and Edom*, eds. J. F. A. Sawyer and D. J. A. Clines. *JSOT* Supplement Series 24. Sheffield: JSOT Press.

Battista, A., and Bagatti, B.

1976 *La Fortezza Saracena del Monte Tabor (AH 609-15: A.D. 1212-18)*. *SBF*, Collectio Minor, 18. Jerusalem: Franciscan Printing Press.

Beck, P.

1975 The Pottery of the Middle Bronze Age IIA at Tel Aphek. *Tel Aviv* 2: 45-85.

Beit-Arieh, I.

1983 Central-Southern Sinai in the Early Bronze Age II and its Relationship with Palestine. *Levant* 15: 39-48.

Ben-Arieh, S., and Edelstein, G.

1977 Akko: Tombs near the Persian Garden. *ᶜAtiqot* 12.

Ben-Dor, I.

1950 A Middle Bronze-Age Temple at Nahariya. *QDAP* 14: 1-41.

Bennett, C. -M.

1965 Tombs of the Roman Period. Pp. 516-45 in *Excavations at Jericho II, The Tombs Excavated in 1955-8*, ed. K. Kenyon. London: The British School of Archaeology in Jerusalem.

1966 Fouilles d'Umm el-Biyara. *RB* 73: 372-403.

1973 Excavations at Buseirah, Southern Jordan 1971: A Preliminary Report. *Levant* 5: 1-11.

1974 Excavations at Buseirah, Southern Jordan 1972: Preliminary Report. *Levant* 6: 1-24.

1975 Excavations at Buseirah, Southern Jordan, 1973: Third Preliminary Report. *Levant* 7: 1-19.

1978 Excavations at the Citadel (el Qalᶜah), Amman, Jordan. *Levant* 10: 1-9.

1982 Neo-Assyrian Influences in Transjordan. Pp. 181-87 in *Studies in the History and Archaeology of Jordan, I*, ed. A. Hadidi. Amman: Department of Antiquities.

Bennett, C. -M., and Northedge, A. E.
1977-78 Excavations at the Citadel, Amman, 1976: Second Preliminary Report. *ADAJ* 22: 172-79.

Bennett, M. A.
1972 *Byzantine and Islamic Ceramics from Hebron (El-Khalil): The Common Wares*. Ph.D. dissertation, University of Utah. Ann Arbor: University Microfilms.

Ben-Tor, A.
1966 Excavations at Ḥorvat Usa. *'Atiqot* 3: 1-24 (Hebrew series).
1975a Two Burial Caves of the Proto-Urban Period at Azor, 1971. *QMIA* 1: 1-54.
1975b The First Season of Excavations at Tell-Yarmuth, 1970. *QMIA* 1: 55-87.
1978 *Cylinder Seals of Third Millennium Palestine*. *BASOR* Supplement Series 22. Philadelphia: American Schools of Oriental Research.

Ben-Tor, A., and Rosenthal, R.
1978 The First Season of Excavations at Tel Yoqne[c]am, 1977. *IEJ* 28: 57-82.

Biran, A. R., and Gophna, R.
1970 An Iron Age Burial Cave at Tel Ḥalif. *IEJ* 20: 151-69.

Berthier, S.
1985 Sondage dans le secteur des thermes sud a Buṣrā (Syria) 1985. *Berytus* 33: 5-45.

Bisheh, G.
1972 A Cave Burial from Jabal Jofeh El-Sharqi in Amman. *ADAJ* 27: 81-83.
1980 Excavations at Qasr al-Hallabat, 1979. *ADAJ* 24: 69-77.

Blau, J.
1979-80 Short Philological Notes on the Inscription of Meša[c]. *Maarav* 2: 143-57.

Bliss, F. J.
1895 Narrative of an Expedition to Moab and Gilead in March 1895. *PEFQS*: 203-34.

Boling, R. G.
1975 Excavations at Tananir, 1968. Pp. 25-85 in *Report on Archaeological Work at Suwwânet Eth-Thanîya, Tananir, and Khirbet Minḥa (Munḥata)*, ed. G. M. Landes. *BASOR* Supplemental Studies 21. Missoula, Montana: Scholars Press.

Boraas, R.
1971 A Preliminary Sounding at Rujum el-Malfuf, 1969. *ADAJ* 16: 31-45.

Boraas, R. S., and Geraty, L. T.
1976 *Heshbon 1974: The Fourth Campaign At Tell Ḥesbân*. Andrews University Monographs: Studies in Religion 9. Berrien Springs, Mich.: Andrews University.
1978 *Heshbon 1976: The Fifth Campaign At Tell Ḥesbân*. Andrews University Monographs: Studies in Religion 10. Berrien Springs, Mich.: Andrews University.

Boraas, R. S., and Horn, S. H.
1975 *Heshbon 1973: The Third Campaign At Tell Ḥesbân*. Andrews University Monographs: Studies in Religion 8. Berrien Springs, Mich.: Andrews University.

Borée, W.
1968 *Die alten Ortsnamen Palästinas*. 2nd ed. Hildesheim: Olms.

Bowersock, G. W.
1983 *Roman Arabia*. Cambridge, MA: Harvard University.

Briend, J., and Humbert, J. -B.
1980 *Tell Keisan (1971-76): Une Cité Phénicienne en Galilée*. Orbis Biblicus et Orientalis, Series Archaeologica 1. Paris: J. Gabalda.

Brooker, C. H., and Knauf, E. A.
1988 Review of J. Prawer (1980). *ZDPV* 104: 184-88.

Brosh, N.
1986 Ceramic Remains: Pottery of the 8th-13th Centuries (Strata 1-3). Pp. 66-89 in *Excavations at Caesarea Maritima 1975, 1976, 1979 –Final Report* by L. I. Levine and E. Netzer. *QMIA* 21.

Broshi, M., and Tsafrir, Y.
1977 Excavations at the Zion Gate, Jerusalem. *IEJ* 27: 28-37.

Brown, R. M.
1983 The 1976 ASOR Soundings. Pp. 105-32 in Vol. 1 of *The Excavations at Araq El-Emir*, ed. N. Lapp. *AASOR* 47.

1984 *Late Islamic Settlement Patterns on the Kerak Plateau, Trans-Jordan*. Unpublished M. A. Thesis, State University of New York at Binghamton.

1987 A 12th Century A. D. Sequence from Southern Transjordan: Crusader and Ayyubid Occupation at el-Wu^ceira. *ADAJ* 31: 267-88.

1988 Late Islamic Shobak: Summary Report of the 1986 Excavations. *ADAJ* 32: 225-45.

1989 Excavations in the 14th Century A.D. Mamluk Palace at Kerak. *ADAJ* 33: 287-304.

n.d.a. Report of the 1987 Excavation at Kerak Castle: The Mamluk Palace Reception Hall. Report on file, Amman: Department of Antiquities.

n.d.b. The Development of Ceramic Folk-art in Modern Jordan. On file with author.

Brünnow, R. E.

1895-99 Reisebericht. *MuNDPV* 1895: 65-73, 81-88; 1896: 1-5, 17-24; 1899: 23-29, 40-42, 56-61, 65-91.

Brünnow, R. E., and von Domaszewski, A.

1904-9 *Die Provincia Arabia. auf Grund Zweier in den Jahre 1897 und 1898 unternommenen Reisen und der Berichte früherer Reisender*, 3 vols. Strassburg: Karl J. Trübner.

Bull, R. J., and Campbell, E. F., Jr.

1968 The Sixth Campaign at Balāṭah (Shechem). *BASOR* 190: 2-41.

Bull, R. J., et al.

1965 The Fifth Campaign at Balāṭah (Shechem). *BASOR* 180: 7-41.

Burckhardt, J. L.

1822 *Travels in Syria and the Holy Land*, ed. William Martin Leake, for the Association for Promoting the Discovery of the Interior Parts of Africa. London: John Murray.

Callaway, J. A.

1972 *The Early Bronze Sanctuary at ^cAi (et-Tell)*, Vol. 1. London: Quadritch.

1980 *The Early Bronze Age Citadel and Lower City at Ai (et-Tell)*. Philadelphia: American Schools of Oriental Research.

Canova, R.

1954 *Iscrizioni e monumenti protocristiani del Paese di Moab*. Rome: Pontifical Institute.

Caskel, W.

1966 *Gamharat an-nasab. Das genealogische Werk des Hisam ibn Muhammad al-Kalbi, II: Erläuterungen zu den Tafeln. Das Register*. Leiden: Brill.

Chafe, W., and Tannen, D.

1987 The Relation between Written and Spoken Language. *ARA*. 16: 383-407.

Clark, V. A.

1979 Investigations in a Prehistoric Necropolis near Bab edh-Dhra^c. *ADAJ* 23: 57-77.

1987 The Desert Survey. Pp. 107-63 in Vol. 1 of *The Roman Frontier in Central Jordan: Interim Report on the Limes Arabicus Project, 1980-1985*, ed. S. T. Parker. BAR International Series 340. Oxford: British Archaeological Reports.

Cleveland, R. L.

1960 *Excavation of the Conway High Place (Petra) and Soundings at Khirbet Ader*. *AASOR* 34-35.

Cohen, R., and Dever, W. G.

1978 Preliminary Report of the Pilot Season of the "Central Negev Highlands Project." *BASOR* 232: 29-45.

1979 Preliminary Report of the Second Season of the "Central Negev Highlands Project." *BASOR* 236: 41-60.

1981 Preliminary Report of the Third and Final Season of the "Central Negev Highlands Project." *BASOR* 243: 57-77.

Cole, D. P.

1984 *Shechem I: The Middle Bronze IIB Pottery*. Excavation Reports. Philadelphia: American Schools of Oriental Research.

Conder, C. R.

1882 Lieutenant Conder's Report. *PEFQS*: 7-15, 69-112.

1889 *Heth and Moab*. London: A. P. Watt (Originally published in 1883 by R. Bentley and Son).

1889 *The Survey of Eastern Palestine*. London: The Committee of the Palestine Exploration Fund.

de Contenson, H.

1956 La céramique chalcolithique de Beersheba; étude typologique. *IEJ* 6: 163-79, 226-38.

1960 Three Soundings in the Jordan Valley. *ADAJ* 4-5: 12-98.

Coogan, M. D.

1975 A Cemetery from the Persian Period at Tell el-Ḥesi. *BASOR* 220: 37-46.

Corbo, P. V.

1955 *Gli Scavi di Kh. Siyar el-Ghanam (Campo Dei Pastori) e i Monasteri Dei Dintorni*. *SBF* 11. Jerusalem: Franciscan Printing Press.

Coughenour, R. A.

1976 Preliminary Report on the Exploration and Excavation of Mugharat el-Wardeh and Abu Thawab. *ADAJ* 21: 71-78.

Crowfoot, G. M.

1932 Pots Ancient and Modern. *PEFQS*: 179-87.

1936 The Nabataean Ware of Sbaita. *PEFQS*: 14-27.

Crowfoot, J. W.

1934 An Expedition to Bālûᶜah. *PEFQS*: 76-84.

Crowfoot, J. W., and Fitzgerald, G. M.

1929 Excavations in the Tyropoeon Valley, Jerusalem 1927. *PEFA* 5.

Crowfoot, J. W.; Crowfoot, G. M.; and Kenyon, K. M.

1957 *The Objects from Samaria*. Vol. 3 of *Samaria Sebaste. Reports of the Joint Expedition in 1931-1933 and of the British Expedition in 1935*. London: Palestine Exploration Fund.

Dajani, R. W.

1964 Iron Age Tombs from Irbed. *ADAJ* 8-9: 99-101.

1966a Four Iron Age Tombs from Irbed. *ADAJ* 11: 88-106.

1966b Jabal Nuzha Tomb at Amman. *ADAJ* 11: 48-52.

1966c An Iron Age Tomb from Amman (Jabal el-Jofeh al-Sharqi). *ADAJ* 11: 41-47.

1970 A Late Bronze-Iron Age Tomb Excavated at Sahab, 1968. *ADAJ* 15: 29-34.

Dalman, G.

1964 *Brot, Öl und Wein*. Vol. 4 of *Arbeit und Sitte in Palästina*. Reprinted. Hildesheim: Georg Olms. Originally published 1933, Gutersloh: C. Bertelsmann.

1971 *Das Haus, Hühnerzucht, Taubenzucht, Bienenzucht*. Vol. 7 of *Arbeit und Sitte in Palästina*. Reprinted. Hildesheim and New York: George Olms. Originally published 1942, Gutersloh: C. Bertelsmann.

Dayan, Y.

1969 Tell Turmus in the Huleh Valley. *IEJ* 19: 65-78.

Dearman, J. A., ed.

1989 *Studies in the Mesha Inscription and Moab*. Archaeology and Biblical Studies 2. Atlanta: Scholars Press.

Degen , R.

1977 Review of S. Wild (1973) in *Göttingische Gelehrte Anzeigen* 229: 228-35.

Delougaz, P., and Haines, R. C.

1960 *A Byzantine Church at Khirbat al-Karak*. Oriental Institute Publications 85. Chicago: The University of Chicago.

Denizeau, C.

1960 *Dictionnaire des parlers arabes de Syrie, Liban et Palestine*. Paris: G. -P. Maisonneuve.

Dentzer, J-M.; Villenevue, F.; and Larché, F.

1983 The Monumental Gateway and the Princely Estate of Araq el-Emir. Pp. 133-48 in Vol. 1 of *The Excavations at Araq el-Emir*, ed. N. Lapp. *AASOR* 47.

Desreumaux, A., and Humbert, J. -B.

1981 Ḫirbet Es-Samra. *ADAJ* 25: 33-84.

Dever, W. G.

1972 Middle Bronze Age I Cemeteries at Mirzbāneh and ᶜAin-Samiya. *IEJ* 22: 95-112.

1973 The EBIV-MBI Horizon in Transjordan and Southern Palestine. *BASOR* 210: 37-63.

1975 MBIIA Cemeteries at ᶜAin es-Sāmiyeh and Sinjil. *BASOR* 217: 23-36.

1976 The Beginning of the Middle Bronze Age in Syria-Palestine. Pp. 3-38 in *Magnalia Dei: The Mighty Acts of God. Essays on the Bible and Archaeology in Memory of G. Ernest Wright*, ed. F. M. Cross, W. E. Lenke, and P. D. Miller, Jr. Garden City, New York: Doubleday.

1980 New Vistas on the EBIV ("MBI") Horizon in Syria- Palestine. *BASOR* 237: 35-64.

Dever, W. G., and Richard, S.

1977 A Reevaluation of Tell Beit Mirsim Stratum J. *BASOR* 226: 1-14.

Dever, W. G.; Lance, H. D.; and Wright, G. E.

1970 *Gezer I: Preliminary Report of the 1964-66 Seasons; Annual of the Hebrew Union College Biblical and Archaeological School in Jerusalem*, Vol 1. Jerusalem: Keter.

Dever, W. G., *et al.*

1974 *Gezer II: Report of the 1967-70 Seasons in Fields I and II. Annual of the Hebrew Union College/Nelson Glueck School of Biblical Archaeology*, Vol. 2. Jerusalem: Keter.

Donahue, J., and Beynon, D. E.

1988 Geologic History of the Wadi el Ḥesā Survey Area. Pp. 26-39 in *The Wadi el Hasa Archaeological Survey 1979-1983, West-Central Jordan* by B. MacDonald et al. Waterloo, Canada: Wilfrid Laurier University.

Donner, H.

1957 Neue Quellen zur Geschichte des Staates Moab in der zweiten Hälfte des 8. Jahrh. v. Chr. *Mitteilungen des Instituts für Orientsforschung* 5: 155-84.

1964 Remarks and Observations on the Historical Topography of Jordan. *ADAJ* 8-9: 88-92.

1982 Mitteilungen zur Topographie des Ostjordanlandes anhand der Mosaikkarte von Madeba. *ZDPV* 98: 174-91.

Donner, H., and Cüppers, H.

1977 *Die Mosaikkarte von Madeba. Tafelband.* Wiesbaden: Harrassowitz.

Dothan, M.

1955 The Excavation at ᶜAfula. *ᶜAtiqot* 1: 19-70.

1959a Excavations at Horvat Beter (Beersheva). *ᶜAtiqot* 2: 1-42.

1959b Excavations at Meṣer, 1957: Preliminary Report on the Second Season. *IEJ* 9: 13-29.

1964 Ashdod: Preliminary Report on the Excavations in Seasons 1962/1963. *IEJ* 14: 79-95.

1965 The Fortress at Kadesh-Barnea. *IEJ* 15: 134-51.

1976 Akko: Interim Excavation Report: First Season, 1973/4. *BASOR* 224: 1-48.

Dothan, M., and Freedman, D. N.

1967 Ashdod I: The First Season of Excavations, 1962. *ᶜAtiqot* 7.

Doughty, C. M.

1888 *Travels in Arabia Deserta*, 2 vols. Cambridge: Cambridge University.

Drioton, E.

1933 A propos de Stèle du Balouᶜa. *RB* 42: 353-65.

Duncan, J. G.

1930 *Corpus of Palestinian Pottery*. London: British School of Archaeology in Egypt.

Elliot, C.

1978 The Ghassulian Culture in Palestine: Origins, Influences and Abandonment. *Levant* 10: 37-54.

Epstein, C.

1978 A New Aspect of Chalcolithic Culture. *BASOR* 229: 27-45.

Ernoul,

1871 *Chronique d'Ernoul et de Bernard le Trésorier*, ed. L. de Mas-Latrie. Paris: Mme Ve Jules Renouard.

Ettinghausen, R.

1965 The Uses of Sphero-conical Vessels in the Muslim East. *JNES* 23: 218-29.

Eusebius

1904 *Das Onomastikon der biblischen Ortsnamen*, ed. Ed. E. Klostermann. Reprint. Hildesheim: Georg Olms.

Falconer, S. E.

1987 Village Pottery Production and Exchange: A Jordan Valley Perspective. Pp. 251-59 in *Studies in the History and Archaeology of Jordan III*, ed. A. Hadidi. Amman: Department of Antiquities.

Falconer, S. E., and Magness-Gardiner, B.

1983 The 1982 Excavations at Tell el-Hayyāt. *ADAJ* 27: 87-104.

1984 Preliminary Report of the First Season of the Tell el-Hayyat Project. *BASOR* 255: 49-74.

Fargo, V.
1979 Early Bronze Age Pottery at Tell el-Ḥesi. *BASOR* 226: 1-14.

Ferembach, D.; Furshpan, A.; and Perrot, J.
1975 Une sepulture collective du bronze moyen II AB à Kh. Minha (Munhata), Israel. Pp. 87-117 in *Report on Archaeological Work at Ṣuwwânet eth-Thanîya, Tananir, and Khirbet Minḥa (Munḥata), Israel*, ed. G. M. Landes. *BASOR* Supplemental Studies 21. Missoula, Montana: Scholars Press.

Fisher, S., and McCown, C.
1931 *Jerash-Gerasa, 1930*. *AASOR* 11.

Fitzgerald, G. M.
1931 *Beth-Shan Excavations 1921-1923: The Arab and Byzantine Levels*. Philadelphia: University of Pennsylvania.
1935 The Earliest Pottery of Beth-Shan. *The Museum Journal* 24: 5-22.

Forder, A.
1902 *With the Arabs in Tent and Town*. London: Marshall Brothers.

Franken, H. J.
1969 *Excavations at Tell Deir 'Allâ: A Stratigraphical and Analytical Study of the Early Iron Age Pottery*. Leiden: E. J. Brill.
1974 *In Search of the Jericho Potters*. North Holland Ceramic Studies in Archaeology 1. Amsterdam: North Holland Publishing Company.
1982 A Technological Study of Iron Age Pottery from Tell Deir ᶜAllā. Pp. 141-44 in *Studies in the History and Archaeology of Jordan, I*, ed. A. Hadidi. Amman: Department of Antiquities.

Franken, H. J., and Kalsbeek, J.
1975 *Potters of a Medieval Village in the Jordan Valley*. North Holland Ceramic Studies in Archaeology, Vol. 3. Amsterdam and Oxford: North Holland Publishing Company.

Freedman, D. N.
1964 A Second Mesha Inscription. *BASOR* 175: 50-51.

Gabrieli, F.
1969 *Arab Historians of the Crusades*. Trans. E. J. Costello. Berkeley and Los Angeles: University of California Press.

Garstang, J.
1932 Jericho: City and Necropolis. *AAA* 19: 3-22, 35-54.
1933 Jericho: City and Necropolis. *AAA* 20: 3-42.
1935 Jericho: City and Necropolis, Fifth Report. *AAA* 22: 143-84.
1936 Jericho: City and Necropolis, Report for Sixth and Concluding Season, 1936. *AAA* 23: 67-100.

Gatt, G.
1885 Industrielles aus Gaza. *ZDPV* 8: 69-79.

Gaube, H.
1974 *Hirbet el-Baida. Ein arabischer Palast in Südsyrien*. Beirut: Orient-Institut der DMG.

Gaudefroy-Demombynes, M.
1923 *La Syrie à l' Époque des Mamelouks*. Paris: Paul Geuthner.

Gautier, L.
1901 *Autour de la Mer Morte. Avec 34 Illustrations d'après les photographies de l'auteur et une Carte*. Geneva: Ch. Eggimann & Eie.

Gawlikowski, M.
1986 A Residential Area by the South Decumanus. Pp. 107-36 in *Jerash Archaeological Project 1981-1983, I*, ed. F. Zayadine. Amman: Department of Antiquities.

Germer-Durand, J.
1897 Mélanges I: La Voie Romaine de Petra a Madaba. *RB* 6: 574-92.

Gerstenblith, P.
1980 A Reassessment of the Beginning of the Middle Bronze Age in Syria-Palestine. *BASOR* 237: 65-84.
1983 *The Levant at the Beginning of the Middle Bronze Age*. *ASOR* Dissertation Series 5. Philadelphia: American Schools of Oriental Research.

Gitin, S.
1979 *An Abstract of a Ceramic Typology of the Late Iron II, Persian and Hellenistic Periods at Tell*

Gezer. Cincinnati: Hebrew Union College-Jewish Institute of Religion.

Glock, A. E.
1975 *Homo Faber*: the Pot and the Potter at Taanach. *BASOR* 219: 9-28.

Glueck, N.
1933 Further Explorations in Eastern Palestine. *BASOR* 51: 9-19.
1934 Explorations in Eastern Palestine I. Pp. 1-113 in *AASOR* 14.
1935 *Explorations in Eastern Palestine II*. *AASOR* 15.
1939 *Explorations in Eastern Palestine III*. *AASOR* 18-19: 60-138.
1940 *The Other Side of the Jordan*. New Haven: American Schools of Oriental Studies (Revised ed., Cambridge, Mass.: American Schools of Oriental Research, 1970).
1943 Some Ancient Towns in the Plains of Moab. *BASOR* 91: 7-26.
1945 A Chalcolithic Settlement in the Jordan Valley. *BASOR* 97: 10-22.
1946 Band-Slip Ware in the Jordan Valley and Northern Gilead. *BASOR* 101: 3-20.
1951 *Explorations in Eastern Palestine, IV, Parts 1 and 2*. *AASOR* 25-28.
1965 *Deities and Dolphins*. New York: Farrar, Straus and Giroux.
1970 *The Other Side of the Jordan*. Cambridge, Massachusetts: American Schools of Oriental Research.

Grabar, O.; Perrot, J.; Ravani, B.; and Rosen, M.
1960 Sondages à Khirbet el-Minyeh. *IEJ* 10: 226-45.

Grabar, O.; Holod, R.; Knustad, J.; and Trousdale, W.
1978 *City in the Desert: Qasr al-Hayr East*. Harvard Middle Eastern Monographs 23-24. Cambridge, Massachusetts: Harvard University.

Graham, M. P.
1989 The Discovery and Reconstruction of the Mesha Inscription. Pp. 41-92 in *Studies in the Mesha Inscription and Moab*, ed. J. A. Dearman. Archaeology and Biblical Studies 2. Atlanta: Scholars Press.

Grant, E.
1929 Beth Shemesh 1928. *AASOR* 9: 1-16.

Grohman, E. D.
1958 *A History of Moab*. Unpublished Ph.D. dissertation, Johns Hopkins University.

Gubser, P.
1973 *Politics and Change in al-Karak, Jordan: A Study of a Small Arab Town and its District*. London: Oxford University.

Gutwein, K.
1981 *Third Palestine: A Regional Study in Byzantine Urbanization*. Washington: University Press of America.

Guy, P. L. O.
1938 *Megiddo Tombs*. Oriental Institute Publications 33. Chicago: University of Chicago.

Hadidi, A.
1970 Pottery from the Roman Forum at Amman. *ADAJ* 15: 11-15.

Hamilton, C.
1875 *Oriental Zigzag, or Wanderings in Syria, Moab, Abyssinia, and Egypt. With Illustrations by Fritz Wallis from Original Sketches by the Author*. London: Chapman and Hall.

Hamilton, R. W.
1931 Jerusalem: Ancient Street Levels in the Tyropoeon Valley within the Walls. *QDAP* 1: 105-10.
1935a Excavations at Tell Abu Hawam. *QDAP* 4: 1-69.
1935b A Note on Excavations at Bishop Gobat School 1933. *PEFQS*: 141-43.
1944 Excavations Against the North Wall of Jerusalem, 1937-38. *QDAP* 10: 1-53.

Hammond, P. C.
1959 Pattern Families in Nabataean Painted Ware. *AJA* 63: 371-82.
1962 A Classification of Nabataean Fine Ware. *AJA* 66: 169-80.
1965 *The Excavation of the Main Theater at Petra 1961-1962: Final Report*. London: Quadritch.
1973 Pottery from Petra. *PEQ* 105: 27-49.

Hankey, V.
1974 A Late Bronze Age Temple at Amman. *Levant* 6: 131-78.

Al-Harawī, Abū l-Ḥasan ᵓAlī b. Abī Bakr (d. 611/1215)
1957 *Kitâb az-Ziyârât*. Trans. J. Sourdel-Thomine. Damascus: Institut Française de Damas.

Harding, G. L.
1948 An Iron-Age Tomb at Sahab. *QDAP* 13: 92-102.
1950a An Iron-Age Tomb at Meqabelein. *QDAP* 14: 44-48.
1950b A Roman Family Vault on Jebel Jofeh, ᶜAmman. *QDAP* 14: 81-94.
1951a Two Iron-Age Tombs in Amman. *ADAJ* 1: 37-38.
1951b Excavations on the Citadel, Amman. *ADAJ* 1: 7-16.
1953a An Early Bronze Age Cave at el Husn. *PEFA* 6: 1-4.
1953b A Middle Bronze Age Tomb at Amman. *PEFA* 6: 14-18.
1953c An Early Iron Age Tomb at Madaba. *PEFA* 6: 27-33.
1953d The Tomb of Adoni Nur in Amman. *PEFA* 6: 48-65.

Harlan, J. R.
1985 The Early Bronze Age Environment of the Southern Ghor and the Moab Plateau. Pp. 125-29 in *Studies in the History and Archaeology of Jordan, II*, ed. A. Hadidi. Amman: Department of Antiquities.

Hart, S.
1987 Five Soundings in Southern Jordan. *Levant* 19: 33-47.

Hayes, J.
1972 *Late Roman Pottery*. London: The British School at Rome.

Helms, S.
1975 Jawa 1973: A Preliminary Report. *Levant* 7: 20-38.
1976 Jawa Excavations 1974: A Preliminary Report. *Levant* 8: 1-29.

Hennessy, J. B.
1966a An Early Bronze Age Tomb Group from Beit Sahur. *ADAJ* 11: 19-40.
1966b Excavation of a Late Bronze Age Temple. *PEQ* 98: 155-62.
1967 *The Foreign Relations of Palestine during the Early Bronze Age*. London: Colt Archaeological Publications.
1969 Preliminary Report on a First Season of Excavations at Teleilat Ghassul. *Levant* 1: 1-24.

Hennessy, J. B., *et al.*
1981 Preliminary Report on a Second Season of Excavation at Pella, Jordan. *ADAJ* 25: 267-309.

Herr, L. G., ed.
1983 *The Amman Airport Excavations, 1976. AASOR* 48.

Hill, Gray
1891 *With the Beduins. A Narrative of Journeys and Adventures in Unfrequented Parts of Syria*. London: T. Fisher Unwin.
1896 A Journey East of the Jordan and the Dead Sea, 1895. *PEFQS*: 24-46.

Hill, G. F.
1922 *Catalogue of the Greek Coins of Arabia, Mesopotamia and Persia*. London: British Museum.

Homès-Fredericq, D., and Franken, J.
1986 *Pottery and Potters–Past and Present: 7000 Years of Ceramic Art in Jordan*. Ausstellungskataloge der Universität Tübingen Nr. 20. Tübingen: Attempto.

Homès-Fredericq, D., and Naster, P.
1979 *Lehun. District de Madaba. Rapport préliminaire sur la première campagne de fouilles belges en Jordanie (Automne 1979)*. Brussels: unpublished manuscript.
1980 *Lehun. District de Madaba. Rapport préliminaire sur la deuxième campagne de fouilles belges en Jordanie (Automne 1980)*. Brussels: unpublished manuscript.

Hornstein, A.
1898 A Visit to Kerak and Petra. *PEFQS*: 94-103.

Horsfield G., and Horsfield, A.
1941 Selah-Petra, the Rock, of Edom and Nabatene IV: The Finds. *QDAP* 9: 105-205.

Horsfield, G., and Vincent, L.-H.
1932 Chronique: Une Stèle Égypto-Moabite au Balouᶜa. *RB* 41: 417-44.

Hübner, U.
1990 Der erste moabitische Palast. *BN* 51: 13-18.

Huot, J. L.
1967 Typologie et chronologie relative de la céramique du bronze ancien a Tell el-Fârᶜah. *RB* 74: 517-54.

Husseini, S. A. S.
1937 A Rock-Cut Tomb-Chamber at ᶜAin Yabrūd. *QDAP* 6: 54-55.

Hütteroth, W. -D.
1975 The Pattern of Settlement in Palestine in the Sixteenth Century: Geographical Research on Turkish Defter-i Mufassal. In *Studies on Palestine During the Ottoman Period*, ed. M. Maᶜoz. Jerusalem: Magnes.
1978 *Palästina und Transjordanien im 16 Jahrhundert. Wirtschaftsstruktur ländlicher Siedlungen nach osmanischen Steuerregistern. BTAVO* 19. Wiesbaden: Ludwig Reichert.

Hütteroth, W. -D., and Abdulfattah, K.
1977 *Historical Geography of Palestine, Transjordan and Southern Syria in the Late 16th Century.* Erlangen: Fränkische Geographische Gesellschaft.

Huss, W.
1985 *Geschichte der Karthager* = *HAW* 3.8. Munich: Beck.

Ibach, R. D. Jr.
1987 *Archaeological Survey of the Hesban Region: Catalogue of Sites and Characterizations of Periods. Hesban 5.* Berrien Springs, MI: Andrews University.

Ibrahim, M.
1971 Accidental Digs. *ADAJ* 16: 114-15.

Ibrahim, M.; Sauer, J.; and Yassine, K.
1976 The East Jordan Valley Survey, 1975. *BASOR* 222: 41-66.

Iliffe, J. H.
1936 Pottery from Râs el-ᶜAin. *QDAP* 5: 113-26.

Irby, C. L., and Mangles, J.
1823 *Travels in Egypt and Nubia, Syria, and Asia Minor; During the Years 1817 & 1818.* London: Printed for private distribution. *Travels in Egypt and Nubia, Syria, and the Holy Land. Including a Journey Round the Dead Sea, and Through the Country East of the Jordan.* (2nd ed. of the above; London: John Murray).

Isserlin, B. S. J.
1953a Notes and Comparisons. *PEFA* 6: 5-8.
1953b Notes and Comparisons. *PEFA* 6: 19-22.
1953c Notes and Comparisons. *PEFA* 6: 34-41.
1956 Place Name Provinces in the Semitic-speaking Ancient Near East. Pp. 83-110 in *Proceedings of the Leeds Philosophical and Literary Society, A VIII*, part 2.
1986a Arabian place name types. Pp. 45-50 in *Proceedings of the Seminar for Arabian Studies* 16.
1986b Phoenician and Arabic Place Names in North Africa. A Comparative and Historical Study. Pp. 145-51 in *Gli Interscambi culturali e socio-economici fra l'Africa settentrionale e l'Europa mediterranea*. Napoli.

Jacobs, L. K.
1983 Survey of the South Ridge of Wadi ᵓIsal, 1981. *ADAJ* 27: 245-74, figs. 1-15.

James, F. W.
1966 *The Iron Age at Beth Shan: A Study of Levels VI-IV.* Museum Monographs. Philadelphia: University of Pennsylvania Museum.

Jenkins, M.
1984 Mamluk Underglaze-painted Pottery: Foundations for Future Study. *Muqarnas* 2: 95-114. New Haven and London: Yale University.

Johns, C. N.
1934 Medieval Slip-Ware from Pilgrims' Castle, ᶜAtlīt (1930-1). *QDAP* 3: 137-44.
1936 Excavations at Pilgrims' Castl, ᶜAtlīt (1932-3); Stables at the South-West of the Suburb. *QDAP* 5: 31-60.

Johns, J.
f.c. Settlement and Land Exploitation Strategies in the Ard al-Karak During the Islamic Period. Forthcoming in *Studies in the History and Archaeology of Jordan, IV.* Amman: Department of Antiquities.

Johns, J., and McQuitty, A.
1989 The Fâris Project: Supplementary Report Upon the 1986 and 1988 Seasons: The Coins and the Glass. *ADAJ* 33: 245-58.

Johns, J.; McQuitty, A.; and Falkner, R.
1989 The Fâris Project: Preliminary Report Upon the 1986 and 1988 Seasons. *Levant* 21:63-95.

Johnston, R. H., and Schaub, R. T.
1978 Selected Pottery from Bâb edh-Dhrâᶜ, 1975. Pp. 33-49 in *Preliminary Excavation Reports:*

Bâb edh-Dhrâʻ, Sardis, Meiron, Tell el Hesi, Carthage (Punic), ed. D. N. Freedman. *AASOR* 43.

Josephus, F.
1926 *The Jewish War*. Trans. H. St. J. Thackery. *The Loeb Classical Library*. New York: G. P. Putnam's Sons.

Kedar, B. Z., and Pringle, D.
1985 La Fève: a Crusader Castle in the Jezreel Valley. *IEJ* 35 (2-3): 164-79.

Kafafi, Z.
1983 The Local Pottery. Pp. 33-45 in *The Amman Airport Excavations, 1976*, ed. L. G. Herr. *AASOR* 48.
1985 Egyptian Topographical Lists of the Late Bronze Age in Jordan (East Bank). *BN* 29: 17-21.

Kampffmeyer, G.
1892 *Alte Namen im heutigen Palästina und Syrien: I. Namen des Alten Testaments*. Leipzig: Hinrichs (also published in *ZDPV* 15: 1-33, 16: 1-71).

Kaplan, J.
1958 Excavations in the Wadi Rabah. *IEJ* 8: 149-60.
1959 Excavations at the White Mosque in Ramla. *ᶜAtiqot* 2: 106-15.
1969 ᶜEin el Jarba: Chalcolithic Remains in the Plain of Esdraelon. *BASOR* 194: 2-38.

Kautz, J.
1981 Tracking the Ancient Moabites. *BA* 44: 27-35.

Kelso, J. L.
1968 *The Excavation of Bethel (1934-1960)*. *AASOR* 39.

Kelso, J. L., and Baramki, D. C.
1955 *Excavations at New Testament Jericho and Khirbet en-Nitla*. *AASOR* 29-30.

Kempinski, A., and Fritz, V.
1977 Excavations at Tel Masos (Khirbet el-Meshâsh): Preliminary Report of the Third Season, 1975. *Tel Aviv* 4: 136-58.

Kenyon, K.
1952 Excavations at Jericho, 1952. *PEQ*: 62-82.
1956 Tombs of the Intermediate Early Bronze-Middle Bronze Age at Tell Ajjul. *ADAJ* 3: 41-55.
1960 *Excavations at Jericho I, The Tombs Excavated in 1952-4*. Jerusalem: British School of Archaeology.
1965 *Excavations at Jericho II, The Tombs Excavated in 1955-8*. Jerusalem: British School of Archaeology.
1966 *Amorites and Canaanites*. London: Oxford University.
1969 The Middle and Late Bronze Age Strata at Megiddo. *Levant* 1: 25-60.

Khairy, N. I.
1983 Technical Aspects of Fine Nabataean Pottery. *BASOR* 250: 17-40.

Kieppert, H.
1841 Map published in *Biblical Researches in Palestine, Mount Sinai, and Arabia Petraia* by E. Robinson. Boston: Crocker and Brewster.
1856 Map published in revised edition of the above.

Kislev, M. E.
1985 Reference to the Pistachio Tree in Near East Geographical Names. *PEQ* 117: 133-38.

Kitchen, K.
1964 Some New Light on the Asiatic Wars of Ramesses II. *JEA* 50: 47-70.
1982 *Pharaoh Triumphant: the Life and Times of Ramesses II*. Warminster: Aris & Phillips.

Klein, F. A.
1869 Missionary Tour into a Portion of the Transjordanic Countries. *The Church Missionary Intelligencer* 5: 60-64, 92-96, 123-28.
1879 Notizen über eine Reise nach Moab im Jahre 1872. *ZDPV*: 124-34 (trans. Notes on a Journey to Moab. *PEFQS* 1880: 249-55).

Knauf, E. A.
1983 Midianites and Ishmaelites. Pp. 147-62 in *Midian, Moab and Edom. The History and Archaeology of Late Bronze and Early Iron Age Jordan and North-West Arabia*, ed. J. F. A. Sawyer & D. J. A. Clines = *JSOT* Suppl. 24. Sheffield: JSOT Press.
1984a Zum Vordringen des Arabischen im Libanon vor dem Islam. *WO* 15: 119-22.
1984b Supplementa Ismaelitica 6. Tall Hira —eine Ituräer-Burg. *BN* 25: 19-21.
1984c Arsapolis. Eine epigraphische Bemerkung. *LA* 34: 353-56.
1985a Bwtrt and Batora. *Göttinger Miszellen* 87: 45-48.
1985b Die Braut im Hohenlied. Pp. 128-32, 841 in *Geliebt-verkauft-getauscht-geraubt. Die Rolle der Frau im Kulturvergleich = Materialienband zur Ausstellung im Rautenstrauch-Joest-*

Museum, 16. Juli - 13. Oktober 1985, eds. G. Völger & K. von Welck. Köln: Rautenstrauch -Joest-Museum für Völkerkunde.

1985c Alter und Herkunf der edomitischen Königsliste Gen 36, 31-39. *ZAW* 97: 245-53.

1987a Supplementa Ismaelitica 9. Phinon-Feinan und das westarabische Orts-namenkontinuum. *BN* 36: 37-50.

1987b Berg und Tal, Stadt und Stamm —Grundzüge der Geschichte Palästinas in den letzten fünftausend Jahren. Pp. 26-35, 417-18 in *Pracht und Geheimnis. Kleidung und Schmuck aus Palästina und Jordanien. Katalog der Sammlung Widad Kawar anlässlich einer Ausstellung des Rautenstrauch-Joest-Museums*, eds. G. Völger, K. von Welck, and K. Hackstein. Köln: Rautenstrauch-Joest Museum.

1988 The West Arabian Place Name Province: Its Origin and Significance. *Proceedings of the Seminar for Arabian Studies* 18.

1989 Aššūr, Šūah und der stimmlose Sibilant des Assyrischen. *BN* 49: 13-16.

Kochavi, M.

1974 Khirbet Rabud = Debir. *Tel Aviv* 1: 2-33.

Koeppel, R., et al.

1940 *Teleilat Ghassul II. Compte Rendu des Fouilles de l'Institut Biblique Pontifical, 1932-1936.* Rome: Pontifical Biblical Institute.

Koucky, F. L.

1987a The Regional Environment. Pp. 11-40 in Vol. 1 of *The Roman Frontier in Central Jordan*, ed. S. Thomas Parker. *BAR International Series* 340. Oxford: British Archaeological Reports.

1987b Survey of the *Limes* Zone. Pp. 41-106 in Vol. 1 of *The Roman Frontier in Central Jordan*, ed. S. Thomas Parker. *BAR International Series* 340. Oxford: British Archaeological Reports.

Kraeling, C.

1938 *Gerasa: City of the Decapolis*. New Haven: American Schools of Oriental Research.

Kruse, Fr., *et al.*

1859 *Commentare zu Ulrich Jasper Seetzen's Reisen durch Syrien U.S.W.* = Vol. 4 of Seetzen, *Reisen durch Syrien, Palästina, Phönicien, die Transjordan-Länder, Arabia Petraea und Unter Aegypten*, ed. Fr. Kruse et al. Berlin: G. Reimer.

Kuschke, A.

1977 Historisch-topographische Bemerkungen zu Stefan Wilds "Libanesische Ortsnamen." Pp. 75-82 in *La Toponymie antique. Actes du Colloque de Strasbourg, 12 - 14 juin 1975.* Leiden: Brill.

Lagrange, M. -J.

1897 Notre Exploration de Pétra. *RB* 6: 208-30.

Lane, A.

1937 Medieval Finds at Al-Mina in North Syria. *Archaeologia* 87: 19-78.

Lapidus, I. M.

1984 *Muslim Cities in the Later Middle Ages*. Cambridge, Massachusetts: Harvard University.

Lapp, N.

1964 Pottery from some Hellenistic Loci at Balâṭah (Shechem). *BASOR* 175: 14-26.

Lapp, N., ed.

1981 *The Third Campaign at Tell el-Fûl: The Excavations of 1964. AASOR* 45.

1983 *The Excavations at Araq el-Emir*, Vol. 1. *AASOR* 47.

Lapp, P. W.

1961 *Palestinian Ceramic Chronology 200 B.C.-A.D. 70*. New Haven: American Schools of Oriental Research.

1964 The 1963 Excavation at Taᶜannek. *BASOR* 173: 4-44.

1966 Chronique Archéologique: Bâb edh-Dhrâᶜ. *RB* 73: 556-61.

1968a Chronique Archéologique: Bâb edh-Dhrâᶜ. *RB* 75: 86-93.

1968b Bâb edh-Dhrâᶜ Tomb A 76 and Early Bronze I in Palestine. *BASOR* 189: 12-41.

1970a Palestine in the Early Bronze Age. Pp. 101-31 in *Near Eastern Archaeology in the Twentieth Century: Essays in Honor of Nelson Glueck*, ed. J. A. Sanders. New York: Doubleday.

1970b The Pottery of Palestine in the Persian Period. Pp. 179-97 in *Archaeologie und Altes Testament: Festschrift für Kurt Galling*, eds. A. Kuschke and E. Kutsch. Tübingen: Mohr.

Lapp, P., and Lapp, N.

1968 Iron II-Hellenistic Pottery Groups. Pp. 54-79 in *The 1957 Excavation at Beth-Zur*, ed. O. Sellers et al. *AASOR* 38.

Lapp, P. W., and Lapp, N. L., eds.
1974 *Discoveries in the Wâdi ed-Dâliyeh. AASOR* 41.

Layard, H.
1887 *Early Adventures in Persia, Susiana, and Babylonia*. London: John Murray.

Lenzen, C. J.
1989 The Pottery. Pp. 231ff. in *Ar-Risha: A Bedouin Station of the Early Islamic Period*. Edinburgh: University of Edinburgh.

Lenzen, C. J., and Knauf, E. A.
1987 Notes on Syrian Toponyms in Egyptian Sources I: 1. *Gintot and *Qart ḏnab. 2. *Buşruna - Buşra š-Šam. *Göttinger Miszellen* 96: 59-64.

Leonard, A., Jr.
1979 Kataret es-Samra: a Late Bronze Age Cemetery in Transjordan? *BASOR* 234: 53-65.
1983 The Proto-Urban/Early Bronze I Utilization of the Kataret es-Samra Plateau. *BASOR* 251: 37-60.

Le Strange, G.
1890 *Palestine Under the Moslems. A Description of Syria and the Holy Land From A.D. 650 to 1500*. Khayats Oriental Reprints 14. Beirut: Khayats, 1965.

Levy, S.
1960 The Ancient Synagogue at Maᶜon (Nirim). A. Excavation Report. *EI* 6: 6-13.

Levy, S., and Edelstein, G.
1972 Cinq années de fouilles à Tel ᶜAmal (Nir David). *RB* 79: 325-67.

Lewis, N. H.
1987 *Nomads and Settlers in Syria and Jordan, 1800-1980*. Cambridge: Cambridge University.

Libby, W. and Hoskins, F. E.
1905 *The Jordan Valley and Petra*. 2 Vols. New York/London: G. P. Putnam's Sons /Knickerbocker.

Liebowitz, H.
1981 Excavations at Tel Yinᶜam: the 1976 and 1977 Seasons, Preliminary Report. *BASOR* 234: 53-65.

Lipínski, E.
1971 Etymological and Exegetical Notes on the Mešaᶜ Inscription. *Orientalia* 40: 325-40.

Loffreda, S.
1969 Due tombe a Betania presso le suore della nigrizia. *LA* 19: 349-66.
1974 *La Ceramica: Cafarnao II. SBF* 19. Jerusalem: Franciscan Printing Press.
1976 Alcune osservazioni sulla ceramici di Magdala. Pp. 338-54 in *Studia Hierosolymitana, in Onore del P. Bellarmino Bagatti, I. SBF* 22. Jerusalem: Franciscan Printing Press.
1979 Potsherds from a Sealed Level of the Synagogue at Capharnaum. *LA* 29: 215-20.

Loud, G., et al.
1948 *Megiddo II: Seasons of 1935-39, Vol. I Text, Vol. II Plates*. Oriental Institute Publications 62. Chicago: University of Chicago.

Luckenbill, D. D.
1926-27 *Ancient Records of Assyria and Babylonia*. 2 vols. Chicago: University of Chicago Press.

Lugenbeal, E. N., and Sauer, J. A.
1972 Seventh-Sixth Century B.C. Pottery from Area B at Heshbon. *AUSS* 10: 21-69.

Lux, U.
1972 Vorläufiger Bericht über die Ausgrabung unter der Erlöserkirche im Muristan in der Altstade von Jerusalem in den Jahren 1970 und 1971. *ZDPV* 88: 185-201.

Luynes, A. Duc de.
1871-76 *Voyage d'exploration à la Mer Morte, à Petra et sur la rive gauche du Jourdain*, 3 vols. Paris: Arthur Bertrand.

Lynch, W. F.
1848 *Narrative of the United States' Expedition to the River Jordan and the Dead Sea*. Philadelphia: Lea & Blanchard.

MacDonald, B.
1981a The Wâdī el-Ḥasā Survey. *BA* 44: 60-61.
1981b The Wâdī el-Ḥasā Survey, 1981. *ASOR Newsletter* 3: 8-15.
1982 The Wâdī el-Ḥasā Survey 1979 and Previous Archaeological Work in Southern Jordan. *BASOR* 245: 35-52.

MacDonald, B., *et al.*
1988 *The Wadi el Hasa Archaeological Survey 1979-1983, West-Central Jordan*. Waterloo, Ontario: Wilfrid Laurier University.

MacDonald, B.; Rollefson, G.; and Roller, D. W.
1982 The Wadi el-Ḥasa Survey 1981. A Preliminary Report. *ADAJ* 26: 117-31.

Macmichael, W.
1819 *Journey from Moscow to Constantinople, in the Years 1817, 1818*. London: John Murray (See esp. pp. 195-249).

Maisler, B.
1951 The Excavations at Tell Qasîle: Preliminary Report. *IEJ* 1: 194-218.

Mallet, J.
1974 Tell el-Far^{c}ah prés de Naplouse: remarques sur la tombe a et le cylindre-sceau. *RB* 81: 423-31.

Mallon, A.
1932 La civilisation du IIIe millénaire dans la vallée du Jourdain. Les fouilles de Teleilāt Ghassūl. *Syria* 13: 334-44.

Mallon, A., *et al.*
1934 *Teleilāt Ghassūl I. Compte rendu des fouilles de l'Institut Biblique Pontifical, 1929-1932.* Rome: Pontifical Institute.

Marmardji, A.-S.
1951 *Textes géographiques Arabes sur la Palestine. Recueillis, Mis en Ordre alphabétique et Traduits en Français*. Etudes Bibliques. Paris: J. Gabalda.

Marquet-Krause, J.
1949 *Les Fouilles de 'Ai (et-Tell) 1933-1935: La Résurrection d'Une Grande Cité Biblique*. *BAH* 45. Paris: Guethner.

Mattingl y, G. L.
1980 *A Reconstruction of Early Bronze Age Cultural Patterns in Central Moab*. Unpublished Ph.D. dissertation, Southern Baptist Theological Seminary, Louisville, Ky.
1983a Nelson Glueck and Early Bronze Age Moab. *ADAJ* 27: 481-89.
1983b The Natural Environment of Central Moab. *ADAJ* 27: 597-605.
1984 The Early Bronze Age Sites of Central and Southern Moab. *NEASB* 23: 69-98.
1987 Moabite Religion. Pp. 1-3 in Vol. 10 of *Encyclopedia of Religion*, ed. Mircea Eliade. New York: Macmillan.

Mauss, C., and Sauvaire, H.
1867 De Karak à Chaubak. extrait d'un journal de voyage. *Bulletin de la Société de Geographie* 14: 449-522.
1871-76 Voyage de Jérusalem à Karak et a Chaubak. Pp. 83-178 in Vol. 2 of A. Duc de Luynes, *Voyage d'exploration à la Mer Morte, à Petra et sur la rive gauche du Jourdain*. Paris: Arthur Bertrand.

Mazar, B., *et al.*
1964 ^{c}Ein Gev Excavations in 1961. *IEJ* 14: 1-49.

McCown, C. C.
1947 *Tell en Naṣbeh I: Archaeological and Historical Results*. Berkeley: Palestine Institute of Pacific School of Religion.

McGovern, P. E.
1986 *The Late Bronze/Early Iron Age of Central Transjordan: The Baq'ah Valley Project, 1977-1981*. Museum Monographs. Philadelphia: University of Pennsylvania Museum.

McNicoll, A. W., and Smith, R. H.
1980 The 1979 Season at Pella of the Decapolis. *BASOR* 240: 63-84.

Menéndez, M.
1983 The Iron I Structures in the Area Surrounding Medeineh Al Ma^{c}arradjeh (Smakieh). *ADAJ* 27: 179-84.

Merrill, S.
1881 *East of the Jordan*. New York: Charles Scribner's Sons.

Mershen, B.
1985 Recent Hand-made Pottery from Northern Jordan. *Berytus* 33: 75-87.
1987 Töperferin, Flechterin, Weberin und Gerberin. Zum Haushaltshandwerk im Ostjordanland. Pp. 100-5 in *Pracht und Geheimnis. Kleidung und Schmuck aus Palästina und Jordanien. Katalog der Sammlung Widad Kawar anlässlich einer Ausstellung des Rautenstrauch-Joest-Museums*, ed. G. Völger, K. von Welck, and K. Hackstein. Köln: Rautenstrauch-Joest Museum.

Meshel, Z.
1977 Ḥorvat Ritma —An Iron Age Fortress in the Negev Highlands. *Tel Aviv* 4: 110-35.

Meyer, R., and Donner, H.
1987 *Wilhelm Gesenius Hebräisches und Aramäisches Handwörterbuch über das Alte Testament*, 18 ed., 1. Lieferung. Berlin: Springer.

Meyers, E. M.; Kraabel, A. T.; and Strange, J. F.
1976 *Ancient Synagogue Excavations at Khirbet Shema^c, Upper Galilee, Israel 1970-1972*. *AASOR* 42. Durham, North Carolina: Duke University.

Meyers, E. M.; Strange, J. F.; and Groh, D. E.
1978 The Meiron Excavation Project: Archaeological Survey in Galilee and Golan, 1976. *BASOR* 230: 1-24.

Meyers, E. M.; Strange, J. F.; and Meyers, C. L.
1981 *Excavations at Ancient Meiron, Upper Galilee, Israel 1971-72, 1974-75, 1977*. Cambridge, Massachusetts: American Schools of Oriental Research.

Milik, J. T.
1958-59 Inscription araméenne de l'époque perse. *LA* 9: 331-41.

Miller, J. M.
1967 The Fall of the House of Ahab. *VT* 17: 307-24.
1974 The Moabite Stone as a Memorial Stele. *PEQ* 106: 9-18.
1979a Archaeological Survey of Central Moab: 1978. *BASOR* 234: 43-52.
1979b Archaeological Survey South of Wadi Mūjib: Glueck's Sites Revisited. *ADAJ* 23: 79-92.
1980 Reviews and Reports. *PEQ* 112: 69.
1981 Renewed Interest in Ancient Moab. *Perspectives in Religious Studies* 8: 219-29.
1982 Recent Archaeological Developments Relevant to Ancient Moab. Pp. 169-73 in *Studies in the History and Archaeology of Jordan I*, ed. A. Hadidi. Amman: Department of Antiquities of Jordan.
1983 Site Identification: A Problem Area in Contemporary Biblical Scholarship. *ZDPV* 99: 119-29.
1989a Moab and the Moabites. Pp. 1-40 in *Studies in the Mesha Inscription and Moab*, ed. J. A. Dearman. Archaeology and Biblical Studies 2. Atlanta: Scholars Press.
1989b The Israelite Journey Through (Around?) Moab and Moabite Toponymy. *JBL* 108: 577-95.
1990 Six Khirbet el-Medeinehs in the Region East of the Dead Sea. *BASOR* 276: 25-28.

Miller, J. M., and Hayes, J. H.
1986 *A History of Ancient Israel and Judah*. Philadelphia: Westminster.

Miller, P. D.
1969 A Note on the Meša^c Inscription. *Orientalia* 38: 461-64.

Mittmann, S.
1970 *Beiträge zur Siedlungs- und Territorialgeschichte des Nordlichen Ostjordanlandes*. Wiesbaden: Harrassowitz
1973 Das sudliche Ostjordanland im Lichte eines neuassyrischen Keilschriftbriefes aus Nimrūd. *ZDPV* 93: 15-25.
1982 The Ascent of Luhith. Pp. 175-80 in *Studies in the History and Archaeology of Jordan I*, ed. A. Hadidi. Amman: Department of Antiquities of Jordan.

Morton, W. H.
1955 Report of the Director of the School in Jerusalem. *BASOR* 140: 47.
1957 Dhībān. *RB* 64: 221-23.
1989 The 1954, 55 and 65 Excavations at Dhiban in Jordan. Pp. 239-46 in *Studies in the Mesha Inscription and Moab*, ed. J. A. Dearman. Archaeology and Biblical Studies 2. Atlanta: Scholars Press.

Moulton, W. J.
1928 The American Palestine Exploration Society. *AASOR* 8: 55-69.

Mousa, S.
1982 Jordan: Towards the End of the Ottoman Empire 1841-1918. Pp. 385-91 in *Studies in the History and Archaeology of Jordan I*, ed. A. Hadidi. Amman: Department of Antiquities of Jordan.

Mukaddasi,
1896 *Description of Syria, Including Palestine*. Trans. Guy le Strange. *PPTS*. London: Palestine Pilgrim Text Society.

Müller, W. W.
1977 Rez. M. Höfner, Inschriften aus Sirwah, Haulan. Teil 1. Sammlung Eduard Glaser 8 = *Sitzungsberichte der Österreichischen Akademie der Wissenschaften, Philosophisch-historische Klasse*, Bd. 291, 1. Wien: Österreichische Akademie der Wissenschaften, 1973, in *ZDMG* 127: 125-28.

Munsell
1975 *Munsell Soil Color Charts*. Baltimore: Munsell Color Company.

Murphy, R. E.
1952 A Fragment of an Early Moabite Inscription from Dibon. *BASOR* 125: 20-23.

Musil, A.
1907-8 *Arabia Petraea*. Kaiserliche Akademie der Wissenschaften, 2 vols. Wien: Alfred Hölder.

Naveh, J.
1962 The Excavations at Meṣad Ḥashavyahu: Preliminary Report. *IEJ* 12: 89-113.

Negev, A.
1969 Seal Impressions from Tomb 107 at Kurnub (Mampsis). *IEJ* 19: 89-106.
1977 The Nabataeans and the Provincia Arabia. Pp. 520-686 in *Aufstieg und Niedergang der Römischen Welt: Geschichte und Kultur Roms im Spiegel der Neuren Forschung*, 2, part 8, ed. H. Temporini and W. Haase. Berlin and New York: Walter de Gruyter.

Netzer, E., and Meyers, E. M.
1977 Preliminary Report on the Joint Jericho Excavation Project. *BASOR* 228: 15-27.

Neuville, R., and Mallon, A.
1931 Les débuts de l'age métaux dans les grottes du Désert de Judée. *Syria* 12: 24-47.

Nöldeke, Th.
1952-54 *Belegwörterbuch zur Klassischen Arabischen Sprache*, ed. J. Kraemer. Berlin: de Gruyter.

North, R., S. J.
1979 *A History of Biblical Map Making*. *BTAVO* B/32. Wiesbaden: Ludwig Reichert.

Northedge, A. E.
1984 *Qalᶜat ᶜAmman in the Early Islamic Period*. Unpublished Ph.D dissertation, School of Oriental and African Studies, University of London.

Olávarri, E.
1965 Sondages à ᶜArôᶜer sur l'Arnon. *RB* 72: 77-94.
1969 Fouilles à ᶜArôᶜer sur l'Arnon. *RB* 76: 230-59.
1977-78 Sondeo Arquelogico en Khirbet Medeineh junto a Smakieh (Jordania). *ADAJ* 22: 136-49.
1983 La Campagne de fouilles 1982 à Khirbet Medeinet al-Muᶜarradjeh prés de Smakieh (Kerak). *ADAJ* 27: 165-78.

Olávarri-Goicoechea, E.
1985 *El Palacio Omeya de Amman, II: La Arqueologia*. Valencia: Institucion San Jeronimo.

Olivier, H.
1986 Nineteenth-Century Travelogues and the Land of Moab. Pp. 80-95 in *Pillars of Smoke and Fire: The Holy Land in History and Thought*, ed. M. Sharon. Johannesburg: Southern Book Publishers.
1989a Archaeological Evidence Pertaining to a Possible Identification of Ar-Moab and er-Rabbah. *Nederduitse Gereformeerde Teologiese Tydskrift* 30: 179-89.
1989b The Location of Jahaz Reconsidered. *Old Testament Essays* 1/3: 43-55.

Oppenheim, M. Frhr. v.
1943 *Die Beduinen, II: Die Beduinenstämme in Palästina, Transjordanien, Sinai, Hedjaz*. Leipzig: Harrassowitz/Hildesheim: Olms, 1983.

Oren, E.
1973a The Early Bronze IV Period in Northern Palestine and its Cultural and Chronological Setting. *BASOR* 210: 20-37.
1973b *The Northern Cemetery of Beth Shan*. Leiden: E. J. Brill.
1975 The Pottery from the Achzib Defence System, Area D: 1963 and 1964 Seasons. *IEJ* 25: 211-25.

Ory, J.
1948 A Bronze Age Cemetery at Dhahrat el Humraiya. *QDAP* 13: 75-89.

Palmer, E. H.
1871a The Desert of the Tíh and the Country of Moab. *PEFQS*: 3-73.
1871b *The Desert of the Exodus. Journeys on Foot in the Wilderness of the Forty Years Wanderings*. Cambridge: Deighton, Bell, and Co.

Parker, S. T.
1976 Archaeological Survey of the *Limes Arabicus*: A Preliminary Report. *ADAJ* 21: 19-31.
1981 The Central *Limes Arabicus* Project: the 1980 Campaign. *ADAJ* 25: 171-78.
1982 Preliminary Report on the 1980 Season of the Central *Limes Arabicus* Project. *BASOR* 247: 1-26.
1983 The Central *Limes Arabicus* Project: The 1982 Campaign. *ADAJ* 27: 213-30.
1985 Preliminary Report on the 1982 Season of the Central *Limes Arabicus* Project. *BASOR Supplement* 23: 1-34.
1986a The *Limes Arabicus* Project: the 1985 Campaign. *ADAJ* 30: 233-52.
1986b *Romans and Saracens: A History of the Arabian Frontier*. ASOR Dissertation Series 6. Winona Lake, IN: Eisenbrauns.

1987a Preliminary Report on the 1985 Season of the *Limes Arabicus* Project. *BASOR Supplement* 25: 131-74.

1987b The Pottery. Pp. 525-619 in *The Roman Frontier in Central Jordan. Interim Report on the Limes Arabicus Project, 1980-1985*, ed. S. T. Parker. BAR International Series 340. Oxford: British Archaeological Reports.

1987c Peasants, Pastoralists, and Pax Romana: A Different View. *BASOR* 265: 35-51.

1987d The Roman Limes in Jordan. Pp. 151-64 in *Studies in the History and Archaeology of Jordan III*, ed. A. Hadidi. London: Routledge and Kegan Paul.

1988a The *Limes Arabicus* Project: the 1987 Campaign. *ADAJ* 32: 171-87.

1988b Preliminary Report on the 1985 Season of the *Limes Arabicus* Project. *BASOR Supplement* 25: 131-174.

1990a New Light on the Roman Frontier in Arabia. Pp. 215-30 in *Akten des 14. Internationalen Limes-kongresses 1986 in Carnuntum*, eds. H. Vetters and M. Kandler. Vienna: Österreichische Akademie der Wissenschaften.

1990b Preliminary Report on the 1987 Season of the *Limes Arabicus* Project. *BASOR Supplement* 26: 89-136.

fc a Preliminary Report on the 1989 Season of the *Limes Arabicus* Project. Forthcoming in *BASOR Supplement* 27.

fc b The Pottery. Forthcoming in *The Roman Frontier in Central Jordan: Final Report on the Limes Arabicus Project 1980-1989*, ed. S. T. Parker. Baltimore: American Schools of Oriental Research.

fc c The *Limes* and Settlement Patterns in Central Jordan during the Roman and Byzantine Periods. Forthcoming in *Studies in the History and Archaeology of Jordan IV*, ed. Ghazi Bisheh. Amman: Department of Antiquities of Jordan.

fc d The Pottery from the 1977 Season. Forthcoming in *Umm el-Jemal*, Vol. 1, ed. B. de Vries.

Parker, S. T., ed.

1987 *The Roman Frontier in Central Jordan. Interim Report on the Limes Arabicus Project, 1980-1985*. BAR International Series 340. 2 Vols. Oxford: British Archaeological Reports.

Parr, P. J.

1956 A Cave at Arqub el Dhahr. *ADAJ* 3: 61-73.

1960 Excavations at Khirbet Iskander. *ADAJ* 4-5: 128-33.

1970 A Sequence of Pottery from Petra. Pp. 348-81 in *Near Eastern Archaeology in the Twentieth Century: Essays in Honor of Nelson Glueck*, ed. J. A. Sanders. Garden City, New York: Doubleday.

Peake, F. G.

1958 *A History of Jordan and Its Tribes*. Coral Gables, FL: University of Miami.

Peleg, M.

1989 Domestic Pottery. Pp. 31-113 in *Excavations at Capernaum, Volume I 1978-1982*, ed. V. Tzaferis. Winona Lake, IN: Eisenbrauns.

Perrot, J.

1957 Les fouilles d'Abou Matar près de Beersheba. *Syria* 34: 1-38.

1964 Les deux premières campagnes de fouilles à Munḥatta (1962-1963); premieres resultats. *Syria* 41: 323-45.

Perrot, J.; Zori, N.; and Reich, Y.

1967 Neve Ur; un novel aspect du Ghassoulien. *IEJ* 17(4): 201-32.

Petrie, W. M. F.

1891 *Tell el Ḥesy (Lachish)*. London: Watt.

Piccirillo, M.

1975 Una tomba del Ferro I a Madaba. *LA* 25: 199-224.

1976 Una tomba del Ferro I a Mafraq (Giordania). *LA* 26: 27-30.

1982 A Church at Shunat Nimrin. *ADAJ* 26: 335-42.

Pierobon, R.

1983-84 Sanctuary of Artemis: Soundings in the Temple-Terrace, 1978-1980. *Mesopotamia* 18-19: 85-111.

Pinkerton, J. M.

1979 *An Examination of Glueck's Conclusions Concerning Central Moab in the Light of the Miller-Pinkerton 1978 Archaeological Survey of Central Moab*. Unpublished M.T.S. thesis. Atlanta: Emory University, Candler School of Theology.

Polotsky, H. J.

1962 The Greek Papyri from the Cave of the Letters. *IEJ* 12: 258-62.

Posener, G.
1940 *Princes et pays d'Asie et de Nubie*. Bruxelles: Fondation égyptologique Reine Elisabeth.

Prag, K.
1974 The Intermediate Early Bronze-Middle Bronze Age: An Interpretation of the Evidence from Transjordan, Syria and Lebanon. *Levant* 6: 69-116.

Prausnitz, M. W.; Avi-Yonah, M.; and Barag, D.
1967 *Excavations at Shavei Zion: The Early Christian Church*. Rome: Centro per le Antichita e la Storia dell'arte del Vicino Oriente.

Prawer, J.
1980 *Crusader Institutions*. Oxford: Clarendon.

Pringle, D.
1981 The Medieval Pottery of Palestine and Transjordan (A.D. 636-1500): an Introduction, Gazetteer and Bibliography. *Medieval Ceramics* 5: 45-60.
1984 Thirteenth-Century Pottery from the Monastery of St. Mary of Carmel. *Levant* 16: 91-111.
1985 Medieval Pottery from Caesarea: the Crusader Period. *Levant* 17: 171-202.
1986 *The Red Tower (al-Burj al-Ahmar): Settlement in the Plain of Sharon at the time of the Crusaders and Mamluks A.D. 1099-1516*. London: British School of Archaeology in Jerusalem.

Pritchard, J. B.
1955 *Ancient Near Eastern Texts Relating to the Old Testament*. 2nd ed. Princeton: Princeton University Press.
1958 *The Excavation at Herodian Jericho, 1951*. *AASOR* 29-30.
1961 *The Water System at Gibeon*. Museum Monographs. Philadelphia: University of Pennsylvania Museum.
1963 *The Bronze Age Cemetery at Gibeon*. Museum Monographs. Philadelphia: University of Pennsylvania Museum.
1968 New Evidence on the Role of the Sea Peoples in Canaan at the Beginning of the Iron Age. Pp. 99-112 in *The Role of the Phoenicians in the Interaction of Mediterranean Civilizations*, ed. W. Ward. Papers Presented to the Archaeological Symposium at the American University of Beirut, March, 1967. Beirut: American University of Beirut.
1980 *The Cemetery at Tell es-Saᶜidiyeh, Jordan*. University Monographs 41. Philadelphia: University of Pennsylvania Museum.

Ptolemy, C.
1843-45 *Claudii Ptolemaei Geographia*, ed. C. F. A. Nobbe. Leipzig:

Rainey, A. F.
1978 The Toponymics of Eretz-Israel. *BASOR* 231: 1-17.

Rahmani, L. Y.
1967 Jason's Tomb. *IEJ* 17: 61-100.

Rast, W.
1978 *Taanach I: Studies in the Iron Age Pottery*. Excavation Reports. Philadelphia: American Schools of Oriental Research.

Rast, W. E., and Schaub, R. T.
1974 Survey of the Southeastern Plain of the Dead Sea, 1973. *ADAJ* 19: 5-53.
1978 A Preliminary Report of Excavations at Bâb edh-Dhrâʾ, 1975. *AASOR* 43: 1-32.
1980 Preliminary Report of the 1979 Expedition to the Dead Sea Plain, Jordan. *BASOR* 240: 21-61.
1981 The Southeastern Dead Sea Plain Expedition: An Interim Report of the 1977 Season. *AASOR* 46.

Redford, D. B.
1982a Contacts Between Egypt and Jordan in the New Kingdom: Some Comments on Sources. Pp. 115-20 in *Studies in the History and Archaeology of Jordan I*, ed. Adnan Hadidi. Amman: Department of Antiquities of Jordan.
1982b A Bronze Age Itinerary in Transjordan. *Journal for the Study of Egyptian Archaeology* 12: 55-74.

Reed, W. L.
1972 The Archaeological History of Elealeh in Moab. Pp. 18-28 in *Studies on the Ancient Palestinian World*, Festschrift for F. V. Winnett, ed. J. W. Wevers and D. B. Redford. Toronto Texts and Studies 2. Toronto: University of Toronto.

Reed, W. L., and Winnett, F. V.
1963 A Fragment of an Early Moabite Inscription from Kerak. *BASOR* 172: 1-9.

Richard, S.

1980 Toward a Consensus of Opinion on the End of the Early Bronze Age in Palestine-Transjordan. *BASOR* 237: 5-34.

Richard, S., and Boraas, R. S.

1984 Preliminary Report of the 1981-82 Seasons of the Expedition to Khirbet Iskander and its Vicinity. *BASOR* 254: 63-87.

Riis, P. J., and Poulsen, V.

1957 *Les Verreries et Poteries Médiévales. Hama Fouilles et Recherches 1931-38*, Vol. 4.2. Copenhague: Nationalmusset.

Riley, J. A.

1975 The Pottery from the First Session of Excavation in the Caesarea Hippodrome. *BASOR* 218: 25-63.

Robinson, E.

1856a *Biblical Researches in Palestine, and in the Adjacent Regions. A Journal of Travels in the Year 1838*. 2 vols. Boston: Crocker & Brewster.

1858b *Later Biblical Researches in Palestine, and in the Adjacent Regions. A Journal of Travels in the Year 1852*. Boston: Crocker & Brewster.

Rogers, J. M.

1984 Mediaeval Pottery at Apamaea in the 1976 and 1977 Seasons. Pp. 261-85 in *Apamée de Syrie, Bilan des Recherches Archéologiques 1973-1979: Aspects de l'Architechture Domestique d'Apamée*. Brussels: Centre Belge de Recherches Archéologiques à Apamée de Syrie.

Roller, D. W.

1980 Hellenistic Pottery from Caesarea Maritima: A Preliminary Study. *BASOR* 238: 35-42.

Rosenthal, U.

1986 Eine Weinpresse im antiken Moab. *BN* 34: 25-29.

Roth, J. B.

1858 Prof. Dr. J. B. Roth's Reisen in Palästina. IV Abschnitt: Erste Ausflüge in die Ost-Jordan-Länder, 17 März bis 4 April 1858. Pp. 267-72 in *Petermann's Mittheilungen*.

Rye, O. S.

1981 *Pottery Technology: Principles and Reconstruction*. Manuals on Archaeology 4. Washington, D.C.: Taraxacum.

Saᶜad, Y.

1964 A Bronze Age Tomb Group from Hablet el Amud, Silwan Village Lands. *ADAJ* 8-9: 77-80.

Safar, Z.

1974 Excavations at Basseh Cave. *ADAJ* 19: 5-10. (Arabic)

Saggs, W. F.

1955 The Nimrud Letters–II: Relations with the West. *Iraq* 17: 126-60.

Saller, S.

1941 *The Memorial of Moses on Mount Nebo. Part II. The Plates. SBF* 1. Jerusalem: Franciscan Printing Press.

1957 *Excavations at Bethany (1949-1953). SBF* 12. Jerusalem: Franciscan Printing Press.

Sartre, M.

1982 *Trois études sur l'Arabie romaine et byzantine*. Revue d'études latines Collection Latomus, vol. 178.

Sauer, J. A.

1973 *Heshbon Pottery 1971: A Preliminary Report on the Pottery from the 1971 Excavations at Tell Heshbân*. Berrien Springs, Michigan: Andrews University.

1974 Review of R. H. Smith (1973). *ADAJ* 19: 169-72.

1975 Review of A. D. Tushingham (1972). *ADAJ* 20: 103-9.

1976 Pottery Techniques at Tell Deir ᶜAllā. Review of H. J. Franken and J. Kalsbeek (1975). *BASOR* 224: 91-94.

1979a A Review of *Gezer II (HUC)*. *BASOR* 233: 70-74.

1979b Iron I Pillared House in Moab. *BA* 42: 9.

1982 The Pottery of Jordan in the Early Islamic Periods. Pp. 329-37 in *Studies in the History and Archaeology of Jordan, I*, ed. A. Hadidi. Amman: Department of Antiquities.

Saulcy, F. de

1853 *Voyage autour de la Mer Morte et dans les Terres Bibliques. exécuté de Décembre 1850 à Avril 1851*. 2 vols. Paris: Gide et J. Baudry. (trans. *Narrative of a Journey round the Dead Sea and in the Bible Lands*. London: Bentley).

Savignac, M. -R.

1936 Chronique. Sur les pistes de Transjordanie méridionale. *RB* 45: 235-62.

Scanlon, G.
1971 The Fustat Mounds: A Shard Count, 1968. *Archaeology* 24.3: 220-33.
1984 Mamluk Pottery: More Evidence from Fustat. *Muqarnas* 2: 115-26.

Schäfer, B.
1971 *Beitrage zur Mamlukischen Historiographie nach dem Tode al-Malik en-Nasirs*. Freiburg: Klaus Schwartz.

Schaefer, J.
1989 Archaeological Remains from the Medieval Islamic Occupation of the Northwest Negev Desert. *BASOR* 274: 33-60.

Schaefer, J., and Falkner, R. K.
1986 An Umayyad Potters' Complex in the North Theater, Jerash. Pp. 411-60 in *Jerash Archaeological Project 1981-1983, I*, ed. F. Zayadine. Amman: Department of Antiquities.

Schaub, R. T.
1973 An Early Bronze IV Tomb from Bâb edh-Dhrâ^{c}. *BASOR* 210: 2-19.
1981 Ceramic Sequences in the Tomb Groups at Bab edh Dhra. Pp. 69-118 in *The South-eastern Dead Sea Plain Expedition: An Interim Report of the 1977 Season*, eds. W. Rast and R. T. Schaub. *AASOR* 46.

Schiffmann, I.
1965 Eine neue moabitische Inschrift aus Karcha. *ZAW* 77: 324-25.

Schmitt-Korte, K.
1970 Die Bemalte Nabätaische Keramik: Verbreitung, Typologie und Chronologie. Pp. 174-97 in *Petra und das Königreich der Nabatäer: Lebensraum, Geschichte und Kultur eines Arabischen Volkes der Antike*, ed. M. Linder. Nürnberg: Delp.

Schneider, H.
1950 *The Memorial of Moses on Mount Nebo. Part III. The Pottery. SBF* 1. Jerusalem: Franciscan Printing Press.

Schottroff, W.
1966 Horonaim, Nimrim, Luhith und der Westrand des Landes Ataroth. *ZDPV* 82: 163-208.

Seetzen, U. J.
1810 *A Brief Account of the Countries Adjoining the Lake Tiberias, the Jordan and the Dead Sea*. London: Palestine Association of London.
1854-55 *Reisen durch Syrien, Palästina, Phönicien, die Transjordan-Länder, Arabia Petraea und Unter Aegypten*, ed. Fr. Kruse, et al. 3 vols. Berlin: G. Reimer. Vol. 4 = *Commentare zu Ulrich Jasper Seetzen's Reisen durch Syrien U.S.W.*, ed. Fr. Kruse, et al., Berlin: G. Reimer, 1859.

Seger, J. D.
1974 The Middle Bronze IIC Date of the East Gate at Shechem. *Levant* 6: 117-30.

Segert, S.
1961 Die Sprache der moabitischen Königsinschrift. *AOr* 29: 197-267.

Sellers, O. R.
1933 *The Citadel of Beth-Zur*. Philadelphia: Westminster.

Sellers, O. R., and Baramki, D. C.
1953 A Roman-Byzantine Burial Cave in Northern Palestine. *BASOR* Supplementary Studies 15-16.

Sellers, O., et al.
1968 *The 1957 Excavation at Beth-Zur*. *AASOR* 38.

Shipton, G.
1939 *Notes on the Megiddo Pottery of Strata VI-XX*. *SAOC* 17. Chicago: University of Chicago.

Simons, J.
1937 *Handbook for the Study of Egyptian Topographical Lists Relating to Western Asia*. Leiden: E. J. Brill.

Sinclair, L. A.
1960 *An Archaeological Study of Gibeah (Tell el-Fûl)*. *AASOR* 34-35.

Sivan, R.
1977 Notes on Some Nabatean Pottery Vessels. *IEJ* 27: 138-44.

Smith, G. A.
1904-5 The Roman Road between Kerak and Madeba. *PEFQS* 1904: 367-77; 1905: 39-48.

Smith, R. H.
1973 *Pella of the Decapolis, Vol. I: The 1967 Season of the College of Wooster Expedition to Pella*. Wooster, Ohio: The College of Wooster.

Smith, R. H.; McNicoll, A. W.; and Hennessy, J. B.
1980 Preliminary Report on the 1979 Season of the Sydney-Wooster Joint Expedition to Pella. *ADAJ* 24: 13-40.
1981 The 1980 Season at Pella of the Decapolis. *BASOR* 243: 1-30.
1983 The 1981 Season at Pella of the Decapolis. *BASOR* 249: 45-78.

von Soden, W.
1965-81 *Akkadisches Handwörterbuch*. 3 vols. Wiesbaden: Harrassowitz.

Spijkermann, A.
1978 *The Coins of the Decapolis and Provincia Arabia*, ed. M. Piccirillo. *SBF*, Collectio Maior 25. Jerusalem: Franciscan Printing Press.
1984 Unknown Coins of Rabbath Moba-Areopolis. *LA* 34: 347-52.

Steele, C. S.
1983 *Early Bronze Age Socio-Political Organization in Southwestern Jordan*. M.A. thesis, State University of New York at Binghamton.

Stern, E.
1978 Excavations at Tel Mevorakh. *QMIA* 9.
1982 *The Material Culture of the Land of the Bible in the Persian Period 538-332 B.C.* Jerusalem: Israel Exploration Society.

Stern, E., and Magen, Y.
1984 A Pottery Group of the Persian Period from Qadum in Samaria. *BASOR* 253: 9-27.

Strange, J.
1975 Late Hellenistic and Herodian Ossuary Tombs at French Hill, Jerusalem. *BASOR* 219: 39-67.

Strabo,
1917 *The Geography of Strabo*. Trans. H. L. Jones. *The Loeb Classical Library*. New York: G. P. Putnam's Sons.

Sukenik, E. L.
1948 Archaeological Investigations at ᶜAffûla. *JPOS* 21: 1-79.

Suleiman, E., and Betts, A.
1981 Rescue Excavations at Tell Sahl es-Sarabet. *ADAJ* 25: 227-34.

al-Ṭabarī, Abū Jaᶜfar ibn Jarīr
1879-1901 *Taʾrikh al-rusul wa-al-muluk*. Ed. M. J. de Goeje, et al., Leiden: Brill. Also ed. M. A. Ibrahim, Cairo: Dār al-Maᶜārif, 1960-79.

Thalmann, J. -P.
1978 Tell ᶜArqa̧ (Liban nord) campagnes I-II (1972-1974): rapport préliminaire. *Syria* 55: 1-152.

Thilo, U.
1958 *Die Ortsnamen in der altarabischen Poesie*. Wiesbaden: Harrassowitz.

Thompson, H. A.
1934 Two Centuries of Hellenistic Pottery. The American Excavations in the Athenian Agora: Fifth Report. *Hesperia* 3(4): 311-476.

Thomsen, P.
1907 *Loca Sancta. Verzeichnis der im 1. bis 6. Jahrhundert n. Chr. erwähnten Ortschaften Palästinas mit besonderer Berücksichtigung der Lokalisierung der biblischen Stätten*. Halle: Rudolf Haupt.

Timm, S.
1989 *Moab zwischen den Mächten. Studien zu historischen Denkmälern und Texten*. *Ägypten und Altes Testament*. *Studien zu Geschichte, Kultur und Religion Ägyptens und des Alten Testaments* 17. Wiesbaden: Harrassowitz.

Toombs, L. E., and Wright, G. E.
1963 The Fourth Campaign at Balâṭah (Shechem). *BASOR* 160: 1-60.

Tristram, H. B.
1873 *The Land of Moab: Travels and Discoveries on the East Side of the Dead Sea and the Jordan*. New York: Harper.

Tufnell, O.
1953 *Lachish III: The Iron Age*. 2 Vols. London: Oxford University.
1958 *Lachish IV (Tell ed-Duweir): The Bronze Age*. London: Oxford University.

Tufnell, O.; Inge, C. H.; and Harding, G. L.
1940 *Lachish II: The Fosse Temple*. London: Oxford University.

Tushingham, A. D.
1965 Tombs of the Early Iron Period. Pp. 479-515 in *Excavations at Jericho Vol. II: Tombs Excavated in 1955-8*, ed. K. Kenyon. Jerusalem: The British School of Archaeology.
1972 *The Excavations at Dibon (Dhībân) in Moab: The Third Campaign 1952-53*. *AASOR* 40.

Tzaferis, V.
1975 The Archaeological Excavation at Shepherds' Field. *LA* 25: 5-52.

Tzori, N.
1973 The House of Kyrios Leontis at Beth Shean. *EI* 11: 229-47 (Heb.).

Vailhé, S.
1899 Voyage a Pétra. *Échos d'Orient* 3: 100-2.

Van de Velde, C.W.M.
1866 *Karte von Palästina*.

Van Zyl, A. H.
1960 *The Moabites*. Pretoria Oriental Series 3. Leiden: E. J. Brill.

de Vaux, R.
1952 La quatrième campagne de fouilles à Tell el-Fâr^cah, près Naplouse. *RB* 59: 551-83.
1953 Fouille au Khirbet Qumrân: rapport préliminaire. *RB* 60: 83-106.
1954 Fouilles au Khirbet Qumrân: rapport préliminaire sur la deuzieme campagne. *RB* 61: 206-36.
1956 Fouilles au Khirbet Qumrân: rapport préliminaire sur les 3, 4, et 5 Campagnes. *RB* 63: 537-77.
1959 Fouilles de Feshka: rapport préliminaire. *RB* 66: 225-55.
1961 Les fouilles de Tell el-Fâr[c]ah: Rapport préliminaire sur les 7, 8, 9 campagnes, 1958-1960. *RB* 68: 557-92.

de Vaux, R. and Stève, A. M.
1947 La première campagne de fouilles à Tell el-Fār[c]ah, près Naplouse. *RB* 54: 394-433.
1949 La deuxième campagne de fouilles à Tell el-Fār[c]ah, près Naplouse. *RB* 56: 102-38.
1950 *Fouilles à Qaryet el-[c]Enab, Abū Gôsh, Palestine*. Paris: J. Gabalda et Cie.

Vincent, L.-H.
1898 Notes de voyage. *RB* 7: 424-51.
1911 *Underground Jerusalem*. English translation of *Jerusalem Sous Terre: Les Recentes Fouilles d'Ophel*. London: Horace Cox.

de Vries, S. J.
1978 *Prophet against Prophet: the Role of the Micaiah Narrative (1 Kings 22) in the Development of Early Prophetic Tradition*. Grand Rapids: Eerdmans.

Vriezen, K. J. H.
1975 Hirbet Kefire —eine Oberflächenuntersuchung. *ZDPV* 91: 135-58.

Wagner, K.
1967 *Echte und unechte Ortsnamen*. Abhandlungen der geistes- und sozialwissenschaftlichen Klasse 1967, 3. Mainz: Akademie der Wissenschaften und der Literatur.

Wagner, N. E.
1972 Early Bronze Age Houses at [c]Ai (Et-Tell). *PEQ*: 5-25.

Walmsley, A. G.
1982 The Umayyad Pottery and its Antecedents. Pp. 143-157 in *Pella in Jordan 1: an Interim Report on the Joint University of Sydney and the College of Wooster Excavations at Pella 1979-1981*, eds. A. McNicoll, R. H. Smith, and B. Hennessy. Canberra: Australian National Gallery.
1987 *The Administrative Structure and Urban Geography of the Jund of Filastin and the Jund of al-Urdunn: The Cities and Districts of Palestine and East Jordan During the Early Islamic, Abbasid and Early Fatimid Periods*. Ph.D. thesis submitted at the University of Sidney.
1988 Pella/Fiḥl After the Islamic Conquest (A.D. 635 - c. 900): a Convergence of Literary and Archaeological Evidence. *Mediterranean Archaeology* 1: 142-59.

Wampler, J. C.
1940 Triangular Impressed Design in Palestinian Pottery. *BASOR* 80: 25-43.
1941 Three Cistern Groups from Tell en-Naṣbeh. *BASOR* 82: 25-43.

Ward, W. A., and Martin, M. F.
1964 The Bālū[c]a Stele: A New Transcription with Palaeographical and Historical Notes. *ADAJ* 8-9: 5-35.

Warmenbol, E.
1983 La stèle de Ruğm el-[c]Abd (Louvre AO 5055). Une Image de Divinité Moabite du IXème-VIIIème Siècle av. N. E. *Levant* 15: 63-75.

Wehr, H., and Cowan, J. M.
1976 *A Dictionary of Modern Written Arabic*. Ithaca, NY: Spoken Language Services Inc.

Weinberg, S. S.
1971 Tel Anafa: The Hellenistic Town. *IEJ* 21: 86-109.

Weippert, H.
1985 Amos: Seine Bilder und ihr Milieu. Pp. 1-29 in *Beiträge zur prophetischen Bildersprache in Israel und Assyrien* by H. Weippert, K. Seybold, and M. Weippert. Freiburg /Schweiz: Universitätsverlag and Göttingen: Vandenhoeck & Ruprecht.
1988 *Palästina in vorhellenistischer Zeit. Handbuch der Archäologie: Vorderasien II,1*, München: C. H. Beck.

Weippert, M.
1979a Nabatäisch-römische Keramik aus Hirbet Dor im südlichen Jordanian. *ZDPV* 95: 87-110.
1979b The Israelite 'Conquest' and the Evidence from Transjordan. Pp.15-34 in *Symposia Celebrating the Seventy-fifth Anniversary of the Founding of the American Schools of Oriental Research (1900-1975)*, ed. F. M. Cross. Cambridge, MA: ASOR.
1982a Remarks on the History of Settlement in Southern Jordan during the Early Iron Age. Pp. 153-62 in *Studies in the History and Archaeology of Jordan I*, ed. A. Hadidi. Amman: Department of Antiquities.
1982b Edom und Israel. Pp. 291-99 in Vol. 9 of *Theologische Realenzyklopädie*, ed. G. Krause, G. Müller, et al. Berlin: de Gruyter.
1987 The Relations of the States East of the Jordan with the Mesopotamian Powers during the First Millennium BC. Pp. 97-105 in *Studies in the History and Archaeology of Jordan III*, ed. A. Hadidi. Amman: Department of Antiquities of Jordan.

Weippert, M. and Knauf, E. A.
1988 Zu den Namen der omajjadischen Töpfer von Ğaraš. *ZDPV* 104: 150-51.

Whitcomb, D.
1987 Excavations in ʿAqaba: First Preliminary Report. *ADAJ* 31: 247-66.
1988a Khirbet al-Mafjar Reconsidered: the Ceramic Evidence. *BASOR* 271: 51-67.
1988b A Fatimid Residence at Aqaba, Jordan. *ADAJ* 32: 207-24.
1989a Mahesh Ware: Evidence of Early Abbassid Occupation from Southern Jordan. *ADAJ* 33: 269-85.
1989b Evidence of the Umayyad Period from the Aqaba Excavations. Pp. 164-84 in *The Fourth International Conference on the History of Bilad al-Sham during the Umayyad Period, Proceedings of the Third Symposium, Vol. II*, eds. M. A. Bakhit and R. Schick. Amman: University of Jordan.
fc a Islamic Period Sites. Forthcoming in *Archaeological Survey of the Southern Ghors and Northeast ʿArabah*, ed. B. MacDonald. Waterloo, Ontario: Wilfrid Laurier University.
fc b Reassessing the Archaeology of Jordan of the Abbasid Period. Forthcoming in *Studies in the History and Archaeology of Jordan, IV*. Amman: Department of Antiquities.

Whitcomb, D. S., and Johnson, J.
1979 *Quseir al-Qadim 1978: Preliminary Report*. Cairo: American Research Center in Egypt.

Wiemken, R. C., and Holum, K. G.
1981 The Joint Expedition to Caesarea Maritima: Eighth Season, 1979. *BASOR* 244: 27-52.

Wightman, G. J.
1989 *The Damascus Gate, Jerusalem: Excavations by C. -M. Bennett and J. B. Hennessy at the Damascus Gate, Jerusalem, 1964-66. BAR International Series* 519. Oxford: British Archaeological Reports.

Wild, S.
1973 *Libanesische Ortsnamen. Typologie und Deutung*. Beiruter Texte und Studien 9. Wiesbaden: Steiner.

Wilkinson, C. K.
1973 *Nishapur: Pottery of the Early Islamic Period*. Greenwich, Connecticut: New York Graphic Society.

Williams, D. P.
1977 *The Tombs of the Middle Bronze Age II Period from the '500' Cemetery at Tell Fara (South)*. Institute of Archaeology Occasional Publications No. 1. University of London. London: Institute of Archaeology.

Wilson, C. W.
1899 Address Delivered at the Annual Meeting of the Fund. *PEFQS*: 304-16.

Wilson, J.
1847 *The Lands of the Bible*. Edinburgh: William Whyte (Map prepared by W. & A. K. Johnston).

Winnett, F. V., and Reed, W. L.
1964 *The Excavations at Dībon(Dhibân) in Moab*. *AASOR* 36-37. New Haven.

Wissmann, H. von
1976 Die Geschichte des Sabäerreichs und der Felzug des Aelius Gallus. Pp. 308-544 in *Aufstieg und Niedergang der Römischen Welt*, Vol. 2, 9/1, ed. W. Haase und H. Temporini. Berlin: de Gruyter.

Worschech, Udo F.
1984 Archäologischer Survey der nördlichen Arḍ el-Kerak 1984. *LA* 34: 445-47.

1985a *Northwest Ard el-Kerak 1983 and 1984: A Preliminary Report*. *BN* Beiheft 2. Munchen: Manfred Gorg.
1985b Preliminary Report on the Third Survey Season in the North-west Arḍ el-Kerak, 1985. *ADAJ* 29: 161-73.
1985c Die Šehburgen am Wādī Ibn Ḥammād. Eine Studie zu einer Gruppe von Bauten im antiken Moab. *BN* 28: 66-88.
1986 Die sozio-ökologische Bedeutung früh-bronzezeitlicher Ortslagen in der nord-westlichen Arḍ el-Kerak. *ZDPV* 102: 40-52.
1990 *Die Beziehungen Moabs zu Israel und Ägypten in der Eisenzeit. Siedlungsarchäologische und siedlungshistorische Untersuchungen im Kern-land Moabs (Ard el-Kerak). Ägypten und Altes Testament. Studien zu Geschichte, Kultur und Religion Ägyptens und des Alten Testaments* 18. Wiesbaden: Otto Harrassoswitz.

Worschech, Udo F., and Knauf, E. A.
1985 Alte Straßen in der nordwestlichen Arḍ el-Kerak: Ein Vorbericht. *ZDPV* 101/2: 128-33.
1986 Diamon und Horonaim. *BN* 31: 70-94.

Worschech, Udo F.; Rosenthal, U.; and Zayadine, F.
1986 The Fourth Survey Season in the North-west Arḍ el-Kerak, and Soundings at Baluᶜ 1986. *ADAJ* 30: 285-309.

Wright, G. E.
1965 *Shechem: The Biography of a Biblical City*. New York: McGraw-Hill.

Yadin, Y., *et al.*
1958 *Hazor I: An Account of the First Season of Excavations, 1955*. Jerusalem: Magnes.
1960 *Hazor II: An Account of the Second Season of Excavations, 1956*. Jerusalem: Magnes.
1961 *Hazor III-IV: An Account of the Third and Fourth Seasons of Excavations, 1957-1958*. Jerusalem: Magnes Press.

Yāqūt,
1957 *Muᶜjam al-buldan*. Vol. 1-5. Beirut: Dār Bayrūt.

Yassine, K.
1984 *Tell el Mazar I: Cemetery*. Amman: A. Shukayr & Akasheh and the University of Jordan.

Yassine, K.; Ibrahim, I.; and Sauer, J.
1988 The East Jordan Valley Survey, 1976 (Second Part). Pp. 189-207 in *Archaeology of Jordan: Essays and Reports* by K. Yassine. Amman: Khair Yassine.

Yeivin, S.
1961 *First Preliminary Report on the Excavations at Tell Gat (Tell Sheykh 'Ahmed el-'Areyny), Seasons 1956-1958*. Jerusalem: The Gat Expedition.

Zayadine, F.
1970 Une Tombé Nabatéene près de Dhat-Râs. *Syria* 47: 117-35.
1971a Deux Inscriptions Grecques de Rabbat Moab (Areopolis). *ADAJ* 16: 71-76.
1971b Un séisme à Rabbat Moab (Jordanie) d'après une inscription grecque du VIe s. *Berytus* 10: 139-41.
1973 Recent Excavations on the Citadel of Amman. *ADAJ* 18: 7-35.
1974 Excavations at Petra (1973-1974). *ADAJ* 19: 135-50.
1977-78 Excavations on the Upper Citadel of Amman —Area A (1975-77). *ADAJ* 22: 20-56.
1978 An EB-MB Bilobate Tomb at Amman. Pp. 59-66 in *Archaeology in the Levant: Essays for Kathleen Kenyon*, eds. R. Moorey and P. Parr. Warminster, England: Aris and Phillips.
1979 Excavations at Petra (1976-1978). *ADAJ* 23: 185-97.
1986 The Moabite Inscription. *ADAJ* 30: 302-4

Zori, N.
1966 The House of Kyrios Leontis at Beth Shean. *IEJ* 16: 123-34.